The
WILEY
advantage

Dear Valued Customer,

We realize you're a busy professional with deadlines to hit. Whether your goal is to learn a new technology or solve a critical problem, we want to be there to lend you a hand. Our primary objective is to provide you with the insight and knowledge you need to stay atop the highly competitive and ever-changing technology industry.

Wiley Publishing, Inc. offers books on a wide variety of technical categories, including security, data warehousing, software development tools, and networking - everything you need to reach your peak. Regardless of your level of expertise, the Wiley family of books has you covered.

- For Dummies – The **_fun_** and **_easy_** way to learn
- The Weekend Crash Course –The **_fastest_** way to learn a new tool or technology
- Visual – For those who prefer to learn a new topic **_visually_**
- The Bible – The **_100% comprehensive_** tutorial and reference
- The Wiley Professional list – **_Practical_** and **_reliable_** resources for IT professionals

The book you hold now, *The CISSP Prep Guide: Gold Edition,* is the all-in-one update to the first edition, *CISSP Prep Guide. The CISSP Prep Guide: Gold Edition* gives you the ultimate in CISSP Prep content. Updated to include more than 660 question and answers including 100 bonus questions, and a new advanced question and answer tutorial, this book is your one-stop source for comprehensive CISSP exam prep. Plus, the interactive Boson-powered CD provides you with a unique opportunity to simulate the test-taking experience.

Our commitment to you does not end at the last page of this book. We'd like to open a dialog with you to see what other solutions we can provide. Please be sure to visit us at www.wiley.com/compbooks to review our complete title list and explore the other resources we offer. If you have a comment, suggestion or any other inquiry, please locate the "contact us" link at www.wiley.com.

Thank you for your support and we look forward to hearing from you and serving your needs again in the future.

Sincerely,

Richard K. Swadley

Richard K. Swadley
Vice President & Executive Group Publisher
Wiley Publishing, Inc.

15 HOUR WEEKEND CRASH COURSE

Visual

Bible

DUMMIES FOR

WILEY
Independent Thinkers

The CISSP® Prep Guide:
Gold Edition

The CISSP® Prep Guide:
Gold Edition

Ronald L. Krutz
Russell Dean Vines

Wiley Publishing, Inc.

Publisher: Robert Ipsen
Executive Editor: Carol Long
Managing Editor: Angela Smith
Text Design & Composition: D&G Limited, LLC

Designations used by companies to distinguish their products are often claimed as trademarks. In all instances where Wiley Publishing, Inc., is aware of a claim, the product names appear in initial capital or ALL CAPITAL LETTERS. Readers, however, should contact the appropriate companies for more complete information regarding trademarks and registration.

This book is printed on acid-free paper. ∞

Published by Wiley Publishing, Inc., Indianapolis, Indiana
Published simultaneously in Canada.

Limit of Liability/Disclaimer of Warranty: While the publisher and author have used their best efforts in preparing this book, they make no representations or warranties with respect to the accuracy or completeness of the contents of this book and specifically disclaim any implied warranties of merchantability or fitness for a particular purpose. No warranty may be created or extended by sales representatives or written sales materials. The advice and strategies contained herein may not be suitable for your situation. You should consult with a professional where appropriate. Neither the publisher nor author shall be liable for any loss of profit or any other commercial damages, including but not limited to special, incidental, consequential, or other damages.

For general information on our other products and services please contact our Customer Care Department within the United States at (800) 762-2974, outside the United States at (317) 572-3993 or fax (317) 572-4002.

Wiley also publishes its books in a variety of electronic formats. Some content that appears in print may not be available in electronic versions.

For more information about Wiley products, visit our Web site at www.wiley.com.

Library of Congress Cataloging-in-Publication Data:

ISBN 0-471-26802-X

Printed in the United States of America.

10 9 8 7 6 5 4 3

Contents

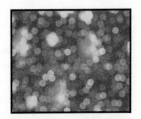

Acknowledgments

I would like to express my appreciation to my soul mate, Hilda, for her patience and support during the writing of this guide.

RLK

I would especially like to thank my best friend and wife, Elzy Kolb, for her continual support and guidance.

RDV

The authors would especially like to thank those who contributed changes, updates, corrections, and ideas for this Gold Edition, and the help and support of the excellent Wiley team.

Foreword

One day last year, the *chief executive officer* (CEO) of a large media company received an alarming e-mail. The sender said that he had gained access to the computer system of the CEO's company. If the CEO were willing to pay a large sum of money, the sender would reveal the weaknesses that he had found in the company's computer system. Just to ensure that they took him seriously, he attached to the e-mail several sensitive files (including photographs) that could only have come from the company's network. This occurrence was not a drill—it was reality.

As you might expect, this kind of problem went straight to the top of the to-do list for the victimized company. The CEO needed many immediate answers and solutions: the true source of the e-mail, the accuracy of the sender's claims, the possible weaknesses that he might have used to break into the system, why the intrusion detection system did not trigger, the steps that they could take to further tighten security, the legal actions that might be possible, and the best way to deal with an adversary living halfway around the world.

For several months, many people—including computer security professionals—worked to gather information and evidence, to secure the system, and to track down the source of the attack. Ultimately, undercover officers from New Scotland Yard and the *Federal Bureau of Investigation* (FBI) met the unsuspecting "cyberextortionists" at a designated location in London, where they arrested them. They are currently in jail, awaiting extradition to the United States.

For anyone who has information security experience, this case brings many thoughts to mind about some of the tools of the trade: logging, packet sniffers, firewalls and their rule sets, and legal access rights to e-mail communications. We cover these concepts in this book. Also, this incident raises questions about how an adversary in a remote location can gain access to a computer network without detection.

As those of us who have been involved in this field for years know, you achieve information systems security through intelligent risk management rather than risk elimination. Computer information security professionals find themselves at the core of a collaborative decision-making process. They must be able to provide answers and explanations anchored in sound methodology.

Not all security issues that arise in the daily course of business are as intense as the case study cited here, and many will be quite subtle. As many of the finest minds in technology focus more on the topic of security, there is a growing consensus that security is ensured through a process, rather than a blind reliance on software or hardware products. No one in this field disputes that a computer security professional must be armed with training and experience to be effective.

As you read this book, keep in mind that those people who are closest to the business operations of an organization are in a great position to help notice anomalies. I often point out to clients that a violation of computer security might only be apparent to someone who is intimately familiar with the features of a given network and its file structure. It is not just what you see but what you know.

For example, if you went home tonight and found that someone had switched around your family photographs on your bedroom nightstand, yet everything else in the house was still in its place, you would immediately know that someone had been in your home. Would a security guard who does not intimately know your home be able to notice this kind of difference, even if he or she took the time to look at your nightstand? The answer is probably not. Similarly, an intruder could disturb many computer network features that no one would notice except for an expert who is familiar with your system.

It is sometimes necessary to point out to clients that the most serious threat to information systems security comes from people, not machines. A person who is an insider and has a user account on a computer system has an enormous advantage in targeting an attack on that system. Computer crime statistics consistently show that insiders do greater damage to systems as opposed to outside hackers. As brilliant as they might be, computer criminals are a poor choice as computer security professionals.

Think of it this way: While the fictional criminal Dr. Hannibal Lechter in the movie "Silence of the Lambs" was brilliant in many ways, I would not trust him with my family. I respect the knowledge that smart people possess, but when you bring one onto the team you get their knowledge and their ethics—a package deal.

As you study the depth of material provided in this book, keep in mind that the information systems security professional of today is just that: a professional. Professionals must abide by rigorous standards yet provide something that computers cannot: human judgment. For this reason (and others), the (ISC)^2 requires strict adherence to its Code of Ethics before granting *Certified Information System Security Professional* (CISSP) certifications.

If you are beginning your CISSP certification, this book provides the framework to help you become a Certified Information System Security Professional. If you are a harried *information technology* (IT) manager for whom security is an increasingly daily concern, this book gives you the fundamental concepts and a solid foundation to implement effective security controls. If you are already a CISSP or an active security practitioner, the "CISSP Prep Guide" will help you succeed in a field that has become crucial to the success of business and the security of a nation's economy.

—Edward M. Stroz

Ed Stroz is president of Stroz Associates, LLC, a consulting firm specializing in helping clients detect and respond to incidents of computer crime. He was an agent with the FBI, where he formed and supervised the computer crime squad in its New York office. You can reach him at www.strozassociates.com.

Introduction

You hold in your hand a key—a key unlocking the secrets of the world of information systems security. This world presents you with many new challenges and rewards, because information systems security is the latest frontier in man's continuing search for communication. This communication has taken many forms over the centuries; the Internet and electronic communications being only our most recent attempt. But for this communication to survive and prosper, it needs reliability, confidence, and security. It needs security professionals who can provide the secure foundation for the growth of this new communication. It needs professionals like you.

With the increasing use of the World Wide Web for e-business, we must protect transaction information from compromise. Threats to networks and information systems in general come from sources that are internal and external to the organization. These threats materialize in the form of stolen intellectual proprietary, *denial of service* (DoS) to customers, an unauthorized use of critical resources, and malicious code that destroys or alters valuable data.

The need to protect information resources has produced a demand for information systems security professionals. Along with this demand came a need to ensure that these professionals possess the knowledge to perform the required job functions. To address this need, the *Certified Information Systems Security Professional* (CISSP) certification emerged. This certification guarantees to all parties that the certified individual meets the standard criteria of knowledge and continues to upgrade that knowledge in the field of information systems security. The CISSP initiative also serves to enhance the recognition and reputation of the field of information security.

The (ISC)² Organization

The CISSP certification is the result of cooperation among a number of North American professional societies in establishing the *International Information Systems Security Certification Consortium* (ISC)² in 1989. The (ISC)² is a nonprofit corporation whose sole function is to develop and administer the certification program. The organization defined a *common body of knowledge* (CBK) that defines a common set of terms for information security professionals to use to communicate with each other and to establish a dialogue in the field. This guide was created based on the most recent CBK and skills, as described by (ISC)² for security professionals. At this time, the domains in alphabetical order are as follows:

- Access Control Systems and Methodology
- Application and Systems Development Security
- Business Continuity and Disaster Recovery Planning
- Cryptography
- Law, Investigation, and Ethics
- Operations Security
- Physical Security
- Security Architecture and Models
- Security Management Practices
- Telecommunications and Networking Security

The (ISC)² conducts review seminars and administers examinations for information security practitioners who seek the CISSP certification. Candidates for the examination must attest that they have three to five years' experience in the information security field and that they subscribe to the (ISC)² Code of Ethics. The seminars cover the CBK from which the examination questions originate. The seminars are not intended to teach the examination.

New Candidate Requirements

Beginning June 1, 2002, the (ISC)² has divided the credentialing process into two steps: examination and certification. Once a CISSP candidate has been notified of passing the examination, he or she must have the application endorsed by a qualified third party before the CISSP credential is awarded. Another CISSP, the candidate's employer, or any licensed, certified, or commissioned professional can endorse a CISSP candidate.

After the examination scoring and the candidate receiving a passing grade, a notification letter advises the candidate of his or her status. The candidate has 90 days from the date of the letter to submit an endorsement form. If the endorsement form is not received before the 90-day period expires, the application is void and the candidate must resubmit to the entire process. Also, a percentage of the candidates who pass the examination and submit endorsements are randomly subjected to audit and are required to submit a resume for formal review and investigation.

You can find more information regarding this process at www.isc2.org.

The Examination

The examination questions are from the CBK and aim at the level of a three to five-year practitioner in the field. It consists of 250 English language questions, of which 25 are not counted. The 25 are trial questions that might be used on future exams. The 25 are not identified, so there is no way to tell which questions they are. The questions are not ordered according to domain but are randomly arranged. There is no penalty for candidates answering questions of which they are unsure. Candidates have six hours for the examination.

The examination questions are multiple choice with four possible answers. No acronyms appear without an explanation. It is important to read the questions carefully and thoroughly and to choose the *best* possible answer of the four. As with any conventional test-taking strategy, a good approach is to eliminate two of the four answers and then choose the best answer of the remaining two. The questions are of not of exceptional difficulty for a knowledgeable person who has been practicing in the field. Most professionals are not usually involved with all 10 domains in their work, however. It is uncommon for an information security practitioner to work in all the diverse areas that the CBK covers. For example, specialists in physical security might not be required to work in depth in the areas of computer law or cryptography as part of their job descriptions. The examination questions also do not refer to any specific products or companies. Approximately 70 percent of the people taking the examination score a passing grade.

ONE-STOP, UP-TO-DATE PREPARATION

This text is truly a one-stop source of information that emphasizes the areas of knowledge associated with the CBK and avoids the extraneous mathematical derivations and irrelevant material that serve to distract the candidate during his or her intensive period of preparation for the examination. It covers the breadth of the CBK material and is independent of the breakdown of the domains or the possible merger of domains. Thus, although the domains of the CBK might eventually be reorganized, the fundamental content is still represented in this text. Also of equal importance, we added material that reflects recent advances in the information security arena that will be valuable to the practicing professional and might be future components of the CBK.

The Approach of This Book

Based on the experience of the authors, who have both taken and passed the CISSP examination, there is a need for a single, high-quality reference source that the candidate can use to prepare for the examination and to use if the candidate is taking the (ISC)² CISSP training seminar. Prior to this text, the candidate's choices were the following:

1. To buy numerous expensive texts and use a small portion of each in order to cover the breadth of the 10 domains
2. To purchase a so-called single source book that focused on areas in the domains not emphasized in the CBK or that left gaps in the coverage of the CBK

Organization of the Book

We organize the text into the following parts:

Chapter 1—Security Management Practices

Chapter 2—Access Control Systems and Methodology

Chapter 3—Telecommunications and Network Security

Chapter 4—Cryptography

Chapter 5—Security Architecture and Models

Chapter 6—Operations Security

Chapter 7—Applications and Systems Development

Chapter 8—Business Continuity Planning/Disaster Recovery Planning

Chapter 9—Law, Investigation, and Ethics

Chapter 10—Physical Security

Appendix A—A Process Approach to HIPAA Compliance through a HIPAA-CMM©

Appendix B—The InfoSec Assessment Methodology

Appendix C—The Case for Ethical Hacking

Appendix D—The Common Criteria

Appendix E—British Standard 7799

Appendix F—HIPAA Informational Updates

Appendix G—References for Further Study

Appendix H—Answers to the Sample and Bonus Questions

Appendix I—Answers to the Advanced Sample QuestionsA series of sample practice questions that are of the same format as those in the CISSP examination accompany each domain of the CBK. Answers are provided to each question along with explanations of the answers.

The appendices include valuable reference material and advanced topics. For example, Appendix B summarizes the National Security Agency's IAM, Information Security Assessment Methodology, and Appendix D provides an excellent overview of the Common Criteria, which is replacing a number of U.S. and international evaluation criteria guidelines, including the *Trusted Computer System Evaluation Criteria* (TCSEC). The Common Criteria is the result of the merging of a number of criteria in order to establish one evaluation guideline that the International community accepts and uses.

In Appendix A, we cover emerging process approaches to information systems security as well as their application to the recent *Health Insurance Portability and Accountability Act* (HIPAA). These methodologies include the *Systems Security Engineering Capability Maturity Model* (SSE-CMM©) and a newly proposed HIPAA-CMM©. This appendix gives a brief history of the CMM culminating in the HIPAA-CMM. Appendix F provides an overview of the HIPAA Administrative Simplification Standards including updated Security and Privacy information.

Who Should Read This Book?

There are three main categories of readers for this comprehensive guide:

1. Candidates for the CISSP examination who are studying on their own or those who are taking the CISSP review seminar will find this text a valuable aid in their preparation plan. The guide provides a no-

nonsense way of obtaining the information needed without having to sort through numerous books covering portions of the CBK domains and then filtering their content to acquire the fundamental knowledge needed for the exam. The sample questions provided will acclimate the reader to the type of questions that he or she will encounter on the exam, and the answers serve to cement and reinforce the candidate's knowledge.

2. Students attending information system security certification programs offered in many of the major universities will find this text a valuable addition to their reference library. For the same reasons cited for the candidate preparing for the CISSP exam, this book is a single source repository of fundamental and emerging information security knowledge. It presents the information at the level of the experienced information security professional and thus is commensurate with the standards that universities require for their certificate offerings.

3. The material contained in this book is of practical value to information security professionals in performing their job functions. The professional, certified or not, will refer to the text as a refresher for information security basics as well as for a guide to the application of emerging methodologies.

Summary

The authors sincerely believe that this text will provide a more cost-effective and timesaving means of preparing for the CISSP certification examination. By using this reference, the candidate can focus on the fundamentals of the material instead of spending time deciding upon and acquiring numerous expensive texts that might turn out to be, on the whole, inapplicable to the desired domain. It also provides the breadth and depth of coverage to avoid gaps in the CBK that are present in other "single" references.

We present the information security material in the text in an organized, professional manner that is a primary source of information for students in the information security field as well as for practicing professionals.

New Revisions for the Gold Edition

We have made several additions and revisions in this new CISSP Prep Guide: Gold Edition. In addition to corrections and updates, we include new security information—especially in the areas of law, cryptography, and wireless technology. Also, we have created additional bonus questionsand expanded and updated the glossary.

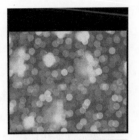

About the Authors

RONALD L. KRUTZ, Ph.D., P.E., CISSP. Dr. Krutz is director of privacy at Corbett Technologies, Inc. He also directs the *Capability Maturity Model* (CMM) engagements for Corbett Technologies and led the development of Corbett's HIPAA-CMM assessment methodology. He has more than 40 years of experience in distributed computing systems, computer architectures, real-time systems, information assurance methodologies, and information security training. He has been an information security consultant at REALTECH Systems Corporation, an associate director of the *Carnegie Mellon Research Institute* (CMRI), and a professor in the Carnegie Mellon University Department of Electrical and Computer Engineering. Dr. Krutz founded the CMRI Cybersecurity Center and was founder and director of the CMRI Computer, Automation, and Robotics Group. He is a former instructor for the ISC2 CISSP Common Body of Knowledge review seminars. Dr. Krutz is also a Distinguished Special Lecturer in the Center for Forensic Computer Investigation at the University of New Haven and a Registered Professional Engineer.

Dr. Krutz conducted sponsored, applied research and development in the areas of computer security, artificial intelligence, networking, modeling and simulation, robotics, and real-time computer applications. He is the author of three textbooks in the areas of microcomputer system design, computer interfacing, and computer architecture and co-author of the CISSP Prep Guide. Dr. Krutz holds seven patents in the area of digital systems. He is a Distinguished Visiting Lecturer in the University of New Haven Computer Forensics Program and is a part-time instructor in the University of Pittsburgh Computer Engineering Program, where he teaches courses in information system security and computer organization. Dr. Krutz is a *Certified Information Systems Security Professional* (CISSP) and a Registered Professional Engineer.

RUSSELL DEAN VINES, CISSP, CCNA, MCSE, MCNE. President and founder of The RDV Group Inc., a New York City-based security consulting services firm, Mr. Vines has been active in the prevention, detection, and remediation of security vulnerabilities for international corporations, including government, finance, and new media organizations, for many years.

He is co-author of the bestselling *CISSP Prep Guide: Mastering the 10 Domains of Computer Security* and *Wireless Security Essentials*, both published by John Wiley and Sons. He frequently addresses classes, professional groups, and corporate clients on topics of privacy, security awareness, and best practices in the information industry.

Mr. Vines has been active in computer engineering since the start of the personal computer revolution. He holds high-level certifications in Cisco, 3Com, Ascend, Microsoft, and Novell technologies and istrained in the National Security Agency's ISSO Information Assessment Methodology. He has headed computer security departments and managed worldwide information systems networks for prominent technology, entertainment, and nonprofit corporations based in New York. He formerly directed the Security Consulting Services Group for Realtech Systems Corporation, designed, implemented, and managed international information networks for CBS/Fox Video, Inc., and was director of MIS for the Children's Aid Society in New York City.

Mr. Vines' early professional years were illuminated not by the flicker of a computer monitor but by the bright lights of Nevada casino show rooms. After receiving a *Down Beat* magazine scholarship to Boston's Berklee College of Music, he performed as a sideman for a variety of well-known entertainers, including George Benson, John Denver, Sammy Davis Jr., and Dean Martin. Mr. Vines composed and arranged hundreds of pieces of jazz and contemporary music that his own big band and others have recorded and performed; he also founded and managed a scholastic music publishing company and worked as an artist-in-residence for the *National Endowment for the Arts* (NEA) in communities throughout the West. He still performs and teaches music in the New York City area and is a member of the American Federation of Musicians Local #802.

CHAPTER 1

Security Management Practices

In our first chapter, we enter the domain of Security Management. Through-out this book, you will see that many Information Systems Security (InfoSec) domains have several elements and concepts that overlap. While all other security domains are clearly focused, this domain, for example, introduces concepts that we extensively touch upon in both the Operations Security (Chapter 6, "Operations Security") and Physical Security (Chapter 10, "Physi-cal Security") domains. We will try to point out those occasions where the material is repetitive, but be aware that if we describe a concept in several domains, you need to understand it.

From the published (ISC)² goals for the Certified Information Systems Secu-rity Professional candidate:

"The candidate will be expected to understand the planning, organization, and roles of individuals in identifying and securing an organization's information assets; the devel-opment and use of policies stating management's views and position on particular topics and the use of guidelines standards, and procedures to support the polices; security awareness training to make employees aware of the importance of information security, its significance, and the specific security-related requirements relative to their position; the importance of confidentiality, proprietary and private information; employment

agreements; employee hiring and termination practices; and the risk management practices and tools to identify, rate, and reduce the risk to specific resources."

A professional will be expected to know the following:

- *Basic information about security management concepts*
- *The difference between policies, standards, guidelines, and procedures*
- *Security awareness concepts*
- *Risk management (RM) practices*
- *Basic information on classification levels*

Our Goals

We will examine the InfoSec domain of Security Management by using the following elements:

- Concepts of Information Security Management
- The Information Classification process
- Security Policy implementation
- The roles and responsibilities of Security Administration
- Risk Management Assessment tools (including Valuation Rationale)
- Security Awareness training

Domain Definition

The InfoSec domain of Security Management incorporates the identification of the information data assets with the development and implementation of policies, standards, guidelines, and procedures. It defines the management practices of data classification and risk management. It also addresses confidentiality, integrity, and availability by identifying threats, classifying the organization's assets, and rating their vulnerabilities so that effective security controls can be implemented.

Management Concepts

Under the heading of Information Security Management concepts, we will discuss the following:

- The big three: Confidentiality, Integrity, and Availability
- The concepts of identification, authentication, accountability, authorization, and privacy
- The objective of security controls –(to reduce the impact of threats and the likelihood of their occurrence)

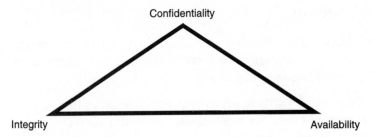

Figure 1.1 The C.I.A. triad.

The Big Three

Throughout this book, you will read about the three tenets of InfoSec: Confidentiality, Integrity, and Availability (C.I.A.), as shown in Figure 1.1. These concepts represent the three fundamental principles of information security. All of the information security controls and safeguards and all of the threats, vulnerabilities, and security processes are subject to the CIA yardstick.

Confidentiality. The concept of confidentiality attempts to prevent the intentional or unintentional unauthorized disclosure of a message's contents. Loss of confidentiality can occur in many ways, such as through the intentional release of private company information or through a misapplication of network rights.

Integrity. The concept of integrity ensures that:

- Modifications are not made to data by unauthorized personnel or processes
- Unauthorized modifications are not made to data by authorized personnel or processes
- The data are internally and externally consistent; in other words, that the internal information is consistent among all subentities and that the internal information is consistent with the real-world, external situation

Availability. The concept of availability ensures the reliable and timely access to data or computing resources by the appropriate personnel. In other words, availability guarantees that the systems are up and running when needed. In addition, this concept guarantees that the security services that the security practitioner needs are in working order.

NOTE D.A.D. is the reverse of C.I.A.
The reverse of confidentiality, integrity, and availability is disclosure, alteration, and destruction (D.A.D.).

Other Important Concepts

There are also several other important concepts and terms that a CISSP candidate must fully understand. These concepts include identification, authentication, accountability, authorization, and privacy:

Identification. The means by which users claim their identities to a system. Most commonly used for access control, identification is necessary for authentication and authorization.

Authentication. The testing or reconciliation of evidence of a user's identity. It establishes the user's identity and ensures that the users are who they say they are.

Accountability. A system's capability to determine the actions and behaviors of a single individual within a system, and to identify that particular individual. Audit trails and logs support accountability.

Authorization. The rights and permissions granted to an individual (or process) that enable access to a computer resource. Once a user's identity and authentication are established, authorization levels determine the extent of system rights that an operator can hold.

Privacy. The level of confidentiality and privacy protection given to a user in a system. This is often an important component of security controls. Privacy not only guarantees the fundamental tenet of confidentiality of a company's data, but also guarantees the data's level of privacy, which is being used by the operator.

Objectives of Security Controls

The prime objective of security controls is to reduce the effects of security threats and vulnerabilities to a level that an organization can tolerate. This goal entails determining the impact that a threat might have on an organization and the likelihood that the threat could occur. The process that analyzes the threat scenario and produces a representative value of the estimated potential loss is called Risk Analysis (RA).

A small matrix can be created by using an x-y graph, where the y-axis represents the level of impact of a realized threat and the x-axis represents the likelihood of the threat being realized, both set from low to high. When the matrix is created, it produces the graph shown in Figure 1.2. Remember, the goal here is to reduce both the level of impact and the likelihood of a threat or disastrous event by implementing the security controls. A properly implemented control should move the plotted point from the upper right—the threat value defined before the control was implemented—to the lower left

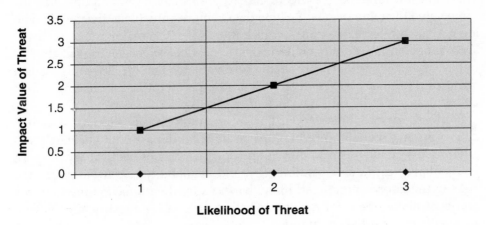

Figure 1.2 The threat versus likelihood matrix.

(that is, toward 0,0), after the control was implemented. This concept is also very important when determining a control's cost/benefit ratio.

Therefore, an improperly designed or implemented control will show very little to no movement in the point before and after the control's implementation. The point's movement toward the 0,0 range could be so small (or in the case of badly designed controls, in the opposite direction) that it does not warrant the expense of implementation. In addition, the 0,0 point (no threat with no likelihood) is impossible to achieve because a very unlikely threat could still have a measurement of .000001. Thus, it would still exist and possibly have a measurable impact. For example, the possibility that a flaming pizza delivery van will crash into the operations center is extremely unlikely; however, this potentially dangerous situation could still occur and have a fairly serious impact on the availability of computing resources.

A matrix with more than four subdivisions can be used for a more detailed categorization of threats and impacts.

Information Classification Process

The first major InfoSec process that we examine in this chapter is the concept of Information Classification. The Information Classification process is related to the domains of Business Continuity Planning and Disaster Recovery Planning because both focus on business risk and data valuation, yet it is still a fundamental concept in its own right—one that a CISSP candidate must understand.

Information Classification Objectives

There are several good reasons to classify information. Not all data has the same value to an organization. Some data is more valuable to the people who are making strategic decisions because it aids them in making long-range or short-range business direction decisions. Some data, such as trade secrets, formulas, and new product information, is so valuable that its loss could create a significant problem for the enterprise in the marketplace by creating public embarrassment or by causing a lack of credibility.

For these reasons, it is obvious that information classification has a higher, enterprise-level benefit. Information can have an impact on a business globally, not just on the business unit or line operation levels. Its primary purpose is to enhance confidentiality, integrity, and availability and to minimize the risks to the information. In addition, by focusing the protection mechanisms and controls on the information areas that need it the most, you achieve a more efficient cost-to-benefit ratio.

Information classification has the longest history in the government sector. Its value has long been established, and it is a required component when securing trusted systems. In this sector, information classification is primarily used to prevent the unauthorized disclosure and the resultant failure of confidentiality.

You can also use information classification to comply with privacy laws or to enable regulatory compliance. A company might wish to employ classification to maintain a competitive edge in a tough marketplace. There might also be sound legal reasons for a company to employ information classification, such as to minimize liability or to protect valuable business information.

Information Classification Benefits

In addition to the reasons we mentioned previously, employing information classification has several clear benefits to an organization. Some of these benefits are as follows:

- Demonstrates an organization's commitment to security protections
- Helps identify which information is the most sensitive or vital to an organization
- Supports the tenets of confidentiality, integrity, and availability as it pertains to data
- Helps identify which protections apply to which information
- Might be required for regulatory, compliance, or legal reasons

Information Classification Concepts

The information that an organization produced or processed must be classified according to the organization's sensitivity to its loss or disclosure. These data owners are responsible for defining the sensitivity level of the data. This approach enables the security controls to be properly implemented according to the classification scheme.

Classification Terms

The following definitions describe several governmental data classification levels ranging from the lowest level of sensitivity to the highest:

1. *Unclassified.* Information designated as neither sensitive nor classified. The public release of this information does not violate confidentiality.

2. *Sensitive but Unclassified* (SBU). Information designated as a minor secret but might not create serious damage if disclosed. Answers to tests are an example of this kind of information. Health care information is another example of SBU data.

3. *Confidential.* Information designated to be of a confidential nature. The unauthorized disclosure of this information could cause some damage to the country's national security. This level applies to documents labeled between SBU and Secret in sensitivity.

4. *Secret.* Information designated of a secret nature. The unauthorized disclosure of this information could cause serious damage to the country's national security.

5. *Top Secret.* The highest level of information classification (actually, the President of the United States has a level only for him). The unauthorized disclosure of Top Secret information will cause exceptionally grave damage to the country's national security.

In all of these categories, in addition to having the appropriate clearance to access the information, an individual or process must have a "need to know" the information. Thus, an individual cleared for Secret or below is not authorized to access Secret material that is not needed for him or her to perform assigned job functions.

In addition, the following classification terms are also used in the private sector (see Table 1.1):

Table 1.1 A Simple Private/Commercial Sector Information Classification Scheme

DEFINITION	DESCRIPTION
Public Use	Information that is safe to disclose publicly
Internal Use Only	Information that is safe to disclose internally but not externally
Company Confidential	The most sensitive need-to-know information

1. *Public.* Information that is similar to unclassified information; all of a company's information that does not fit into any of the next categories can be considered public. This information should probably not be disclosed. If it is disclosed, however, it is not expected to seriously or adversely impact the company.

2. *Sensitive.* Information that requires a higher level of classification than normal data. This information is protected from a loss of confidentiality as well as from a loss of integrity due to an unauthorized alteration.

3. *Private.* Information that is considered of a personal nature and is intended for company use only. Its disclosure could adversely affect the company or its employees. For example, salary levels and medical information are considered private.

4. *Confidential.* Information that is considered very sensitive and is intended for internal use only. This information is exempt from disclosure under the Freedom of Information Act. Its unauthorized disclosure could seriously and negatively impact a company. For example, information about new product development, trade secrets, and merger negotiations is considered confidential.

Classification Criteria

We use several criteria to determine the classification of an information object:

Value. Value is the number one commonly used criteria for classifying data in the private sector. If the information is valuable to an organization or its competitors, it needs to be classified.

Age. The classification of the information might be lowered if the information's value decreases over time. In the Department of Defense, some classified documents are automatically declassified after a predetermined time period has passed.

Useful Life. If the information has been made obsolete due to new information, substantial changes in the company, or other reasons, the information can often be declassified.

Personal Association. If information is personally associated with specific individuals or is addressed by a privacy law, it might need to be classified. For example, investigative information that reveals informant names might need to remain classified.

Information Classification Procedures

There are several steps in establishing a classification system. We list the following primary procedural steps in priority order:

1. Identify the administrator/custodian.

2. Specify the criteria of how to classify and label the information.

3. Classify the data by its owner, who is subject to review by a supervisor.

4. Specify and document any exceptions to the classification policy.

5. Specify the controls that will be applied to each classification level.

6. Specify the termination procedures for declassifying the information or for transferring custody of the information to another entity.

7. Create an enterprise awareness program about the classification controls.

Distribution of Classified Information

External distribution of classified information is often necessary, and the inherent security vulnerabilities will need to be addressed. Some of the instances when this distribution is necessary are as follows:

Court order. Classified information might need to be disclosed to comply with a court order.

Government contracts. Government contractors might need to disclose classified information *in accordance with* (IAW) the procurement agreements that are related to a government project.

Senior-level approval. A senior-level executive might authorize the release of classified information to external entities or organizations. This release might require the signing of a confidentiality agreement by the external party.

Information Classification Roles

The roles and responsibilities of all participants in the information classification program must be clearly defined. A key element of the classification scheme is the role that the users, owners, or custodians of the data play in regard to the data. These roles are important to remember.

Owner

An *information owner* might be an executive or manager of an organization. This person is responsible for the asset of information that must be protected. An owner is different from a custodian. The owner has the final corporate responsibility of data protection, and under the concept of due care the owner might be liable for negligence because of the failure to protect this data. The actual day-to-day function of protecting the data, however, belongs to a custodian.

The responsibilities of an information owner could include the following:

■ Making the original decision about what level of classification the information requires, which is based upon the business needs for the protection of the data

- Reviewing the classification assignments periodically and making alterations as the business needs change
- Delegating the responsibility of the data protection duties to the custodian

Custodian

The owner of information delegates the responsibility of protecting that information to the *information custodian*. IT systems personnel commonly execute this role. The duties of a custodian might include the following:

- Running regular backups and routinely testing the validity of the backup data
- Performing data restoration from the backups when necessary
- Maintaining those retained records IAW the established information classification policy

In addition, the custodian might also have additional duties, such as being the administrator of the classification scheme.

User

In the information classification scheme, an *end user* is considered to be anyone (such as an operator, employee, or external party) who routinely uses the information as part of his or her job. This person can also be considered a consumer of the data—someone who needs daily access to the information to execute tasks. The following are a few important points to note about end users:

- Users must follow the operating procedures defined in an organization's security policy, and they must adhere to the published guidelines for its use.
- Users must take "due care" to preserve the information's security during their work (as outlined in the corporate information use policies). They must prevent "open view" from occurring (see sidebar).
- Users must use company computing resources only for company purposes and not for personal use.

OPEN VIEW

The term "open view" refers to the act of leaving classified documents in the open where an unauthorized person can see them, thus violating the information's confidentiality. Procedures to prevent "open view" should specify that information is to be stored in locked areas or transported in properly sealed containers, for example.

Security Policy Implementation

Security policies are the basis for sound security implementation. Often, organizations will implement technical security solutions without first creating a foundation of policies, standards, guidelines, and procedures, which results in unfocused and ineffective security controls.

We discuss the following questions in this section:

- What are polices, standards, guidelines, and procedures?
- Why do we use polices, standards, guidelines, and procedures?
- What are the common policy types?

Policies, Standards, Guidelines, and Procedures

Policies

A *policy* is one of those terms that can mean several things in InfoSec. For example, there are security policies on firewalls, which refer to the access control and routing list information. Standards, procedures, and guidelines are also referred to as policies in the larger sense of a global information security policy.

A good, well-written policy is more than an exercise created on white paper—it is an essential and fundamental element of sound security practice. A policy, for example, can literally be a lifesaver during a disaster, or it might be a requirement of a governmental or regulatory function. A policy can also provide protection from liability due to an employee's actions or can form a basis for the control of trade secrets.

Policy Types

When we refer to specific polices rather than a group "policy," we generally refer to those policies that are distinct from the standards, procedures, and guidelines. As you can see from the policy hierarchy chart in Figure 1.3, policies are considered the first and highest level of documentation, from which the lower level elements of standards, procedures, and guidelines flow. This order, however, does not mean that policies are more important than the lower elements. These higher-level policies, which are the more general policies and statements, should be created first in the process for strategic reasons, and then the more tactical elements can follow.

> **Senior Management Statement of Policy.** The first policy of any policy creation process is the Senior Management Statement of Policy. This is a general, high-level statement of a policy that contains the following elements:

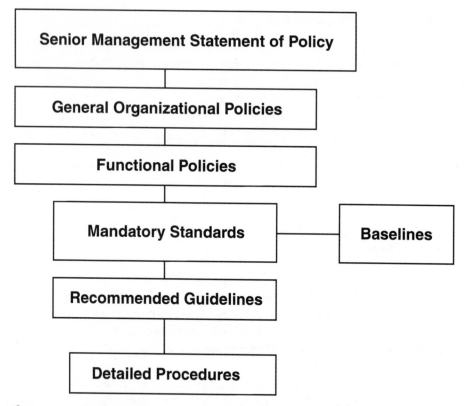

Figure 1.3 Policy hierarchy.

- An acknowledgment of the importance of the computing resources to the business model
- A statement of support for information security throughout the enterprise
- A commitment to authorize and manage the definition of the lower-level standards, procedures, and guidelines

Regulatory. Regulatory policies are security policies that an organization must implement due to compliance, regulation, or other legal requirements. These companies might be financial institutions, public utilities, or some other type of organization that operates in the public interest. These policies are usually very detailed and are specific to the industry in which the organization operates.

Regulatory polices commonly have two main purposes:

1. To ensure that an organization is following the standard procedures or base practices of operation in its specific industry

SENIOR MANAGEMENT COMMITMENT

Fundamentally important to any security program's success is the senior management's high-level statement of commitment to the information security policy process and a senior management's understanding of how important security controls and protections are to the enterprise's continuity. Senior management must be aware of the importance of security implementation to preserve the organization's viability (and for their own "due care" protection) and must publicly support that process throughout the enterprise.

2. To give an organization the confidence that it is following the standard and accepted industry policy

Advisory. Advisory policies are security polices that are not mandated to be followed but are strongly suggested, perhaps with serious consequences defined for failure to follow them (such as termination, a job action warning, and so forth). A company with such policies wants most employees to consider these policies mandatory. Most policies fall under this broad category.

These policies can have many exclusions or application levels. Thus, these policies can control some employees more than others, according to their roles and responsibilities within that organization. For example, a policy that requires a certain procedure for transaction processing might allow for an alternative procedure under certain, specified conditions.

Informative. Informative policies are policies that exist simply to inform the reader. There are no implied or specified requirements, and the audience for this information could be certain internal (within the organization) or external parties. This does not mean that the policies are authorized for public consumption, but that they are general enough to be distributed to external parties (vendors accessing an extranet, for example) without a loss of confidentiality.

Penalties might be defined for the failure to follow a policy, however, such as the failure to follow a defined authorization procedure without stating what that policy is and then referring the reader to another more detailed and confidential policy.

Standards, Guidelines, and Procedures

The next level down from policies is the three elements of policy implementation: *standards*, *guidelines*, and *procedures*. These three elements contain the actual details of the policy, such as how they should be implemented and what standards and procedures should be used. They are published throughout the organization via manuals, the intranet, handbooks, or awareness classes.

It is important to know that standards, guidelines, and procedures are separate yet linked documents from the general polices (especially the senior-level statement). Unfortunately, companies will often create one document that satisfies the needs of all of these elements. This situation is not good. There are a few good reasons why they should be kept separate:

- Each of these elements serves a different function and focuses on a different audience. Also, physical distribution of the policies is easier.

- Security controls for confidentiality are different for each policy type. For example, a high-level security statement might need to be available to investors, but the procedures for changing passwords should not be available to anyone who is not authorized to perform the task.

- Updating and maintaining the policy is much more difficult when all the policies are combined into one voluminous document. Mergers, routine maintenance, and infrastructure changes all require that the policies be routinely updated. A modular approach to a policy document will keep the revision time and costs down.

Standards. *Standards* specify the use of specific technologies in a uniform way. This standardization of operating procedures can be a benefit to an organization by specifying the uniform methodologies to be used for the security controls. Standards are usually compulsory and are implemented throughout an organization for uniformity.

Guidelines. *Guidelines* are similar to standards—they refer to the methodologies of securing systems, but they are recommended actions only and are not compulsory. Guidelines are more flexible than standards and take into consideration the varying nature of the information systems. Guidelines can be used to specify the way standards should be developed, for example, or to guarantee the adherence to general security principles. The Rainbow Series described in Appendix B, and the Common Criteria discussed in Appendix G, are considered guidelines.

Procedures. *Procedures* embody the detailed steps that are followed to perform a specific task. Procedures are the detailed actions that personnel must follow. They are considered the lowest level in the policy chain. Their purpose is to provide the detailed steps for implementing the policies, standards, and guidelines previously created. *Practices* is also a term that is frequently used in reference to procedures.

Baselines. We mention *baselines* here because they are similar to standards, yet are a little different. Once a consistent set of baselines has been created, we can design the security architecture of an organization and develop standards. Baselines take into consideration the difference between various operating systems, for example, to assure that the security is being uniformly implemented throughout the enterprise. If adopted by the organization, baselines are compulsory.

Roles and Responsibilities

The phrase "roles and responsibilities" pops up quite frequently in InfoSec. InfoSec controls are often defined by the job or role an employee plays in an organization. Each of these roles has data security rights and responsibilities. Roles and responsibilities are central to the "separation of duties" concept— the concept that security is enhanced through the division of responsibilities in the production cycle. It is important that individual roles and responsibilities are clearly communicated and understood (see Table 1.2).

We discuss these concepts briefly here:

Senior Management. Executive or senior-level management is assigned the overall responsibility for the security of information. Senior management might delegate the function of security, but they are viewed as the end of the food chain when liability is concerned.

Information Systems Security Professionals. Information systems security professionals are delegated the responsibility for implementing and maintaining security by the senior-level management. Their duties

Table 1.2 Roles and Responsibilities

ROLE	DESCRIPTION
Senior Manager	Has the ultimate responsibility for security
InfoSec Officer	Has the functional responsibility for security
Owner	Determines the data classification
Custodian	Preserves the information's CIA
User/Operator	Performs IAW the stated policies
Auditor	Examines security

include the design, implementation, management, and review of the organization's security policy, standards, guidelines, and procedures.

Data Owners. As we previously discussed in the section titled "Information Classification Roles," data owners are primarily responsible for determining the data's sensitivity or classification levels. They can also be responsible for maintaining the information's accuracy and integrity.

Users. As we previously discussed in the section titled "Information Classification Roles," users are responsible for following the procedures set out in the organization's security policy during the course of their normal daily tasks.

Information Systems Auditors. Information systems auditors are responsible for providing reports to the senior management on the effectiveness of the security controls by conducting regular, independent audits. They also examine whether the security policies, standards, guidelines, and procedures effectively comply with the company's stated security objectives.

Risk Management

A major component of InfoSec is Risk Management (RM). RM's main function is to *mitigate* risk. Mitigating risk means to reduce the risk until it reaches a level that is acceptable to an organization. We can define RM as the identification, analysis, control, and minimization of loss that is associated with events.

The identification of risk to an organization entails defining the following basic elements:

- The actual threat
- The possible consequences of the realized threat
- The probable frequency of the occurrence of a threat
- The extent of how confident we are that the threat will happen

Many formulas and processes are designed to help provide some certainty when answering these questions. We should point out, however, that because life and nature are constantly evolving and changing, we cannot consider every possibility. RM tries as much as possible to see the future and to lower the possibility of threats impacting a company.

> **NOTE** **Mitigating Risk**
> It's important to remember that the risk to an enterprise—can never be totally eliminated—that would entail ceasing operations. Risk Mitigation means finding out what level of risk the enterprise can safely tolerate and still continue to function effectively.

Principles of Risk Management

The RM task process has several elements, primarily including the following:

- Performing a Risk Analysis, including the cost-benefit analysis of protections
- Implementing, reviewing, and maintaining protections

To enable this process, you will need to determine some properties of the various elements, such as the value of assets, threats, and vulnerabilities and the likelihood of events. A primary part of the RM process is assigning values to threats and estimating how often (or how likely) that threat will occur. To perform this task, several formulas and terms have been developed, and the CISSP candidate must fully understand them. The terms and definitions listed in the following section are ranked in the order that they are defined during the Risk Analysis (RA).

The Purpose of Risk Analysis

The main purpose of performing a Risk Analysis is to quantify the impact of potential threats—to put a price or value on the cost of a lost business functionality. The two main results of an RA—the identification of risks and the cost/benefit justification of the countermeasures—are vitally important to the creation of a risk mitigation strategy.

There are several benefits to performing an RA. It creates a clear cost-to-value ratio for security protections. It also influences the decision-making process dealing with hardware configuration and software systems design. In addition, it also helps a company focus its security resources where they are needed most. Furthermore, it can influence planning and construction decisions, such as site selection and building design.

Terms and Definitions

The following are RA terms that the CISSP candidate will need to know:

Asset. An *asset* is a resource, process, product, computing infrastructure, and so forth that an organization has determined must be protected. The loss of the asset could affect C.I.A., confidentiality, integrity, or availability or have an overall effect, or it could have a discrete dollar value—tangible or intangible. It could also affect the full ability of an organization to continue in business. The value of an asset is composed of all of the elements that are related to that asset—its creation, development, support, replacement, public credibility, considered costs, and ownership values.

Threat. Simply put, the presence of any potential event that causes an undesirable impact on the organization is called a *threat*. As we will discuss in the Operations Domain, a threat could be man-made or natural and have a small or large effect on a company's security or viability.

Vulnerability. The absence or weakness of a safeguard constitutes a *vulnerability*. A minor threat has the potential to become a greater threat, or a more frequent threat, because of a vulnerability. Think of a vulnerability as the threat that gets through a safeguard into the system. Combined with the terms asset and threat, vulnerability is the third part of an element that is called a *triple* in risk management.

Safeguard. A *safeguard* is the control or countermeasure employed to reduce the risk associated with a specific threat or group of threats.

Exposure Factor (EF). The *EF* represents the percentage of loss that a realized threat event would have on a specific asset. This value is necessary to compute the *Single Loss Expectancy* (SLE), which in turn is necessary to compute the *Annualized Loss Expectancy* (ALE). The EF can be a small percentage, such as the effect of a loss of some hardware, or a very large percentage, such as the catastrophic loss of all computing resources.

Single Loss Expectancy (SLE). An *SLE* is the dollar figure that is assigned to a single event. It represents an organization's loss from a single threat and is derived from the following formula:

Asset Value (\$) × *Exposure Factor* (EF) = SLE

For example, an asset valued at \$100,000 that is subjected to an exposure factor of 30 percent would yield an SLE of \$30,000. While this figure is primarily defined in order to create the *Annualized Loss Expectancy* (ALE), it is occasionally used by itself to describe a disastrous event for a *Business Impact Assessment* (BIA).

Annualized Rate of Occurrence (ARO). The *ARO* is a number that represents the estimated frequency with which a threat is expected to occur. The range for this value can be from 0.0 (never) to a large number (for minor threats, such as misspellings of names in data entry). How this number is derived can be very complicated. It is usually created based upon the likelihood of the event and the number of employees that could make that error occur. The loss incurred by this event is not a concern here, only how often it does occur.

For example, a meteorite damaging the data center could be estimated to occur only once every 100,000 years and will have an ARO of .00001. In contrast, 100 data entry operators attempting an unauthorized access attempt could be estimated at six times a year per operator and will have an ARO of 600.

Annualized Loss Expectancy (ALE). The *ALE*, a dollar value, is derived from the following formula:

Single Loss Expectancy (SLE) × *Annualized Rate of Occurrence* (ARO) = ALE

In other words, an ALE is the annually expected financial loss to an

Table 1.3 Risk Analysis Formulas

CONCEPT	DERIVATION FORMULA
Exposure Factor (EF)	Percentage of asset loss caused by threat
Single Loss Expectancy (SLE)	Asset Value x *Exposure Factor* (EF)
Annualized Rate of Occurrence (ARO)	Frequency of threat occurrence per year
Annualized Loss Expectancy (ALE)	*Single Loss Expectancy* (SLE) x *Annualized Rate of Occurrence* (ARO)

organization from a threat. For example, a threat with a dollar value of $100,000 (SLE) that is expected to happen only once in 1,000 years (ARO of .001) will result in an ALE of $100. This example helps to provide a more reliable cost-benefit analysis. Remember that the SLE is derived from the asset value and the Exposure Factor (EF). Table 1.3 shows these formulas.

Overview of Risk Analysis

We now discuss the four basic elements of the Risk Analysis process:

1. Quantitative Risk Analysis
2. Qualitative Risk Analysis
3. Asset Valuation Process
4. Safeguard Selection

Quantitative Risk Analysis

The difference between quantitative and qualitative RA is fairly simple: Quantitative RA attempts to assign independently objective numeric values (hard dollars, for example) to the components of the risk assessment and to the assessment of potential losses. Qualitative RA addresses more intangible values of a data loss and focuses on the other issues, rather than on the pure, hard costs.

When all elements (asset value, impact, threat frequency, safeguard effectiveness, safeguard costs, uncertainty, and probability) are measured, rated, and assigned values, the process is considered to be fully quantitative. Fully quantitative risk analysis is not possible, however, because qualitative measures must be applied. Thus, you should be aware that just because the figures look hard on paper does not mean it is possible to foretell the future with any certainty.

A quantitative risk analysis process is a major project, and as such it requires a project or program manager to manage the main elements of the analysis. A major part of the initial planning for the quantitative RA is the estimation of the time required to perform the analysis. In addition, you must also create a detailed process plan and assign roles to the RA team.

Preliminary Security Examination **(PSE).** A PSE is often conducted before the actual quantitative RA. The PSE helps to gather the elements that you will need when the actual RA takes place. A PSE also helps to focus an RA. Elements that are defined during this phase include asset costs and values, a listing of various threats to an organization (in terms of threats to both the personnel and the environment), and documentation of the existing security measures. The PSE is normally then subject to a review by an organization's management before the RA begins.

Risk Analysis Steps

The three primary steps in performing a risk analysis are similar to the steps in performing a Business Impact Assessment (see Chapter 6, "Operations Security"). A risk analysis is commonly much more comprehensive, however, and is designed to be used to quantify complicated, multiple-risk scenarios.

The three primary steps are as follows:

1. Estimate the potential losses to assets by determining their value.
2. Analyze potential threats to the assets.
3. Define the Annualized Loss Expectancy (ALE).

Estimate Potential Losses

To estimate the potential losses incurred during the realization of a threat, the assets must be valued by commonly using some sort of standard asset valuation process (we describe this task in more detail later). This process results in an assignment of an asset's financial value by performing the EF and the SLE calculations.

AUTOMATED RISK ANALYSIS PRODUCTS

There are several good automated risk analysis products on the market. The main objectives of these products is to minimize the manual effort that you must expend to create the risk analysis and to provide a company with the capability to forecast its expected losses quickly with different input variations. The creation of a database during an initial automated process enables the operator to rerun the analysis by using different parameters to create a what-if scenario. These products enable the users to perform calculations quickly in order to estimate future expected losses, thereby determining the benefit of their implemented safeguards.

Analyze Potential Threats

Here, we determine what the threats are and how likely and often they are to occur. To define the threats, we must also understand the asset's vulnerabilities and perform an ARO calculation for the threat and vulnerabilities.

All types of threats should be considered in this section, no matter whether they seem likely or not. It might be helpful to organize the threat listing into the types of threats by source or by their expected magnitude. In fact, some organizations can provide statistics on the frequency of various threats that occur in your area. In addition, the other domains of InfoSec discussed in this book have several varied listings of the categories of threats.

Some of the following categories of threats could be included in this section:

Data Classification. Data aggregation or concentration that results in data inference, covert channel manipulation, a malicious code/virus/Trojan horse/worm/logic bomb, or a concentration of responsibilities (lack of separation of duties).

Information Warfare. Technology-oriented terrorism, malicious code or logic, or emanation interception for military or economic espionage.

Personnel. Unauthorized or uncontrolled system access, the misuse of technology by authorized users, tampering by disgruntled employees, or falsified data input.

Application/Operational. An ineffective security application that results in procedural errors or incorrect data entry.

Criminal. Physical destruction or vandalism, the theft of assets or information, organized insider theft, armed robbery, or physical harm to personnel.

Environmental. Utility failure, service outage, natural disasters, or neighboring hazards.

Computer Infrastructure. Hardware/equipment failure, program errors, operating system flaws, or a communications system failure.

Delayed Processing. Reduced productivity or a delayed funds collection that results in reduced income, increased expenses, or late charges.

Define the Annualized Loss Expectancy (ALE)

Once we have determined the SLE and ARO, we can estimate the ALE by using the formula that we previously described.

Results

After performing the Risk Analysis, the final results should contain the following:

- Valuations of the critical assets in hard costs
- A detailed listing of significant threats
- Each threat's likelihood and possible occurrence rate
- Loss potential by a threat—the dollar impact that the threat will have on an asset
- Recommended remedial measures and safeguards or countermeasures

Remedies

There are three generic remedies to risk that might take the form of either one or a combination of the following three:

Risk Reduction. Taking measures to alter or improve the risk position of an asset throughout the company.

Risk Transference. Assigning or transferring the potential cost of a loss to another party (like an insurance company).

Risk Acceptance. Accepting the level of loss that will occur and absorbing that loss.

The remedy chosen will usually be the one that results in the greatest risk reduction while retaining the lowest annual cost necessary to maintain a company.

Qualitative Risk Analysis

As we mentioned previously, a qualitative RA does not attempt to assign hard and fast costs to the elements of the loss. It is more scenario-oriented, and as opposed to a quantitative RA, a purely qualitative risk analysis is possible. Threat frequency and impact data are required to do a qualitative RA, however.

In a qualitative risk assessment, the seriousness of threats and the relative sensitivity of the assets are given a ranking, or qualitative grading, by using a scenario approach and creating an exposure rating scale for each scenario.

During a scenario description, we match various threats to identified assets. A scenario describes the type of threat and the potential loss to which assets and selects the safeguards to mitigate the risk.

Qualitative Scenario Procedure

After the threat listing has been created, the assets for protection have been defined, and an exposure level rating is assigned, the qualitative risk assessment scenario begins. See Table 1.4 for a simple exposure rating scale.

The procedures in performing the scenario are as follows:

- A scenario is written that addresses each major threat.
- The scenario is reviewed by business unit managers for a reality check.

Table 1.4 Simple Exposure Rating Level Scale

RATING LEVEL	EXPOSURE PERCENTAGE
Blank or 0	No measurable loss
1	20% loss
2	40% loss
3	60% loss
4	80% loss
5	100% loss

- The RA team recommends and evaluates the various safeguards for each threat.
- The RA team works through each finalized scenario by using a threat, asset, and safeguard.
- The team prepares their findings and submits them to management.

After the scenarios have all been played out and the findings are published, management must implement the safeguards that were selected as being acceptable and begin to seek alternatives for the safeguards that did not work.

Asset Valuation Process

There are several elements of a process that determine the value of an asset. Both quantitative and qualitative RA (and Business Impact Assessment) procedures require a valuation made of the asset's worth to the organization. This valuation is a fundamental step in all security auditing methodologies. A common universal mistake made by organizations is not accurately identifying the information's value before implementing the security controls. This situation often results in a control that either is ill suited for asset protection, not financially effective, or protective of the wrong asset. Table 1.5 discusses quantitative versus qualitative RA.

Reasons for Determining the Value of an Asset

Here are some additional reasons to define the cost or value that we previously described:

- The asset valuation is necessary to perform the cost-benefit analysis.
- The asset's value might be necessary for insurance reasons.
- The asset's value supports safeguard selection decisions.
- The asset valuation might be necessary to satisfy "due care" and prevent negligence and legal liability.

Table 1.5 Quantitative versus Qualitative RA

PROPERTY	QUANTITATIVE	QUALITATIVE
Cost/benefit analysis	Yes	No
Financial hard costs	Yes	No
Can be automated	Yes	No
Guesswork involved	Low	High
Complex calculations	Yes	No
Volume of information required	High	Low
Time/work involved	High	Low
Ease of communication	High	Low

Elements that Determine the Value of an Asset

Three basic elements determine an information asset's value:

1. The initial and ongoing cost (to an organization) of purchasing, licensing, developing, and supporting the information asset
2. The asset's value to the organization's production operations, research and development, and business model viability
3. The asset's value established in the external marketplace and the estimated value of the intellectual property (trade secrets, patents, copyrights, and so forth)

Safeguard Selection Criteria

Once the risk analysis has been completed, safeguards and countermeasures must be researched and recommended. There are several standard principles that are used in the selection of safeguards to ensure that a safeguard is properly matched to a threat and to ensure that a safeguard most efficiently implements the necessary controls. Important criteria must be examined before selecting an effective countermeasure.

Cost-Benefit Analysis

The number one safeguard selection criteria is the cost effectiveness of the control to be implemented, which is derived through the process of the cost-benefit analysis. To determine the total cost of the safeguard, many elements need to be considered (including the following):

■ The purchase, development, and/or licensing costs of the safeguard

- The physical installation costs and the disruption to normal production during the installation and testing of the safeguard
- Normal operating costs, resource allocation, and maintenance/repair costs

The simplest calculation to compute a cost-benefit for a given safeguard is as follows:

(ALE before safeguard implementation) – (ALE after safeguard implementation) – (annual safeguard cost) = value of safeguard to the organization

For example, if an ALE of a threat has been determined to be $10,000, the ALE after the safeguard implementation is $1,000, and the annual cost to operate the safeguard totals $500, then the value of a given safeguard is thought to be $8,500 annually. This amount is then compared against the startup costs, and the benefit or lack of benefit is determined.

This value can be derived for a single safeguard or can be derived for a collection of safeguards though a series of complex calculations. In addition to the financial cost-benefit ratio, other factors can influence the decision of whether to implement a specific security safeguard. For example, an organization is exposed to legal liability if the cost to implement a safeguard is less than the cost resulting from the threat realized and the organization does not implement the safeguard.

Level of Manual Operations

The amount of manual intervention required to operate the safeguard is also a factor in the choice of a safeguard. In case after case, vulnerabilities are created due to human error or an inconsistency in application. In fact, automated systems require fail-safe defaults to allow for manual shutdown capability in case a vulnerability occurs. The more automated a process, the more sustainable and reliable that process will be.

In addition, a safeguard should not be too difficult to operate, and it should not unreasonably interfere with the normal operations of production. These characteristics are vital for the acceptance of the control by operating personnel and for acquiring the all-important management support required for the safeguard to succeed.

Auditability and Accountability Features

The safeguard must allow for the inclusion of auditing and accounting functions. The safeguard must also have the capability for auditors to audit and test it, and its accountability must be implemented to effectively track each individual who accesses the countermeasure or its features.

Recovery Ability

The safeguard's countermeasure should be evaluated with regard to its functioning state after activation or reset. During and after a reset condition, the safeguard must provide the following:

BACK DOORS

A back door, maintenance hook, or trap door is a programming element that gives application maintenance programmers access to the internals of the application, thereby bypassing the normal security controls of the application. While this function is valuable for the support and maintenance of a program, the security practitioner must be aware of these doors and provide a means of control and accountability during their use.

- No asset destruction during activation or reset
- No covert channel access to or through the control during reset
- No security loss or increase in exposure after activation or reset
- Defaults to a state that does not give any operator access or rights until the controls are fully operational

Vendor Relations

The credibility, reliability, and past performance of the safeguard vendor must be examined. In addition, the openness (open source) of the application programming should also be known in order to avoid any design secrecy that prevents later modifications or allows unknown application to have a back door into the system. Vendor support and documentation should also be considered.

Security Awareness

Although this section is our last for this chapter, it is not the least important. Security awareness is often an overlooked element of security management, because most of a security practitioner's time is spent on controls, intrusion detection, risk assessment, and proactively or reactively administering security.

It should not be that way, however. People are often the weakest link in a security chain because they are not trained or generally aware of what security is all about. Employees must understand how their actions, even seemingly insignificant actions, can greatly impact the overall security position of an organization.

Employees must be aware of the need to secure information and to protect the information assets of an enterprise. Operators need training in the skills that are required to fulfill their job functions securely, and security practitioners need training to implement and maintain the necessary security controls.

All employees need education in the basic concepts of security and its benefits to an organization. The benefits of the three pillars of security awareness training—awareness, training, and education—will manifest themselves through an improvement in the behavior and attitudes of personnel and through a significant improvement in an enterprise's security.

Awareness

As opposed to training, security awareness refers to the general, collective awareness of an organization's personnel of the importance of security and security controls. In addition to the benefits and objectives we previously mentioned, security awareness programs also have the following benefits:

- Make a measurable reduction in the unauthorized actions attempted by personnel.
- Significantly increase the effectiveness of the protection controls.
- Help to avoid the fraud, waste, and abuse of computing resources.

Personnel are considered "security aware" when they clearly understand the need for security, how security impacts viability and the bottom line, and the daily risks to computing resources.

It is important to have periodic awareness sessions to orient new employees and refresh senior employees. The material should always be direct, simple, and clear. It should be fairly motivational and should not contain a lot of techno-jargon, and you should convey it in a style that the audience easily understands. The material should show how the security interests of the organization parallel the interest of the audience and how they are important to the security protections.

Let's list a few ways that security awareness can be improved within an organization, and without a lot expense or resource drain:

Live/interactive presentations. Lectures, videos, and computer-based training (CBT).

Publishing/distribution. Posters, company newsletters, bulletins, and the intranet.

Incentives. Awards and recognition for security-related achievement.

Reminders. Login banner messages and marketing paraphernalia such as mugs, pens, sticky notes, and mouse pads.

One caveat here: It is possible to oversell security awareness and to inundate personnel with a constant barrage of reminders. This will most likely have the effect of turning off their attention. It is important to find the right balance of selling security awareness. An awareness program should be creative and frequently altered to stay fresh.

Training and Education

Training is different from awareness in that it utilizes specific classroom or one-on-one training. The following types of training are related to InfoSec:

- Security-related job training for operators and specific users
- Awareness training for specific departments or personnel groups with security-sensitive positions
- Technical security training for IT support personnel and system administrators
- Advanced InfoSec training for security practitioners and information systems auditors
- Security training for senior managers, functional managers, and business unit managers

In-depth training and education for systems personnel, auditors, and security professionals is very important and is considered necessary for career development. In addition, specific product training for security software and hardware is also vital to the protection of the enterprise.

A good starting point for defining a security training program could be the topics of policies, standards, guidelines, and procedures that are in use at an organization. A discussion of the possible environmental or natural hazards or a discussion of the recent common security errors or incidents—without blaming anyone publicly—could work. Motivating the students is always the prime directive of any training, and their understanding of the value of the security's impact to the bottom line is also vital. A common training technique is to create hypothetical security vulnerability scenarios and to get the students' input on the possible solutions or outcomes.

THE NEED FOR USER SECURITY TRAINING

All personnel using a system should have some kind of security training that is either specific to the controls employed or general security concepts. Training is especially important for those users who are handling sensitive or critical data. The advent of the microcomputer and distributed computing has created an opportunity for the serious failures of confidentiality, integrity, and availability.

Sample Questions

You can find the answers to the following questions in Appendix H.

1. Which formula accurately represents an Annualized Loss Expectancy (ALE) calculation?

   a. SLE × ARO

   b. Asset Value (AV) × EF

   c. ARO × EF – SLE

   d. % of ARO × AV

2. What is an ARO?

   a. A dollar figure assigned to a single event

   b. The annual expected financial loss to an organization from a threat

   c. A number that represents the estimated frequency of an occurrence of an expected threat

   d. The percentage of loss that a realized threat event would have on a specific asset

3. Which choice MOST accurately describes the difference between the role of a data owner versus the role of a data custodian?

   a. The custodian implements the information classification scheme after the initial assignment by the owner.

   b. The data owner implements the information classification scheme after the initial assignment by the custodian.

   c. The custodian makes the initial information classification assignments, and the operations manager implements the scheme.

   d. The custodian implements the information classification scheme after the initial assignment by the operations manager.

4. Which choice is NOT an accurate description of C.I.A.?

   a. C stands for confidentiality.

   b. I stands for integrity.

   c. A stands for availability.

   d. A stands for authorization.

5. Which group represents the MOST likely source of an asset loss through inappropriate computer use?

   a. Crackers

   b. Hackers

    c. Employees

    d. Saboteurs

6. Which choice is the BEST description of authentication as opposed to authorization?

    a. The means by which a user provides a claim of his or her identity to a system

    b. The testing or reconciliation of evidence of a user's identity

    c. A system's capability to determine the actions and behavior of a single individual within a system

    d. The rights and permissions granted to an individual to access a computer resource

7. What is a non-compulsory recommendation on how to achieve compliance with published standards called?

    a. Procedures

    b. Policies

    c. Guidelines

    d. Standards

8. Place the following four information classification levels in their proper order, from the least-sensitive classification to the most sensitive:

    _____ a. SBU

    _____ b. Top secret

    _____ c. Unclassified

    _____ d. Secret

9. How is an SLE derived?

    a. (Cost – benefit) $\times$ (% of Asset Value)

    b. AV $\times$ EF

    c. ARO $\times$ EF

    d. % of AV – implementation cost

10. What are the detailed instructions on how to perform or implement a control called?

    a. Procedures

    b. Policies

    c. Guidelines

    d. Standards

11. What is the BEST description of risk reduction?

    a. Altering elements of the enterprise in response to a risk analysis

    b. Removing all risk to the enterprise at any cost

   c. Assigning any costs associated with risk to a third party

   d. Assuming all costs associated with the risk internally

12. Which choice MOST accurately describes the differences between standards, guidelines, and procedures?

   a. Standards are recommended policies, and guidelines are mandatory policies.

   b. Procedures are step-by-step recommendations for complying with mandatory guidelines.

   c. Procedures are the general recommendations for compliance with mandatory guidelines.

   d. Procedures are step-by-step instructions for compliance with mandatory standards.

13. A purpose of a security awareness program is to improve:

   a. The security of vendor relations

   b. The performance of a company's intranet

   c. The possibility for career advancement of the IT staff

   d. The company's attitude about safeguarding data

14. What is the MOST accurate definition of a safeguard?

   a. A guideline for policy recommendations

   b. A step-by-step instructional procedure

   c. A control designed to counteract a threat

   d. A control designed to counteract an asset

15. What does an Exposure Factor (EF) describe?

   a. A dollar figure that is assigned to a single event

   b. A number that represents the estimated frequency of the occurrence of an expected threat

   c. The percentage of loss that a realized threat event would have on a specific asset

   d. The annual expected financial loss to an organization from a threat

16. Which choice would be an example of a cost-effective way to enhance security awareness in an organization?

   a. Train every employee in advanced InfoSec.

   b. Create an award or recognition program for employees.

   c. Calculate the cost-benefit ratio of the asset valuations for a risk analysis.

   d. Train only managers in implementing InfoSec controls.

17. What is the prime directive of Risk Management?

   a. Reduce the risk to a tolerable level.

   b. Reduce all risk regardless of cost.

   c. Transfer any risk to external third parties.

   d. Prosecute any employees that are violating published security policies.

18. Which choice MOST closely depicts the difference between qualitative and quantitative risk analysis?

   a. A quantitative RA does not use the hard costs of losses, and a qualitative RA does.

   b. A quantitative RA uses less guesswork than a qualitative RA.

   c. A qualitative RA uses many complex calculations.

   d. A quantitative RA cannot be automated.

19. Which choice is NOT a good criterion for selecting a safeguard?

   a. The ability to recover from a reset with the permissions set to "allow all"

   b. Comparing the potential dollar loss of an asset to the cost of a safeguard

   c. The ability to recover from a reset without damaging the asset

   d. Accountability features for tracking and identifying operators

20. Which policy type is MOST likely to contain mandatory or compulsory standards?

   a. Guidelines

   b. Advisory

   c. Regulatory

   d. Informative

21. What are high-level policies?

   a. They are recommendations for procedural controls.

   b. They are the instructions on how to perform a Quantitative Risk Analysis.

   c. They are statements that indicate a senior management's intention to support InfoSec.

   d. They are step-by-step procedures to implement a safeguard.

Bonus Questions

You can find the answers to the following questions in Appendix H.

1. Place the general information classification procedures below in their proper order:
   _____ a. Classify the data.
   _____ b. Specify the controls.
   _____ c. Specify the classification criteria.
   _____ d. Publicize awareness of the classification controls.

2. Which choice below is NOT considered an information classification role?
   a. Data owner
   b. Data custodian
   c. Data alterer
   d. Data user

3. Which choice below is NOT an example of the appropriate external distribution of classified information?
   a. Compliance with a court order
   b. Upon senior-level approval after a confidentiality agreement
   c. IAW contract procurement agreements for a government project
   d. To influence the value of the company's stock price

4. Which choice below is usually the number one-used criterion to determine the classification of an information object?
   a. Value
   b. Useful life
   c. Age
   d. Personal association

5. Which choice below is the BEST description of a vulnerability?
   a. A weakness in a system that could be exploited
   b. A company resource that could be lost due to an incident
   c. The minimization of loss associated with an incident
   d. A potential incident that could cause harm

6. Which choice below is NOT a common result of a risk analysis?
   a. A detailed listing of relevant threats
   b. Valuations of critical assets

    c. Likelihood of a potential threat

    d. Definition of business recovery roles

7. Which choice below is the BEST definition of advisory policies?

    a. Nonmandated policies, but strongly suggested

    b. Policies implemented for compliance reasons

    c. Policies implemented due to public regulation

    d. Mandatory policies implemented as a consequence of legal action

8. Which statement below BEST describes the primary purpose of risk analysis?

    a. To create a clear cost-to-value ratio for implementing security controls

    b. To influence the system design process

    c. To influence site selection decisions

    d. To quantify the impact of potential threats

9. Put the following steps in the qualitative scenario procedure in order:

    _____ a. The team prepares its findings and presents them to management.

    _____ b. A scenario is written to address each identified threat.

    _____ c. Business unit managers review the scenario for a reality check.

    _____ d. The team works through each scenario by using a threat, asset, and safeguard.

10. Which statement below is NOT correct about safeguard selection in the risk analysis process?

    a. Maintenance costs need to be included in determining the total cost of the safeguard.

    b. The best possible safeguard should always be implemented, regardless of cost.

    c. The most commonly considered criteria is the cost effectiveness of the safeguard.

    d. Many elements need to be considered in determining the total cost of the safeguard.

Advanced Sample Questions

You can find the answers to the following questions in Appendix I.

These questions are supplemental to and coordinated with Chapter 1 and are at a level on par with that of the CISSP examination.

We assume that the reader has a basic knowledge of the material contained in Chapter 1. In the security management questions areas, we will discuss data classification, security awareness, risk analysis, information system policies, and roles in information protection.

1. Which choice below most accurately reflects the goals of risk mitigation?
   a. Defining the acceptable level of risk the organization can tolerate, and reducing risk to that level
   b. Analyzing and removing all vulnerabilities and threats to security within the organization
   c. Defining the acceptable level of risk the organization can tolerate, and assigning any costs associated with loss or disruption to a third party, such as an insurance carrier
   d. Analyzing the effects of a business disruption and preparing the company's response

2. Which answer below is the BEST description of a Single Loss Expectancy (SLE)?
   a. An algorithm that represents the magnitude of a loss to an asset from a threat
   b. An algorithm that expresses the annual frequency with which a threat is expected to occur
   c. An algorithm used to determine the monetary impact of each occurrence of a threat
   d. An algorithm that determines the expected annual loss to an organization from a threat

3. Which choice below is the BEST description of an Annualized Loss Expectancy (ALE)?
   a. The expected risk factor of an annual threat event, derived by multiplying the SLE by its ARO
   b. An estimate of how often a given threat event may occur annually
   c. The percentile of the value of the asset expected to be lost, used to calculate the SLE
   d. A value determined by multiplying the value of the asset by its exposure factor

4. Which choice below is NOT an example of appropriate security management practice?

    a. Reviewing access logs for unauthorized behavior

    b. Monitoring employee performance in the workplace

    c. Researching information on new intrusion exploits

    d. Promoting and implementing security awareness programs

5. Which choice below is an accurate statement about standards?

    a. Standards are the high-level statements made by senior management in support of information systems security.

    b. Standards are the first element created in an effective security policy program.

    c. Standards are used to describe how policies will be implemented within an organization.

    d. Standards are senior management's directives to create a computer security program.

6. Which choice below is a role of the Information Systems Security Officer?

    a. The ISO establishes the overall goals of the organization's computer security program.

    b. The ISO is responsible for day-to-day security administration.

    c. The ISO is responsible for examining systems to see whether they are meeting stated security requirements.

    d. The ISO is responsible for following security procedures and reporting security problems.

7. Which statement below is NOT true about security awareness, training, and educational programs?

    a. Awareness and training help users become more accountable for their actions.

    b. Security education assists management in determining who should be promoted.

    c. Security improves the users' awareness of the need to protect information resources.

    d. Security education assists management in developing the in-house expertise to manage security programs.

8. Which choice below is NOT an accurate description of an information policy?

    a. Information policy is senior management's directive to create a computer security program.

    b. An information policy could be a decision pertaining to use of the organization's fax.

c. Information policy is a documentation of computer security decisions.

d. Information policies are created after the system's infrastructure has been designed and built.

9. Which choice below MOST accurately describes the organization's responsibilities during an unfriendly termination?

   a. System access should be removed as quickly as possible after termination.

   b. The employee should be given time to remove whatever files he needs from the network.

   c. Cryptographic keys can remain the employee's property.

   d. Physical removal from the offices would never be necessary.

10. Which choice below is NOT an example of an issue-specific policy?

    a. E-mail privacy policy

    b. Virus-checking disk policy

    c. Defined router ACLs

    d. Unfriendly employee termination policy

11. Who has the final responsibility for the preservation of the organization's information?

    a. Technology providers

    b. Senior management

    c. Users

    d. Application owners

12. Which choice below is NOT a generally accepted benefit of security awareness, training, and education?

    a. A security awareness program can help operators understand the value of the information.

    b. A security education program can help system administrators recognize unauthorized intrusion attempts.

    c. A security awareness and training program will help prevent natural disasters from occurring.

    d. A security awareness and training program can help an organization reduce the number and severity of errors and omissions.

13. Which choice below is NOT a common information-gathering technique when performing a risk analysis?

    a. Distributing a questionnaire

    b. Employing automated risk assessment tools

    c. Reviewing existing policy documents

    d. Interviewing terminated employees

14. Which choice below is an incorrect description of a control?

    a. Detective controls discover attacks and trigger preventative or corrective controls.

    b. Corrective controls reduce the likelihood of a deliberate attack.

    c. Corrective controls reduce the effect of an attack.

    d. Controls are the countermeasures for vulnerabilities.

15. Which statement below is accurate about the reasons to implement a layered security architecture?

    a. A layered security approach is not necessary when using COTS products.

    b. A good packet-filtering router will eliminate the need to implement a layered security architecture.

    c. A layered security approach is intended to increase the work-factor for an attacker.

    d. A layered approach doesn't really improve the security posture of the organization.

16. Which choice below represents an application or system demonstrating a need for a high level of confidentiality protection and controls?

    a. Unavailability of the system could result in inability to meet payroll obligations and could cause work stoppage and failure of user organizations to meet critical mission requirements. The system requires 24-hour access.

    b. The application contains proprietary business information and other financial information, which if disclosed to unauthorized sources, could cause an unfair advantage for vendors, contractors, or individuals and could result in financial loss or adverse legal action to user organizations.

    c. Destruction of the information would require significant expenditures of time and effort to replace. Although corrupted information would present an inconvenience to the staff, most information, and all vital information, is either backed up by paper documentation or on disk.

    d. The mission of this system is to produce local weather forecast information that is made available to the news media forecasters and the general public at all times. None of the information requires protection against disclosure.

17. Which choice below is an accurate statement about the difference between monitoring and auditing?

    a. Monitoring is a one-time event to evaluate security.

    b. A system audit is an ongoing "real-time" activity that examines a system.

    c. A system audit cannot be automated.

    d. Monitoring is an ongoing activity that examines either the system or the users.

18. Which statement below is accurate about the difference between issue-specific and system-specific policies?

    a. Issue-specific policy is much more technically focused.

    b. System-specific policy is much more technically focused.

    c. System-specific policy is similar to program policy.

    d. Issue-specific policy commonly addresses only one system.

19. Which statement below MOST accurately describes the difference between security awareness, security training, and security education?

    a. Security training teaches the skills that will help employees to perform their jobs more securely.

    b. Security education is required for all system operators.

    c. Security awareness is not necessary for high-level senior executives.

    d. Security training is more in depth than security education.

20. Which choice below BEST describes the difference between the System Owner and the Information Owner?

    a. There is a one-to-one relationship between system owners and information owners.

    b. One system could have multiple information owners.

    c. The Information Owner is responsible for defining the system's operating parameters.

    d. The System Owner is responsible for establishing the rules for appropriate use of the information.

21. Which choice below is NOT an accurate statement about an organization's incident-handling capability?

    a. The organization's incident-handling capability should be used to detect and punish senior-level executive wrong-doing.

    b. It should be used to prevent future damage from incidents.

c. It should be used to provide the ability to respond quickly and effectively to an incident.

d. The organization's incident-handling capability should be used to contain and repair damage done from incidents.

22. Place the data classification scheme in order, from the least secure to the most:

____ a. Sensitive

____ b. Public

____ c. Private

____ d. Confidential

23. Place the five system security life-cycle phases in order:

____ a. Implementation phase

____ b. Development/acquisition phase

____ c. Disposal phase

____ d. Operation/maintenance phase

____ e. Initiation phase

24. How often should an independent review of the security controls be performed, according to OMB Circular A-130?

a. Every year

b. Every three years

c. Every five years

d. Never

25. Which choice below is NOT one of NIST's 33 IT security principles?

a. Implement least privilege.

b. Assume that external systems are insecure.

c. Totally eliminate any level of risk.

d. Minimize the system elements to be trusted.

26. Which choice below would NOT be considered an element of proper user account management?

a. Users should never be rotated out of their current duties.

b. The users' accounts should be reviewed periodically.

c. A process for tracking access authorizations should be implemented.

d. Periodically re-screen personnel in sensitive positions.

27. Which question below is NOT accurate regarding the process of Risk Assessment?

    a. The likelihood of a threat must be determined as an element of the risk assessment.

    b. The level of impact of a threat must be determined as an element of the risk assessment.

    c. Risk assessment is the first process in the risk management methodology.

    d. Risk assessment is the final result of the risk management methodology.

28. Which choice below is NOT an accurate statement about the visibility of IT security policy?

    a. The IT security policy should not be afforded high visibility.

    b. The IT security policy could be visible through panel discussions with guest speakers.

    c. The IT security policy should be afforded high visibility.

    d. Include the IT security policy as a regular topic at staff meetings at all levels of the organization.

29. According to NIST, which choice below is not an accepted security self-testing technique?

    a. War Dialing

    b. Virus Distribution

    c. Password Cracking

    d. Virus Detection

30. Which choice below is NOT a concern of policy development at the high level?

    a. Identifying the key business resources

    b. Identifying the types of firewalls to be used for perimeter security

    c. Defining roles in the organization

    d. Determining the capability and functionality of each role.

Access Control Systems

The information security professional should be aware of access control requirements and their means of implementation to ensure a system's availability, confidentiality, and integrity. In the world of networked computers, this professional should understand the use of access control in distributed as well as centralized architectures.

The professional should also understand the threats, vulnerabilities, and risks associated with the information system's infrastructure and the preventive and detective measures that are available to counter them.

Rationale

Controlling access to information systems and associated networks is necessary for the preservation of their *confidentiality, integrity,* and *availability*. Confidentiality assures that the information is not disclosed to unauthorized persons or processes. We address integrity through the following three goals:

1. Prevention of the modification of information by unauthorized users

2. Prevention of the unauthorized or unintentional modification of information by authorized users

3. Preservation of the internal and external consistency

   a. Internal consistency ensures that internal data is consistent. For example, assume that an internal database holds the number of units of a particular item in each department of an organization. The sum of the number of units in each department should equal the total number of units that the database has recorded internally for the whole organization.

   b. External consistency ensures that the data stored in the database is consistent with the real world. Using the example previously discussed in (a), external consistency means that the number of items recorded in the database for each department is equal to the number of items that physically exist in that department.

Availability assures that a system's authorized users have timely and uninterrupted access to the information in the system. The additional access control objectives are reliability and utility.

These and other related objectives flow from the organizational security policy. This policy is a high-level statement of management intent regarding the control of access to information and the personnel who are authorized to receive that information.

Three things that you must consider for the planning and implementation of access control mechanisms are the threats to the system, the system's vulnerability to these threats, and the risk that the threat might materialize. We further define these concepts as follows:

Threat. An event or activity that has the potential to cause harm to the information systems or networks

Vulnerability. A weakness or lack of a safeguard that can be exploited by a threat, causing harm to the information systems or networks

Risk. The potential for harm or loss to an information system or network; the probability that a threat will materialize

Controls

Controls are implemented to mitigate risk and reduce the potential for loss. Controls can be *preventive*, *detective*, or *corrective*. Preventive controls are put in place to inhibit harmful occurrences; detective controls are established to discover harmful occurrences; and corrective controls are used to restore systems that are victims of harmful attacks.

To implement these measures, controls can be *administrative*, *logical* or *technical*, and *physical*.

■ Administrative controls include policies and procedures, security awareness training, background checks, work habit checks, a review of vacation history, and increased supervision.

■ Logical or technical controls involve the restriction of access to systems and the protection of information. Examples of these types of controls are encryption, smart cards, access control lists, and transmission protocols.

■ Physical controls incorporate guards and building security in general, such as the locking of doors, the securing of server rooms or laptops, the protection of cables, the separation of duties, and the backing up of files.

Controls provide accountability for individuals who are accessing sensitive information. This accountability is accomplished through access control mechanisms that require identification and authentication and through the audit function. These controls must be in accordance with and accurately represent the organization's security policy. Assurance procedures ensure that the control mechanisms correctly implement the security policy for the entire life cycle of an information system.

In general, a group of processes that share access to the same resources is called a *protection domain*.

Models for Controlling Access

Controlling access by a *subject* (an active entity such as an individual or process) to an *object* (a passive entity such as a file) involves setting up access rules. These rules can be classified into three categories or models:

Mandatory Access Control. The authorization of a subject's access to an object depends upon *labels*, which indicate the subject's *clearance*, and the *classification* or *sensitivity* of the object. For example, the military classifies documents as unclassified, confidential, secret, and top secret. Similarly, an individual can receive a clearance of confidential, secret, or top secret and can have access to documents classified at or below his or her specified clearance level. Thus, an individual with a clearance of "secret" can have access to secret and confidential documents with a restriction. This restriction is that the individual must have a *need to know* relative to the classified documents involved. Therefore, the documents must be necessary for that individual to complete an assigned task. Even if the individual is cleared for a classification level of information, unless there is a need to know the individual should not access the information. *Rule-based* access control is a type of mandatory access control because rules determine this access (such as the correspondence of clearance labels to classification labels), rather than the identity of the subjects and objects alone.

Discretionary Access Control. The subject has authority, within certain limitations, to specify what objects are accessible. For example, access control lists can be used. An *access control list* (ACL) is a list denoting which users have what privileges to a particular resource. For example, a tabular listing would show the subjects or users who have access to the object, FILE X, and what privileges they have with respect to that file. An access control *triple* consists of the user, program, and file with the corresponding access privileges noted for each user. This type of access control is used in local, dynamic situations where the subjects must have the discretion to specify what resources certain users are permitted to access. When a user within certain limitations has the right to alter the access control to certain objects, this is termed as *user-directed* discretionary access control. An *identity-based* access control is a type of discretionary access control based on an individual's identity. In some instances, a *hybrid* approach is used, which combines the features of user-based and identity-based discretionary access control.

Non-Discretionary Access Control. A central authority determines what subjects can have access to certain objects based on the organizational security policy. The access controls might be based on the individual's role in the organization (*role-based*) or the subject's responsibilities and duties (*task-based*). In an organization where there are frequent personnel changes, non-discretionary access control is useful because the access controls are based on the individual's role or title within the organization. These access controls do not need to be changed whenever a new person takes over that role. Another type of non-discretionary access control is *lattice-based* access control. In this type of control, a lattice model is applied. In a lattice model, there are pairs of elements that have the least upper bound of values and greatest lower bound of values. To apply this concept to access control, the pair of elements is the subject and object, and the subject has the greatest lower bound and the least upper bound of access rights to an object.

Access control can also be characterized as context-dependent or content-dependent. *Context-dependent* access control is a function of factors such as location, time of day, and previous access history. It is concerned with the environment or context of the data. In *content-dependent* access control, access is determined by the information contained in the item being accessed.

Control Combinations

By combining preventive and detective control types with the administrative, technical (logical), and physical means of implementation, the following pairings are obtained:

- Preventive/administrative
- Preventive/technical
- Preventive/physical
- Detective/administrative
- Detective/technical
- Detective/physical

Next, we discuss these six pairings and the key elements that are associated with their control mechanisms.

Preventive/Administrative

In this pairing, we place emphasis on "soft" mechanisms that support the access control objectives. These mechanisms include organizational policies and procedures, pre-employment background checks, strict hiring practices, employment agreements, friendly and unfriendly employee termination procedures, vacation scheduling, labeling of sensitive materials, increased supervision, security awareness training, behavior awareness, and sign-up procedures to obtain access to information systems and networks.

Preventive/Technical

The preventive/technical pairing uses technology to enforce access control policies. These technical controls are also known as logical controls and can be built into the operating system, can be software applications, or can be supplemental hardware/software units. Some typical preventive/technical controls are protocols, encryption, smart cards, biometrics (for *authentication*), local and remote access control software packages, call-back systems, passwords, constrained user interfaces, menus, shells, database views, limited keypads, and virus scanning software. *Protocols, encryption,* and *smart cards* are technical mechanisms for protecting information and passwords from disclosure. *Biometrics* apply technologies such as fingerprint, retina, and iris scans to authenticate individuals requesting access to resources, and *access control software packages* manage access to resources holding information from subjects local to the information system or from those at remote locations. *Callback* systems provide access protection by calling back the number of a previously authorized location, but this control can be compromised by call forwarding. *Constrained user interfaces* limit the functions that a user can select. For example, some functions might be "grayed-out" on the user menu and cannot be chosen. *Shells* limit the system-level commands that an individual or process can use. *Database views* are mechanisms that restrict the information that a user can access in a database. *Limited keypads* have a small number of keys that the user can select. Thus, the functions that are intended not to be accessible by the user are not represented on any of the available keys.

Preventive/Physical

Many preventive/physical measures are intuitive. These measures are intended to restrict the physical access to areas with systems holding sensitive information. A circular *security perimeter* that is under access control defines the area or zone to be protected. Preventive/physical controls include fences, badges, multiple doors (a man-trap that consists of two doors physically separated so that an individual can be "trapped" in the space between the doors after entering one of the doors), magnetic card entry systems, biometrics (*for identification*), guards, dogs, environmental control systems (temperature, humidity, and so forth), and building and access area layout. Preventive/physical measures also apply to areas that are used for storage of the backup data files.

Detective/Administrative

Several detective/administrative controls overlap with preventive/administrative controls because they can be applied for the prevention of future security policy violations or to detect existing violations. Examples of such controls are organizational policies and procedures, background checks, vacation scheduling, the labeling of sensitive materials, increased supervision, security awareness training, and behavior awareness. Additional detective/administrative controls are job rotation, the sharing of responsibilities, and reviews of audit records.

Detective/Technical

The detective/technical control measures are intended to reveal the violations of security policy by using technical means. These measures include intrusion detection systems and automatically generated violation reports from audit trail information. These reports can indicate variations from "normal" operation or detect known signatures of unauthorized access episodes. In order to limit the amount of audit information flagged and reported by automated violation analysis and reporting mechanisms, *clipping levels* can be set. Using clipping levels refers to setting allowable thresholds on a reported activity. For example, a clipping level of three can be set for reporting failed logon attempts at a workstation. Thus, three or fewer logon attempts by an individual at a workstation are not reported as a violation, thus eliminating the need for reviewing normal logon entry errors.

Due to the importance of the audit information, audit records should be protected at the highest level of sensitivity in the system.

Detective/Physical

Detective/physical controls usually require a human to evaluate the input from sensors or cameras to determine whether a real threat exists. Some of these control types are motion detectors, thermal detectors, and video cameras.

Identification and Authentication

Identification and authentication are the keystones of most access control systems. *Identification* is the act of a user professing an identity to a system, usually in the form of a logon ID to the system. Identification establishes user accountability for the actions on the system. *Authentication* is verification that the user's claimed identity is valid, and is usually implemented through a user password at logon time. Authentication is based on the following three factor types:

Type 1. Something you know, such as a personal identification number (PIN) or password

Type 2. Something you have, such as an ATM card or smart card

Type 3. Something you are (physically), such as a fingerprint or retina scan

Sometimes a fourth factor, something you do, is added to this list. Something you do might be typing your name or other phrases on a keyboard. Conversely, something you do can be considered something you are.

Two-Factor Authentication refers to the act of requiring two of the three factors to be used in the authentication process. For example, withdrawing funds from an ATM machine requires a two-factor authentication in the form of the ATM card (something you have) and a PIN number (something you know).

Passwords

Passwords can be compromised and must be protected. In the ideal case, a password should only be used once. This *"one-time password"* provides maximum security because a new password is required for each new logon. A password that is the same for each logon is called a *static password*. A password that changes with each logon is termed a *dynamic password*. The changing of passwords can also fall between these two extremes. Passwords can be required to change monthly, quarterly, or at other intervals, depending on the criticality of the information needing protection and the password's frequency of use. Obviously, the more times a password is used, the more chance there is of it being compromised. A *passphrase* is a sequence of characters that is usually longer than the allotted number for a password. The passphrase is converted into a virtual password by the system.

Tokens in the form of credit card-sized memory cards or smart cards, or those resembling small calculators, supply static and dynamic passwords. These types of tokens are examples of something you have. An ATM card is a memory card that stores your specific information. Smart cards provide even more capability by incorporating additional processing power on the card. The following are the four types of smart cards:

- Static password tokens
  - The owner authenticates himself to the token.
  - The token authenticates the owner to an information system.
- Synchronous dynamic password tokens
  - The token generates a new, unique password value at fixed time intervals (this password could be the time of day encrypted with a secret key).
  - The unique password is entered into a system or workstation along with an owner's PIN.
  - The authentication entity in a system or workstation knows an owner's secret key and PIN, and the entity verifies that the entered password is valid and that it was entered during the valid time window.
- Asynchronous dynamic password tokens
  - This scheme is similar to the synchronous dynamic password scheme, except the new password is generated asynchronously and does not have to fit into a time window for authentication.
- Challenge-response tokens
  - A workstation or system generates a random challenge string, and the owner enters the string into the token along with the proper PIN.
  - The token generates a response that is then entered into the workstation or system.
  - The authentication mechanism in the workstation or system then determines whether the owner should be authenticated.

In all these schemes, a front-end authentication device and a back-end authentication server, which services multiple workstations or the host, can perform the authentication.

Biometrics

An alternative to using passwords for authentication in logical or technical access control is biometrics. Biometrics are based on the Type 3 authentication mechanism: something you are. *Biometrics are defined as an automated means of identifying or authenticating the identity of a living person based on physiological or behavioral characteristics.* In biometrics, *identification* is a "one-to-many" search of an individual's characteristics from a database of stored images. Authentication in biometrics is a "one-to-one" search to verify a claim to an identity made by a person. *Biometrics is used for identification in physical controls and for authentication in logical controls.*

There are three main performance measures in biometrics:

False Rejection Rate **(FRR) or Type I Error.** The percentage of valid subjects that are falsely rejected

False Acceptance Rate **(FAR) or Type II Error.** The percentage of invalid subjects that are falsely accepted

Crossover Error Rate **(CER).** The percent in which the FRR equals the FAR

Almost all types of detection permit a system's sensitivity to be increased or decreased during an inspection process. If the system's sensitivity is increased, such as in an airport metal detector, the system becomes increasingly selective and has a higher FRR. Conversely, if the sensitivity is decreased, the FAR will increase. Thus, to have a valid measure of the system performance, the CER is used. We show these concepts in Figure 2.1.

In addition to the accuracy of the biometric systems, there are other factors that must also be considered. These factors include the *enrollment time*, the *throughput rate*, and *acceptability*. Enrollment time is the time that it takes to initially "register" with a system by providing samples of the biometric characteristic to be evaluated. An acceptable enrollment time is around two minutes. For example, in fingerprint systems the actual fingerprint is stored and requires approximately 250KB per finger for a high-quality image. This level of information is required for one-to-many searches in forensics applications on very large databases. In finger-scan technology, a full fingerprint is not stored; rather, the features extracted from this fingerprint are stored by using a small template that requires approximately 500 to 1,000 bytes of storage. The original fingerprint cannot be reconstructed from this template. Finger-scan technology is used for one-to-one verification by using smaller databases. Updates of the enrollment information might be required because some biometric characteristics, such as voice and signature, might change with time.

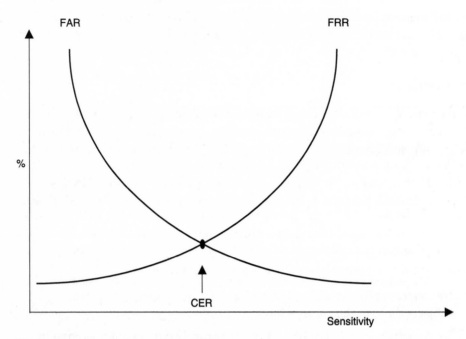

Figure 2.1   Crossover Error Rate (CER).

The throughput rate is the rate at which the system processes and identifies or authenticates individuals. Acceptable throughput rates are in the range of 10 subjects per minute. Acceptability refers to considerations of privacy, invasiveness, and psychological and physical comfort when using the system. For example, a concern with retina scanning systems might be the exchange of body fluids on the eyepiece. Another concern would be the retinal pattern that could reveal changes in a person's health, such as diabetes or high blood pressure.

Collected biometric images are stored in an area referred to as a *corpus*. The corpus is stored in a database of images. Potential sources of error are the corruption of images during collection and mislabeling or other transcription problems associated with the database. Therefore, the image collection process and storage must be performed carefully with constant checking. These images are collected during the enrollment process and thus are critical to the correct operation of the biometric device.

The following are typical biometric characteristics that are used to uniquely authenticate an individual's identity:

- Fingerprints
- Retina scans
- Iris scans

- Facial scans
- Palm scans
- Hand geometry
- Voice
- Handwritten signature dynamics

Single Sign-On (SSO)

Single Sign-On (SSO) addresses the cumbersome situation of logging on multiple times to access different resources. A user must remember numerous passwords and IDs and might take shortcuts in creating passwords that might be open to exploitation. In SSO, a user provides one ID and password per work session and is automatically logged on to all the required applications. For SSO security, the passwords should not be stored or transmitted in the clear. SSO applications can run either on a user's workstation or on authentication servers. The advantages of SSO include having the ability to use stronger passwords, easier administration of changing or deleting the passwords, and requiring less time to access resources. The major disadvantage of many SSO implementations is that once a user obtains access to the system through the initial logon, the user can freely roam the network resources without any restrictions.

The Open Group has defined functional objectives in support of a user SSO interface. These objectives include the following:

- The interface shall be independent of the type of authentication information handled.
- It shall not predefine the timing of secondary sign-on operations.
- Support shall be provided for a subject to establish a default user profile.

Authentication mechanisms include items such as smart cards and magnetic badges. Strict controls must be placed to prevent a user from changing configurations that another authority sets. The scope of the Open Group SSO Standards is to define services in support of the following:

- "The development of applications to provide a common, single end-user sign-on interface for an enterprise"
- "The development of applications for the coordinated management of multiple user account management information bases maintained by an enterprise"

SSO can be implemented by using scripts that replay the users' multiple logins or by using authentication servers to verify a user's identity and encrypted authentication tickets to permit access to system services.

Enterprise Access Management (EAM) provides access control management services to Web-based enterprise systems that include SSO. SSO can be provided in a number of ways. For example, SSO can be implemented on Web applications in the same domain residing on different servers by using non-persistent, encrypted cookies on the client interface. This task is accomplished by providing a cookie to each application that the user wishes to access. Another solution is to build a secure credential for each user on a reverse proxy that is situated in front of the Web server. The credential is then presented at each instance of a user attempting to access protected Web applications.

Kerberos, SESAME, KryptoKnight, and NetSP are authentication server systems with operational modes that can implement SSO.

Kerberos

Kerberos is a trusted, third-party authentication protocol developed under Project Athena at the Massachusetts Institute of Technology (MIT). In Greek mythology, Kerberos is a three-headed dog that guards the entrance to the underworld.

Using symmetric key cryptography, Kerberos authenticates clients to other entities on a network of which a client requires services. The rationale and architecture behind Kerberos can be illustrated by using a university environment as an example. In such an environment, there are thousands of locations for workstations, local networks, and PC computer clusters. Client locations and computers are not secure; thus, one cannot assume that the cabling is secure. Messages, therefore, are not secure from interception. A few specific locations and servers can be secured, however, and can serve as trusted authentication mechanisms for every client and service on that network. These centralized servers implement the Kerberos-trusted Key Distribution Center (KDC), Kerberos Ticket Granting Service (TGS), and Kerberos Authentication Service (AS). Windows 2000 provides Kerberos implementations.

The basic principles of Kerberos operation are as follows:

1. The KDC knows the secret keys of all clients and servers on the network.

2. The KDC initially exchanges information with the client and server by using these secret keys.

3. Kerberos authenticates a client to a requested service on a server through TGS and by issuing temporary symmetric session keys for communications between the client and KDC, the server and the KDC, and the client and server.

4. Communication then takes place between the client and the server by using those temporary session keys.

Table 2.1 Kerberos Items and Symbols

KERBEROS ITEM	SYMBOL
Client	C
Client secret key	K_c
Client network address	A
Server	S
Client/TGS session key	$K_{c, tgs}$
TGS secret key	K_{tgs}
Server secret key	K_s
Client/server session key	$K_{c, s}$
Client/TGS ticket	$T_{c, tgs}$
Client to server ticket	$T_{c, s}$
Client to server authenticator	$A_{c, s}$
Starting and ending time ticket is valid	V
Timestamp	T
M encrypted in secret key of x	$[M] K_x$
Ticket Granting Ticket	TGT
Optional, additional session key	Key

Table 2.1 explains this detailed procedure using the Kerberos terminology and symbols.

Kerberos Operation

Next, we examine in more detail the exchange of messages among the client, TGS Server, Authentication Server, and the server that is providing the service.

Client-TGS Server: Initial Exchange

To initiate a request for service from a server (or servers), the user enters an ID and password on the client workstation. The client temporarily generates the client's secret key (K_c) from the password by using a one-way hash function. (The one-way hash function performs a mathematical encryption operation on the password that cannot be reversed.) The client sends a request for authentication to the TGS server by using the client's ID in the clear. Note that no password or secret key is sent. If the client is in the Authentication Server database, the TGS server returns a client/TGS session key ($K_{c, tgs}$), which is encrypted in the secret key of the client, and a *Ticket Granting Ticket* (TGT) encrypted in the secret key (K_{tgs}) of the TGS server. Thus, neither the client nor any other entity except the TGS server can read the contents of the TGT, because only the TGS server knows the K_{tgs}. The TGT consists of the client ID, the client network address, the starting and ending time that the ticket is valid (v), and the client/TGS session key. Symbolically, these initial messages from the TGS server to the client are represented as follows:

$[K_{c, tgs}]K_c$

$TGT = [c, a, v, K_{c, tgs}] K_{tgs}$

The client decrypts the message containing the session key ($K_{c, tgs}$) with its secret key (K_c) and now uses this session key to communicate with the TGS server. Then, the client erases its stored secret key to avoid compromising the secret key.

Client to TGS Server: Request for Service

When requesting access to a specific service on the network from the TGS server, the client sends two messages to the TGS server. In one message, the client submits the previously obtained TGT, which is encrypted in the secret key (K_{tgs}) of the TGS server, and an identification of the server (s) from which service is requested. The other message is an authenticator that is encrypted in the assigned session key ($K_{c, tgs}$). The authenticator contains the client ID, a timestamp, and an optional additional session key. These two messages are as follows:

$TGT = s, [c, a, v, K_{c, tgs}] K_{tgs}$
$Authenticator = [c, t, key] K_{c, tgs}$

TGS Server to Client: Issuing of Ticket for Service

After receiving a valid TGT and an authenticator from the client requesting a service, the TGS server issues a ticket ($T_{c, s}$) to the client that is encrypted in the server's secret key (K_s) and a client/server session key ($K_{c, s}$) that is encrypted in the client/TGS session key ($K_{c, tgs}$). These two messages are as follows:

$Ticket\ T_{c, s} = s, [c, a, v, K_{c, s}] K_s$
$[K_{c, s}] K_{c, tgs}$

Client to Server Authentication: Exchange and Providing of Service

To receive service from the server (or servers), the client sends the ticket ($T_{c, s}$) and an authenticator to the server. The server decrypts the message with its secret key (K_s) and checks the contents. The contents contain the client's address, the valid time window (v), and the client/server session key ($K_{c,s}$), which will now be used for communication between the client and server. The server also checks the authenticator, and if that timestamp is valid, it provides the requested service to the client. The client messages to the server are as follows:

Ticket $T_{c,s}$ = s, [c, a, v, $K_{c,s}$]K_s
Authenticator = [c, t, key] $K_{c,s}$

Kerberos Vulnerabilities

Kerberos addresses the confidentiality and integrity of information. It does not directly address availability and attacks, such as frequency analysis. Furthermore, because all the secret keys are held and authentication is performed on the Kerberos TGS and the authentication servers, these servers are vulnerable to both physical attacks and attacks from malicious code. Replay can be accomplished on Kerberos if the compromised tickets are used within an allotted time window. Because a client's password is used in the initiation of the Kerberos request for the service protocol, password guessing can be used to impersonate a client.

The keys used in the Kerberos exchange are also vulnerable. A client's secret key is stored temporarily on the client workstation and can be compromised as well as the session keys that are stored at the client's computer and at the servers.

SESAME

To address some of the weaknesses in Kerberos, the *Secure European System for Applications in a multi-vendor Environment* (SESAME) project uses public key cryptography for the distribution of secret keys and provides additional access control support. It uses the Needham-Schroeder protocol and a trusted authentication server at each host to reduce the key management requirements. SESAME employs the MD5 and crc32 one-way hash functions. In addition, SESAME incorporates two certificates or tickets. One certificate provides authentication as in Kerberos, and the other certificate defines the access privileges assigned to a client. One weakness in SESAME is that it authenticates by using the first block of a message only and not the complete message. SESAME is also subject to password guessing (like Kerberos).

KryptoKnight

The IBM KryptoKnight system provides authentication, SSO, and key distribution services. It was designed to support computers with widely varying computational capabilities. KryptoKnight uses a trusted Key Distribution Center (KDC) that knows the secret key of each party. One of the differences between Kerberos and KrytpoKnight is that there is a peer-to-peer relationship among the parties and the KDC. To implement SSO, the KDC has a party's secret key that is a one-way hash transformation of their password. The initial exchange from the party to the KDC is the user's name and a value, which is a function of a nonce (a randomly-generated, one-time use authenticator) and the password. The KDC authenticates the user and sends the user a ticket encrypted with the user's secret key. The user decrypts this ticket and can use it for authentication to obtain services from other servers on the system. NetSP is a product that is based on KryptoKnight and uses a workstation as an authentication server. NetSP tickets are compatible with a number of access control services, including the Resource Access Control Facility (RACF).

Access Control Methodologies

Access control implementations are as diverse as their requirements. However, access control can be divided into two domains: centralized access control and decentralized/distributed access control. In the following sections, we summarize the mechanisms to achieve both types.

Centralized Access Control

Dial-up users can use the standard Remote Authentication and Dial-In User Service (*RADIUS*). RADIUS incorporates an authentication server and dynamic passwords. Users can also use *Callback*. In Callback, a remote user dials in to the authentication server, provides an ID and password, and then hangs up. The authentication server looks up the caller's ID in a database of authorized users and obtains a phone number at a fixed location. (Note that the remote user must be calling from that location.) The authentication server then calls the phone number, the user answers, and then the user has access to the system. In some Callback implementations, the user must enter another password upon receiving a Callback. The disadvantage of this system is that the user must be at a fixed location whose phone number is known to the authentication server. A threat to Callback is that a cracker can arrange to have the call automatically forwarded to their number, enabling access to the system.

Another approach to remote access is the Challenge Handshake Authentication Protocol (CHAP). CHAP protects the password from eavesdroppers and supports the encryption of communication.

For networked applications, the Terminal Access Controller Access Control System (TACACS) employs a user ID and a static password for network access. *TACACS+* provides even stronger protection through the use of tokens for two-factor, dynamic password authentication.

Decentralized/Distributed Access Control

A powerful approach to controlling the access of information in a decentralized environment is through the use of databases. In particular, the relational model developed by E. F. Codd of IBM (circa 1970) has been the focus of much research in providing information security. Other database models include models that are hierarchical, network, object-oriented, and object-relational. The relational and object-relational database models support queries while the traditional file systems and the object-oriented database model do not. The object-relational and object-oriented models are better suited to managing complex data, such as what is required for computer-aided design and imaging. Because the bulk of information security research and development has focused on relational databases, this section emphasizes the relational model.

Relational Database Security

A relational database model has three parts:

- Data structures called tables or relations
- Integrity rules on allowable values and value combinations in the tables
- Operators on the data in the tables

A *database* can be defined as a persistent collection of interrelated data items. Persistency is obtained through the preservation of integrity and through the use of non-volatile storage media. The description of the database is a *schema*, and a Data Description Language (DDL) defines the schema. A database management system (DBMS) is the software that maintains and provides access to the database. For security, you can set up the DBMS so that only certain subjects are permitted to perform certain operations on the database. For example, a particular user can be restricted to certain information in the database and will not be allowed to view any other information.

A *relation* is the basis of a relational database and is represented by a two-dimensional table. The rows of the table represent *records* or *tuples,* and the columns of the table represent the *attributes*. The number of rows in the relation is referred to as the *cardinality*, and the number of columns is the *degree*. The *domain* of a relation is the set of allowable values that an attribute can take. For example, a relation might be PARTS, as shown in Table 2.2, or ELECTRICAL ITEMS, as shown in Table 2.3.

Table 2.2 PARTS Relation

PART NUMBER	PART NAME	PART TYPE	LOCATION
E2C491	Alternator	Electrical	B261
M4D326	Idle Gear	Mechanical	C418
E5G113	Fuel Gauge	Electrical	B561

Table 2.3 ELECTRICAL ITEMS Relation

SERIAL NUMBER	PART NUMBER	PART NAME	PART COST
S367790	E2C491	Alternator	$200
S785439	E5D667	Control Module	$700
S677322	E5W459	Window Motor	$300

In each table, a *primary key* is required. A primary key is a unique identifier in the table that unambiguously points to an individual tuple or record in the table. A primary key is a subset of candidate keys within the table. A *candidate key* is an attribute that is a unique identifier within a given table. In Table 2.2, for example, the primary key would be the Part Number. If the Location of the part in Table 2.2 were unique to that part, it might be used as the primary key. Then, the Part Numbers and Locations would be considered candidate keys and the primary key would be taken from one of these two attributes. Now, assume that the Part Number attributes in Table 2.2 are the primary keys. If an attribute in one relation has values matching the primary key in another relation, this attribute is called a *foreign key*. A foreign key does not have to be the primary key of its containing relation. For example, the Part Number attribute E2C491 in Table 2.3 is a foreign key because its value corresponds to the primary key attribute in Table 2.2.

Entity and Referential Integrity

Continuing with the example, if we designate the Part Number as the primary key in Table 2.2, then each row in the table must have a Part Number attribute. If the Part Number attribute is NULL, then *Entity Integrity* has been violated. Similarly, the *Referential Integrity* requires that for any foreign key attribute, the referenced relation must have a tuple with the same value for its primary key. Thus, if the attribute E2C491 of Table 2.3 is a foreign key of Table 2.2, then E2C491 must be a primary key in Table 2.2 to hold the referential integrity.

Foreign key to primary key matches are important because they represent references from one relation to another and establish the connections among these relations.

Relational Database Operations

A number of operations in a relational algebra are used to build relations and operate on the data. Five of these operations are primitives, and the other operations can be defined in terms of those five. Later, we discuss in greater detail some of the more commonly applied operations. The operations include the following:

- Select (primitive)
- Project (primitive)
- Union (primitive)
- Difference (primitive)
- Product (primitive)
- Join
- Intersection
- Divide
- Views

For clarification, the Select operation defines a new relation based on a formula (for example, all the electrical parts whose cost exceed $300 in Table 2.3). The Join operation selects tuples that have equal numbers for some attributes—for example, in Tables 2.2 and 2.3, Serial Numbers and Locations can be joined by the common Part Number. The Union operation forms a new relation from two other relations (for example, for relations that we call X and Y, the new relation consists of each tuple that is in either X or Y or both).

An important operation related to controlling the access of database information is the View. A *View* is defined from the operations of Join, Project, and Select. A View does not exist in a physical form, and can be considered as a virtual table that is derived from other tables. (A relation that actually exists in the database is called a *base relation*.) These other tables could be tables that exist within the database or previously defined Views. You can think of a View as a way to develop a table that is going to be frequently used although it might not physically exist within the database. Views can be used to restrict access to certain information within the database, to hide attributes, and to implement content-dependent access restrictions. Thus, an individual requesting access to information within a database will be presented with a View containing the information that the person is allowed to see. The View will then hide the information that individual is not allowed to see. In this way, the View can be thought of as implementing *Least Privilege*.

In developing a query of the relational database, an optimization process is performed. This process includes generating query plans and selecting the best (lowest in cost) of the plans. A *query plan* is comprised of implementation procedures that correspond to each of the low-level operations in that query. The selection of the lowest-cost plan involves assigning costs to the plan. Costs might be a function of disk accesses and CPU usage.

In statistical database queries, a protection mechanism that is used to limit inferencing of information is the specification of a minimum query set size, but prohibiting the querying of all but one of the records in the database. This control thwarts an attack of gathering statistics on a query set size M, equal to or greater than the minimum query set size, and then requesting the same statistics on a query set size of M + 1. The second query set would be designed to include the individual whose information is being sought surreptitiously. When querying a database for statistical information, individually identifiable information should be protected. Thus, requiring a minimum size for the query set (greater than one) offers protection against gathering information on one individual.

A bind is also applied in conjunction with a plan to develop a query. A *bind* creates the plan and fixes or resolves the plan. *Bind variables* are placeholders for literal values in a Structured Query Language (SQL) query being sent to the database on a server. The SQL statement is sent to the server for parsing, and then later values are bound to the placeholders and sent separately to the server. This separate binding step is the origin of the term *bind variable*.

Data Normalization

Normalization is an important part of database design that ensures that attributes in a table depend only on the primary key. This process makes it easier to maintain data and have consistent reports.

Normalizing data in the database consists of three steps:

1. Eliminating any repeating groups by putting them into separate tables
2. Eliminating redundant data (occurring in more than one table)
3. Eliminating attributes in a table that are not dependent on the primary key of that table

SQL

Developed at IBM, SQL is a standard data manipulation and relational database definition language. The SQL Data Definition Language creates and deletes views and relations (tables). SQL commands include Select, Update, Delete, Insert, Grant, and Revoke. The latter two commands are used in access control to grant and revoke privileges to resources. Usually, the owner of an object can withhold or transfer GRANT privileges related to an object to another subject. If the owner intentionally does not transfer the GRANT privileges, however, which are relative to an object to the individual A, A cannot pass on the GRANT privileges to another subject. In some instances, however, this security control can be circumvented. For example, if A copies the object, A essentially becomes the owner of that object and thus can transfer the GRANT privileges to another user, such as user B.

SQL security issues include the granularity of authorization and the number of different ways you can execute the same query.

Object-Oriented Databases (OODB)

Relational database models are ideal for business transactions where most of the information is in text form. Complex applications involving multimedia, computer-aided design, video, graphics, and expert systems are more suited to an object-oriented database (OODB). For example, an OODB places no restrictions on the types or sizes of data elements, as is the case with relational databases. An OODB has the characteristics of ease of reusing code and analysis, reduced maintenance, and an easier transition from analysis of the problem to design and implementation. Its main disadvantages are a steep learning curve, even for experienced traditional programmers, and a high overhead of hardware and software required for development and operation.

Object-Relational Databases

The object-relational database is the marriage of object-oriented and relational technologies and combines the attributes of both. This model was introduced in 1992 with the release of the UniSQL/X unified relational and object-oriented database system. Hewlett Packard then released OpenODB (later called Odapter), which extended its AllBase relational Database Management System.

Intrusion Detection

An Intrusion Detection System (IDS) is a system that monitors network traffic or monitors host audit logs in order to determine whether any violations of an organization's security policy have taken place. An IDS can detect intrusions that have circumvented or passed through a firewall or that are occurring within the local area network behind the firewall.

A truly effective IDS will detect common attacks as they occur, which includes distributed attacks. This type of IDS is called a *network-based* IDS because it monitors network traffic in real time. Conversely, a *host-based* IDS resides on centralized hosts.

A Network-Based IDS

A network-based IDS usually provides reliable, real-time information without consuming network or host resources. A network-based IDS is passive when acquiring data. Because a network-based IDS reviews packets and headers, it can also detect *denial of service* (DoS) attacks. Furthermore, because this IDS is monitoring an attack in real time, it can also respond to an attack in progress to limit damage.

A problem with a network-based IDS system is that it will not detect attacks against a host made by an intruder who is logged in at the host's terminal. If a network IDS along with some additional support mechanism determines that an attack is being mounted against a host, it is usually not capable of determining the type or effectiveness of the attack being launched.

A Host-Based IDS

A host-based IDS can review the system and event logs in order to detect an attack on the host and to determine whether the attack was successful. (It is also easier to respond to an attack from the host.) Detection capabilities of host-based ID systems are limited by the incompleteness of most host audit log capabilities.

IDS Detection Methods

An IDS detects an attack through two major mechanisms: a signature-based ID or a statistical anomaly-based ID. These approaches are also termed Knowledge-based and Behavior-based ID, respectively, and are reinforced in Chapter 3, "Telecommunications and Network Security."

A Signature-Based ID

In a signature-based ID, signatures or attributes, which characterize an attack, are stored for reference. Then, when data about events are acquired from host audit logs or from network packet monitoring, this data is compared with the attack signature database. If there is a match, a response is initiated. A weakness of this approach is the failure to characterize slow attacks that extend over a long time period. To identify these types of attacks, large amounts of information must be held for extended time periods.

Another issue with signature-based IDs is that only attack signatures that are stored in their database are detected.

A Statistical Anomaly-Based ID

With this method, an IDS acquires data and defines a "normal" usage profile for the network or host that is being monitored. This characterization is accomplished by taking statistical samples of the system over a period of normal use. Typical characterization information used to establish a normal profile includes memory usage, CPU utilization, and network packet types. With this approach, new attacks can be detected because they produce abnormal system statistics. Some disadvantages of a statistical anomaly-based ID are that it will not detect an attack that does not significantly change the system operating characteristics, or it might falsely detect a non-attack event that had caused a momentary anomaly in the system.

Some Access Control Issues

As we discussed earlier in this chapter, the cost of access control must be commensurate with the value of the information being protected. The value of this information is determined through qualitative and quantitative methods. These methods incorporate factors such as the cost to develop or acquire the information, the importance of the information to an organization and its competitors, and the effect on the organization's reputation if the information is compromised.

Access control must offer protection from an unauthorized, unanticipated, or unintentional modification of information. This protection should preserve the data's internal and external consistency. The confidentiality of the information must also be similarly maintained, and the information should be available on a timely basis. These factors cover the integrity, confidentiality, and availability components of information system security.

Accountability is another facet of access control. Individuals on a system are responsible for their actions. This accountability property enables system activities to be traced to the proper individuals. Accountability is supported by audit trails that record events on the system and on the network. Audit trails can be used for intrusion detection and for the reconstruction of past events. Monitoring individual activities, such as keystroke monitoring, should be accomplished in accordance with the company policy and appropriate laws. Banners at logon time should notify the user of any monitoring being conducted.

The following measures compensate for both internal and external access violations:

- Backups
- RAID (Redundant Array of Independent Disks) technology
- Fault tolerance
- Business continuity planning
- Insurance

Sample Questions

You can find the answers to the following questions in Appendix H.

1. The goals of integrity do NOT include:
   a. Accountability of responsible individuals
   b. Prevention of the modification of information by unauthorized users
   c. Prevention of the unauthorized or unintentional modification of information by authorized users
   d. Preservation of internal and external consistency

2. Kerberos is an authentication scheme that can be used to implement:
   a. Public key cryptography
   b. Digital signatures
   c. Hash functions
   d. Single Sign-On (SSO)

3. The fundamental entity in a relational database is the:
   a. Domain
   b. Relation
   c. Pointer
   d. Cost

4. In a relational database, security is provided to the access of data through:
   a. Candidate keys
   b. Views
   c. Joins
   d. Attributes

5. In biometrics, a "one-to-one" search to verify an individual's claim of an identity is called:
   a. Audit trail review
   b. Authentication
   c. Accountability
   d. Aggregation

6. Biometrics is used for identification in the physical controls and for authentication in the:
   a. Detective controls
   b. Preventive controls

    c. Logical controls

    d. Corrective controls

7. Referential integrity requires that for any foreign key attribute, the referenced relation must have:

    a. A tuple with the same value for its primary key

    b. A tuple with the same value for its secondary key

    c. An attribute with the same value for its secondary key

    d. An attribute with the same value for its other foreign key

8. A password that is the same for each logon is called a:

    a. Dynamic password

    b. Static password

    c. Passphrase

    d. One-time pad

9. The number of times a password should be changed is NOT a function of:

    a. The criticality of the information to be protected

    b. The frequency of the password's use

    c. The responsibilities and clearance of the user

    d. The type of workstation used

10. The description of a relational database is called the:

    a. Attribute

    b. Record

    c. Schema

    d. Domain

11. A statistical anomaly-based intrusion detection system:

    a. Acquires data to establish a normal system operating profile

    b. Refers to a database of known attack signatures

    c. Will detect an attack that does not significantly change the system's operating characteristics

    d. Does not report an event that caused a momentary anomaly in the system

12. Intrusion detection systems can be all of the following types EXCEPT:

    a. Signature-based

    b. Statistical anomaly-based

    c. Network-based

    d. Defined-based

13. In a relational database system, a primary key is chosen from a set of:
    a. Foreign keys
    b. Secondary keys
    c. Candidate keys
    d. Cryptographic keys

14. A standard data manipulation and relational database definition language is:
    a. OOD
    b. SQL
    c. SLL
    d. Script

15. An attack that can be perpetrated against a remote user's callback access control is:
    a. Call forwarding
    b. A Trojan horse
    c. A maintenance hook
    d. Redialing

16. The definition of CHAP is:
    a. Confidential Hash Authentication Protocol
    b. Challenge Handshake Authentication Protocol
    c. Challenge Handshake Approval Protocol
    d. Confidential Handshake Approval Protocol

17. Using symmetric key cryptography, Kerberos authenticates clients to other entities on a network and facilitates communications through the assignment of:
    a. Public keys
    b. Session keys
    c. Passwords
    d. Tokens

18. Three things that must be considered for the planning and implementation of access control mechanisms are:
    a. Threats, assets, and objectives
    b. Threats, vulnerabilities, and risks
    c. Vulnerabilities, secret keys, and exposures
    d. Exposures, threats, and countermeasures

19. In mandatory access control, the authorization of a subject to have access to an object is dependent upon:

    a. Labels

    b. Roles

    c. Tasks

    d. Identity

20. The type of access control that is used in local, dynamic situations where subjects have the ability to specify what resources certain users can access is called:

    a. Mandatory access control

    b. Rule-based access control

    c. Sensitivity-based access control

    d. Discretionary access control

21. Role-based access control is useful when:

    a. Access must be determined by the labels on the data.

    b. There are frequent personnel changes in an organization.

    c. Rules are needed to determine clearances.

    d. Security clearances must be used.

22. Clipping levels are used to:

    a. Limit the number of letters in a password.

    b. Set thresholds for voltage variations.

    c. Reduce the amount of data to be evaluated in audit logs.

    d. Limit errors in callback systems.

23. Identification is:

    a. A user being authenticated by the system

    b. A user providing a password to the system

    c. A user providing a shared secret to the system

    d. A user professing an identity to the system

24. Authentication is:

    a. The verification that the claimed identity is valid

    b. The presentation of a user's ID to the system

    c. Not accomplished through the use of a password

    d. Only applied to remote users

25. An example of two-factor authentication is:
    a. A password and an ID
    b. An ID and a PIN
    c. A PIN and an ATM card
    d. A fingerprint

26. In biometrics, a good measure of performance of a system is the:
    a. False detection
    b. Crossover Error Rate (CER)
    c. Positive acceptance rate
    d. Sensitivity

27. In finger scan technology,
    a. The full fingerprint is stored.
    b. Features extracted from the fingerprint are stored.
    c. More storage is required than in fingerprint technology.
    d. The technology is applicable to large, one-to-many database searches.

28. An acceptable biometric throughput rate is:
    a. One subject per two minutes
    b. Two subjects per minute
    c. Ten subjects per minute
    d. Five subjects per minute

29. In a relational database, the *domain* of a relation is the set of allowable values:
    a. That an attribute can take
    b. That tuples can take
    c. That a record can take
    d. Of the primary key

30. Object-Oriented Database (OODB) systems:
    a. Are ideally suited for text-only information
    b. Require minimal learning time for programmers
    c. Are useful in storing and manipulating complex data, such as images and graphics
    d. Consume minimal system resources

Bonus Questions

You can find the answers to the following questions in Appendix H.

1. An important element of database design that ensures that the attributes in a table depend only on the primary key is:

    a. Database management

    b. Data normalization

    c. Data integrity

    d. Data reuse

2. A database View operation implements the principle of:

    a. Least privilege

    b. Separation of duties

    c. Entity integrity

    d. Referential integrity

3. Which of the following is NOT a technical (logical) mechanism for protecting information from unauthorized disclosure?

    a. Smart cards

    b. Encryption

    c. Labeling (of sensitive materials)

    d. Protocols

4. A token that generates a unique password at fixed time intervals is called:

    a. An asynchronous dynamic password token

    b. A time-sensitive token

    c. A synchronous dynamic password token

    d. A challenge-response token

5. In a biometric system, the time it takes to register with the system by providing samples of a biometric characteristic is called:

    a. Setup time

    b. Login time

    c. Enrollment time

    d. Throughput time

6. Which of the following is NOT an assumption of the basic Kerberos paradigm?

    a. Client computers are not secured and are easily accessible.

    b. Cabling is not secure.

    c. Messages are not secure from interception.

    d. Specific servers and locations cannot be secured.

7. Which one of the following statements is TRUE concerning the Terminal Access Controller Access Control System (TACACS) and TACACS+?

    a. TACACS supports prompting for a password change.

    b. TACACS+ employs tokens for two-factor, dynamic password authentication.

    c. TACACS+ employs a user ID and static password.

    d. TACACS employs tokens for two-factor, dynamic password authentication.

8. Identity-based access control is a subset of which of the following access control categories?

    a. Discretionary access control

    b. Mandatory access control

    c. Non-discretionary access control

    d. Lattice-based access control

9. Procedures that ensure that the access control mechanisms correctly implement the security policy for the entire life cycle of an information system are known as:

    a. Accountability procedures

    b. Authentication procedures

    c. Assurance procedures

    d. Trustworthy procedures

10. Which of the following is NOT a valid database model?

    a. Hierarchical

    b. Relational

    c. Object-relational

    d. Relational-rational

Advanced Sample Questions

You can find answers to the following questions in Appendix I.

The following questions are supplemental to and coordinated with Chapter 2, "Access Control Systems and Methodology," and are at a level commensurate with that of the CISSP examination.

These questions cover advanced material relative to trusted networks, remote access, biometrics, database security (including relational and object models), operating system security, Kerberos, SSO, authentication (including mobile authentication), and *Enterprise Access Management* (EAM).

We assume that the reader has a basic knowledge of the material contained in Chapter 2. These questions and answers build upon the questions and answers covered in that chapter.

1. The concept of limiting the routes that can be taken between a workstation and a computer resource on a network is called:

   a. Path limitation

   b. An enforced path

   c. A security perimeter

   d. A trusted path

2. An important control that should be in place for external connections to a network that uses call back schemes is:

   a. Breaking of a dial-up connection at the remote user's side of the line

   b. Call forwarding

   c. Call enhancement

   d. Breaking of a dial-up connection at the organization's computing resource side of the line

3. When logging on to a workstation, the log-on process should:

   a. Validate the log-on only after all input data has been supplied.

   b. Provide a Help mechanism that provides log-on assistance.

   c. Place no limits on the time allotted for log-on or on the number of unsuccessful log-on attempts.

   d. Not provide information on the previous successful log-on and on previous unsuccessful log-on attempts.

4. A group of processes that share access to the same resources is called:

    a. An access control list

    b. An access control triple

    c. A protection domain

    d. A Trusted Computing Base (TCB)

5. What part of an access control matrix shows capabilities that one user has to multiple resources?

    a. Columns

    b. Rows

    c. Rows and columns

    d. Access control list

6. A type of preventive/physical access control is:

    a. Biometrics for authentication

    b. Motion detectors

    c. Biometrics for identification

    d. An intrusion detection system

7. In addition to accuracy, a biometric system has additional factors that determine its effectiveness. Which one of the following listed items is NOT one of these additional factors?

    a. Throughput rate

    b. Acceptability

    c. Corpus

    d. Enrollment time

8. Access control that is a function of factors such as location, time of day, and previous access history is called:

    a. Positive

    b. Content-dependent

    c. Context-dependent

    d. Information flow

9. A persistent collection of data items that form relations among each other is called a:

    a. Database management system (DBMS)

    b. Data description language (DDL)

    c. Schema

    d. Database

10. A relational database can provide security through *view* relations. Views enforce what information security principle?

    a. Aggregation

    b. Least privilege

    c. Separation of duties

    d. Inference

11. A software interface to the operating system that implements access control by limiting the system commands that are available to a user is called a(n):

    a. Restricted shell

    b. Interrupt

    c. Physically constrained user interface

    d. View

12. Controlling access to information systems and associated networks is necessary for the preservation of their confidentiality, integrity, and availability. Which of the following is NOT a goal of integrity?

    a. Prevention of the modification of information by unauthorized users

    b. Prevention of the unauthorized or unintentional modification of information by authorized users

    c. Prevention of authorized modifications by unauthorized users

    d. Preservation of the internal and external consistency of the information

13. In a Kerberos exchange involving a message with an authenticator, the authenticator contains the client ID and which of the following?

    a. Ticket Granting Ticket (TGT)

    b. Timestamp

    c. Client/TGS session key

    d. Client network address

14. Which one of the following security areas is directly addressed by Kerberos?

    a. Confidentiality

    b. Frequency analysis

    c. Availability

    d. Physical attacks

15. The Secure European System for Applications in a Multivendor Environment (SESAME) implements a Kerberos-like distribution of secret keys. Which of the following is NOT a characteristic of SESAME?

    a. Uses a trusted authentication server at each host

    b. Uses secret key cryptography for the distribution of secret keys

    c. Incorporates two certificates or tickets, one for authentication and one defining access privileges

    d. Uses public key cryptography for the distribution of secret keys

16. Windows 2000 uses which of the following as the primary mechanism for authenticating users requesting access to a network?

    a. Hash functions

    b. Kerberos

    c. SESAME

    d. Public key certificates

17. A protection mechanism to limit inferencing of information in statistical database queries is:

    a. Specifying a maximum query set size

    b. Specifying a minimum query set size

    c. Specifying a minimum query set size, but prohibiting the querying of all but one of the records in the database

    d. Specifying a maximum query set size, but prohibiting the querying of all but one of the records in the database

18. In SQL, a relation that is actually existent in the database is called a(n):

    a. Base relation

    b. View

    c. Attribute

    d. Domain

19. A type of access control that supports the management of access rights for groups of subjects is:

    a. Role-based

    b. Discretionary

    c. Mandatory

    d. Rule-based

20. The Simple Security Property and the Star Property are key principles in which type of access control?

    a. Role-based

    b. Rule-based

    c. Discretionary

    d. Mandatory

21. Which of the following items is NOT used to determine the types of access controls to be applied in an organization?

    a. Least privilege

    b. Separation of duties

    c. Relational categories

    d. Organizational policies

22. Kerberos provides an integrity check service for messages between two entities through the use of:

    a. A checksum

    b. Credentials

    c. Tickets

    d. A trusted, third-party authentication server

23. The Open Group has defined functional objectives in support of a user single sign-on (SSO) interface. Which of the following is NOT one of those objectives and would possibly represent a vulnerability?

    a. The interface shall be independent of the type of authentication information handled.

    b. Provision for user-initiated change of non-user configured authentication information.

    c. It shall not predefine the timing of secondary sign-on operations.

    d. Support shall be provided for a subject to establish a default user profile.

24. There are some correlations between relational database terminology and object-oriented database terminology. Which of the following relational model terms, respectively, correspond to the object model terms of class, attribute, and instance object?

    a. Domain, relation, and column

    b. Relation, domain, and column

    c. Relation, tuple, and column

    d. Relation, column, and tuple

25. A *reference monitor* is a system component that enforces access controls on an object. Specifically, the *reference monitor concept* is an abstract machine that mediates all access of subjects to objects. The hardware,

firmware, and software elements of a trusted computing base that implement the reference monitor concept are called:

a. The authorization database

b. Identification and authentication (I & A) mechanisms

c. The auditing subsystem

d. The security kernel

26. Authentication in which a random value is presented to a user, who then returns a calculated number based on that random value is called:

a. Man-in-the-middle

b. Challenge-response

c. One-time password

d. Personal identification number (PIN) protocol

27. Which of the following is NOT a criterion for access control?

a. Identity

b. Role

c. Keystroke monitoring

d. Transactions

28. Which of the following is typically NOT a consideration in the design of passwords?

a. Lifetime

b. Composition

c. Authentication period

d. Electronic monitoring

29. A distributed system using passwords as the authentication means can use a number of techniques to make the password system stronger. Which of the following is NOT one of these techniques?

a. Password generators

b. Regular password reuse

c. Password file protection

d. Limiting the number or frequency of log-on attempts

30. Enterprise Access Management (EAM) provides access control management services to Web-based enterprise systems. Which of the following functions is NOT normally provided by extant EAM approaches?

    a. Single sign-on

    b. Accommodation of a variety of authentication mechanisms

    c. Role-based access control

    d. Interoperability among EAM implementations

31. The main approach to obtaining the true biometric information from a collected sample of an individual's physiological or behavioral characteristics is:

    a. Feature extraction

    b. Enrollment

    c. False rejection

    d. Digraphs

32. In a wireless General Packet Radio Services (GPRS) Virtual Private Network (VPN) application, which of the following security protocols is commonly used?

    a. SSL

    b. IPSEC

    c. TLS

    d. WTP

33. How is authentication implemented in GSM?

    a. Using public key cryptography

    b. It is not implemented in GSM

    c. Using secret key cryptography

    d. Out of band verification

CHAPTER

Telecommunications and Network Security

This section is the most detailed and comprehensive domain of study for the CISSP test. Although it is just one domain in the Common Book of Knowledge (CBK) of Information Systems Security, due to its size and complexity it is taught in two sections at the (ISC)² CISSP CBK Study Seminar.

From the published (ISC)² goals for the Certified Information Systems Security Professional candidate:

The professional should fully understand the following:

- *Communications and network security as it relates to voice, data, multimedia, and facsimile transmissions in terms of local area, wide area, and remote access*
- *Communications security techniques to prevent, detect, and correct errors so that integrity, availability, and the confidentiality of transactions over networks may be maintained*
- *Internet/intranet/extranet in terms of firewalls, routers, gateways, and various protocols*
- *Communications security management and techniques, which prevent, detect, and correct errors so that the integrity, availability, and confidentiality of transactions over networks may be maintained*

This is one reason why we feel the CISSP certification favors those candidates with engineering backgrounds rather than, say, auditing backgrounds. It is easier to learn the Legal, Risk Management, and Security Management domains if you have a science or engineering background than the reverse (that is, learning cryptology and telecommunications with a non-engineering or non-science background). While more advanced telecommunications or data communications specialists will find the domain rather basic, it is fairly comprehensive in its subject matter and in this case, can help fill in the gaps that a full-time, working engineer may have missed conceptually. And, of course, the focus here is security methodology: How does each element of Telecommunications (TC) and Data Communications affect the basic structure of Confidentiality, Integrity, and Availability (C.I.A.)? To that end, remember (as in every domain) that the purpose of the CBK seminar series and the CISSP test is not to teach or test a candidate on the latest and greatest technological advances in Telecommunications/Data Communications, but to examine how standard Telecommunications/Data Communications practices affect InfoSec. Enclosed is an outline of recommended study areas for this domain. Even an advanced Telecommunications/Data Communications engineer must clearly understand these concepts and terminology.

Our Goals

We have divided this chapter into two sections: Management Concepts and Technology Concepts. These are the concepts a CISSP candidate needs to understand for the exam. We have laid out the areas of study so that you can quickly go to an area that you feel you need to brush up on, or you can "take it from the top" and read the chapter in this order:

The *Management Concepts* section examines the following areas:

- The C.I.A. Triad
- Remote Access Management
- Intrusion Detection and Response
    - Intrusion Detection Systems
    - Computer Incident Response Teams
- Network Availability
    - RAID
    - Backup Concepts
    - Managing Single Points of Failure
- Network Attacks and Abuses
- Trusted Network Interpretation (TNI)

In the *Technology Concepts* section, we will examine the following:

- Protocols
    - The Layered Architecture Concept
    - Open Systems Interconnect (OSI) Model
    - Transmission Control Protocol/Internet Protocol (TCP/IP) Model
    - Security-Enhanced and Security-Focused Protocols
- Firewall Types and Architectures
- Virtual Private Networks (VPNs)
    - VPN Protocol Standards
    - VPN Devices
- Data Networking Basics
    - Data Network Types
    - Common Data Network Services
    - Data Networking Technologies
    - Local Area Network (LAN) Technologies
    - Wide Area Network (WAN) Technologies
    - Remote Access Technologies
    - Remote Identification and Authentication Technologies

Domain Definition

The Telecommunications and Network Security domain includes the structures, transmission methods, transport formats, and security measures that provide integrity, availability, authentication, and confidentiality for transmissions over private and public communications networks and media. This domain is the information security domain that is concerned with protecting data, voice, and video communications, and ensuring the following:

Confidentiality. Making sure that only those who are supposed to access the data can access it. Confidentiality is the opposite of "disclosure."

Integrity. Making sure that the data has not been changed unintentionally, due to an accident or malice. Integrity is the opposite of "alteration."

Availability. Making sure that the data is accessible when and where it is needed. Availability is the opposite of "destruction."

The Telecommunications Security Domain of information security is also concerned with the prevention and detection of the misuse or abuse of systems, which poses a threat to the tenets of Confidentiality, Integrity, and Availability (C.I.A.).

Management Concepts

This section describes the function of the Telecommunications and Network Security management, which includes the management of networks, communications systems, remote connections, and security systems.

The C.I.A. Triad

The fundamental information systems security concept of C.I.A. relates to the Telecommunications domain in the following three ways.

Confidentiality

Confidentiality is the prevention of the intentional or unintentional unauthorized disclosure of contents. Loss of confidentiality can occur in many ways. For example, loss of confidentiality can occur through the intentional release of private company information or through a misapplication of network rights.

Some of the elements of telecommunications used to ensure confidentiality are:

- Network security protocols
- Network authentication services
- Data encryption services

Integrity

Integrity is the guarantee that the message sent is the message received, and that the message was not intentionally or unintentionally altered. Loss of integrity can occur either through an intentional attack to change information (for example, a Web site defacement) or by the most common type (data is altered accidentally by an operator). Integrity also contains the concept of *non-repudiation* of a message source, which we will describe later.

Some of the elements used to ensure integrity are:

- Firewall services
- Communications Security Management
- Intrusion detection services

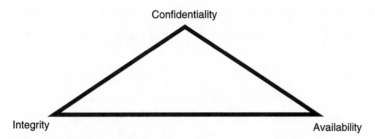

Figure 3.1 The C.I.A. triad.

Availability

This concept refers to the elements that create reliability and stability in networks and systems, which assures that connectivity is accessible when needed, allowing authorized users to access the network or systems. Also included in that assurance is the guarantee that security services for the security practitioner are usable when they are needed. The concept of availability also tends to include areas in Information Systems (IS) that are traditionally not thought of as pure security (such as guarantee of service, performance, and up time), yet are obviously affected by an attack like a Denial of Service (DoS).

Some of the elements that are used to ensure availability are:

- Fault tolerance for data availability, such as backups and redundant disk systems
- Acceptable logins and operating process performances
- Reliable and interoperable security processes and network security mechanisms

You should also know another point about availability: The use of ill-structured security mechanisms can also affect availability. Over-engineered or poorly designed security systems can impact the performance of a network or system as seriously as an intentional attack. The C.I.A. triad is often represented by a triangle, as shown in Figure 3.1.

Remote Access Security Management

Remote Access Security Management (RASM) is defined as the management of the elements of the technology of remote computing. Several current remote computing technologies confront a security practitioner:

- Dial-Up, Async, and Remote Internet Connectivity
  - Digital Subscriber Line (xDSL)

- Integrated Services Digital Network (ISDN)
- Wireless computing—mobile and cellular computing, and Personal Digital Assistants (PDAs)
- Cable modems
- Securing Enterprise and Telecommuting Remote Connectivity
  - Securing external connections (such as Virtual Private Networks (VPNs), Secure Sockets Layer (SSL), Secure Shell (SSH-2), and so forth)
  - Remote access authentication systems (such as RADIUS and TACACS)
  - Remote node authentication protocols (such as Password Authentication Protocol (PAP) and Challenge Handshake Authentication Protocol (CHAP))
- Remote User Management Issues
  - Justification for and the validation of the use of remote computing systems
  - Hardware and software distribution
  - User support and remote assistance issues

Intrusion Detection (ID) and Response

Intrusion Detection (ID) and Response is the task of monitoring systems for evidence of an intrusion or an inappropriate usage. This includes notifying the appropriate parties to take action in order to determine the extent of the severity of an incident and to remediate the incident's effects. This function is not preventative; it exists after the fact of intrusion (which it detects) and entails the following two major concepts:

- Creation and maintenance of intrusion detection systems and processes for the following:
  - Host or network monitoring
  - Event notification
- Creation of a Computer Incident Response Team (CIRT) for the following:
  - Analysis of an event notification
  - Response to an incident if the analysis warrants it
  - Escalation path procedures
  - Resolution, post-incident follow-up, and reporting to the appropriate parties

ID Systems

Various types of Intrusion Detection Systems exist from many vendors. A CISSP candidate should remember the two fundamental variations on the way they work: a) network- versus host-based systems, and b) knowledge- versus behavior-based systems. A short description of the differences has been provided, along with some of the pros and cons of each.

Network- versus Host-Based ID Systems

The two most common implementations of Intrusion Detection are Network-based and Host-based. Their differences are as follows:

- Network-based ID systems
    - Commonly reside on a discrete network segment and monitor the traffic on that network segment
    - Usually consist of a network appliance with a Network Interface Card (NIC) that is operating in promiscuous mode and is intercepting and analyzing the network packets in real time
- Host-based ID systems
    - Use small programs (intelligent agents), which reside on a host computer, and monitor the operating system continually
    - Write to log files and trigger alarms
    - Detect inappropriate activity only on the host computer—they do not monitor the entire network segment

Knowledge- versus Behavior-Based ID Systems

The two current conceptual approaches to Intrusion Detection methodology are knowledge-based ID systems and behavior-based ID systems, sometimes referred to as signature-based ID and statistical anomaly-based ID, respectively.

Knowledge-based ID. Systems use a database of previous attacks and known system vulnerabilities to look for current attempts to exploit their vulnerabilities, and trigger an alarm if an attempt is found. These systems are more common than behavior-based ID systems.

The following are the advantages of a knowledge-based ID system:

- This system is characterized by low false alarm rates (or positives).
- Their alarms are standardized and are clearly understandable by security personnel.

The following are the disadvantages of knowledge-based ID systems:

- This system is resource-intensive; the knowledge database continually needs maintenance and updates.
- New, unique, or original attacks often go unnoticed.

Behavior-based ID. Systems dynamically detect deviations from the learned patterns of user behavior, and an alarm is triggered when an activity that is considered intrusive (outside of normal system use) occurs. Behavior-based ID systems are less common than knowledge-based ID systems.

The following are the advantages of a behavior-based ID system:

- The system can dynamically adapt to new, unique, or original vulnerabilities.
- A behavior-based ID system is not as dependent upon specific operating systems as a knowledge-based ID system.

The following are the disadvantages of a behavior-based ID system:

- The system is characterized by high false alarm rates. High positives are the most common failure of ID systems and can create data noise that makes the system unusable.
- The activity and behavior of the users while in the networked system might not be static enough to effectively implement a behavior-based ID system.

NOTE Remember: Intrusion detection is Detective rather than Preventative.

Computer Incident Response Team

As part of a structured program of Intrusion Detection and Response, a Computer Emergency Response Team (CERT) or Computer Incident Response Team (CIRT) is commonly created. Because "CERT" is copyrighted, "CIRT" is more often used.

The prime directive of every CIRT is Incident Response Management, which manages a company's response to events that pose a risk to its computing environment.

This management often consists of the following:

- Coordinating the notification and distribution of information pertaining to the incident to the appropriate parties (those with a need to know) through a predefined escalation path
- Mitigating risk to the enterprise by minimizing the disruptions to normal business activities and the costs associated with remediating the incident (including public relations)

■ Assembling teams of technical personnel to investigate the potential vulnerabilities and to resolve specific intrusions

Additional examples of CIRT activities are:

■ Management of the network logs, including collection, retention, review, and analysis of data

■ Management of the resolution of an incident, management of the remediation of a vulnerability, and post-event reporting to the appropriate parties

Network Availability

This section defines those elements that can provide for or threaten network availability. Network availability can be defined as an area of the Telecommunications and Network Security domain that directly affects the Information Systems Security tenet of Availability. Later, we will examine the areas of these networks that are required to provide redundancy and fault tolerance. A more techno-focused description of these topologies and devices can be found in the *Technology Concepts* section later in this chapter.

Now, we will examine the following:

■ RAID

■ Backup concepts

■ Managing single points of failure

RAID

RAID stands for Redundant Array of Inexpensive Disks. It is also commonly referred to as the Redundant Array of Independent Disks. Its primary purpose is to provide fault tolerance and protection against file server hard disk crashes. Some RAID types secondarily improve system performance by caching and distributing disk reads from multiple disks that work together to save files simultaneously. Basically, RAID separates the data into multiple units and stores it on multiple disks by using a process called "striping." It can be implemented either as a hardware or a software solution, but as we will see in the following *Hardware versus Software* section, each type of implementation has its own issues and benefits.

The RAID Advisory Board has defined three classifications of RAID: Failure Resistant Disk Systems (FRDSs), Failure Tolerant Disk Systems, and Disaster Tolerant Disk Systems. As of this writing, only the first one, FRDS, is an existing standard, and the others are still pending. We will now discuss the various implementation levels of an FRDS.

Failure Resistant Disk System

The basic function of an FRDS is to protect file servers from data loss and a loss of availability due to disk failure. It provides the capability to reconstruct the contents of a failed disk onto a replacement disk and provides the added protection against data loss due to the failure of many hardware parts of the server. One feature of an FRDS is that it enables the continuous monitoring of these parts and the alerting of their failure.

Failure Resistant Disk System Plus

An update to the FRDS standard is called FRDS+. This update adds the capability to automatically *hot swap* (swapping while the server is still running) failed disks. It also adds protection against environmental hazards (such as temperature, out-of-range conditions, and external power failure) and includes a series of alarms and warnings of these failures.

Overview of the Levels of RAID

RAID Level 0 creates one large disk by using several disks. This process is called *striping*. It stripes data across all disks (but provides no redundancy) by using all of the available drive space to create the maximum usable data volume size and to increase the read/write performance. One problem with this level of RAID is that it actually lessens the fault tolerance of the disk system rather than increasing it——the entire data volume is unusable if one drive in the set fails.

RAID Level 1 is commonly called *mirroring*. It mirrors the data from one disk or set of disks by duplicating the data onto another disk or set of disks. This process is often implemented by a one-for-one disk-to-disk ratio: Each drive is mirrored to an equal drive partner that is continually being updated with current data. If one drive fails, the system automatically gets the data from the other drive. The main issue with this level of RAID is that the one-for-one ratio is very expensive—resulting in the highest cost per megabyte of data capacity. This level effectively doubles the amount of hard drives you need; therefore, it is usually best for smaller-capacity systems.

RAID Level 2 consists of bit-interleaved data on multiple disks. The parity information is created by using a *hamming code* that detects errors and establishes which part of which drive is in error. It defines a disk drive system with 39 disks: 32 disks of user storage and seven disks of error recovery coding. This level is not used in practice and was quickly superseded by the more flexible levels of RAID that follow.

RAID Levels 3 and 4 are discussed together because they function in the same way. The only difference is that level 3 is implemented at the *byte level* and level 4 is usually implemented at the *block level*. In this scenario, data is striped across several drives and the parity check bit is written to a dedicated parity drive. This process is similar to RAID 0. They both have a large data volume, but the addition of a dedicated parity drive provides redundancy. If a hard disk fails, the data can be reconstructed by using the bit information on the parity drive. The main issue with this level of RAID is that the constant writes to the parity drive can create a performance hit. In this implementation, spare drives can be used to replace crashed drives.

RAID Level 5 stripes the data and the parity information at the block level across all the drives in the set. It is similar to RAID 3 and 4 except that the parity information is written to the next-available drive rather than to a dedicated drive by using an *interleave* parity. This feature enables more flexibility in the implementation and increases fault tolerance because the parity drive is not a single point of failure, as it is in RAID 3 or 4. The disk reads and writes are also performed concurrently, thereby increasing performance over levels 3 and 4. The spare drives that replace the failed drives are usually hot swappable, meaning they can be replaced on the server while the system is up and running. This is probably the most popular implementation of RAID today.

RAID Level 7 is a variation of RAID 5 wherein the array functions as a *single virtual disk* in the hardware. This is sometimes simulated by software running over a RAID level 5 hardware implementation, which enables the drive array to continue to operate if any disk or any path to any disk fails. It also provides parity protection.

Vendors create various other implementations of RAID to combine the features of several RAID levels, although these levels are common. Level 6 is an extension of Level 5 which allows for additional fault tolerance by using a second independent distributed parity scheme, i.e., two-dimensional parity. Level 10 is created by combining level 0 (striping) with level 1 (mirroring). Level 15 is created by combining level 1 (mirroring) with level 5 (interleave). Level 51 is created by mirroring entire level 5 arrays. Table 3.1 shows the various levels of RAID with terms you will need to remember.

Other Types of Server Fault-Tolerant Systems

Redundant Servers. A redundant server implementation takes the concept of RAID 1 (mirroring) and applies it to a pair of servers. A primary server mirrors its data to a secondary server, thus enabling the primary to "roll over" to the secondary in the case of primary server failure (the secondary server steps in and takes over for the primary server). This rollover can be hot or warm (that is, the rollover may or may not be transparent to the user), depending upon the vendor's implementation of this redundancy. This process is also commonly known as *server fault tolerance*. Common vendor implementations of this are Novell's SFTIII, Octopus, and Vinca's Standby Server. Figure 3.2 shows a common redundant server implementation.

Table 3.1 RAID Level Descriptions

RAID LEVEL	DESCRIPTION
0	Striping
1	Mirroring
2	Hamming Code Parity
3	Byte Level Parity
4	Block Level Parity
5	Interleave Parity
6	Second Independent Parity
7	Single Virtual Disk
10	Striping Across Multiple Pairs (1+0)
15	Striping With Parity Across RAID 5 Pairs (1+5)
51	Mirroring RAID 5 Arrays With Parity (5+1)

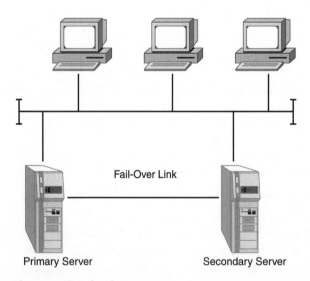

Figure 3.2 Redundant servers.

Server Clustering. A server cluster is a group of independent servers, which are managed as a single system, that provides higher availability, easier manageability, and greater scalability. The concept of server clustering is similar to the redundant server implementation previously dis-

> ### HARDWARE VERSUS SOFTWARE RAID
>
> RAID can be implemented in either hardware or software. Each type has its own issues and benefits. A hardware RAID implementation is usually platform-independent. It runs below the *operating system* (OS) of the server and usually does not care if the OS is Novell, NT, or Unix. The hardware implementation uses its own Central Processing Unit (CPU) for calculations on an intelligent controller card. There can be more than one of these cards installed to provide hardware redundancy in the server. RAID levels 3 and 5 run faster on hardware. A software implementation of RAID means that it runs as part of the operating system on the file server. Often RAID levels 0, 1, and 10 run faster on software RAID because of the need for the server's software resources. Simple striping or mirroring can run faster on the operating system because neither use the hardware-level parity drives.

cussed, except that all the servers in the cluster are online and take part in processing service requests. By enabling the secondary servers to provide processing time, the cluster acts as an intelligent entity and balances the traffic load to improve performance. The cluster looks like a single server from the user's point of view. If any server in the cluster crashes, processing continues transparently; however, the cluster suffers some performance degradation. This implementation is sometimes called a "server farm." Examples of this type of vendor implementation are Microsoft Cluster Server ("Wolfpack"), Oracle Parallel Server, and Tandem NonStop. Figure 3.3 shows a type of server clustering.

Backup Concepts

A CISSP candidate will also need to know the basic concepts of data backup. The candidate might be presented with questions regarding file selection methods, tape format types, and common problems.

Tape Backup Methods

The purpose of a tape backup method is to protect and/or restore lost, corrupted, or deleted information—thereby preserving the data integrity and ensuring network availability.

There are several varying methods of selecting files for backup. Some have odd names, like Grandfather/Father/Son, Towers of Hanoi, and so forth. The three most basic, common methods are as follows:

1. *Full Backup Method.* This backup method makes a complete backup of every file on the server every time it is run. The method is primarily run

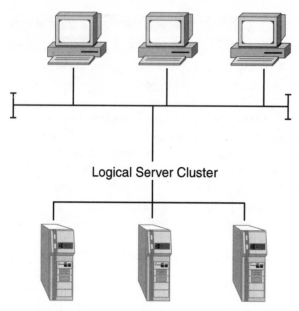

Figure 3.3 Server clustering.

when time and tape space permits, and is used for system archive or baselined tape sets.

2. *Incremental Backup Method.* This backup method only copies files that have been recently added or changed (that day) and ignores any other backup set. It is usually accomplished by resetting the archive bit on the files after they have been backed up. This method is used if time and tape space is at an extreme premium; however, this method has some inherent vulnerabilities, which we will discuss later.

3. *Differential Backup Method.* This backup method only copies files that have changed since a full backup was last performed. This type of backup is additive because the time and tape space required for each night's backup grows during the week as it copies the day's changed files and the previous days' changed files up to the last full backup. In this scenario, each file's archive bit is not reset until the next full backup.

NOTE A Full Backup must be made regardless of whether Differential or Incremental methods are used.

Tape Format Types

The following are the four most common backup tape format technologies:

1. *Digital Audio Tape (DAT).* Digital Audio Tape can be used to back up data systems in addition to its original intended audio uses.

Table 3.2 Tape Format Technology Comparison

PROPERTIES	DAT	QIC	8MM	DLT
Capacity	4GB/12GB	13GB	20GB	20/35GB
Max. Transfer Rate	1MBps	1.5MBps	3MBps	5MBps
Cost	Medium	Low	Medium	High

2. *Quarter Inch Cartridge (QIC) drives.* This format is mostly used for home/small office backups, has a small capacity, and is slow but inexpensive.

3. *8mm Tape.* This format was commonly used in Helical Scan tape drives, but was superseded by *Digital Linear Tape* (DLT).

4. *Digital Linear Tape (DLT).* The tape is 4mm in size, yet the compression techniques and head scanning process make it a large capacity and fast tape.

The criteria for selecting which of these tape formats to use is usually based upon a comparison of the tradeoff of performance versus capacity versus cost. The bottom line is, "How big is the data that you need to back up, and how long can you operate until it is recovered?" Table 3.2 is a quick reference of the major types of backup tape formats.

Other Backup Media

Compact Disc (CD) optical media types. Write once, read many (WORM) optical disk "jukeboxes" are used for archiving data that does not change. This is a very good format to use for a permanent backup. Companies use this format to store data in an accessible format that may need to be accessed at a much later date, such as legal data. The shelf life of a CD is also longer than a tape. Rewritable and erasable (CDR/W) optical disks are sometimes used for backups that require short-time storage for changeable data, but require faster file access than tape. This format is used more often for very small data sets.

Zip/Jaz drives, SyQuest, and Bernoulli boxes. These types of drives are frequently used for the individual backups of small data sets of specific application data. These formats are very transportable and are often the standard for data exchange in many businesses.

Tape Arrays. A Tape Array is a large hardware/software system that uses the RAID technology we discussed earlier. It uses a large device with multiple (sometimes 32 or 64) tapes that are configured as a single array. These devices require very specific hardware and software to operate,

---

BACKUP METHOD EXAMPLE

A full backup was made on Friday night. This full backup is just what it says—it copied every file on the file server to the tape regardless of the last time any other backup was made. This type of backup is common for creating full copies of the data for off-site archiving or in preparation for a major system upgrade. On Monday night, another backup is made. If the site uses the Incremental Backup Method, Monday, Tuesday, Wednesday, and Thursday's backup tapes contain only those files that were altered during that day (Monday's incremental backup tape has only Monday's data on it, Tuesday's backup tape has only Tuesday's on it, and so on). All backup tapes might be required to restore a system to its full state after a system crash, because some files that changed during the week might only exist on one tape. If the site is using the Differential Backup Method, Monday's tape backup has the same files that the Incremental tape has (Monday is the only day that the files have changed so far). However, on Tuesday, rather than only backing up that day's files, it also backs up Monday's files—creating a longer backup. Although this increases the time required to perform the backup and increases the amount of tapes needed, it does provide more protection from tape failure and speeds up recovery time.

---

but provide a very fast backup and a multi-tasking backup of multiple targets with considerable fault tolerance.

Hierarchical Storage Management (HSM). HSM provides a continuous online backup by using optical or tape "jukeboxes," similar to WORMs. It appears as an infinite disk to the system, and can be configured to provide the closest version of an available real-time backup. This is commonly employed in very large data retrieval systems.

Common Backup Issues and Problems

All backup systems share common issues and problems, whether they use a tape or a CD-ROM format. There are three primary backup concerns:

Slow data transfer of the backup. All backups take time, especially tape backup. Depending upon the volume of data that needs to be copied, full backups to tape can take an incredible amount of time. In addition, the time required to restore the data must also be factored into any disaster recovery plan. Backups that pass data through the network infrastructure must be scheduled during periods of low network utilization, which are commonly overnight, over the weekend, or during holidays. This also requires off-hour monitoring of the backup process.

Server disk space utilization expands over time. As the amount of data that needs to be copied increases, the length of time to run the backup proportionally increases and the demand on the system grows as more tapes are required. Sometimes the data volume on the hard drives expands very quickly, thus overwhelming the backup process. Therefore, this process must be monitored regularly.

The time the last backup was run is never the time of the server crash. With non-continuous backup systems, data that was entered after the last backup prior to a system crash will have to be recreated. Many systems have been designed to provide online fault tolerance during backup (the old Vortex Retrochron was one), yet because backup is a post-processing batch process, some data re-entry will need to be performed.

NOTE Physically securing the tapes from unauthorized access is obviously a security concern and is considered a function of the Operations Security Domain.

Managing Single Points of Failure

A Single Point of Failure is an element in the network design that, if it fails or is compromised, can negatively affect the entire network. Network design methodologies expend a lot of time and resources to search for these points; here, we provide only a few. We discuss the technological aspects of cabling and networking topologies in more detail in the *Technology Concepts* section later in this chapter. Now, we will discuss how they can contribute to creating a single point of failure.

Cabling Failures

Coaxial. These are coaxial cables with many workstations or servers attached to the same segment of cable, which creates a single point of failure if it is broken. Exceeding the specified effective cable length is also a source of cabling failures.

Twisted Pair. Twisted Pair cables currently have two categories in common usage: CAT3 and CAT5. The fundamental difference between these two types is how tightly the copper wires are wound. This tightness determines the cable's resistance to interference, the allowable distance it can be pulled between points, and the data's transmission speed before attenuation begins to affect the signal. CAT3 is an older specification with a shorter effective distance. Cable length is the most common failure issue with twisted pair cabling.

Fiber Optic. Fiber-Optic cable is immune to the effects of electromagnetic interference (EMI) and therefore has a much longer effective usable length (up to 2 kilometers in some cases). It can carry a heavy load of activity much more easily than the copper types, and as such it is commonly used for infrastructure backbones, server farms, or connections that need large amounts of bandwidth. The primary drawbacks of this cable type are its cost of installation and the high level of expertise needed to have it properly terminated.

Topology Failures

Ethernet. Ethernet is currently the most popular topology. The older coaxial cable has been widely replaced with twisted pair, which is extremely resistant to failure, especially in a star-wired configuration.

Token Ring. Token ring was designed to be a more fault-tolerant topology than Ethernet, and can be a very resilient topology when properly implemented. Because a token is passed by every station on the ring, a NIC that is set to the wrong speed or that is in an error state can bring down the entire ring.

Fiber Distributed Data Interface (FDDI). FDDI is a token-passing ring scheme like a token ring, yet it also has a second ring that remains dormant until an error condition is detected on the primary ring. The primary ring is then isolated and the secondary ring begins working, thus creating an extremely fault-tolerant network. This fault tolerance is occasionally overridden in certain implementations that use both rings to create a faster performance.

Leased Lines. Leased lines, such as T1 connections and Integrated Services Digital Network (ISDN) lines, can be a single point of failure and have no built-in redundancy like the Local Area Network (LAN) topologies. A common way to create fault tolerance with leased lines is to group several T1s together with an inverse multiplexer placed at both ends of the connection. Having multiple vendors can also help with redundancy; the T1 lines are not all supplied by one carrier.

Frame Relay. Frame relay uses a public switched network to provide Wide Area Network (WAN) connectivity. Frame relay is considered extremely fault-tolerant because any segment in the frame relay cloud that is experiencing an error or failure diverts traffic to other links. Sometimes fault tolerance is achieved by a client using multiple vendors for this service, such as in leased lines.

Other Single Points of Failure

Other single points of failure can be unintentionally created by not building redundancy into the network design. For example, network devices can create

---

SAVING CONFIGURATION FILES AND TRIVIAL FILE TRANSFER PROTOCOL

Sometimes when a network device fails, the configuration programmed into it is also lost. This can especially happen to routers. The procedure that is used to prevent this from occurring consists of capturing the configuration files by logging a terminal session during a configuration session, and then storing that configuration on floppies, or installing a Trivial File Transfer Protocol (TFTP) server. The TFTP server is then accessed during the configuration session to save or retrieve configuration information to the network device. This server can be located in a secure area. If the network is very large, a TFTP server is considered mandatory. Many networking devices now support TFTP.

---

a single point of failure when all network traffic in or out of the network passes through this single device. This can happen with firewalls, routers, hubs, and switches. All single devices should have redundant units installed and/or redundant power supplies and parts. Dial-up or ISDN Basic Rate Interface (BRI) connections are often created as backup routes for faster leased lines.

POWER FAILURE

Blackouts, brownouts, surges, and spikes are all examples of power fluctuations that can seriously harm any electronic equipment. Servers, firewalls, routers, and mission-critical workstations are network devices that should have their own Uninterruptible Power Supply (UPS) attached. A UPS can provide a source of clean, filtered, steady power, unlike a battery backup. Intelligent UPS systems can shut down devices gracefully (without a hard crash), notify personnel that a power outage has occurred, and restart the system after the outage has been remedied. For example, in New York, the supplied power wattage range varies widely throughout the day and can be very damaging on electronics without a UPS. Network Operations Centers (NOC) and other providers of carrier services commonly install their own Direct Current (DC) power generators as part of their network infrastructure design. You can find a more thorough description of electrical power failures and controls in Chapter 10, "Physical Security."

Network Attacks and Abuses

The CISSP candidate will need to know in general the various types of attacks on and abuses of networked systems. In current practice, these attacks are constantly evolving. This is probably the most dynamic area of InfoSec today. Large teams and huge amounts of money and resources are dedicated to reacting to the latest twists and turns of intrusions into networked systems, particularly on the

Internet. We describe attacks and abuses in almost every chapter; here we focus on those attacks and abuses that commonly apply to networked systems.[1]

This area is also a constant source of fodder for the media. Arguments can be made as to whether internal versus external intrusions are more serious or common. A recent study estimated that about 60 percent of unauthorized network intrusions originated internally, and this figure is on a downward trend. With the Internet economy so visible, external C.I.A. failures can create some very serious credibility and PR problems that will negatively affect the bottom line.

General Classes of Network Abuses

We will now explain several classes of network attacks a CISSP candidate should know. These classes are grouped very generally, and should not be considered a complete listing of network attacks or abuses.

Class A: Unauthorized Access of Restricted Network Services by the Circumvention of Security Access Controls

This type of usage is called *logon abuse*. It refers to legitimate users accessing networked services that would normally be restricted to them. Unlike network intrusion, this type of abuse focuses primarily on those users who might be internal to the network, legitimate users of a different system, or users who have a lower security classification. *Masquerading* is the term used when one user pretends to be another user. An attacker socially engineering passwords from an Internet Service Provider (ISP) would be an example of this type of masquerading.

Class B: Unauthorized Use of a Network for Non-Business Purposes

This style of network abuse refers to the non-business or personal use of a network by otherwise authorized users, such as Internet surfing to inappropriate content sites (travel, pornography, sports, and so forth). As per the (ISC)[2] Code of Ethics and the *Internet Advisory Board* (IAB) recommendations, the use of networked services for other than business purposes can be considered abuse of the system. While most employers do not enforce extremely strict Web surfing rules, occasional harassment litigation resulting from employees accessing pornography sites and employees operating private Web businesses using the company's infrastructure can constitute unauthorized use.

---

[1] Two books that are excellent sources of detailed information on network hacks and intrusions are "*Hack Attacks Encyclopedia*" by John Chirillo (Wiley, 2001), and "*Counter Hack*," by Ed Skoudis (Prentice Hall PTR, 2002).

Class C: Eavesdropping

This type of network attack consists of the unauthorized interception of network traffic. Eavesdropping attacks occur through the interception of network traffic. Certain network transmission methods, such as by satellite, wireless, mobile, PDAs, and so on, are vulnerable to eavesdropping attacks. *Tapping* refers to the physical interception of a transmission medium (like the splicing of the cable or the creation of an induction loop to pick up electromagnetic emanations from copper).

Passive Eavesdropping. Covertly monitoring or listening to transmissions that are unauthorized by either the sender or receiver.

Active Eavesdropping. Tampering with a transmission to create a covert signaling channel, or actively *probing* the network for infrastructure information.

An active variation on eavesdropping is called Covert Channel eavesdropping, which consists of using a hidden unauthorized network connection to communicate unauthorized information. A Covert Storage Channel operates by writing information to storage by one process and then reading by using another process from a different security level. A Covert Timing Channel signals information to another process by modulating its own resource use to affect the response time of another.

Eavesdropping and probing are often the preliminary steps to session hijacking and other network intrusions.

Class D: Denial of Service and Other Service Disruptions

These types of attacks create service outages due to the saturation of networked resources. This saturation can be aimed at the network devices, servers, or infrastructure bandwidth—whatever network area that unusual traffic volumes can seriously degrade. For example, the Distributed Denial of Service (DDoS) attack that occurred in February 2000 is not specifically considered a hack because the attack's primary goal was not to gather information (confidentiality or integrity is not intentionally compromised), but rather to halt service by overloading the system. This attack, however, can be used as a diversion to enable an intentional hack to gain information from a different part of the system by diverting the company's Information Technology (IT) resources elsewhere. We provide detailed examples of DoS attacks later in the text.

Class E: Network Intrusion

This type of attack refers to the use of unauthorized access to break into a network primarily from an external source. Unlike a login abuse attack, the intruders are not considered to be known to the company. Most common conceptions of hacks reside in this category. Also known as a penetration attack, it exploits known security vulnerabilities in the security perimeter.

Spoofing. Refers to an attacker deliberately inducing a user (subject) or device (object) into taking an incorrect action by giving it incorrect information.

Piggy-backing. Refers to an attacker gaining unauthorized access to a system by using a legitimate user's connection. A user leaves a session open or incorrectly logs off, enabling an attacker to resume the session.

Back-door attacks. Commonly refers to intrusions via dial-up or async external network connections.

Class F: Probing

Probing is an active variation of eavesdropping. It is usually used to give an attacker a road map of the network in preparation for an intrusion or a DoS attack. It can give the eavesdropper a list of available services. Traffic analysis through the use of a "Sniffer" is one probing type of eavesdropping, where scans of the hosts for various enabled services document what systems are active on a network and what ports are open.

Probing can be performed either manually or automatically. Manual vulnerability checks are performed by using tools such as Telnet to connect to a remote service to see what is listening. Automated vulnerability scanners are software programs that automatically perform all the probing and scanning steps and report the findings back to the user. Due to its free availability on the Internet, the number of this type of automated probing has skyrocketed recently.

Denial of Service (DoS) Attacks

The DoS attack might use some of the following techniques to overwhelm a target's resources:

- Filling up a target's hard drive storage space by using huge e-mail attachments or file transfers
- Sending a message, which resets a target host's subnet mask, causing a disruption of the target's subnet routing
- Using up all of a target's resources to accept network connections, resulting in additional network connections being denied

Next, we list additional specific types of DoS attacks:

Buffer Overflow Attack. A basic *buffer overflow* attack occurs when a process receives much more data than expected. If the process has no programmed routine to deal with this excessive amount of data, it acts in an unexpected way that the intruder can exploit. A Ping of Death exploits ICMP by sending an illegal ECHO packet of >65K octets of data, which can cause an overflow of system variables and lead to a system crash.[2]

SYN Attack. A *SYN attack* occurs when an attacker exploits the use of the buffer space during a Transmission Control Protocol (TCP) session initialization handshake. The attacker floods the target system's small "in-process" queue with connection requests, but it does not respond when a target system replies to those requests. This causes the target system to time out while waiting for the proper response, which makes the system crash or become unusable.

Teardrop Attack. A *Teardrop attack* consists of modifying the length and fragmentation offset fields in sequential Internet Protocol (IP) packets. The target system then becomes confused and crashes after it receives contradictory instructions on how the fragments are offset on these packets.

Smurf. A *Smurf attack* uses a combination of IP spoofing and ICMP to saturate a target network with traffic, thereby launching a DoS attack. It consists of three elements: the source site, the bounce site, and the target site. The attacker (the source site) sends a spoofed ping packet to the broadcast address of a large network (the bounce site). This modified packet contains the address of the target site, which causes the bounce site to broadcast the misinformation to all of the devices on its local network. All of these devices now respond with a reply to the target system, which is then saturated with those replies.

Session Hijacking Attacks

IP Spoofing Attacks. Unlike a Smurf attack, where spoofing creates a DoS attack, IP spoofing convinces a system that it is communicating with a known entity that gives an intruder access. *IP spoofing* involves an alteration of a packet at the TCP level, which is used to attack Internet-connected systems that provide various TCP/IP services. The attacker sends a packet with an IP source address of a known, trusted host. This target host might accept the packet and act upon it.

TCP Sequence Number Attacks. *TCP sequence number attacks* exploit the communications session, which was established between the target and

---

[2]Andress, Mandy. "*Surviving Security: How to Integrate People, Process, and Technology*" (Sams Publishing, 2001).

the trusted host that initiated the session. The intruder tricks the target into believing it is connected to a trusted host and then hijacks the session by predicting the target's choice of an initial TCP sequence number. This session is then often used to launch various attacks on other hosts.

Other Fragmentation Attacks

IP fragmentation attacks use varied IP datagram fragmentation to disguise its TCP packets from a target's IP filtering devices. The following are some examples of these types of attacks:

- A *tiny fragment attack* occurs when the intruder sends a very small fragment that forces some of the TCP header field into a second fragment. If the target's filtering device does not enforce minimum fragment size, this illegal packet can then be passed on through the target's network.

- An *overlapping fragment attack* is another variation on a datagram's zero-offset modification (like the teardrop attack). Subsequent packets overwrite the initial packet's destination address information, and then the second packet is passed by the target's filtering device. This can happen if the target's filtering device does not enforce a minimum fragment offset for fragments with non-zero offsets.

Trusted Network Interpretation

One of the most important documents of the 20 or so books in the Rainbow series is the Trusted Network Interpretation (TNI), which is also called the "Red Book." The National Institute of Standards and Technology (NIST) developed these books and the resulting standards.

The Red Book interprets the criteria described in the *Trusted Computer Security Evaluation Criteria* (TCSEC, called the "Orange Book") for networks and network components, so it is applicable for this chapter. The reader should note that time and technological changes lessen the relevancy of the TNI to contemporary networking.

To deal with technical issues that are outside the scope of the Orange Book, the Red Book examines an interpretation of the Orange Book as it relates to networks and examines other security services that the Orange Book does not address. The TNI provides Orange Book interpretations for trusted computer and communications network systems under the areas of assurance requirements. It creates rating structures for this assurance and describes and defines additional security services for networks in the areas of communications integrity, DoS, and transmission security. It also assumes that the physical, administrative, and procedural protection measures are already in place. The primary purpose of these interpretations is to provide a standard to manufacturers who are incorporating security features, which operate at defined

Table 3.3 TNI Evaluation Classes

CLASS	DESCRIPTION
D:	Minimal protection
C:	Discretionary protection
C1:	Discretionary security protection
C2:	Controlled access protection
B:	Mandatory protection
B1:	Labeled security protection
B2:	Structured protection
B3:	Security domains
A1:	Verified protection

TNI ISSUES

The TNI is restricted to a limited class of networks; namely, centralized networks with a single accreditation authority. It addresses network issues, which the Orange Book does not address, and in a way it competes with the ISO architecture. Because the distributed network model is becoming the standard (including the rise of the Internet), you can think of the TNI as a bridge between the Orange Book and these newer network classes.

assurance levels that provide a measurable degree of trust. Table 3.3 is a short introduction to the various TNI evaluation classes.

Technology Concepts

This section describes the functions of various Telecommunications and Network technologies.

Protocols

Here is where we get into the meat of networking, and can understand the layered model and the protocols that accompany it. In this section, we will examine the OSI and the TCP/IP layered models, and the protocols that accompany each of these models.

> **LAYERED MODELS**
>
> Layered models serve to enhance the development and management of a network architecture. While they primarily address issues of data communications, they also include some data processing activities at the upper layers. These upper layers address applications software processes, the presentation format, and the establishment of user sessions. Each independent layer of a network architecture addresses different functions and responsibilities. All of these layers work together to maximize the performance of the process and interoperability. Examples of the various functions addressed are data transfer, flow control, sequencing, error detection, and notification.

A protocol is a standard set of rules that determine how computers communicate with each other across networks. When computers communicate with one another, they exchange a series of messages. A protocol describes the format that a message must take and the way in which computers must exchange messages. Protocols enable different types of computers such as Macintosh, PC, UNIX, and so on to communicate in spite of their differences. They communicate by describing a standard format and communication method by adhering to a layered architecture model.

The Layered Architecture Concept

Layered architecture is a conceptual blueprint of how communications should take place. It divides communication processes into logical groups called layers.

There are many reasons to use a layered architecture:

- To clarify the general functions of a communications process, rather than focusing on the specifics of how to do it
- To break down complex networking processes into more manageable sublayers
- Using industry-standard interfaces enables interoperability
- To change the features of one layer without changing all of the programming code in every layer
- Easier troubleshooting

How Data Moves through a Layered Architecture

Data is sent from a source computer to a destination computer. In a layered architecture model, the data passes downward through each layer from the highest layer (the Application Layer 7 in the OSI model) to the lowest layer (the Physical Layer 1 of the OSI model) of the source. It is then transmitted across the medium (cable) and is received by the destination computer, where it is passed up the layers in the opposite direction from the lowest (Layer 1) to the highest (Layer 7).

Each of the various protocols operates at specific layers. Each protocol in the source computer has a job to do: Each one is responsible for attaching its own unique information to the data packet when it comes through its own layer. When the data reaches the destination computer, it moves up the model. Each protocol on the destination computer also has a job to do: Each protocol detaches and examines only the data that was attached by its protocol counterpart at the source computer, then it sends the rest of the packet up the protocol stack to the next highest layer. Each layer at each destination sees and deals only with the data that was packaged by its counterpart on the sending side.

Open Systems Interconnect (OSI) Model

In the early 1980s, the Open Systems Interconnection (OSI) reference model was created by the International Standards Organization (ISO) to help vendors create interoperable network devices. The OSI reference model describes how data and network information is communicated from one computer through a network media to another computer. The OSI reference model breaks this approach into seven distinct layers. Layering divides a problem into functional groups that permit an easier understanding of each piece of the problem. Each layer has a unique set of properties and directly interacts with its adjacent layers.

The OSI model was expected to become the standard, yet it did not prevail over TCP/IP. Actually, in some cases, they have been joined at the Application Level to obtain the benefits of each.

The Seven Layers of the OSI Reference Model

The OSI reference model is divided into seven layers (see Figure 3.4), which we will examine here.

NOTE As we describe these OSI layers, you will notice that we do not equally discuss all of the layers—we will focus on some layers more than others. The OSI layers that we are most concerned with are the Application, Network, Transport, Data Link, and Physical layers.

Application Layer (Layer 7). The *Application Layer* of the OSI model supports the components that deal with the communication aspects of an application. The Application Layer is responsible for identifying and

DATA ENCAPSULATION

Data Encapsulation is the process in which the information from one data packet is wrapped around or attached to the data of another packet. In the OSI reference model, each layer encapsulates the layer immediately above it as the data flows down the protocol stack. The logical communication, which happens at each layer of the OSI reference model, does not involve several physical connections because the information that each protocol needs to send is encapsulated within the protocol layer.

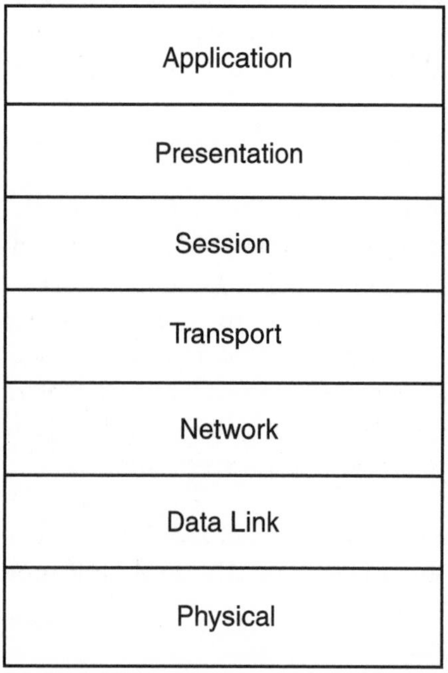

Application
Presentation
Session
Transport
Network
Data Link
Physical

Figure 3.4 The OSI seven-layer reference model.

establishing the availability of the intended communication partner. It is also responsible for determining whether sufficient resources exist for the intended communication. This layer is the highest level and is the interface to the user.

The following are some examples of Application Layer applications:

- *World Wide Web* (WWW)
- *File Transfer Protocol* (FTP)
- *Trivial File Transfer Protocol* (TFTP)

- *Line Printer Daemon* (LPD)
- *Simple Mail Transfer Protocol* (SMTP)

Presentation Layer (Layer 6). The *Presentation Layer* presents data to the Application Layer. It functions essentially as a translator, such as Extended Binary-Coded Decimal Interchange Code (EBCDIC)[3] or American Standard Code for Information Interchange (ASCII)[4]. Tasks like data compression, decompression, encryption, and decryption are all associated with this layer. This layer defines how the applications can enter a network.

When you are surfing the Web, most likely you are frequently encountering some of the following Presentation Layer standards:

- *Hypertext Transfer Protocol* (HTTP)
- *Tagged Image File Format* (TIFF). A standard graphics format.
- *Joint Photographic Experts Group* (JPEG). Standard for graphics defined by the Joint Photographic Experts Group.
- *Musical Instrument Digital Interface* (MIDI). A format used for digitized music.
- *Motion Picture Experts Group* (MPEG). The Motion Picture Experts Group's standard for the compression and coding of motion video.

Session Layer (Layer 5). The *Session Layer* makes the initial contact with other computers and sets up the lines of communication. It formats the data for transfer between end nodes, provides session restart and recovery, and performs the general maintenance of the session from end to end. The Session Layer offers three different modes: simplex, half duplex, and full duplex. It also splits up a communication session into three different phases: connection establishment, data transfer, and connection release.

Some examples of Session Layer protocols are:

- *Network File System* (NFS)
- *Structured Query Language* (SQL)
- *Remote Procedure Call* (RPC)

Transport Layer (Layer 4). The *Transport Layer* defines how to address the physical locations and/or devices on the network, how to make connections between nodes, and how to handle the networking of messages. It

---

[3] IBM's 8-bit extension of the 4-bit Binary Coded Decimal encoding of digits 0-9.
[4] 7-bit American National Standard Code for information interchange.

is responsible for maintaining the end-to-end integrity and control of the session. Services located in the Transport Layer both segment and reassemble the data from upper-layer applications and unite it onto the same data stream, which provides end-to-end data transport services and establishes a logical connection between the sending host and destination host on a network. The Transport Layer is also responsible for providing mechanisms for multiplexing upper-layer applications, session establishment, and the teardown of virtual circuits.

Examples of Transport Layer protocols are:

- *Transmission Control Protocol* (TCP)
- *User Datagram Protocol* (UDP)
- *Sequenced Packet Exchange* (SPX)

Network Layer (Layer 3). The *Network Layer* defines how the small packets of data are routed and relayed between end systems on the same network or on interconnected networks. At this layer, message routing, error detection, and control of node data traffic are managed. The Network Layer's primary function is the job of sending packets from the source network to the destination network.

Examples of Network Layer protocols are:

- *Internet Protocol* (IP)
- *Open Shortest Path First* (OSPF)
- *Internet Control Message Protocol* (ICMP)
- *Routing Information Protocol* (RIP)

Data Link Layer (Layer 2). The *Data Link Layer* defines the protocol that computers must follow in order to access the network for transmitting and receiving messages. Token Ring and Ethernet operate within this layer. This layer establishes the communications link between individual devices over a physical link or channel. It also ensures that messages are delivered to the proper device and translates the messages from layers above into bits for the Physical Layer to transmit. It also formats the message into data frames and adds a customized header that contains the hardware destination and source address. The Data Link Layer contains the *Logical Link Control Sublayer*[5] and the *Media Access Control*[6] (MAC) *Sublayer*.

---

[5] The Logical Link Control Sublayer is the part of the *link level* that supports *medium*-independent *data link* functions and uses the services of the *medium access control sublayer* to provide services to the *network layer*.

[6] The Media Access Control Layer is one of two sublayers that make up the Data Link Layer of the *OSI* model. The MAC layer is responsible for moving data *packets to* and from one *Network Interface Card* (NIC) to another across a shared *channel*.

Examples of Data Link Layer protocols are:

- Address Resolution Protocol (ARP)
- Serial Line Internet Protocol (SLIP)
- Point-to-Point Protocol (PPP)

Physical Layer (Layer 1). The *Physical Layer* defines the physical connection between a computer and a network and converts the bits into voltages or light impulses for transmission. It also defines the electrical and mechanical aspects of the device's interface to a physical transmission medium, such as twisted pair, coax, or fiber. Communications hardware and software drivers are found at this layer as well as electrical specifications such as EIA-232 (RS-232) and Synchronous Optical NETwork (SONET). The Physical Layer has only two responsibilities: It sends bits and receives bits.

The Physical Layer defines the following standard interfaces:

- EIA/TIA-232 and EIA/TIA-449
- X.21
- High-Speed Serial Interface (HSSI)

OSI Security Services and Mechanisms

OSI defines six basic security services to secure OSI communications. A *security service* is a collection of security mechanisms, files, and procedures that help protect the network.

These are the six basic security services:

1. Authentication
2. Access control
3. Data confidentiality
4. Data integrity
5. Nonrepudiation
6. Logging and monitoring

In addition, the OSI model also defines eight security mechanisms. A *security mechanism* is a control that is implemented in order to provide the six basic security services.

These are the eight security mechanisms:

1. Encipherment
2. Digital signature
3. Access control
4. Data integrity

5. Authentication

6. Traffic padding

7. Routing control

8. Notarization

Transmission Control Protocol/Internet Protocol (TCP/IP) Model

Transmission Control Protocol/Internet Protocol (TCP/IP) is the common name for the suite of protocols developed by the Department of Defense (DoD) in the 1970s to support the construction of the Internet. The Internet is based on TCP/IP. A CISSP candidate should be familiar with the major properties of TCP/IP and should know which protocols operate at which layers of the TCP/IP protocol suite. TCP and IP are the two most well known protocols in the suite.

The TCP/IP Protocol Model (see Figure 3.5) is similar to the OSI model, but it defines only the following four layers instead of seven:

- *Application Layer.* Consists of the applications and processes that use the network.

- *Host-to-Host Transport Layer.* Provides end-to-end data delivery service to the Application Layer.

- *Internet Layer.* Defines the IP datagram and handles the routing of data across networks.

- *Network Access or Link Layer.* Consists of routines for accessing physical networks and the electrical connection.

The *Application Layer* is roughly similar to the top three layers of the OSI model—the Application, Presentation, and Session layers—and performs most of the same functions. It is sometimes called the Process/Application Layer in some DoD definitions.

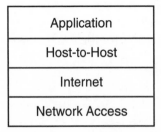

Figure 3.5 The TCP/IP Protocol Model.

The *Host-to-Host Layer* is comparable to OSI's Transport Layer. It defines the protocols for setting up the level of transmission service. It also provides for reliable end-to-end communications, ensures the data's error-free delivery, handles the data's packet sequencing, and maintains the data's integrity.

The *Internet Layer* corresponds to the OSI's Network Layer. It designates the protocols that are related to the logical transmission of packets over the network. This layer gives network nodes an IP address and handles the routing of packets among multiple networks. It also controls the communication flow between hosts.

At the bottom of the TCP/IP model, the *Network Access Layer* monitors the data exchange between the host and the network. The equivalent of the Data Link and Physical layers of the OSI model, it oversees hardware addressing and defines protocols for the physical transmission of data.

TCP/IP Protocols

The functional protocols can be grouped by the TCP/IP layer that they inhabit. Next, we list the main protocols that we are concerned with in the Telecommunications domain (and the corresponding layer). We describe each one in the following text.

Host-to-Host Transport Layer Protocols:

- Transmission Control Protocol (TCP)
- User Datagram Protocol (UDP)

Internet Layer Protocols:

- Internet Protocol (IP)
- Address Resolution Protocol (ARP)
- Reverse Address Resolution Protocol (RARP)
- Internet Control Message Protocol (ICMP)

Host-to-Host Transport Layer Protocols

Transmission Control Protocol (TCP). TCP provides a full-duplex, *connection-oriented, reliable,* virtual circuit. Incoming TCP packets are sequenced to match the original transmission sequence numbers. Because any lost or damaged packets are retransmitted, TCP is very costly in terms of network overhead and is slower than UDP.

Reliable data transport is addressed by TCP to ensure that the following goals are achieved:

- An acknowledgment is sent back to the sender upon the reception of delivered segments.
- Any unacknowledged segments are retransmitted.

- Segments are sequenced back in their proper order upon arrival at their destination.

- A manageable data flow is maintained in order to avoid congestion, overloading, and data loss.

TCP and UDP must use port numbers to communicate with the upper layers. Port numbers are used to keep track of the different conversations that are simultaneously crossing the network. Originating source port numbers dynamically assigned by the source host are usually some number greater than 1,023.

User Datagram Protocol (UDP). UDP is a scaled-down version of TCP. UDP is used like TCP, yet it only gives a "best effort" delivery. It does not offer error correction, does not sequence the packet segments, and does not care about the order in which the packet segments arrive at their destination. Thus, it is referred to as an *unreliable* protocol.

UDP does not create a virtual circuit and does not contact the destination before delivering the data. Thus, it is also considered a *connectionless* protocol. UDP imposes much less overhead, however, which makes it faster than TCP for applications that can afford to lose a packet now and then, such as streaming video or audio. Table 3.4 lists the main differences between TCP and UDP.

Table 3.4 TCP versus UDP Protocols

TCP	UDP
Acknowledged	Unacknowledged
Sequenced	Unsequenced
Connection-oriented	Connectionless
Reliability	Unreliable
High Overhead (slower)	Low overhead (faster)

CONNECTION-ORIENTED VERSUS CONNECTIONLESS NETWORK SERVICES

The traditional telephone versus letter example might help you to understand the difference between a TCP and a UDP. Calling someone on the phone is like TCP, because you have established a virtual circuit with the party at the other end. That party may or may not be the person you want to speak to (or might be an answering machine), but you know whether or not you spoke to them. Alternatively, using UDP is like sending a letter. You write your message, address it, and mail it. This process is like UDP's connectionless property. You are not really sure it will get there, but you assume the post office will provide its "best effort" to deliver it.

The Internet Layer Protocols

Internet Protocol (IP). IP is the Big Daddy of all the protocols. All hosts on a network have a logical ID called an IP address. This software address contains the information that aids in simplifying routing. Each data packet is assigned the IP address of the sender and the IP address of the recipient. Each device then receives the packet and makes routing decisions based upon the packet's destination IP address.

IP provides an "unreliable datagram service." It supplies a) no guarantees that the packet will be delivered, b) no guarantees that it will be delivered only once, and c) no guarantees that it will be delivered in the order in which it was sent.

Address Resolution Protocol (ARP). IP needs to know the hardware address of the packet's destination so that it can send it. ARP matches an IP address to an Ethernet address. An Ethernet address is a 48-bit address that is hard-wired into the NIC of the network node. ARP matches up the 32-bit IP address with this hardware address, which is technically referred to as the Media Access Control (MAC) address or the physical address.

ARP interrogates the network by sending out a broadcast seeking a network node that has a specific IP address, and asking it to reply with its hardware address. ARP maintains a dynamic table of these translations between IP addresses and Ethernet addresses, so that it only has to broadcast a request to every host the first time it is needed.

Reverse Address Resolution Protocol (RARP). In some cases, the reverse is required: The MAC address is known, but the IP address needs to be discovered. This is sometimes the case when diskless machines are booted onto the network. The RARP protocol sends out a packet, which includes its MAC address and a request to be informed of the IP address that should be assigned to that MAC address. A RARP server then responds with the answer.

Internet Control Message Protocol (ICMP). ICMP is a management protocol and messaging service provider for IP. Its primary function is to send messages between network devices regarding the health of the network. It also informs hosts of a better route to a destination if there is trouble with an existing route. It can also help identify the problem with that route.

Other TCP/IP Protocols

Telnet. Telnet's function is terminal emulation. It enables a user on a remote client machine to access the resources of another machine.

Telnet's capabilities are limited to running applications—it cannot be used for downloading files.

File Transfer Protocol (FTP). FTP is the protocol that facilitates file transfer between two machines. FTP is also employed to perform file tasks. It enables access for both directories and files, and can also accomplish certain types of directory operations. However, FTP cannot execute remote files as programs.

Trivial File Transfer Protocol (TFTP). TFTP is a stripped-down version of FTP. TFTP has no directory-browsing abilities; it can do nothing but send and receive files. Unlike FTP, authentication does not occur, so it is insecure. Some sites choose not to implement TFTP due to the inherent security risks.

Network File System (NFS). NFS is the protocol that supports file sharing. It enables two different types of file systems to interoperate.

Simple Mail Transfer Protocol (SMTP). SMTP is the protocol that we use every day to send and receive Internet email. When a message is sent, it is sent to a mail queue. The SMTP server regularly checks the mail queue for messages and delivers them when they are detected.

Line Printer Daemon (LPD). The LPD daemon, along with the Line Printer (LPR) program, enables print jobs to be spooled and sent to a network's shared printers.

X Window. X Window defines a protocol for the writing of graphical user interface-based client/server applications.

Simple Network Management Protocol (SNMP). SNMP is the protocol that provides for the collection of network information by polling the devices on the network from a management station. This protocol can also notify network managers of any network events by employing agents that send an alert called a trap to the management station. The databases of these traps are called *Management Information Bases* (MIBs).

Bootstrap Protocol (BootP). When a diskless workstation is powered on, it broadcasts a BootP request to the network. A BootP server hears the request and looks up the client's MAC address in its BootP file. If it finds an appropriate entry, it responds by telling the machine its IP address and the file from which it should boot. BootP is an Internet Layer protocol.

Security-Enhanced and Security-Focused Protocols

The following are two types of security-enhanced protocol extensions:

- Security enhancements to the Telnet protocol, such as Remote Terminal Access and Secure Telnet

- Security enhancements to the Remote Procedure Call protocol, such as Secure RPC Authentication (SRA)

The following protocols are two examples of security-focused protocols that were primarily created to support Internet transactions and authentication:

Secure Electronic Transaction (SET). Originated by Visa and MasterCard as an Internet credit card protocol, SET supports the authentication of both the sender and receiver and ensures content privacy in an effort to reduce merchant fraud on public networks. Although SET is still widely in use, SSL is overtaking it.

Secure HTTP (S-HTTP). An early standard for encrypting HTTP documents; the HTTP server caches and secures stored S-HTTP documents. SSL is also overtaking this protocol.

SET and S-HTTP operate at the Application Layer of the OSI model. The following are three protocols that provide security services at the Transport Layer. SSH and SSL are very heavily used for protecting Internet transactions. These are the three security-focused protocols:

Secure Shell (SSH-2). SSH is a strong method of performing client authentication. Because it supports authentication, compression, confidentiality, and integrity, SSH is used frequently on the Internet. SSH has two important components: RSA certificate exchange for authentication and Triple DES for session encryption.

Secure Sockets Layer (SSL). An encryption technology that is used to provide secure transactions such as the exchange of credit card numbers. SSL is a socket layer security protocol and is a two-layered protocol that contains the SSL Record Protocol and the SSL Handshake Protocol. Similar to SSH, SSL uses symmetric encryption for private connections and asymmetric or public key cryptography for peer authentication. It also uses a Message Authentication Code for message integrity checking.

Simple Key Management for Internet Protocols (SKIP). A security technology that provides high availability in encrypted sessions (for example, crashed gateways). SKIP is similar to SSL, except that it requires no prior communication in order to establish or exchange keys on a session-by-session basis. Therefore, no connection setup overhead exists and new key values are not continually generated.

Firewall Types and Architectures

A CISSP candidate will need to know the basic types of firewalls and their functions, which firewall operates at which protocol layer, and the basic variations of firewall architectures.

Firewall Types

We will begin by looking at the various types of firewalls. We have ordered them here by generation (in what order they were developed).

Packet Filtering Firewalls

The first type of firewall that we examine is the packet filtering firewall, which we can also call a screening router. This type of firewall examines both the source and destination address of the incoming data packet. This firewall either blocks or passes the packet to its intended destination network, which is usually the local network segment where it resides. The firewall can then deny access to specific applications and/or services based on the Access Control Lists (ACLs), which are database files that reside on the firewall, that are maintained by the firewall administrator, and that tell the firewall specifically which packets can and cannot be forwarded to certain addresses. The firewall can also enable access for only authorized application port or service numbers.

A packet filtering firewall looks at the data packet to get information about the source and destination addresses of an incoming packet, the session's communications protocol (TCP, UDP, or ICMP), and the source and destination application port for the desired service. This type of firewall system is considered a first-generation firewall and can operate at either the Network or Transport Layer of the OSI model.

Application Level Firewalls

Another type of firewall is known as an Application Level Firewall (see Figure 3.6). This firewall is commonly a host computer that is running proxy server software, which makes it a Proxy Server. This firewall works by transferring a copy of each accepted data packet from one network to another, thereby masking the data's origin. This can control which services a workstation uses (FTP and so on), and it also aids in protecting the network from outsiders who may be trying to get information about the network's design.

This type of firewall is considered a second-generation firewall. It is also called an Application Layer Proxy, and is commonly used with a Dual-Homed Host. It operates at the OSI protocol Layer Seven, the Application Layer. One drawback of this type of firewall is that it reduces network performance due

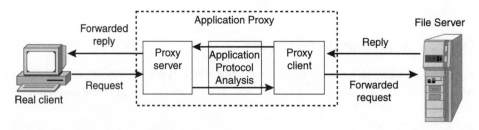

Figure 3.6 An Application Level Firewall.

to the fact that it must analyze every packet and decide what to do with each packet.

A variation of the application proxy firewall is called a Circuit Level Firewall. Like an application level firewall, this firewall is used as a proxy server. However, this firewall creates a virtual circuit between the workstation client (destination) and the server (host). It also provides security for a wide variety of protocols and is easier to maintain.

Stateful Inspection Firewalls

Another type of firewall is known as a Stateful Inspection Firewall. In a Stateful Inspection Firewall, data packets are captured by an inspection engine that is operating at the faster Network Layer. It maintains a "state" table which is constantly updated. The packets are queued and then analyzed at all OSI layers. This boosts performance over the pure application level firewall, and also provides a more complete inspection of the data. By examining the "state" and "context" of the incoming data packets, it helps to track the protocols that are considered "connectionless," such as UDP-based applications and Remote Procedure Calls (RPCs). This type of firewall system is used in third-generation firewall systems.

Dynamic Packet Filtering Firewalls

A Dynamic Packet Filtering Firewall is a *fourth-generation firewall* technology that enables the modification of the firewall security rule. This type of technology is mostly used for providing limited support for UDP. For a short period of time, this firewall remembers all of the UDP packets that have crossed the network's perimeter, and it decides whether to enable packets to pass through the firewall.

Kernel Proxy

A *Kernel Proxy* is a *fifth-generation firewall* architecture that provides a modular, kernel-based, multi-layer session evaluation and runs in the Windows NT Executive, which is the kernel mode of Windows NT. It is a specialized firewall architecture that uses dynamic and custom TCP/IP-based stacks to inspect the network packets and to enforce security policies. Unlike normal TCP/IP stacks, these stacks are constructed out of kernel-level proxies.

Firewall Architectures

Now we will discuss the four types of firewall architectures: packet filtering, screened hosts, dual-homed hosts, and screened-subnet firewalls. Keep in mind that some of these architectures are specifically associated with one of the previously discussed firewall generation types while other architectures can be a combination of generation types.

Figure 3.7 A Packet-Filtering Router.

Packet-Filtering Routers

The most common and oldest firewall device in use is the *Packet-Filtering Router* (see Figure 3.7). A packet-filtering router sits between the private "trusted" network and the "untrusted" network or network segment, and is sometimes used as a *boundary router*. A packet-filtering router uses Access Control Lists (ACLs). This firewall protects against standard generic external attacks; however, one problem with this type of firewall is that ACLs can be manually difficult to maintain.

This type of firewall has several drawbacks: It lacks strong user authentication, employs minimal auditing, and its complex ACLs negatively impact network performance. This packet filtering router is sometimes used to directly manage the access to a *demilitarized zone* (DMZ) network segment.

Screened-Host Firewall Systems

This firewall architecture employs both a packet-filtering router and a bastion host and is called a *Screened-Host Firewall* (see Figure 3.8). It commonly provides both network-layer (routing) and application-layer (proxy) services. This type of firewall system is considered safer because it requires an intruder to penetrate two separate systems before he or she can compromise the trusted network. The bastion host is configured on the local "trusted" network with a packet-filtering router between the "untrusted" network and the bas-

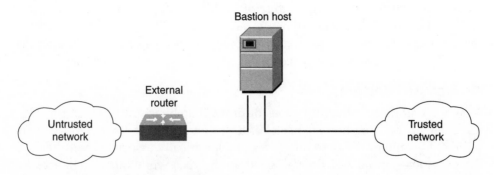

Figure 3.8 A Screened-Host Firewall.

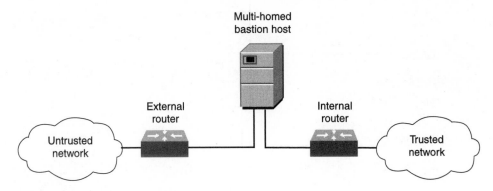

Figure 3.9 A Dual-Homed Firewall.

tion host. Because the bastion host is commonly the focus of external attacks, it is sometimes called the sacrificial host.

Dual-Homed Host Firewalls

Another very common firewall architecture configuration is the *Dual-Homed Host* (see Figure 3.9). It is also called a dual-homed or multi-homed bastion host. This architecture is a simple configuration that consists of a single computer (the host) with two NICs: One is connected to the local "trusted" network and the other is connected to the Internet or an "untrusted" external network. A dual-homed host firewall usually acts to block or filter some or all of the traffic trying to pass between the networks. IP traffic forwarding is usually disabled or restricted—all traffic between the networks and the traffic's destination must pass through some kind of security inspection mechanism. A multi-homed bastion host can translate between two network access layer protocols, such as Ethernet to Token Ring, for example.

A design issue with this firewall is that the host's routing capabilities must be disabled so that it does not unintentionally enable internal routing, which will connect the two networks together transparently and negate the firewall's function.

Screened-Subnet Firewalls (with a Demilitarized Zone)

One of the most secure implementations of firewall architectures is the *Screened-Subnet Firewall* (see Figure 3.10). It employs two packet-filtering routers and a bastion host. Like a screened-host firewall, this firewall supports both packet-filtering and proxy services, yet it also defines a demilitarized zone (DMZ). This creates a small network between the untrusted network and the trusted network where the bastion host and other public Web services

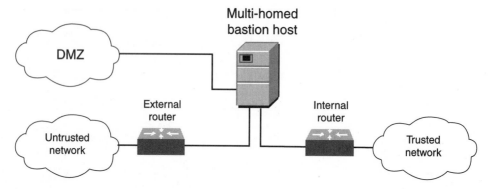

Figure 3.10 A Screened-Subnet Firewall with a DMZ.

exist. The outside router provides protection against external attacks while the inside router manages the private network access to a DMZ by routing it through the bastion host. This provides more layers of security. An issue with this configuration is its complex configuration and maintenance.

SOCKS Gateway

Another variation of firewall protection is provided by a proprietary firewall called a SOCKS server. This is a circuit-level proxy server that does not require the server resource overhead of conventional proxy servers. It does, however, require proprietary SOCKS client software to be loaded on every workstation. This firewall is mostly used for outbound Internet access by a workstation. The problem with this type of firewall configuration is that it is IT support-intensive (due to the individual workstation configurations) and uses proprietary software.

NETWORK ADDRESS TRANSLATION

Network Address Translation (NAT) is a very important concept in data networking, especially when it pertains to firewalls (see Figure 3.11). As a firewall administrator, you do not really want to let remote systems know the true IP addresses of your internal systems. The *Internet Assigned Numbers Authority* (IANA) has reserved the following three blocks of the IP address space for private Internets: 10.0.0.0 to 10.255.255.255, 172.16.0.0 to 172.31.255.255, and 192.168.0.0 to 192.168.255.255. These are known as global, non-routable addresses. NAT is a tool that is used for masking true IP addresses by employing these internal addresses. NAT converts a private IP address to a registered "real" IP address. Most firewall systems now include NAT capability. NAT is also used when corporations use private addressing ranges for internal networks (these ranges are not allowed to be routed on the Internet).

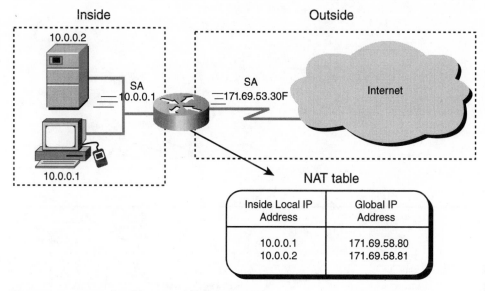

Figure 3.11 *Network Address Translation* (NAT).

Virtual Private Networks

A Virtual Private Network (VPN) is created by dynamically building a secure communications link between two nodes by using a *secret encapsulation method* (see Figure 3.12). This link is commonly called a secure encrypted tunnel, although it is more accurately defined as an encapsulated tunnel because encryption may or may not be used.

This tunnel can be created by using methods such as the following:

- Installing software or hardware agents on the client or a network gateway

- Implementing various user or node authentication systems

- Implementing key and certificate exchange systems

VPN Protocol Standards

The following are the three most common VPN communications protocol standards:

Point-to-Point Tunneling Protocol (PPTP). PPTP works at the Data Link Layer of the OSI model. Designed for individual client to server connections, it enables only a single point-to-point connection per session. This standard is very common with asynchronous connections that use Win9x or NT clients. PPTP uses native *Point-to-Point Protocol* (PPP) authentication and encryption services.

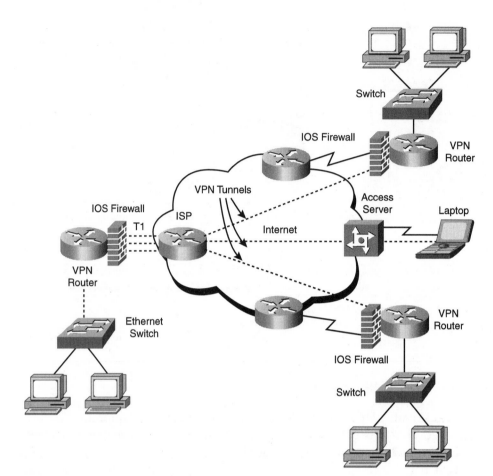

Figure 3.12 Example of a Cisco VPN.

Layer 2 Tunneling Protocol (L2TP). L2TP is a combination of PPTP and the earlier *Layer 2 Forwarding* (L2F) Protocol that works at the Data Link Layer like PPTP. It has become an accepted tunneling standard for VPNs. In fact, dial-up VPNs use this standard quite frequently. Like PPTP, this standard was designed for single point-to-point client to server connections. Note that multiple protocols can be encapsulated within the L2TP tunnel, but do not use encryption like PPTP. Also, L2TP supports TACACS+ and RADIUS, but PPTP does not.

IPSec. IPSec operates at the Network Layer and it enables multiple and simultaneous tunnels, unlike the single connection of the previous standards. IPSec has the functionality to encrypt and authenticate IP data. It is built into the new IPv6 standard, and is used as an add-on to the current IPv4. While PPTP and L2TP are aimed more at dial-up VPNs, IPSec focuses more on network-to-network connectivity. We describe the elements of IPSec in more detail in Chapter 4, "Cryptography."

VPN Devices

VPN devices are hardware or software devices that utilize the previously discussed VPN standards to create a secure tunnel. The VPN devices should be grouped into two types: *IPSec-compatible* and *non-IPSec-compatible*.

IPSec-Compatible VPN Devices

IPSec-compatible VPN devices are installed on a network's perimeter and encrypt the traffic between networks or nodes by creating a secure tunnel through the unsecured network. Because they employ IPSec encryption, they only work with IP (thus, they are not multi-protocol). These devices operate at the Network Layer (Layer Three). These devices have two operational modes:

1. Tunnel mode. The entire data packet is encrypted and encased in an IPSec packet.
2. Transport mode. Only the datagram is encrypted, leaving the IP address visible.

Non-IPSec-Compatible VPN Devices

Common VPN devices that are not compatible with IPSec include SOCKS-based proxy servers, PPTP-compatible devices, and devices that use SSH.

SOCKS-based proxy servers can be used in a VPN configuration as well as in a firewall configuration. In this implementation, they provide access to the internal network from the outside instead of enabling internal workstations access to the external Internet through a proxy firewall (described earlier in the "Firewall Architectures" section). While not a traditional VPN protocol, SOCKS-based systems contain authentication and encryption features, which are similar to strong VPN protocols. SOCKS operates at the OSI Layer 7.

As we previously described, PPTP is most frequently implemented in Win9x clients and/or WinNT Servers and clients. It is multi-protocol, uses PAP or CHAP user authentication, compresses data for efficient transmissions, and employs end-to-end encryption. *Dial-up VPNs* are LAN Remote Access Servers that have multi-protocol VPN services implemented and use PPTP. Internet Service Providers (ISPs) commonly use them.

Secure Shell (SSH-2) is not strictly a VPN product, but it can be used like one. SSH opens a secure, encrypted shell (command line) session from the Internet through a firewall to the SSH server. After the connection is established, it can be used as a terminal session or for tunneling other protocols.

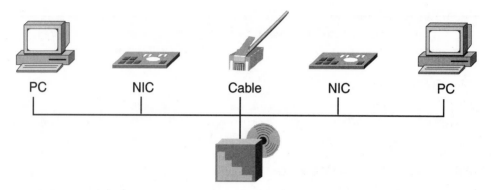

Figure 3.13 Data networking components.

Firewall-Based VPNs

Firewall-based VPNs are frequently available on third-generation firewalls. These devices employ a VPN system, which is integrated into a firewall and often uses proprietary or non-standard VPN protocols. These VPNs operate at the application layer in the tunnel mode. Because they commonly use user-based authentication and end-to-end encryption, performance degradation is often a problem with these devices.

Data Networking Basics

A CISSP candidate will also need to know the basics of the data network structures—the types of cabling, the various network access methods and topologies, and the differences between various LANs and WANs.

A Data Network consists of two or more computers that are connected for the purpose of sharing files, printers, exchanging data, and so forth. To communicate on the network, every workstation must have an NIC inserted into the computer, a transmission medium (such as copper, fiber, or wireless), a *Network Operating System* (NOS), and a LAN device of some sort (such as a hub, bridge, router, or switch) to physically connect the computers together. Figure 3.13 shows common data networking components.

Data Network Types

We will examine the following Data Network types:

- Local Area Networks (LAN)
- Wide Area Networks (WAN)
- Internet, intranet, and extranet

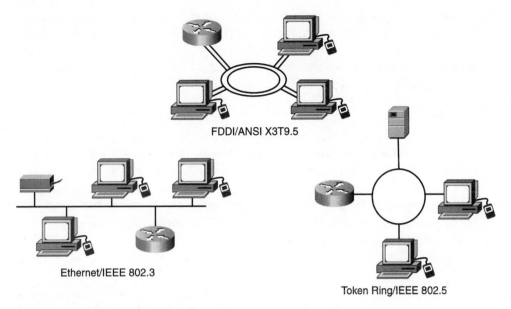

Figure 3.14 Local Area Networks (LANs).

Local Area Networks

A *Local Area Network (LAN)* (see Figure 3.14) is a discrete network that is designed to operate in a specific, limited geographic area like a single building or floor. LANs connect workstations and file servers together so that they can share network resources like printers, email, and files. LAN devices are connected by using a type of connection medium (such as copper wire or fiber optics), and they use various LAN protocols and access methods to communicate through LAN devices (such as bridges or routers). LANs can also be connected to a public switched network.

Two common types of LANs are as follows:

- Campus Area Network (CAN). A typically large campus network that connects multiple buildings with each other across a high-performance, switched backbone on the main campus

- Metropolitan Area Network (MAN). Although not often used as a description, essentially a LAN that extends over a city-wide metropolitan area

Both CANs and MANs can have connections to a WAN.

Wide Area Networks

Think of a *Wide Area Network* (WAN) as a network of subnetworks that physically or logically interconnect LANs over a large geographic area. A WAN is basically everything outside of a LAN. A WAN might be privately operated for a specific user community, might support multiple communication protocols, or might provide network connectivity and services via interconnected network segments (extranets, intranets, and VPNs). We will describe WAN technologies later in more detail.

Internet

The *Internet* is a WAN that was originally funded by the DoD, which uses TCP/IP for data interchange. The term "Internet" is used to refer to any and all kinds of *Advanced Research Projects Agency Network* (ARPANET), *Department of Defense Research Projects Agency Network* (DARPANET), *Defense Data Network* (DDN), or DoD Internets. It specifically refers to the global network of public networks and ISPs throughout the world. Either public or private networks (with a VPN) can utilize the Internet.

Intranet

An intranet is an Internet-like logical network that uses a firm's internal, physical network infrastructure. Because it uses TCP/IP and HTTP standards, it can use low-cost Internet products like Web browsers. A common example of an intranet would be a company's human resource department publishing employee guidelines that are accessible by all company employees on the intranet. An intranet provides more security and control than a public posting on the Internet.

Extranet

Like an intranet, an extranet is a private network that uses Internet protocols. Unlike an intranet, users outside the company (partners, vendors, and so forth) can access an extranet but the general public cannot. An example of this type of network is a company's supplier, who can access a company's private network (via a VPN or Internet connection with some kind of authentication) but only has access to the information that he or she needs.

In addition, a CISSP candidate should know the difference between asynchronous versus synchronous communications and analog versus digital technologies. Figure 3.15 shows the difference between an analog and digital signal while Table 3.5 shows the difference between analog and digital technologies.

Common Data Network Services

The following are some of the common services that a data network provides:

File services. They share data files and subdirectories on file servers.

Mail services. They send and receive email internally or externally through an email gateway device.

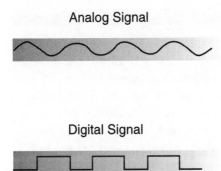

Figure 3.15 Examples of analog and digital signals.

Table 3.5 Analog versus Digital Technologies

ANALOG	DIGITAL
Infinite wave form	Saw-tooth wave form
Continuous signal	Pulses
Varied by amplification	On-off only

ASYNCHRONOUS VERSUS SYNCHRONOUS COMMUNICATIONS

Asynchronous Communication transfers data by sending bits of data sequentially. Start and stop bits mark the beginning and the end of each transfer. Communications devices must operate at the same speed to communicate. Asynchronous Communication is the basic language of modems and dial-up remote access systems. Synchronous Communication is characterized by very high-speed transmission rates governed by electronic clock timing signals.

Print services. They print documents to a shared printer or a print queue/spooler.

Client/Server services. They allocate computing power resources among workstations with some shared resources centralized in a file server.

Domain Name Service (DNS). It matches Internet Uniform Resource Locator (URL) requests with the actual address or location of the server that provides that URL. It is a distributed database system that maps host names to IP addresses. The Domain Name System (DNS) is a global network of servers that provide these Domain Name Services (DNSs).

A WORD ABOUT NETWORK ARCHITECTURES

Network Architecture refers to the communications products and services, which ensure that the various components of a network (such as devices, protocols, and access methods) work together. Originally, a manufacturer's network system often did not interoperate within its own product line, much less enable connectivity with the products of other manufacturers. While IBM's *Systems Network Architecture* (SNA) and Digital Equipment Corporation's DECnet were seen as an advance in solving these problems within the vendor's product line, they still did not interoperate outside of that product line. The Open Systems Interconnection (OSI) model by the International Standardization Organizations (ISO) was a big step in solving this problem. Other network architecture examples include the Xerox Networking System (XNS) and the Advanced Research Projects Agency Network (ARPANET), the originator of the Internet. These and other standard computer network architectures divide and subdivide the various functions of data communications into isolated layers, which makes it easier to create products and standards that can interoperate.

Figure 3.16 Cabling types.

Data Networking Technologies

In this section, we examine the basic components of LAN and WAN technologies, including cabling, transmission protocols, and topologies.

LAN Technologies

To become more familiar with the various types of LAN technologies, we need to examine LAN cabling, protocols, transmission and access methods, topologies, and devices.

LAN Cabling Types

Network cabling comes in three flavors—twisted pair, coaxial, and fiber-optic—as shown in Figure 3.16.

Twisted Pair Cabling. Twisted pair cabling is a relatively low-speed transmission medium, which consists of two insulated wires that are arranged in a regular spiral pattern. The wires can be shielded (STP) or unshielded (UTP). UTP cabling is a four-pair wire medium used in a variety of networks. UTP does not require the fixed spacing between connections that is necessary with coaxial-type connections.

UTP comes in several categories. The category rating is based on how tightly the copper cable is wound within the shielding: the tighter the wind, the higher the rating and its resistance against interference and attenuation. In fact, UTP Category 3 wire was often used for phone lines, but now the Category 5 wire is the standard, and even higher categories are available. Eavesdroppers can more easily tap this UTP cabling than the other cable types.

The categories of UTP are as follows:

- *Category 1 UTP.* Used for telephone communications and is not suitable for transmitting data.

- *Category 2 UTP.* Specified in the EIA/TIA-586 standard to be capable of handling data rates of up to 4 *million bits per second* (Mbps).

- *Category 3 UTP.* Used in 10BaseT networks and is specified to be capable of handling data rates of up to 10 Mbps.

- *Category 4 UTP.* Used in Token Ring networks and can transmit data at speeds of up to 16 Mbps.

- *Category 5 UTP.* Specified to be capable of handling data rates of up to 100 Mbps, and is currently the UTP standard for new installations.

- *Category 6 UTP.* Specified to be capable of handling data rates of up to 155 Mbps.

- *Category 7 UTP.* Specified to be capable of handling data rates of up to 1 *billion bits per second* (Gbps).

Coaxial Cable (Coax). Coax consists of a hollow outer cylindrical conductor that surrounds a single, inner wire conductor. Two types of coaxial cable are currently used in LANs: 50-ohm cable, which is used for digital signaling, and 75-ohm cable, which is used for analog signaling and high-speed digital signaling.

Coax is more expensive, yet it is more resistant to Electromagnetic Interference (EMI) than twisted pair cabling and can transmit at a greater bandwidth and distance. However, twisted pair cabling is so ubiquitous that most installations rarely use coax except in special cases, such as broadband communications.

Coax can come in two types for LANs:

1. Thinnet (RG58 size)
2. Thicknet (RG8 or RG11 size)

The following are the two common types of coaxial cable transmission methods:

1. *Baseband.* The cable carries only a single channel.
2. *Broadband.* The cable carries several usable channels, such as data, voice, audio, and video.

Fiber Optic Cable. Fiber optic cable is a physical medium that is capable of conducting modulated light transmission. Fiber optic cable carries signals as light waves, thus creating higher transmission speeds and greater distances due to less attenuation. This type of cabling is much more difficult to tap than other cabling and is the most resistant to interference, especially EMI. It is sometimes called *optical fiber*.

Fiber optic cable is usually reserved for the connections between backbone devices in larger networks. In some very demanding environments, however, fiber optic cable connects desktop workstations to the network or links to adjacent buildings. Fiber optic cable is the most reliable cable type, but it is also the most expensive to install and terminate.

LAN Transmission Protocols

LAN Transmission Protocols are the rules for communication between computers on a LAN. These rules oversee the various steps in communicating, such as the formatting of the data frame, the timing and sequencing of packet delivery, and the resolution of error states.

Carrier Sense Multiple Access (CSMA). The foundation of the Ethernet communications protocol. It has two functional variations: CSMA/CA and CSMA/CD, which is the Ethernet standard. In CSMA, a workstation continuously monitors a line while waiting to send a packet, then transmits the packet when it thinks the line is free. If the workstation doesn't receive an acknowledgment from the destination to which it sent the packet, it assumes a collision has occurred and it resends the packet. This is defined as persistent carrier sense. Another version of CSMA is called non-persistent carrier sense where a workstation waits a random amount of time before resending a packet, thus resulting in fewer errors.

Carrier-Sense Multiple Access with Collision Avoidance (CSMA/CA). In this variation of CSMA, workstations are attached to two coaxial cables. Each coax cable carries data signals in one direction only. A workstation monitors its receive cable to determine whether the carrier is busy. It then communicates on its transmit cable if it detected no carrier. Thus, the workstation transmits its intention to send when it feels the line is clear due to a precedence that is based upon pre-established tables. Pure

CSMA does not have a feature to avoid the problem of one workstation dominating a conversation.

Carrier-Sense Multiple Access with Collision Detection (CSMA/CD). Under the Ethernet CSMA/CD media-access process, any computer on a CSMA/CD LAN can access the network at any time. Before sending data, CSMA/CD hosts listen for traffic on the network. A host wanting to send data waits until it does not detect any traffic before it transmits. Ethernet enables any host on a network to transmit whenever the network is quiet. In addition, the transmitting host also constantly monitors the wire to make sure that no other hosts begin transmitting. If the host detects another signal on the wire, it then sends out an extended jam signal that causes all nodes on the segment to stop sending data. These nodes respond to that jam signal by waiting a bit before attempting to transmit again.

CSMA/CD was created to overcome the problem of collisions that occur when packets are simultaneously transmitted from different nodes. Collisions occur when two hosts listen for traffic, and upon hearing none they both transmit simultaneously. In this situation, both transmissions are damaged and the hosts must retransmit at a later time.

Polling. In the polling transmission method, a primary workstation checks a secondary workstation regularly at predetermined times to determine whether it has data to transmit. Secondary workstations cannot transmit until the primary host gives them permission. Polling is commonly used in large mainframe environments where hosts are polled to determine whether they need to transmit. Because polling is very inexpensive, networks that are low-level and peer-to-peer types also use it.

Token-Passing. Used in Token Ring, FDDI, and Attached Resource Computer Network (ARCnet) networks, stations in token-passing networks cannot transmit until they receive a special frame called a token. This arrangement prevents the collision problems that are present in CSMA. Token-passing networks will work well if large, bandwidth-consuming applications are commonly used on the network.

Token Ring and IEEE 802.5 are two principal examples of token-passing networks. Token-passing networks move a small frame, called a token, around the network. Possession of this token grants the right to transmit. If a node that is receiving the token has no information to send, it passes the token to the next end station. Each station can then hold the token for a maximum period of time, as determined by the 802.5 specification.

Unlike CSMA/CD networks (such as Ethernet), token-passing networks are deterministic, which means that it is possible to calculate the maximum time that will pass before any end station can transmit. This feature and the fact that collisions cannot occur make Token Ring networks ideal for applications where the transmission delay must be predictable and robust network operation is important. Factory automation environments are examples of such applications.

LAN Transmission Methods

There are three flavors of LAN transmission methods:

Unicast. The packet is sent from a single source to a single destination address.

Multicast. The source packet is copied and sent to specific multiple destinations on the network.

Broadcast. The packet is copied and sent to all of the nodes on a network or segment of a network.

LAN Topologies

A network topology defines the manner in which the network devices are organized to facilitate communications. A LAN topology defines this transmission manner for a Local Area Network.

There are five common LAN topologies: BUS, RING, STAR, TREE, and MESH.

BUS Topology. In a BUS topology, all the transmissions of the network nodes travel the full length of cable and are received by all other stations (see Figure 3.17). Ethernet primarily uses this topology. This topology does have some faults. For example, when any station on the bus experiences cabling termination errors, the entire bus can cease to function.

RING Topology. In a RING topology, the network nodes are connected by unidirectional transmission links to form a closed loop (see Figure 3.18). Token Ring and FDDI both use this topology.

STAR Topology. In a STAR topology, the nodes of a network are connected to a central LAN device directly (see Figure 3.19). Here is where it gets a little confusing: The logical BUS and RING topologies that we previously described are often implemented physically in a STAR topology. Although Ethernet is logically thought of as a BUS topology (its first implementations were Thinnet and Thicknet on a BUS), 10BaseT is actually wired as a STAR topology, which provides more resiliency for the entire topology when a station experiences errors.

TREE Topology. The TREE topology (as shown in Figure 3.20) is a BUS-type topology where branches with multiple nodes are possible.

Figure 3.17 A BUS topology.

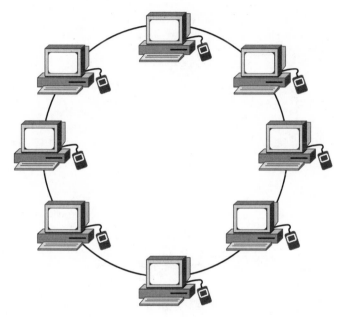

Figure 3.18 A RING topology.

> **MESH Topology.** In a MESH topology, all the nodes are connected to every other node in a network (see Figure 3.21). This topology may be used to create backbone-redundant networks. A full MESH topology has every node connected to every other node. A partial MESH topology may be used to connect multiple full MESH networks together.

LAN Media Access Methods

LAN media access methods control the use of a network (its physical and data link layers). Now, we will discuss the basic characteristics of Ethernet, ARC-net, Token Ring, and FDDI—the LAN technologies that account for virtually all deployed LANs.

> **Ethernet.** The Ethernet media access method transports data to the LAN by using CSMA/CD. Currently, this term is often used to refer to all CSMA/CD LANs. Ethernet was designed to serve on networks with sporadic, occasionally heavy traffic requirements.

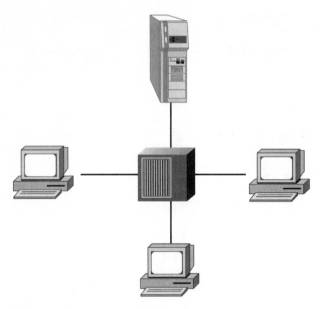

Figure 3.19 A STAR topology.

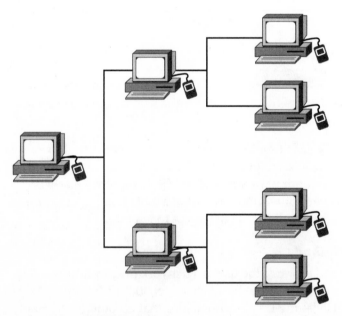

Figure 3.20 A TREE topology.

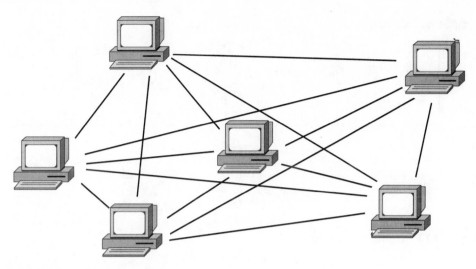

Figure 3.21 A MESH topology.

Ethernet defines a BUS-topology LAN with three cable standards:

1. *Thinnet.* Known as 10Base2, it is a coaxial cable with segments of up to 185 meters.

2. *Thicknet.* Known as 10BaseS, it is a coaxial cable with segments of up to 500 meters.

3. *Unshielded Twisted Pair.* In UTP, all hosts are connected by using an unshielded twisted pair cable connected to a central device (such as a hub or switch). UTP has three common variations: 10BaseT operates at 10 Mbps, 100BaseT (Fast Ethernet) operates at 100 Mbps, and 1000BaseT (Gigabit Ethernet) operates at 1 Gbps.

Figure 3.22 shows an Ethernet network segment.

ARCnet. ARCnet is one of the earliest LAN technologies. It uses a token-passing access method in a STAR technology on coaxial cable. ARCnet provides predictable (if not slow) network performance. One issue with ARCnet stations is that the node address of each station has to be manually set during installation, thus creating the possibility of duplicate and conflicting nodes.

Token Ring. IBM originally developed the Token Ring network in the 1970s. It is second only to Ethernet in general LAN popularity. The term Token Ring refers to both IBM's Token Ring network and IEEE 802.5 networks. All end stations are attached to a device called a Multistation Access Unit (MSAU). One station on a Token Ring network is designated the Active Monitor. The Active Monitor makes sure that there is

Ethernet Segment

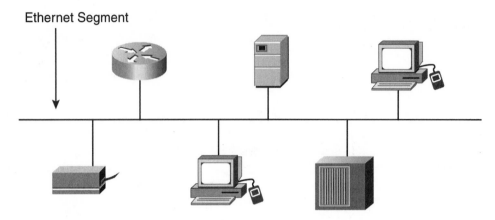

Figure 3.22 An Ethernet segment.

DUELING ETHERNETS

Digital, Intel, and Xerox teamed up to create the original Ethernet I standard in 1980. In 1984, they followed up with the release of Ethernet II. The Institute of Electrical and Electronic Engineers (IEEE) founded the 802.3 subcommittee to create an Ethernet standard that was almost identical to the Ethernet II version. These two standards differ only in their descriptions of the Data Link Layer: Ethernet II has a "Type" field, whereas 802.3 has a "Length" field. Otherwise, both are the same in their Physical Layer specifications and MAC addressing.

---

not more than one token on the Ring at any given time. If a transmitting station fails, it probably cannot remove a token as it makes it way back onto the ring. In this case, the Active monitor will step in and remove the token and generate a new one.

Fiber Distributed Data Interface (FDDI). Like Token Ring, FDDI is a token-passing media access topology. It consists of a dual Token Ring LAN that operates at 100 Mbps over Fiber Optic cabling. FDDI employs a token-passing media access with dual counter-rotating rings, with only one ring active at any given time. If a break or outage occurs, the ring will then wrap back the other direction, keeping the ring intact.

The following are the major advantages of FDDI:

■ It can operate over long distances, at high speeds, and with minimal electromagnetic or radio frequency interference present.

■ It provides predictable, deterministic delays and permits several tokens to be present on the ring concurrently.

The major drawbacks of FDDI are its expense and the expertise needed to implement it properly.

Copper Distributed Data Interface (CDDI) can be used with a UTP cable to connect servers or other stations into the ring instead of using fiber optic cable. Unfortunately, this introduces the basic problems that are inherent with the use of copper cabling (length and interference problems).

LAN Devices

Repeaters. *Repeaters* amplify the data signals to extend the length of a network segment, and they help compensate for signal deterioration due to attenuation. They do not add any intelligence to the process, however. They do not filter packets, examine addressing, or change anything in the data.

Hubs. *Hubs* are often used to connect multiple LAN devices (such as servers and workstations) into a device called a concentrator. Hubs can be considered as *multi-port repeaters*. See Figure 3.23.

Repeaters and Hubs operate at the Physical Layer of the OSI model.

Bridges. *Bridges* also amplify the data signals and add some intelligence. A bridge forwards the data to all other network segments if the Media Access Control (MAC) or hardware address of the destination computer is not on the local network segment. If the destination computer is on the local network segment, it does not forward the data. Because bridges operate at the Data Link Layer, Layer 2, they do not use IP addresses due to the fact that the information is attached in the Network Layer, Layer 3. One issue with bridges is that because a bridge automatically forwards all broadcast traffic, an error state known as a broadcast storm can develop, bringing all of the devices to a halt. Figure 3.24 shows a bridged network.

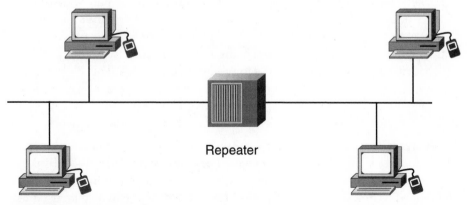

Repeater

Figure 3.23 A repeater or hub.

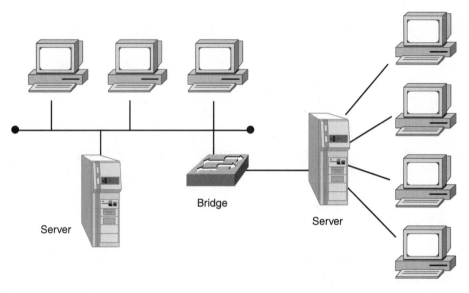

Figure 3.24 A bridged network.

Switches. A *switch* is similar to a bridge or a hub, except that a switch will only send the data packet to the specific port where the destination MAC address is located, rather than to all ports that are attached to the hub or bridge. A switch can be thought of as a fast, *multi-port bridge*. Switches primarily operate at the Data Link Layer, Layer 2, although intelligent, extremely fast Layer 3 switching techniques (combing, switching, and routing) are being used more frequently. Tag Switching, Netflow Switching, and Cisco Express Forwarding are some examples. Figure 3.25 shows a switched network.

Routers. *Routers* add even more intelligence to the process of forwarding data packets. A router opens up a data packet, reads either the hardware or network address (IP address) before forwarding it, and then forwards only the packet to the network to which the packet was destined. This prevents unnecessary network traffic from being sent over the network by blocking broadcast information and traffic to unknown addresses. This blocking does, however, create more overhead in the routing device than exists in a bridge. Routers operate at the Network Layer, Layer 3, and at the lower levels of the OSI protocol model. Figure 3.26 shows a routed network.

Gateways. *Gateways* are primarily software products that you can run on computers or other network devices. They can be multi-protocol (link different protocols) and can examine the entire packet. Mail gateways are used to link dissimilar mail programs. Gateways can also be used to translate between two dissimilar network protocols.

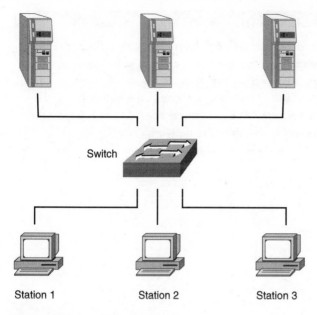

Figure 3.25 A switched network.

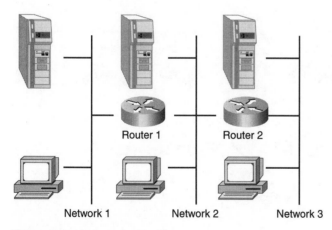

Figure 3.26 A routed network.

Asynchronous Transfer Mode (ATM) Switches. Although ATM switches are more commonly used for WANs, they are beginning to be used extensively in CANs. ATM switches use a cell relay technology that combines the advantages of both conventional circuit and packet-based systems, thus providing high-speed cell switching. We will describe ATM in greater detail later when dealing with WAN technology.

BROADCASTS

A broadcast is a data packet that is sent to all network stations at the same time. Broadcasts are an essential function built into all protocols. When servers need to send data to all the other hosts on the network segment, network broadcasts are useful. If a lot of broadcasts are occurring on a network segment, however, network performance can be seriously degraded. It is important to use these devices properly and to segment the network correctly.

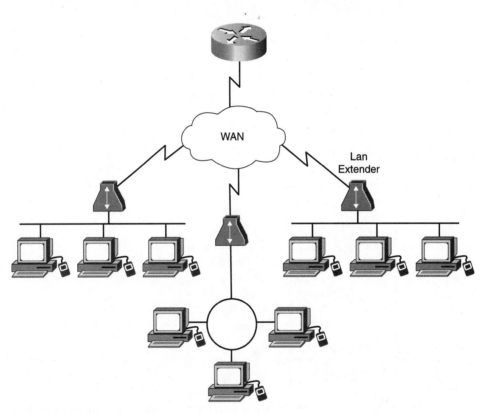

Figure 3.27 A LAN extender.

LAN Extenders. A LAN extender is a remote-access, multi-layer switch that connects to a host router (see Figure 3.27). LAN extenders forward traffic from all the standard network-layer protocols (such as IP, IPX, and Appletalk), and filter traffic based on the MAC address or network-layer protocol type. LAN extenders scale well because the host router filters out unwanted broadcasts and multicasts. LAN extenders, however, are not capable of segmenting traffic or creating security firewalls.

WAN Technologies

To become more familiar with the various types of WAN technologies, you must understand WAN protocols, topologies, and devices.

WAN Protocols and Topologies

Like LAN protocols, WAN protocols are the rules for communicating between computers on a WAN. Because the WAN is more often used for connecting networks together than a LAN, these protocols address the issues involved with communications between many large and disparate networks. Almost every WAN protocol is designed to run on a specific WAN topology. While some topologies can combine protocols, the list in the next section shows which protocol is native to and runs on which topology.

Private Circuit Technologies

Private circuits evolved before packet-switching networks. A private circuit network is a dedicated analog or digital point-to-point connection joining geographically diverse networks. Examples of private circuit networks are dedicated lines, leased lines, *Serial Line Internet Protocol* (SLIP), *Point-to-Point Protocol* (PPP), ISDN, and xDSL.

Dedicated Line. A dedicated line is a communications line that is indefinitely and continuously reserved for transmissions, rather than being switched on and off as transmission is required. A dedicated link can be a leased line or a point-to-point link.

Leased Line. A communications carrier can reserve a dedicated line for a customer's private use. A leased line is a type of dedicated line.

Types and speeds of standard leased lines are as follows:

- Digital Signal Level 0 *(DS-0)*. The framing specification used in transmitting digital signals over a single channel at 64 Kbps on a T1 facility.
- Digital Signal Level 1 *(DS-1)*. The framing specification used in transmitting digital signals at 1.544 Mbps on a T1 facility (in the United States) or at 2.108 Mbps on an E1 facility (in Europe).
- Digital Signal Level 3 (DS-3). The framing specification used for transmitting digital signals at 44.736 Mbps on a T3 facility.
- *T1*. Transmits DS-1-formatted data at 1.544 Mbps through a telephone-switching network.

■ *T3.* Transmits DS-3-formatted data at 44.736 Mbps through a telephone-switching network.

■ *E1.* A wide-area digital transmission scheme predominantly used in Europe that carries data at a rate of 2.048 Mbps.

■ *E3.* The same as E1 (both can be leased for private use from common carriers), but it carries data at a rate of 34.368 Mbps.

Serial Line IP (SLIP). SLIP is an industry standard that was developed in 1984 to support TCP/IP networking over low-speed serial interfaces in Berkeley Unix computers. Using the Windows NT RAS service, Windows NT computers can use TCP/IP and SLIP to communicate with remote hosts.

Point-to-Point Protocol (PPP). PPP is a specification used by data communications equipment for transmitting over dial-up and dedicated links. It enables multi-vendor operability and was originally proposed as a standard to improve on SLIP, which only supported IP. PPP takes the specifications of SLIP and builds on them by adding login, password, and error correction capabilities. PPP is a Data Link Layer protocol and has built-in security mechanisms such as CHAP and PAP.

Integrated Services Digital Network (ISDN). ISDN is a combination of digital telephony and data transport services that telecommunications carriers offer. ISDN consists of a digitization of the telephone network by permitting voice and other digital services (data, music, video, and so forth) to be transmitted over existing telephone wires. The more popular xDSL types have recently overtaken it.

Digital Subscriber Line (xDSL). *Digital Subscriber Line* (xDSL) uses existing twisted pair telephone lines to transport high bandwidth data to remote subscribers. It consists of a point-to-point public network that is accessed through an in-home copper phone wire. It is rapidly becoming the standard for inexpensive remote connectivity.

The following are examples of the types of xDSL:

■ *Asymmetric Digital Subscriber Line (ADSL).* ADSL is designed to deliver more bandwidth downstream (from the central office to the customer site) than upstream. Downstream rates range from 1.5 to 9 Mbps while upstream bandwidth ranges from 16 to 640 Kbps. ADSL transmissions work at distances of up to 18,000 feet over a single copper twisted pair (although 14,400 feet is the maximum practical length).

■ *Single-Line Digital Subscriber Line (SDSL).* SDSL delivers 1.544 Mbps both downstream and upstream over a single copper twisted pair. This use of a single twisted pair limits the operating range of SDSL to 10,000 feet.

■ *High-Rate Digital Subscriber Line (HDSL).* HDSL delivers 1.544 Mbps of bandwidth each way over two copper twisted pairs. Because HDSL provides T1 speed, telephone companies have been using HDSL to provide local access to T1 services whenever possible. The operating range of HDSL is limited to 12,000 feet.

■ *Very-High Data Rate Digital Subscriber Line (VDSL).* VDSL delivers 13 to 52 Mbps downstream and 1.5 to 2.3 Mbps upstream over a single twisted copper pair. The operating range of VDSL is limited to 1,000 to 4,500 feet.

Circuit-Switched Versus Packet-Switched Networks

Circuit-Switched Networks. *Circuit switching* is defined as a switching system in which a dedicated physical circuit path must exist between the sender and receiver for the duration of the transmission or the "call." A *circuit-switched network* describes a type of WAN that consists of a physical, permanent connection from one point to another. This technology is older than packet switching, which we discuss next, but it is the main choice for communications that need to be "on" constantly and have a limited scope of distribution (one transmission path only). This network type is used heavily in telephone company networks.

Packet-Switched Networks. *Packet-switching* is defined as a networking method where nodes share bandwidth with each other by sending small data units called packets. A *packet-switched network* (PSN) or PSDN is a network that uses packet-switching technology for data transfer. Unlike circuit-switched networks, the data in packet-switched networks is broken up into packets and then sent to the next destination based on the router's understanding of the best available route. At that destination, the packets are reassembled based on their originally assigned sequence numbers. Although the data is manhandled a lot in this process, it creates a network that is very resistant to error. Table 3.6 is a list of the basic differences between circuit and packet switching.

Table 3.6 Circuit Switching versus Packet Switching

CIRCUIT SWITCHING	PACKET SWITCHING
Constant traffic	Bursty traffic
Fixed delays	Variable delays
Connection-oriented	Connectionless
Sensitive to loss of connection	Sensitive to loss of data
Voice-oriented	Data-oriented

Packet-Switched Technologies

Packet-switched networks can be far more cost effective than dedicated circuits because they create virtual circuits, which are used as needed, rather than supplying a continuous dedicated circuit. Examples of packet-switching networks are X.25, *Link Access Procedure-Balanced* (LAPB), Frame Relay, *Switched Multimegabit Data Systems* (SMDS), *Asynchronous Transfer Mode* (ATM), and *Voice over IP* (VoIP).

X.25. The first packet-switching network, X.25, defines the point-to-point communication between *Data Terminal Equipment* (DTE), *Data Circuit-Terminating Equipment* (DCE, commonly a modem), or a *Data Service Unit/Channel Service Unit* (DSU/CSU), which supports both *switched virtual circuits* (SVCs) and *permanent virtual circuits* (PVCs). X.25 defines how WAN devices are established and maintained. X.25 was designed to operate effectively regardless of the type of systems that are connected to the network. It has become an international standard and is currently much more prevalent overseas than in the United States.

Link Access Procedure-Balanced (LAPB). Created for use with X.25, LAPB defines frame types and is capable of retransmitting, exchanging, and acknowledging frames as well as detecting out-of-sequence or missing frames.

Frame Relay. Frame Relay is a high-performance WAN protocol that operates at the Data Link layer of the OSI model. Originally designed for use across ISDN interfaces, it is currently used with a variety of other interfaces and is a major standard for high-speed WAN communications. Frame Relay is an upgrade from X.25 and LAPB. It is the fastest of the WAN protocols listed because of its simplified framing approach, which utilizes no error correction. Frame Relay uses SVCs, PVCs, and *Data Link Connection Identifiers* (DLCIs) for addressing. Because it requires access to a high-quality digital network infrastructure, it is not available everywhere.

Switched Multi-megabit Data Service (SMDS). SMDS is a high-speed technology used over public switched networks. It is provided for companies that need to exchange large amounts of data with other enterprises over WANs on a bursty or non-continuous basis, by providing connectionless bandwidth upon demand.

Asynchronous Transfer Mode (ATM). ATM is a high-bandwidth, low-delay technology that uses both switching and multi-plexing. It uses 53-byte, fixed-size cells instead of frames like Ethernet. It can allocate bandwidth upon demand, making it a solution for bursty applications. ATM requires a high-speed, high-bandwidth medium like fiber optics. ATM is taking the place of FDDI in the campus backbone arena because it can run in both WAN and LAN environments at tremendous speeds.

VIRTUAL CIRCUITS

Switched virtual circuits (SVCs) are virtual circuits that are dynamically established on demand and are torn down when transmission is complete. SVCs are used in situations where data transmission is sporadic. SVCs have three phases: circuit establishment, data transfer, and circuit termination (teardown). *Permanent virtual circuits* (PVCs) are virtual circuits that are permanently connected. PVCs save the bandwidth that is associated with circuit establishment and teardown.

Voice over IP (VoIP). VoIP is one of several digital, multi-service access IP technologies that combine many types of data (such as voice, audio, and video) into a single IP packet, which provides major benefits in the areas of cost, interoperability, and performance.

Other Important WAN Protocols

Synchronous Data Link Control (SDLC). SDLC is a protocol that IBM created to make it easier for its mainframes to connect to the remote offices. SDLC defines and uses a polling media-access method. It consists of a primary station, which controls all communications, and one or more secondary stations. SDLC is based on dedicated, leased lines with permanent physical connections, and it has evolved into the HDLC and Link Access Procedure-Balanced (LAPB) protocols. This protocol operates at the Data Link Layer.

High-Level Data Link Control (HDLC). Derived from SDLC, HDLC specifies the data encapsulation method on synchronous serial links by using frame characters and checksums. The ISO created the HDLC standard to support both point-to-point and multi-point configurations. Vendors often implement HDLC in different ways, which sometimes makes the HDLC protocol incompatible. It also operates at the Data Link Layer.

High-Speed Serial Interface (HSSI). HSSI is a DTE/DCE interface that was developed to address the need for high-speed communications over WAN links. It defines the electrical and physical interfaces that DTE/DCEs use and operates at the Physical Layer of the OSI model.

WAN Devices

WAN devices are the elements that enable the use of WAN protocols and topologies. The following are examples of these device types:

- *Routers.* Although previously described as a LAN device, in the WAN environment, routers are extremely important—especially for IP Internet traffic.

■ *Multiplexers.* Commonly referred to as a mux, a multiplexer is a device that enables more than one signal to be sent out simultaneously over one physical circuit.

■ *WAN Switches.* WAN Switches are multi-port, networking devices that are used in carrier networks. They operate at the Data Link Layer and typically switch Frame Relay, X.25, and SMDS. These switches connect private data over public data circuits by using digital signals.

■ *Access Servers.* An Access Server is a server that provides dial-in and dial-out connections to the network. These are typically asynchronous servers that enable users to dial in and attach to the LAN. Cisco's AS5200 series of communication servers are an example of such devices.

■ *Modems.* A modem is a device that interprets digital and analog signals, which enables data to be transmitted over voice-grade telephone lines. The digital signals are then converted to an analog form, which is suitable for transmission over an analog communications medium. These signals are then converted back to their digital form at the destination.

■ *Channel Service Unit (CSU)/Data Service Unit (DSU).* This digital interface device terminates the physical interface on a DTE device (such as a terminal) to the interface of a DCE device (such as a switch) in a switched carrier network. These devices connect to the closest telephone company switch in a *central office (CO)*.

Figure 3.28 shows a network that allows Internet access with several different devices.

Remote Access Technologies

Remote Access Technologies can be defined as those data networking technologies that are uniquely focused on providing the remote user (telecommuter, Internet/intranet user, or extranet user/partner) with access into a network, while striving to maintain the principle tenets of Confidentiality, Availability, and Integrity.

There are many obvious advantages to employing secure remote network access, such as the following:

■ Reducing networking costs by using the Internet to replace expensive dedicated network lines

■ Providing employees with flexible work styles such as telecommuting

■ Building more efficient ties with customers, suppliers, and employees

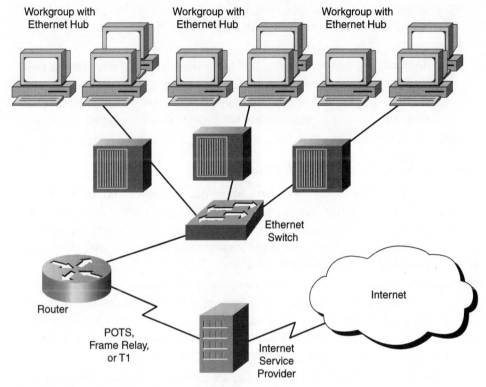

Figure 3.28 Shared Internet access with WAN and LAN devices.

Remote Access Types

While several of these Remote Access Types share common WAN protocols, we list them here to indicate their importance in the area of remote access security.

Asynchronous Dial-Up Access. This method is how most everyone accesses the Internet. It is the most common remote access method for personal remote users because it uses the existing public switched telephone network to access an ISP.

Integrated Services Digital Network (ISDN). Described in the section *WAN Technologies*, ISDN is a communications protocol, which is offered by telephone companies, and permits telephone networks to carry data, voice, and other source traffic. ISDN has two interface types: *Basic Rate Interface* (BRI), which is composed of two B channels and one D channel, and *Primary Rate Interface* (PRI), which consists of a single 64 Kbps D channel plus 23 (T1) or 30 (E1) B channels for voice or data.

xDSL. Described in the section *WAN Technologies*, xDSL uses regular telephone lines for high-speed digital access.

Cable Modems. A cable modem provides high-speed access to the Internet by the cable company. All cable modems share a single coax line to the Internet; therefore, throughput varies according to how many users are currently using the service. It is also considered one of the most insecure of the remote access types because the local segment is typically not filtered or firewalled.

Some Remote Access Security Methods

Restricted Address. This procedure filters out unauthorized users based on their source protocol address (IP or other LAN protocol). It enables incoming calls only from specific addresses on an approved list. You should remember, however, that this procedure authenticates the node; it is not a user authentication method.

Caller ID. Caller ID checks the incoming phone number of the caller against an approved phone list before accepting the session. This is one of the most common security methods because it is very hard to defeat. Its major drawback is that it is hard to administer for traveling users (such as users calling from a different hotel every night).

Callback. In a callback scenario, a user attempting to initiate the session supplies a password or some type of identifying code. The Access Server then hangs up and calls the user back at a predetermined phone number. Again, this procedure authenticates the node, not the user, and is difficult to administer in traveling situations.

Remote Identification and Authentication Technologies

Remote Identification and Authentication technologies are the processes that are necessary to securely verify who is remotely communicating. Because remote access presents security professionals with many issues, a variety of technologies have been developed to provide solutions to these concerns. Identification embodies the concept of identifying who is attempting the connection, and Authentication embodies the concept of establishing a level of trust, which includes non-repudiation of the network session.

Remote Node Security Protocols

The following are the two most common remote node security protocols:

- *Password Authentication Protocol* (PAP)
- *Challenge Handshake Authentication Protocol* (CHAP)

Password Authentication Protocol (PAP). PAP is a remote security protocol that provides identification and authentication of the node attempting to initiate the remote session. PAP uses a static, replayable password for this authentication, which is now considered a weak process. In addition, PAP also does not encrypt the User ID or password during communication.

Challenge Handshake Authentication Protocol (CHAP). CHAP is the next evolution of PAP, which uses a stronger authentication process: a non-replayable, challenge/response dialog that verifies the identity of the node attempting to initiate the remote session. CHAP is often used to enable network-to-network communications and is commonly used by remote access servers and xDSL, ISDN, and cable modems.

Remote Access Authentication Systems

As the demand for large remote access networks increased, two security administration systems, TACACS and RADIUS, emerged to provide security professionals with more resources. These systems provide a centralized database, which maintains user lists, passwords, and user profiles that remote access equipment on a network can access. These systems are "standards-based," which means that they are interoperable with other systems of the same type.

Common Remote Access Authentication Systems include the following:

- *Terminal Access Controller Access Control System* (TACACS)
- TACACS+ (TACACS with additional features, including the use of two-factor authentication)
- *Remote Authentication Dial-In User Server* (RADIUS)

Terminal Access Controller Access Control System (TACACS). TACACS is an authentication protocol that provides remote access authentication and related services, such as event logging. In a TACACS system, user passwords are administered in a central database rather than in individual routers, which provides an easily scalable network security solution. A TACACS-enabled network device prompts the remote user for a username and static password, then the TACACS-enabled device queries a TACACS server to verify that password. TACACS does not support prompting for a password change or for the use of dynamic password tokens.

TACACS+ superseded TACACS. TACACS+ is a proprietary Cisco enhancement to TACACS that provides the following additional features:

- The use of two-factor password authentication
- The user can change his or her password.
- The capability for resynchronizing security tokens
- Better audit trails and session accounting

TACACS and TACACS+ software is free and is often bundled in the operating systems of TACACS network devices.

RADIUS. The IETF adopted RADIUS as a standard protocol. It provides similar user authentication (including the use of dynamic passwords) and password management as a TACACS+-enabled system. RADIUS is often used as a stepping-stone to a more robust TACACS+ system.

RADIUS is a distributed client/server system wherein the clients send their authentication requests to a central RADIUS server that contains all of the user authentication and network service access information (network ACLs). RADIUS is a fully open protocol, is distributed in source code format, and can be modified to work with any security system that is currently available on the market. It can also be used with TACACS+ and Kerberos and provides CHAP remote node authentication.

RADIUS does *not* support the following protocols:

- AppleTalk Remote Access Protocol (ARAP)
- NetBIOS Frame Protocol Control Protocol (NBFCP)
- NetWare Asynchronous Services Interface (NASI)
- X.25 PAD connections

In addition, RADIUS also does not provide two-way authentication and therefore is not commonly used for router-to-router authentication.

Wireless Technologies

Wireless technology is probably the fastest-growing area of network connectivity. Experts estimate that the number of Internet-connected PDAs, such as the Palm Pilot, will eclipse the number of personal computers in use in a few years. Security is an extreme concern here, because all wireless technologies (mobile phones, satellite transmissions, and so forth) are inherently susceptible to interception and eavesdropping. Encryption standards are rapidly being developed to combat this problem.

Let's look at some common wireless standards and technologies.

IEEE Wireless Standards

IEEE 802.11 refers to a family of specifications for *wireless local area networks* (WLANs) developed by a working group of the IEEE. This standards effort began in 1989 with the focus on deployment in large enterprise networking environments, effectively a wireless equivalent to Ethernet. The IEEE accepted the specification in 1997.

The 802.11 specification identifies an over-the-air interface between a mobile device wireless client and a base station or between two mobile device wireless clients. To date, there are four completed specifications in the family: 802.11, 802.11a, 802.11b, and 802.11g with a fifth, 802.11e, in development as a draft standard. All four existing standards use the Ethernet protocol and CSMA/CA for path sharing.

802.11—The original IEEE wireless LAN standard that provides 1 or 2 Mbps transmission speed in the 2.4 GHz band, using either FHSS or DSSS (see *Spread Spectrum Technologies*). The modulation used in 802.11 is commonly *phase-shift keying* (PSK).

802.11b—An extension to the 802.11 wireless LAN standard, it provides 11 Mbps transmission speed (but that automatically slows down to 5.5 Mbps, 2 Mbps, or 1 Mbps speeds in the 2.4 GHz band based upon the strength of the signal). 802.11b uses only DSSS. 802.11b, a 1999 ratification to the original 802.11 standard, provides wireless functionality comparable to Ethernet; it is also referred to as 802.11 High Rate or Wi-Fi.

802.11a—An extension to the original IEEE 802.11 wireless LAN standard that provides up to 54 Mbps in the 5 GHz band. 802.11a uses an orthogonal frequency division multiplexing encoding scheme rather than FHSS or DSSS.

802.11g—A new IEEE wireless standard that applies to wireless LANs, 802.11g provides 20 Mbps to 54 Mbps in the 2.4 GHz band. As of this writing, this standard has not yet been approved, so it is not available in the marketplace (unlike 802.11b or 802.11a).

802.11e—The latest IEEE draft extension to provide QoS features and multimedia support for home and business wireless environments.

802.16—Another wireless 802 standard called IEEE 802 Broadband Wireless Access (802.WBA or 802.16) is under development. IEEE 802.16 standardizes the air interface and related functions associated with the *wireless local loop* (WLL) for wireless broadband subscriber access. Three working groups have been chartered to produce 802.16 standards: IEEE 802.16.1, air interface for 10 to 66 GHz; IEEE 802.16.2, coexistence of broadband wireless access systems; and IEEE 802.16.3, air interface for licensed frequencies, 2 to 11 GHz.

Spread-Spectrum Technologies

The de facto communication standard for wireless LANs is *spread spectrum*, a wideband radio frequency technique originally developed by the military for use in secure, mission-critical communications systems. Spread spectrum uses a radio transmission mode that broadcasts signals over a range of frequencies. The receiving mobile device must know the correct frequency of the spread-spectrum signal being broadcast.

Two different spread spectrum technologies for 2.4 GHz wireless LANs currently exist: *direct-sequence spread spectrum* (DSSS) and *frequency-hopping spread spectrum* (FHSS).

Direct Sequence Spread Spectrum (DSSS)

DSSS is a wideband spread-spectrum transmission technology that generates a redundant bit pattern for each bit to be transmitted. DSSS spreads the signal over a wide frequency band in which the source transmitter maps each bit of data into a pattern of chips. At the receiving mobile device, the original data is recreated by mapping the chips back into a data bit. The DSSS transmitter and receiver must be synchronized to operate properly. A DSSS signal appears as low-power wideband noise to a non-DSSS receiver and therefore is ignored by most narrowband receivers.

Because DSSS spreads across the spectrum, the number of independent, non-overlapping channels in the 2.4 GHz band is small (typically only three); therefore, only a very limited number of colocated networks can operate without interference. Some DSSS products enable users to deploy more than one channel in the same area by separating the 2.4 GHz band into multiple sub-bands, each of which contains an independent DSSS network.

Frequency-Hopping Spread Spectrum (FHSS)

FHSS uses a narrowband carrier that continually changes frequency in a known pattern. The FHSS algorithm spreads the signal by operating on one frequency for a short duration and then "hopping" to another frequency. The minimum number of frequencies engaged in the hopping pattern and the maximum frequency dwell time (how long it stays on each frequency before it changes) are restricted by the FCC, which requires that 75 or more frequencies be used with a maximum dwell time of 400 ms.

The source mobile device's transmission and the destination mobile device's transmission must be synchronized so that they are on the same frequency at the same time. When the transmitter and receiver are properly synchronized, it maintains a single logical communications channel. Similar to DSSS, FHSS appears to be noise of a short duration to a non-FHSS receiver and hence is ignored.

FHSS makes it possible to deploy many non-overlapping channels. Because there are a large number of possible sequences in the 2.4 GHz band, FHSS products enable users to deploy more than one channel in the same area by implementing separate channels with different hopping sequences.

WLAN Operational Modes

The IEEE 802.11 wireless networks operate in one of two operational modes: *ad hoc* or *infrastructure* mode. Ad hoc mode is a peer-to-peer type of networking, whereas infrastructure mode uses access points to communicate between the mobile devices and the wired network.

Ad Hoc Mode

In ad hoc mode, each mobile device client communicates directly with the other mobile device clients within the network. That is, no access points are used to connect the ad hoc network directly with any WLAN. Ad hoc mode is designed so that only the clients within transmission range (within the same cell) of each other can communicate. If a client in an ad hoc network wants to communicate outside the cell, a member of the cell must operate as a gateway and a perform routing service.

Infrastructure Mode

Each mobile device client in infrastructure mode sends all of its communications to a network device called an *access point* (AP). The access point acts as an Ethernet bridge and forwards the communications to the appropriate network, either the WLAN or another wireless network.

The Wireless Application Protocol (WAP)

Wireless Application Protocol (WAP) was developed as a set of technologies related to HTML but tailored to the small screens and limited resources of handheld, wireless devices. The most notable of these technologies is the Handheld Device Markup Language (HDML). HDML looks similar to HTML but has a feature set and programming paradigm tailored to wireless devices with small screens. HDML and other elements of this architecture eventually became the Wireless Markup Language (WML) and the architecture of WAP.

Since its initial release, WAP has evolved twice. Releases 1.1 and 1.2 of the specification have the same functionality as 1.0 but with added features to align with what the rest of the industry is doing. Version 1.3 is used most often in WAP products as of this writing.

In August 2001, the WAP Forum approved and released the specifications for WAP 2.0 for public review, and Ericsson, Nokia, and Motorola all announced support for WAP 2.0. The WAP 2.0 specification contains new functionality that enables users to send sound and moving pictures over their telephones, among other things. WAP 2.0 will also provide a toolkit for easy development and deployment of new services, including XHTML.

The WAP architecture is loosely based on the OSI model, but unlike the seven layers of OSI or the four layers of the TCP/IP model, WAP has five layers: application, session, transaction, security, and transport.

Application layer

The WAP application layer is the direct interface to the user and contains the wireless application environment (WAE). This top layer consists of several elements, including a microbrowser specification for Internet access, the Wireless Markup Language (WML), WMLScript, and wireless telephony applications (WTA).

It encompasses devices, content, development languages (WML and WMLScript), wireless telephony APIs (WTA) for accessing telephony functionality from within WAE programs, and some well-defined content formats for phone book records, calendar information, and graphics.

Session Layer

The WAP session layer contains the Wireless Session Protocol (WSP), which is similar to the Hypertext Transfer Protocol (HTTP) because it is designed for low-bandwidth, high-latency wireless networks. WSP facilitates the transfer of content between WAP clients and WAP gateways in a binary format. Additional functionalities include content push and the suspension/resumption of connections.

The WSP layer provides a consistent interface to WAE for two types of session services: a connection mode and a connectionless service. This layer provides the following:

- Connection creation and release between the client and server
- Data exchange between the client and server by using a coding scheme that is much more compact than traditional HTML text
- Session suspend and release between the client and server

Transaction Layer

The WAP transaction layer provides the Wireless Transactional Protocol (WTP), which provides the functionality similar to TCP/IP in the Internet model. WTP is a lightweight transactional protocol that provides reliable request and response transactions and supports unguaranteed and guaranteed push.

WTP provides transaction services to WAP. It handles acknowledgments so that users can determine whether a transaction has succeeded. It also provides a retransmission of transactions in case they are not successfully received and removes duplicate transactions. WTP manages different classes of transactions for WAP devices: unreliable one-way requests, reliable one-way requests, and reliable two-way requests. An unreliable request from a WAP device means that no precautions are taken to guarantee that the request for information makes it to the server.

Security Layer

The security layer contains Wireless Transport Layer Security (WTLS). WTLS is based on Transport Layer Security (TLS, similar to the Secure Sockets Layer, or SSL) and can be invoked similar to HTTPS in the Internet world. It provides data integrity, privacy, authentication, and DoS protection mechanisms.

WAP privacy services guarantee that all transactions between the WAP device and gateway are encrypted. Authentication guarantees the authenticity of the client and application server. DoS protection detects and rejects data that comes in the form of unverified requests.

Transport Layer

The bottom WAP layer, the transport layer, supports the Wireless Datagram Protocol (WDP), which provides an interface to the bearers of transportation.

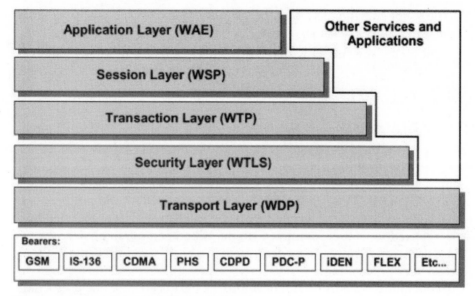

Figure 3.29 The Wireless Application Protocol.

It supports the CDPD, GSM, *Integrated Digital Enhanced Network* (iDEN), CDMA, TDMA, SMS, and FLEX protocols.

WDP provides a consistent interface to the higher layers of the WAP architecture, meaning that it does not matter which type of wireless network on which the application is running. Among other capabilities, WDP provides data error correction. The bearers, or wireless communications networks, are at WAP's lowest level.

Figure 3.29 shows the layers of WAP.

Wired Equivalent Privacy (WEP) Encryption

An option in IEEE 802.11b, Wired Equivalent Privacy, uses a 40-bit shared secret key, a *Rivest Code 4* (RC4) *pseudorandom number generator* (PRNG) encryption algorithm, and a 24-bit *initialization vector* (IV) to provide data encryption. The basic process works as follows:

1. A checksum of the message is computed and appended to the message.

2. A shared secret key and the IV are fed to the RC4 algorithm to produce a key stream.

3. An exclusive OR (XOR) operation of the key stream with the message and checksum grouping produces ciphertext.

4. The IV is appended to the ciphertext to form the encrypted message, which is sent to the intended recipient.

5. The recipient, who has a copy of the same shared key, uses it to generate an identical key stream.

6. XORing the key stream with the ciphertext yields the original plaintext message.

You can find more details about WEP in Chapter 4, "Cryptography."

Personal Digital Assistant Security

PDAs have not been designed to the same standards nor exposed to the same rigorous examination as desktop operating systems. OS security requirements for military systems are derived from AR 380-19 and DoD 5200.28-STD of the "Orange Book." Techniques to evaluate and test products against security functional requirements are spelled out in the ISO standard 15408, referred to as the Common Criteria. When compared against the OS against security requirements described in these standards, most PDAs receive a very poor rating.

PDA operating systems do not have provisions to separate one user's data from another (required to support discretionary access control, or DAC); they lack audit capabilities; they have no support for object reuse control through the implementation of *identification and authentication* (I&A); and they do not provide data integrity protection. Even if a PDA is password-protected, a malicious user can retrieve the password of a target PDA by using the Palm debug mode. The password can then be decoded by using simple tools such as the PalmCrypt tool. Another problem is that even when the OS is password-locked, applications can still be installed onto the PalmOS without the owner's knowledge.

Obviously, the result is compromise of the integrity of the data. Once the password has been bypassed, all of the information on the PDA is fully readable by the malicious user. Security administrators currently do not have the ability to determine whether this type of attack has occurred, nor do they have any method to determine who was responsible for the attack.

Probably the most common threat to a PDA is caused by the physical loss of the device. Although some technical solutions are available to protect against some of the OS security deficiencies we just mentioned, none provide a countermeasure to the physical security concerns associated with the use of PDAs. The devices are so small and portable that loss of the device and any information contained on it is common. They are smaller, lighter, and have fewer connections to the physical environment—and their mode of use puts them at a greater risk because they are generally used in uncontrolled environments.

Sample Questions

You can find the answers to the following questions in Appendix H.

1. Which of the following is NOT a type of data network?
   a. LAN
   b. WAN
   c. MAN
   d. GAN

2. Which of the following is NOT a network cabling type?
   a. Twisted pair
   b. Token Ring
   c. Fiber Optic
   d. Coaxial

3. Which of the following is NOT a property of a Packet Filtering Firewall?
   a. Considered a first-generation firewall
   b. Uses ACLs
   c. Operates at the Application Layer
   d. Examines the source and destination addresses of the incoming packet

4. Which of the following is NOT a remote computing technology?
   a. PGP
   b. ISDN
   c. Wireless
   d. xDSL

5. A firewall that performs stateful inspection of the data packet across all layers is considered a:
   a. First-generation firewall
   b. Second-generation firewall
   c. Third-generation firewall
   d. Fourth-generation firewall

6. RAID refers to the:
   a. Redundant Arrays of Intelligent Disks
   b. Redundant And fault tolerant Internetworking Devices
   c. Rapid And Inexpensive Digital tape backup
   d. Remote Administration of Internet Domains

7. Which of the following is NOT a true statement about Network Address Translation (NAT)?

    a. NAT is used when corporations want to use private addressing ranges for internal networks.

    b. NAT is designed to mask the true IP addresses of internal systems.

    c. Private addresses can easily be routed globally.

    d. NAT translates private IP addresses to registered "real" IP addresses.

8. What does LAN stand for?

    a. Local Arena News

    b. Local Area Network

    c. Layered Addressed Network

    d. Local Adaptive Network

9. What does CSMA stand for?

    a. Carrier Station Multi-port Actuator

    b. Carrier Sense Multiple Access

    c. Common Systems Methodology Applications

    d. Carrier Sense Multiple Attenuation

10. Which is NOT a property of a packet-switched network?

    a. Packets are assigned sequence numbers

    b. Characterized by "bursty" traffic

    c. Connection-oriented network

    d. Connectionless network

11. Which is NOT a layer in the OSI architecture model?

    a. Transport

    b. Internet

    c. Data Link

    d. Session

12. Which is NOT a layer in the TCP/IP architecture model?

    a. Internet

    b. Application

    c. Host-to-host

    d. Session

13. Which is NOT a backup method type?

    a. Differential

    b. Full

    c. Reactive

    d. Incremental

14. What does TFTP stand for?

    a. Trivial File Transport Protocol

    b. Transport for TCP/IP

    c. Trivial File Transfer Protocol

    d. Transport File Transfer Protocol

15. What does the Data Encapsulation in the OSI model do?

    a. Creates seven distinct layers

    b. Wraps data from one layer around a data packet from an adjoining layer

    c. Provides "best effort" delivery of a data packet

    d. Makes the network transmission deterministic

16. What is NOT a feature of TACACS+?

    a. Enables two-factor authentication

    b. Replaces older Frame Relay-switched networks

    c. Enables a user to change passwords

    d. Resynchronizes security tokens

17. What is NOT true of a star-wired topology?

    a. Cabling termination errors can crash the entire network.

    b. The network nodes are connected to a central LAN device.

    c. It has more resiliency than a BUS topology.

    d. 10BaseT Ethernet is star-wired.

18. FDDI uses what type of network topology?

    a. BUS

    b. RING

    c. STAR

    d. MESH

19. What does the protocol ARP do?

    a. Takes a MAC address and finds an IP address to match

    b. Sends messages to the devices regarding the health of the network

    c. Takes an IP address and finds out the MAC address to which it belongs

    d. Facilitates file transfers

20. What does the protocol RARP do?
    a. Takes a MAC address and finds an IP address to match
    b. Sends messages to the devices regarding the health of the network
    c. Takes an IP address and finds out the MAC address to which it belongs
    d. Facilitates file transfers

21. What is the protocol that supports sending and receiving email?
    a. SNMP
    b. SMTP
    c. ICMP
    d. RARP

22. Which of the following is NOT a VPN remote computing protocol?
    a. PPTP
    b. L2F
    c. L2TP
    d. UTP

23. Which of the following is NOT a property of CSMA?
    a. The workstation continuously monitors the line.
    b. The workstation transmits the data packet when it thinks that the line is free.
    c. Workstations are not permitted to transmit until they are given permission from the primary host.
    d. It does not have a feature to avoid the problem of one workstation dominating the conversation.

24. Which of the following is NOT a property of Token Ring networks?
    a. Workstations cannot transmit until they receive a token.
    b. These networks were originally designed to serve large, bandwidth-consuming applications.
    c. These networks were originally designed to serve sporadic and only occasionally heavy traffic.
    d. All end stations are attached to an MSAU.

25. Which is NOT a property of Fiber Optic cabling?
    a. Carries signals as light waves
    b. Transmits at higher speeds than copper cable
    c. Easier to tap than copper cabling
    d. Very resistant to interference

26. Which is NOT a property of a bridge?

    a. Forwards the data to all other segments if the destination is not on the local segment

    b. Operates at Layer 2, the Data Link Layer

    c. Operates at Layer 3, the Network Layer

    d. Can create a broadcast storm

27. Which is NOT a standard type of DSL?

    a. ADSL

    b. FDSL

    c. VDSL

    d. HDSL

28. Which is a property of a circuit-switched network as opposed to a packet-switched network?

    a. Physical, permanent connections exist from one point to another in a circuit-switched network.

    b. The data is broken up into packets.

    c. The data is sent to the next destination, which is based on the router's understanding of the best available route.

    d. Packets are reassembled according to their originally assigned sequence numbers.

29. Which is NOT a packet-switched technology?

    a. SMDS

    b. T1

    c. Frame Relay

    d. X.25

30. Which is NOT a remote security method?

    a. VoIP

    b. Callback

    c. Caller ID

    d. Restricted Address

31. To what does covert channel eavesdropping refer?

    a. Using a hidden, unauthorized network connection to communicate unauthorized information

    b. Nonbusiness or personal use of the Internet

    c. Socially engineering passwords from an ISP

    d. The use of two-factor passwords

32. To what does logon abuse refer?
    a. Breaking into a network primarily from an external source
    b. Legitimate users accessing networked services that would normally be restricted to them
    c. Nonbusiness or personal use of the Internet
    d. Intrusions via dial-up or asynchronous external network connections

33. What is probing used for?
    a. To induce a user into taking an incorrect action
    b. To give an attacker a road map of the network
    c. To use up all of a target's resources
    d. To covertly listen to transmissions

34. Which is NOT a property of or issue with tape backup?
    a. Slow data transfer during backups and restores
    b. Server disk space utilization expands.
    c. The possibility that some data re-entry might need to be performed after a crash
    d. One large disk created by using several disks

35. What is a server cluster?
    a. A primary server that mirrors its data to a secondary server
    b. A group of independent servers that are managed as a single system
    c. A tape array backup implementation
    d. A group of WORM optical jukeboxes

36. In which OSI layer does the MIDI digital music protocol standard reside?
    a. Application Layer
    b. Presentation Layer
    c. Session Layer
    d. Transport Layer

Bonus Questions

You can find the answers to the following questions in Appendix H.

1. Which statement about a VPN tunnel below is incorrect?

    a. It can be created by implementing IPSec devices only.

    b. It can be created by installing software or hardware agents on the client or network.

    c. It can be created by implementing key and certificate exchange systems.

    d. It can be created by implementing node authentication systems.

2. Which answer below is true about the difference between FTP and TFTP?

    a. FTP does not have a directory browsing ability, whereas TFTP does.

    b. FTP enables print job spooling, whereas TFTP does not.

    c. TFTP is less secure because session authentication does not occur.

    d. FTP is less secure because session authentication does not occur.

3. Which answer below is true about the difference between TCP and UDP?

    a. UDP is considered a connectionless protocol, and TCP is connection-oriented.

    b. TCP is considered a connectionless protocol, and UDP is connection-oriented.

    c. UDP acknowledges the receipt of packets, and TCP does not.

    d. TCP is sometimes referred to as an unreliable protocol.

4. Which TCP/IP protocol operates at the OSI Network layer?

    a. FTP

    b. IP

    c. TCP

    d. UDP

5. Which IEEE standard defines wireless networking in the 5 GHz band with speeds of up to 54 Mbps?

    a. 802.5

    b. 802.11a

    c. 802.11b

    d. 802.3

6. Which UTP cable category is rated for 16 Mbps?

   a. Category 4

   b. Category 5

   c. Category 6

   d. Category 7

7. Which statement below about the difference between analog and digital signals is incorrect?

   a. An analog signal produces an infinite waveform.

   b. Analog signals cannot be used for data communications.

   c. An analog signal can be varied by amplification.

   d. A digital signal produces a saw-tooth waveform.

8. Which choice below BEST describes coaxial cable?

   a. Coax consists of two insulated wires wrapped around each other in a regular spiral pattern.

   b. Coax consists of a hollow outer cylindrical conductor surrounding a single, inner conductor.

   c. Coax does not require a fixed spacing between connections that UTP requires.

   d. Coax carries signals as light waves.

9. Which LAN transmission method below describes a packet sent from a single source to multiple specific destinations?

   a. Unicast

   b. Multicast

   c. Broadcast

   d. Anycast

10. To what does 10Base-5 refer?

   a. 10 Mbps thinnet coax cabling rated to 185 meters maximum length

   b. 10 Mbps thicknet coax cabling rated to 500 meters maximum length

   c. 10 Mbps baseband optical fiber

   d. 100 Mbps unshielded twisted pair cabling

Advanced Sample Questions

You can find the answers to the following questions in Appendix I.

The following questions are supplemental to and coordinated with Chapter 3 and are at a level on par with that of the CISSP Examination. We assumed that the reader has a basic knowledge of the material contained in Chapter 3.

1. Which of the choices below is NOT an OSI reference model Session Layer protocol, standard, or interface?
   a. SQL
   b. RPC
   c. MIDI
   d. ASP
   e. DNA SCP

2. Which part of the 48-bit, 12-digit hexadecimal number known as the Media Access Control (MAC) address identifies the manufacturer of the network device?
   a. The first three bytes
   b. The first two bytes
   c. The second half of the MAC address
   d. The last three bytes

3. Which IEEE protocol defines the Spanning Tree protocol?
   a. IEEE 802.5
   b. IEEE 802.3
   c. IEEE 802.11
   d. IEEE 802.1D

4. Which choice below is NOT one of the legal IP address ranges specified by RFC1976 and reserved by the Internet Assigned Numbers Authority (IANA) for non-routable private addresses?
   a. 10.0.0.0–10.255.255.255
   b. 127.0.0.0–127.0.255.255
   c. 172.16.0.0–172.31.255.255
   d. 192.168.0.0–192.168.255.255

5. Which statement is correct about ISDN Basic Rate Interface?
   a. It offers 23 B channels and 1 D channel.
   b. It offers 2 B channels and 1 D channel.
   c. It offers 30 B channels and 1 D channel.
   d. It offers 1 B channel and 2 D channels.

6. In the DoD reference model, which layer conforms to the OSI transport layer?

    a. Process/Application Layer

    b. Host-to-Host Layer

    c. Internet Layer

    d. Network Access Layer

7. What is the Network Layer of the OSI reference model primarily responsible for?

    a. Internetwork packet routing

    b. LAN bridging

    c. SMTP Gateway services

    d. Signal regeneration and repeating

8. Which IEEE protocol defines wireless transmission in the 5 GHz band with data rates up to 54 Mbps?

    a. IEEE 802.11a

    b. IEEE 802.11b

    c. IEEE 802.11g

    d. IEEE 802.15

9. Which category of UTP wiring is rated for 100BaseT Ethernet networks?

    a. Category 1

    b. Category 2

    c. Category 3

    d. Category 4

    e. Category 5

10. Which choice below is the earliest and the most commonly found Interior Gateway Protocol?

    a. RIP

    b. OSPF

    c. IGRP

    d. EAP

11. The data transmission method in which data is sent continuously and doesn't use either an internal clocking source or start/stop bits for timing is known as:

    a. Asynchronous

    b. Synchronous

    c. Isochronous

    d. Pleisiochronous

12. Which level of RAID is commonly referred to as "disk mirroring"?

    a. RAID 0

    b. RAID 1

    c. RAID 3

    d. RAID 5

13. Which network attack below would NOT be considered a Denial of Service attack?

    a. Ping of Death

    b. SMURF

    c. Brute Force

    d. TCP SYN

14. Which choice below is NOT an element of IPSec?

    a. Authentication Header

    b. Layer Two Tunneling Protocol

    c. Security Association

    d. Encapsulating Security Payload

15. Which statement below is NOT true about the difference between cut-through and store-and-forward switching?

    a. A store-and-forward switch reads the whole packet and checks its validity before sending it to the next destination.

    b. Both methods operate at layer two of the OSI reference model.

    c. A cut-through switch reads only the header on the incoming data packet.

    d. A cut-through switch introduces more latency than a store-and-forward switch.

16. Which statement is NOT true about the SOCKS protocol?

    a. It is sometimes referred to as an application-level proxy.

    b. It uses an ESP for authentication and encryption.

    c. It operates in the transport layer of the OSI model.

    d. Network applications need to be SOCKS-ified to operate.

17. Which choice below does NOT relate to analog dial-up hacking?

    a. War Dialing

    b. War Walking

    c. Demon Dialing

    d. ToneLoc

18. Which choice below is NOT a way to get Windows NT passwords?

    a. Obtain the backup SAM from the repair directory.

    b. Boot the NT server with a floppy containing an alternate operating system.

    c. Obtain root access to the /etc/passwd file.

    d. Use pwdump2 to dump the password hashes directly from the registry.

19. A "back door" into a network refers to what?

    a. Socially engineering passwords from a subject

    b. Mechanisms created by hackers to gain network access at a later time

    c. Undocumented instructions used by programmers to debug applications

    d. Monitoring programs implemented on dummy applications to lure intruders

20. Which protocol below does NOT pertain to e-mail?

    a. SMTP

    b. POP

    c. CHAP

    d. IMAP

21. The IP address, 178.22.90.1, is considered to be in which class of address?

    a. Class A

    b. Class B

    c. Class C

    d. Class D

22. What type of firewall architecture employs two network cards and a single screening router?

    a. A screened-host firewall

    b. A dual-homed host firewall

    c. A screened-subnet firewall

    d. An application-level proxy server

23. What is one of the most common drawbacks to using a dual-homed host firewall?

    a. The examination of the packet at the Network layer introduces latency.

    b. The examination of the packet at the Application layer introduces latency.

   c. The ACLs must be manually maintained on the host.

   d. Internal routing may accidentally become enabled.

24. Which firewall type below uses a dynamic state table to inspect the content of packets?

   a. A packet-filtering firewall

   b. An application-level firewall

   c. A circuit-level firewall

   d. A stateful-inspection firewall

25. Which attack type below does NOT exploit TCP vulnerabilities?

   a. Sequence Number attack

   b. SYN attack

   c. Ping of Death

   d. land.c attack

26. Which utility below can create a server-spoofing attack?

   a. DNS poisoning

   b. C2MYAZZ

   c. Snort

   d. BO2K

27. Which LAN topology below is MOST vulnerable to a single point of failure?

   a. Ethernet Bus

   b. Physical Star

   c. FDDI

   d. Logical Ring

28. Which choice below does NOT accurately describe the difference between multi-mode and single-mode fiber optic cabling?

   a. Multi-mode fiber propagates light waves through many paths, single-mode fiber propagates a single light ray only.

   b. Multi-mode fiber has a longer allowable maximum transmission distance than single-mode fiber.

   c. Single-mode fiber has a longer allowable maximum transmission distance than multi-mode fiber.

   d. Both types have a longer allowable maximum transmission distance than UTP Cat 5.

29. Which statement below is correct regarding VLANs?

   a. A VLAN restricts flooding to only those ports included in the VLAN.

   b. A VLAN is a network segmented physically, not logically.

c. A VLAN is less secure when implemented in conjunction with private port switching.

d. A "closed" VLAN configuration is the least secure VLAN configuration.

30. Which choice below denotes a packet-switched connectionless wide area network (WAN) technology?

a. X.25

b. Frame Relay

c. SMDS

d. ATM

31. Which statement below is accurate about the difference between Ethernet II and 802.3 frame formats?

a. 802.3 uses a "Length" field, whereas Ethernet II uses a "Type" field.

b. 802.3 uses a "Type" field, whereas Ethernet II uses a "Length" field.

c. Ethernet II uses a 4-byte FCS field, whereas 802.3 uses an 8-byte Preamble field.

d. Ethernet II uses an 8-byte Preamble field, whereas 802.3 uses a 4-byte FCS field.

32. Which standard below does NOT specify fiber optic cabling as its physical media?

a. 100BaseFX

b. 1000BaseCX

c. 1000BaseLX

d. 1000BaseSX

33. Which type of routing below commonly broadcasts its routing table information to all other routers every minute?

a. Static Routing

b. Distance Vector Routing

c. Link State Routing

d. Dynamic Control Protocol Routing

34. Which protocol is used to resolve a known IP address to an unknown MAC address?

a. ARP

b. RARP

c. ICMP

d. TFTP

35. Which statement accurately describes the difference between 802.11b WLAN ad hoc and infrastructure modes?

    a. The ad hoc mode requires an Access Point to communicate to the wired network.

    b. Wireless nodes can communicate peer-to-peer in the infrastructure mode.

    c. Wireless nodes can communicate peer-to-peer in the ad hoc mode.

    d. Access points are rarely used in 802.11b WLANs.

36. Which type of cabling below is the most common type for recent Ethernet installations?

    a. ThickNet

    b. ThinNet

    c. Twinax

    d. Twisted Pair

37. Which choice below most accurately describes SSL?

    a. It's a widely used standard of securing e-mail at the Application level.

    b. It gives a user remote access to a command prompt across a secure, encrypted session.

    c. It uses two protocols, the Authentication Header and the Encapsulating Security Payload.

    d. It allows an application to have authenticated, encrypted communications across a network.

38. Which backup method listed below will probably require the backup operator to use the most number of tapes for a complete system restoration, if a different tape is used every night in a five-day rotation?

    a. Full Backup Method

    b. Differential Backup Method

    c. Incremental Backup Method

    d. Ad Hoc Backup Method

39. Which choice below is NOT an element of a fiber optic cable?

    a. Core

    b. BNC

    c. Jacket

    d. Cladding

40. Given an IP address of 172.16.0.0, which subnet mask below would allow us to divide the network into the maximum number of subnets with at least 600 host addresses per subnet?

    a. 255.255.224.0

    b. 255.255.240.0

    c. 255.255.248.0

    d. 255.255.252.0

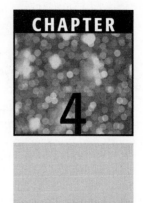

CHAPTER

4

Cryptography

The information system professional should have a fundamental comprehension of the following areas in cryptography:

- Definitions
- History
- Cryptology Fundamentals
- Symmetric Key Cryptosystem Fundamentals
- Asymmetric Key Cryptosystem Fundamentals
- Key Distribution and Management Issues
- Public Key Infrastructure (PKI) Definitions and Concepts

This chapter will address each of these areas to the level required of a practicing information system security professional.

Introduction

The purpose of cryptography is to protect transmitted information from being read and understood by anyone except the intended recipient. In the ideal sense, unauthorized individuals can never read an enciphered message. In practice, reading an enciphered communication can be a function of time—the effort and corresponding time, which is required for an unauthorized individual to decipher an encrypted message may be so large that it can be impractical. By the time the message is decrypted, the information within the message may be of minimal value.

Definitions

Block Cipher. Obtained by segregating plaintext into blocks of n characters or bits and applying the identical encryption algorithm and key, K, to each block. For example, if a plaintext message, M, is divided into blocks M1, M2, . . . Mp, then

$$E(M, K) = E(M1, K)\ E(M2, K) \ldots E(Mp, K)$$

where the blocks on the right-hand side of the equation are concatenated to form the ciphertext.

Cipher. A cryptographic transformation that operates on characters or bits.

Ciphertext or Cryptogram. An unintelligible message.

Clustering. A situation in which a plaintext message generates identical ciphertext messages by using the same transformation algorithm, but with different cryptovariables or keys.

Codes. A cryptographic transformation that operates at the level of words or phrases.

Cryptanalysis. The act of obtaining the plaintext or key from the ciphertext that is used to obtain valuable information to pass on altered or fake messages in order to deceive the original intended recipient; breaking the ciphertext.

Cryptographic Algorithm. A step-by-step procedure used to encipher plaintext and decipher ciphertext.

Cryptography. The art and science of hiding the meaning of a communication from unintended recipients. The word cryptography comes from the Greek words kryptos (hidden) and graphein (to write).

Cryptology. Encompasses cryptography and cryptanalysis.

Cryptosystem. A set of transformations from a message space to a ciphertext space. For example, if M = Plaintext, C = Ciphertext, E = the encryption transformation, and D = the decryption transformation,

$E(M) = C$

$D[E(M)] = M$

To specifically show the dependence of the encipherment and decipherment transformation on the cryptovariable or key, K,

$E(M, K) = C$
$D(C, K) = D[E(M, K), K] = M$

Decipher. To undo the encipherment process and make the message readable.

Encipher. To make the message unintelligible to all but the intended recipients.

End-to-End Encryption. Encrypted information that is sent from the point of origin to the final destination. In symmetric key encryption, this process requires the sender and receiver to have the identical key for the session.

Exclusive Or. Boolean operation that essentially performs binary addition without carry on the input bits, as shown in Table 4.1. For two binary input variables, A and B, the Exclusive Or function produces a binary 1 output when A and B are not equal and a binary 0 when A and B are equal. The symbol ⊗ or the acronym XOR indicates the Exclusive Or operation.

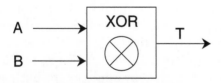

Table 4.1 Exclusive OR (XOR)

| INPUTS | | OUTPUT |
A	B	T
0	0	0
0	1	1
1	0	1
1	1	0

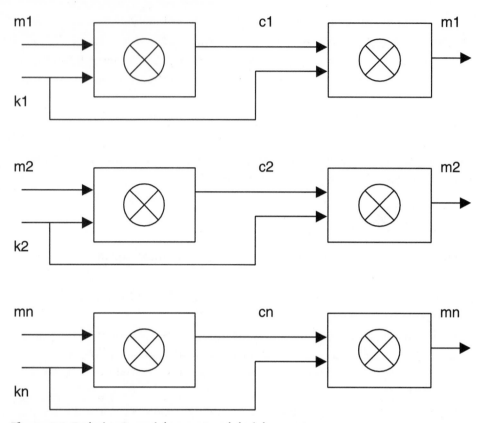

Figure 4.1 Exclusive Or encipherment and decipherment.

The Exclusive Or function is easily implemented in hardware and therefore can be executed at hardware speeds. A valuable property of the Exclusive Or function is that the inverse of the function can be obtained by performing another Exclusive Or on the output. For example, assume that a transformation is performed on a stream cipher by applying the Exclusive Or operation, bit by bit, on the plaintext bits with the bits of a keystream. Then, the decipherment of the enciphered stream is accomplished by applying the Exclusive Or of the keystream, bit by bit, to the enciphered stream. This property is illustrated in Figure 4.1.

If the bits of the message stream M are m1, m2, . . ., mn, the bits of the keystream K are k1, k2, . . ., kn, and the bits of the cipherstream C are c1, c2, . . ., cn, then

E(M,K) = M XOR K = C, and

D(C) = D[M XOR K] = [M XOR K] XOR K

Schematically, the process is illustrated in Figure 4.2.

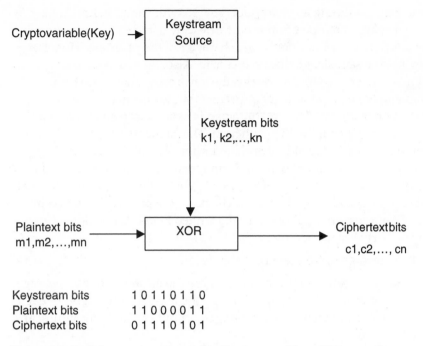

Keystream bits	1 0 1 1 0 1 1 0
Plaintext bits	1 1 0 0 0 0 1 1
Ciphertext bits	0 1 1 1 0 1 0 1

Figure 4.2 Encipherment process using Keystream with an XOR operation.

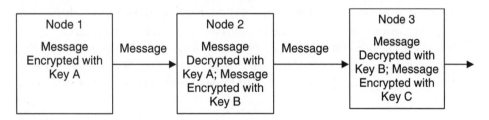

Figure 4.3 Link encryption.

Key or Cryptovariable. Information or a sequence that controls the enciphering and deciphering of messages.

Link Encryption. Each entity has keys in common with its two neighboring nodes in the transmission chain. Thus, a node receives the encrypted message from its predecessor (the neighboring node), decrypts it, and then re-encrypts it with another key that is common to the successor node. Then, the encrypted message is sent on to the successor node, where the process is repeated until the final destination is reached. Obviously, this mode does not provide protection if the nodes along the transmission path can be compromised. A general representation of link encryption is shown in Figure 4.3.

One Time Pad. Assuming an encryption key, K, with components k1, k2, . . ., kn, the encipherment operation is performed by using each component ki of the key, K, to encipher exactly one character of the plaintext. Therefore, the key has the same length as the message. Also, the key is used only once and is never used again. Ideally, the key's components are truly random and have no periodicity or predictability, thus making the ciphertext unbreakable. The one-time pad is usually implemented as a stream cipher by using the XOR function. The elements k1, k2, . . ., kn of the key stream are independent and are uniformly distributed, random variables. This requirement of a single, independently chosen value of ki to encipher each plaintext character is stringent and might not be practical for most commercial IT applications. The one-time pad was invented in 1917 by Major Joseph Mauborgne of the United States Army Signal Corps and by Gilbert Vernam of AT&T.

Plaintext. A message in cleartext readable form.

Steganography. Secret communications where the existence of the message is hidden. For example, in a digital image the least-significant bit of each word can be used to comprise a message without causing any significant change in the image.

Work Function (Factor). The difficulty in recovering the plaintext from the ciphertext as measured by cost and/or time. A system's security is directly proportional to the value of the work function. The work function only needs to be large enough to suffice for the intended application. If the message to be protected loses its value after a short time period, the work function only needs to be large enough to ensure that the decryption would be highly infeasible in that period of time.

History

Secret writing can be traced back to 3,000 B.C. when it was used by the Egyptians. They employed hieroglyphics to conceal writings from unintended recipients. Hieroglyphics is derived from the Greek word hieroglyphica, which means sacred carvings. Hieroglyphics evolved into hieratic, which was a stylized script that was easier to use. Around 400 B.C., military cryptography was employed by the Spartans in the form of a strip of papyrus or parchment wrapped around a wooden rod. This system is called a Scytale and is shown in Figure 4.4.

The message to be encoded was written lengthwise down (or up) the rod on the wrapped material. Then, the material was unwrapped and carried to the recipient. In its unwrapped form, the writing appeared to be random characters. When the material was rewound on a rod of the same diameter, d, and

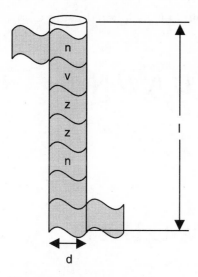

Figure 4.4 A Spartan Scytale.

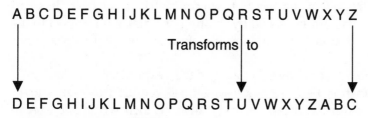

Figure 4.5 Caesar C3 substitution cipher.

minimum length, l, the message could be read. Thus, as shown in Figure 4.4, the keys to deciphering the message are d and l.

Around 50 B.C., Julius Caesar, the emperor of Rome, used a substitution cipher to transmit messages to Marcus Tullius Cicero. In this cipher, letters of the alphabet are substituted for other letters of the same alphabet. Because only one alphabet was used, this cipher was a monoalphabetic substitution. This particular cipher involved shifting the alphabet by three letters and substituting those letters. This substitution, sometimes known as C3 (for Caesar shifting three places) is shown in Figure 4.5.

In general, the Caesar system of ciphers can be written as follows:

$$Zi = Cn\ (Pi),$$

where the Zi are ciphertext characters, Cn is a monoalphabetic substitution transformation, n is the number of letters shifted, and the Pi are plaintext characters.

Thus, the message ATTACK AT DAWN would be enciphered using C3 as follows:

ATTACK AT DAWN

DWWDFN DW GDZQ

Disks have played an important part in cryptography for the past 500 years. In Italy around 1460, Leon Battista Alberti developed cipher disks for encryption (Figure 4.6). His system consisted of two concentric disks. Each disk had an alphabet around its periphery, and by rotating one disk with respect to the other, a letter in one alphabet could be transformed to a letter in another alphabet.

The Arabs invented cryptanalysis because of their expertise in mathematics, statistics and linguistics. Because every Muslim is required to seek knowledge, they studied earlier civilizations and translated their writings into Arabic. In 815, the Caliph al-Mámun established the House of Wisdom in Baghdad that was the focal point of translation efforts. In the ninth century, the Arab philosopher al-Kindi wrote a treatise (rediscovered in 1987) entitled, "A Manuscript on Deciphering Cryptographic Messages."

In 1790, Thomas Jefferson developed an encryption device by using a stack of 26 disks that could be rotated individually. A message was assembled by rotating each disk to the proper letter under an alignment bar that ran the length of the disk stack. Then, the alignment bar was rotated through a specific angle, A, and the letters under the bar were the encrypted message. The

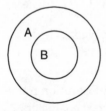

Figure 4.6 Cipher disks.

Figure 4.7 Jefferson disks.
(Courtesy of the National Cryptologic Museum)

recipient would align the enciphered characters under the alignment bar, rotate the bar back through the angle A and read the plaintext message. This Jeffersonian system is shown in Figure 4.7.

Disk systems were used extensively during the U.S. Civil War. A Federal Signal Officer obtained a patent on a disk system similar to the one invented by Leon Battista Alberti in Italy, and he used it to encode and decode flag signals among units.

Unix systems use a substitution cipher called ROT 13 that shifts the alphabet by 13 places. Another shift of 13 places brings the alphabet back to its original position, thus decoding the message.

A mechanical cryptographic machine called the Hagelin Machine, shown in Figure 4.8, was developed in 1920 by Boris Hagelin in Stockholm, Sweden. In the United States, the Hagelin Machine is known as the M-209.

In the 1920s, Herbert O. Yardley was in charge of the secret U.S. MI-8 organization, also known as the "Black Chamber." MI-8 cracked the codes of a number of nations. During the 1921–1922 Washington Naval Conference, the United States had an edge in the Japanese negotiations because MI-8 was supplying the U.S. Secretary of State with the intercepted Japanese negotiating plans. The U.S. State Department closed MI-8 in 1929, much to the chagrin of Yardley. In retaliation, Yardley published the book *The American Black Chamber* (Yardley, Herbert O., Laguna Hills, CA: Aegean Park Press, 1931), which described to the world the secrets of MI-8. As a consequence, the Japanese installed new codes. Because of his pioneering contributions to the field, Yardley is known as the "father of

Figure 4.8 The Hagelin Machine.

Figure 4.9 Herbert Yardley's Black Chamber.
(Courtesy of the National Cryptologic Museum)

American Cryptology." Figure 4.9 shows a display concerning Yardley in the U.S. National Cryptologic Museum at the National Security Agency (NSA) site near Baltimore, Maryland.

The Japanese Purple Machine

Following Yardley's departure, William F. Friedman resumed cryptanalysis efforts for the U.S. Army. Friedman's team broke the new Japanese diplomatic cipher.

Yardley's counterpart in the U.S. Navy was Laurance Stafford. Stafford headed the team that broke the Japanese Purple Machine naval codes during World War II. A group of these code breakers worked in dark basement rooms at Naval District Headquarters in Pearl Harbor. Commander Joseph J. Rochefort led this group in the spring of 1942 when his cryptanalysts intercepted and deciphered a Japanese coded message. This message described a forthcoming major Japanese attack on a location known as AF. Rochefort believed that AF referred to the U.S.-held Midway Island. Midway was a key U.S. base that projected U.S. power into the mid-Pacific.

Rochefort could not convince his superiors that AF was Midway Island. As a ruse, Rochefort asked Midway personnel to transmit a message that Midway was having a water problem. The message was sent in the clear and in weak code that was sure to be intercepted and broken by the Japanese. Later on May 22, Japanese Naval intelligence transmitted a message read by the United States that AF was having a water problem. As a result of this brilliant effort in code breaking, Admiral Chester W. Nimitz authorized the strategy for the U.S. fleet to surprise the Japanese fleet at Midway. This bold undertaking resulted in a resounding U.S. victory that was the turning point of the war in the Pacific.

The German Enigma Machine

The German military used a polyalphabetic substitution cipher machine called the Enigma as its principal encipherment system during World War II. The Enigma incorporated mechanical rotors for encipherment and decipherment. A Dutchman, Hugo Koch, developed the machine in 1919, and it was produced for the commercial market in 1923 by Arthur Scherbius. Sherbius obtained a U.S. patent on the Enigma machine for the Berlin firm of Chiffriermasschinen Aktiengesellschaft. Polish cryptanalyst Marian Rejewski, working with the French from 1928 to 1938, solved the wiring of the three-rotor system that was used by the Germans at the time and created a card file that could anticipate the 6 times 17,576 possible rotor positions. The Germans changed the indicator system and the number of rotors to six in 1938, thus tremendously increasing the difficulty of breaking the Enigma cipher. In their work in 1938, the Polish and French constructed a prototype machine called "The Bombe" for use in breaking the Enigma cipher. The name was derived from the ticking noises that the machine made.

The work on breaking the Enigma cipher was then taken over by the British at Bletchley Park in England and was led by many distinguished scientists, including Alan Turing. The Turing prototype Bombe appeared in 1940, and high-speed Bombes were developed by the British and Americans in 1943.

The Enigma machine, as shown in Figure 4.10, consists of a plugboard, three rotors, and a reflecting rotor.

The three rotors' rotational positions changed with encipherments. A rotor is illustrated in Figure 4.11. It is constructed of an insulating material and has 26 electrical contacts that are evenly spaced around the circumference on both sides. A conductor through the disk connects a contact on one side of the disk to a non-corresponding contact on the other side of the disk, effecting a monoalphabetic substitution. This connection is illustrated in Figure 4.12.

Turning the rotor places the results in another substitution. These substitutions come from rotor to rotor. The rotors are turned 360/26 degrees for each increment.

Figure 4.10 Enigma Machine.
(Courtesy of the National Cryptologic Museum)

Figure 4.11 An Enigma rotor.

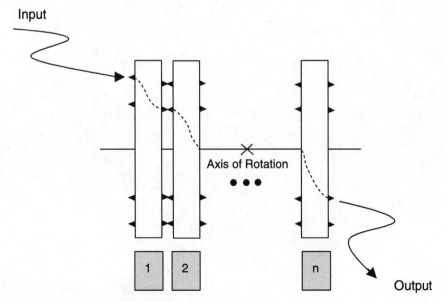

Figure 4.12 An illustration of Enigma rotor connections.

Thus, current entering the input point on rotor 1 travels through the subsequent rotors and emerges at the output. This traverse implements a monoalphabetic substitution. To further complicate the decryption, the position of the rotor is changed after the encryption of each letter. Actually, when one rotor makes a complete revolution, it increments the next "higher-position" rotor in much the same manner as counters increment on a gasoline pump. This rotation accomplishes a polyalphabetic substitution because the plaintext is being transformed into a different alphabet. The rotational displacements were implemented by gears in the World War II Enigma machine. In practice, the rotors had an initial rotational displacement. These rotors were the primary key and the rotational displacement was the secondary key. An initial permutation was performed on the plaintext by means of the plugboard prior to its being passed through the three substitution rotors. Then, this result was further enciphered by the reflecting rotor, which has contacts only on one side. The path was then returned through the three rotors in this backward direction. The final resulting ciphertext was subjected to the inverse permutation of the initial plaintext permutation.

Rotor systems are also referred to as Hebern Machines. In addition to the German Enigma, the Japanese Red and Purple Machines and the American SIGABA (Big Machine) (Figure 4.13) were rotor machines. As far as it is known, SIGABA ciphers were never broken.

Figure 4.13 American SIGABA "Big Machine."
(Courtesy of National Cryptographic Museum)

Cryptographic Technologies

The two principal types of cryptographic technologies are symmetric key (secret key or private key) cryptography and asymmetric (public key) cryptography. In symmetric key cryptography, both the receiver and sender share a common secret key. In asymmetric key cryptography, the sender and receiver respectively share a public and private key. The public and private keys are related mathematically, and in an ideal case, they have the characteristic where an individual who has the public key cannot derive the private key.

Because of the amount of computation involved in public key cryptography, private key cryptography is on the order of 1,000 times faster than public key cryptography.

Classical Ciphers

In this section, the basic encipherment operations are discussed in detail in order to provide a basis for understanding the evolution of encryption methods and the corresponding cyptanalysis efforts.

Substitution

The Caesar Cipher, as we discussed earlier in this chapter, is a simple substitution cipher that involves shifting the alphabet three positions to the right. The Caesar Cipher is a subset of the Vigenère polyalphabetic cipher. In the Caesar cipher, the message's characters and repetitions of the key are added together, modulo 26. In modulo 26 addition, the letters A to Z of the alphabet are given a value of 0 to 25, respectively. Two parameters have to be specified for the key:

D, the number of repeating letters representing the key

K, the key

In the following example, D = 3 and K = BAD.

The message is: ATTACK AT DAWN

Assigning numerical values to the message yields

```
0 19 19 0 2 10    0 19    3  0  22 13
A  T  T A C  K     A  T    D  A  W  N
```

The numerical values of K are

```
1  0  3
B  A  D
```

Now, the repetitive key of 103 is added to the letters of the message as follows:

1	0	3	1	0	3	1	0	3	1	0	3	Repeating Key
0	19	19	0	2	10	0	19	3	0	22	13	Message
1	19	22	1	2	13	1	19	6	1	22	16	Ciphertext Numerical Equivalents
B	T	W	B	C	N	B	T	G	B	W	Q	Ciphertext

Converting the numbers back to their corresponding letters of the alphabet produces the ciphertext as shown.

For the special case of the Caesar Cipher, D is 1 and the Key is D (2).

Taking the same message as an example using the Caesar cipher yields the following:

2	2	2	2	2	2	2	2	2	2	2	2	Repeating Key
0	19	19	0	2	10	0	19	3	0	22	13	Message
2	21	21	2	4	12	2	21	5	2	24	15	Ciphertext Numerical Equivalents
C	V	V	C	E	M	C	V	F	C	Y	P	Ciphertext

Converting the numbers back to their corresponding letters of the alphabet produces the ciphertext, which is the letters of the original message text shifted three positions to the right.

If the sum of any of the additions yields a result greater than or equal to 26, the additions would be modulo 26, in which the final result is the remainder over 26. The following examples illustrate modulo 26 addition:

14	12	22	24	
12	22	8	5	
26	32	30	29	Apparent Sum
0	6	4	3	Result of modulo 2 addition

These ciphers can be described by the general equation,

$C = (M + b) \bmod N$ where

b is a fixed integer

N is the size of the alphabet

M is the Plaintext message in numerical form

C is the Ciphertext in numerical form

This representation is a special case of an Affine Cryptosystem, which is described in the following equation:

C = (aM + b)mod N where

a and b comprise the key

Recall that the following transformation is implemented by the Caesar Cipher:

A B C D E F G H I J K L M N O P Q R S T U V W X Y Z

Transforms | to

D E F G H I J K L M N O P Q R S T U V W X Y Z A B C

This type of cipher can be attacked by using frequency analysis. In frequency analysis, the frequency characteristics shown in the use of the alphabet's letters in a particular language are used. This type of cryptanalysis is possible because the Caesar cipher is a monoalphabetic or simple substitution cipher, where a character of ciphertext is substituted for each character of the plaintext. A polyalphabetic cipher is accomplished through the use of multiple substitution ciphers. For example, using the alphabets shown in Figure 4.14, a Caesar cipher with D =3, and the Key =BAD (103), the plaintext EGGA is enciphered into YGZR. Blaise de Vigenère, a French diplomat born in 1523, consolidated the cryptographic works of Alberti, Trithemius, and Porta to develop the very strong polyalphabetic cipher at that time. Vigenère's cipher used 26 alphabets.

Because multiple alphabets are used, this approach counters frequency analysis. It can, however, be attacked by discovery of the periods—when the substitution repeats.

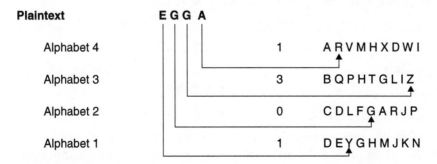

Figure 4.14 Polyalphabetic substitution.

```
NOWISTHE
TIMEFORA
LLGOODME
NTOCOMET
OTHEAIDO
FTHEIRPA
RTY
```

Figure 4.15 A columnar transposition cipher.

Transposition (Permutation)

Another type of cipher is the transposition cipher. In this cipher, the letters of the plaintext are permuted.

For example, the letters of the plaintext A T T A C K A T D A W N could be permuted to D C K A A W N A T A T T.

A columnar transposition cipher is one where the plaintext is written horizontally across the paper and is read vertically, as shown in Figure 4.15.

Reading the ciphertext vertically yields: NTLNOFROILTTTTWMGOHHY . . .

The transposition cipher can be attacked through frequency analysis, but it hides the statistical properties of letter pairs and triples, such as IS and TOO.

Vernam Cipher (One-Time Pad)

The one-time pad or Vernam cipher is implemented through a key that consists of a random set of non-repeating characters. Each key letter is added modulo 26 to a letter of the plaintext. In the one-time pad, each key letter is used one time for only one message and is never used again. The length of the key character stream is equal to the length of the message. For megabyte and gigabyte messages, this one-time pad is not practical, but it is approximated by shorter random sets of characters with very long periods.

An example of a one-time pad encryption is as follows:

Plaintext	HOWAREYOU	7	14	22	0	17	4	24	14	20
One-time pad key	XRAQZTBCN	23	17	0	16	25	19	1	2	13
Apparent sum		30	31	22	16	42	23	25	16	33
Sum Mod 26		4	5	22	16	16	23	25	16	7
Ciphertext		E	F	W	Q	Q	X	Z	Q	H

The Vernam machine (shown in Figure 4.16) was developed at AT&T, and the original system performed an XOR of the message bits in a Baudot code with the key bits.

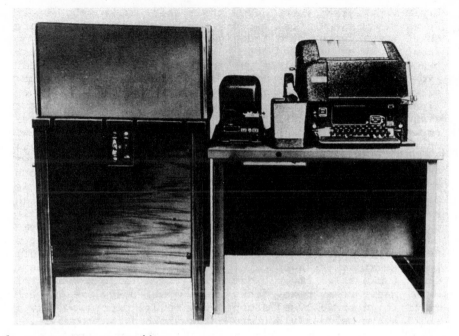

Figure 4.16 A Vernam machine.

Book or Running Key Cipher

This cipher uses text from a source (say, a book) to encrypt the plaintext. The key, known to the sender and the intended receiver, might be the page and line number of text in the book. This text is matched character for character with the plaintext, and modulo 26 addition is performed to effect the encryption.

The Running Key Cipher eliminates periodicity, but it is attacked by exploiting the redundancy in the key.

Codes

Codes deal with words and phrases and relate these words as phrases to corresponding groups of numbers or letters. For example, the numbers 526 might mean "Attack at Dawn."

Steganography

Steganography is the art of hiding the existence of a message. The word steganography comes from the Greek words steganos, meaning "covered," and graphein, meaning "to write." An example is the microdot, which compresses a message into the size of a period or dot. Steganography can be used to make a digital "watermark" to detect the illegal copying of digital images.

Secret Key Cryptography (Symmetric Key)

Secret key cryptography is the type of encryption that is familiar to most people. In this type of cryptography, the sender and receiver both know a secret key. The sender encrypts the plaintext message with the secret key, and the receiver decrypts the message with the same secret key. Obviously, the challenge is to make the secret key available to both the sender and receiver without compromising it. For increased security, the secret key should be changed at frequent intervals. Ideally, a particular secret key should only be used once.

Figure 4.17 illustrates a secret (symmetric) key cryptographic system.

A secret key cryptographic system is comprised of information that is public and private. The public information usually consists of the following:

■ The algorithm for enciphering the plaintext copy of the enciphered message

■ Possibly, a copy of the plaintext and an associated ciphertext

■ Possibly, an encipherment of the plaintext that was chosen by an unintended receiver

Private information is:

■ The key or cryptovariable

■ One particular cryptographic transformation out of many possible transformations

An important property of any secret key cryptographic system is that the same key can encipher and decipher the message. If large key sizes (> 128 bits)

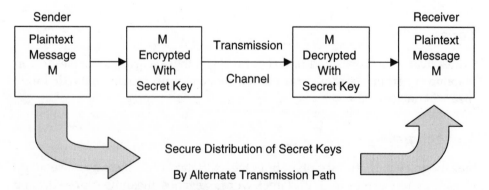

Figure 4.17 A symmetric (secret) key cryptographic system.

are used, secret key systems are very difficult to break. These systems are also relatively fast and are used to encrypt large volumes of data. There are many symmetric key algorithms available because of this feature. One problem with using a symmetric key system is that because the sender and receiver must share the same secret key, the sender requires a different key for each intended receiver. One commonly used approach is to use public key cryptography to transmit a symmetric session key that can be used for a session between the sender and receiver. Time stamps can be associated with this session key so that it is valid only for a specified period of time. Time stamping is a counter to replay, wherein a session key is somehow intercepted and used at a later time. Symmetric key systems, however, do not provide mechanisms for authentication and non-repudiation. The best-known symmetric key system is probably the *Data Encryption Standard* (DES). DES evolved from the IBM Lucifer cryptographic system in the early 1970s for commercial use.

Data Encryption Standard (DES)

DES is a symmetric key cryptosystem that was devised in 1972 as a derivation of the Lucifer algorithm developed by Horst Feistel at IBM. He obtained a patent on the technique (H. Feistel, "Block Cipher Cryptographic System," U.S. Patent #3,798,539, March, 19, 1974.) DES is used for commercial and non-classified purposes. DES describes the *Data Encryption Algorithm* (DEA) and is the name of the *Federal Information Processing Standard* (FIPS) 46-1 that was adopted in 1977 [Data Encryption Standard, FIPS PUB 46-1 (Washington, D.C.: National Bureau of Standards, January 15, 1977)]. DEA is also defined as the ANSI Standard X3.92 [ANSI X3.92 American National Standard for Data Encryption Algorithm, (DEA)," American National Standards Institute, 1981]. The *National Institute of Standards and Technology* (NIST) recertified DES in 1993. DES will not be recertified again. It will, however, be replaced by the *Advanced Encryption Standard* (AES).

DEA uses a 64-bit block size and uses a 56-bit key. It begins with a 64-bit key and strips off eight parity bits. DEA is a 16-round cryptosystem and was originally designed for implementation in hardware. With a 56-bit key, one would have to try 2^{56} or 70 quadrillion possible keys in a brute force attack. Although this number is huge, large numbers of computers cooperating over the Internet could try all possible key combinations. Due to this vulnerability, the U.S. government has not used DES since November 1998. Triple DES-three encryptions using the DEA has replaced DES and will be used until the AES is adopted.

As previously stated, DES uses 16 rounds of transposition and substitution. It implements the techniques that were suggested by Claude Shannon, the father of Information Theory. Shannon proposed two techniques, confusion and diffusion, for improving the encryption of plaintext. Confusion conceals the statistical connection between ciphertext and plaintext. It is accomplished in DES through a substitution by means of non-linear substitution S-boxes. An S-box is non-linear because it generates a 4-bit output string from a 6-bit input string.

The purpose of diffusion is to spread the influence of a plaintext character over many ciphertext characters. Diffusion can be implemented by means of a Product Cipher. In a Product Cipher, a cryptosystem (E1) is applied to a message (M) to yield ciphertext (C1). Then, another cryptosystem (E2) is applied to ciphertext (C1) to yield ciphertext C2. Symbolically, this product is generated by E1(M) = C1; E2(C1) = C2. DES implements this product 16 times. Diffusion is performed in DES by permutations in P-Boxes.

DES operates in four modes:

1. *Cipher Block Chaining* (CBC)
2. *Electronic Code Book* (ECB)
3. *Cipher Feedback* (CFB)
4. *Output Feedback* (OFB)

Cipher Block Chaining

Cipher Block Chaining (CBC) operates with plaintext blocks of 64 bits. A randomly generated 64-bit initialization vector is XORed with the first block of plaintext used to disguise the first part of the message that might be predictable (such as Dear Sir). The result is encrypted by using the DES key. The first ciphertext will then XOR with the next 64-bit plaintext block. This encryption continues until the plaintext is exhausted. Note that in this mode, errors propagate.

A schematic diagram of CBC is shown in Figure 4.18.

Electronic Code Book (ECB)

Electronic Code Book (ECB) is the "native" mode of DES and is a block cipher. ECB is best suited for use with small amounts of data. It is usually applied to encrypt initialization vectors or encrypting keys. ECB is applied to 64-bit blocks of plaintext, and it produces corresponding 64-bit blocks of ciphertext. ECB operates by dividing the 64-bit input vector into two 32-bit blocks called a Right Block and a Left Block. The bits are then recopied to produce two 48-bit blocks. Then, each of these 48-bit blocks is XORed with a 48-bit encryption key. The nomenclature "code book" is derived from the notion of a code book in manual encryption, which has pairs of plaintext and the corresponding code. For example, the word "RETREAT" in the code book might have the corresponding code 5374.

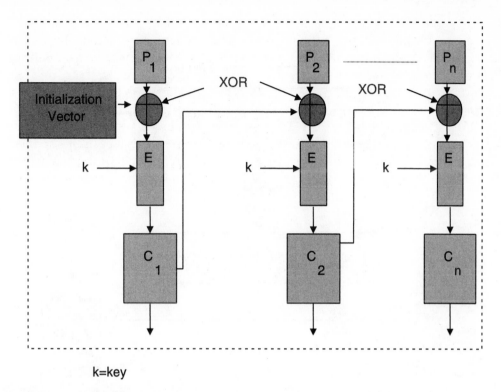

k=key

Figure 4.18 Cipher block chaining.

Cipher Feedback (CFB)

The Cipher Feedback (CFB) mode of DES is a stream cipher where the ciphertext is used as feedback into the key generation source to develop the next key stream. The ciphertext generated by performing an XOR of the plaintext with the key stream has the same number of bits as the plaintext. In this mode, errors will propagate. A diagram of the CFB is shown in Figure 4.19.

Output Feedback

The DES Output Feedback (OFB) mode is also a stream cipher that generates the ciphertext key by XORing the plaintext with a key stream. In this mode, errors will not propagate. Feedback is used to generate the key stream; therefore, the key stream varies. An initialization vector is required in OFB. OFB is depicted in Figure 4.20.

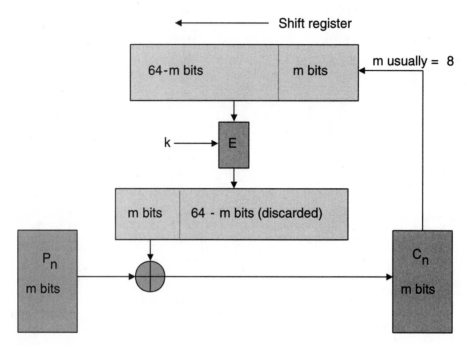

Figure 4.19 DES Cipher Feedback operation.

DES Security

Due to the increase in computing power that is capable of being integrated onto Very Large Scale Integration (VLSI) chips and the corresponding decrease in cost, DES has been broken. Through the use of the Internet, a worldwide network of PCs was used to crack DES.

The consensus of the information security community is that DES is vulnerable to attack by an exhaustive research for the 56-bit key. Therefore, DES is being replaced by Triple DES, and then by the Advanced Encryption Standard (AES).

Triple DES

It has been shown that encrypting plaintext with one DES key and then encrypting it with a second DES key is no more secure than using a single DES key. It would seem at first glance that if both keys have n bits, a brute force attack of trying all possible keys will require trying $2^n \times 2^n$ or 2^{2n} different combinations. However, Merkle and Hellman showed that a known plaintext,

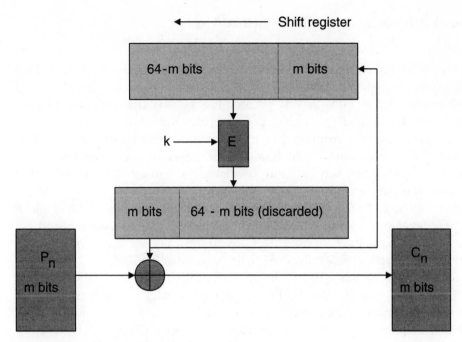

Figure 4.20 DES Output Feedback operations.

Meet-in-the-Middle attack could break the double encryption in 2^{n+1} attempts. This type of attack is achieved by encrypting from one end, decrypting from the other, and comparing the results in the middle. Therefore, Triple DES is used to obtain stronger encryption.

Triple DES encrypts a message three times. This encryption can be accomplished in several ways. For example, the message can be encrypted with Key 1, decrypted with Key 2 (essentially another encryption), and encrypted again with Key 1:

[E{D[E(M,K1)], K2}, K1]

A Triple DES encryption in this manner is denoted as DES–EDE2. If three encryptions are performed using the two keys, it is referred to as DES–EEE2:

[E{E[E(M, K1)], K2}, K1]

Similarly,

E{E[E(M, K1)], K2}, K3]

describes a triple encryption DES–EEE3 with three different keys. This encryption is the most secure form of Triple DES.

The Advanced Encryption Standard (AES)

AES is a block cipher that will replace DES, but it is anticipated that Triple DES will remain an approved algorithm for U.S. Government use. Triple DES and DES are specified in FIPS 46-3. The AES initiative was announced in January 1997 by NIST, and candidate encryption algorithm submissions were solicited. On August 29, 1998, a group of 15 AES candidates were announced by NIST. In 1999, NIST announced five finalist candidates. These candidates were MARS, RC6, Rijndael, Serpent, and Twofish. NIST closed Round 2 of public analyses of these algorithms on May 15, 2000.

On October 2, 2000, NIST announced the selection of the Rijndael Block Cipher, developed by the Belgian cryptographers Dr. Joan Daemen and Dr. Vincent Rijmen, as the proposed AES algorithm. Rijndael was formalized as the *Advanced Encryption Standard* (AES) on November 26, 2001, as *Federal Information Processing Standard Publication* (FIPS PUB 197). FIPS PUB 197 states that "This standard may be used by Federal departments and agencies when an agency determines that sensitive (unclassified) information (as defined in P.L. 100-235) requires cryptographic protection. Other FIPS-approved cryptographic algorithms may be used in addition to, or in lieu of, this standard." Depending upon which of the three keys is used, the standard might be referred to as "AES-128," "AES-192," or "AES-256." It is expected that AES will be adopted by other private and public organizations inside and outside the United States.

The Rijndael Block Cipher

The Rijndael algorithm was designed to have the following properties:

- Resistance against all known attacks
- Design simplicity
- Code compactness and speed on a wide variety of platforms

The Rijndael cipher can be categorized as an iterated block cipher with a variable block length and key length that can be independently chosen as 128, 192, or 256 bits.

In decimal terms, there are approximately 3.4×10^{38} possible 128-bit keys, 6.2×10^{57} possible 192-bit keys, and 1.1×10^{77} possible 256-bit keys.

AES specifies three key sizes—128, 192, and 256 bits—with a fixed block size of 128 bits.

As a measure of the relative strength of the Rijndael encryption algorithm, if a computer could crack the DES encryption by trying 2^{56} keys in one second, the same computer would require 149 trillion (149×10^{12}) years to crack Rijndael. For a comparison, the universe is estimated to be fewer than 20 billion (20×10^9) years old.

Rijndael defines an intermediate cipher result as a State upon which the transformations that are defined in the cipher operate.

Instead of a Feistel network that takes a portion of the modified plaintext and transposes it to another position, the Rijndael Cipher employs a round transformation that is comprised of three layers of distinct and invertible transformations. These transformations are also defined as uniform, which means that every bit of the State is treated the same. Each of the layers has the following respective functions:

The non-linear layer. The parallel application of S-boxes that have optimum worst-case non-linearity properties.

The linear mixing layer. Layer that provides a guarantee of a high diffusion of multiple rounds.

The key addition layer. An Exclusive Or of the Round Key to the intermediate State.

Round keys are derived from the Cipher key through a key schedule, which consists of a key expansion and Round key selection—defined as follows in the Rijndael Block Cipher AES Proposal (AES Proposal: Rijndael, Joan Daemen and Vincent Rijmen, version 2, 9/8/99), submitted to NIST:

The total number of Round key bits is equal to block length multiplied by the number of rounds plus 1, (e.g., for a block length of 128 bits and 10 rounds, 1408 Round Key bits are needed.) The Cipher Key is expanded into an Expanded Key. Round Keys are taken from the Expanded Key . . . .

The number of rounds used in the Rijndael cipher is a function of the key size as follows:

- 256-bit key → 14 rounds
- 192-bit key → 12 rounds
- 128-bit key → 10 rounds

The Rijndael Block Cipher is suited for the following types of implementations:

- High-speed chips with no area restrictions
- A compact co-processor on a smart card

The Twofish Algorithm

Another example of the evolution of cryptographic technology is found in the Twofish algorithm, one of the finalists in the AES competition.

In summary, Twofish is a symmetric block cipher that operates on 128-bit blocks in 16 rounds that works in all standard modes. It can accept key lengths up to 256 bits.

Twofish is a Feistel network in that in each round, one-half of the 128-bit block of plaintext or modified plaintext is fed into an element called the F Function box and then is XORed with the other half of the text in the network. This one-half block is broken into two 32-bit units that are, in turn, broken into four bytes. These four bytes are fed into four different, key-dependent S-boxes and emerge from the S-boxes as four transformed output bytes.

The four output bytes of the S-boxes are combined in a Maximum Distance Separable (MDS) matrix to form two 32-bit units. These two 32-bit units are then combined by using a Pseudo-Hadamard Transform (PHT) and are added to two round subkeys. The PHT is a linear operation of the form

$d_1 = (2b_1 + b_2) \bmod 256$

where b_1 and b_2 are the inputs, and d_1 is the output.

These results are XORed with the right half of the 64 bits of the plaintext. In addition, 1-bit rotations are performed before and after the XOR. These operations are then repeated for 15 more rounds.

Twofish also employs what is termed as "prewhitening" and "postwhitening," where additional subkeys are XORed with the plaintext before the first round and after the 16th round. This approach makes cryptanalysis more difficult, because the whitening subkeys have to be determined in addition to the algorithm key.

In the Twofish algorithm, the MDS matrix, the PHT, and key additions provide diffusion.

The IDEA Cipher

The *International Data Encryption Algorithm* (IDEA) cipher is a secure, secret, key block encryption algorithm that was developed by James Massey and Xuejia Lai (X. Lai, "On the Design and Security of Block Ciphers," *ETH Series on Information Processing*, v. 1, Konstanz: Hartung-Gorre Verlag, 1992). It evolved in 1992 from earlier algorithms called the Proposed Encryption Standard and the Improved Proposed Encryption Standard. IDEA operates on 64-bit Plaintext blocks and uses a 128-bit key. It applies both confusion and diffusion.

The IDEA algorithm performs eight rounds and operates on 16-bit sub-blocks by using algebraic calculations that are amenable to hardware implementation. These operations are modulo 2^{16} addition, modulo $2^{16} + 1$ multiplication, and the Exclusive Or.

With its 128-bit key, an IDEA cipher is much more difficult to crack than DES. IDEA operates in the modes described for DES and is applied in the

Pretty Good Privacy (PGP) e-mail encryption system that was developed by Phil Zimmerman.

RC5

RC5 is a family of cryptographic algorithms invented by Ronald Rivest in 1994. It is a block cipher of variable block length and encrypts through integer addition, the application of a bit-wise Exclusive Or, and variable rotations. The key size and number of rounds are also variable. Typical block sizes are 32, 64, or 128 bits. The number of rounds can range from 0 to 255 and the key size can range from 0 to 2048 bits. RC5 was patented by RSA Data Security in 1997.

Public (Asymmetric) Key Cryptosystems

Unlike secret key cryptosystems, which make use of a single key that is known to a sender and receiver, public key systems employ two keys: a public key and a private key. The public key is made available to anyone wanting to encrypt and send a message. The private key is used to decrypt the message. Thus, the need to exchange secret keys is eliminated. The following are the important points to note:

- The public key cannot decrypt the message that it encrypted.
- Ideally, the private key cannot be derived from the public key.
- A message that is encrypted by one of the keys can be decrypted with the other key.
- The private key is kept private.

When Kp is the public key and Ks is the private key, the process is illustrated as follows:

$$C = Kp(P) \text{ and } P = Ks(C)$$

where C is the ciphertext and P is the plaintext.

In addition, the reverse is also true:

$$C = Ks(P) \text{ and } P = Kp(C)$$

One-Way Functions

Public key cryptography is possible through the application of a one-way function. A one-way function is a function that is easy to compute in one direction, yet is difficult to compute in the reverse direction. For such a function, if $y = 5 f(x)$, it would be easy to compute y if given x, yet it would be very difficult to derive x when given y. A simple example would be the telephone directory. It is easy to find a number when given a name, but it is difficult to find the name when given a number. For a one-way function to be useful in the context of public key cryptography, it should have a trap door. A trap door is a secret mechanism that enables you to easily accomplish the reverse function in a one-way function. Thus, if you know the trap door, you can easily derive x in the previous example when given y.

In the context of public key cryptography, it is very difficult to calculate the private key from the public key unless you know the trap door.

Public Key Algorithms

A number of public key algorithms have been developed. Some of these algorithms are applicable to digital signatures, encryption, or both. Because there are more calculations associated with public key cryptography, it is 1,000 to 10,000 times slower than secret key cryptography. Thus, hybrid systems have evolved that use public key cryptography to safely distribute the secret keys used in symmetric key cryptography.

Some of the important public key algorithms that have been developed include the Diffie-Hellman key exchange protocol, RSA, El Gamal, Knapsack, and Elliptic Curve.

RSA

RSA is derived from the last names of its inventors, Rivest, Shamir, and Addleman (R. L. Rivest, A. Shamir, and L. M. Addleman, "A Method for Obtaining Digital Signatures and Public-Key Cryptosystems," Communications of the ACM, v. 21, n. 2, Feb 1978, pp. 120–126). This algorithm is based on the difficulty of factoring a number, N, which is the product of two large prime numbers. These numbers might be 200 digits each. Thus, the difficulty in obtaining the private key from the public key is a hard, one-way function that is equivalent to the difficulty of finding the prime factors of N.

In RSA, public and private keys are generated as follows:

- Choose two large prime numbers, p and q, of equal length and compute $p \times q = n$, which is the public modulus.
- Choose a random public key, e, so that e and $(p - 1)(1q - 1)$ are relatively prime.
- Compute $e \times d = 1 \mod (p - 1)(q - 1)$, where d is the private key.
- Thus, $d = e^{-1} \mod [(p - 1)(q - 1)]$.

From these calculations, (d, n) is the private key and (e, n) is the public key. The plaintext, P, is thus encrypted to generate ciphertext C as follows:

$C = P^e \bmod n,$

and is decrypted to recover the plaintext, P, as

$P = C^d \bmod n$

Typically, the plaintext will be broken into equal length blocks, each with fewer digits than n, and each block will be encrypted and decrypted as shown.

RSA can be used for encryption, key exchange, and digital signatures.

Diffie-Hellman Key Exchange

The Diffie-Hellman Key Exchange is a method where subjects exchange secret keys over a non-secure medium without exposing the keys. The method was disclosed by Dr. W. Diffie and Dr. M. E. Hellman in their seminal 1976 paper entitled "New Directions in Cryptography" (Whitfield Diffie and Martin Hellman, "New Directions in Cryptography," *IEEE Transactions on Information Theory*, Vol. IT-22, November 1976, pp. 644–654).

The method enables two users to exchange a secret key over an insecure medium without an additional session key. It has two system parameters, p and g. Both parameters are public and can be used by all the system's users. Parameter p is a prime number, and parameter g (which is usually called a generator) is an integer less than p that has the following property: For every number n between 1 and p − 1 inclusive, there is a power k of g such that $g^k = n \bmod p$.

For example, when given the following public parameters:

p = prime number

g = generator

Generating equation $y = g^x \bmod p$

Alice and Bob can securely exchange a common secret key as follows:

Alice can use her private value "a" to calculate:

$y_a = g^a \bmod p$

Also, Bob can use his private value "b" to calculate the following:

$y_b = g^b \bmod p.$

Alice can now send y_a to Bob, and Bob can send y_b to Alice. Knowing her private value, a, Alice can calculate $(y_b)^a$, which yields the following:

$g^{ba} \bmod p$

Similarly, with his private value, b, Bob can calculate $(y_a)^b$ as such:

$g^{ab} \bmod p.$

Because $g^{ba}modp$ is equal to $g^{ab}modp$, Bob and Alice have securely exchanged the secret key.

In their paper, Diffie and Hellman primarily described key exchange, yet they also provided a basis for the further development of public key cryptography.

El Gamal

Dr. T. El Gamal extended the Diffie-Hellman concepts to apply to encryption and digital signatures (T. El Gamal, "A Public-Key Crypto System and a Signature Scheme Based on Discrete Logarithms," *Advances in Cryptography: Proceedings of CRYPTO 84*, Springer-Verlag, 1985, pp. 10-18). The El Gamal system is a non-patented public-key cryptosystem that is based on the discrete logarithm problem. Encryption with El Gamal is illustrated in the following example:

Given the prime number, p, and the integer, g, Alice uses her private key, a, to compute her public key as $y_a = g^a modp$.

For Bob to send message M to Alice:

Bob generates random #b < p.

Bob computes $y_b = g^b modp$ and $y_m = M$ XOR $y_a{}^b = M$ XOR $g^{ab}modp$.

Bob sends y_b, y_m to Alice, and Alice computes $y_b{}^a = g^{ab}modp$.

Therefore, $M = y_b{}^a$ XOR $y_m = g^{ab}modp$ XOR M XOR $g^{ab}modp$.

Merkle-Hellman Knapsack

The Merkle-Hellman Knapsack (R.C. Merkle and M. Hellman, "Hiding Information and Signatures in Trapdoor Knapsacks," IEEE Transactions on Information Theory, v. 24, n. 5, Sep. 1978, pp. 525-530) is based on the problem of having a set of items with fixed weights and determining which of these items can be added in order to obtain a given total weight.

This concept can be illustrated by using a superincreasing set of weights. Superincreasing means that each succeeding term in the set is greater than the sum of the previous terms. The set [2, 3, 6, 12, 27, 52] has these properties. If we have a knapsack with a total weight of 69 for this example, the problem would be to find the terms whose sum is equal to 69. The solution to this simple example is that terms 52, 12, 3, and 2 would be in the knapsack. Or equivalently, if we represent the terms that are in the knapsack by 1s and those that are not by 0s, the "ciphertext" representing the "plaintext 69" is 110101.

Elliptic Curve (EC)

Elliptic curves are another approach to public key cryptography. This method was developed independently by Neal Koblitz (N. Koblitz, "Elliptic Curve

Cryptosystems," *Mathematics of Computation*, v. 48, n. 177, 1987, pp. 203-209) and V.S. Miller (V.S. Miller, "Use of Elliptic Curves in Cryptography," *Advances in Cryptology—CRYPTO '85 Proceedings*, Springer-Verlag, 1986, pp. 417-426). Elliptic curves are usually defined over finite fields, such as real and rational numbers, and implement an analog to the discreet logarithm problem.

An elliptic curve is defined by the following equation:

$y^2 = x^3 + ax + b$ along with a single point O, the point at infinity.

The space of the elliptic curve has properties where:

- Addition is the counterpart of modular multiplication.
- Multiplication is the counterpart of modular exponentiation.

Thus, given two points, P and R, on an elliptic curve where P = KR, finding K is the hard problem that is known as the elliptic curve discreet logarithm problem.

Because it is more difficult to compute elliptic curve discreet logarithms than conventional discreet logarithms or to factor the product of large prime numbers, smaller key sizes in the elliptic curve implementation can yield higher levels of security. For example, an elliptic curve key of 160 bits is equivalent to a 1024-bit RSA key. This characteristic means fewer computational and memory requirements. Therefore, elliptic curve cryptography is suited to hardware applications such as smart cards and wireless devices. Elliptic curves can be used to implement digital signatures, encryption, and key management capabilities.

Public Key Cryptosystems Algorithm Categories

Public key encryption utilizes hard, one-way functions. The calculations associated with this type of encryption are as follows:

- Factoring the product of large prime numbers
  - RSA
- Finding the discreet logarithm in a finite field
  - El Gamal
  - Diffie-Hellman
  - Schnorr's signature algorithm
  - Elliptic curve
  - Nybergrueppel's signature algorithm

Table 4.2 Equivalent Strengths of Asymmetric and Symmetric Key Sizes

ASYMMETRIC KEY SIZE	SYMMETRIC KEY SIZE
512 Bits	64 Bits
1792 Bits	112 Bits
2304 Bits	128 Bits

Asymmetric and Symmetric Key Length Strength Comparisons

A comparison of the approximate equivalent strengths of public and private key cryptosystems is provided in Table 4.2.

Digital Signatures

The purpose of digital signatures is to detect unauthorized modifications of data and to authenticate the identity of the signatories and non-repudiation. These functions are accomplished by generating a block of data that is usually smaller than the size of the original data. This smaller block of data is bound to the original data and to the identity of the sender. This binding verifies the integrity of data and provides non-repudiation. To quote the NIST Digital Signature Standard (DSS) [National Institute of Standards and Technology, NIST FIPS PUB 186, "Digital Signature Standard," U.S. Department of Commerce, May 1994]:

Digital signatures are used to detect unauthorized modifications to data and to authenticate the identity of the signatory. In addition, the recipient of signed data can use a digital signature in proving to a third party that the signature was in fact generated by the signatory.

To generate a digital signature, the digital signal program passes the file to be sent through a one-way hash function. This hash function produces a fixed size output from a variable size input. The output of the hash function is called a message digest. The message digest is uniquely derived from the input file, and if the hash algorithm is strong, the message digest has the following characteristics:

- The hash function is considered one-way because the original file cannot be created from the message digest.
- Two files should not have the same message digest.
- Given a file and its corresponding message digest, it should not be feasible to find another file with the same message digest.
- The message digest should be calculated by using all of the original file's data.

After the message digest is calculated, it is encrypted with the sender's private key. The encrypted message digest is then attached to the original file and is sent to the receiver. The receiver then decrypts the message digest by using the sender's public key. If this public key opens the message digest and it is the true public key of the sender, verification of the sender is then accomplished. Verification occurs because the sender's public key is the only key that can decrypt the message digest encrypted with the sender's private key. Then, the receiver can compute the message digest of the received file by using the identical hash function as the sender. If this message digest is identical to the message digest that was sent as part of the signature, the message has not been modified.

Digital Signature Standard (DSS) and Secure Hash Standard (SHS)

NIST announced the *Digital Signature Standard* (DSS) *Federal Information Processing Standard* (FIPS) 186-1. This standard enables the use of the RSA digital signature algorithm or the *Digital Signature Algorithm* (DSA). The DSA is based on a modification of the El Gamal digital signature methodology and was developed by Claus Schnorr (C.P. Schnorr, "Efficient Signature Generation for Smart Cards," *Advances in Cryptology—CRYPTO '89 Proceedings*, Springer-Verlag, 1990, pp. 239–252).

Both of these digital signature algorithms use the *Secure Hash Algorithm* (SHA-1) as defined in FIPS 180 (NIST, NIST FIPS PUB 180, "Secure Hash Standard," U.S. Department of Commerce, May 1993).

SHA-1 computes a fixed-length message digest from a variable length input message. This message digest is then processed by the DSA to either generate or verify the signature. Applying this process to the shorter message digest is more efficient than applying it to the longer message.

As previously discussed, any modification to the message being sent to the receiver results in a different message digest being calculated by the receiver. Thus, the signature will not be verified.

SHA-1 produces a message digest of 160 bits when any message less than 264 bits is used as an input.

SHA-1 has the following properties:

- It is computationally infeasible to find a message that corresponds to a given message digest.

- It is computationally infeasible to find two different messages that produce the same message digest.

For SHA-1, the length of the message is the number of bits in a message. Padding bits are added to the message to make the total length of the message, including padding, a multiple of 512. To quote from the NIST DSS/SHS document:

The SHA-1 sequentially processes blocks of 512 bits when computing a message digest. The following specifies how the padding shall be performed. As a summary, a "1" followed by m "0's" followed by a 64-bit integer are applied to the end of the message to produce a padded message of length 512*n. The 64-bit integer is l, the length of the original message. The padded message is then processed by the SHA-1 as n 512-bit blocks.

MD5

MD5 is a message digest algorithm that was developed by Ronald Rivest in 1991. MD5 takes a message of an arbitrary length and generates a 128-bit message digest. In MD5, the message is processed in 512-bit blocks in four distinct rounds.

Sending a Message with a Digital Signature

In summary, to send a message:

1. A hash algorithm is used to generate the message digest from the message.
2. The message digest is fed into the digital signature algorithm that generates the signature of the message. The signing of the message is accomplished by encrypting the message digest with the sender's private key and attaching the result to the message. Thus, the message is a signed message.
3. The message and the attached message digest are sent to the receiver. The receiver then decrypts the attached message digest with the sender's public key.

   The receiver also calculates the message digest of the received message by using the identical hash function as the sender. The two message digests should be identical. If they are not identical, the message was modified in transmission. If the two message digests are identical, then the message sent is identical to the message received, the sender is verified, and the sender cannot repudiate the message.

Hashed Message Authentication Code (HMAC)

An HMAC is a hash algorithm that uses a key to generate a *Message Authentication Code* (MAC). A MAC is a type of checksum that is a function of the information in the message. The MAC is generated before the message is sent, appended to the message, and then both are transmitted.

At the receiving end, a MAC is generated from the message alone by using the same algorithm as used by the sender, and this MAC is compared to the MAC sent with the message. If they are not identical, the message was modified en route. Hashing algorithms can be used to generate the MAC and hash algorithms using keys that provide stronger protection than an ordinary MAC generation.

Hash Function Characteristics

As described in the previous section, a hash function (H) is used to condense a message of an arbitrary length into a fixed-length message digest. This message digest should uniquely represent the original message, and it will be used to create a digital signature. Furthermore, it should not be computationally possible to find two messages, M1 and M2, such that H(M1) = H(M2). If this situation were possible, then an attacker could substitute another message (M2) for the original message (M1) and the message digest would not change. Because the message digest is the key component of the digital signature authentication and integrity process, a false message could be substituted for the original message without detection. Specifically, it should not be computationally possible to find:

- A message (M2) that would hash to a specific message digest generated by a different message (M1)
- Two messages that hash to any common message digest

These two items refer to an attack against the hash function known as a birthday attack. This attack relates to the paradoxes that are associated with the following questions:

1. If you were in a room with other people, what would be the sample size, n, of individuals in the room to have a better than 50/50 chance of someone having the same birthday as you? (The answer is 253.)

2. If you were in a room with other people, what would be the sample size, n, of individuals in the room to have a better than 50/50 chance of at least two people having a common birthday? (The answer is 23, because with 23 people in a room, there are $n(n-1)/2$ or 253 pairs of individuals in the room.)

Cryptographic Attacks

As defined earlier, cryptanalysis is the act of obtaining the plaintext or key from the ciphertext. Cryptanalysis is used to obtain valuable information and to pass on altered or fake messages in order to deceive the original intended recipient. This attempt at "cracking" the cipher is also known as an attack. The following are examples of some common attacks:

Brute Force. Trying every possible combination of key patterns; the longer the key length, the more difficult it is to find the key with this method.

Known Plaintext. The attacker has a copy of the plaintext corresponding to the ciphertext.

Chosen Plaintext. Chosen plaintext is encrypted and the output ciphertext is obtained.

Adaptive Chosen Plaintext. A form of a chosen plaintext attack where the selection of the plaintext is altered according to the previous results.

Ciphertext Only. Only the ciphertext is available.

Chosen Ciphertext. Portions of the ciphertext are selected for trial decryption while having access to the corresponding decrypted plaintext.

Adaptive Chosen Ciphertext. A form of a chosen ciphertext attack where the selection of the portions of ciphertext for the attempted decryption is based on the results of previous attempts.

Birthday Attack. Usually applied to the probability of two different messages using the same hash function that produces a common message digest; or given a message and its corresponding message digest, finding another message that when passed through the same hash function generates the same specific message digest. The term "birthday" comes from the fact that in a room with 23 people, the probability of two or more people having the same birthday is greater than 50 percent.

Meet-in-the-Middle. Is applied to double encryption schemes by encrypting known plaintext from one end with each possible key (K) and comparing the results "in the middle" with the decryption of the corresponding ciphertext with each possible K.

Man-in-the-Middle. An attacker taking advantage of the store-and-forward nature of most networks by intercepting messages and forwarding modified versions of the original message while in-between two parties attempting secure communications.

Differential Cryptanalysis. Is applied to private key cryptographic systems by looking at ciphertext pairs, which were generated through the encryption of plaintext pairs, with specific differences and analyzing the effect of these differences.

Linear Cryptanalysis. Using pairs of known plaintext and corresponding ciphertext to generate a linear approximation of a portion of the key.

Differential Linear Cryptanalysis. Using both differential and linear approaches.

Factoring. Using a mathematical approach to determine the prime factors of large numbers.

Statistical. Exploiting the lack of randomness in key generation.

Public Key Certification Systems

A source that could compromise a public key cryptographic system is an individual (A) who is posting a public key under the name of another individual (B). In this scenario, the people who are using this public key to encrypt the messages that were intended for individual B will actually be sending messages to individual A. Because individual A has the private key that corresponds to the posted public key, individual A can decrypt the messages that were intended for individual B.

Digital Certificates

To counter this type of attack, a certification process can be used to bind individuals to their public keys. A Certificate Authority (CA) acts as notary by verifying a person's identity and issuing a certificate that vouches for a public key of the named individual. This certification agent signs the certificate with its own private key. Therefore, the individual is verified as the sender if that person's public key opens the data. The certificate contains the subject's name, the subject's public key, the name of the certificate authority, and the period in which the certificate is valid. To verify the CA's signature, its public key must be cross-certified with another CA. (The X.509 standard defines the format for public key certificates.) This Certificate is then sent to a Repository, which holds the Certificates and Certificate Revocation Lists (CRLs) that denote the revoked certificates. The diagram shown in Figure 4.21 illustrates the use of digital certificates in a transaction between a subscribing entity and a transacting party.

Public Key Infrastructure (PKI)

The integration of digital signatures and certificates, and the other services required for E-commerce is called the Public Key Infrastructure (PKI). These services provide integrity, access control, confidentiality, authentication, and non-repudiation for electronic transactions. The PKI includes the following elements:

- Digital certificates
- Certificate Authority (CA)
- Registration authorities
- Policies and procedures
- Certificate revocation
- Non-repudiation support
- Timestamping
- Lightweight Directory Access Protocol (LDAP)

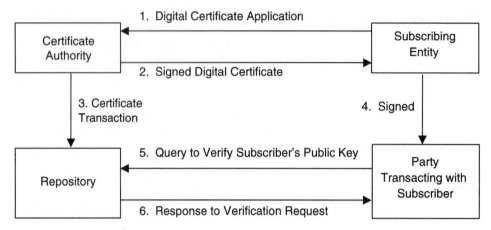

Figure 4.21 A transaction with digital certificates.

- Security-enabled applications
- Cross certification

The Lightweight Directory Access Protocol (LDAP) provides a standard format to access the certificate directories. These directories are stored on LDAP servers on a network and the servers on these networks provide public keys and corresponding X.509 certificates for the enterprise. A directory contains information such as the individuals' names, addresses, phone numbers, and public key certificates. LDAP enables a user to search these directories over the Internet. A series of standards under X.500 defines the protocols and information models for computer directory services that are independent of the platforms and other related entities.

The primary security concerns relative to LDAP servers are availability and integrity. For example, denial of service attacks on an LDAP server could prevent access to the Certification Revocation Lists and, thus, permit the use of a revoked certificate for transactions.

Approaches to Escrowed Encryption

In some instances, there is a need for law enforcement agencies to have access to information transmitted electronically over computer networks. To have this access, law enforcement agencies need the encryption keys to read the enciphered messages. At the same time, the privacy of citizens must be protected from illegal and unauthorized surveillance of their digital communications. This section describes two approaches to this issue.

The Escrowed Encryption Standard

This standard (National Institute of Standards and Technology, NIST FIPS PUB 185, "Escrowed Encryption Standard," U.S. Department of Commerce, Feb 1994) strives to achieve individual privacy and, at the same time, strives to provide for legal monitoring of the encrypted transmissions. The idea is to divide the key into two parts, and to escrow two portions of the key with two separate "trusted" organizations. Then, law enforcement officials, after obtaining a court order, can retrieve the two pieces of the key from the organizations and decrypt the message. The Escrowed Encryption Standard is embodied in the U.S. Government's Clipper Chip, which is implemented in tamper-proof hardware. The Skipjack Secret Key algorithm performs the encryption. Figure 4.22 is a block diagram of the clipper chip and the components of a transmitted message.

Each Clipper Chip has a unique serial number and an 80-bit unique unit or secret key. The unit key is divided into two parts and is stored at two separate organizations with the serial number that uniquely identifies that particular Clipper Chip. Initially, two parties that wish to exchange information agree on a session key, Ks. Ks can be exchanged using a Diffie-Hellman or an RSA key exchange. The plaintext message, M, is encrypted with the session key, Ks. Ks is not escrowed. In addition, a Law Enforcement Access Field (LEAF) is also transmitted along with the encrypted message, M. The LEAF is encrypted with the family key, which is common to all Clipper Chips, and contains the following:

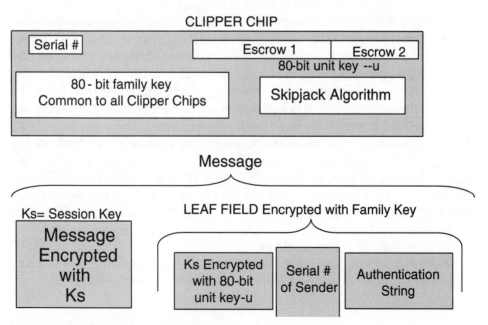

Figure 4.22 A Clipper Chip block diagram.

- Ks encrypted with secret key, u
- The serial number of sender Clipper Chip
- An authentication string

When the intended individual receives the transmitted items, this person decrypts the message with the mutually known session key, Ks.

A law enforcement agency can obtain the session key as follows:

1. Decrypt the LEAF with a family key to obtain the particular Clipper Chip serial number and encrypted session key. Ks is still encrypted with the secret family key, u.

2. Present an authorization court order to the two escrow agencies and obtain the two portions of the key, u.

3. Decrypt Ks with the key, u.

4. Decrypt the message, M, with Ks.

The 80-bit key of the Clipper Chip is weak. In fact, concerns exist over the escrow agencies' abilities to protect the escrowed keys, and whether these agencies may divulge them in unauthorized ways.

Key Escrow Approaches Using Public Key Cryptography

Another key escrow approach is Fair Cryptosystems.

In 1992, Sylvio Micali introduced the concept of Fair Cryptosystems (S. Micali, "Fair Cryptosystems," MIT/LCS/TR-579.b, MIT Laboratory for Computer Science, Nov 1993) where the private key of a public/private key pair is divided into multiple parts and distributed to different trustees. In 1994, Micali obtained patents on this approach that were eventually purchased by Banker's Trust. One valuable characteristic of Micali's approach is that each portion of the secret key can be verified as correct without having to reconstruct the entire key. This is accomplished by giving each trustee a piece of each public key and private key. Micali also developed calculations, which can be used on each trustee's private/public key pieces to verify that they are correct. If authorities have the legal permission to decrypt a message that is encrypted with the secret key, they can obtain all the portions of the private key and read the message. Micali also proposed a threshold approach where some subset of the trustee's set would be sufficient to recover the entire secret key.

Micali's approach can be applied by voluntary trustees in different countries or business areas rather than by a controlled, governmental entity.

Key Management Issues

Obviously, when dealing with encryption keys, the same precautions must be used as with physical keys to secure the areas or the combinations to the safes. These precautions include the following:

- Key control measures
- Key recovery
- Key storage
- Key retirement/destruction
- Key change
- Key generation
- Key theft
- Frequency of key use

Email Security Issues and Approaches

The main objectives of email security are to ensure the following:

- Non-repudiation
- Messages are read only by their intended recipients
- Integrity of the message
- Authentication of the source
- Verification of delivery
- Labeling of sensitive material
- Control of access

The following "standards" have been developed to address some or all of these issues.

Secure Multi-purpose Internet Mail Extensions (S/MIME)

S/MIME is a specification that adds secure services to email in a MIME format. S/MIME provides authentication through digital signatures and the confidentiality of encryption. S/MIME follows the Public Key Cryptography Standards (PKCS) and uses the X.509 standard for its digital certificates.

MIME Object Security Services (MOSS)

MOSS provides flexible email security services by supporting different trust models. Introduced in 1995, MOSS provides authenticity, integrity, confidentiality, and non-repudiation to email. It uses MD2/MD5, RSA Public Key, and DES. MOSS also permits user identification outside of the X.509 Standard.

Privacy Enhanced Mail (PEM)

Privacy Enhanced Mail (PEM) is a standard that was proposed by the IETF to be compliant with the Public Key Cryptography Standards (PKCS), which were developed by a consortium that included Microsoft, Novell, and Sun Microsystems. PEM supports the encryption and authentication of Internet email. For message encryption, PEM applies Triple DES-EDE using a pair of symmetric keys. RSA Hash Algorithms MD2 or MD5 are used to generate a message digest, and RSA public key encryption implements digital signatures and secure key distribution. PEM employs certificates that are based on the X.509 standard and are generated by a formal CA.

Pretty Good Privacy (PGP)

In order to bring email security to the "masses," Phil Zimmerman developed the Pretty Good Privacy (PGP) software (Zimmerman, Philip R., *The Official PGP User's Guide*. Cambridge, MA: MIT Press, 1995). Zimmerman derived the PGP name from Ralph's Pretty Good Groceries, which sponsored Garrison Keillor's *Prairie Home Companion* radio show. In PGP, the symmetric cipher IDEA is used to encipher the message, and RSA is used for symmetric key exchange and for digital signatures.

Instead of using a CA, PGP uses a Web of Trust. Users can certify each other in a mesh model, which is best applied to smaller groups (as shown in Figure 4.23).

Internet Security Applications

With the growing use of the Internet and World Wide Web for commercial transactions, there is a need for providing confidentiality, integrity, and authentication of information. This section describes some of the approaches to obtain secure Internet and World Wide Web e-commerce.

Message Authentication Code (MAC) or the Financial Institution Message Authentication Standard (FIMAS)

In order to protect against fraud in electronic fund transfers, the Message Authentication Code (MAC), ANSI X9.9, was developed. The MAC is a check

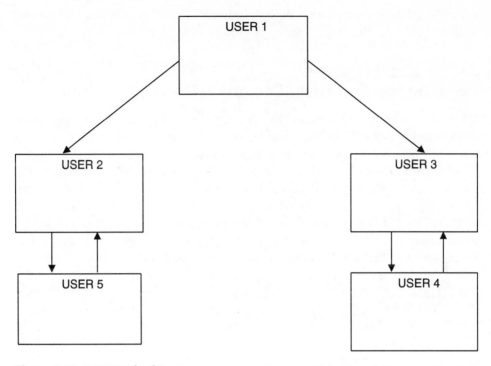

Figure 4.23 A PGP Web of Trust.

value derived from the contents of the message itself that is sensitive to the bit changes in a message. It is similar to a Cyclic Redundancy Check (CRC). A MAC is appended to the message before it is transmitted. At the receiving end, a MAC is generated from the received message and is compared to the MAC of an original message. A match indicates that the message was received without any modification occurring while en route.

To strengthen the MAC algorithm, a keyed MAC can be generated using a symmetric key encryption, such as DES. Typically, the Exclusive Or function of the DES key with a message is performed on the sequential, 8-byte blocks of the message to generate the MAC. As with all symmetric key applications, the key must be distributed securely so that sender and receiver have the same key.

Secure Electronic Transaction (SET)

A consortium including MasterCard and Visa developed SET in 1997 as a means of preventing fraud from occurring during electronic payments. SET provides confidentiality for purchases by encrypting the payment information. Thus, the seller cannot read this information. SET uses a DES symmetric key system for encryption of the payment information and uses RSA for the symmetric key exchange and digital signatures. SET covers the end-to-end transactions from the cardholder to the financial institution.

Secure Sockets Layer (SSL)/Transaction Layer Security (TLS)

The SSL protocol was developed by Netscape in 1994 to secure Internet client-server transactions. The SSL protocol authenticates the server to the client using public key cryptography and digital certificates. In addition, this protocol also provides for optional client-to-server authentication. It supports the use of RSA public key algorithms, IDEA, DES, and 3DES private key algorithms, and the MD5 hash function. Web pages using the SSL protocol start with HTTPs. SSL 3.0 and its successor, the Transaction Layer Security (TLS) 1.0 protocol are de facto standards, but they do not provide the end-to-end capabilities of SET. TLS implements confidentiality, authentication, and integrity above the Transport Layer, and it resides between the application and TCP layer. Thus, TLS, as with SSL, can be used with applications such as Telnet, FTP, HTTP, and email protocols. Both SSL and TLS use certificates for public key verification that are based on the X.509 standard.

Internet Open Trading Protocol (IOTP)

IOTP is an Internet protocol that is aimed at the consumer-to-business transactions. It provides a buyer with the same options as in the ordinary, non-e-commerce marketplace. IOTP is similar to shopping in the real world because it gives buyers the option to choose their method of payment. It supports public and private encryption key algorithms and can use digital certificates. IOTP is designed to be flexible and to accommodate other payment models that may emerge in the future.

MONDEX

The MONDEX International Corporation operates the MONDEX payment system. This system is an example of a cash smart card application. The value of the amount of currency is stored in smart cards and a proprietary encryption algorithm provides security. Because the algorithm is not subject to public scrutiny, its strength and vulnerabilities are not known. The smart card, then, can be used in financial transactions instead of cash. Funds can be transferred among cards using digital signatures. The smart cards are designed to preclude tampering and modifying the stored currency amount. However, if a card is lost, the finder can use it as cash.

IPSec

IPSec is a standard that provides encryption, access control, non-repudiation, and authentication of messages over IP. It is designed to be functionally compatible with IPv6. The two main protocols of IPSec are the Authentication Header (AH) and the Encapsulating Security Payload (ESP). The AH provides integrity, authentication, and non-repudiation. An ESP primarily provides encryption, but it can also provide limited authentication.

At the heart of IPSec is the Security Association (SA). An SA is required for communication between two entities. It provides a one-way (simplex) connection and is comprised of a Security Parameter Index (SPI), destination IP address, and the identity of the security protocol (AH or ESP). The SPI is a 32-bit number that is used to distinguish among various SAs terminating at the receiving station. Because an SA is simplex, two SAs are required for bi-directional communication between entities. Thus, if the AH protocol is used and bi-directional communication is required, two SAs must be established. Similarly, if both the AH and ESP protocols are to be employed bi-directionally, four SAs are needed.

IPSec in a VPN implementation can operate in either the transport or tunnel mode. In the transport mode, the data in the IP packet is encrypted, but the header is not encrypted. In the tunnel mode, the original IP header is encrypted and a new IP header is added to the beginning of the packet. This additional IP header has the address of the VPN gateway, and the encrypted IP header points to the final destination on the internal network behind the gateway.

The hashing algorithms HMAC-MD5 and HMAC-SHA-1 are used for authentication and integrity, and the IPSEC standard enables the use of a variety of symmetric key systems.

Security Associations (SAs) can be combined into "bundles" to provide authentication, confidentiality, and layered communication. An SA bundle can be developed using transport adjacency or iterated tunneling. Transport adjacency uses the transport mode for communication wherein iterated tunneling provides for the multiple levels of encapsulation as the protocol stack is being traversed.

In order to set up and manage SAs on the Internet, a standard format called the Internet Security Association and Key Management Protocol (ISAKMP) was established. ISAKMP provides for secure key exchange and data authentication. However, ISAKMP is independent of the authentication protocols, security protocols, and encryption algorithms. Strictly speaking, a combination of three protocols is used to define the key management for IPSEC. These protocols are ISAKMP, Secure Key Exchange Mechanism

(SKEME) and Oakley. When combined and applied to IPSEC, these protocols are called the Internet Key Exchange (IKE) protocol. In general, ISAKMP defines the phases for establishing a secure relationship, SKEME describes a secure exchange mechanism, and Oakley defines the modes of operation needed to establish a secure connection.

An initiative to specify a standard IPSEC implementation for VPNs on the Internet is known as Secure Wide Area Network (S/WAN). By defining a common set of IPSEC algorithms and modes of operation, S/WAN promotes the widespread use of VPNs on the Internet.

Secure Hypertext Transfer Protocol (S-HTTP)

S-HTTP is an alternative to SSL for providing security for World Wide Web (WWW) transactions. While SSL is applied to an entire session, S-HTTP can be used to protect individual WWW documents, and it provides authentication, confidentiality, integrity, and non-repudiation. S-HTTP supports a variety of encryption algorithms.

Secure Shell (SSH-2)

Secure Shell (SSH-2) is a set of protocols that are primarily used for remote access over a network by establishing an encrypted tunnel between an SSH client and an SSH server. This protocol can be used to authenticate the client to the server. In addition, it can also provide confidentiality and integrity services. It is comprised of a Transport Layer protocol, a User Authentication protocol, and a Connection protocol.

Wireless Security

With the increasing use and popularity of Personal Digital Assistants (PDAs) and cellular telephones to access the Internet, wireless security is important. Because information is broadcast like radio transmissions, it is susceptible to interception and can be compromised. As storage and processor technologies improve, Mobile Commerce (M-commerce) will be more common. Issues that are associated with wireless security include

- Physical security of wireless devices
- Proliferation of many different platforms
- Protection of sensitive financial transactions
- Limitations of processing power and memory due to space and weight considerations

- No standard method for securing wireless transactions
- Public Key Infrastructure (PKI)

Wireless Application Protocol (WAP)

The Wireless Application Protocol (WAP) is widely used by mobile devices to access the Internet. Because it is aimed at small displays and systems with limited bandwidth, it is not designed to display large volumes of data on a small, mobile display. In addition to cellular phones and PDAs, WAP is applied to network browsing through TV and in automotive displays. It has analogies to TCP/IP, IP, and HTML in wired Internet connections and is actually a set of protocols that cover layer 7 to layer 3 of the OSI model. Due to the memory and processor limitations on mobile devices, WAP has less overhead than TCP/IP. The WAP protocol stack contains the following:

- Wireless Markup Language (WML) and Script
- Wireless Application Environment (WAE)
- Wireless Session Protocol (WSP)
- Wireless Transaction Protocol (WTP)
- Wireless Transport Layer Security Protocol (WTLS)
- Wireless Datagram Protocol (WDP)

For wireless security, WAP uses the Wireless Transport Layer Security Protocol (WTLS). WTLS provides the following three classes of security:

1. Class 1 (*Anonymous Authentication*). The client logs on to the server, but, in this mode, neither the client nor the server can be certain of the identity of the other.
2. *Class 2 (Server Authentication).* The server is authenticated to the client, but the client is not authenticated to the server.
3. *Class 3 (Two-Way Client and Server Authentication).* The server is authenticated to the client and the client is authenticated to the server.

Authentication and authorization can be performed on the mobile device using smart cards to execute PKI-enabled transactions.

A specific security issue that is associated with WAP is the "WAP GAP." A WAP GAP results from the requirement to change security protocols at the carrier's WAP gateway from the wireless WTLS to SSL for use over the wired network. At the WAP gateway, the transmission, which is protected by WTLS, is decrypted and then re-encrypted for transmission using SSL. Thus, the data is temporarily in the clear on the gateway and can be compromised if the gateway is not adequately protected. In order to address this issue, the WAP

Forum has put forth specifications that will reduce this vulnerability and thus support e-commerce applications. These specifications are defined in WAP 1.2 as WMLScript Crypto Library and the WAP Identity Module (WIM). The WMLScript Crypto Library supports end-to-end security by providing for cryptographic functions to be initiated on the WAP client from the Internet content server. These functions include digital signatures originating with the WAP client and encryption and decryption of data. The WIM is a tamper-resistant device, such as a smart card, that cooperates with WTLS and provides cryptographic operations during the handshake phase.

The WAP Forum is also considering another alternative to providing the end-to-end encryption for WAP. This alternative, described in WAP specification 1.3, is the use of a client proxy server that communicates authentication and authorization information to the wireless network server.

The Handheld Device Markup Language (HDML) is a simpler alternative to WML that actually preceded the Wireless Markup Language (WML). HDML contains minimal security features, however. A direct competitor to WAP is Compact HTML (C-HTML). Used primarily in Japan through NTT DoCoMo's I-mode service, C-HTML is essentially a stripped-down version of HTML. Due to this approach, C-HTML can be displayed on a standard Internet browser.

The Public Key Infrastructure (PKI) for mobile applications provides for the encryption of communications and mutual authentication of the user and application provider. One concern associated with the "mobile PKI" relates to the possible time lapse between the expiration of a public key certificate and the re-issuing of a new valid certificate and associated public key.

This "dead time" may be critical in disasters or in time-sensitive situations. One solution to this problem is to generate one-time keys for use in each transaction.

The IEEE 802.11 Wireless Standard

The IEEE 802.11 specification is a wireless LAN standard that specifies an interface between a wireless client and a base station or access point, as well as among wireless clients. Work on the standard began in 1990 and has evolved from various draft versions; approval of the final draft occurred on June 26, 1997.

802.11 Layers

The IEEE 802.11 standard places specifications on the parameters of both the physical (PHY) and medium access control (MAC) layers of the network. The PHY Layer is responsible for the transmission of data among nodes. It can use direct sequence (DS) spread spectrum, frequency-hopping (FH) spread spectrum, or infrared (IR) pulse position modulation. The standard supports data rates of 1 Mbps or 2 Mbps, 2.4-2.4835 GHz frequency band for spread-spectrum transmission, and 300-428,000 GHz for IR transmission. Infrared is generally considered to be more secure to eavesdropping than multi-directional radio transmissions, because infrared requires direct line-of-sight paths.

The MAC Layer is a set of protocols responsible for maintaining order in the use of a shared medium. The 802.11 standard specifies a carrier sense multiple access with collision avoidance (CSMA/CA) protocol as described in Chapter 3, "Telecommunications and Network Security," for LANs. The MAC Layer provides the following services:

Data transfer. CSMA/CA media access.

Association. Establishment of wireless links between wireless clients and access points in infrastructure networks.

Reassociation. This action takes place in addition to association when a wireless client moves from one Basic Service Set (BSS) to another, such as in roaming.

Authentication. The process of proving a client identity through the use of the 802.11 option, Wired Equivalent Privacy (WEP). In WEP, a shared key is configured into the access point and its wireless clients. Only those devices with a valid shared key will be allowed to be associated to the access point.

Privacy. In the 802.11 standard, data is transferred in the clear by default. If confidentiality is desired, the WEP option encrypts data before it is sent wirelessly. The WEP algorithm of the 802.11 Wireless LAN Standard uses a secret key that is shared between a mobile station (for example, a laptop with a wireless Ethernet card) and a base station access point to protect the confidentiality of information being transmitted on the LAN. The transmitted packets are encrypted with a secret key and an Integrity Check (IC) field comprised of a CRC-32 checksum that is attached to the message. WEP uses the RC4 variable key-size stream cipher encryption algorithm. RC4 was developed in 1987 by Ron Rivest and operates in output feedback mode.

Researchers at the University of California at Berkeley (wep@isaac.cs.berkeley.edu) have found that the security of the WEP algorithm can be compromised, particularly with the following attacks:

- Passive attacks to decrypt traffic based on statistical analysis
- Active attack to inject new traffic from unauthorized mobile stations based on known plaintext
- Active attacks to decrypt traffic based on tricking the access point
- Dictionary-building attack that, after an analysis of about a day's worth of traffic, allows real-time automated decryption of all traffic

The Berkeley researchers have found that these attacks are effective against both the 40-bit and the so-called 128-bit versions of WEP using inexpensive off-the-shelf equipment. These attacks can also be used against networks that use the 802.11b Standard, which is the extension to 802.11 to support higher data rates, but does not change the WEP algorithm.

The weaknesses in WEP and 802.11 are being addressed by the IEEE 802.11i Working Group. WEP will be upgraded to WEP2 with the following proposed changes:

- Modifying the method of creating the initialization vector (IV)
- Modifying the method of creating the encryption key
- Protection against replays
- Protection against IV collision attacks
- Protection against forged packets

In the longer term, it is expected that the Advanced Encryption Standard (AES) will replace the RC4 encryption algorithm currently used in WEP.

Power management. Two power modes are defined in the IEEE 802.11 standard: an active mode used in transmitting and receiving, and a power save mode that conserves power but does not enable the user to transmit or receive.

The 802.11 standard has been ratified for IR, FH, and DH spread spectrum at 2.4 GHz. As of this writing, the IEEE 802.11 committee is addressing higher speed PHYs beyond the 2 Mbps data rate.

Sample Questions

You can find answers to the following questions in Appendix H.

1. The Secure Hash Algorithm (SHA) is specified in the:

   a. Data Encryption Standard

   b. Digital Signature Standard

   c. Digital Encryption Standard

   d. Advanced Encryption Standard

2. What does Secure Sockets Layer (SSL)/Transaction Security Layer (TSL) do?

   a. Implements confidentiality, authentication, and integrity above the Transport Layer

   b. Implements confidentiality, authentication, and integrity below the Transport Layer

   c. Implements only confidentiality above the Transport Layer

   d. Implements only confidentiality below the Transport Layer

3. What are MD4 and MD5?

   a. Symmetric encryption algorithms

   b. Asymmetric encryption algorithms

   c. Hashing algorithms

   d. Digital certificates

4. Elliptic curves, which are applied to public key cryptography, employ modular exponentiation that characterizes the:

   a. Elliptic curve discrete logarithm problem

   b. Prime factors of very large numbers

   c. Elliptic curve modular addition

   d. Knapsack problem

5. Which algorithm is used in the Clipper Chip?

   a. IDEA

   b. DES

   c. SKIPJACK

   d. 3 DES

6. The hashing algorithm in the Digital Signature Standard (DSS) generates a message digest of:

   a. 120 bits

   b. 160 bits

   c. 56 bits

   d. 130 bits

7. The protocol of the Wireless Application Protocol (WAP), which performs functions similar to SSL in the TCP/IP protocol, is called the:

   a. Wireless Application Environment (WAE)

   b. Wireless Session Protocol (WSP)

   c. Wireless Transaction Protocol (WTP)

   d. Wireless Transport Layer Security Protocol (WTLS)

8. A Security Parameter Index (SPI) and the identity of the security protocol (AH or ESP) are the components of:

   a. SSL

   b. IPSec

   c. S-HTTP

   d. SSH-1

9. When two different keys encrypt a plaintext message into the same ciphertext, this situation is known as:

   a. Public key cryptography

   b. Cryptanalysis

   c. Key clustering

   d. Hashing

10. What is the result of the Exclusive Or operation, 1XOR 0?

   a. 1

   b. 0

   c. Indeterminate

   d. 10

11. A block cipher:

   a. Encrypts by operating on a continuous data stream

   b. Is an asymmetric key algorithm

   c. Converts a variable-length of plaintext into a fixed length ciphertext

   d. Breaks a message into fixed length units for encryption

12. In most security protocols that support authentication, integrity and confidentiality,

   a. Public key cryptography is used to create digital signatures.

   b. Private key cryptography is used to create digital signatures.

   c. DES is used to create digital signatures.

   d. Digital signatures are not implemented.

13. Which of the following is an example of a symmetric key algorithm?

   a. Rijndael

   b. RSA

   c. Diffie-Hellman

   d. Knapsack

14. Which of the following is a problem with symmetric key encryption?

   a. It is slower than asymmetric key encryption.

   b. Most algorithms are kept proprietary.

   c. Work factor is not a function of the key size.

   d. It provides secure distribution of the secret key.

15. Which of the following is an example of an asymmetric key algorithm?

   a. IDEA

   b. DES

   c. 3 DES

   d. ELLIPTIC CURVE

16. In public key cryptography,

   a. Only the private key can encrypt and only the public key can decrypt.

   b. Only the public key can encrypt and only the private key can decrypt.

   c. The public key is used to encrypt and decrypt.

   d. If the public key encrypts, then only the private key can decrypt.

17. In a hybrid cryptographic system, usually:

   a. Public key cryptography is used for the encryption of the message.

   b. Private key cryptography is used for the encryption of the message.

   c. Neither public key nor private key cryptography is used.

   d. Digital certificates cannot be used.

18. What is the block length of the Rijndael Cipher?

   a. 64 bits

   b. 128 bits

   c. Variable

   d. 256 bits

19. A polyalphabetic cipher is also known as:
    a. One-time pad
    b. Vigenère cipher
    c. Steganography
    d. Vernam cipher

20. The classic Caesar cipher is a:
    a. Polyalphabetic cipher
    b. Monoalphabetic cipher
    c. Transposition cipher
    d. Code group

21. In steganography,
    a. Private key algorithms are used.
    b. Public key algorithms are used.
    c. Both public and private key algorithms are used.
    d. The fact that the message exists is not known.

22. What is the key length of the Rijndael Block Cipher?
    a. 56 or 64 bits
    b. 512 bits
    c. 128, 192, or 256 bits
    d. 512 or 1024 bits

23. In a block cipher, diffusion:
    a. Conceals the connection between the ciphertext and plaintext
    b. Spreads the influence of a plaintext character over many ciphertext characters
    c. Is usually implemented by non-linear S-boxes
    d. Cannot be accomplished

24. The NIST Advanced Encryption Standard uses the:
    a. 3 DES algorithm
    b. Rijndael algorithm
    c. DES algorithm
    d. IDEA algorithm

25. The modes of DES do NOT include:
    a. Electronic Code Book
    b. Cipher Block Chaining
    c. Variable Block Feedback
    d. Output Feedback

26. Which of the following is true?
    a. The work factor of triple DES is the same as for double DES.
    b. The work factor of single DES is the same as for triple DES.
    c. The work factor of double DES is the same as for single DES.
    d. No successful attacks have been reported against double DES.

27. The Rijndael Cipher employs a round transformation that is comprised of three layers of distinct, invertible transformations. These transformations are also defined as uniform, which means that every bit of the State is treated the same. Which of the following is NOT one of these layers?
    a. The non-linear layer, which is the parallel application of S-boxes that have the optimum worst-case non-linearity properties
    b. The linear mixing layer, which provides a guarantee of the high diffusion of multiple rounds
    c. The key addition layer, which is an Exclusive OR of the Round Key to the intermediate State
    d. The key inversion layer, which provides confusion through the multiple rounds

28. The Escrowed Encryption Standard describes the:
    a. Rijndael Cipher
    b. Clipper Chip
    c. Fair Public Key Cryptosystem
    d. Digital certificates

29. Enigma was:
    a. An English project created to break German ciphers
    b. The Japanese rotor machine used in WWII
    c. Probably the first programmable digital computer
    d. The German rotor machine used in WWII

30. Which of the following characteristics does a one-time pad have if used properly?
    a. It can be used more than once.
    b. The key does not have to be random.
    c. It is unbreakable.
    d. The key has to be of greater length than the message to be encrypted.

31. The DES key is:
    a. 128 bits
    b. 64 bits

   c. 56 bits

   d. 512 bits

32. In a digitally-signed message transmission using a hash function,

   a. The message digest is encrypted in the private key of the sender.

   b. The message digest is encrypted in the public key of the sender.

   c. The message is encrypted in the private key of the sender.

   d. The message is encrypted in the public key of the sender.

33. The strength of RSA public key encryption is based on the:

   a. Difficulty in finding logarithms in a finite field

   b. Difficulty of multiplying two large prime numbers

   c. Fact that only one key is used

   d. Difficulty in finding the prime factors of very large numbers

34. Elliptic curve cryptosystems:

   a. Have a higher strength per bit than an RSA

   b. Have a lower strength per bit than an RSA

   c. Cannot be used to implement digital signatures

   d. Cannot be used to implement encryption

35. Which of the following is NOT a key management issue?

   a. Key recovery

   b. Key storage

   c. Key change

   d. Key exchange

Bonus Questions

You can find answers to the following questions in Appendix H.

1. A cryptographic attack in which portions of the ciphertext are selected for trial decryption while having access to the corresponding decrypted plaintext is known as what type of attack?

    a. Known plaintext

    b. Chosen ciphertext

    c. Chosen plaintext

    d. Adaptive chosen plaintext

2. For a given hash function H, to prevent substitution of a message M1 for a message M2, it is necessary that:

    a. $H(M1) \neq H(M2)$

    b. $H(M1) = H(M2)$

    c. $H(M1) > H(M2)$

    d. $H(M1) < H(M2)$

3. The Secure Hash Algorithm (SHA-1) of the Secure Hash Standard (NIST FIPS PUB 180) processes data in block lengths of:

    a. 128 bits

    b. 256 bits

    c. 512 bits

    d. 1024 bits

4. The technique of confusion, proposed by Claude Shannon, is used in block ciphers to:

    a. Spread the influence of a plaintext character over many ciphertext characters

    b. Limit the influence of a plaintext character across ciphertext characters

    c. Implement transposition to obtain the ciphertext

    d. Conceal the statistical connection between ciphertext and plaintext

5. The Advanced Encryption Standard, the Rijndael cipher, can be described as:

    a. A recursive, sequential cipher

    b. A Feistel network

    c. A streaming block cipher

    d. An iterated block cipher

6. The Rijndael cipher employs a *round* transformation that is, itself, comprised of three layers of transformations. Which of the following is NOT one of these layers?

   a. Key addition layer

   b. Linear mixing layer

   c. Nonlinear mixing layer

   d. Nonlinear layer

7. A secret mechanism that enables the implementation of the reverse function in a one-way function is called a:

   a. Trap door

   b. View

   c. Open door

   d. Data diode

8. Which of the following is NOT a symmetric key algorithm?

   a. Advanced Encryption Standard (AES)

   b. Data Encryption Standard (DES)

   c. International Data Encryption Algorithm (IDEA)

   d. MD5

9. The following elements comprise a portion of what services?

   ■ Digital certification

   ■ Certification authority

   ■ Timestamping

   ■ Lightweight Directory Access Protocol (LDAP)

   ■ Non-repudiation support

   a. IPSec

   b. Public Key Infrastructure (PKI)

   c. Transaction Layer Security (TLS)

   d. Wireless Application Protocol (WAP)

10. The vulnerability associated with the requirement to change security protocols at a carriers' Wireless Application Protocol (WAP) gateway from the Wireless Transport Layer Security Protocol (WTLS) to SSL or TLS over the wired network is called:

    a. Wireless Transaction Protocol (WTP) Gap

    b. Wired Equivalency Privacy (WEP) Gap

    c. Wireless Application Protocol (WAP) Gap

    d. Wireless Transport Layer Security Protocol (WTLS) Gap

Advanced Sample Questions

You can find answers to the following questions in Appendix I.

The following questions are supplemental to and coordinated with Chapter 4 and are at a level commensurate with that of the CISSP Examination.

Topics covered in this chapter include the following:

- British Standard 7799/ISO Standard 17799
- Digital cash
- Digital certificates
- Digital signatures
- Elliptic curves
- Escrowed encryption
- Quantum computing
- The 802.11 Wireless LAN Standard
- The Advanced Encryption Standard (Rijndael)
- The Wireless Application Protocol (WAP)
- Transport Layer Security (TLS)
- Triple DES
- Wired Equivalency Privacy (WEP)It
- Wireless Transport Layer Security (WTLS)

It is assumed that the reader has a basic knowledge of the material contained in Chapter 4. These questions and answers build upon the cryptography questions and answers listed earlier.

1. A cryptographic algorithm is also known as:
    a. A cryptosystem
    b. Cryptanalysis
    c. A cipher
    d. A key

2. Which of the following is NOT an issue with secret key cryptography?
    a. Security of the certification authority.
    b. A networked group of m users with separate keys for each pair of users will require m (m-1)/2 keys.
    c. Secure distribution of the keys.
    d. Compromise of the keys can enable the attacker to impersonate the key owners and, therefore, read and send false messages.

3. Which of the following is NOT a characteristic of the ElGamal public key cryptosystem?

   a. It can perform encryption.

   b. It can be used to generate digital signatures.

   c. It is based on the discrete logarithm problem.

   d. It can perform encryption, but not digital signatures.

4. The Transport Layer Security (TLS) 1.0 protocol is based on which Protocol Specification?

   a. SSH-2

   b. SSL-3.0

   c. IPSEC

   d. TCP/IP

5. The primary goal of the TLS Protocol is to provide:

   a. Privacy and authentication between two communicating applications

   b. Privacy and data integrity between two communicating applications

   c. Authentication and data integrity between two communicating applications

   d. Privacy, authentication, and data integrity between two communicating applications

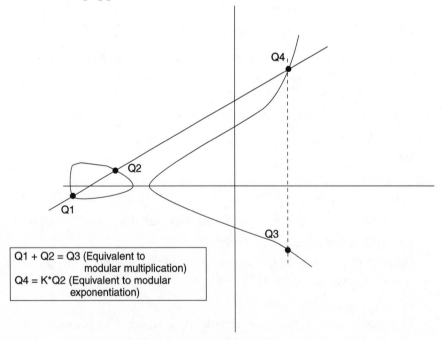

Figure 4.1 Graph of the function $y^2 = x^3 + ax + b$.

6. The graph in Figure 4.1, which depicts the equation $y^2 = x^3 + ax + b$, denotes the:

   a. Elliptic curve and the elliptic curve discrete logarithm problem

   b. RSA Factoring problem

   c. ElGamal discrete logarithm problem

   d. Knapsack problem

7. In communications between two parties, encrypting the hash function of a message with a symmetric key algorithm is equivalent to:

   a. Generating a digital signature

   b. Providing for secrecy of the message

   c. Generating a one-way function

   d. Generating a keyed Message Authentication Code (MAC)

8. Which of the following is NOT a characteristic of a cryptographic hash function, H (m), where m denotes the message being hashed by the function H?

   a. H (m) is collision-free.

   b. H (m) is difficult to compute for any given m.

   c. The output is of fixed length.

   d. H (m) is a one-way function.

9. Which one of the following statements BEST describes the operation of the Digital Signature Algorithm (DSA) (National Institute of Standards and Technology, NIST FIPS PUB 186, "Digital Signature Standard," U.S. Department of Commerce, May 1994) at the transmitting end of a communication between two parties?

   a. A message of $< 2^{64}$ bits is input to the DSA, and the resultant message digest of 160 bits is fed into the Secure Hash Algorithm (SHA), which generates the digital signature of the message.

   b. A message of $< 2^{64}$ bits is input to the Secure Hash Algorithm (SHA), and the resultant message digest of 128 bits is fed into the DSA, which generates the digital signature of the message.

   c. A message of $< 2^{64}$ bits is input to the Secure Hash Algorithm (SHA), and the resultant message digest of 160 bits is used as the digital signature of the message.

   d. A message of $< 2^{64}$ bits is input to the Secure Hash Algorithm (SHA), and the resultant message digest of 160 bits is fed into the DSA, which generates the digital signature of the message.

10. If the application of a hash function results in an m-bit fixed length output, an attack on the hash function that attempts to achieve a collision after $2^{m/2}$ possible trial input values is called a(n):

    a. Adaptive-chosen-plaintext attack

    b. Chosen-ciphertext attack

    c. Birthday attack

    d. Meet-in-the-middle attack

11. The minimum information necessary on a digital certificate is:

    a. Name, expiration date, digital signature of the certifier

    b. Name, expiration date, public key

    c. Name, serial number, private key

    d. Name, public key, digital signature of the certifier

12. What do the message digest algorithms MD2, MD4, and MD5 have in common?

    a. They all take a message of arbitrary length and produce a message digest of 160 bits.

    b. They all take a message of arbitrary length and produce a message digest of 128 bits.

    c. They are all optimized for 32-bit machines.

    d. They are all used in the Secure Hash Algorithm (SHA).

13. What is the correct sequence which enables an authorized agency to use the Law Enforcement Access Field (LEAF) to decrypt a message sent by using the Clipper Chip? (The following designations are used for the respective keys involved—K_f, the family key; K_s, the session key; U, a unique identifier for each Clipper Chip, and K_u, the unit key that is unique to each Clipper Chip.)

    a. Obtain a court order to acquire the two halves of K_u, the unit key. Recover K_u. Decrypt the LEAF with K_u and then recover K_s, the session key. Use the session key to decrypt the message.

    b. Decrypt the LEAF with the family key, K_f; recover U; obtain a court order to obtain the two halves of K_u; recover K_u; and then recover K_s, the session key. Use the session key to decrypt the message.

    c. Decrypt the LEAF with the family key, K_f; recover U; obtain a court order to obtain K_s, the session key. Use the session key to decrypt the message.

    d. Obtain a court order to acquire the family key, K_f; recover U and K_u; then recover K_s, the session key. Use the session key to decrypt the message.

14. What BEST describes the National Security Agency-developed Capstone?

    a. A device for intercepting electromagnetic emissions

    b. The PC Card implementation of the Clipper Chip system

    c. A chip that implements the U. S. Escrowed Encryption Standard

    d. A one-way function for implementation of public key encryption

15. Which of the following BEST describes a block cipher?

    a. A symmetric key algorithm that operates on a variable-length block of plaintext and transforms it into a fixed-length block of ciphertext

    b. A symmetric key algorithm that operates on a fixed-length block of plaintext and transforms it into a fixed-length block of ciphertext

    c. An asymmetric key algorithm that operates on a variable-length block of plaintext and transforms it into a fixed-length block of ciphertext

    d. An asymmetric key algorithm that operates on a fixed-length block of plaintext and transforms it into a fixed-length block of ciphertext

16. An iterated block cipher encrypts by breaking the plaintext block into two halves and, with a subkey, applying a "round" transformation to one of the halves. Then, the output of this transformation is XORed with the remaining half. The round is completed by swapping the two halves. This type of cipher is known as:

    a. RC4

    b. Diffie-Hellman

    c. RC6

    d. Feistel

17. A key schedule is:

    a. A list of cryptographic keys to be used at specified dates and times

    b. A method of generating keys by the use of random numbers

    c. A set of subkeys derived from a secret key

    d. Using distributed computing resources to conduct a brute force attack on a symmetric algorithm

18. The Wireless Transport Layer Security (WTLS) Protocol in the Wireless Application Protocol (WAP) stack is based on which Internet Security Protocol?

    a. S-HTTP

    b. TLS

    c. SET

    d. IPSEC

19. The Advanced Encryption Standard (Rijndael) block cipher requirements regarding keys and block sizes have now evolved to which configuration?

   a. Both the key and block sizes can be 128, 192, and 256 bits each.

   b. The key size is 128 bits, and the block size can be 128, 192, or 256 bits.

   c. The block size is 128 bits, and the key can be 128, 192, or 256 bits.

   d. The block size is 128 bits, and the key size is 128 bits.

20. The Wireless Transport Layer Security Protocol (WTLS) in the Wireless Application Protocol (WAP) stack provides for security:

   a. Between the WAP gateway and the content server

   b. Between the WAP client and the gateway

   c. Between the Internet and the content server

   d. Between the WAP content server and the WAP client

21. What is a protocol that adds digital signatures and encryption to Internet MIME (Multipurpose Internet Mail Extensions)?

   a. IPSEC

   b. PGP

   c. S/MIME

   d. SET/MIME

22. Digital cash refers to the electronic transfer of funds from one party to another. When digital cash is referred to as anonymous or identified, it means that:

   a. Anonymous—the identity of the cash holder is not known; Identified—the identity of the cash holder is known

   b. Anonymous—the identity of merchant is withheld; Identified—the identity of the merchant is not withheld

   c. Anonymous—the identity of the bank is withheld; Identified—the identity of the bank is not withheld

   d. Anonymous—the identity of the cash holder is not known; Identified—the identity of the merchant is known

23. Which of the following is NOT a key recovery method?

   a. A message is encrypted with a session key and the session key is, in turn, encrypted with the public key of a trustee agent. The encrypted session key is sent along with the encrypted message. The trustee, when authorized, can then decrypt the message by recovering the session key with the trustee's private key.

   b. A message is encrypted with a session key. The session key, in turn, is broken into parts and each part is encrypted with the public key of a different trustee agent. The encrypted parts of the session key are sent along with the encrypted message. The trustees, when authorized, can then decrypt their portion of the session key and provide their respective parts of the session key to a central agent. The central agent can then decrypt the message by reconstructing the session key from the individual components.

c. A secret key or a private key is broken into a number of parts and each part is deposited with a trustee agent. The agents can then provide their parts of the key to a central authority, when presented with appropriate authorization. The key can then be reconstructed and used to decrypt messages encrypted with that key.

d. A message is encrypted with a session key and the session key is, in turn, encrypted with the private key of a trustee agent. The encrypted session key is sent along with the encrypted message. The trustee, when authorized, can then decrypt the message by recovering the session key with the trustee's public key.

24. Theoretically, quantum computing offers the possibility of factoring the products of large prime numbers and calculating discreet logarithms in polynomial time. These calculations can be accomplished in such a compressed time frame because:

a. Information can be transformed into quantum light waves that travel through fiber optic channels. Computations can be performed on the associated data by passing the light waves through various types of optical filters and solid-state materials with varying indices of refraction, thus drastically increasing the throughput over conventional computations.

b. A quantum bit in a quantum computer is actually a linear superposition of both the one and zero states and, therefore, can theoretically represent both values in parallel. This phenomenon allows computation that usually takes exponential time to be accomplished in polynomial time since different values of the binary pattern of the solution can be calculated simultaneously.

c. A quantum computer takes advantage of quantum tunneling in molecular scale transistors. This mode permits ultra high-speed switching to take place, thus exponentially increasing the speed of computations.

d. A quantum computer exploits the time-space relationship that changes as particles approach the speed of light. At that interface, the resistance of conducting materials effectively is zero and exponential speed computations are possible.

25. Which of the following statements BEST describes the Public Key Cryptography Standards (PKCS)?

    a. A set of public-key cryptography standards that supports algorithms such as Diffie-Hellman and RSA as well as algorithm-independent standards

    b. A set of public-key cryptography standards that supports only "standard" algorithms such as Diffie-Hellman and RSA

    c. A set of public-key cryptography standards that supports only algorithm-independent implementations

    d. A set of public-key cryptography standards that supports encryption algorithms such as Diffie-Hellman and RSA, but does not address digital signatures

26. An interface to a library of software functions that provide security and cryptography services is called:

    a. A security application programming interface (SAPI)

    b. An assurance application programming interface (AAPI)

    c. A cryptographic application programming interface (CAPI)

    d. A confidentiality, integrity, and availability application programming interface (CIAAPI)

27. The British Standard 7799/ISO Standard 17799 discusses cryptographic policies. It states, "An organization should develop a policy on its use of cryptographic controls for protection of its information. . . . When developing a policy, the following should be considered:" (Which of the following items would most likely NOT be listed?)

    a. The management approach toward the use of cryptographic controls across the organization

    b. The approach to key management, including methods to deal with the recovery of encrypted information in the case of lost, compromised or damaged keys

    c. Roles and responsibilities

    d. The encryption schemes to be used

28. The Number Field Sieve (NFS) is a:

    a. General purpose factoring algorithm that can be used to factor large numbers

    b. General purpose algorithm to calculate discreet logarithms

    c. General purpose algorithm used for brute force attacks on secret key cryptosystems

    d. General purpose hash algorithm

29. DESX is a variant of DES in which:

    a. Input plaintext is bitwise XORed with 64 bits of additional key material before encryption with DES.

    b. Input plaintext is bitwise XORed with 64 bits of additional key material before encryption with DES, and the output of DES is also bitwise XORed with another 64 bits of key material.

    c. The output of DES is bitwise XORed with 64 bits of key material.

    d. The input plaintext is encrypted X times with the DES algorithm using different keys for each encryption.

30. The ANSI X9.52 standard defines a variant of DES encryption with keys k1, k2, and k3 as:

    $C = E_{k3} [D_{k2} [E_{k1} [M]]]$

    What is this DES variant?

    a. DESX

    b. Triple DES in the EEE mode

    c. Double DES with an encryption and decryption with different keys

    d. Triple DES in the EDE mode

31. Using a modulo 26 substitution cipher where the letters A to Z of the alphabet are given a value of 0 to 25, respectively, encrypt the message "OVERLORD BEGINS." Use the key K = NEW and D = 3 where D is the number of repeating letters representing the key. The encrypted message is:

    a. BFAEQKEH XRKFAW

    b. BFAEPKEH XRKFAW

    c. BFAEPKEH XRKEAW

    d. BFAERKEH XRKEAW

32. The algorithm of the 802.11 Wireless LAN Standard that is used to protect transmitted information from disclosure is called:

    a. Wireless Application Environment (WAE)

    b. Wired Equivalency Privacy (WEP)

    c. Wireless Transaction Protocol (WTP)

    d. Wireless Transport Layer Security Protocol (WTLS)

33. The Wired Equivalency Privacy algorithm (WEP) of the 802.11 Wireless LAN Standard uses which of the following to protect the confidentiality of information being transmitted on the LAN?

    a. A secret key that is shared between a mobile station (e.g., a laptop with a wireless Ethernet card) and a base station access point

    b. A public/private key pair that is shared between a mobile station (e.g., a laptop with a wireless Ethernet card) and a base station access point

c. Frequency shift keying (FSK) of the message that is sent between a mobile station (e.g., a laptop with a wireless Ethernet card) and a base station access point

d. A digital signature that is sent between a mobile station (e.g., a laptop with a wireless Ethernet card) and a base station access point

34. In a block cipher, diffusion can be accomplished through:

a. Substitution

b. XORing

c. Non-linear S-boxes

d. Permutation

35. The National Computer Security Center (NCSC) is:

a. A division of the National Institute of Standards and Technology (NIST) that issues standards for cryptographic functions and publishes them as Federal Information Processing Standards (FIPS)

b. A branch of the National Security Agency (NSA) that initiates research and develops and publishes standards and criteria for trusted information systems

c. A joint enterprise between the NSA and NIST for developing cryptographic algorithms and standards

d. An activity within the U.S. Department of Commerce that provides information security awareness training and develops standards for protecting sensitive but unclassified information

36. A portion of a Vigenère cipher square is given below using five (1, 2, 14, 16, 22) of the possible 26 alphabets. Using the key word bow, which of the following is the encryption of the word "advance" using the Vigenère cipher in Table 4.1?

a. b r r b b y h

b. b r r b j y f

c. b r r b b y f

d. b r r b c y f

37. There are two fundamental security protocols in IPSEC. These are the Authentication Header (AH) and the Encapsulating Security Payload (ESP). Which of the following correctly describes the functions of each?

a. ESP—data encrypting protocol that also validates the integrity of the transmitted data; AH—source authenticating protocol that also validates the integrity of the transmitted data

b. ESP—data encrypting and source authenticating protocol; AH—source authenticating protocol that also validates the integrity of the transmitted data

Table 4.1 Vigenère Cipher

PLAINTEXT	A	B	C	D	E	F	G	H	I	J	K	L	M	N	O	P	Q	R	S	T	U	V	W	X	Y	Z
1	b	c	d	e	f	g	h	i	j	k	l	m	n	o	p	q	r	s	t	u	v	w	x	y	z	a
2	c	d	e	f	g	h	i	j	k	l	m	n	o	p	q	r	s	t	u	v	w	x	y	z	a	b
14	o	p	q	r	s	t	u	v	w	x	y	z	a	b	c	d	e	f	g	h	i	j	k	l	m	n
16	q	r	s	t	u	v	w	x	y	z	a	b	c	d	e	f	g	h	i	j	k	l	m	n	o	p
22	w	x	y	z	a	b	c	d	e	f	g	h	i	j	k	l	m	n	o	p	q	r	s	t	u	v

c. ESP—data encrypting and source authenticating protocol that also validates the integrity of the transmitted data; AH—source authenticating protocol

d. ESP—data encrypting and source authenticating protocol that also validates the integrity of the transmitted data; AH—source authenticating protocol that also validates the integrity of the transmitted data

38. Which of the following is NOT an advantage of a stream cipher?

a. The same equipment can be used for encryption and decryption.

b. It is amenable to hardware implementations that result in higher speeds.

c. Since encryption takes place bit by bit, there is no error propagation.

d. The receiver and transmitter must be synchronized.

39. Which of the following is NOT a property of a public key cryptosystem? (Let P represent the private key, Q represent the public key, and M the plaintext message.)

a. $Q[P(M)] = M$

b. $P[Q(M)] = M$

c. It is computationally infeasible to derive P from Q.

d. P and Q are difficult to generate from a particular key value.

40. A form of digital signature where the signer is not privy to the content of the message is called a:

a. Zero knowledge proof

b. Blind signature

c. Masked signature

d. Encrypted signature

41. The following compilation represents what facet of cryptanalysis?

A 8.2	J 0.2	S 6.3
B 1.5	K 0.8	T 9.1
C 2.8	L 4.0	U 2.8
D 4.3	M 2.4	V 1.0
E 12.7	N 6.7	W 2.4
F 2.2	O 7.5	X 0.2
G 2.0	P 1.9	Y 2.0
H 6.1	Q 0.1	Z 0.1
I 7.0	R 6.0	

a. Period analysis
b. Frequency analysis
c. Cilly analysis
d. Cartouche analysis

CHAPTER

5

Security Architecture and Models

Security Architecture

The security architecture of an information system is fundamental to enforcing the organization's information security policy. Therefore, it is important for security professionals to understand the underlying computer architectures, protection mechanisms, distributed environment security issues, and formal models that provide the framework for the security policy. In addition, professionals should have knowledge of the assurance evaluation, certification and accreditation guidelines, and standards. We address the following topics in this chapter:

- Computer organization
- Hardware components
- Software/firmware components
- Open systems
- Distributed systems

- Protection mechanisms
- Evaluation criteria
- Certification and accreditation
- Formal security models
- Confidentiality models
- Integrity models
- Information flow models

Computer Architecture

The term *computer architecture* refers to the organization of the fundamental elements comprising the computer. From another perspective, it refers to the view that a programmer has of the computing system when viewed through its instruction set. The main hardware components of a digital computer are the *Central Processing Unit* (CPU), memory, and input/output devices. A basic CPU of a general-purpose digital computer consists of an Arithmetic Logic Unit (ALU), control logic, one or more accumulators, multiple general-purpose registers, an instruction register, a program counter, and some on-chip local memory. The ALU performs arithmetic and logical operations on the binary words of the computer.

A group of conductors called a *bus* interconnects these computer elements. The bus runs in a common plane with the different computer elements connected to the bus. A bus can be organized into subunits, such as the *address bus*, the *data bus*, and the *control bus*. A diagram of the organization of a bus is shown in Figure 5.1.

Memory

Several types of memory are used in digital computer systems. The principal types of memory and their definitions are as follows:

Cache memory. A relatively small amount (when compared to primary memory) of very high-speed RAM, which holds the instructions and data from primary memory that have a high probability of being accessed during the currently executing portion of a program. Cache logic attempts to predict which instructions and data in main memory will be used by a currently executing program. It then moves these items to the higher-speed cache in anticipation of the CPU requiring these programs and data. Properly designed caches can significantly reduce the apparent main memory access time and thus increase the speed of program execution.

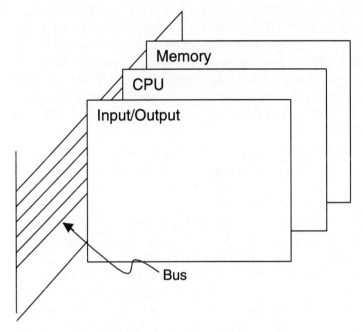

Figure 5.1 A computer bus.

Random Access Memory (RAM). Memory where locations can be directly addressed and the data that is stored can be altered. RAM is *volatile* due to the fact that the data is lost if power is removed from the system. *Dynamic RAM* (DRAM) stores the information on parasitic capacitance that decays over time. Therefore, the data on each RAM bit must be periodically refreshed. Refreshing is accomplished by reading and rewriting each bit every few milliseconds. Conversely, Static RAM (SRAM) uses latches to store the bits and does not need to be refreshed. Both types of RAM, however, are volatile.

RDRAM Memory (Rambus DRAM). Based on Rambus Signaling Level (RSL) technology introduced in 1992, RSL RDRAM devices provide systems with 16MB to 2GB of memory capacity at speeds of up to 1066MHz. The RDRAM channel achieves high speeds through the use of separate control and address buses, a highly efficient protocol, low-voltage signaling, and precise clocking to minimize skew between clock and data lines. At this writing, RSL technology is approaching 1200 MHz speeds.

Programmable Logic Device (PLD). An integrated circuit with connections or internal logic gates that can be changed through a programming process. Examples of a PLD are a *Read Only Memory* (ROM), a *Programmable Array*

Logic (PAL) device, the *Complex Programmable Logic Device* (CPLD), and the *Field Programmable Gate Array* (FPGA). Programming of these devices is accomplished by blowing fuse connections on the chip, using an *antifuse* that makes a connection when a high voltage is applied to the junction, through mask programming when a chip is fabricated, and by using SRAM latches to turn a *Metal Oxide Semiconductor* (MOS) transistor on or off. This last technology is volatile because the power to the chip must be maintained for the chip to operate.

Read Only Memory (ROM). Non-volatile storage where locations can be directly addressed. In a basic ROM implementation, data cannot be altered dynamically. Non-volatile storage retains its information even when it loses power. Some ROMs are implemented with one-way fusible links, and their contents cannot be altered. Other types of ROMs—such as *Erasable, Programmable Read-Only Memories* (EPROMs), *Electrically Alterable Read Only Memories* (EAROMs), *Electrically Erasable Programmable Read Only Memories* (EEPROMs), Flash memories, and their derivatives—can be altered by various means, but only at a relatively slow rate when compared to normal computer system reads and writes. ROMs are used to hold programs and data that should normally not be changed or that are changed infrequently. Programs stored on these types of devices are referred to as *firmware*.

Real or primary memory. The memory directly addressable by the CPU and used for the storage of instructions and data associated with the program that is being executed. This memory is usually high-speed *Random Access Memory* (RAM).

Secondary memory. This type of memory is a slower memory (such as magnetic disks) that provides non-volatile storage.

Sequential memory. Memory from which information must be obtained by sequentially searching from the beginning rather than directly accessing the location. A good example of a sequential memory access is reading information from a magnetic tape.

Virtual memory. This type of memory uses secondary memory in conjunction with primary memory to present a CPU with a larger, apparent address space of the real memory locations.

A typical memory hierarchy is shown in Figure 5.2.

There are a number of ways that a CPU can address memory. These options provide flexibility and efficiency when programming different types of applications, such as searching through a table or processing a list of data items. The following are some of the commonly used addressing modes:

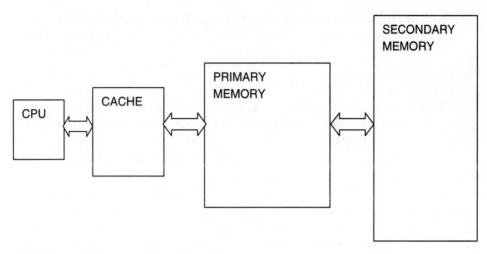

Figure 5.2 A computer memory hierarchy.

Register addressing. Addressing the registers within a CPU or other special purpose registers that are designated in the primary memory.

Direct addressing. Addressing a portion of primary memory by specifying the actual address of the memory location. The memory addresses are usually limited to the memory page that is being executed or page zero.

Absolute addressing. Addressing all of the primary memory space.

Indexed addressing. Developing a memory address by adding the contents of the address defined in the program's instruction to that of an index register. The computed, effective address is used to access the desired memory location. Thus, if an index register is incremented or decremented, a range of memory locations can be accessed.

Implied addressing. Used when operations that are internal to the processor must be performed, such as clearing a carry bit that was set as a result of an arithmetic operation. Because the operation is being performed on an internal register that is specified within the instruction itself, there is no need to provide an address.

Indirect addressing. Addressing where the address location that is specified in the program instruction contains the address of the final desired location.

An associated definition is the definition of memory protection.

Memory protection. Preventing one program from accessing and modifying the memory space contents that belong to another program.

Memory protection is implemented by the operating system or by hardware mechanisms.

Instruction Execution Cycle

A basic machine cycle consists of two phases: fetch and execute. In the fetch phase, the CPU presents the address of the instruction to memory, and it retrieves the instruction located at that address. Then, during the execute phase, the instruction is decoded and executed. This cycle is controlled by and synchronized with the CPU clock signals. Because of the need to refresh dynamic RAM, multiple clock signals known as *multi-phase clock signals* are needed. Static RAM does not require refreshing and uses *single-phase* clock signals. In addition, some instructions might require more than one machine cycle to execute, depending on their complexity. A typical machine cycle showing a single-phase clock is shown in Figure 5.3. Note that in this example, four clock periods are required to execute a single instruction.

A computer can be in a number of different states during its operation. When a computer is executing instructions, this situation is sometimes called the *run* or *operating state*. When application programs are being executed, the machine is in the *application* or *problem* state because it is hopefully calculating the solution to a problem. For security purposes, users are permitted to access only a subset of the total instruction set that is available on the computer in this state. This subset is known as the *non-privileged* instructions. *Privileged*

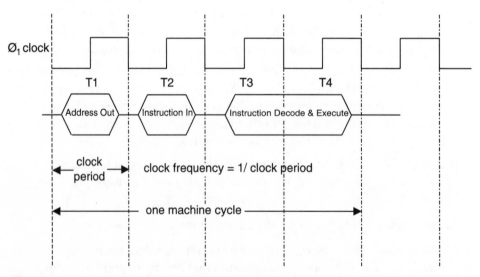

Figure 5.3 A typical machine cycle.

instructions are executed by the system administrator or by an individual who is authorized to use those instructions. A computer is in a *supervisory* state when it is executing these privileged instructions. The computer can be in a *wait* state, for example, if it is accessing a slow memory relative to the instruction cycle time, which causes it to extend the cycle.

After examining a basic machine cycle, it is obvious that there are opportunities for enhancing the speed of retrieving and executing instructions. Some of these methods include overlapping the fetch and execute cycles, exploiting opportunities for parallelism, anticipating instructions that will be executed later, fetching and decoding instructions in advance, and so on. Modern computer design incorporates these methods and their key approaches are provided in the following definitions:

Pipelining. Increases the performance of a computer by overlapping the steps of different instructions. For example, if the instruction cycle is divided into three parts—fetch, decode, and execute—instructions can be overlapped (as shown in Figure 5.4) to increase the execution speed of the instructions.

Complex Instruction Set Computer (CISC). Uses instructions that perform many operations per instruction. This concept was based on the fact that in earlier technologies, the instruction fetch was the longest part of the cycle. Therefore, by packing the instructions with several operations, the number of fetches could be reduced.

Reduced Instruction Set Computer (RISC). Uses instructions that are simpler and require fewer clock cycles to execute. This approach was a result of the increase in the speed of memories and other processor components, which enabled the fetch part of the instruction cycle to be no longer than any other portion of the cycle. In fact, performance was limited by the decoding and execution times of the instruction cycle.

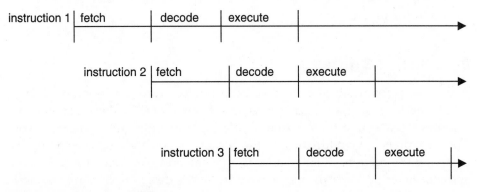

Figure 5.4 Instruction pipelining.

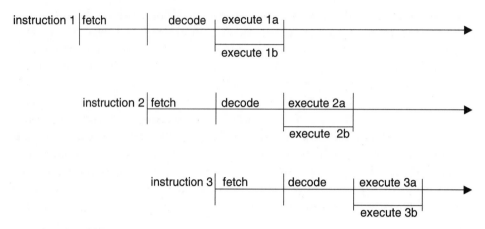

Figure 5.5 Very-Long Instruction Word (VLIW) processing.

Scalar Processor. A processor that executes one instruction at a time.

Superscalar Processor. A processor that enables the concurrent execution of multiple instructions in the same pipeline stage as well as in different pipeline stages.

Very-Long Instruction Word (VLIW) Processor. A processor in which a single instruction specifies more than one concurrent operation. For example, the instruction might specify and concurrently execute two operations in one instruction. VLIW processing is illustrated in Figure 5.5.

Multi-programming. Executes two or more programs simultaneously on a single processor (CPU) by alternating execution among the programs.

Multi-tasking. Executes two or more subprograms or tasks at the same time on a single processor (CPU) by alternating execution among the tasks.

Multi-processing. Executes two or more programs at the same time on multiple processors.

Input/Output Structures

A processor communicates with outside devices through interface devices called *input/output* (I/O) *interface adapters*. In many cases, these adapters are complex devices that provide data buffering and timing and interrupt controls. Adapters have addresses on the computer bus and are selected by the computer instructions. If an adapter is given an address in the memory space and thus takes up a specific memory address, this design is known as *memory-mapped I/O*. The advantage of this approach is that a CPU sees no difference in instructions for the I/O adapter and any other memory location. Therefore, all the computer instructions that are associated with memory can be used for the I/O device. On the other hand, in *isolated I/O* a special signal on the bus indicates that an I/O operation is being executed. This signal distinguishes an address for an I/O device from an address to memory. The signal is generated as a result of the execution of a few selected I/O instructions in the computer instructions' set. The advantage of an isolated I/O is that its addresses do not use up any addresses that could be used for memory. The disadvantage is that the I/O data accesses and manipulations are limited to a small number of specific I/O instructions in the processor's instruction set. Both memory-mapped and isolated I/Os are termed *programmed* I/Os.

In a programmed I/O, data transfers are a function of the speed of the instruction's execution, which manipulates the data that goes through a CPU. A faster alternative is *direct memory access* (DMA). With DMA, data is transferred directly to and from memory without going through a CPU. DMA controllers accomplish this direct transfer in the time interval between the instruction executions. The data transfer rate in DMA is limited primarily by the memory cycle time. The path of the data transfer between memory and a peripheral device is sometimes referred to as a *channel*.

Another alternative to moving data into and out of a computer is through the use of *interrupts*. In *interrupt processing*, an external signal interrupts the normal program flow and requests service. The service might consist of reading data or responding to an emergency situation. Adapters provide the interface for handling the interrupts and the means for establishing priorities among multiple interrupt requests. When a CPU receives an interrupt request, it will save the current state of the information related to the program that is currently running, and it will then jump to another program that services the interrupt. When the interrupt service is completed, the CPU restores the state of the original program and continues processing. Multiple interrupts can be handled concurrently by *nesting* the interrupt service routines. Interrupts can be turned off or *masked* if a CPU is executing high-priority code and does not want to be delayed in its processing.

Software

The CPU of a computer is designed to support the execution of a set of instructions associated with that computer. This set consists of a variety of instructions such as ADD WITH CARRY, ROTATE BITS LEFT, MOVE DATA, and JUMP TO LOCATION X. Each instruction is represented as a binary code that the instruction decoder of the CPU is designed to recognize and execute. These instructions are referred to as *machine language instructions*. The code of each machine language instruction is associated with an English-like mnemonic to make it easier for people to work with the codes. This set of mnemonics for the computer's basic instruction set is called its *assembly language*, which is specific to that particular computer. Thus, there is a one-to-one correspondence of each assembly language instruction to each machine language instruction. For example, in a simple 8-bit instruction word computer, the binary code for the ADD WITH CARRY machine language instruction might be 10011101, and the corresponding mnemonic could be ADC. A programmer who is writing this code at the machine language level would write the code using mnemonics for each instruction. Then, the mnemonic code would be passed through another program called an *assembler* that would perform the one-to-one translation of the assembly language code to the machine language code. The code generated by the assembler running on the computer is called the *object code*, and the original assembly code is called the *source code*. The assembler software can be resident on the computer being programmed and thus is called a *resident assembler*. If the assembler is being run on another computer, the assembler is called a *cross assembler*. Cross assemblers can run on various types and models of computers. A *disassembler* reverses the function of an assembler by translating machine language into assembly language.

If a group of assembly language statements is used to perform a specific function, they can be defined to the assembler with a name called a *MACRO*. Then, instead of writing the list of statements, the MACRO can be called, causing the assembler to insert the appropriate statements.

Because it is desirable to write software in higher-level, English-like statements, *high-level* or *high-order languages* are employed. In these languages, one statement usually requires a number of machine language instructions for its implementation. Therefore, unlike assembly language, there is a one-to-many relationship of high-level language instructions to machine language instructions. Pascal, FORTRAN, BASIC, and Java are examples of high-level languages. High-level languages are converted to the appropriate machine language instructions through either an *interpreter* or *compiler* programs. An interpreter operates on each high-level language source statement individually and performs the indicated operation by executing a predefined sequence of machine language instructions. Thus, the instructions are executed immediately. Java and BASIC are examples of interpreted languages. In contrast, a compiler translates the entire software program into its corresponding machine language instructions. These instructions are then loaded in the computer's memory and are executed as a program package. FORTRAN is an example of a compiled language. From a security standpoint, a compiled program is less desirable than an interpreted one because malicious code can be resident somewhere in the compiled code, and it is difficult to detect in a very large program.

High-level languages have been grouped into five generations, and they are labeled as a Generation Language (GL). The following is a list of these languages:

- *1 GL.* A computer's machine language
- *2 GL.* An assembly language
- *3 GL.* FORTRAN, BASIC, PL/1, and C languages
- *4 GL.* NATURAL, FOCUS, and database query languages
- *5 GL.* Prolog, LISP, and other artificial intelligence languages that process symbols or implement predicate logic

The program (or set of programs) that controls the resources and operations of the computer is called an *operating system* (OS). Operating systems perform process management, memory management, system file management, and I/O management. Windows XP, Windows 2000, Linux, and Unix are some examples of these operating systems.

An OS communicates with I/O systems through a *controller*. A controller is a device that serves as an interface to the peripheral and runs specialized software to manage communications with another device. For example, a disk controller is used to manage the information exchange and operation of a disk drive.

Open and Closed Systems

Open systems are vendor-independent systems that have published specifications and interfaces in order to permit operations with the products of other suppliers. One advantage of an open system is that it is subject to review and evaluation by independent parties. Usually, this scrutiny will reveal any errors or vulnerabilities in that product.

A *closed system* uses vendor-dependent proprietary hardware (and/or software) that is usually not compatible with other systems or components. Closed systems are not subject to independent examination and might have vulnerabilities that are not known or recognized.

Distributed Architecture

The migration of computing from the centralized model to the client-server model has created a new set of issues for information system security professionals. In addition, this situation has also been compounded by the proliferation of desktop PCs and workstations. A PC on a user's desktop might contain documents that are sensitive to the business of an organization and that can be compromised. In most operations, a user also functions as the systems administrator, programmer, and operator of the desktop platform. The major concerns in this scenario are as follows:

- Desktop systems can contain sensitive information that might be at risk of being exposed.
- Users might generally lack security awareness.
- A desktop PC or workstation can provide an avenue of access into critical information systems of an organization.
- Modems that are attached to a desktop machine can make the corporate network vulnerable to dial-in attacks.
- Downloading data from the Internet increases the risk of infecting corporate systems with a malicious code or an unintentional modification of the databases.
- A desktop system and its associated disks might not be protected from physical intrusion or theft.
- A lack of proper backup might exist.

Security mechanisms can be put into place to counter these security vulnerabilities that can exist in a distributed environment. Such mechanisms are as follows:

- E-mail and download/upload policies
- Robust access control, which includes biometrics to restrict access to desktop systems
- Graphical user interface (GUI) mechanisms to restrict access to critical information
- File encryption
- Separation of the processes that run in privileged or non-privileged processor states
- Protection domains
- Protection of sensitive disks by locking them in non-movable containers and by physically securing the desktop system or laptop
- Distinct labeling of disks and materials according to their classification or an organization's sensitivity
- A centralized backup of desktop system files
- Regular security awareness training sessions
- Control of software installed on desktop systems
- Encryption and hash totals for use in sending and storing information

- Logging of transactions and transmissions
- Application of other appropriate physical, logical, and administrative access controls
- Database management systems restricting access to sensitive information
- Protection against environmental damage to computers and media
- Use of formal methods for software development and application, which includes libraries, change control, and configuration management
- Inclusion of desktop systems in disaster recovery and business continuity plans

Protection Mechanisms

In a computational system, multiple processes might be running concurrently. Each process has the capability to access certain memory locations and to execute a subset of the computer's instruction set. The execution and memory space assigned to each process is called a *protection domain*. This domain can be extended to virtual memory, which increases the apparent size of real memory by using disk storage. The purpose of establishing a protection domain is to protect programs from all unauthorized modification or executional interference.

Security professionals should also know that a Trusted Computing Base (TCB) is the total combination of protection mechanisms within a computer system, which includes the hardware, software, and firmware that are trusted to enforce a security policy. The *security perimeter* is the boundary that separates the TCB from the remainder of the system. A *trusted path* must also exist so that a user can access the TCB without being compromised by other processes or users. A *trusted computer system* is one that employs the necessary hardware and software assurance measures to enable its use in processing multiple levels of classified or sensitive information. This system meets the specified requirements for reliability and security.

Resources can also be protected through the principle of *abstraction*. Abstraction involves viewing system components at a high level and ignoring or segregating its specific details. This approach enhances the system's capability to understand complex systems and to focus on critical, high-level issues. In object-oriented programming, for example, methods (programs), and data are *encapsulated* in an object that can be viewed as an abstraction. This concept is called *information hiding* because the object's functioning details are hidden. Communication with this object takes place through messages to which the object responds as defined by its internal method.

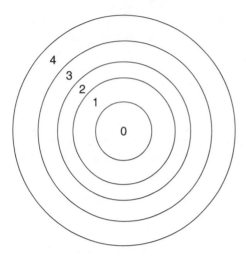

Figure 5.6 Protection rings.

Rings

One scheme that supports multiple protection domains is the use of *protection rings*. These rings are organized with the most privileged domain located in the center of the ring and the least-privileged domain in the outermost ring. This approach is shown in Figure 5.6.

The operating system security kernel is usually located at Ring 0 and has access rights to all domains in that system. A *security kernel* is defined as the hardware, firmware, and software elements of a trusted computing base that implement the reference monitor concept. A *reference monitor* is a system component that enforces access controls on an object. Therefore, the *reference monitor concept* is an abstract machine that mediates all access of subjects to objects. The security kernel must:

- Mediate all accesses
- Be protected from modification
- Be verified as correct

In the ring concept, access rights decrease as the ring number increases. Thus, the most trusted processes reside in the center rings. System components are placed in the appropriate ring according to the principle of least privilege. Therefore, the processes only have the minimum privileges necessary to perform their functions.

The ring protection mechanism was implemented in MIT's MULTICS time-shared operating system that was enhanced for secure applications by the Honeywell Corporation. MULTICS was initially targeted for use on specific hardware platforms because some of its functions could be implemented through the hardware's customization. It was designed to support 64 rings, but in practice only eight rings were defined.

There are also other related kernel-based approaches to protection:

■ Using a separate hardware device that validates all references in a system

■ Implementing a *virtual machine* monitor, which establishes a number of virtual machines isolated from each other that are running on the actual computer. The virtual machines mimic the architecture of a real machine in addition to establishing a multi-level security environment; each virtual machine can run at a different security level.

■ Using a software security kernel that operates in its own hardware protection domain

Security Labels

A security label is assigned to a resource to denote a type of classification or designation. This label can then indicate special security handling, or it can be used for access control. Once labels are assigned, they usually cannot be altered and are an effective access control mechanism. Because labels must be compared and evaluated in accordance with the security policy, they incur additional processing overhead when used.

Security Modes

An information system operates in different security modes that are determined by an information system's classification level and the clearance of the users. A major distinction in its operation is between the system high mode and the multi-level security mode. In the *system high mode of operation*, a system operates at the highest level of information classification, where all users must have clearances for the highest level. However, not all users may have a need to know for all the data. The *multi-level mode of operation* supports users who have different clearances and data at multiple classification levels. Additional modes of operation are defined as follows:

Dedicated. All users have a clearance or an authorization and a need to know for all information that is processed by an information system; a system might handle multiple classification levels.

Compartmented. All users have a clearance for the highest level of information classification, but they do not necessarily have the authorization and a need to know for all the data handled by the computer system.

Controlled. It is a type of multi-level security where a limited amount of trust is placed in the system's hardware/software base along with the corresponding restrictions on the classification of the information levels that can be processed.

Limited access. It is a type of system access where the minimum user clearance is not cleared and the maximum data classification is unclassified but sensitive.

Additional Security Considerations

Vulnerabilities in the system security architecture can lead to violations of the system's security policy. Typical vulnerabilities that are architecturally related vulnerabilities include the following:

Covert channel. An unintended communication path between two or more subjects sharing a common resource, which supports the transfer of information in such a manner that it violates the system's security policy. The transfer usually takes place through common storage areas or through access to a common path that can use a timing channel for the unintended communication.

Lack of parameter checking. The failure to check the size of input streams specified by parameters. Buffer overflow attacks exploit this vulnerability in certain operating systems and programs.

Maintenance hook. A hardware or software mechanism that was installed to permit system maintenance and to bypass the system's security protections. This vulnerability is sometimes referred to as a *trap door*.

Time of Check to Time of Use (TOC/TOU) attack. An attack that exploits the difference in the time that security controls were applied and the time the authorized service was used.

Recovery Procedures

Whenever a hardware or software component of a trusted system fails, it is important that the failure does not compromise the security policy requirements of that system. In addition, the recovery procedures should not also provide an opportunity for violation of the system's security policy. If a system restart is required, the system must restart in a secure state. Startup should occur in the *maintenance mode* that permits access only by privileged users from privileged terminals. This mode supports the restoring the system state and the security state.

When a computer or network component fails and the computer or the network continues to function, it is called a *fault-tolerant* system. For fault tolerance to operate, the system must be capable of detecting that a fault has occurred, and the system must then have the capability to correct the fault or operate around it. In a *failsafe* system, program execution is terminated and the system is protected from being compromised when a hardware or software failure occurs and is detected. In a system that is *fail soft* or *resilient*, selected, non-critical processing is terminated when a hardware or software failure occurs and is detected. The computer or network then continues to function in a degraded mode. The term *failover* refers to switching to a duplicate "hot" backup component in real time when a hardware or software failure occurs, which enables the system to continue processing.

A *cold start* occurs in a system when there is a TCB or media failure and the recovery procedures cannot return the system to a known, reliable, secure state. In this case, the TCB and portions of the software and data might be inconsistent and require external intervention. At that time, the maintenance mode of the system usually has to be employed.

Assurance

Assurance is simply defined as the degree of confidence in satisfaction of security needs. The following sections summarize guidelines and standards that have been developed to evaluate and accept the assurance aspects of a system.

Evaluation Criteria

In 1985, the *Trusted Computer System Evaluation Criteria* (TCSEC) was developed by the *National Computer Security Center* (NCSC) to provide guidelines for evaluating vendors' products for the specified security criteria. TCSEC provides the following:

- A basis for establishing security requirements in the acquisition specifications
- A standard of the security services that should be provided by vendors for the different classes of security requirements
- A means to measure the trustworthiness of an information system

The TCSEC document, called the Orange Book because of its color, is part of a series of guidelines with covers of different coloring called the Rainbow Series. The Rainbow Series is covered in detail in Appendix B. In the Orange Book, the basic control objectives are security policy, assurance, and accountability. TCSEC addresses confidentiality but does not cover integrity. Also, functionality (security controls applied) and assurance (confidence that security controls are functioning as expected) are not separated in TCSEC as they are in other evaluation criteria developed later. The Orange Book defines the major hierarchical classes of security by the letters D through A as follows:

- *D.* Minimal protection
- *C.* Discretionary protection (C1 and C2)
- *B.* Mandatory protection (B1, B2, and B3)
- *A.* Verified protection; formal methods (A1)

The DoD *Trusted Network Interpretation* (TNI) is analogous to the Orange Book. It addresses confidentiality and integrity in trusted computer/communications network systems and is called the Red Book. The Trusted Database Management System Interpretation (TDI) addresses the trusted database management systems.

The European Information Technology Security Evaluation Criteria (ITSEC) address C.I.A. issues. The product or system to be evaluated by ITSEC is defined as the Target of Evaluation (TOE). The TOE must have a security target, which includes the security enforcing mechanisms and the system's security policy.

ITSEC separately evaluates functionality and assurance, and it includes 10 functionality classes (F), eight assurance levels (Q), seven levels of correctness (E), and eight basic security functions in its criteria. It also defines two kinds of assurance. One assurance measure is of the correctness of the security functions' implementation, and the other is the effectiveness of the TOE while in operation.

The ITSEC ratings are in the form F-X,E, where functionality and assurance are listed. The ITSEC ratings that are equivalent to TCSEC ratings are as follows:

F-C1, E1 = C1

F-C2, E2 = C2

F-B1, E3 = B1

F-B2, E4 = B2

F-B3, E5 = B3

F-B3, E6 = A1

The other classes of the ITSEC address high integrity and high availability.

TCSEC, ITSEC, and the *Canadian Trusted Computer Product Evaluation Criteria* (CTCPEC) have evolved into one evaluation criteria called the *Common Criteria*. The Common Criteria define a Protection Profile (PP), which is an implementation-independent specification of the security requirements and protections of a product that could be built. The Common Criteria terminology for the degree of examination of the product to be tested is the Evaluation Assurance Level (EAL). EALs range from EA1 (functional testing) to EA7 (detailed testing and formal design verification). The Common Criteria TOE refers to the product to be tested. A Security Target (ST) is a listing of the security claims for a particular IT security product. Also, the Common Criteria describe an intermediate grouping of security requirement components as a package. Functionality in the Common Criteria refers to standard and well-understood functional security requirements for IT systems. These functional requirements are organized around TCB entities that include physical and logical controls, startup and recovery, reference mediation, and privileged states.

The Common Criteria are discussed in Appendix G. As with TCSEC and ITSEC, the ratings of the Common Criteria are also hierarchical.

Certification and Accreditation

In many environments, formal methods must be applied to ensure that the appropriate information system security safeguards are in place and that they are functioning per the specifications. In addition, an authority must take responsibility for putting the system into operation. These actions are known as certification and accreditation.

Formally, the definitions are as follows:

Certification. The comprehensive evaluation of the technical and non-technical security features of an information system and the other safeguards, which are created in support of the accreditation process to establish the extent to which a particular design and implementation meets the set of specified security requirements

Accreditation. A formal declaration by a *Designated Approving Authority* (DAA) where an information system is approved to operate in a particular security mode by using a prescribed set of safeguards at an acceptable level of risk

The certification and accreditation of a system must be checked after a defined period of time or when changes occur in the system and/or its environment. Then, recertification and re-accreditation are required.

DITSCAP and NIACAP

Two U.S. defense and government certification and accreditation standards have been developed for the evaluation of critical information systems. These standards are the Defense Information Technology Security Certification and Accreditation Process (DITSCAP) and the National Information Assurance Certification and Accreditation Process (NIACAP).

DITSCAP

The DITSCAP establishes a standard process, a set of activities, general task descriptions, and a management structure to certify and accredit the IT systems that will maintain the required security posture. This process is designed to certify that the IT system meets the accreditation requirements and that the system will maintain the accredited security posture throughout its life cycle. These are the four phases to the DITSCAP:

Phase 1, Definition. Phase 1 focuses on understanding the mission, the environment, and the architecture in order to determine the security requirements and level of effort necessary to achieve accreditation.

Phase 2, Verification. Phase 2 verifies the evolving or modified system's compliance with the information agreed on in the System Security Authorization Agreement (SSAA). The objective is to use the SSAA to establish an evolving yet binding agreement on the level of security required before system development begins or changes to a system are made. After accreditation, the SSAA becomes the baseline security configuration document.

Phase 3, Validation. Phase 3 validates the compliance of a fully integrated system with the information stated in the SSAA.

Phase 4, Post Accreditation. Phase 4 includes the activities that are necessary for the continuing operation of an accredited IT system in its computing environment and for addressing the changing threats that a system faces throughout its life cycle.

NIACAP

The NIACAP establishes the minimum national standards for certifying and accrediting national security systems. This process provides a standard set of activities, general tasks, and a management structure to certify and accredit systems that maintain the information assurance and the security posture of a system or site. The NIACAP is designed to certify that the information system meets the documented accreditation requirements and will continue to maintain the accredited security posture throughout the system's life cycle.

There are three types of NIACAP accreditation:

A site accreditation. Evaluates the applications and systems at a specific, self-contained location.

A type accreditation. Evaluates an application or system that is distributed to a number of different locations.

A system accreditation. Evaluates a major application or general support system.

The NIACAP is composed of four phases: Definition, Verification, Validation, and Post Accreditation. These are essentially identical to those of the DITSCAP.

Currently, the Commercial Information Security Analysis Process (CIAP) is being developed for the evaluation of critical commercial systems using the NIACAP methodology.

The Systems Security Engineering Capability Maturity Model (SSE-CMM)

The *Systems Security Engineering Capability Maturity Model* (SSE-CMM; copyright 1999 by the Systems Security Engineering Capability Maturity Model [SSE-CMM] Project) is based on the premise that if you can guarantee the quality of the processes that are used by an organization, then you can guarantee the quality of the products and services generated by those processes. It was developed by a consortium of government and industry experts and is now under the auspices of the International Systems Security Engineering Association (ISSEA) at www.issea.org. The SSE-CMM has the following salient points:

- Describes those characteristics of security engineering processes essential to ensure good security engineering
- Captures industry's best practices
- Accepted way of defining practices and improving capability
- Provides measures of growth in capability of applying processes

The SSE-CMM addresses the following areas of security:

- Operations Security
- Information Security
- Network Security
- Physical Security
- Personnel Security
- Administrative Security
- Communications Security
- Emanations Security
- Computer Security

The SSE-CMM methodology and metrics provide a reference for comparing existing systems' security engineering best practices against the essential systems security engineering elements described in the model. It defines two dimensions that are used to measure the capability of an organization to perform specific activities. These dimensions are *domain* and *capability*. The domain dimension consists of all the practices that collectively define security engineering. These practices are called Base Practices (BPs). Related BPs are grouped into Process Areas (PAs). The capability dimension represents practices that indicate process management and institutionalization capability. These practices are called Generic Practices (GPs) because they apply across a wide range of domains. The GPs represent activities that should be performed as part of performing BPs.

For the domain dimension, the SSE-CMM specifies 11 security engineering PAs and 11 organizational and project-related PAs, each consisting of BPs. BPs are mandatory characteristics that must exist within an implemented security engineering process before an organization can claim satisfaction in a given PA. The 22 PAs and their corresponding BPs incorporate the best practices of systems security engineering. The PAs are as follows:

SECURITY ENGINEERING

- PA01 Administer Security Controls
- PA02 Assess Impact
- PA03 Assess Security Risk
- PA04 Assess Threat
- PA05 Assess Vulnerability
- PA06 Build Assurance Argument
- PA07 Coordinate Security
- PA08 Monitor Security Posture
- PA09 Provide Security Input
- PA10 Specify Security Needs
- PA11 Verify and Validate Security

PROJECT AND ORGANIZATIONAL PRACTICES

- PA12—Ensure Quality
- PA13—Manage Configuration
- PA14—Manage Project Risk
- PA15—Monitor and Control Technical Effort
- PA16—Plan Technical Effort
- PA17—Define Organization's Systems Engineering Process
- PA18—Improve Organization's Systems Engineering Process

- PA19—Manage Product Line Evolution
- PA20—Manage Systems Engineering Support Environment
- PA21—Provide Ongoing Skills and Knowledge
- PA22—Coordinate with Suppliers

The GPs are ordered in degrees of maturity and are grouped to form and distinguish among five levels of security engineering maturity. The attributes of these five levels are as follows:

- Level 1

    1.1 BPs Are Performed
- Level 2

    2.1 Planning Performance

    2.2 Disciplined Performance

    2.3 Verifying Performance

    2.4 Tracking Performance
- Level 3

    3.1 Defining a Standard Process

    3.2 Perform the Defined Process

    3.3 Coordinate the Process
- Level 4

    4.1 Establishing Measurable Quality Goals

    4.2 Objectively Managing Performance
- Level 5

    5.1 Improving Organizational Capability

    5.2 Improving Process Effectiveness

The corresponding descriptions of the five levels are given as follows ("The Systems Security Engineering Capability Maturity Model v2.0," 1999):

- Level 1, "Performed Informally," focuses on whether an organization or project performs a process that incorporates the BPs. A statement characterizing this level would be, "You have to do it before you can manage it."
- Level 2, "Planned and Tracked," focuses on project-level definition, planning, and performance issues. A statement characterizing this level would be, "Understand what's happening on the project before defining organization-wide processes."

■ Level 3, "Well Defined," focuses on disciplined tailoring from defined processes at the organization level. A statement characterizing this level would be, "Use the best of what you've learned from your projects to create organization-wide processes."

■ Level 4, "Quantitatively Controlled," focuses on measurements being tied to the business goals of the organization. Although it is essential to begin collecting and using basic project measures early, measurement and use of data is not expected organization-wide until the higher levels have been achieved. Statements characterizing this level would be, "You can't measure it until you know what 'it' is" and "Managing with measurement is only meaningful when you're measuring the right things."

■ Level 5, "Continuously Improving," gains leverage from all the management practice improvements seen in the earlier levels and then emphasizes the cultural shifts that will sustain the gains made. A statement characterizing this level would be, "A culture of continuous improvement requires a foundation of sound management practice, defined processes, and measurable goals."

Information Security Models

Models are used in information security to formalize security policies. These models might be abstract or intuitive and will provide a framework for the understanding of fundamental concepts. In this section, three types of models are described: access control models, integrity models, and information flow models.

Access Control Models

Access control philosophies can be organized into models that define the major and different approaches to this issue. These models are the access matrix, the Take-Grant model, the Bell-LaPadula confidentiality model, and the state machine model.

The Access Matrix

The access matrix is a straightforward approach that provides access rights to subjects for objects. Access *rights* are of the type read, write, and execute. A *subject* is an active entity that is seeking rights to a resource or object. A subject can be a person, a program, or a process. An *object* is a passive entity, such as a file or a storage resource. In some cases, an item can be a subject in one context and an object in another. A typical access control matrix is shown in Figure 5.7.

Subject Object	File Income	File Salaries	Process Deductions	Print Server A
Joe	Read	Read/Write	Execute	Write
Jane	Read/Write	Read	None	Write
Process Check	Read	Read	Execute	None
Program Tax	Read/Write	Read/Write	Call	Write

Figure 5.7 Example of an access matrix.

The columns of the access matrix are called *Access Control Lists* (ACLs), and the rows are called *capability lists*. The access matrix model supports discretionary access control because the entries in the matrix are at the discretion of the individual(s) who have the authorization authority over the table. In the access control matrix, a subject's capability can be defined by the triple (object, rights, and random #). Thus, the triple defines the rights that a subject has to an object along with a random number used to prevent a replay or spoofing of the triple's source. This triple is similar to the Kerberos tickets previously discussed in Chapter 2, "Access Control Systems."

Take-Grant Model

The Take-Grant model uses a directed graph to specify the rights that a subject can transfer to an object or that a subject can take from another subject. For example, assume that Subject A has a set of rights (S) that includes Grant rights to Object B. This capability is represented in Figure 5.8a. Then, assume that Subject A can transfer Grant rights for Object B to Subject C and that Subject A has another set of rights, (Y), to Object D. In some cases, Object D acts as an object, and in other cases it acts as a subject. Then, as shown by the heavy arrow in Figure 5.8b, Subject C can grant a subset of the Y rights to Subject/Object D because Subject A passed the Grant rights to Subject C.

The Take capability operates in an identical fashion as the Grant illustration.

Bell-LaPadula Model

The Bell-LaPadula Model was developed to formalize the U.S. *Department of Defense* (DoD) multi-level security policy. The DoD labels materials at different levels of security classification. As previously discussed, these levels are Unclassified, Confidential, Secret, and Top Secret—from least sensitive to

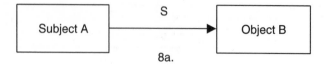

8a.

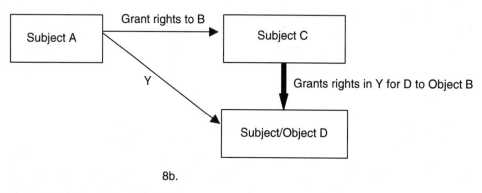

8b.

Figure 5.8 Take-Grant model illustration.

most sensitive. An individual who receives a clearance of Confidential, Secret, or Top Secret can access materials at that level of classification or below. An additional stipulation, however, is that the individual must have a need-to-know for that material. Thus, an individual cleared for Secret can only access the Secret-labeled documents that are necessary for that individual to perform an assigned job function. The Bell-LaPadula model deals *only* with the confidentiality of classified material. It does not address integrity or availability.

The Bell-LaPadula model is built on the state machine concept. This concept defines a set of allowable states (A_i) in a system. The transition from one state to another upon receipt of an input(s) (X_j) is defined by transition functions (f_k). The objective of this model is to ensure that the initial state is secure and that the transitions always result in a secure state. The transitions between two states are illustrated in Figure 5.9.

The Bell-LaPadula model defines a secure state through three multi-level properties. The first two properties implement mandatory access control, and the third one permits discretionary access control. These properties are defined as follows:

1. *The Simple Security Property* (ss Property). States that reading of information by a subject at a lower sensitivity level from an object at a higher sensitivity level is not permitted (no read up).

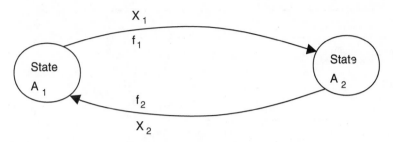

Figure 5.9 State transitions defined by the function f with an input X.

2. *The * (star) Security Property.* States that writing of information by a subject at a higher level of sensitivity to an object at a lower level of sensitivity is not permitted (no write-down).

3. *The Discretionary Security Property.* Uses an access matrix to specify discretionary access control.

There are instances where the * (Star) property is too restrictive and it interferes with required document changes. For instance, it might be desirable to move a low-sensitivity paragraph in a higher-sensitivity document to a lower-sensitivity document. This transfer of information is permitted by the Bell-LaPadula model through a *Trusted Subject*. A Trusted Subject can violate the * property, yet it cannot violate its intent. These concepts are illustrated in Figure 5.10.

In some instances, a property called the *Strong * Property* is cited. This property states that reading or writing is permitted at a particular level of sensitivity but not to either higher or lower levels of sensitivity.

This model defines requests (R) to the system. A request is made while the system is in the state v1; a decision (d) is made upon the request, and the system changes to the state v2. (R, d, v1, v2) represents this tuple in the model. Again, the intent of this model is to ensure that there is a transition from one secure state to another secure state.

The discretionary portion of the Bell-LaPadula model is based on the access matrix. The system security policy defines who is authorized to have certain privileges to the system resources. *Authorization* is concerned with how access rights are defined and how they are evaluated. Some discretionary approaches are based on context-dependent and content-dependent access control. *Content-dependent* control makes access decisions based on the data contained in the object, whereas *context-dependent* control uses subject or object attributes or environmental characteristics to make these decisions. Examples of such characteristics include a job role, earlier accesses, and file creation dates and times.

As with any model, the Bell-LaPadula model has some weaknesses. These are the major ones:

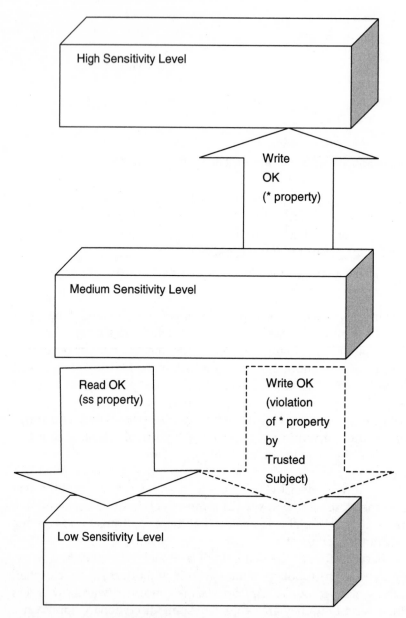

Figure 5.10 The Bell-LaPadula Simple Security and * properties.

- The model considers normal channels of the information exchange and does not address covert channels.
- The model does not deal with modern systems that use file sharing and servers.

- The model does not explicitly define what it means by a secure state transition.
- The model is based on multi-level security policy and does not address other policy types that might be used by an organization.

Integrity Models

In many organizations, both governmental and commercial, integrity of the data is as important or more important than confidentiality for certain applications. Thus, formal integrity models evolved. Initially, the integrity model was developed as an analog to the Bell-LaPadula confidentiality model and then became more sophisticated to address additional integrity requirements.

The Biba Integrity Model

Integrity is usually characterized by the three following goals:

1. The data is protected from modification by unauthorized users.
2. The data is protected from unauthorized modification by authorized users.
3. The data is internally and externally consistent; the data held in a database must balance internally and correspond to the external, real-world situation.

To address the first integrity goal, the Biba model was developed in 1977 as an integrity analog to the Bell-LaPadula confidentiality model. The Biba model is lattice-based and uses the less-than or equal-to relation. A lattice structure is defined as a partially ordered set with a *least upper bound* (LUB) and a *greatest lower bound* (GLB.) The lattice represents a set of *integrity classes* (ICs) and an ordered relationship among those classes. A lattice can be represented as (IC, ≤, LUB, GUB).

Similar to the Bell-LaPadula model's classification of different sensitivity levels, the Biba model classifies objects into different levels of integrity. The model specifies the three following integrity axioms:

1. *The Simple Integrity Axiom.* States that a subject at one level of integrity is not permitted to observe (read) an object of a lower integrity (no read-down).
2. *The * (star) Integrity Axiom.* States that an object at one level of integrity is not permitted to modify (write to) an object of a higher level of integrity (no write-up).
3. A subject at one level of integrity cannot invoke a subject at a higher level of integrity.

These axioms and their relationships are illustrated in Figure 5.11.

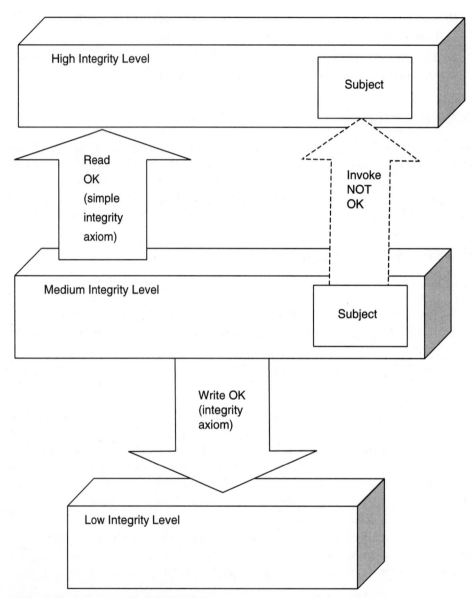

Figure 5.11 The Biba model axioms.

The Clark-Wilson Integrity Model

The approach of the Clark-Wilson model (1987) was to develop a framework for use in the real-world, commercial environment. This model addresses the three integrity goals and defines the following terms:

Constrained data item (CDI). A data item whose integrity is to be preserved.

Integrity verification procedure (IVP). Confirms that all CDIs are in valid states of integrity.

Transformation procedure (TP). Manipulates the CDIs through a well-formed transaction, which transforms a CDI from one valid integrity state to another valid integrity state.

Unconstrained data item. Data items outside the control area of the modeled environment, such as input information.

The Clark-Wilson model requires integrity labels to determine the integrity level of a data item and to verify that this integrity was maintained after an application of a TP. This model incorporates mechanisms to enforce internal and external consistency, a separation of duty, and a mandatory integrity policy.

Information Flow Models

An information flow model is based on a state machine, and it consists of objects, state transitions, and lattice (flow policy) states. In this context, objects can also represent users. Each object is assigned a security class and value, and information is constrained to flow in the directions that are permitted by the security policy. An example is shown in Figure 5.12.

In Figure 5.12, information flows from Unclassified to Confidential in Tasks in Project X and to the combined tasks in Project X. This information can flow in only one direction.

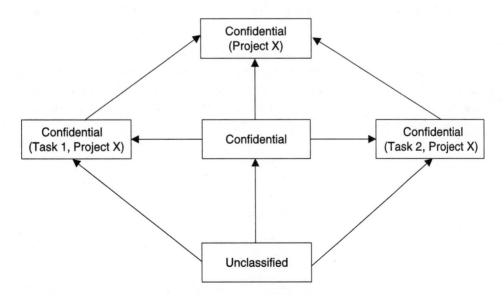

Figure 5.12 An information flow model.

Non-Interference Model

This model is related to the information flow model with restrictions on the information flow. The basic principle of this model is that a group of users (A), who are using the commands (C), do not interfere with the user group (B), who are using commands (D). This concept is written as A, C: | B, D. Restating this rule, the actions of Group A who are using commands C are not seen by users in Group B using commands D.

Composition Theories

In most applications, systems are built by combining smaller systems. An interesting situation to consider is whether the security properties of component systems are maintained when they are combined to form a larger entity.

John McClean studied this issue in 1994 (McLean, J. "A General Theory of Composition for Trace Sets Closed Under Selective Interleaving Functions," Proceedings of 1994 IEEE Symposium on Research in Security and Privacy, IEEE Press, 1994").

He defined two compositional constructions: external and internal. The following are the types of external constructs:

Cascading. One system's input is obtained from the output of another system.

Feedback. One system provides the input to a second system, which in turn feeds back to the input of the first system.

Hookup. A system that communicates with another system as well as with external entities

The internal composition constructs are intersection, union, and difference.

The general conclusion of this study was that the security properties of the small systems were maintained under composition (in most instances) in the cascading construct yet are also subject to other system variables for the other constructs.

Sample Questions

You can find answers to the following questions in Appendix H.

1. What does the Bell-LaPadula model NOT allow?
   a. Subjects to read from a higher level of security relative to their level of security
   b. Subjects to read from a lower level of security relative to their level of security
   c. Subjects to write to a higher level of security relative to their level of security
   d. Subjects to read at their same level of security

2. In the * (star) property of the Bell-LaPadula model,
   a. Subjects cannot read from a higher level of security relative to their level of security.
   b. Subjects cannot read from a lower level of security relative to their level of security.
   c. Subjects cannot write to a lower level of security relative to their level of security.
   d. Subjects cannot read from their same level of security.

3. The Clark-Wilson model focuses on data's:
   a. Integrity.
   b. Confidentiality.
   c. Availability.
   d. Format.

4. The * (star) property of the Biba model states that:
   a. Subjects cannot write to a lower level of integrity relative to their level of integrity.
   b. Subjects cannot write to a higher level of integrity relative to their level of integrity.
   c. Subjects cannot read from a lower level of integrity relative to their level of integrity.
   d. Subjects cannot read from a higher level of integrity relative to their level of integrity.

5. Which of the following does the Clark-Wilson model NOT involve?
   a. Constrained data items
   b. Transformational procedures

    c. Confidentiality items

    d. Well-formed transactions

6. The Take-Grant model:

    a. Focuses on confidentiality.

    b. Specifies the rights that a subject can transfer to an object.

    c. Specifies the levels of integrity.

    d. Specifies the levels of availability.

7. The Biba model addresses:

    a. Data disclosure.

    b. Transformation procedures.

    c. Constrained data items.

    d. Unauthorized modification of data.

8. Mandatory access controls first appear in the Trusted Computer System Evaluation Criteria (TCSEC) at the rating of:

    a. D

    b. C

    c. B

    d. A

9. In the access control matrix, the rows are:

    a. Access Control Lists (ACLs).

    b. Tuples.

    c. Domains.

    d. Capability lists.

10. Superscalar computer architecture is characterized by a:

    a. Computer using instructions that perform many operations per instruction.

    b. Computer using instructions that are simpler and require fewer clock cycles to execute.

    c. Processor that executes one instruction at a time.

    d. Processor that enables the concurrent execution of multiple instructions in the same pipeline stage.

11. A Trusted Computing Base (TCB) is defined as:

    a. The total combination of protection mechanisms within a computer system that are trusted to enforce a security policy.

    b. The boundary separating the trusted mechanisms from the remainder of the system.

c. A trusted path that permits a user to access resources.

d. A system that employs the necessary hardware and software assurance measures to enable processing of multiple levels of classified or sensitive information to occur.

12. Memory space insulated from other running processes in a multi-processing system is part of a:

a. Protection domain.

b. Security perimeter.

c. Least upper bound.

d. Constrained data item.

13. The boundary separating the TCB from the remainder of the system is called the:

a. Star property.

b. Simple security property.

c. Discretionary control boundary.

d. Security perimeter.

14. The system component that enforces access controls on an object is the:

a. Security perimeter.

b. Trusted domain.

c. Reference monitor.

d. Access control matrix.

15. In the discretionary portion of the Bell-LaPadula model that is based on the access matrix, how the access rights are defined and evaluated is called:

a. Authentication.

b. Authorization.

c. Identification.

d. Validation.

16. A computer system that employs the necessary hardware and software assurance measures to enable it to process multiple levels of classified or sensitive information is called a:

a. Closed system.

b. Open system.

c. Trusted system.

d. Safe system.

17. For fault-tolerance to operate, a system must be:

a. Capable of detecting and correcting the fault.

b. Capable of only detecting the fault.

c. Capable of terminating operations in a safe mode.

d. Capable of a cold start.

18. Which of the following choices describes the four phases of the National Information Assurance Certification and Accreditation Process (NIACAP)?

    a. Definition, Verification, Validation, and Confirmation

    b. Definition, Verification, Validation, and Post Accreditation

    c. Verification, Validation, Authentication, and Post Accreditation

    d. Definition, Authentication, Verification, and Post Accreditation

19. What is a programmable logic device (PLD)?

    a. A volatile device

    b. Random Access Memory (RAM) that contains the software to perform specific tasks

    c. An integrated circuit with connections or internal logic gates that can be changed through a programming process

    d. A program resident on disk memory that executes a specific function

20. The termination of selected, non-critical processing when a hardware or software failure occurs and is detected is referred to as:

    a. Fail safe.

    b. Fault tolerant.

    c. Fail soft.

    d. An exception.

21. Which of the following are the three types of NIACAP accreditation?

    a. Site, type, and location

    b. Site, type, and system

    c. Type, system, and location

    d. Site, type, and general

22. Content-dependent control makes access decisions based on:

    a. The object's data.

    b. The object's environment.

    c. The object's owner.

    d. The object's view.

23. The term failover refers to:

    a. Switching to a duplicate, "hot" backup component.

    b. Terminating processing in a controlled fashion.

  c. Resiliency.

  d. A fail-soft system.

24. Primary storage is the:

  a. Memory directly addressable by the CPU, which is for storage of instructions and data that are associated with the program being executed.

  b. Memory, such as magnetic disks, that provide non-volatile storage.

  c. Memory used in conjunction with real memory to present a CPU with a larger, apparent address space.

  d. Memory where information must be obtained by sequentially searching from the beginning of the memory space.

25. In the Common Criteria, a Protection Profile:

  a. Specifies the mandatory protection in the product to be evaluated.

  b. Is also known as the Target of Evaluation (TOE).

  c. Is also known as the Orange Book.

  d. Specifies the security requirements and protections of the products to be evaluated.

26. Context-dependent control uses which of the following to make decisions?

  a. Subject or object attributes or environmental characteristics

  b. Data

  c. Formal models

  d. Operating system characteristics

27. What is a computer bus?

  a. A message sent around a Token Ring network

  b. Secondary storage

  c. A group of conductors for the addressing of data and control

  d. A message in object-oriented programming

28. In a ring protection system, where is the security kernel usually located?

  a. Highest ring number

  b. Arbitrarily placed

  c. Lowest ring number

  d. Middle ring number

29. Increasing performance in a computer by overlapping the steps of different instructions is called:

  a. A reduced instruction set computer.

  b. A complex instruction set computer.

    c. Vector processing.

    d. Pipelining.

30. Random access memory is:

    a. Non-volatile.

    b. Sequentially addressable.

    c. Programmed by using fusible links.

    d. Volatile.

31. The addressing mode in which an instruction accesses a memory location whose contents are the address of the desired data is called:

    a. Implied addressing.

    b. Indexed addressing.

    c. Direct addressing.

    d. Indirect addressing.

32. Processes are placed in a ring structure according to:

    a. Least privilege.

    b. Separation of duty.

    c. Owner classification.

    d. First in, first out.

33. The MULTICS operating system is a classic example of:

    a. An open system.

    b. Object orientation.

    c. Database security.

    d. Ring protection system.

34. What are the hardware, firmware, and software elements of a Trusted Computing Base (TCB) that implement the reference monitor concept called?

    a. The trusted path

    b. A security kernel

    c. An Operating System (OS)

    d. A trusted computing system

Bonus Questions

You can find the answers to the following questions in Appendix H.

1. The memory hierarchy in a typical digital computer, in order, is:

   a. CPU, secondary memory, cache, primary memory.

   b. CPU, primary memory, secondary memory, cache.

   c. CPU, cache, primary memory, secondary memory.

   d. CPU, cache, secondary memory, primary memory.

2. Which one of the following is NOT a typical bus designation in a digital computer?

   a. Secondary

   b. Address

   c. Data

   d. Control

3. The addressing mode in a digital computer in which the address location that is specified in the program instructions contains the address of the final desired location is called:

   a. Indexed addressing.

   b. Implied addressing.

   c. Indirect addressing.

   d. Absolute addressing.

4. A processor in which a single instruction specifies more than one CONCURRENT operation is called a:

   a. Pipelined processor.

   b. Superscalar processor.

   c. Very-Long Instruction Word processor.

   d. Scalar processor.

5. Which one of the following is NOT a security mode of operation in an information system?

   a. System high

   b. Dedicated

   c. Multi-level

   d. Contained

6. The standard process to certify and accredit U.S. defense critical information systems is called:

   a. DITSCAP.

   b. NIACAP.

    c. CIAP.

    d. DIACAP.

7. What information security model formalizes the U.S. Department of Defense multi-level security policy?

    a. Clark-Wilson

    b. Stark-Wilson

    c. Biba

    d. Bell-LaPadula

8. The Biba model axiom, "An object at one level of integrity is not permitted to modify (write to) an object of a higher level of integrity (no write up)" is called:

    a. The Constrained Integrity Axiom.

    b. The * (star) Integrity Axiom.

    c. The Simple Integrity Axiom.

    d. The Discretionary Integrity Axiom.

9. The property that states, "Reading or writing is permitted at a particular level of sensitivity, but not to either higher or lower levels of sensitivity" is called the:

    a. Strong * (star) Property.

    b. Discretionary Security Property.

    c. Simple * (star) Property.

    d. * (star) Security Property.

10. Which one of the following is NOT one of the three major parts of the Common Criteria (CC)?

    a. Introduction and General Model

    b. Security Evaluation Requirements

    c. Security Functional Requirements

    d. Security Assurance Requirements

11. In the Common Criteria, an implementation-independent statement of security needs for a set of IT security products that *could be built* is called a:

    a. Security Target (ST).

    b. Package.

    c. Protection Profile (PP).

    d. Target of Evaluation (TOE).

12. In Part 3 of the Common Criteria, *Security Assurance Requirements*, seven predefined Packages of assurance components "that make up the CC scale for rating confidence in the security of IT products and systems" are called:

    a. Evaluation Assurance Levels (EALs).

    b. Protection Assurance Levels (PALs).

    c. Assurance Levels (ALs).

    d. Security Target Assurance Levels (STALs).

13. Which one of the following is NOT a component of a CC Protection Profile?

    a. Target of Evaluation (TOE) description

    b. Threats against the product that must be addressed

    c. Product-specific security requirements

    d. Security objectives

Advanced Sample Questions

You can find the answers to the following questions in Appendix I.

The following questions are supplemental to and coordinated with Chapter 5 and are at a level commensurate with that of the CISSP Examination.

These questions include advanced material relative to computer architectures, computer hardware, the Java security model, multi-level security, security models and their properties, trusted computer systems, Common Criteria, ITSEC, TCSEC, HIPAA privacy, HIPAA security, HIPAA transactions, HIPAA code sets, the Gramm-Leach-Bliley Act, privacy, NIACAP, DITSCAP, P3P, and FedCIRC.

We assume that the reader has a basic knowledge of the material contained in Chapter 5. These questions and answers build upon the questions and answers covered in Chapter 5.

1. When microcomputers were first developed, the instruction fetch time was much longer than the instruction execution time because of the relatively slow speed of memory accesses. This situation led to the design of the:

    a. Reduced Instruction Set Computer (RISC).

    b. Complex Instruction Set Computer (CISC).

    c. Superscalar processor.

    d. Very-long instruction word (VLIW) processor.

2. The main objective of the Java Security Model (JSM) is to:

    a. Protect the user from hostile, network mobile code.

    b. Protect a web server from hostile, client code.

    c. Protect the local client from hostile, user-input code.

    d. Provide accountability for events.

3. Which of the following would NOT be a component of a general enterprise security architecture model for an organization?

    a. Information and resources to ensure the appropriate level of risk management

    b. Consideration of all the items that comprise information security, including distributed systems, software, hardware, communications systems and networks

    c. A systematic and unified approach for evaluating the organization's information systems security infrastructure and defining approaches to implementation and deployment of information security controls

    d. IT system auditing

4. In a multi-level security system (MLS), the Pump is:

   a. A two-way information flow device.

   b. A one-way information flow device.

   c. Compartmented Mode Workstation (CMW).

   d. A device that implements role-based access control.

5. The Bell-LaPadula model addresses which one of the following items?

   a. Covert channels

   b. The creation and destruction of subjects and objects

   c. Information flow from high to low

   d. Definition of a secure state transition

6. In order to recognize the practical aspects of multi-level security in which, for example, an unclassified paragraph in a Secret document has to be moved to an Unclassified document, the Bell-LaPadula model introduces the concept of a:

   a. Simple security property.

   b. Secure exchange.

   c. Data flow.

   d. Trusted subject.

7. In a refinement of the Bell-LaPadula model, the *strong tranquility property* states that:

   a. Objects never change their security level.

   b. Objects never change their security level in a way that would violate the system security policy.

   c. Objects can change their security level in an unconstrained fashion.

   d. Subjects can read up.

8. As an analog of confidentiality labels, integrity labels in the Biba model are assigned according to which of the following rules?

   a. Objects are assigned integrity labels identical to the corresponding confidentiality labels.

   b. Objects are assigned integrity labels according to their trustworthiness; subjects are assigned classes according to the harm that would be done if the data were modified improperly.

   c. Subjects are assigned classes according to their trustworthiness; objects are assigned integrity labels according to the harm that would be done if the data were modified improperly.

   d. Integrity labels are assigned according to the harm that would occur from unauthorized disclosure of the information.

9. The Clark-Wilson Integrity Model (D. Clark, D. Wilson, "A Comparison of Commercial and Military Computer Security Policies," *Proceedings of the 1987 IEEE Computer Society Symposium on Research in Security and Privacy, Los Alamitos, CA, IEEE Computer Society Press, 1987*) focuses on what two concepts?

   a. Separation of duty and well-formed transactions

   b. Least privilege and well-formed transactions

   c. Capability lists and domains

   d. Well-formed transactions and denial of service

10. The model that addresses the situation wherein one group is not affected by another group using specific commands is called the:

    a. Information flow model.

    b. Non-interference model.

    c. Composition model.

    d. Clark-Wilson model.

11. The secure path between a user and the Trusted Computing Base (TCB) is called:

    a. Trusted distribution.

    b. Trusted path.

    c. Trusted facility management.

    d. The security perimeter.

12. The Common Criteria terminology for the degree of examination of the product to be tested is:

    a. Target of Evaluation (TOE).

    b. Protection Profile (PP).

    c. Functionality (F).

    d. Evaluation Assurance Level (EAL).

13. A difference between the Information Technology Security Evaluation Criteria (ITSEC) and the Trusted Computer System Evaluation Criteria (TCSEC) is:

    a. TCSEC addresses availability as well as confidentiality.

    b. ITSEC addresses confidentiality only.

    c. ITSEC addresses integrity and availability as well as confidentiality.

    d. TCSEC separates functionality and assurance .

14. Which of the following items BEST describes the standards addressed by Title II, Administrative Simplification, of the Health Insurance

Portability and Accountability Act (U.S. *Kennedy-Kassebaum Health Insurance and Portability Accountability Act—HIPAA—Public Law 104-19)*?

a. Transaction Standards, to include Code Sets; Unique Health Identifiers; Security and Electronic Signatures and Privacy

b. Transaction Standards, to include Code Sets; Security and Electronic Signatures and Privacy

c. Unique Health Identifiers; Security and Electronic Signatures and Privacy

d. Security and Electronic Signatures and Privacy

15. Which one of the following is generally NOT considered a covered entity under Title II, Administrative Simplification, of the HIPAA law?

a. Health care providers who transmit health information electronically in connection with standard transactions

b. Health plans

c. Employers

d. Health care clearinghouses

16. The principles of Notice, Choice, Access, Security, and Enforcement refer to which of the following?

a. Authorization

b. Privacy

c. Nonrepudiation

d. Authentication

17. The simple security property of which one of the following models is described as:

"A user has access to a client company's information, c, if and only if for all other information, o, that the user can read, either $x(c) \neq z(o)$ or $x(c) = x(o)$, where $x(c)$ is the client's company and $z(o)$ are the competitors of $x(c)$."

a. Biba

b. Lattice

c. Bell-LaPadula

d. Chinese wall

18. The two categories of the policy of *separation of duty* are:

a. Span of control and functional separation.

b. Inference control and functional separation.

c. Dual control and functional separation.

d. Dual control and aggregation control.

19. In the National Information Assurance Certification and Accreditation Process (NIACAP), a *type accreditation* performs which one of the following functions?

    a. Evaluates a major application or general support system

    b. Verifies the evolving or modified system's compliance with the information agreed on in the System Security Authorization Agreement (SSAA)

    c. Evaluates an application or system that is distributed to a number of different locations

    d. Evaluates the applications and systems at a specific, self-contained location

20. Which of the following processes establishes the minimum national standards for certifying and accrediting national security systems?

    a. CIAP

    b. DITSCAP

    c. NIACAP

    d. Defense audit

21. Which of the following terms is NOT associated with a Read Only Memory (ROM)?

    a. Flash memory

    b. Field Programmable Gate Array (FPGA)

    c. Static RAM (SRAM)

    d. Firmware

22. Serial data transmission in which information can be transmitted in two directions, but only one direction at a time is called:

    a. Simplex.

    b. Half-duplex.

    c. Synchronized.

    d. Full-duplex.

23. The ANSI ASC X12 (American National Standards Institute Accredited Standards Committee X12) Standard version 4010 applies to which one of the following HIPAA categories?

    a. Privacy

    b. Code sets

    c. Transactions

    d. Security

24. A 1999 law that addresses privacy issues related to health care, insurance, and finance and that will be implemented by the states is:

    a. Gramm-Leach-Bliley (GLB).

    b. Kennedy-Kassebaum.

    c. the Medical Action Bill.

    d. the Insurance Reform Act.

25. The Platform for Privacy Preferences (P3P) was developed by the World Wide Web Consortium (W3C) for what purpose?

    a. To implement public key cryptography for transactions

    b. To evaluate a client's privacy practices

    c. To monitor users

    d. To implement privacy practices on Web sites

26. What process is used to accomplish high-speed data transfer between a peripheral device and computer memory, bypassing the Central Processing Unit (CPU)?

    a. Direct memory access

    b. Interrupt processing

    c. Transfer under program control

    d. Direct access control

27. An associative memory operates in which one of the following ways?

    a. Uses indirect addressing only

    b. Searches for values in memory exceeding a specified value

    c. Searches for a specific data value in memory

    d. Returns values stored in a memory address location specified in the CPU address register

28. The following concerns usually apply to what type of architecture?

    ■ Desktop systems can contain sensitive information that may be at risk of being exposed.

    ■ Users may generally lack security awareness.

    ■ Modems present a vulnerability to dial-in attacks.

    ■ Lack of proper backup may exist.

    a. Distributed

    b. Centralized

    c. Open system

    d. Symmetric

29. The definition "A relatively small amount (when compared to primary memory) of very high speed RAM, which holds the instructions and data from primary memory, that has a high probability of being accessed during the currently executing portion of a program" refers to what category of computer memory?

    a. Secondary

    b. Real

    c. Cache

    d. Virtual

30. The organization that "establishes a collaborative partnership of computer incident response, security and law enforcement professionals who work together to handle computer security incidents and to provide both proactive and reactive security services for the U.S. Federal government" is called:

    a. CERT/CC.

    b. Center for Infrastructure Protection.

    c. Federal CIO Council.

    d. Federal Computer Incident Response Center.

Operations Security

The Operations Security Domain of Information Systems Security contains many elements that are important for a CISSP candidate to remember. In this domain, we will describe the controls that a computing operating environment needs to ensure the three pillars of information security: Confidentiality, Integrity, and Availability (C.I.A.). Examples of these elements of control are controlling the separation of job functions, controlling the hardware and media that are used, and controlling the exploitation of common I/O errors.

This domain somewhat overlaps the Physical Security domain. In fact, there has been discussion as to whether the Physical domain should be removed altogether and merged with the Operations domain. We will point out the areas that overlap in this chapter.

Operations Security can be described as the controls over the hardware in a computing facility, the data media used in a facility, and the operators using these resources in a facility.

From the published (ISC)² goals for the Certified Information Systems Security Professional candidate:

A CISSP candidate will be expected to know the resources that must be protected, the privileges that must be restricted, the control mechanisms that are available, the potential for access abuse, the appropriate controls, and the principles of good practice.

Our Goals

We will approach this material from the three following directions:

1. *Controls and Protections.* We will describe the categories of operational controls needed to ensure C.I.A.
2. *Monitoring and Auditing.* We will describe the need for monitoring and auditing these controls.
3. *Threats and Vulnerabilities.* We will discuss threats and violations that are applicable to the Operations domain.

Domain Definition

Operations Security refers to the act of understanding the threats to and vulnerabilities of computer operations in order to routinely support operational activities that enable computer systems to function correctly. It also refers to the implementation of security controls for normal transaction processing, system administration tasks, and critical external support operations. These controls can include resolving software or hardware problems along with the proper maintenance of auditing and monitoring processes.

Triples

Like the other domains, the Operations Security domain is concerned with triples—threats, vulnerabilities, and assets. We will now look at what constitutes a triple in the Operations Security domain:

Threat. A *threat* in the Operations Security domain can be defined as the presence of any potential event that could cause harm by violating security. An example of an operations threat would be an operator's abuse of privileges, thereby violating confidentiality.

Vulnerability. A *vulnerability* is defined as a weakness in a system that enables security to be violated. An example of an operations vulnerability would be a weak implementation of the separation of duties.

Asset. An *asset* is considered anything that is a computing resource or ability, such as hardware, software, data, and personnel.

C.I.A.

The following are the effects of operations controls on C.I.A.:

Confidentiality. Operations controls affect the sensitivity and secrecy of the information.

Integrity. How well the operations controls are implemented directly affects the data's accuracy and authenticity.

Availability. Like the Physical Security domain, these controls affect the organization's level of fault tolerance and its capability to recover from failure.

Controls and Protections

The Operations Security domain is concerned with the controls that are used to protect hardware, software, and media resources from the following:

- Threats in an operating environment
- Internal or external intruders
- Operators who are inappropriately accessing resources

A CISSP candidate should know the resources to protect, how privileges should be restricted, and the controls to implement.

In addition, we will also discuss the following two critical aspects of operations controls:

1. Resource protection, which includes hardware control
2. Privileged-entity control

Categories of Controls

The following are the major categories of operations security controls:

Preventative Controls. In the Operations Security domain, preventative controls are designed to achieve two things: to lower the amount and impact of unintentional errors that are entering the system and to prevent unauthorized intruders from internally or externally accessing the system. An example of these controls might be prenumbered forms or a data validation and review procedure to prevent duplications.

Detective Controls. Detective controls are used to detect an error once it has occurred. Unlike preventative controls, these controls operate after the fact and can be used to track an unauthorized transaction for prosecution, or to lessen an error's impact on the system by identifying it quickly. An example of this type of control is an audit trail.

Corrective (or Recovery) Controls. Corrective controls are implemented to help mitigate the impact of a loss event through data recovery procedures. They can be used to recover after damage, such as restoring data that was inadvertently erased from floppy diskettes.

The following are additional control categories:

Deterrent Controls. Deterrent controls are used to encourage compliance with external controls, such as regulatory compliance. These controls are meant to complement other controls, such as preventative and detective controls. Deterrent controls are also known as directive controls.

Application Controls. Application controls are the controls that are designed into a software application to minimize and detect the software's operational irregularities. In addition, the following controls are also examples of the various types of application controls.

Transaction Controls. Transaction controls are used to provide control over the various stages of a transaction—from initiation to output through testing and change control. There are several types of transaction controls:

■ *Input Controls*. Input controls are used to ensure that transactions are properly input into the system only once. Elements of input controls might include counting the data and timestamping it with the date it was entered or edited.

■ *Processing Controls*. Processing controls are used to guarantee that transactions are valid and accurate and that wrong entries are reprocessed correctly and promptly.

■ *Output Controls*. Output controls are used for two things: for protecting the confidentiality of an output and for verifying the integrity of an output by comparing the input transaction with the output data. Elements of proper output controls would involve ensuring that the output reaches the proper users, restricting access to the printed output storage areas, printing heading and trailing banners, requiring signed receipts before releasing sensitive output, and printing "no output" banners when a report is empty.

■ *Change Controls*. Change controls are implemented to preserve data integrity in a system while changes are made to the configuration. Procedures and standards have been created to manage these changes and modifications to the system and its configuration. Change control and configuration management control is thoroughly described later in this chapter.

■ *Test Controls*. Test controls are put into place during the testing of a system to prevent violations of confidentiality and to ensure a transaction's integrity. An example of this type of control is the proper use of sanitized test data. Test controls are often part of the change control process.

Orange Book Controls

The *Trusted Computer Security Evaluation Criteria* (TCSEC, the Orange Book) defines several levels of assurance requirements for secure computer operations. Assurance is a level of confidence that ensures that a TCB's security policy has been correctly implemented and that the system's security features have accurately implemented that policy.

The Orange Book defines two types of assurance—*operational assurance* and *life cycle assurance*. Operational assurance focuses on the basic features and architecture of a system while life cycle assurance focuses on the controls and standards that are necessary for building and maintaining a system. An example of an operational assurance would be a feature that separates a security-sensitive code from a user code in a system's memory.

The operational assurance requirements specified in the Orange Book (found in Appendix B) are as follows:

■ System architecture

■ System integrity

■ Covert channel analysis

■ Trusted facility management

■ Trusted recovery

Life cycle assurance ensures that a TCB is designed, developed, and maintained with formally controlled standards that enforce protection at each stage in the system's life cycle. *Configuration management*, which carefully monitors and protects all changes to a system's resources, is a type of life cycle assurance.

The life cycle assurance requirements specified in the Orange Book are as follows:

■ Security testing

■ Design specification and testing

■ Configuration management

■ Trusted distribution

In the Operations Security domain, the operations assurance areas of covert channel analysis, trusted facility management and trusted recovery, and the life cycle assurance area of configuration management are covered.

Covert Channel Analysis

A *covert channel* is an information path that is not normally used for communication within a system; therefore, it is not protected by the system's normal security mechanisms. Covert channels are a secret way to convey information to another person or program.

There are two types of covert channels: *covert storage channels* and *covert timing channels*. Covert storage channels convey information by changing a system's stored data. For example, a program can convey information to a less-secure program by changing the amount or the patterns of free space on a hard disk. Changing the characteristics of a file is also another example of creating a covert channel.

Covert timing channels convey information by altering the performance of or modifying the timing of a system resource in some measurable way. Timing channels often work by taking advantage of some kind of system clock or timing device in a system. Information is conveyed by using elements such as the elapsed time required to perform an operation, the amount of CPU time expended, or the time occurring between two events.

Noise and traffic generation are effective ways to combat the use of covert channels. Table 6.1 describes the primary covert channel classes.

Trusted Facility Management

Trusted facility management is defined as the assignment of a specific individual to administer the security-related functions of a system. Although trusted facility management is an assurance requirement only for highly secure systems (B2, B3, and A1), many systems evaluated at lower security levels are structured to try to meet this requirement (see Table 6.2).

Trusted facility management is closely related to the concept of least privilege, and it is also related to the administrative concept of *separation of duties* and *need to know*.

Table 6.1 Covert Channel Classes

CLASS	DESCRIPTION
B2	The system must protect against covert storage channels. It must perform a covert channel analysis for all covert storage channels.
B3 and A1	The system must protect against both covert storage and covert timing channels. It must perform a covert channel analysis for both types.

Table 6.2 Trusted Facility Management Classes

CLASS	REQUIREMENTS
B2	Systems must support separate operator and system administrator roles.
B3 and A1	Systems must clearly identify the functions of the security administrator to perform the security-related functions.

Separation of Duties

Separation of duties (also called *segregation of duties*) assigns parts of tasks to different personnel. Thus, if no single person has total control of the system's security mechanisms, the theory is that no single person can completely compromise the system. This concept is related to the principle of *least privilege*. In this context, least privilege means that a system's users should have the lowest level of rights and privileges necessary to perform their work and should only have them for the shortest length of time.

In many systems, a system administrator has total control of the system's administration and security functions. This consolidation of power is not allowed in a secure system because security tasks and functions should not automatically be assigned to the role of the system administrator. In highly secure systems, three distinct administrative roles might be required: a system administrator, a security administrator who is usually an Information System Security Officer (ISSO), and an enhanced operator function.

The security administrator, system administrator, and operator might not necessarily be different personnel, which is often the case. However, whenever a system administrator assumes the role of the security administrator, this role change must be controlled and audited. Because the security administrator's job is to perform security functions, the performance of non-security tasks must be strictly limited. This separation of duties reduces the likelihood of loss that results from users abusing their authority by taking actions outside of their assigned functional responsibilities. While it might be cumbersome for the person to switch from one role to another, the roles are functionally different and must be executed as such.

In the concept of *two-man control*, two operators review and approve the work of each other. The purpose of two-man control is to provide accountability and to minimize fraud in highly sensitive or high-risk transactions. The concept of *dual control* means that both operators are needed to complete a sensitive task.

Typical system administrator or enhanced operator functions can include the following:

- Installing system software
- Starting up (booting) and shutting down a system
- Adding and removing system users
- Performing back-ups and recovery
- Handling printers and managing print queues

Typical security administrator functions might include the following:

- Setting user clearances, initial passwords, and other security characteristics for new users
- Changing security profiles for existing users
- Setting or changing file sensitivity labels
- Setting the security characteristics of devices and communications channels
- Reviewing audit data

An operator might perform some system administrator roles, such as back-ups. This may happen in facilities where personnel resources are constrained.

Rotation of Duties

Another variation on the separation of duties is called *rotation of duties*. It is defined as the process of limiting the amount of time that an operator is assigned to perform a security-related task before being moved to a different task with a different security classification. This control lessens the opportunity for collusion between operators for fraudulent purposes. Like a separation of duties, a rotation of duties might be difficult to implement in small organizations but can be an effective security control procedure.

THE SYSTEM ADMINISTRATOR'S MANY HATS

It is not just small organizations anymore that require a system administrator to function as a security administrator. The LAN/Internet Network administrator role creates security risks due to the inherent lack of the separation of duties. With the current pullback in the Internet economy, a network administrator has to wear many hats—and performing security-related tasks is almost always one of them (along with various operator functions). The sometimes cumbersome yet very important concept of separation of duties is vital to preserve operations controls.

Trusted Recovery

Trusted recovery ensures that security is not breached when a system crash or other system failure (sometimes called a "discontinuity") occurs. It must ensure that the system is restarted without compromising its required protection scheme and that it can recover and roll back without being compromised after the failure. Trusted recovery is required only for B3 and A1 level systems. A system failure represents a serious security risk because the security controls might be bypassed when the system is not functioning normally.

For example, if a system crashes while sensitive data is being written to a disk (where it would normally be protected by controls), the data might be left unprotected in memory and might be accessible by unauthorized personnel.

Trusted recovery has two primary activities: preparing for a system failure and recovering the system.

Failure Preparation

Under trusted recovery, preparing for a system failure consists of backing up all critical files on a regular basis. This preparation must enable the data recovery in a protected and orderly manner while ensuring the continued security of the system. These procedures might also be required if a system problem, such as a missing resource, an inconsistent database, or any kind of compromise, is detected, or if the system needs to be halted and rebooted.

System Recovery

While specific, trusted recovery procedures depend upon a system's requirements, general, secure system recovery procedures include the following:

- Rebooting the system into a *single user mode*—an operating system loaded without the security front end activated—so that no other user access is enabled at this time
- Recovering all file systems that were active at the time of the system failure
- Restoring any missing or damaged files and databases from the most recent backups
- Recovering the required security characteristics, such as file security labels
- Checking security-critical files, such as the system password file

After all of these steps have been performed and the system's data cannot be compromised, operators can then access the system.

In addition, the Common Criteria also describes three hierarchical recovery types:

1. *Manual Recovery.* System administrator intervention is required to return the system to a secure state after a crash.

2. *Automated Recovery.* Recovery to a secure state is automatic (without system administrator intervention) when resolving a single failure; however, manual intervention is required to resolve any additional failures.

3. *Automated Recovery without Undue Loss.* Similar to automated recovery, this type of recovery is considered a higher level of recovery defining prevention against the undue loss of protected objects.

Configuration/Change Management Control

Configuration management is the process of tracking and approving changes to a system. It involves identifying, controlling, and auditing all changes made to the system. It can address hardware and software changes, networking changes, or any other change affecting security. Configuration management can also be used to protect a trusted system while it is being designed and developed.

The primary security goal of configuration management is to ensure that changes to the system do not unintentionally diminish security. For example, configuration management might prevent an older version of a system from being activated as the production system. Configuration management also makes it possible to accurately roll back to a previous version of a system in case a new system is found to be faulty. Another goal of configuration management is to ensure that system changes are reflected in current documentation to help mitigate the impact that a change might have on the security of other systems, while either in the production or planning stages.

Although configuration management is a requirement only for B2, B3, and A1 systems, it is recommended for systems that are evaluated at lower levels. Most developers use some type of configuration management because it is common sense.

The following are the primary functions of configuration or change control:

- To ensure that the change is implemented in a orderly manner through formalized testing

- To ensure that the user base is informed of the impending change

- To analyze the effect of the change on the system after implementation

- To reduce the negative impact that the change might have had on the computing services and resources

Five generally accepted procedures exist to implement and support the change control process:

1. Applying to introduce a change
2. Cataloging the intended change
3. Scheduling the change
4. Implementing the change
5. Reporting the change to the appropriate parties

Table 6.3 shows the two primary configuration management classes.

Administrative Controls

Administrative controls can be defined as the controls that are installed and maintained by administrative management to help reduce the threat or impact of violations on computer security. We separate them from the operations controls because these controls have more to do with human resources personnel administration and policy than they do with hardware or software controls.

The following are some examples of administrative controls:

Personnel Security. These controls are administrative human resources controls that are used to support the guarantees of the quality levels of the personnel performing the computer operations. These are also explained in the Physical Security domain. Elements of these include the following:

■ *Employment screening or background checks.* Pre-employment screening for sensitive positions should be implemented. For less-sensitive positions, post-employment background checks might be suitable.

■ *Mandatory taking of vacation in one-week increments.* This practice is common in financial institutions or other organizations where an operator has access to sensitive financial transactions. Some institutions require a two-week vacation, during which the operator's accounts, processes, and procedures are audited carefully to uncover any evidence of fraud.

Table 6.3 Configuration Management Classes

CLASS	REQUIREMENT
B2 and B3	Configuration management procedures must be enforced during development and maintenance of a system.
A1	Configuration management procedures must be enforced during the entire system's life cycle.

■ *Job action warnings or termination.* These are the actions taken when employees violate the published computer behavior standards.

Separation of Duties and Responsibilities. Separation (or Segregation) of Duties and Responsibilities is the concept of assigning parts of security-sensitive tasks to several individuals. We described this concept earlier in this chapter.

Least Privilege. Least privilege requires that each subject be granted the most restricted set of privileges needed for the performance of their task. We describe this concept later in more detail.

Need to Know. Need to know refers to the access to, knowledge of, or possession of specific information that is required to carry out a job function. It requires that the subject is given only the amount of information required to perform an assigned task. We also describe this concept later in more detail.

Change/Configuration Management Controls. The function of Change Control or Configuration Control is to protect a system from problems and errors that might result from improperly executed or tested changes to a system. We described this concept earlier in this chapter.

Record Retention and Documentation. The administration of security controls on documentation and the procedures implemented for record retention have an impact on operational security. We describe these concepts later in more detail.

Least Privilege

It might be necessary to separate the levels of access based on the operator's job function. A very effective approach is *least privilege*. An example of least privilege is the concept of computer operators who are not allowed access to computer resources at a level beyond what is absolutely needed for their specific job tasks. Operators are organized into privilege-level groups. Each group is then assigned the most restrictive level that is applicable.

The three basic levels of privilege are defined as follows:

Read Only. This level is the lowest level of privilege and the one to which most operators should be assigned. Operators are allowed to view data but are not allowed to add, delete, or make changes to the original or copies of the data.

Read/Write. The next higher privilege level is read/write access. This level enables operators to read, add to, or write over any data for which they have authority. Operators usually only have read/write access to data copied from an original location; they cannot access the original data.

Access Change. The third and highest level is access change. This level gives operators the right to modify data directly in its original location, in addition to data copied from the original location. Operators might also have the right to change file and operator access permissions in the system (a supervisor right).

These privilege levels are commonly much more granular than we have stated here. Privilege levels in a large organization can, in fact, be very complicated.

Operations Job Function Overview

In a large shop, job functions and duties might be divided among a very large base of IT personnel. In many IT departments, the following roles are combined into fewer positions. The following listing, however, gives a nice overview of the various task components of the operational functions.

Computer Operator. Responsible for backups, running the system console, mounting and unmounting reel tapes and cartridges, recording and reporting operational problems with hardware devices and software products, and maintaining environmental controls

Operations Analyst. Responsible for working with application software developers, maintenance programmers, and computer operators

Job Control Analyst. Responsible for the overall quality of the production job control language and conformance to standards

Production Scheduler. Responsible for planning, creating, and coordinating computer processing schedules for all production and job streams in conjunction with the established processing periods and calendars

Production Control Analyst. Responsible for the printing and distribution of computer reports and microfiche/microfilm records

Tape Librarian. Responsible for collecting input tapes and scratch tapes, sending tapes to and receiving returns from offsite storage and third parties, and for maintaining tapes

Record Retention

Record retention refers to how long transactions and other types of records (legal, audit trails, e-mail, and so forth) should be retained according to management, legal, audit, or tax compliance requirements. In the Operations Security domain, record retention deals with retaining computer files, directories, and libraries. The retention of data media (tapes, diskettes, and backup media) can be based on one or more criteria, such as the number of days elapsed, number of days since creation, hold time, or other factors. An example of record retention issues could be the mandated retention periods for trial documentation or financial records.

Data Remanence

Data remanence refers to the data left on the media after the media has been erased. After erasure, there might be some physical traces left, which could enable the data to be reconstructed that could contain sensitive material.

Systems administrators and security administrators should be informed of the risks involving the issues of object reuse, declassification, destruction, and disposition of storage media. Data remanence, object reuse, and the proper disposal of data media are discussed thoroughly in Chapter 10, "Physical Security."

Due Care and Due Diligence

The concepts of *due care* and *due diligence* require that an organization engage in good business practices relative to the organization's industry. Training employees in security awareness could be an example of due care, unlike simply creating a policy with no implementation plan or follow-up. Mandating statements from the employees stating that they have read and understood appropriate computer behavior is also an example of due care.

Due diligence might be mandated by various legal requirements in the organization's industry or through compliance with governmental regulatory standards. Due care and due diligence are described in more detail in Chapter 9, "Law, Investigation, and Ethics."

NOTE Due care and due diligence are becoming serious issues in computer operations today. In fact, the legal system has begun to hold major partners liable for the lack of due care in the event of a major security breach. Violations of security and privacy are hot-button issues that are confronting the Internet community, and standards covering the best practices of due care are necessary for an organization's protection.

Documentation

A security system needs documentation controls. Documentation can include several things: security plans, contingency plans, risk analyses, and security policies and procedures. Most of this documentation must be protected from unauthorized disclosure, and it must also be available in the event of a disaster.

Operations Controls

Operations Controls embody the day-to-day procedures used to protect computer operations. The concepts of resource protection, hardware/software control, and privileged entity must be understood by a CISSP candidate.

The following are the most important aspects of operations controls:

- Resource protection
- Hardware controls
- Software controls
- Privileged-entity controls
- Media controls
- Physical access controls

Resource Protection

Resource protection is just what it sounds like—the concept of protecting an organization's computing resources and assets from loss or compromise. Computing resources are defined as any hardware, software, or data that is owned and used by the organization. Resource protection is designed to help reduce the possibility of damage that can result from the unauthorized disclosure and/or alteration of data by limiting the opportunities for its misuse.

Resources that Require Protection

These are various examples of resources that require protection.

HARDWARE RESOURCES

- Communications, which includes routers, firewalls, gateways, switches, modems, and access servers
- Storage media, which includes floppies, removable drives, external hard drives, tapes, and cartridges
- Processing systems, which includes file servers, mail servers, Internet servers, backup servers, and tape drives
- Standalone computers, which includes workstations, modems, disks, and tapes
- Printers and fax machines

SOFTWARE RESOURCES

- Program libraries and source code
- Vendor software or proprietary packages
- Operating system software and systems utilities

DATA RESOURCES

- Backup data
- User data files
- Password files
- Operating Data Directories
- System logs and audit trails

Hardware Controls

Hardware Maintenance. System maintenance requires physical or logical access to a system by support and operations staff, vendors, or service providers. Maintenance might be performed on-site, or it might be transported to a repair site. It might also be remotely performed. Furthermore, background investigations of the service personnel might be necessary. Supervising and escorting the maintenance personnel when they are on-site is also necessary.

Maintenance Accounts. Many computer systems provide *maintenance accounts*. These supervisor-level accounts are created at the factory with preset and widely known passwords. It is critical to change these passwords or at least disable the accounts until these accounts are needed. If an account is used remotely, authentication of the maintenance provider can be performed by using callback or encryption.

TRANSPARENCY OF CONTROLS

One important aspect of controls is the need for their transparency. Operators need to feel that security protections are reasonably flexible and that the security protections do not get in the way of doing their jobs. Ideally, the controls should not require users to perform extra steps, although realistically this result is hard to achieve. Transparency also aids in preventing users from learning too much about the security controls.

Diagnostic Port Control. Many systems have diagnostic ports through which trouble-shooters can directly access the hardware. These ports should only be used by authorized personnel and should not enable either internal or external unauthorized access. *Diagnostic port attacks* is the term that describes this type of abuse.

Hardware Physical Control. Many data processing areas that contain hardware might require locks and alarms. The following are some examples:

- Sensitive operator terminals and keyboards
- Media storage cabinets or rooms
- Server or communications equipment data centers
- Modem pools or telecommunication circuit rooms

Locks and alarms are described in Chapter 10.

Software Controls

An important element of operations controls is software support—controlling what software is used in a system. Elements of controls on software are as follows:

Anti-Virus Management. If personnel can load or execute any software on a system, the system is more vulnerable to viruses, unexpected software interactions, and to the subversion of security controls.

Software Testing. A rigid and formal software testing process is required to determine compatibility with custom applications or to identify other unforeseen interactions. This procedure should also apply to software upgrades.

Software Utilities. Powerful systems utilities can compromise the integrity of operations systems and logical access controls. Their use must be controlled by security policy.

Safe Software Storage. A combination of logical and physical access controls should be implemented to ensure that the software and copies of backups have not been modified without proper authorization.

Backup Controls. Not only do support and operations personnel back up software and data, but in a distributed environment users may also back up their own data. It is very important to routinely test the restore accuracy of a backup system. A backup should also be stored securely to protect from theft, damage, or environmental problems. A description of the types of backups is in Chapter 3, "Telecommunications and Network Security."

Privileged Entity Controls

Privileged entity access, which is also known as *privileged operations functions*, is defined as an extended or special access to computing resources given to operators and system administrators. Many job duties and functions require privileged access.

Privileged entity access is most often divided into classes. Operators should be assigned to a class based on their job title.

The following are some examples of privileged entity operator functions:

- Special access to system commands
- Access to special parameters
- Access to the system control program

Media Resource Protection

Media resource protection can be classified into two areas: media security controls and media viability controls. Media security controls are implemented to prevent any threat to C.I.A. by the intentional or unintentional exposure of sensitive data. Media viability controls are implemented to preserve the proper working state of the media, particularly to facilitate the timely and accurate restoration of the system after a failure.

Media Security Controls

Media security controls should be designed to prevent the loss of sensitive information when the media is stored outside the system.

A CISSP candidate needs to know several of the following elements of media security controls:

Logging. Logging the use of data media provides accountability. Logging also assists in physical inventory control by preventing tapes from walking away and facilitating their recovery process.

RESTRICTING HARDWARE INSTRUCTIONS

A *system control program* restricts the execution of certain computing functions and permits them only when a processor is in a particular functional state, known as *privileged* or *supervisor* state. Applications can run in different states, during which different commands are permitted. To be authorized to execute privileged instructions, a program should be running in a restrictive state that enables these commands.

Access Control. Physical access control to the media is used to prevent unauthorized personnel from accessing the media. This procedure is also a part of physical inventory control.

Proper Disposal. Proper disposal of the media after use is required to prevent data remanence. The process of removing information from used data media is called *sanitization*. Three techniques are commonly used for sanitization: overwriting, degaussing, and destruction. These are described in Chapter 10.

Media Viability Controls

Many physical controls should be used to protect the viability of the data storage media. The goal is to protect the media from damage during handling and transportation or during short-term or long-term storage. Proper marking and labeling of the media is required in the event of a system recovery process.

Marking. All data storage media should be accurately marked or labeled. The labels can be used to identify media with special handling instructions or to log serial numbers or bar codes for retrieval during a system recovery.

There is a difference between this kind of physical storage media marking for inventory control and the logical data labeling of sensitivity classification for mandatory access control, which we described in other chapters, so please do not get them confused.

Handling. Proper handling of the media is important. Some issues with the handling of media include cleanliness of the media and the protection from physical damage to the media during transportation to the archive sites.

Storage. Storage of the media is very important for both security and environmental reasons. A proper heat- and humidity-free, clean storage environment should be provided for the media. Data media is sensitive to temperature, liquids, magnetism, smoke, and dust.

MEDIA LIBRARIAN

It is the job of a media librarian to control access to the media library and to regulate the media library environment. All media must be labeled in a human- and machine-readable form that should contain information such as the date and who created the media, the retention period, a volume name and version, and security classification.

Physical Access Controls

The control of physical access to the resources is the major tenet of the Physical Security domain. Obviously, the Operations Security domain requires physical access control, and the following list contains examples of some of the elements of the operations resources that need physical access control.

HARDWARE

- Control of communications and the computing equipment
- Control of the storage media
- Control of the printed logs and reports

SOFTWARE

- Control of the backup files
- Control of the system logs
- Control of the production applications
- Control of the sensitive/critical data

Obviously, all personnel require some sort of control and accountability when accessing physical resources, yet some personnel will require special physical access to perform their job functions. The following are examples of this type of personnel:

- IT department personnel
- Cleaning staff
- Heating Ventilation and Air Conditioning (HVAC) maintenance personnel
- Third-party service contract personnel
- Consultants, contractors, and temporary staff

Special arrangements for supervision must be made when external support providers are entering a data center.

NOTE Physical piggybacking describes when an unauthorized person goes through a door behind an authorized person. The concept of a "man trap" (described in Chapter 10) is designed to prevent physical piggybacking.

Monitoring and Auditing

Problem identification and problem resolution are the primary goals of monitoring. The concept of monitoring is integral to almost all of the domains of information security. In Chapter 3 we described the technical aspects of monitoring and intrusion detection. Chapter 10 will also describe intrusion de-tection and monitoring from a physical access perspective. In this chapter, we are more concerned with monitoring the controls implemented in an operational facility in order to identify abnormal computer usage, such as inappropriate use or intentional fraud. Failure recognition and re-sponse, which includes reporting mechanisms, is an important part of monitoring.

Monitoring

Monitoring contains the mechanisms, tools, and techniques that permit the identification of security events that could impact the operation of a computer facility. It also includes the actions to identify the important elements of an event and to report that information appropriately.

The concept of monitoring includes monitoring for illegal software installation, monitoring the hardware for faults and error states, and monitoring operational events for anomalies.

Monitoring Techniques

To perform this type of monitoring, an information security professional has several tools at his or her disposal:

- Intrusion detection
- Penetration testing
- Violation processing using clipping levels

Intrusion Detection (ID)

Intrusion Detection (ID) is a useful tool that can assist in the detective analysis of intrusion attempts. ID can be used not only for the identification of intruders, but it can also be used to create a sampling of traffic patterns. By analyzing the activities occurring outside of normal clipping levels, a security practitioner can find evidence of events such as in-band signaling or other system abuses. More in-depth descriptions of the types of common intrusion detection are provided in Chapters 3 and 10.

Penetration Testing

Penetration testing is the process of testing a network's defenses by attempting to access the system from the outside by using the same techniques that an external intruder (for example, a cracker) would use. This testing gives a security professional a better snapshot of the organization's security posture.

Among the techniques used to perform a penetration test are:

Scanning and Probing. Various scanners, like a port scanner, can reveal information about a network's infrastructure and enable an intruder to access the network's unsecured ports.

Demon Dialing. Demon (or "war") dialers automatically test every phone line in an exchange to try to locate modems that are attached to the network. Information about these modems can then be used to attempt external unauthorized access.

Sniffing. A protocol analyzer can be used to capture data packets that are later decoded to collect information such as passwords or infrastructure configurations.

Other techniques that are not solely technology-based can be used to complement the penetration test. The following are examples of such techniques:

Dumpster Diving. Searching paper disposal areas for unshredded or otherwise improperly disposed of reports.

Social Engineering. The most commonly used technique of all: getting information (like passwords) just by asking for them.

Violation Analysis

One of the most-used techniques to track anomalies in user activity is *violation tracking*, *processing*, and *analysis*. To make violation tracking effective, *clipping levels* must be established. A clipping level is a baseline of user activity that is considered a routine level of user errors. A clipping level is used to enable a system to ignore normal user errors. When the clipping level is exceeded, a violation record is then produced. Clipping levels are also used for *variance detection*.

Using clipping levels and *profile-based anomaly detection*, the following are the types of violations that should be tracked, processed, and analyzed:

- Repetitive mistakes that exceed the clipping level number
- Individuals who exceed their authority
- Too many people with unrestricted access
- Patterns indicating serious intrusion attempts

INDEPENDENT TESTING

It is important to note that in most cases, external penetration testing should be performed by a reputable, experienced firm that is independent of an organization's IT or Audit departments. This independence guarantees an objective, non-political report on the state of the company's defenses.

NOTE Profile-based anomaly detection uses profiles to look for abnormalities in user behavior. A profile is a pattern that characterizes the behavior of users. Patterns of usage are established according to the various types of activities the users engage in, such as processing exceptions, resource utilization, and patterns in actions performed, for example. The ways in which the various types of activity are recorded in the profile are referred to as profile metrics.

Auditing

The implementation of regular system audits is the foundation of operational security controls monitoring. In addition to enabling internal and external compliance checking, regular auditing of audit (transaction) trails and logs can assist the monitoring function by helping to recognize patterns of abnormal user behavior.

Security Auditing

Information Technology (IT) auditors are often divided into two types: internal and external. Internal auditors typically work for a given organization while external auditors do not. External auditors are often Certified Public Accountants (CPAs) or other audit professionals who are hired to perform an independent audit of an organization's financial statements. Internal auditors, on the other hand, usually have a much broader mandate—checking for compliance and standards of due care, auditing operational cost efficiencies, and recommending the appropriate controls.

IT auditors typically audit the following functions:

- Backup controls
- System and transaction controls
- Data library procedures
- Systems development standards
- Data center security
- Contingency plans

In addition, IT auditors might also recommend improvement to controls, and they often participate in a system's development process to help an organization avoid costly re-engineering after the system's implementation.

Audit Trails

An audit (or transaction) trail enables a security practitioner to trace a transaction's history. This transaction trail provides information about additions, deletions, or modifications to the data within a system. Audit trails enable the enforcement of individual accountability by creating a reconstruction of events. Like monitoring, one purpose of an audit trail is to assist in a problem's identification that leads to a problem's resolution. An effectively implemented audit trail also enables the data to be retrieved and easily certified by an auditor. Any unusual activity and variations from the established procedures should be identified and investigated.

The audit logs should record the following:

- The transaction's date and time
- Who processed the transaction
- At which terminal the transaction was processed
- Various security events relating to the transaction

In addition, an auditor should also examine the audit logs for the following:

- Amendments to production jobs
- Production job reruns
- Computer operator practices

Other important security issues regarding the use of audit logs are as follows:

- Retention and protection of the audit media and reports when their storage is off-site
- Protection against the alteration of audit or transaction logs
- Protection against the unavailability of an audit media during an event

Problem Management Concepts

Effective auditing embraces the concepts of problem management. Problem management is a way to control the process of problem isolation and problem

---

ELECTRONIC AUDIT TRAILS

Maintaining a proper audit trail is more difficult now because more transactions are not recorded to paper media, and thus they will always stay in an electronic form. In the old paper system, a physical purchase order might be prepared with multiple copies, initiating a physical, permanent paper trail. An auditor's job is now more complicated because digital media is more transient and a paper trail might not exist.

resolution. An auditor might use problem management to resolve the issues arising from an IT security audit, for example.

The goal of problem management is threefold:

1. To reduce failures to a manageable level
2. To prevent the occurrence or reoccurrence of a problem
3. To mitigate the negative impact of problems on computing services and resources

The first step in implementing problem management is to define the potential problem areas and the abnormal events that should be investigated. Some examples of potential problem areas are:

- The performance and availability of computing resources and services
- The system and networking infrastructure
- Procedures and transactions
- The safety and security of personnel

Some examples of abnormal events that could be discovered during an audit are as follows:

- Degraded hardware or software resource availability
- Deviations from the standard transaction procedures
- Unexplained occurrences in a processing chain

Of course, the final objective of problem management is resolution of the problem.

Threats and Vulnerabilities

A *threat* is simply any event that, if realized, can cause damage to a system and create a loss of confidentiality, availability, or integrity. Threats can be malicious, such as the intentional modification of sensitive information, or they can be accidental—such as an error in a transaction calculation or the accidental deletion of a file.

A *vulnerability* is a weakness in a system that can be exploited by a threat. Reducing the vulnerable aspects of a system can reduce the risk and impact of threats on the system.

For example, a password-generation tool, which helps users choose robust passwords, reduces the chance that users will select poor passwords (the vulnerability) and makes the password more difficult to crack (the threat of external attack).

Threats

We have grouped the threats into several categories, and we will describe some of the elements of each category.

Accidental Loss

Accidental loss is a loss that is incurred unintentionally, through either the lack of operator training or proficiency or by the malfunctioning of an application processing procedure. The following are some examples of the types of accidental loss:

Operator input errors and omissions. Manual input transaction errors, entry or data deletion, and faulty data modification.

Transaction processing errors. Errors that are introduced into the data through faulty application programming or processing procedures.

Inappropriate Activities

Inappropriate activity is computer behavior that, while not rising to the level of criminal activity, might be grounds for job action or dismissal.

Inappropriate Content. Using the company systems to store pornography, entertainment, political, or violent content.

Waste of Corporate Resources. Personal use of hardware or software, such as conducting a private business with a company's computer system.

Sexual or Racial Harassment. Using email or other computer resources to distribute inappropriate material.

Abuse of Privileges or Rights. Using unauthorized access levels to violate the confidentiality of sensitive company information.

Illegal Computer Operations and Intentional Attacks

Under this heading, we have grouped the areas of computer activities that are considered as intentional and illegal computer activity for personal financial gain for destruction.

Eavesdropping. Data scavenging, traffic or trend analysis, social engineering, economic or political espionage, sniffing, dumpster diving, keystroke monitoring, or shoulder surfing are all types of eavesdropping to gain information or to create a foundation for a later attack. Eavesdropping is a primary cause of the failure of confidentiality.

Fraud. Examples of the types of fraud are collusion, falsified transactions, data manipulation, and other altering of data integrity for gain.

Theft. Examples of the types of theft are the theft of information or trade secrets for profit or unauthorized disclosure, and hardware or software physical theft.

Sabotage. Sabotage includes Denial of Service (DoS), production delays, and data integrity sabotage.

External Attack. Examples of external attacks are malicious cracking, scanning, and probing to gain infrastructure information, demon dialing to locate an unsecured modem line, and the insertion of a malicious code or virus.

Vulnerabilities

Traffic/Trend Analysis. *Traffic analysis*, which is sometimes called *trend analysis*, is a technique employed by an intruder that involves analyzing data characteristics (message length, message frequency, and so forth) and the patterns of transmissions (rather than any knowledge of the actual information transmitted) to infer information that is useful to an intruder.

Countermeasures to traffic analysis are similar to the countermeasures to crypto-attacks:

- *Padding messages*. Creating all messages to be a uniform data size by filling empty space in the data

- *Sending noise*. Transmitting non-informational data elements mixed in with real information to disguise the real message

- *Covert channel analysis*. Previously described in the "Orange Book Controls" section of this chapter

Maintenance Accounts. See Hardware Controls. It is a method used to break into computer systems by using maintenance accounts that still have factory-set or easily guessed passwords. Physical access to the hardware by maintenance personnel can also constitute a security violation.

Data-Scavenging Attacks. Data scavenging is the technique of piecing together information from found bits of data. There are two common types of data-scavenging attacks:

1. *Keyboard Attacks.* Data scavenging through the resources that are available to normal system users who are sitting at the keyboard and using normal utilities and tools to glean information.

2. *Laboratory Attacks.* Data scavenging by using very precise electronic equipment; it is a planned, orchestrated attack.

IPL Vulnerabilities. The start of a system, the Initial Program Load (IPL), presents very specific system vulnerabilities whether the system is a centralized mainframe type or a distributed LAN type. During the IPL, the operator brings up the facility's system. This operator has the ability to put a system into a single user mode, without full security features, which is a very powerful ability. In this state, an operator could load unauthorized programs or data, reset passwords, rename various resources, or reset the system's time and date. The operator could also reassign the data ports or communications lines to transmit information to a confederate outside of the data center.

In a LAN, a system administrator could start the bootup sequence from a tape, CD-ROM, or floppy disk—bypassing the operating system's security on the hard drive.

Network Address Hijacking. It might be possible for an intruder to reroute data traffic from a server or network device to a personal machine, either by device address modification or network address "hijacking." This diversion enables the intruder to capture traffic to and from the devices for data analysis or modification or to steal the password file from the server and gain access to user accounts. By rerouting the data output, the intruder can obtain supervisory terminal functions and bypass the system logs.

Sample Questions

You can find answers to the following questions in Appendix H.

1. What does IPL stand for?

   a. Initial Program Life Cycle

   b. Initial Program Load

   c. Initial Post-Transaction Logging

   d. Internet Police League

2. Which of the following is NOT a use of an audit trail?

   a. Provides information about additions, deletions, or modifications to the data

   b. Collects information such as passwords or infrastructure configurations

   c. Assists the monitoring function by helping to recognize patterns of abnormal user behavior

   d. Enables the security practitioner to trace a transaction's history

3. Why is security an issue when a system is booted into "single-user mode"?

   a. The operating system is started without the security front end loaded.

   b. The users cannot log in to the system, and they will complain.

   c. Proper forensics cannot be executed while in single-user mode.

   d. Backup tapes cannot be restored while in single-user mode.

4. Which of the following examples is the best definition of Fail Secure?

   a. Access personnel have security clearance, but they do not have a "need to know."

   b. The operating system is started without the security front end loaded.

   c. The system fails to preserve a secure state during and after a system crash.

   d. The system preserves a secure state during and after a system crash.

5. Which of the following would NOT be an example of compensating controls being implemented?

   a. Sensitive information requiring two authorized signatures to release

   b. A safety deposit box needing two keys to open

    c. Modifying the timing of a system resource in some measurable way to covertly transmit information

    d. Signing in or out of a traffic log and using a magnetic card to access an operations center

6. "Separation of duties" embodies what principle?

    a. An operator does not know more about the system than the minimum required to do the job.

    b. Two operators are required to work in tandem to perform a task.

    c. The operators' duties are frequently rotated.

    d. The operators have different duties to prevent one person from compromising the system.

7. Which is NOT true about Covert Channel Analysis?

    a. It is an operational assurance requirement that is specified in the Orange Book.

    b. It is required for B2 class systems in order to protect against covert storage channels.

    c. It is required for B2 class systems to protect against covert timing channels.

    d. It is required for B3 class systems to protect against both covert storage and covert timing channels.

8. An audit trail is an example of what type of control?

    a. Deterrent control

    b. Preventative control

    c. Detective control

    d. Application control

9. Using pre-numbered forms to initiate a transaction is an example of what type of control?

    a. Deterrent control

    b. Preventative control

    c. Detective control

    d. Application control

10. Which of the following is a reason to institute output controls?

    a. To preserve the integrity of the data in the system while changes are being made to the configuration

    b. To protect the output's confidentiality

    c. To detect irregularities in the software's operation

    d. To recover damage after an identified system failure

11. Covert Channel Analysis, Trusted Facility Management, and Trusted Recovery are parts of which book in the TCSEC Rainbow Series?

    a. Red Book

    b. Orange Book

    c. Green Book

    d. Dark Green Book

12. How do covert timing channels convey information?

    a. By changing a system's stored data characteristics

    b. By generating noise and traffic with the data

    c. By performing a covert channel analysis

    d. By modifying the timing of a system resource in some measurable way

13. Which of the following is the best example of "need to know"?

    a. An operator does not know more about the system than the minimum required to do the job.

    b. Two operators are required to work together to perform a task.

    c. The operators' duties are frequently rotated.

    d. An operator cannot generate and verify transactions alone.

14. Which of the following is an example of "least privilege"?

    a. An operator does not know more about the system than the minimum required to do the job.

    b. An operator does not have more system rights than the minimum required to do the job.

    c. The operators' duties are frequently rotated.

    d. An operator cannot generate and verify transactions alone.

15. Which of the following would be the BEST description of clipping levels?

    a. A baseline of user errors above which violations will be recorded

    b. A listing of every error made by users to initiate violation processing

    c. Variance detection of too many people with unrestricted access

    d. Changes a system's stored data characteristics

16. Which of the following is NOT a proper media control?

    a. The data media should be logged to provide a physical inventory control.

    b. All data storage media should be accurately marked.

    c. A proper storage environment should be provided for the media.

    d. The media that is reused in a sensitive environment does not need sanitization.

17. Configuration management control best refers to:

    a. The concept of "least control" in operations

    b. Ensuring that changes to the system do not unintentionally diminish security

    c. The use of privileged-entity controls for system administrator functions

    d. Implementing resource-protection schemes for hardware control

18. Which of the following would NOT be considered a penetration testing technique?

    a. War dialing

    b. Sniffing

    c. Data manipulation

    d. Scanning

19. Inappropriate computer activities could be described as:

    a. Computer behavior that might be grounds for a job action or dismissal

    b. Loss incurred unintentionally through the lack of operator training

    c. Theft of information or trade secrets for profit or unauthorized disclosure

    d. Data scavenging through the resources available to normal system users

20. Why are maintenance accounts a threat to operations controls?

    a. Maintenance personnel could slip and fall and sue the organization.

    b. Maintenance accounts are commonly used by hackers to access network devices.

    c. Maintenance account information could be compromised if printed reports are left out in the open.

    d. Maintenance might require physical access to the system by vendors or service providers.

Bonus Questions

You can find the answers to these questions in Appendix H.

1. Which choice below is NOT an example of intentionally inappropriate operator activity?

   a. Making errors when manually inputting transactions

   b. Using the company's system to store pornography

   c. Conducting private business on the company system

   d. Using unauthorized access levels to violate information confidentiality

2. Which choice below would NOT be a common element of a transaction trail?

   a. The date and time of the transaction

   b. Who processed the transaction

   c. Why the transaction was processed

   d. At which terminal the transaction was processed

3. Which choice below is NOT an element of proper media control?

   a. Accurately and promptly marking all data storage media

   b. Assuring the accuracy of the backup data

   c. The safe and clean handling of the media

   d. The proper environmental storage of the media

3. Which choice below best describes the function of change control?

   a. To ensure that system changes are implemented in an orderly manner

   b. To guarantee that an operator is only given the privileges needed for the task

   c. To guarantee that transaction records are retained IAW compliance requirements

   d. To assign parts of security-sensitive tasks to more than one individual

4. Which task below would normally be a function of the security administrator, not the system administrator?

   a. Installing system software

   b. Adding and removing system users

   c. Reviewing audit data

   d. Managing print queues

5. Which choice below BEST describes the type of control that a firewall exerts on a network infrastructure?

   a. Corrective control

   b. Preventative control

   c. Detective control

   d. Application control

6. Which choice below BEST describes a threat as defined in the Operations Security domain?

   a. A potential incident that could cause harm

   b. A weakness in a system that could be exploited

   c. A company resource that could be lost due to an incident

   d. The minimization of loss associated with an incident

7. Which choice below is considered the HIGHEST level of operator privilege?

   a. Read/Write

   b. Read Only

   c. Access Change

   d. Write Only

8. Which choice below is NOT a common example of exercising due care or due diligence in security practices?

   a. Implementing security awareness and training programs

   b. Implementing employee compliance statements

   c. Implementing controls on printed documentation

   d. Implementing employee casual Friday

9. Which choice below is NOT an example of a software control?

   a. Controlling diagnostic ports on networked equipment

   b. Employing anti-virus management and tools

   c. Implementing a formal application upgrade process

   d. Routinely testing the backup data for accuracy

Advanced Sample Questions

You can find the answers to the following questions in Appendix I.

The following questions are supplemental to and coordinated with Chapter 6 and are at a level on par with that of the CISSP Examination.

We assume that the reader has a basic knowledge of the material contained in Chapter 6.

1. Which book of the Rainbow series addresses the Trusted Network Interpretation (TNI)?

   a. Red Book

   b. Orange Book

   c. Green Book

   d. Purple Book

2. Which choice describes the Forest Green Book?

   a. It is a tool that assists vendors in data gathering for certifiers.

   b. It is a Rainbow series book that defines the secure handling of storage media.

   c. It is a Rainbow series book that defines guidelines for implementing access control lists.

   d. It does not exist; there is no "Forest Green Book."

3. Which term below BEST describes the concept of "least privilege"?

   a. Each user is granted the lowest clearance required for their tasks.

   b. A formal separation of command, program, and interface functions.

   c. A combination of classification and categories that represents the sensitivity of information.

   d. Active monitoring of facility entry access points.

4. Which general TCSEC security class category describes that mandatory access policies be enforced in the TCB?

   a. A

   b. B

   c. C

   d. D

5. Which statement below is the BEST definition of "need-to-know"?

   a. Need-to-know ensures that no single individual (acting alone) can compromise security controls.

   b. Need-to-know grants each user the lowest clearance required for their tasks.

   c. Need-to-know limits the time an operator performs a task.

    d. Need-to-know requires that the operator have the minimum knowledge of the system necessary to perform his task.

6. Place the four systems security modes of operation in order, from the most secure to the least:

_____ a. Dedicated Mode

_____ b. Multilevel Mode

_____ c. Compartmented Mode

_____ d. System High Mode

7. Which media control below is the BEST choice to prevent data remanence on magnetic tapes or floppy disks?

    a. Overwriting the media with new application data

    b. Degaussing the media

    c. Applying a concentration of hydriodic acid (55% to 58% solution) to the gamma ferric oxide disk surface

    d. Making sure the disk is re-circulated as quickly as possible to prevent object reuse

8. Which choice below is the BEST description of an audit trail?

    a. Audit trails are used to detect penetration of a computer system and to reveal usage that identifies misuse.

    b. An audit trail is a device that permits simultaneous data processing of two or more security levels without risk of compromise.

    c. An audit trail mediates all access to objects within the network by subjects within the network.

    d. Audit trails are used to prevent access to sensitive systems by unauthorized personnel.

9. Which TCSEC security class category below specifies "trusted recovery" controls?

    a. C2

    b. B1

    c. B2

    d. B3

10. Which choice does NOT describe an element of configuration management?

    a. Configuration management involves information capture and version control.

    b. Configuration management reports the status of change processing.

    c. Configuration management is the decomposition process of a verification system into Configuration Items (CIs).

    d. Configuration management documents the functional and physical characteristics of each configuration item.

11. Which choice below does NOT accurately describe a task of the Configuration Control Board?

    a. The CCB should meet periodically to discuss configuration status accounting reports.

    b. The CCB is responsible for documenting the status of configuration control activities.

    c. The CCB is responsible for assuring that changes made do not jeopardize the soundness of the verification system.

    d. The CCB assures that the changes made are approved, tested, documented, and implemented correctly.

12. Which choice below is NOT a security goal of an audit mechanism?

    a. Deter perpetrators' attempts to bypass the system protection mechanisms

    b. Review employee production output records

    c. Review patterns of access to individual objects

    d. Discover when a user assumes a functionality with privileges greater than his own

13. Which choice below is NOT a common element of user account administration?

    a. Periodically verifying the legitimacy of current accounts and access authorizations

    b. Authorizing the request for a user's system account

    c. Tracking users and their respective access authorizations

    d. Establishing, issuing, and closing user accounts

14. Which element of Configuration Management listed below involves the use of Configuration Items (CIs)?

    a. Configuration Accounting

    b. Configuration Audit

    c. Configuration Control

    d. Configuration Identification

15. Which standard defines the International Standard for the Common Criteria?

    a. IS15408

    b. BS7799

    c. DoD 5200.28-STD

    d. CSC-STD-002-85

16. Which statement below is NOT correct about reviewing user accounts?

    a. User account reviews cannot be conducted by outside auditors.

    b. User account reviews can examine conformity with least privilege.

    c. User account reviews may be conducted on a system-wide basis.

    d. User account reviews may be conducted on an application-by-application basis.

17. Which statement below MOST accurately describes configuration control?

    a. The decomposition process of a verification system into CIs

    b. Assuring that only the proposed and approved system changes are implemented

    c. Tracking the status of current changes as they move through the configuration control process

    d. Verifying that all configuration management policies are being followed

18. Which term below MOST accurately describes the Trusted Computing Base (TCB)?

    a. A computer that controls all access to objects by subjects

    b. A piece of information that represents the security level of an object

    c. Formal proofs used to demonstrate the consistency between a system's specification and a security model

    d. The totality of protection mechanisms within a computer system

19. Which choice below would NOT be considered a benefit of employing incident-handling capability?

    a. An individual acting alone would not be able to subvert a security process or control.

    b. It enhances internal communications and the readiness of the organization to respond to incidents.

    c. It assists an organization in preventing damage from future incidents.

    d. Security training personnel would have a better understanding of users' knowledge of security issues.

20. Which statement below is accurate about Evaluation Assurance Levels (EALs) in the Common Criteria (CC)?

    a. A security level equal to the security level of the objects to which the subject has both read and write access

    b. A statement of intent to counter specified threats

    c. Requirements that specify the security behavior of an IT product or system

    d. Predefined packages of assurance components that make up the security confidence rating scale

21. Which choice below is the BEST description of operational assurance?

    a. Operational assurance is the process of examining audit logs to reveal usage that identifies misuse.

    b. Operational assurance has the benefit of containing and repairing damage from incidents.

    c. Operational assurance is the process of reviewing an operational system to see that security controls are functioning correctly.

    d. Operational assurance is the process of performing pre-employment background screening.

22. Which choice below MOST accurately describes a Covert Storage Channel?

    a. A process that manipulates observable system resources in a way that affects response time

    b. An information transfer path within a system

    c. A communication channel that allows a process to transfer information in a manner that violates the system's security policy

    d. An information transfer that involves the direct or indirect writing of a storage location by one process and the direct or indirect reading of the storage location by another process

23. Which choice below is the BEST description of a Protection Profile (PP), as defined by the Common Criteria (CC)?

    a. A statement of security claims for a particular IT security product

    b. A reusable definition of product security requirements

    c. An intermediate combination of security requirement components

    d. The IT product or system to be evaluated

24. Which choice below is NOT one of the four major aspects of configuration management?

    a. Configuration status accounting

    b. Configuration product evaluation

    c. Configuration auditing

    d. Configuration identification

25. Which choice below MOST accurately describes "partitioned security mode"?

    a. All personnel have the clearance and formal access approval.

    b. All personnel have the clearance but not necessarily formal access approval.

    c. The only state in which certain privileged instructions may be executed.

    d. A system containing information accessed by personnel with different security clearances.

26. Which choice below is NOT an example of a media control?

    a. Sanitizing the media before disposition

    b. Printing to a printer in a secured room

    c. Physically protecting copies of backup media

    d. Conducting background checks on individuals

27. Which statement below is the BEST example of "separation of duties"?

    a. An activity that checks on the system, its users, or the environment.

    b. Getting users to divulge their passwords.

    c. One person initiates a request for a payment and another authorizes that same payment.

    d. A data entry clerk may not have access to run database analysis reports.

28. Which minimum TCSEC security class category specifies "trusted distribution" controls?

    a. C2

    b. B2

    c. B3

    d. A1

29. Which statement is accurate about "trusted facility management"?

    a. The role of a security administrator shall be identified and auditable in C2 systems and above.

    b. The role of a security administrator shall be identified and auditable in B2 systems and above.

    c. The TCB shall support separate operator and administrator functions for C2 systems and above.

    d. The TCB shall support separate operator and administrator functions for B2 systems and above.

30. Which statement below is accurate about the concept of Object Reuse?

    a. Object reuse protects against physical attacks on the storage medium.

    b. Object reuse ensures that users do not obtain residual information from system resources.

    c. Object reuse applies to removable media only.

    d. Object reuse controls the granting of access rights to objects.

CHAPTER 7

Applications and Systems Development

There are information system security issues associated with applications software, whether the software is developed internally or acquired from an external source. This chapter addresses these security issues from the viewpoint of the developer, user, and information system security specialist. Thus, a CISSP professional should understand the following areas:

- The software life cycle development process
- The software process capability maturity model
- Object-oriented systems
- Artificial intelligence systems
- Database systems
    - Database security issues
    - Data warehousing
    - Data mining
    - Data dictionaries
- Application controls

The Software Life Cycle Development Process

Software engineering can be defined as the science and art of specifying, designing, implementing, and evolving programs, documentation, and operating procedures so that computers can be made useful to man. This definition is a combination of popular definitions of engineering and software. One definition of engineering is the application of science and mathematics to the design and construction of artifacts that are useful to man. A definition of software is that it consists of the programs, documentation, and operating procedures by which computers can be made useful to man.

In software engineering, the term *verification* is defined as the process of establishing the truth of correspondence between a software product and its specification. *Validation* establishes the fitness or worth of a software product for its operational mission. *Requirements*, as defined in the Waterfall model (W.W. Royce, "Managing the Development of Large Software Systems: Concepts and Techniques," *Proceedings, WESCON*, August 1970), are a complete, validated specification of the required functions, interfaces, and performance for the software product. *Product design* is a complete, verified specification of the overall hardware-software architecture, control structure, and data structure for the product.

Quality software is difficult to obtain without a development process. As with any project, two principal goals of software development are to produce a quality product that meets the customer's requirements and to stay within the budget and time schedule. A succession of models has emerged over time incorporating improvements in the development process. An early model defined succeeding stages, taking into account the different staffing and planning that was required for each stage. The model was simplistic in that it assumed that each step could be completed and finalized without any effect from the later stages that might require rework. This model is shown in Figure 7.1.

The Waterfall Model

Because subsequent stages such as design, coding, and testing in the development process might require modifying earlier stages in the model, the *Waterfall* model emerged. Under this model, software development can be managed if the developers are limited to going back only one stage to rework. If this limitation is not imposed (particularly on a large project with several team members), then any developer can be working on any phase at any time and the required rework might be accomplished several times. Obviously, this

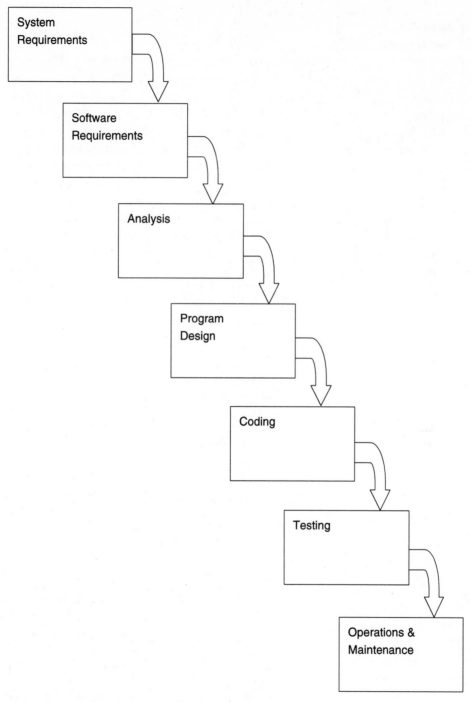

Figure 7.1 Simplistic software development model.

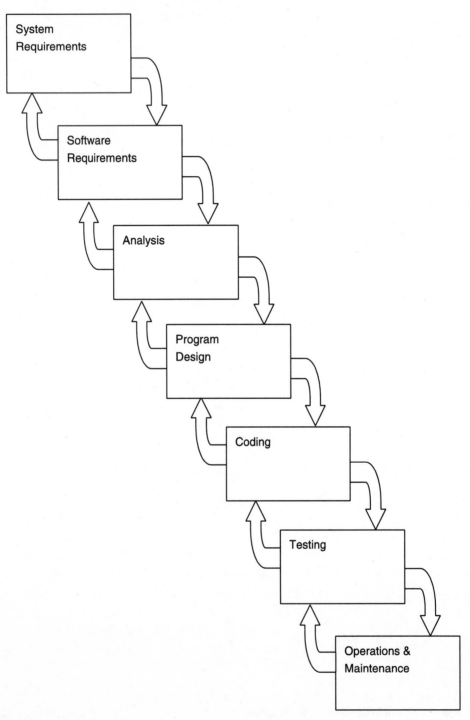

Figure 7.2 The Waterfall model.

approach results in a lack of project control, and it is difficult to manage. The Waterfall model is shown in Figure 7.2.

One fundamental problem with these models is that they assume that a phase or stage ends at a specific time; however, this is not usually the case in real-world applications. If an ending phase is forcibly tied to a project milestone, the situation can be improved. If rework is required in this mode, the phase is not officially pronounced as ending. The rework must then be accomplished and the project milestone met before the phase is officially recognized as completed. In summary, the steps of the Waterfall model are:

- System feasibility
- Software plans and requirements
- Product design
- Detailed design
- Code
- Integration
- Implementation
- Operations and maintenance

In 1976, Barry Boehm reinterpreted the Waterfall model to have phases end at project milestones and to have the backward arrows represent back references for verification and validation (V&V) against defined baselines. Verification evaluates the product during development against the specification, and validation refers to the work product satisfying the real-world requirements and concepts. In simpler terms, Barry Boehm states, "Verification is doing the job right, and validation is doing the right job." These concepts are illustrated in Figure 7.3.

In this modified version of the Waterfall model, the end of each phase is a point in time for which no iteration of phases is provided. Rework can be accomplished within a phase when the phase end review shows that it is required.

The Spiral Model

In 1988 at TRW, Barry Boehm developed the *Spiral* model, which is actually a meta-model that incorporates a number of the software development models. This model depicts a spiral that incorporates the various phases of software development. As shown in Figure 7.4, the angular dimension represents the progress made in completing the phases, and the radial dimension represents cumulative project cost. The model states that each cycle of the spiral involves the same series of steps for each part of the project.

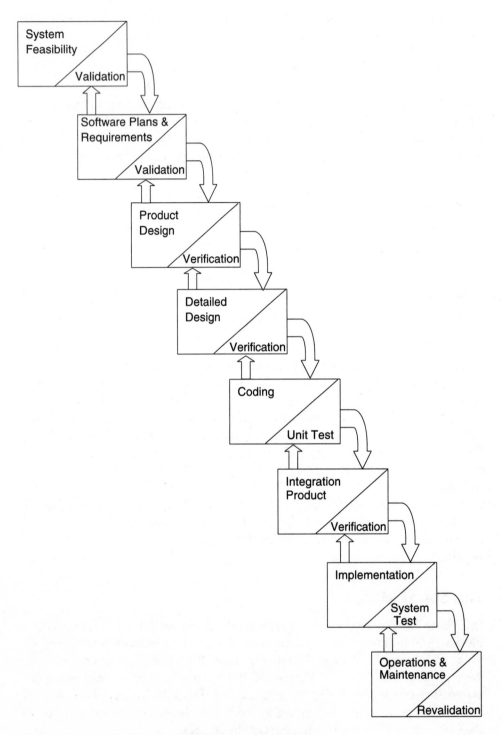

Figure 7.3 A modified Waterfall model incorporating V&V.

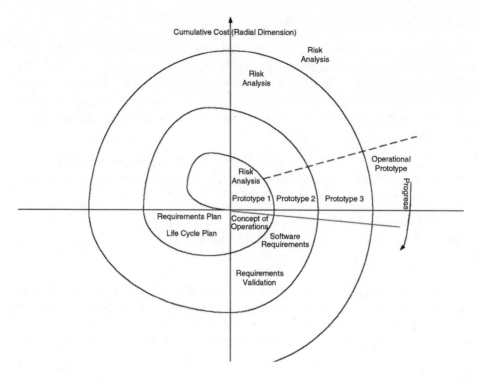

Figure 7.4 The Spiral model.

The lower-left quadrant focuses on developing plans that will be reviewed in the upper quadrants of the diagram prior to finalization of the plans. Then, after a decision to proceed with the project is made, the spiral is initiated in the upper-left quadrant. This particular quadrant defines the objectives of the part of the project being addressed, alternative means of accomplishing this part of the project, and the constraints associated with these alternatives.

The next step involves assessing the alternatives in regard to the project objectives and constraints. This assessment can include prototyping, modeling, and simulation. The purpose of this step is to identify and evaluate the risks involved, and it is shown in the upper-right quadrant of the model. Once these issues are resolved, the next step in this procedure follows the traditional life cycle model approach. The lower-right quadrant of the spiral depicts the final developmental phase for each part of the product. An important concept of the Spiral model is that the left horizontal axis depicts the major review that is required to complete each full cycle.

Cost Estimation Models

An early model for estimating the cost of software development projects was the *Basic COCOMO Model* proposed by Barry Boehm (B.W. Boehm, *Software Engineering Economics*, Prentice-Hall, Englewood Cliffs, New Jersey, 1981). This model estimates software development effort and cost as a function of the size of the software product in source instructions. It develops the following equations:

- "The number of man-months (MM) required to develop the most common type of software product, in terms of the number of thousands of delivered source instructions (KDSI) in the software product"

  $MM = 2.4 (KDSI)^{1.05}$

- "The development schedule (TDEV) in months"

  $TDEV = 2.5(MM)^{0.38}$

In addition, Boehm has developed an *Intermediate COCOMO Model* that also takes into account hardware constraints, personnel quality, use of modern tools and other attributes and their aggregate impact on overall project costs. A *Detailed COCOMO Model* by Boehm accounts for the effects of the additional factors used in the intermediate model on the costs of individual project phases.

Another model, the *function point measurement model*, does not require the user to estimate the number of delivered source instructions. The software development effort is determined by using the following five user functions:

- External input types
- External output types
- Logical internal file types
- External interface file types
- External inquiry types

These functions are tallied and weighted according to complexity and used to determine the software development effort.

A third type of model applies the Rayleigh curve to software development cost and effort estimation. A prominent model using this approach is the *Software Life Cycle Model* (SLIM) estimating method. In this method, estimates based on the number of lines of source code are modified by the following two factors:

- The manpower buildup index (MBI), which estimates the rate of buildup of staff on the project
- A productivity factor (PF), which is based on the technology used

Information Security and the Life Cycle Model

As is the case with most engineering and software development practices, the earlier in the process a component is introduced, the better chance there is for success, lower development costs, and reduced rework. Information security is no exception. Information security controls conception, development, implementation, testing, and maintenance should be conducted concurrently with the system software life cycle phases. This approach is conceptually shown in Figure 7.5.

Testing Issues

Testing of the software modules or unit testing should be addressed when the modules are being designed. Personnel separate from the programmers should conduct this testing. The test data is part of the specifications. Testing should not only check the modules using normal and valid input data, but it should also check for incorrect types, out-of-range values, and other bounds and/or conditions. Live or actual field data is not recommended for use in the testing procedures because both data types might not cover out-of-range situations and the correct outputs of the test are unknown. Special test suites of data that exercise all paths of the software to the fullest extent possible and whose correct resulting outputs are known beforehand should be used.

The Software Maintenance Phase and the Change Control Process

In the life cycle models we have presented, the maintenance phase is listed at the end of the cycle with operations. One way of looking at the maintenance phase is to divide it into the following three subphases:

1. Request control
2. Change control
3. Release control

The request control activity manages the users' requests for changes to the software product and gathers information that can be used for managing this activity. The following steps are included in this activity:

- Establishing the priorities of requests
- Estimating the cost of the changes requested
- Determining the interface that is presented to the user

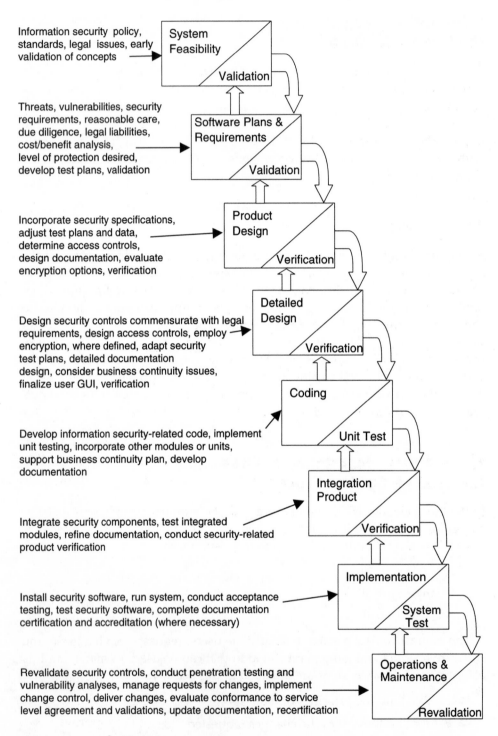

Information security policy, standards, legal issues, early validation of concepts → **System Feasibility** / Validation

Threats, vulnerabilities, security requirements, reasonable care, due diligence, legal liabilities, cost/benefit analysis, level of protection desired, develop test plans, validation → **Software Plans & Requirements** / Validation

Incorporate security specifications, adjust test plans and data, determine access controls, design documentation, evaluate encryption options, verification → **Product Design** / Verification

Design security controls commensurate with legal requirements, design access controls, employ encryption, where defined, adapt security test plans, detailed documentation design, consider business continuity issues, finalize user GUI, verification → **Detailed Design** / Verification

Develop information security-related code, implement unit testing, incorporate other modules or units, support business continuity plan, develop documentation → **Coding** / Unit Test

Integrate security components, test integrated modules, refine documentation, conduct security-related product verification → **Integration Product** / Verification

Install security software, run system, conduct acceptance testing, test security software, complete documentation certification and accreditation (where necessary) → **Implementation** / System Test

Revalidate security controls, conduct penetration testing and vulnerability analyses, manage requests for changes, implement change control, deliver changes, evaluate conformance to service level agreement and validations, update documentation, recertification → **Operations & Maintenance** / Revalidation

Figure 7.5 Security life cycle components.

The change control process is the principal step in the maintenance phase. Issues that are addressed by change control include the following:

- Recreating and analyzing the problem
- Developing the changes and corresponding tests
- Performing quality control

In addition, there are also other considerations such as the following:

- The tool types to be used in implementing the changes
- The documentation of the changes
- The restriction of the changes' effects on other parts of the code
- Recertification and accreditation, if necessary

Release control is associated with issuing the latest release of the software. This step involves deciding which requests will be included in the new release, archiving of the release, configuration management, quality control, distribution, and acceptance testing.

Configuration Management

In order to manage evolving changes to software products and to formally track and issue new versions of software products, configuration management is employed. According to the British Standards Institution (British Standards Institute, U.K., "Information Security Management, British Standard 7799," 1998), configuration management is "the discipline of identifying the components of a continually evolving system for the purposes of controlling changes to those components and maintaining integrity and traceability throughout the life cycle." The following definitions are associated with configuration management:

Configuration Item. A component whose state is to be recorded and against which changes are to be progressed.

Version. A recorded state of the configuration item.

Configuration. A collection of component configuration items that comprise a configuration item in some stage of its evolution (recursive).

Building. The process of assembling a version of a configuration item from versions of its component configuration items.

Build List. The set of the versions of the component configuration items that is used to build a version of a configuration item.

Software Library. A controlled area that is accessible only to approved users who are restricted to the use of approved procedures.

The following procedures are associated with configuration management:

1. Identify and document the functional and physical characteristics of each configuration item (*configuration identification*).
2. Control changes to the configuration items and issue versions of configuration items from the software library (*configuration control*).
3. Record the processing of changes (*configuration status accounting*).
4. Control the quality of the configuration management procedures (*configuration audit*).

The Software Capability Maturity Model (CMM)

The Software CMM is based on the premise that the quality of a software product is a direct function of the quality of its associated software development and maintenance processes. A process is defined by the Carnegie Mellon University Software Engineering Institute (SEI) as "a set of activities, methods, practices, and transformations that people use to develop and maintain systems and associated products"(SEI, "The Capability Maturity Model: Guidelines for Improving the Software Process," Addison Wesley, 1995).

The Software CMM was first developed by the SEI in 1986 with support from the Mitre Corporation. The SEI defines five maturity levels that serve as a foundation for conducting continuous process improvement and as an ordinal scale for measuring the maturity of the organization involved in the software processes. The following are the five maturity levels and their corresponding focuses and characteristics:

Level 1—Initiating. Competent people and heroics; processes are informal and ad hoc.

Level 2—Repeatable. Project management processes; project management practices are institutionalized.

Level 3—Defined. Engineering processes and organizational support; technical practices are integrated with management practices institutionalized.

Level 4—Managed. Product and process improvement; product and process are quantitatively controlled.

Level 5—Optimizing. Continuous process improvement; process improvement is institutionalized.

In the CMM for software, *software process capability* "describes the range of expected results that can be achieved by following a software process." Software process capability is a means of predicting the outcome of the next software project conducted by an organization. *Software process performance* is the result achieved by following a software process. Thus, software capability is aimed at expected results while software performance is focused on results that have been achieved.

Software process maturity, then, provides for the potential for growth in capability of an organization. An immature organization develops software in a crisis mode, usually exceeds budgets and time schedules, and software processes are developed in an ad hoc fashion during the project. In a mature organization, the software process is effectively communicated to staff, the required processes are documented and consistent, software quality is evaluated, and roles and responsibilities are understood for the project.

The Software CMM is a component that supports the concept of continuous process improvement. This concept is embodied in the SEI Process Improvement IDEAL Model and is shown in Figure 7.6.

Phase 1 of the IDEAL Model is the initiation phase in which management support is obtained for process improvement, the objectives and constraints of the process improvement effort are defined, and the resources and plans for the next phase are obtained.

Process Improvement's IDEAL Model

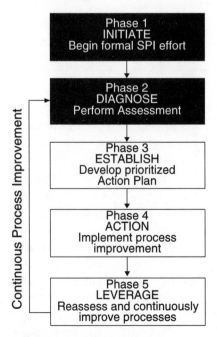

Figure 7.6 The IDEAL model.

Phase 2 identifies the appropriate appraisal method (such as CMM-based), identifies the project(s) to be appraised, trains the appraisal team, conducts the appraisal, and briefs management and the organization on the appraisal results.

In Phase 3, an action plan is developed based on the results of Phase 2, management is briefed on the action plan, and the resources and group(s) are coordinated to implement the action plan.

Phase 4 is the action phase where resources are recruited for implementation of the action plan, the action plan is implemented, the improvement effort is measured, and the plan and implementation are modified based on measurements and feedback.

Phase 5 is the review phase, which ensures that all success criteria have been achieved, all feedback is evaluated, the lessons learned are analyzed, the business plan and process improvement are compared for the desired outcome, and the next stage of the process improvement effort is planned.

The benefits of a long-term, formal software process improvement plan are as follows:

- Improved software quality
- Reduced life cycle time
- More accurate scheduling and meeting of milestones
- Management visibility
- Proactive planning and tracking

Object-Oriented Systems

An object-oriented system has the potential characteristics of being more reliable and capable of reducing the propagation of program change errors, in addition to supporting modeling of the "real world." An object-oriented system can be thought of as a group of independent objects that can be requested to perform certain operations or exhibit specific behaviors. These objects cooperate to provide the system's required functionality. The objects have an *identity* and can be created as the program executes (*dynamic lifetime*). To provide the desired characteristics of object-oriented systems, the objects are *encapsulated*—they can only be accessed through messages sent to them to request performance of their defined operations. The object can be viewed as a "black box" whose internal details are hidden from outside observation and cannot normally be modified. Grady Booch defines encapsulation as "The process of compartmentalizing the elements of an abstraction that constitute its structure and behavior; . . . [it] serves to separate the contractual interface of an abstraction and its implementation." Objects also exhibit the *substitution* property, which means that objects providing compatible operations can be substituted for each other. According to Booch, "An object has a state, behavior, and identity" (Grady Booch, "Object-Oriented Development," *IEEE Transactions on Software Engineering*, Vol. SE-12, No. 2, February 1986, pp. 211–221).

The following definitions are fundamental to object-oriented systems:

Message. A message is the communication to an object to carry out some operation.

Method. A method is the code that defines the actions an object performs in response to a message.

Behavior. Behavior refers to the results exhibited by an object upon receipt of a message.

Class. A class is a collection of the common methods of a set of objects that defines the behavior of those objects. Booch defines a class as "a set of objects that share a common structure and a common behavior."

Instance. Objects are instances of classes that contain their methods.

Inheritance. Methods from a class are inherited by another subclass. Thus, the subclass inherits the behavior of the larger class, or as it is sometimes called, a superclass.

Multiple Inheritance. Multiple inheritance is the situation where a class inherits the behavioral characteristics of more than one parent class.

Delegation. Delegation is the forwarding of a request by an object to another object or *delegate*. This forwarding is necessitated by the fact that the object receiving the request does not have a method to service the request.

Polymorphism. According to Booch, "A name may denote objects of many different classes that are related by some common superclass; thus, any object denoted by this name is able to respond to some common set of operations in a different way."

Polyinstantiation. Polyinstantiation is the development of a detailed version of an object from another object using different values in the new object. In database information security, this term is concerned with the same primary key for different relations at different classification levels being stored in the same database. For example, in a relational database, the name of a military unit may be classified Secret in the database and may have an identification number as the primary key. If another user at a lower classification level attempts to create a confidential entry for another military unit using the same identification number as a primary key, a rejection of this attempt would imply to the lower level user that the same identification number existed at a higher level of classification. To avoid this inference channel of information, the lower level user would be issued the same identification number for their unit and the database management system would manage this situation where the same primary key was used for two different units.

Relative to the software development life cycle phases, object-orientation is applied in different phases as follows:

1. *Object-Oriented Requirements Analysis (OORA).* Defines classes of objects and their interactions

2. *Object-Oriented Analysis (OOA).* In terms of object-oriented concepts, understanding and modeling a particular problem within a problem domain

3. *Domain Analysis (DA).* According to Booch, "Whereas OOA typically focuses upon one specific problem at a time, domain analysis seeks to identify the classes and objects that are common to all applications within a given domain."

4. *Object-Oriented Design (OOD).* Object is the basic unit of modularity; objects are instantiations of a class.

5. *Object-Oriented Programming (OOP).* Emphasizes the employment of objects and methods rather than types or transformations as in other programming approaches

A simple example of a class is the class Airplane. From this class, the object called fighter plane can be created. Other objects called passenger plane, cargo plane, and trainer can also be defined as objects in the class Airplane. The method associated with this class would be carried out when the object received a message. The messages to the object could be Climb, Roll, or Descend.

By reusing tested and reliable objects, applications can be developed in less time and at less cost. These objects can be controlled through an object program library that controls and manages the deposit and issuance of tested objects to users. To provide protection from disclosure and violations of the integrity of objects, security controls must be implemented for the program library. In addition, objects can be made available to users through Object Request Brokers (ORBs). The purpose of the ORB is to support the interaction of objects in heterogeneous, distributed environments. The objects might be on different types of computing platforms. Therefore, ORBs act as the locators and distributors of objects across networks. ORBs are considered *middleware* because they reside between two other entities. ORBs can also provide security features, or the objects can call security services. An ORB is a component of the Object Request Architecture (ORA), which is a high-level framework for a distributed environment. The other components of the ORA are as follows:

■ Object services

■ Application objects

■ Common facilities

The ORA is a product of the Object Management Group (OMG), which is a nonprofit consortium in Framingham, Massachusetts, that was put together in 1989 to promote the use of object technology in distributed computing systems (www.omg.org). *Object Services* support the ORB in creating and tracking objects as well as performing access control functions. *Application Objects* and *Common Facilities* support the end user and use the system services to perform their functions.

The OMG has also developed a Common Object Request Broker Architecture (CORBA), which defines an industry standard that enables programs written in different languages and using different platforms and operating systems to interface and communicate. To implement this compatible interchange, a user develops a small amount of initial code and an *Interface Definition Language* (IDL) file. The IDL file then identifies the methods, classes, and objects that are the interface targets. For example, CORBA can enable a Java code to access and use code written in C++.

Another standard, the Common Object Model (COM), supports the exchange of objects among programs. This capability was formerly known as Object Linking and Embedding (OLE). As in the object-oriented paradigm, COM works with encapsulated objects. Communications with a COM object are through an interface contract between an object and its clients that defines the functions that are available in the object and the behavior of the object when the functions are called. The Distributed Common Object Model (DCOM) defines the standard for sharing objects in a networked environment.

Some examples of object-oriented systems are Simula 67, C++, and Smalltalk. Simula 67 was the first system to support object-oriented programming, but was not widely adopted. However, its constructs influenced other object-oriented languages, including C++. C++ supports classes, multiple inheritance, strict type checking, and user-controlled management of storage. Smalltalk was developed at the Xerox Palo Alto Research Center (PARC) as a complete system. It supports incremental development of programs and run-time type checking.

Object orientation, thus, provides an improved paradigm that represents application domains through basic component definition and interfacing. It supports the reuse of software (objects), reduces the development risks for complex systems, and is natural in its representation of real world entities.

Artificial Intelligence Systems

An alternative approach for using software and/or hardware to solve problems is through the use of artificial intelligence systems. These systems attempt to mimic the workings of the human mind. Two types of artificial intelligence systems are covered in this section:

- Expert systems
- Neural networks

Expert Systems

An expert system exhibits reasoning similar to that of a human expert to solve a problem. It accomplishes this reasoning by building a knowledge base of the domain to be addressed in the form of rules and an inferencing mechanism to determine whether the rules have been satisfied by the system input.

Computer programs are usually defined as:

algorithm + data structures = program

In an expert system, the relationship is

inference engine + knowledge base = expert system

The knowledge base contains facts and the rules concerning the domain of the problem in the form of *if-then* statements. The inference engine compares information it has acquired in memory to the *if* portion of the rules in the knowledge base to see if there is a match. If there is a match, the rule is ready to "fire" and is placed in a list for execution. Certain rules may have a higher priority or *salience*, and the system will fire these rules before others that have a lower salience.

The expert system operates in either a forward-chaining or backward-chaining mode. In a *forward-chaining* mode, the expert system acquires information and comes to a conclusion based on that information. Forward-chaining is the reasoning approach that can be used when there is a small number of solutions relative to the number of inputs. In a *backward-chaining* mode, the expert system backtracks to determine if a given hypothesis is valid. Backward-chaining is generally used when there are a large number of possible solutions relative to the number of inputs.

Another type of expert system is the *blackboard*. A blackboard is an expert system-reasoning methodology in which a solution is generated by the use of a virtual "blackboard," wherein information or potential solutions are placed on the blackboard by a plurality of individuals or expert knowledge sources. As more information is placed on the blackboard in an iterative process, a solution is generated.

As with human reasoning, there is a degree of uncertainty in the conclusions of the expert system. This uncertainty can be handled through a number of approaches such as Bayesian networks, certainty factors, or fuzzy logic.

Bayesian networks are based on Bayes' theorem

$$P\{H \mid E\} = P\{E \mid H\}*P(H) / P(E)$$

that gives the probability of an event (H) given that an event (E) has occurred.

Certainty factors are easy to develop and use. These factors are the probability that a belief is true. For example, a probability of 85 percent can be assigned to Object A occurring under certain conditions.

Fuzzy logic is used to address situations where there are degrees of uncertainty concerning whether something is true or false. This situation is often the case in real world situations. A fuzzy expert system incorporates fuzzy functions to develop conclusions. The inference engine steps in fuzzy logic are as follows:

Fuzzification. The membership functions defined on the input variables are applied to their actual values, to determine the degree of truth for each rule premise.

Inference. The truth value for the premise of each rule is computed and applied to the conclusion part of each rule. This results in one fuzzy subset to be assigned to each output variable for each rule.

Composition. All of the fuzzy subsets assigned to each output variable are combined together to form a single fuzzy subset for each output variable.

Defuzzification. Used when it is useful to convert the fuzzy output set to a quantitative number. One approach to defuzzification is the CENTROID method. With this method, a value of the output variable is computed by finding the variable value of the center of gravity of the membership function for the fuzzy output value.

The Spiral model can be used to build an expert system. The following are the common steps when building a Spiral model:

- Analysis
- Specification
- Development
- Deployment

A key element in this process is the acquisition of knowledge. This activity involves interviewing experts in the domain field and obtaining data from other expert sources. Knowledge acquisition begins in the specification phase and runs into the development phase.

Verification and validation of an expert system are concerned with inconsistencies inherent in conflicting rules, redundant rules, circular chains of rules, and unreferenced values along with incompleteness resulting from unreferenced or unallowable data values.

Neural Networks

A neural network is based on the functioning of biological neurons. In biological neurons, signals are exchanged among neurons through electrical pulses traveling along an *axon*. The electrical pulses arrive at a neuron at points called *synapses*. When a pulse arrives at the synapse, it causes the release of a chemical neurotransmitter that travels across the synaptic cleft to the post-synaptic receptor sites on the dendrite side of the synapse. The neurotransmitter then causes a change in the dendrite membrane post-synaptic-potential (PSP). These PSPs are integrated by the neuron over time. If the integrated PSPs exceed a threshold, the neuron fires and generates an electrical pulse that travels to other neurons.

An analog of the biological neuron system is provided in Figure 7.7. Inputs I_i to the neuron are modified by weights, W_i, and then summed in unit Σ. If the weighted sum exceeds a threshold, unit Σ will produce an output, Z. The functioning of this artificial neural network is shown in the following equation:

$$Z = W_1 I_1 + W_2 I_2 + \ldots + W_n I_n$$

If the sum of the weighted inputs then exceeds the threshold, the neuron will "fire" and there will be an output from that neuron. An alternative approach would be to have the output of the neuron be a linear function of the sum of the artificial neuron inputs.

Because there is only one summing node in Figure 7.7, this network is called a single-layer network. Networks with more than one level of summing nodes are called multi-layer networks. The value of a neural network is its ability to

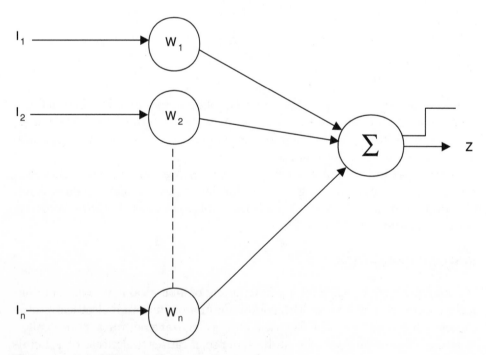

Figure 7.7 A single-layer artificial neural network.

dynamically adjust its weights in order to associate the given input vectors with corresponding output vectors. A "training" period for the neural network has the input vectors repeatedly presented and the weights dynamically adjusted according to the learning paradigm. The delta rule is an example of a learning rule. In the delta rule, the change in weight, $\Delta_{ij} = R^* I_i^* (T_j - Z_j)$ where R is the learning rate, I_i is the input vector, T_j is the target output vector, and Z_j is the actual output of node Σ. For example, if a specific output vector were required for a specific input where the relationship between input and output was non-linear, the neural network would be trained by applying a set of input vectors. Using the delta rule, the neural network would repetitively adjust the weights until it produced the correct output vector for each given input vector. The neural network would then be said to have learned to provide the correct response for each input vector.

Genetic Algorithms

Another type of artificial intelligence technology involves *genetic algorithms*. These algorithms are part of the general class known as *evolutionary computing*. Evolutionary computing uses the Darwinian principles of survival of the fittest, mutation, and the adaptation of successive generations of populations to their environment. The genetic algorithm implements this process through iteration of generations of a constant-size population of items or individuals. Each individual is characterized by a finite string of symbols called *genomes*. The genomes are used to represent possible solutions to a problem in a fixed search space. For example, if the fixed population of the first generation of individuals consists of random binary numbers and the problem is to find the minimum binary number that can be represented by an individual, each binary number is assigned a *fitness value* based on the individual's binary number value. The smaller the binary number represented by a *parent* individual, the higher level of fitness that is assigned to it. Through cross-breeding among the numbers (known as *crossover*), mutations of the numbers, and pairing of the numbers with high fitness ratings, the smallest value that can be represented by the number of bits in the binary number will emerge in later generations.

Database Systems

A database system can be used as a general mechanism for defining, storing, and manipulating data without writing specific programs to perform these functions. A Database Management System (DBMS) provides high-level commands to operate on the data in the database. Some of the different types of databases are as follows:

- Hierarchical
- Mesh
- Object-oriented
- Relational

Much research on information security has been done with relational databases. The information security applications of relational databases are discussed in Chapter 2, "Access Control Systems."

Database Security Issues

In a relational database, security can be provided through the use of *views*. A view is a virtual relation that combines information from other relations. A view can be used to restrict the data made available to users based on their privileges and need to know. A database information security vulnerability can be exploited through the DBMS. Designed to facilitate queries to the database, the DBMS can be a possible source of data compromise by circumventing the normal security controls. The *granularity* of the access to objects in a database refers to the "fineness" in which this access can be controlled or limited. Other database security issues are *aggregation* and *inference*. Aggregation is the act of obtaining information of a higher sensitivity by combining information from lower levels of sensitivity. Inference is the ability of users to infer or deduce information about data at sensitivity levels for which they do not have access privileges. A link that enables inference to occur is called an *inference channel*.

Open Database Connectivity (ODBC) is a Microsoft-developed standard for supporting access to databases through different applications. This access must be controlled to avoid compromising the database.

Data Warehouse and Data Mining

A data warehouse is a repository of information from heterogeneous databases that is available to users for making queries. A more formal definition of a data warehouse is given by Bill Inmon, a pioneer in the field. He defines a data warehouse as a "subject-oriented, integrated, time-variant, non-volatile collection of data in support of management's decision-making process." To create a *data warehouse*, data is taken from an operational database, redundancies are removed, and the data is "cleaned up" in general. This activity is referred to as *normalizing* the data. Then the data is placed into a relational database and can be analyzed by using *On-Line Analytical Processing* (OLAP) and statistical modeling tools. The data warehouse can be used as a Decision Support System (DSS), for example, by performing a time series analysis of the data. The data in the data warehouse must be maintained to ensure that it is timely and valid. The term *data scrubbing* refers to maintenance of the data warehouse by deleting information that is unreliable or no longer relevant. A *data mart* is a database that is comprised of data or relations that have been extracted from the data warehouse. Information in the data mart is usually of interest to a particular group of people. For example, a data mart can be developed for all health care-related data. Searching for data correlations and relationships that were unknown up until now among the data in the warehouse is called *data mining*. The correlations or "data about data" are referred to as *metadata*. The information obtained from the metadata should, however, be sent back for incorporation into the data warehouse to be available for future queries and metadata analyses.

Data mining can be applied to information system security as an intrusion detection tool to discover abnormal system characteristics in order to determine whether there are aggregation or inference problems and for analyzing audit information.

Data Dictionaries

A data dictionary is a database for system developers. It records all the data structures used by an application. Advanced data dictionaries incorporate application generators that use the data stored in the dictionary to automate some of the program production tasks. The data dictionary interacts with the DBMS, the program library, applications, and the information security system. In some instances, the data dictionary system is organized into a primary data dictionary and one or more secondary data dictionaries. The primary data dictionary provides a baseline of data definitions and central control while the secondary data dictionaries are assigned to separate development projects, to provide backup to the primary dictionary and to serve as a partition between the development and test databases.

Application Controls

The goal of application controls is to enforce the organization's security policy and procedures and to maintain the confidentiality, integrity, and availability of the computer-based information. Application security involves the input to the system, the data being processed, and the output of the system. The controls can be classified into preventive, detective, and corrective measures that apply to different security categories. These controls and categories are listed in Table 7.1.

Users running applications require the availability of the system. A *service level agreement* guarantees the quality of a service to a subscriber by a network service provider. Defined service levels provide a basis for measuring the

Table 7.1 Application Control Types

APPLICATION CONTROL TYPE	ACCURACY	SECURITY	CONSISTENCY
Preventive	Data checks, forms, custom screens, validity checks, contingency planning, and backups.	Firewalls, reference monitors, sensitivity labels, traffic padding, encryption, data classification, one-time passwords, contingency planning, separation of development, application and test environments.	Data dictionary, programming standards, and database management system.
Detective	Cyclic redundancy checks, structured walk-throughs, hash totals, and reasonableness checks.	Intrusion detection systems and audit trails.	Comparison controls, relationship tests, and reconciliation controls.
Corrective	Backups, control reports, before/after imaging reporting, and checkpoint restarts.	Emergency response and reference monitor.	Program comments and database controls.

delivered services and are useful in anticipating, identifying, and correcting problems. Some of the metrics in service-level agreements are as follows:

- Turnaround times
- Average response times
- Number of online users
- System utilization rates
- System up times
- Volume of transactions
- Production problems

Distributed Systems

Distributed systems are commonplace and pose special challenges to information systems security implementation. Security in distributed systems should include access control mechanisms, identification, authentication, some type of intrusion detection capability, emergency response plans, logs, and audit trails.

The client/server model implements a type of distributed system. In this model, the client requests services and the server provides the requested service. The client provides the interface to the user, supports the entry of information, and provides the reports. The server provides access to data, holds the databases, provides data to the client, performs backups, and provides security services.

Distributed environments support agents. An *agent* is a surrogate program or process performing services in one environment on behalf of a principal in another environment. This behavior differs from that of a *proxy* in that a proxy acts on behalf of a principal, but it may hide the characteristics of that principal. Similarly, *applets* are small applications that may be written in various languages, which include C++ and Java. Both of these languages are object-oriented. C++ was developed at Bell Laboratories and is an extension of C. Java is a multi-threaded, interpreted language that was developed at Sun Microsystems. A *thread* is considered a "lightweight" process and has a lower overhead for maintaining state and switching contexts. *Multiple threads* run in the protection domain of a task or process, and they share a single address space. An *interpreted* language executes each instruction in real-time. This action is referred to as *run-time binding*. A *compiled* language has all the high-level instructions translated into machine code (object code) by a compiler. Then the computer executes the code. With a compiler, the *binding occurs at compile time*. Compiled code poses more of a security risk than interpreted code because malicious code can be embedded in the compiled code and can be difficult to detect.

Applets can be accessed and downloaded from the *World Wide Web* (WWW) into a web browser such as Netscape. This applet can execute in the network browser and may contain malicious code. These types of downloadable programs are also known as *mobile code*. Java code is designed to run in a constrained space in the client web browser called a *sandbox* for protection of the system. A sandbox is an access control-based protection mechanism and is usually interpreted by a virtual machine such as the Java Virtual Machine (JVM). The Microsoft ActiveX environment also supports the downloading of mobile code written in a language such as Visual BASIC or C++ to Web browsers and thus has the potential for causing harm to a system. ActiveX, however, establishes a trust relationship between the client and the server through the use of digital certificates guaranteeing that the server is trusted. Some security controls that can be applied to mitigate the effects of malicious mobile code are as follows:

■ Configure firewalls to screen applets.

■ Configure Web browsers to restrict or prevent the downloading of applets.

■ Configure Web browsers to only permit the receipt of applets from trusted servers.

■ Provide training to users to make them aware of mobile code threats.

A client/server implementation approach in which any platform can act as a client or server or both is called *peer-to-peer*.

Centralized Architecture

A centralized system architecture is less difficult to protect than a distributed system architecture because, in the latter, the components are interconnected through a network. Centralized systems provide for implementation of the local security and application system controls, whereas distributed systems have to deal with geographically separate entities communicating via a network or through many networks.

Real-Time Systems

Another system classification that is based on temporal considerations rather than on architectural characteristics is real-time systems. Real-time systems operate by acquiring data from transducers or sensors in real time, and then making computations and control decisions in a fixed time window. An example of such a system would be a "fly by wire" control of supersonic aircraft where adjustment of the planes' control surfaces is time-critical. Availability of such systems is crucial, and, as such, can be addressed through Redundant Array of Independent Disks (RAID) technology, disk mirroring, disk duplexing, fault-tolerant systems, and recovery mechanisms to cope with system failures. In *disk mirroring*, a duplicate of the disk is used and in *disk duplexing*, the disk controller is backed up with a redundant controller. A *fault-tolerant* system has to detect a fault and then take action to recover from that fault.

Sample Questions

You can find answers to the following questions in Appendix H.

1. What is a data warehouse?
   a. A remote facility used for storing backup tapes
   b. A repository of information from heterogeneous databases
   c. A table in a relational database system
   d. A hot backup building

2. What does normalizing data in a data warehouse mean?
   a. Redundant data is removed.
   b. Numerical data is divided by a common factor.
   c. Data is converted to a symbolic representation.
   d. Data is restricted to a range of values.

3. What is a neural network?
   a. A hardware or software system that emulates the reasoning of a human expert
   b. A collection of computers that are focused on medical applications
   c. A series of networked PCs performing artificial intelligence tasks
   d. A hardware or software system that emulates the functioning of biological neurons

4. A neural network learns by using various algorithms to:
   a. Adjust the weights applied to the data.
   b. Fire the rules in the knowledge base.
   c. Emulate an inference engine.
   d. Emulate the thinking of an expert.

5. The SEI Software Capability Maturity Model is based on the premise that:
   a. Good software development is a function of the number of expert programmers in the organization.
   b. The maturity of an organization's software processes cannot be measured.
   c. The quality of a software product is a direct function of the quality of its associated software development and maintenance processes.
   d. Software development is an art that cannot be measured by conventional means.

6. In configuration management, a configuration item is:

    a. The version of the operating system that is operating on the work station that provides information security services.

    b. A component whose state is to be recorded and against which changes are to be progressed.

    c. The network architecture used by the organization.

    d. A series of files that contain sensitive information.

7. In an object-oriented system, polymorphism denotes:

    a. Objects of many different classes that are related by some common superclass; thus, any object denoted by this name can respond to some common set of operations in a different way.

    b. Objects of many different classes that are related by some common superclass; thus, all objects denoted by this name can respond to some common set of operations in identical fashion.

    c. Objects of the same class; thus, any object denoted by this name can respond to some common set of operations in the same way.

    d. Objects of many different classes that are unrelated but respond to some common set of operations in the same way.

8. The simplistic model of software life cycle development assumes that:

    a. Iteration will be required among the steps in the process.

    b. Each step can be completed and finalized without any effect from the later stages that might require rework.

    c. Each phase is identical to a completed milestone.

    d. Software development requires reworking and repeating some of the phases.

9. What is a method in an object-oriented system?

    a. The means of communication among objects

    b. A guide to the programming of objects

    c. The code defining the actions that the object performs in response to a message

    d. The situation where a class inherits the behavioral characteristics of more than one parent class

10. What does the Spiral Model depict?

    a. A spiral that incorporates various phases of software development

    b. A spiral that models the behavior of biological neurons

    c. The operation of expert systems

    d. Information security checklists

11. In the software life cycle, verification:
    a. Evaluates the product in development against real-world requirements
    b. Evaluates the product in development against similar products
    c. Evaluates the product in development against general baselines
    d. Evaluates the product in development against the specification

12. In the software life cycle, validation:
    a. Refers to the work product satisfying the real-world requirements and concepts.
    b. Refers to the work product satisfying derived specifications.
    c. Refers to the work product satisfying software maturity levels.
    d. Refers to the work product satisfying generally accepted principles.

13. In the modified Waterfall Model:
    a. Unlimited backward iteration is permitted.
    b. The model was reinterpreted to have phases end at project milestones.
    c. The model was reinterpreted to have phases begin at project milestones.
    d. Product verification and validation are not included.

14. Cyclic redundancy checks, structured walk-throughs, and hash totals are examples of what type of application controls?
    a. Preventive security controls
    b. Preventive consistency controls
    c. Detective accuracy controls
    d. Corrective consistency controls

15. In a system life cycle, information security controls should be:
    a. Designed during the product implementation phase
    b. Implemented prior to validation
    c. Part of the feasibility phase
    d. Specified after the coding phase

16. The software maintenance phase controls consist of:
    a. Request control, change control, and release control
    b. Request control, configuration control, and change control
    c. Change control, security control, and access control
    d. Request control, release control, and access control

17. In configuration management, what is a software library?

    a. A set of versions of the component configuration items

    b. A controlled area accessible to only approved users who are restricted to the use of an approved procedure

    c. A repository of backup tapes

    d. A collection of software build lists

18. What is configuration control?

    a. Identifying and documenting the functional and physical characteristics of each configuration item

    b. Controlling changes to the configuration items and issuing versions of configuration items from the software library

    c. Recording the processing of changes

    d. Controlling the quality of the configuration management procedures

19. What is searching for data correlations in the data warehouse called?

    a. Data warehousing

    b. Data mining

    c. A data dictionary

    d. Configuration management

20. The security term that is concerned with the same primary key existing at different classification levels in the same database is:

    a. Polymorphism

    b. Normalization

    c. Inheritance

    d. Polyinstantiation

21. What is a data dictionary?

    a. A database for system developers

    b. A database of security terms

    c. A library of objects

    d. A validation reference source

22. Which of the following is an example of mobile code?

    a. Embedded code in control systems

    b. Embedded code in PCs

    c. Java and ActiveX code downloaded into a Web browser from the World Wide Web (WWW)

    d. Code derived following the spiral model

23. Which of the following is NOT true regarding software unit testing?

    a. The test data is part of the specifications.

    b. Correct test output results should be developed and known beforehand.

    c. Live or actual field data is recommended for use in the testing procedures.

    d. Testing should check for out-of-range values and other bounds conditions.

Bonus Questions

You can find answers to the following questions in Appendix H.

1. Which of the following is NOT a component of configuration management?

   a. Configuration control

   b. Configuration review

   c. Configuration status accounting

   d. Configuration audit

2. Which one of the following is NOT one of the maturity levels of the Software Capability Maturity Model (CMM)?

   a. Fundamental

   b. Repeatable

   c. Defined

   d. Managed

3. The communication to an object to carry out an operation in an object-oriented system is called a:

   a. Note.

   b. Method.

   c. Behavior.

   d. Message.

4. In an object-oriented system, the situation wherein objects with a common name respond differently to a common set of operations is called:

   a. Delegation.

   b. Polyresponse.

   c. Polymorphism.

   d. Polyinstantiation.

5. What phase of the object-oriented software development life cycle is described as emphasizing the employment of objects and methods rather than types or transformations as in other software approaches?

   a. Object-oriented requirements analysis

   b. Object-oriented programming

   c. Object-oriented analysis

   d. Object-oriented design

6. A system that exhibits reasoning similar to that of humans knowledge-able in a particular field to solve a problem in that field is called:

    a. A "smart" system.

    b. A data warehouse.

    c. A neural network.

    d. An expert system.

7. What type of security controls operate on the input to a computing system, on the data being processed, and the output of the system?

    a. Numerical controls

    b. Data controls

    c. Application controls

    d. Normative controls

8. The Common Object Model (COM) that supports the exchange of objects among programs was formerly known as:

    a. The Distributed Common Object Model (DCOM).

    b. Object Linking and Embedding (OLE).

    c. Object Rationalization and Linking (ORL).

    d. An Object Request Broker (ORB).

9. In a distributed environment, a surrogate program that performs services in one environment on behalf of a principal in another environment is called:

    a. A proxy.

    b. A slave.

    c. A virtual processor.

    d. An agent.

Advanced Sample Questions

You can find answers to the following questions in Appendix I.

The following questions are supplemental to and coordinated with Chapter 7 and are at a level commensurate with that of the CISSP Examination.

These questions include advanced material relative to software engineering, software development, the software *capability maturity model* (CMM), object-oriented systems, expert systems, neural networks, genetic algorithms, databases, the data warehouse, data mining, the *Common Object Model* (COM), client/server architecture and distributed data processing.

It is assumed that the reader has a basic knowledge of the material contained in this chapter. These questions and answers build upon the questions and answers covered in Chapter 7.

1. The definition "the science and art of specifying, designing, implementing and evolving programs, documentation and operating procedures whereby computers can be made useful to man" is that of:

    a. Structured analysis/structured design (SA/SD).

    b. Software engineering.

    c. An object-oriented system.

    d. Functional programming.

2. In software engineering, the term *verification* is defined as:

    a. To establish the truth of correspondence between a software product and its specification.

    b. A complete, validated specification of the required functions, interfaces, and performance for the software product.

    c. To establish the fitness or worth of a software product for its operational mission.

    d. A complete, verified specification of the overall hardware-software architecture, control structure, and data structure for the product.

3. The discipline of identifying the components of a continually evolving system for the purposes of controlling changes to those components and maintaining integrity and traceability throughout the life cycle is called:

    a. Change control.

    b. Request control.

    c. Release control.

    d. Configuration management.

4. The basic version of the Construction Cost Model (COCOMO), which proposes quantitative, life-cycle relationships, performs what function?

   a. Estimates software development effort based on user function categories

   b. Estimates software development effort and cost as a function of the size of the software product in source instructions

   c. Estimates software development effort and cost as a function of the size of the software product in source instructions modified by manpower buildup and productivity factors

   d. Estimates software development effort and cost as a function of the size of the software product in source instructions modified by hardware and input functions

5. A refinement to the basic Waterfall Model that states that software should be developed in increments of functional capability is called:

   a. Functional refinement.

   b. Functional development.

   c. Incremental refinement.

   d. Incremental development.

6. The Spiral Model of the software development process (B.W. Boehm, "A Spiral Model of Software Development and Enhancement," *IEEE Computer*, May, 1988) uses the following metric relative to the spiral:

   a. The radial dimension represents the cost of each phase.

   b. The radial dimension represents progress made in completing each cycle.

   c. The angular dimension represents cumulative cost.

   d. The radial dimension represents cumulative cost.

7. In the Capability Maturity Model (CMM) for software, the definition "describes the range of expected results that can be achieved by following a software process" is that of:

   a. Structured analysis/structured design (SA/SD).

   b. Software process capability.

   c. Software process performance.

   d. Software process maturity.

8. Which of the following is NOT a Software CMM maturity level?

   a. Initial

   b. Repeatable

   c. Behavioral

   d. Managed

9. The main differences between a software process assessment and a software capability evaluation are:

    a. Software process assessments determine the state of an organization's current software process and are used to gain support from within the organization for a software process improvement program; software capability evaluations are used to identify contractors who are qualified to develop software or to monitor the state of the software process in a current software project.

    b. Software capability evaluations determine the state of an organization's current software process and are used to gain support from within the organization for a software process improvement program; software process assessments are used to identify contractors who are qualified to develop software or to monitor the state of the software process in a current software project.

    c. Software process assessments are used to develop a risk profile for source selection; software capability evaluations are used to develop an action plan for continuous process improvement.

    d. Software process assessments and software capability evaluations are, essentially, identical and there are no major differences between the two.

10. Which of the following is NOT a common term in object-oriented systems?

    a. Behavior

    b. Message

    c. Method

    d. Function

11. In object-oriented programming, when all the methods of one class are passed on to a subclass, this is called:

    a. Forward-chaining.

    b. Inheritance.

    c. Multiple Inheritance.

    d. Delegation.

12. Which of the following languages is NOT an object-oriented language?

    a. Smalltalk

    b. Simula 67

    c. Lisp

    d. C++

13. Which of the following items is NOT a component of a knowledge-based system (KBS)?

    a. Knowledge base

    b. Procedural code

    c. Inference Engine

    d. Interface between the user and the system

14. In an expert system, the process of beginning with a possible solution and using the knowledge in the knowledge base to justify the solution based on the raw input data is called:

    a. Dynamic reasoning.

    b. Forward-chaining.

    c. Backward-chaining.

    d. A blackboard solution.

15. An off-the-shelf software package that implements an inference engine, a mechanism for entering knowledge, a user interface and a system to provide explanations of the reasoning used to generate a solution is called:

    a. An expert system shell.

    b. A knowledge base.

    c. A neural network.

    d. A knowledge acquisition system.

16. What key professional or professionals are required to develop an expert system?

    a. Knowledge engineer and object designer

    b. Knowledge engineer and domain expert

    c. Domain expert

    d. Domain expert and object designer

17. An expert system that has rules of the form "If w is low and x is high then y is intermediate," where w and x are input variables and y is the output variable, is called a:

    a. Neural network.

    b. Realistic expert system.

    c. Boolean expert system.

    d. Fuzzy expert system.

18. What is a "subject-oriented, integrated, time-variant, non-volatile collection of data in support of management's decision-making process"?

    a. Data mart

    b. Data warehouse

    c. Data model

    d. Data architecture

19. The process of analyzing large data sets in a data warehouse to find non-obvious patterns is called:

    a. Data mining.

    b. Data scanning.

    c. Data administration.

    d. Derived data.

20. The equation $Z = f[\sum w_n i_n]$, where Z is the output, w_n are weighting functions and i_n is a set of inputs describes:

    a. An expert system.

    b. A knowledge-based system.

    c. An artificial neural network (ANN).

    d. A knowledge acquisition system.

21. A database that comprises tools to support the analysis, design, and development of software and support good software engineering practices is called a:

    a. Data model.

    b. Database management system (DBMS).

    c. Data dictionary.

    d. Data type dictionary.

22. Another type of artificial intelligence technology involves genetic algorithms. Genetic algorithms are part of the general class known as:

    a. Neural networks.

    b. Suboptimal computing.

    c. Evolutionary computing.

    d. Biological computing.

23. The Object Request Architecture (ORA) is a high-level framework for a distributed environment. It consists of four components. Which of the following items is NOT one of those components?

    a. Object Request Brokers (ORBs)

    b. Object Services

    c. Application Objects

    d. Application Services

24. A standard that uses the Object Request Broker (ORB) to implement exchanges among objects in a heterogeneous, distributed environment is called:

    a. The Object Management Group (OMG) Object Model.

    b. A Common Object Request Broker Architecture (CORBA).

    c. Open Architecture.

    d. An Interface Definition Language (IDL).

25. Another model that allows two software components to communicate with each other independent of their platforms' operating systems and languages of implementation is:

    a. Common Object Model (COM).

    b. Sandbox.

    c. Basic Object Model (BOM).

    d. Spiral Model.

26. A distributed object model that has similarities to the Common Object Request Broker Architecture (CORBA) is:

    a. Distributed Component Object Model (DCOM).

    b. The Chinese Wall Model.

    c. Inference Model.

    d. Distributed Data Model.

27. Which of the following is NOT a characteristic of a client in the client/server model?

    a. Extensive user interface

    b. May be diskless

    c. Data entry screens

    d. Systems backup and database protection

28. A client/server implementation approach in which any platform may act as a client or server or both is called:

    a. Simple file transfer.

    b. Peer-to-peer.

    c. Application Programming Interface (API).

    d. Graphical User Interface (GUI).

29. Which of the following is NOT a characteristic of a distributed data processing (DDP) approach?

    a. Consists of multiple processing locations that can provide alternatives for computing in the event of a site becoming inoperative.

    b. Distances from user to processing resource are transparent to the user.

    c. Security is enhanced because of networked systems.

    d. Data stored at multiple, geographically separate locations is easily available to the user.

30. A database management system (DBMS) is useful in situations where:

    a. Rapid development of applications is required and preprogrammed functions can be used to provide those applications along with other support features such as security, error recovery and access control.

    b. Data are processed infrequently and results are not urgently needed.

    c. Large amounts of data are to be processed in time-critical situations.

    d. The operations to be performed on the data are modified infrequently and the operations are relatively straightforward.

CHAPTER

8

Business Continuity Planning and Disaster Recovery Planning

The Business Continuity Planning (BCP) and Disaster Recovery Planning (DRP) domain is all about business. We're not talking about infringements of security policy or unauthorized access; rather, this is about making contingency plans for a business-threatening emergency and continuing the business in the event of a disaster. While the other domains are concerned with preventing risks and protecting the infrastructure against attack, this domain assumes that the worst has happened. It is really two domains in one: BCP is about making the plans and creating the framework to ensure that the business can continue in an emergency; DRP is about quickly recovering from a emergency with the minimum of impact to the organization.

From the published (ISC)² goals for the Certified Information Systems Security Professional candidate:

"The candidate will be expected to know the difference between business continuity planning and disaster recovery; business planning in terms of project scope and planning, business impact analysis, recovery strategies, recovery plan development, and implementation. The candidate should understand disaster recovery in terms of recovery plan development, implementation and restoration."

Our Goals

The CISSP candidate should know the following:

- The basic difference between BCP and DRP
- The difference between natural and manmade disasters
- The four prime elements of BCP
- The reasons for and steps in conducting a Business Impact Assessment (BIA)
- The steps in creating a disaster recovery plan
- The five types of disaster recovery plan tests
- The various types of backup services

We have divided the chapter into two sections, BCP and DRP. Many elements of BCP are also applicable to DRP; we will try to not be too redundant.

Domain Definition

The BCP and DRP domains address the preservation of business in the face of major disruptions to normal operations. Business Continuity Planning and Disaster Recovery Planning involve the preparation, testing, and updating of the actions required to protect critical business processes from the effects of major system and network failures. The CISSP candidate must have an understanding of the preparation of specific actions required to preserve the business in the event of a major disruption to normal business operations.

The BCP process includes the following:

- Scope and plan initiation
- Business Impact Assessment (BIA)
- Business continuity plan development

The DRP process includes the following:

- Disaster Recovery Planning (DRP) processes
- Testing the disaster recovery plan
- Disaster recovery procedures

Business Continuity Planning

Simply put, business continuity plans are created to prevent interruptions to normal business activity. They are designed to protect critical business

---

SO WHAT IS THE DIFFERENCE?

Obviously, these two concepts are so close as to allow combining them into one domain. There are some differences, however. Basically, business continuity planning is the process of making the plans that will ensure that critical business functions can withstand a variety of emergencies. Disaster recovery planning involves making preparations for a disaster but also addresses the procedures to be followed during and after a loss.

---

processes from natural or manmade failures or disasters and the resultant loss of capital due to the unavailability of normal business processes. Business continuity planning is a strategy to minimize the effect of disturbances and to allow for the resumption of business processes.

A disruptive event is any intentional or unintentional security violation that suspends normal operations. The aim of BCP is to minimize the effects of a disruptive event on a company. The primary purpose of business continuity plans is to reduce the risk of financial loss and enhance a company's capability to recover from a disruptive event promptly. The business continuity plan should also help minimize the cost associated with the disruptive event and mitigate the risk associated with it.

Business continuity plans should look at all critical information processing areas of the company, including but not limited to the following:

- LANs, WANs, and servers
- Telecommunications and data communication links
- Workstations and workspaces
- Applications, software, and data
- Media and records storage
- Staff duties and production processes

NOTE The number-one priority of all business continuity and disaster planning is always this: people first. While we talk about the preservation of capital, resumption of normal business processing activities, and other business continuity issues, the main overriding concern of all plans is to get the personnel out of harm's way. If there is at any time a conflict between preserving hardware or data and the threat of physical danger to personnel, the protection of the people always comes first. Personnel evacuation and safety must be the first element of a disaster response plan.

Continuity Disruptive Events

The events that can affect business continuity and require disaster recovery are well documented in the Physical Security domain. Here, we are concerned with those events, either natural or manmade, that are of such a substantial nature as to pose a threat to the continuing existence of the organization. All of the plans and processes in this section are "after the fact"; that is, no preventative controls similar to the controls discussed in the Operations Security domain will be demonstrated here. Business continuity plans are designed to minimize the damage done by the event and facilitate rapid restoration of the organization to its full operational capability.

We can make a simple list of these events, categorized as to whether their origination was natural or human. Examples of natural events that can affect business continuity are as follows:

- Fires, explosions, or hazardous material spills of environmental toxins
- Earthquakes, storms, floods, and fires due to acts of nature
- Power outages or other utility failures

Examples of manmade events that can affect business continuity are as follows:

- Bombings, sabotage, or other intentional attacks
- Strikes and job actions
- Employee or operator unavailability due to emergency evacuation or other issues (these could be either manmade or naturally caused)
- Communications infrastructure failures or testing-related outages (including a massive failure of configuration management controls)

The Four Prime Elements of BCP

There are four major elements of the BCP process:

Scope and Plan Initiation. This phase marks the beginning of the BCP process. It entails creating the scope and the other elements needed to define the parameters of the plan.

Business Impact Assessment. A BIA is a process used to help business units understand the impact of a disruptive event. This phase includes the execution of a vulnerability assessment.

Business Continuity Plan Development. This term refers to using the information collected in the BIA to develop the actual business continuity plan. This process includes the areas of plan implementation, plan testing, and ongoing plan maintenance.

Plan Approval and Implementation. This process involves getting the final senior management signoff, creating enterprise-wide awareness of the plan, and implementing a maintenance procedure for updating the plan as needed.

Scope and Plan Initiation

The Scope and Plan Initiation phase is the first step to creating a business continuity plan. This phase marks the beginning of the BCP process. It entails creating the scope for the plan and the other elements needed to define the parameters of the plan. This phase embodies an examination of the company's operations and support services. Scope activities could include: creating a detailed account of the work required, listing the resources to be used, and defining the management practices to be employed.

NOTE With the advent of the personal computer in the workplace, distributed processing introduces special problems into the BCP process. It's important that the centralized planning effort encompass all distributed processes and systems.

Roles and Responsibilities

The BCP process involves many personnel from various parts of the enterprise. Creation of a BCP committee will represent the first enterprise-wide involvement of the major critical functional business units. All other business units will be involved in some way later, especially during the implementation and awareness phases.

The BCP Committee. A BCP committee should be formed and given the responsibility to create, implement, and test the plan. The committee is made up of representatives from senior management, all functional business units, information systems, and security administration. The committee initially defines the scope of the plan, which should deal with how to recover promptly from a disruptive event and mitigate the financial and resource loss due to a disruptive event.

Senior Management's Role. Senior management has the ultimate responsibility for all phases of the plan, which includes not only initiation of the plan process but also monitoring and management of the plan during testing and supervision and execution of the plan during a disruptive event. This support is essential, and without management being willing to commit adequate tangible and intangible resources, the plan will not be successful.

Because of the concept of due diligence, stockholders might hold senior managers as well as the board of directors personally responsible if a disruptive event causes losses that adherence to base industry standards of due care could have prevented. For this reason and others, it is in the senior managers' best interest to be fully involved in the BCP process.

Also, many elements of the BCP will address senior management, such as the statement of importance and priorities, the statement of organizational responsibility, and the statement of urgency and timing. Table 8.1 shows the roles and responsibilities in the BCP process.

NOTE Senior corporate executives are increasingly being held liable for failure of "due care" in disasters. They can also face civil suits from shareholders and clients for compensatory damages. The definition of "due care" is being updated to include computer functionality outages as more and more people around the world depend upon data information to do their jobs.

Business Impact Assessment

The purpose of a BIA is to create a document to be used to help understand what impact a disruptive event would have on the business. The impact might be financial (quantitative) or operational (qualitative, such as the inability to respond to customer complaints). A *vulnerability assessment* is often part of the BIA process.

BIA has three primary goals:

Criticality Prioritization. Every critical business unit process must be identified and prioritized, and the impact of a disruptive event must be evaluated. Obviously, non-time-critical business processes will require a lower priority rating for recovery than time-critical business processes.

Downtime Estimation. The BIA is used to help estimate the *Maximum Tolerable Downtime* (MTD) that the business can tolerate and still remain

Table 8.1 BCP Department Involvement

WHO	DOES WHAT
Executive management staff	Initiates the project, gives final approval, and gives ongoing support.
Senior business unit management	Identifies and prioritizes time-critical systems.
BCP committee	Directs the planning, implementation, and test processes.
Functional business units	Participate in implementation and testing.

a viable company; that is, what is the longest period of time a critical process can remain interrupted before the company can never recover. It is often found during the BIA process that this time period is much shorter than expected; that is, the company can only tolerate a much briefer period of interruption than was previously thought.

Resource Requirements. The resource requirements for the critical processes are also identified at this time, with the most time-sensitive processes receiving the most resource allocation.

A BIA generally takes the form of these four steps:

1. Gathering the needed assessment materials
2. Performing the vulnerability assessment
3. Analyzing the information compiled
4. Documenting the results and presenting recommendations

Gathering Assessment Materials

The initial step of the BIA is identifying which business units are critical to continuing an acceptable level of operations. Often, the starting point is a simple organizational chart that shows the business units' relationships to each other. Other documents might also be collected at this stage in an effort to define the functional interrelationships of the organization.

As the materials are collected and the functional operations of the business are identified, the BIA will examine these business function interdependencies with an eye toward several factors, such as the business success factors involved, establishing a set of priorities between the units, and what alternate processing procedures can be utilized.

The Vulnerability Assessment

The vulnerability assessment is often part of a BIA. It is similar to a Risk Assessment in that there is a quantitative (financial) section and a qualitative (operational) section. It differs in that it is smaller than a full risk assessment

---

THE FCPA

The Foreign Corrupt Practices Act of 1977 imposes civil and criminal penalties if publicly-held organizations fail to maintain adequate controls over their information systems. Organizations must take reasonable steps to ensure not only the integrity of their data, but also the system controls the organization put in place.

and is focused on providing information that is used solely for the business continuity plan or disaster recovery plan.

A function of a vulnerability assessment is to conduct a loss impact analysis. Because there will be two parts to the assessment, a financial assessment and an operational assessment, it will be necessary to define loss criteria both quantitatively and qualitatively.

Quantitative loss criteria can be defined as follows:

- Incurring financial losses from loss of revenue, capital expenditure, or personal liability resolution
- The additional operational expenses incurred due to the disruptive event
- Incurring financial loss from resolution of violation of contract agreements
- Incurring financial loss from resolution of violation of regulatory or compliance requirements

Qualitative loss criteria can consist of the following:

- The loss of competitive advantage or market share
- The loss of public confidence or credibility, or incurring public embarrassment

During the vulnerability assessment, *critical support* areas must be defined in order to assess the impact of a disruptive event. A critical support area is defined as a business unit or function that must be present to sustain continuity of the business processes, maintain life safety, or avoid public relations embarrassment.

Critical support areas could include the following:

- Telecommunications, data communications, or information technology areas
- Physical infrastructure or plant facilities, transportation services
- Accounting, payroll, transaction processing, customer service, purchasing

The granular elements of these critical support areas will also need to be identified. By granular elements we mean the personnel, resources, and services the critical support areas need to maintain business continuity.

Analyzing the Information

During the analysis phase of the BIA, several activities take place, such as documenting required processes, identifying interdependencies, and determining what an acceptable interruption period would be.

The goal of this section is to clearly describe what support the defined critical areas will require to preserve the revenue stream and maintain predefined processes, such as transaction processing levels and customer service levels. Therefore, elements of the analysis will have to come from many areas of the enterprise.

Documentation and Recommendation

The last step of the BIA entails a full documentation of all of the processes, procedures, analysis, and results and the presentation of recommendations to the appropriate senior management.

The report will contain the previously gathered material, list the identified critical support areas, summarize the quantitative and qualitative impact statements, and provide the recommended recovery priorities generated from the analysis.

Business Continuity Plan Development

Business Continuity Plan development refers to using the information collected in the BIA to create the recovery strategy plan to support these critical business functions. Here we take the information gathered from the BIA and begin to map out a strategy for creating a continuity plan.

This phase consists of two main steps:

1. Defining the continuity strategy
2. Documenting the continuity strategy

Defining the Continuity Strategy

To define the BCP strategy, the information collected from the BIA is used to create a continuity strategy for the enterprise. This task is large, and many

---

THE CRITICALITY SURVEY

A criticality survey is another term for a standardized questionnaire or survey methodology, such as the InfoSec Assessment Method (IAM) promoted by the federal government's *National Security Agency* (NSA), or it could be a subset of the *Security Systems Engineering Capability Maturity Model* (SSE-CMM; see Appendix D). Its purpose is to help identify the most critical business functions by gathering input from management personnel in the various business units. Also, it's very important to obtain senior executive management buy-in and support for the survey, as it requires full disclosure from the business units and a high-level organizational view.

THE INFORMATION TECHNOLOGY DEPARTMENT

The IT department plays a very important role in identifying and protecting the company's internal and external information dependencies. Also, the information technology elements of the BCP should address several vital issues, including:

- Ensuring that the organization employs an adequate data backup and restoration process, including off-site media storage
- Ensuring that the company employs sufficient physical security mechanisms to preserve vital network and hardware components, including file and print servers
- Ensuring that the organization uses sufficient logical security methodologies (authentication, authorization, etc.) for sensitive data
- Ensuring that the department implements adequate system administration, including up-to-date inventories of hardware, software, and media storage

---

elements of the enterprise must be included in defining the continuity strategy, such as:

Computing. A strategy needs to be defined to preserve the elements of hardware, software, communication lines, applications, and data.

Facilities. The strategy needs to address the use of the main buildings or campus and any remote facilities.

People. Operators, management, and technical support personnel will have defined roles in implementing the continuity strategy.

Supplies and equipment. Paper, forms, HVAC, or specialized security equipment must be defined as they apply to the continuity plan.

Documenting the Continuity Strategy

Documenting the continuity strategy simply refers to the creation of documentation of the results of the continuity strategy definition phase. You will see "documentation" a lot in this chapter. Documentation is required in almost all sections, and it is the nature of BCP/DRP to require a lot of paper.

Plan Approval and Implementation

As the last step, the Business continuity plan is implemented. The plan itself must contain a roadmap for implementation. Implementation here doesn't mean executing a disaster scenario and testing the plan, but rather it refers to the following steps:

1. Approval by senior management.
2. Creating an awareness of the plan enterprise-wide.
3. Maintenance of the plan, including updating when needed.

Senior Management Approval. As previously mentioned, senior management has the ultimate responsibility for all phases of the plan. Because they have the responsibility for supervision and execution of the plan during a disruptive event, they must have final approval. When a disaster strikes, senior management must be able to make informed decisions quickly during the recovery effort.

Plan Awareness. Enterprise-wide awareness of the plan is important. There are several reasons for this, including the fact that the capability of the organization to recover from an event will most likely depend on the efforts of many individuals. Also, employee awareness of the plan will emphasize the organization's commitment to its employees. Specific training may be required for certain personnel to carry out their tasks, and quality training is perceived as a benefit that increases the interest and the commitment of personnel in the BCP process.

Plan Maintenance. Business continuity plans often get out of date: a major similarity among recovery plans is how quickly they become obsolete, for many different reasons. The company may reorganize and the critical business units may be different than when the plan was first created. Most commonly, the network or computing infrastructure changes, including the hardware, software, and other components. The reasons might be administrative: cumbersome plans are not easily updated, personnel lose interest or forget, or employee turnover may affect involvement.

Whatever the reason, plan maintenance techniques must be employed from the outset to ensure that the plan remains fresh and usable. It's important to build maintenance procedures into the organization by using job descriptions that centralize responsibility for updates. Also, create audit procedures that can report regularly on the state of the plan. It's also important to ensure that multiple versions of the plan do not exist, because it could create confusion during an emergency. Always replace older versions of the text with updated versions throughout the enterprise when a plan is changed or replaced.

Disaster Recovery Planning

A *disaster recovery plan* is a comprehensive statement of consistent actions to be taken before, during, and after a disruptive event that causes a significant loss of information systems resources. Disaster Recovery Plans are the procedures for responding to an emergency, providing extended backup operations during the interruption, and managing recovery and salvage processes afterwards, should an organization experience a substantial loss of processing capability.

The primary objective of the disaster recovery plan is to provide the capability to implement critical processes at an alternate site and return to the primary site and normal processing within a time frame that minimizes the loss to the organization, by executing rapid recovery procedures.

> **NOTE** It's possible that an organization might not need a disaster recovery plan. While every company may have business units that can withstand lengthy interruptions, perhaps it has been determined that the organization does not have any critical processing areas that require any sort of disaster recovery. In that case, a disaster recovery plan might not need to be implemented; however, we have yet to see a company that doesn't need some type of a contingency plan.

Goals and Objectives of DRP

A major goal of DRP is to provide an organized way to make decisions if a disruptive event occurs. The purpose of the disaster recovery plan is to reduce confusion and enhance the ability of the organization to deal with the crisis.

Obviously, when a disruptive event occurs, the organization will not have the luxury to create and execute a recovery plan on the spot. Therefore, the amount of planning and testing that can be done beforehand will determine the capability of the organization to withstand a disaster.

The objectives of the DRP are multiple, but each is important. They can include the following:

- Protecting an organization from major computer services failure
- Minimizing the risk to the organization from delays in providing services
- Guaranteeing the reliability of standby systems through testing and simulation
- Minimizing the decision-making required by personnel during a disaster

In this section, we will examine the following areas of DRP:

- The DRP process
- Testing the disaster recovery plan
- Disaster recovery procedures

The Disaster Recovery Planning Process

This phase involves the development and creation of the recovery plans, which are similar to the BCP process. However, in BCP we were involved in BIA and loss criteria for identifying the critical areas of the enterprise that the business requires to sustain continuity and financial viability; here, we're assuming that those identifications have been made and the rationale has been created. Now we're defining the steps we will need to perform to protect the business in the event of an actual disaster.

The steps in the disaster planning process phase are as follows:

Data Processing Continuity Planning. Planning for the disaster and creating the plans to cope with it.

Data Recovery Plan Maintenance. Keeping the plans up-to-date and relevant.

Data Processing Continuity Planning

The various means of processing backup services are all important elements to the disaster recovery plan. Here we look at the most common alternate processing types:

- Mutual aid agreements
- Subscription services
- Multiple centers
- Service bureaus
- Other data center backup alternatives

Mutual Aid Agreements

A *mutual aid agreement* (sometimes called a *reciprocal* agreement) is an arrangement with another company that may have similar computing needs. The

---

DISASTER RECOVERY PLAN SOFTWARE TOOLS

There are several vendors that distribute automated tools to create disaster recovery plans. These tools can improve productivity by providing formatted templates customized to the particular organization's needs. Some vendors also offer specialized recovery software focused on a particular type of business or vertical market. Links to these vendors can be found at www.isc2.org.

other company may have similar hardware or software configurations, or may require the same network data communications or Internet access as your organization.

In this type of agreement, both parties agree to support each other in the case of a disruptive event. This arrangement is made on the assumption that each organization's operations area will have the capacity to support the other's in time of need. This is a big assumption.

There are clear advantages to this type of arrangement. It allows an organization to obtain a disaster processing site at very little or no cost, thereby creating an alternate processing site even though a company may have very few financial resources to create one. Also, if the company has very similar processing needs, that is, the same network operating system, the same data communications needs, or the same transaction processing procedures, this type of agreement may be workable.

This type of agreement has serious disadvantages, however, and really should be considered only if the organization has the perfect partner (a subsidiary, perhaps) and has no other alternative to disaster recovery (i.e., a solution would not exist otherwise). One disadvantage is that it is highly unlikely that each organization's infrastructure will have the extra, unused capacity to enable full operational processing during the event. Also, as opposed to a hot or warm site, this type of arrangement severely limits the responsiveness and support available to the organization during an event, and can be used only for short-term outage support.

The biggest flaw in this type of plan is obvious if we ask what happens when the disaster is large enough to affect both organizations. A major outage can easily disrupt both companies, thereby canceling any advantage that this agreement might provide. The capacity and logistical elements of this type of plan make it seriously limited.

Subscription Services

Another type of alternate processing scenario is presented by *subscription services*. In this scenario, third-party, commercial services provide alternate backup and processing facilities. Subscription services are probably the most common of the alternate processing site implementations. They have very specific advantages and disadvantages, as we will see.

There are three basic forms of subscription services with some variations:

- Hot site
- Warm site
- Cold site

Hot Site

This is the Cadillac of disaster recovery alternate backup sites. A hot site is a fully configured computer facility with electrical power, heating, ventilation, and air conditioning (HVAC), and functioning file/print servers and workstations. The applications that are needed to sustain remote transaction processing are installed on the servers and workstations and are kept up-to-date to mirror the production system. Theoretically, personnel and/or operators should be able to walk in and, with a data restoration of modified files from the last backup, begin full operations in a very short time. If the site participates in remote journaling, that is, mirroring transaction processing with a high-speed data line to the hot site, even the backup time may be reduced or eliminated.

This type of site requires constant maintenance of the hardware, software, data, and applications to be sure that the site accurately mirrors the state of the production site. This adds administrative overhead and can be a strain on resources, especially if a dedicated disaster recovery maintenance team does not exist.

The advantages to a hot site are numerous. The primary advantage is that 24/7 availability as well as exclusivity of use are assured. The site is immediately (or within the allowable time tolerances) available after the disruptive event occurs. The site can support an outage for a short time as well as a long-term outage.

Some of the drawbacks of a hot site are as follows:

- It is seriously the most expensive of any alternative. Full redundancy of all processing components (e.g., hardware, software, communications lines, and applications) is expensive, and the services provided to support this function will not be cheap.

- It is common for the service provider to oversell its processing capabilities, betting that not all of its clients would need the facilities simultaneously. This situation could create serious contention for the site's resources if a disaster were large enough to affect a major geographic region.

- There also exists a security issue at the hot site, as the applications may contain mirrored copies of live production data. Therefore, all of the security controls and mechanisms that are required at the primary site must be duplicated at the hot site. Access must be controlled and the organization must be aware of the security methodology implemented by the service organization.

- Also, a hot site might be administratively resource-intensive because controls must be implemented to keep the data up-to-date and the software patched.

Warm Site

A warm site could best be described as a cross between a hot site and cold site. Like a hot site, the warm site is a computer facility readily available with electrical power and HVAC and computers, but the applications may not be installed or configured. It might have file/print servers, but not a full complement of workstations. External communication links and other data elements that commonly take a long time to order and install will be present, however.

To enable remote processing at this type of site, workstations will have to be delivered quickly and applications and their data will need to be restored from backup media.

The advantages to this type of site, as opposed to the hot site, are primarily as follows:

Cost. This type of configuration will be considerably less expensive than a hot site.

Location. Because this type of site requires less extensive control and configuration, more flexibility exists in the choice of site.

Resources. Administrative resource drain is lower than with the maintenance of a hot site.

The primary disadvantage of a warm site, compared to a hot site, is the difference in the amount of time and effort it will take to start production processing at the new site. If extremely urgent critical transaction processing is not needed, this may be an acceptable alternative.

Cold Site

A cold site is the least ready of any of the three choices, but is probably the most common of the three. A cold site differs from the other two in that it is ready for equipment to be brought in during an emergency, but no computer hardware (servers or workstations) resides at the site. The cold site is a room with electrical power and HVAC, but computers must be brought on-site if needed, and communications links may be ready or not. File and print servers have to be brought in, as well as all workstations, and applications will need to be installed and current data restored from backups.

A cold site is not considered an adequate resource for disaster recovery, because of the length of time required to get it going and all of the variables that will not be resolved before the disruptive event. In reality, using a cold site will most likely make effective recovery impossible. It will be next to impossible to perform an in-depth disaster recovery test or to do parallel transaction processing, making it very hard to predict the success of a disaster recovery effort.

There are some advantages to a cold site, however, the primary one being cost. If an organization has very little budget for an alternative backup processing site, the cold site might be better than nothing. Also, resource contention with other organizations will not be a problem, and neither will geographic location likely be an issue.

The big problem with this type of site is that a false sense of security could be engendered by having the cold site. But until a disaster strikes, there's really no way to tell whether it works or not, and by then it will be too late.

Multiple Centers

A variation on the previously listed alternative sites is called *multiple centers*, or dual sites. In a multiple-center concept, the processing is spread over several operations centers, creating a distributed approach to redundancy and sharing of available resources. These multiple centers could be owned and managed by the same organization (in-house sites) or used in conjunction with some sort of reciprocal agreement.

The advantages are primarily financial, because the cost is contained. Also, this type of site will often allow for resource and support sharing among the multiple sites. The main disadvantage is the same as for mutual aid: a major disaster could easily overtake the processing capability of the sites. Also, multiple configurations could be difficult to administer.

Service Bureaus

In rare cases, an organization may contract with a service bureau to fully provide all alternate backup processing services. The big advantage to this type of arrangement is the quick response and availability of the service bureau, testing is possible, and the service bureau may be available for more than backup. The disadvantages of this type of setup are primarily the expense and resource contention during a large emergency.

Other Data Center Backup Alternatives

There are a few other alternatives to the ones we have previously mentioned. Quite often an organization may use some combination of these alternatives in addition to one of the preceding scenarios.

Rolling/mobile backup sites. Contracting with a vendor to provide mobile backup services. This may take the form of mobile homes or flatbed trucks with power and HVAC sufficient to stage the alternate processing required. This is considered a cold site variation.

In-house or external supply of hardware replacements. Vendor re-supply of needed hardware, or internal stockpiling of critical components inventory. The organization may have a subscription service with a vendor to send identified critical components overnight. May be acceptable for a warm site but is not acceptable for a hot site.

Prefabricated buildings. It's not unusual for a company to employ a service organization to construct prefabricated buildings to house the alternate processing functions if a disaster should occur. Not too different from a mobile backup site: a very cold site.

Transaction Redundancy Implementations

The CISSP candidate should understand the three concepts used to create a level of fault tolerance and redundancy in transaction processing. While these processes are not used solely for disaster recovery, they are often elements of a larger disaster recovery plan. If one or more of these processes are employed, the ability of a company to get back on-line is greatly enhanced.

Electronic vaulting. Electronic vaulting refers to the transfer of backup data to an off-site location. This is primarily a batch process of dumping the data through communications lines to a server at an alternate location.

Remote journaling. Remote journaling refers to the parallel processing of transactions to an alternate site, as opposed to a batch dump process like electronic vaulting. A communications line is used to transmit live data as it occurs. This feature enables the alternate site to be fully operational at all times and introduces a very high level of fault tolerance.

Database shadowing. Database shadowing uses the live processing of remote journaling, but creates even more redundancy by duplicating the database sets to multiple servers. See server redundancy in the *Telecommunications* section.

Disaster Recovery Plan Maintenance

Disaster recovery plans often get out of date. A similarity common to all recovery plans is how quickly they become obsolete, for many different reasons. The company may reorganize and the critical business units may be different than when the plan was first created. Most commonly, changes in the network or computing infrastructure may change the location or configuration of hardware, software, and other components. The reasons might be administrative: complex disaster recovery plans are not easily updated, personnel lose interest in the process, or employee turnover might affect involvement.

Whatever the reason, plan maintenance techniques must be employed from the outset to ensure that the plan remains fresh and usable. It's important to build maintenance procedures into the organization by using job descriptions that centralize responsibility for updates. Also, create audit procedures that can report regularly on the state of the plan. It's also important to ensure that multiple versions of the plan do not exist, because it could create confusion during an emergency. Always replace older versions of the text with updated versions throughout the enterprise when a plan is changed or replaced.

Testing the Disaster Recovery Plan

Testing the disaster recovery plan is very important (a tape backup system cannot be considered working until full restoration tests have been conducted); a disaster recovery plan has many elements that are only theoretical until they have actually been tested and certified. The test plan must be created and testing must be carried out in an orderly, standardized fashion and be executed on a regular basis.

Also, there are five specific disaster recovery plan testing types that the CISSP candidate must know. Regular disaster recovery drills and tests are a cornerstone of any disaster recovery plan. No demonstrated recovery capability exists until the plan is tested. The tests must exercise every component of the plan for confidence to exist in the plan's ability to minimize the impact of a disruptive event.

Reasons for Testing

In addition to the general reason for testing we have previously mentioned, there are several specific reasons to test, primarily to inform management of the recovery capabilities of the enterprise. Other specific reasons are as follows:

- Testing verifies the accuracy of the recovery procedures and identifies deficiencies.
- Testing prepares and trains the personnel to execute their emergency duties.
- Testing verifies the processing capability of the alternate backup site.

Creating the Test Document

To get the maximum benefit and coordination from the test, a document outlining the test scenario must be produced, containing the reasons for the test, the objectives of the test, and the type of test to be conducted (see the five following types). Also, this document should include granular details of what will happen during the test, including the following:

- The testing schedule and timing
- The duration of the test

- The specific test steps
- Who will be the participants in the test
- The task assignments of the test personnel
- The resources and services required (supplies, hardware, software, documentation, and so forth)

Certain fundamental concepts will apply to the testing procedure. Primarily, the test must not disrupt normal business functions. Also, the test should start with the easy testing types (see the following section) and gradually work up to major simulations after the recovery team has acquired testing skills.

It's important to remember that the reason for the test is to find weaknesses in the plan. If no weaknesses were found, it was probably not an accurate test. The test is not a graded contest on how well the recovery plan or personnel executing the plan performed. Mistakes will be made, and this is the time to make them. Document the problems encountered during the test and update the plan as needed, then test again.

The Five Disaster Recovery Plan Test Types

There are five types of disaster recovery plan tests. The listing here is prioritized, from the simplest to the most complete testing type. As the organization progresses through the tests, each test is progressively more involved and more accurately depicts the actual responsiveness of the company. Some of the testing types, for example, the last two, require major investments of time, resources, and coordination to implement. The CISSP candidate should know all of these and what they entail.

The following are the testing types:

Checklist test. During a checklist type of disaster recovery plan, copies of the plan are distributed to each business unit's management. The plan is then reviewed to ensure the plan addresses all procedures and critical areas of the organization. In reality, this is considered a preliminary step to a real test, and is not a satisfactory test in itself.

PLAN VIABILITY

Remember: The functionality of the recovery plan will directly determine the survivability of the organization. The plan shouldn't be a document gathering dust in the CIO's bookcase. It has to reflect the actual capability of the organization to recover from a disaster, and therefore needs to be tested regularly.

Structured walk-through test. In this type of test, business unit management representatives meet to walk through the plan. The goal is to ensure that the plan accurately reflects the organization's ability to recover successfully, at least on paper. Each step of the plan is walked-through in the meeting and marked as performed. Major glaring faults with the plan should be apparent during the walk-through.

Simulation test. During a simulation test, all of the operational and support personnel expected to perform during an actual emergency meet in a practice session. The goal here is to test the ability of the personnel to respond to a simulated disaster. The simulation goes to the point of relocating to the alternate backup site or enacting recovery procedures, but does not perform any actual recovery process or alternate processing.

Parallel test. A parallel test is a full test of the recovery plan, utilizing all personnel. The difference between this and the full-interruption test below is that the primary production processing of the business does not stop; the test processing runs parallel to the real processing. The goal of this type of test is to ensure that critical systems will actually run at the alternate processing backup site. Systems are relocated to the alternate site, parallel processing is initiated, and the results of the transactions and other elements are compared. This is the most common type of disaster recovery plan testing.

Full-interruption test. During a full-interruption test, a disaster is replicated even to the point of ceasing normal production operations. The plan is totally implemented as if it were a real disaster, to the point of involving emergency services (although for a major test, local authorities might be informed and help coordinate). This test is a very scary form of test, as it can cause a disaster on its own. It's the absolute best way to test a disaster recovery plan, however, because it either works or it doesn't.

Table 8.2 lists the five disaster recovery plan testing types in priority.

Disaster Recovery Procedures

Like life insurance, these are the procedures that you hope you never have to implement. This part of the plan details what roles various personnel will take on, what tasks must be implemented to recover and salvage the site, how the company interfaces with external groups, and financial considerations.

The primary elements of the disaster recovery process can be separated as follows:

- The recovery team
- The salvage team

Table 8.2 Disaster Recovery Plan Testing Types

LEVEL	TYPE	DESCRIPTION
1	Checklist	Copies of plan are distributed to management for review.
2	Structured walk-through	Business unit management meets to review the plan.
3	Simulation	All support personnel meet in a practice execution session.
4	Parallel Test	Critical systems are run at an alternate site.
5	Full-Interruption Test	Normal production shut down, with real disaster recovery processes.

- Normal operations resume
- Other recovery issues

The Recovery Team

A recovery team will be clearly defined with the mandate to implement the recovery procedures at the declaration of the disaster. The recovery team's primary task is to get the pre-defined critical business functions operating at the alternate backup processing site.

Among the many tasks the recovery team will have will be the retrieval of needed materials from off-site storage, that is, backup tapes, media, workstations, and so on. When this material has been retrieved, the recovery team will install the necessary equipment and communications. The team will also install the critical systems, applications, and data required for the critical business units to resume working.

The Salvage Team

A salvage team, separate from the recovery team, will be dispatched to return the primary site to normal processing environmental conditions. It's advisable to have a different team, because this team will have a different mandate from the recovery team. They are not involved with the same issues the recovery team is concerned with, like creating production processing and determining the criticality of data. The salvage team has the mandate to quickly, and more importantly, safely clean, repair, salvage, and determine the viability of the primary processing infrastructure after the immediate disaster has ended.

Clearly, this cannot begin until all possibility of personal danger has ended. The return to the site might be controlled by fire or police. The salvage team must identify sources of expertise, equipment, and supplies that can make the return to the site possible. The salvage team supervises and expedites the cleaning of equipment or storage media that might have suffered from smoke damage, the removal of standing water, and the drying of water-damaged media and reports.

This team is often also given the authority to declare when the site is up and running again; that is, when the resumption of normal duties can begin at the primary site. This responsibility is large, because many elements of production must be examined before the green light is given to the recovery team that operations can return.

Normal Operations Resume

This job is normally the task of the recovery team, or another, separate resumption team may be created. The plan must have full procedures on how the company will return production processing from the alternate site to the primary site with the minimum of disruption and risk. It's interesting to note that the steps to resume normal processing operations will be different than the steps in the recovery plan; that is, the least critical work should be brought back first to the primary site.

It's important to note that the emergency is not over until all operations are back in full production mode at the primary site (see sidebar).

All three of the implementation elements discussed here involve well-coordinated logistical plans and resources. To manage and dispatch a recovery team, a salvage team, and perhaps a resumption team is a major effort, and the short descriptions we have here should not give the impression that it is not a very serious task.

Other Recovery Issues

Several other issues must be discussed as important elements of a disaster scenario:

- Interfacing with external groups
- Employee relations
- Fraud and crime
- Financial disbursement
- Media relations

Interfacing with External Groups

Quite often the organization might be well equipped to cope with a disaster in relation to its own employees, but it overlooks its relationship with external parties. The external parties could be municipal emergency groups like police, fire, EMS, medical, or hospital staff; they could be civic officials, utility providers, the press, customers, or shareholders. How all personnel, from senior management on down, interact with these groups will impact the success of the disaster recovery effort. The recovery plan must clearly define steps and escalation paths for communications with these external groups.

NOTE One of the elements of the plan will be to identify how close the operations site is to emergency facilities: medical (hospital, clinic), police, and fire. The timeliness of the response of emergency groups will have a bearing on implementation of the plan when a disruptive event occurs.

Employee Relations

Another important facet of the disaster recovery plan is how the organization manages its relationship with its employees and their families. In the event of a major life and/or safety-endangering event, the organization has an inherent responsibility to its employees (and families, if the event is serious enough). The organization must make preparations to be able to continue salaries even when business production has stopped. This salary continuance may be for an extended period of time, and the company should be sure its insurance can cover this cost, if needed. Also, the employees and their families may need funds for various types of emergency assistance for re-location or extended living support, as can happen with a major natural event such as an earthquake or flood.

Fraud and Crime

Other problems related to the event may crop up. Beware of those individuals or organizations that might seek to capitalize financially on the disaster by

---

WHEN IS A DISASTER OVER?

When is a disaster over? The answer is very important. The disaster is not over until all operations have been returned to their normal location and function. A very large window of vulnerability exists when transaction processing returns from the alternate backup site to the original production site. The disaster can be officially called over when all areas of the enterprise are back to normal in their original home, and all data has been certified as accurate.

exploiting security concerns or other opportunities for fraud. In a major physical disaster, vandalism and looting are common occurrences. The plan must consider these contingencies.

Financial Disbursement

An often-overlooked facet of the disaster will be expense disbursement. Procedures for storing signed, authorized checks off-site must be considered in order to facilitate financial reimbursement. Also, the possibility that the expenses incurred during the event may exceed the emergency manager's authority must be addressed.

Media Relations

A major part of any disaster recovery scenario involves the media. An important part of the plan must address dealing with the media and with civic officials. It's important for the organization to prepare an established and unified organizational response that will be projected by a credible, trained, informed spokesperson. The company should be accessible to the media so they don't go to other sources; report your own bad news so as to not appear to be covering up. Tell the story quickly, openly, and honestly to avoid suspicion or rumors. Before the disaster, as part of the plan, determine the appropriate clearance and approval processes for the media. It's important to take control of dissemination of the story quickly and early in the course of the event.

Sample Questions

You can find the answers to the following questions in Appendix H.

1. Which of the following is NOT one of the five disaster recovery plan testing types?
   a. Simulation
   b. Checklist
   c. Mobile
   d. Full Interruption

2. Why is it so important to test disaster recovery plans frequently?
   a. The businesses that provide subscription services might have changed ownership.
   b. A plan is not considered viable until a test has been performed.
   c. Employees might get bored with the planning process.
   d. Natural disasters can change frequently.

3. What is the purpose of the Business Impact Assessment (BIA)?
   a. To create a document to be used to help understand what impact a disruptive event would have on the business.
   b. To define a strategy to minimize the effect of disturbances and to allow for the resumption of business processes.
   c. To emphasize the organization's commitment to its employees and vendors.
   d. To work with executive management to establish a DRP policy.

4. Which of the following is NOT considered an element of a backup alternative?
   a. Electronic vaulting
   b. Remote journaling
   c. Warm site
   d. Checklist

5. Which type of backup subscription service will allow a business to recover quickest?
   a. A hot site
   b. A mobile or rolling backup service
   c. A cold site
   d. A warm site

6. Which of the following would best describe a "cold" backup site?
   a. A computer facility with electrical power and HVAC, all needed applications installed and configured on the file/print servers, and enough workstations present to begin processing
   b. A computer facility with electrical power and HVAC but with no workstations or servers on-site prior to the event and no applications installed
   c. A computer facility with no electrical power or HVAC
   d. A computer facility available with electrical power and HVAC and some file/print servers, although the applications are not installed or configured and all of the needed workstations may not be on-site or ready to begin processing

7. Which of the following is NOT considered a natural disaster?
   a. Earthquake
   b. Sabotage
   c. Tsunami
   d. Flood

8. What could be a major disadvantage to a "mutual aid" or "reciprocal" type of backup service agreement?
   a. It is free or at a low cost to the organization.
   b. The use of prefabricated buildings makes recovery easier.
   c. In a major emergency, the site might not have the capacity to handle the operations required.
   d. Annual testing by the Info Tech department is required to maintain the site.

9. What is considered the major disadvantage to employing a "hot" site for disaster recovery?
   a. Exclusivity is assured for processing at the site.
   b. Maintaining the site is expensive.
   c. The site is immediately available for recovery.
   d. Annual testing is required to maintain the site.

10. When is the disaster considered to be officially over?
    a. When the danger has passed and the disaster has been contained.
    b. When the organization has processing up and running at the alternate site.

   c. When all of the elements of the business have returned to normal functioning at the original site.

   d. When all employees have been financially reimbursed for their expenses.

11. What is the number one priority of disaster response?

   a. Transaction processing

   b. Personnel safety

   c. Protecting the hardware

   d. Protecting the software

12. Put the five disaster recovery testing types in their proper order, from the least extensive to the most:

   a. Full-interruption

   b. Checklist

   c. Structured walk-through

   d. Parallel

   e. Simulation

13. What is the difference between a "parallel" disaster recovery plan test and a "full interruption" disaster recovery plan test?

   a. There is no difference; both terms mean the same thing.

   b. While a full-interruption test tests the processing functionality of the alternate site, the parallel test actually replicates a disaster by halting production.

   c. While a parallel test tests the processing functionality of the alternate site, the full-interruption test actually replicates a disaster by halting production.

   d. Functional business unit representatives meet to review the plan to ensure it accurately reflects the organization's recovery strategy.

14. Which of the following is NOT one of the primary goals of a BIA?

   a. Resource requirements

   b. Personnel safety

   c. Criticality prioritization

   d. Downtime estimation

Bonus Questions

You can find answers to the following questions in Appendix H.

1. Which choice below is the BEST description of the criticality prioritization goal of the Business Impact Assessment (BIA) process?
   a. The identification and prioritization of every critical business unit process
   b. The identification of the resource requirements of the critical business unit processes
   c. The estimation of the maximum downtime the business can tolerate
   d. The presentation of the documentation of the results of the BIA

2. Which choice below is most accurate regarding the information needed to define the continuity strategy?
   a. A strategy needs to be defined to preserve computing elements, such as hardware, software, and networking elements.
   b. The strategy needs to address facility use during a disruptive event.
   c. The strategy needs to define personnel roles in implementing continuity.
   d. All of the above.

3. Which choice below is NOT an element of BCP plan approval and implementation?
   a. Creating an awareness of the plan
   b. Executing a disaster scenario and documenting the results
   c. Obtaining senior management approval of the results
   d. Updating the plan regularly and as needed

4. Which choice below would NOT be a good reason to test the disaster recovery plan?
   a. Testing verifies the processing capability of the alternate backup site.
   b. Testing allows processing to continue at the database shadowing facility.
   c. Testing prepares and trains the personnel to execute their emergency duties.
   d. Testing identifies deficiencies in the recovery procedures.

5. Which statement below is the most accurate about the results of the disaster recovery plan test?
   a. If no deficiencies were found during the test, then the plan is probably perfect.
   b. The results of the test should be kept secret.

    c. If no deficiencies were found during the test, then the test was probably flawed.

    d. The plan should not be changed, no matter what the results of the test.

6. Which statement is true regarding company/employee relations during and after a disaster?

    a. The organization has a responsibility to continue salaries or other funding to the employees and/or families affected by the disaster.

    b. The organization's responsibility to the employee's families ends when the disaster stops the business from functioning.

    c. Employees should seek any means of obtaining compensation after a disaster, including fraudulent ones.

    d. Senior-level executives are the only employees who should receive continuing salaries during the disruptive event.

7. Which statement below is NOT true regarding the relationship of the organization with the media during and after a disaster?

    a. The organization should establish a unified organizational response to the media during and after the disruptive event.

    b. The organization must avoid dealing with the media at all costs during and after the disruptive event.

    c. The company's response should be delivered by a credible, informed spokesperson.

    d. The company should be honest and accurate about what they know about the event and its effects.

8. Which statement is true regarding the disbursement of funds during and after a disruptive event?

    a. Because access to funds is rarely an issue during a disaster, no special arrangements need to be made.

    b. No one but the finance department should ever disburse funds during or after a disruptive event.

    c. In the event senior-level or financial management is unable to disburse funds normally, the company will need to file for bankruptcy.

    d. Authorized, signed checks should be stored securely off-site for access by lower-level managers in the event senior-level or financial management is unable to disburse funds normally.

9. Which statement below is NOT true about the post-disaster salvage team?

    a. The salvage team must return to the site as soon as is possible, regardless of the residual physical danger.

    b. The salvage team manages the cleaning of equipment after smoke damage.

    c. The salvage team identifies sources of expertise to employ in the recovery of equipment or supplies.

    d. The salvage team may be given the authority to declare when operations can resume at the disaster site.

10. Which statement below is NOT correct regarding the role of the recovery team during the disaster?

    a. The recovery team must be the same as the salvage team, as they perform the same function.

    b. The recovery team is often separate from the salvage team, as they perform different duties.

    c. The recovery team's primary task is to get pre-defined critical business functions operating at the alternate processing site.

    d. The recovery team will need full access to all backup media.

Advanced Sample Questions

You can find answers to the following questions in Appendix I.

The following questions are supplemental to and coordinated with Chapter 8 and are at a level on par with that of the CISSP Examination.

It is assumed that the reader has a basic knowledge of the material contained in Chapter 8. Here, we'll discuss business continuity, business resumption, disaster recovery, emergency management, and vulnerability assessments.

1. Which choice below is the MOST accurate description of a warm site?
   a. A backup processing facility with adequate electrical wiring and air conditioning, but no hardware or software installed
   b. A backup processing facility with most hardware and software installed, which can be operational within a matter of days
   c. A backup processing facility with all hardware and software installed and 100% compatible with the original site, operational within hours
   d. A mobile trailer with portable generators and air conditioning

2. Which choice below is NOT an accurate description or element of remote sensing technology?
   a. Photographic, radar, infrared, or multi-spectral imagery from manned or unmanned aircraft.
   b. Photographic, radar, infrared, or multi-spectral imagery from land-based tracking stations.
   c. Photographic, radar, infrared, or multi-spectral imagery from geostationary or orbiting satellites.
   d. RS intelligence may be integrated into geographic information systems (GIS) to produce map-based products.

3. Which disaster recovery/emergency management plan testing type below is considered the most cost-effective and efficient way to identify areas of overlap in the plan before conducting more demanding training exercises?
   a. Full-scale exercise
   b. Walk-through drill
   c. Table-top exercise test
   d. Evacuation drill

4. Which task below would normally be considered a BCP task, rather than a DRP task?
   a. Life safety processes
   b. Project scoping

    c. Restoration procedures

    d. Recovery procedures

5. Which choice below is NOT a role or responsibility of the person designated to manage the contingency planning process?

    a. Providing direction to senior management

    b. Providing stress reduction programs to employees after an event

    c. Ensuring the identification of all critical business functions

    d. Integrating the planning process across business units

6. Which choice below is NOT an emergency management procedure directly relating to financial decision making?

    a. Establishing accounting procedures to track the costs of emergencies

    b. Establishing procedures for the continuance of payroll

    c. Establishing critical incident stress procedures

    d. Establishing program procurement procedures

7. Which choice below is NOT considered an appropriate role for senior management in the business continuity and disaster recovery process?

    a. Delegate recovery roles

    b. Publicly praise successes

    c. Closely control media and analyst communications

    d. Assess the adequacy of information security during the disaster recovery

8. Which choice below is NOT considered a potential hazard resulting from natural events?

    a. Earthquake/land shift

    b. Forest fire

    c. Arson

    d. Urban fire

9. Which choice below represents the most important first step in creating a business resumption plan?

    a. Performing a risk analysis

    b. Obtaining senior management support

    c. Analyzing the business impact

    d. Planning recovery strategies

10. Which choice below would NOT be a valid reason for testing the disaster recovery plan?

    a. Testing provides the contingency planner with recent documentation.

    b. Testing verifies the accuracy of the recovery procedures.

    c. Testing prepares the personnel to properly execute their emergency duties.

    d. Testing identifies deficiencies within the recovery procedures.

11. Which choice below is NOT a commonly accepted definition for a disaster?

    a. An occurrence that is outside the normal computing function

    b. An occurrence or imminent threat to the entity of widespread or severe damage, injury, loss of life, or loss of property

    c. An emergency that is beyond the normal response resources of the entity

    d. A suddenly occurring event that has a long-term negative impact on social life

12. Which choice below is NOT considered an appropriate role for Financial Management in the business continuity and disaster recovery process?

    a. Tracking the recovery costs

    b. Monitoring employee morale and guarding against employee burnout

    c. Formally notifying insurers of claims

    d. Reassessing cash flow projections

13. Which choice below most accurately describes a business continuity program?

    a. Ongoing process to ensure that the necessary steps are taken to identify the impact of potential losses and maintain viable recovery

    b. A program that implements the mission, vision, and strategic goals of the organization

    c. A determination of the effects of a disaster on human, physical, economic, and natural resources

    d. A standard that allows for rapid recovery during system interruption and data loss

14. What is the responsibility of the contingency planner regarding LAN backup and recovery if the LAN is part of a building server environment?

    a. Getting a copy of the recovery procedures from the building server administrator

    b. Recovering client/server systems owned and supported by internal staff

    c. Classifying the recovery time frame of the business unit LAN

    d. Identifying essential business functions

15. Which choice below is the correct definition of a Mutual Aid Agreement?

    a. A management-level analysis that identifies the impact of losing an entity's resources

    b. An appraisal or determination of the effects of a disaster on human, physical, economic, and natural resources

    c. A prearranged agreement to render assistance to the parties of the agreement

    d. Activities taken to eliminate or reduce the degree of risk to life and property

16. In which order should the following steps be taken to create an emergency management plan?

    _____ a. Implement the plan

    _____ b. Form a planning team

    _____ c. Develop a plan

    _____ d. Conduct a vulnerability assessment

17. Place the BRP groups below in their properly tiered organizational structure, from highest to lowest:

    _____ a. Policy group

    _____ b. Senior executives

    _____ c. Emergency response team

    _____ d. Disaster management team

18. Which choice below most accurately describes a business impact analysis (BIA)?

    a. A program that implements the strategic goals of the organization

    b. A management-level analysis that identifies the impact of losing an entity's resources

c. A prearranged agreement between two or more entities to provide assistance

d. Activities designed to return an organization to an acceptable operating condition

19. In which order should the following steps be taken to perform a vulnerability assessment?

_____ a. List potential emergencies

_____ b. Estimate probability

_____ c. Assess external and internal resources

_____ d. Assess potential impact

20. According to FEMA, which choice below is NOT a recommended way to purify water after a disaster?

a. Adding 16 drops per gallon of household liquid bleach to the water

b. Boiling from 3 to 5 minutes

c. Adding water treatment tablets to the water

d. Distilling the water for twenty minutes

21. Which choice below is NOT a recommended step to take when resuming normal operations after an emergency?

a. Re-occupy the damaged building as soon as possible.

b. Account for all damage-related costs.

c. Protect undamaged property.

d. Conduct an investigation.

22. In developing an emergency or recovery plan, which choice below would NOT be considered a short-term objective?

a. Priorities for restoration

b. Acceptable downtime before restoration

c. Minimum resources needed to accomplish the restoration

d. The organization's strategic plan

23. When should security isolation of the incident scene start?

a. Immediately after the emergency is discovered

b. As soon as the disaster plan is implemented

c. After all personnel have been evacuated

d. When hazardous materials have been discovered at the site

24. Place the following backup processing alternatives in order, from the most expensive solution to the least expensive:

_____ a. Warm site

_____ b. Hot site

_____ c. Cold site

_____ d. Mutual aid agreement

25. Which choice below is incorrect regarding when a BCP, DRP, or emergency management plan should be evaluated and modified?

   a. Never; once it has been tested it should not be changed.

   b. Annually, in a scheduled review.

   c. After training drills, tests, or exercises.

   d. After an emergency or disaster response.

26. Which choice below refers to a business asset?

   a. Events or situations that could cause a financial or operational impact to the organization

   b. Protection devices or procedures in place that reduce the effects of threats

   c. Competitive advantage, credibility or good will

   d. Personnel compensation and retirement programs

27. Which choice below is an example of a potential hazard due to a technological event, rather than a human event?

   a. Sabotage

   b. Financial collapse

   c. Mass hysteria

   d. Enemy attack

28. When should the public and media be informed about a disaster?

   a. Whenever site emergencies extend beyond the facility

   b. When any emergency occurs at the facility, internally or externally

   c. When the public's health or safety is in danger

   d. When the disaster has been contained

29. Which choice below is the first priority in an emergency?

   a. Communicating with employees' families the status of the emergency

   b. Notifying external support resources for recovery and restoration

   c. Protecting the health and safety of everyone in the facility

   d. Warning customers and contractors of a potential interruption of service

CHAPTER

9

Law, Investigation, and Ethics

Law, as it applies to information systems security, has multiple facets. A security professional is expected to know and understand what laws apply to computer crimes, how to determine whether a crime has occurred, how to preserve evidence, the basics of conducting an investigation, and the liabilities under the law.

In addition to legal obligations, a security practitioner has ethical responsibilities to the employer, the constituency that is being served, and to the profession as a whole. These ethical factors are delineated by a number of professional organizations, including the International Information Systems Security Certification Consortium (ISC)[2], the Internet Activities Board (IAB), and the Computer Ethics Institute.

Types of Computer Crime

Numerous government and private sector surveys show that computer crimes are increasing. It is difficult to estimate the economic impact of these crimes, however, because many are never detected or reported. It is not unreasonable to assume, however, that computer crimes result in billions of dollars in losses to companies in the worldwide economy. In general, computer crimes fall into two categories—*crimes committed against the computer* and *crimes using the computer*. The following is a general listing of the most prominent types of computer crimes:

- *Denial of Service (DoS) and Distributed Denial of Service*. Overloading or "hogging" a system's resources so that it is unable to provide the required services. In the distributed mode, requests for service from a particular resource can be launched from large numbers of hosts where software has been planted to become active at a particular time or upon receiving a particular command.

- *Theft of passwords*

- *Network Intrusions*. Unauthorized penetrations into networked computer resources

- *Emanation eavesdropping*. Receipt and display of information, which is resident on computers or terminals, through the interception of *Radio Frequency* (RF) signals generated by those computers or terminals. The U.S. government established a program called Tempest that addressed this problem by requiring shielding and other emanation-reducing mechanisms to be employed on computers processing sensitive and classified government information.

- *Social engineering*. Using social skills to obtain information, such as passwords or PIN numbers, to be used in an attack against computer-based systems

- *Illegal content of material*. Pornography is an example of this type of crime.

- *Fraud*. Using computers or the Internet to perpetrate crimes such as auctioning material that will not be delivered after receipt of payment

- *Software piracy*. Illegal copying and use of software

- *Dumpster diving*. Obtaining sensitive data, such as manuals and trade secrets, by gathering information that has been discarded as garbage in dumpsters or at recycling locations

- *Malicious code*. Programs (such as viruses, Trojan horses, and worms) that, when activated, cause DoS or destruction/modification of the information on computers

- *Spoofing of IP addresses*. Inserting a false IP address into a message to disguise the original location of the message or to impersonate an authorized source

- *Information warfare*. Attacking the information infrastructure of a nation—including military/government networks, communication systems, power grids, and the financial community—to gain military and/or economic advantages

- *Espionage*
- *Destruction or the alteration of information*
- *Use of readily available attack scripts on the Internet.* Scripts, which have been developed by others and are readily available through the Internet, that can be employed by unskilled individuals to launch attacks on networks and computing resources
- *Masquerading.* Pretending to be someone else usually to gain higher access privileges to information that is resident on networked systems
- *Embezzlement.* Illegally acquiring funds, usually through the manipulation and falsification of financial statements
- *Data-diddling.* The modification of data
- *Terrorism*

Examples of Computer Crime

The following are some specific instances of computer crimes:

- Klez worm, alias ElKern, Klaz, or Kletz. Klez is a mass-mailer worm that appeared around January 2002 and contains a polymporphic .exe virus called ElKern. In Klez, there is no message text in the body of the email, but the worm portion contains a hidden message aimed at antivirus researchers. KlezH is a later version of the Klez worm that appeared in April 2002 from Asia. Similar to its predecessor, KlezH sends e-mail messages with randomly named attachments and subject fields.
- Distributed DoS attacks against Yahoo!, Amazon.com, and ZDNet in February 2000
- Love Letter (Love Bug) worm released by Onel de Guzman in the Philippines that spread worldwide in May 2000
- Inadvertent transmission of e-mails containing personal client information to 19 unintended recipients by Kaiser Permanente HMO in August 2000
- Penetration of Microsoft Corporation's network in October 2000 by a cracker who gained access to software under development
- Kevin Mitnick's attacks against telephone systems. Mitnick was convicted in 1989 for computer and access device fraud but eluded police and the FBI for more than two years while he was on probation. On Christmas 1995, he broke into the computers of Tsutomu Shimomura in San Diego, California. Tsutomu tracked down Mitnick after a cross-

country electronic pursuit, and he was arrested by the FBI in Raleigh, North Carolina on February 15, 1995.

■ Teenagers in Wisconsin (area code 414) known as the 414 Gang who, in 1982, launched attacks into the Sloan-Kettering Cancer Hospital's medical records systems.

■ The Morris Internet Worm that spread through the Internet in November 1988 and resulted in a DoS. The cause of this disruption was a small program written by Robert Tappan Morris, a 23-year-old doctoral student at Cornell University.

■ Attacks against U.S classified computer systems in 1986 by Germans working for the KGB described in the book *Cuckoo's Egg* written by Clifford Stoll (Clifford Stoll, *The Cuckoo's Egg*, Doubleday, copyright 1989; ISBN 0-385-24946-2). Stoll uncovered this activity after he noticed a 75-cent error in a computer account at the Lawrence Livermore Laboratories.

Laws have been passed in many countries to address these crimes. Obviously, there are jurisdictional problems associated with the international character of the Internet that makes prosecution difficult and sometimes impossible. Some of the international organizations that are addressing computer crime are the United Nations, Interpol, the European Union, and the G8 leading industrial nations.

The rapid development of new technology usually outpaces the law. Thus, law enforcement uses traditional laws against embezzlement, fraud, DoS, and wiretapping to prosecute computer criminals. The issues of digital signatures, e-commerce, and digital currency will certainly have to be addressed by the legal system as these technologies are deployed.

Law

There are many types of legal systems in the world that differ in how they treat evidence, the rights of the accused, and the role of the judiciary. Examples of these different legal systems are Common Law, Islamic and other Religious Law, and Civil Law. The Common Law System is employed in the United States, United Kingdom, Australia, and Canada. Civil Law Systems are used in France, Germany, and Quebec, to name a few.

Example: The United States

Under the Common Law system of the United States, there are three "branches" of government that make the laws. These branches are the legislative branch, the administrative agencies, and the judicial branch. The legislative branch makes the *statutory laws*; the administrative agencies create the *administrative laws*; and the judicial branch makes the *common laws* found in court decisions.

Compilation of Statutory Law

Statutory laws are collected as session laws, which are arranged in order of enactment or as statutory codes that arrange the laws according to subject matter. In the United States at the federal level, the session laws are found in the *Statutes at Large* (Stat.), and the statutory codes are held in the *United States Code* (U.S.C.). The statutory laws for the states are also arranged in these two categories.

Federal statutes are usually cited to the United States Code, and this citation contains the following elements:

- The Code title number (each title is a grouping of statutes dealing with a particular subject matter)
- The abbreviation for the code (U.S.C.)
- The statutory section number within the title
- The date of the edition or supplement

For example, "18 U.S.C. § 1001 (1992)" refers to Section 1001 in Title 18 of the 1992 edition of the United States Code. Title 18 in the United States Code is Crimes and Criminal Procedures, and many computer crimes are prosecuted under this title. The U.S. Computer Fraud and Abuse Act that addresses the use of federal interest computers to commit fraud can be found as "18 U.S.C. § 1030 (1986)" Other titles are as follows:

Title 12. Banks and Banking

Title 15. Commerce and Trade

Title 26. Internal Revenue Code

Title 49. Transportation

Compilation of Administrative Law

Administrative laws are also arranged either chronologically in administrative registers or by subject matter in administrative codes. At the federal level, these arrangements are respectively called the *Federal Register* (Fed. Reg.) and the *Code of Federal Regulations* (C.F.R.). A citation to the Code of Federal Regulations includes the following:

- The number of the C.F.R. title
- The abbreviation for the Code (C.F.R.)
- The section number
- The year of publication

Thus, the reference "12 C.F.R. § 100.4 (1992)" points to Section 100.4 in Title 12 of the 1992 edition of the Code of Federal Regulations.

Compilation of Common Law

Common law is compiled as Case Reporters in chronological fashion and in Case Digests arranged by subject matter.

Common Law System Categories

The main categories of laws under the Common Law system (not to be confused with common law resulting from court decisions) are criminal law, civil (tort) law, and administrative/regulatory law.

Criminal law. Laws about individual conduct that violates government laws enacted for the protection of the public. Punishment can include financial penalties and imprisonment.

Civil law. Laws about a wrong inflicted upon an individual or organization that results in damage or loss. Punishment cannot include imprisonment, but financial awards comprised of punitive, compensatory, or statutory damages can be mandated.

Administrative/regulatory law. Standards of performance and conduct expected by government agencies from industries, organizations, officials, and officers. Violations of these laws can result in financial penalties and/or imprisonment.

Other categories of law under the common law system that relate to information systems are intellectual property and privacy laws.

Intellectual Property Law

The following categories fall under intellectual property law:

Patent. Provides the owner of the patent with a legally enforceable right to exclude others from practicing the invention covered by the patent for a specified period of time. Patent law protects inventions and processes ("utility" patents) and ornamental designs ("design" patents). In the United States, as of June 8, 1995, utility patents are granted for a period of 20 years from the date the application was filed. For patents in force prior to June 8, 1995, and patents granted on applications pending before that date, the patent term is the greater of 17 years from the date of issue (the term under prior law) or 20 years from the date of filing. Design patents are granted for a period of 14 years. Once the patent on an invention or design has expired, anyone is free to make, use, or sell the invention or design.

Copyright. Protects "original works of authorship"; protects the right of the author to control the reproduction, adaptation, public distribution, and performance of these original works; can be applied to software and databases

Trade Secret. Secures and maintains the confidentiality of proprietary technical or business-related information that is adequately protected from disclosure by the owner. Corollaries to this definition are that the owner has invested resources to develop this information, it is valuable to the business of the owner, would be valuable to a competitor, and it is non-obvious.

Trademark. Establishes a word, name, symbol, color, sound, product shape, device, or combination of these that will be used to identify goods and to distinguish them from those made or sold by others

Information Privacy Laws

The protection of information on private individuals from intentional or unintentional disclosure or misuse is the goal of the information privacy laws. The intent and scope of these laws widely varies from country to country. The European Union (EU) has defined privacy principles that in general are more protective of individual privacy than those applied in the United States. Therefore, the transfer of personal information from the EU to the United States, when equivalent personal protections are not in place in the United States, is prohibited. The EU principles include the following:

- Data should be collected in accordance with the law.
- Information collected about an individual cannot be disclosed to other organizations or individuals unless authorized by law or by consent of the individual.
- Records kept on an individual should be accurate and up to date.
- Individuals have the right to correct errors contained in their personal data.
- Data should be used only for the purposes for which it was collected, and it should be used only for reasonable period of time.

- Individuals are entitled to receive a report on the information that is held about them.
- Transmission of personal information to locations where "equivalent" personal data protection cannot be assured is prohibited.

An excellent example of the requirements and application of individual privacy principles is in the area of health care. The protection from disclosure and misuse of a private individual's medical information is a prime example of a privacy law. Some of the common health care security issues are as follows:

- Access controls of most health care information systems do not provide sufficient granularity to implement the principle of least privilege among users.
- Most off-the-shelf applications do not incorporate adequate information security controls.
- Systems must be accessible to outside partners, members, and some vendors.
- Providing users with the necessary access to the Internet creates the potential for enabling violations of the privacy and integrity of information.
- Criminal and civil penalties can be imposed for the improper disclosure of medical information.
- A large organization's misuse of medical information can cause the public to change its perception of the organization.
- Health care organizations should adhere to the following information privacy principles (based on European Union principles):
  - An individual should have the means to monitor the database of stored information about themselves and have the ability to change or correct that information.
  - Information obtained for one purpose should not be used for another purpose.
  - Organizations collecting information about individuals should ensure that the information is provided only for its intended use and should provide safeguards against the misuse of this information.
  - The existence of databases containing personal information should not be kept secret.

The U.S. *Kennedy-Kassebaum Health Insurance Portability and Accountability Act* (HIPAA-Public Law 104–191), effective August 21, 1996, addresses the issues of health care privacy and plan portability in the United States. With respect to privacy, this Act stated, "Not later than the date that is 12 months after the date of the enactment of this Act, the Secretary of Health and Human Services shall submit . . . detailed recommendations on standards with respect to the privacy of individually identifiable health information." This Act further stated "the recommendations . . . shall address at least the following:

- The rights that an individual who is a subject of individually identifiable health information should have:
  - The procedures that should be established for the exercise of such rights
  - The uses and disclosures of such information that should be authorized or required"

The Privacy regulations were reopened for public comment for an additional period that closed on March 30, 2001. In March 2002, HHS proposed changes to the HIPAA Privacy Rule in response to input from health-care related organizations as well as the private sector. The changes were put into effect in August 2002. At the time of this writing, the Security and Electronic Signature Standards are also still in draft form. However, the Privacy regulations state the following in reference to information system security requirements:

"(1) Standard: safeguards. A covered entity must have in place appropriate administrative, technical, and physical safeguards to protect the privacy of protected health information.

(2) Implementation specification: safeguards. A covered entity must reasonably safeguard protected health information from any intentional or unintentional use or disclosure that is in violation of the standards, implementation specifications or other requirements of this subpart."

This information was excerpted as a summary from Appendix D of this text, where additional HIPAA information is provided.

Electronic Monitoring

Additional personal security issues involve keystroke monitoring, email monitoring, surveillance cameras, badges, and magnetic entry cards. Key issues in electronic monitoring are that the monitoring is conducted in a lawful manner and that it is applied in a consistent fashion. With email, for example, an organization monitoring employee email should:

- Inform all that email is being monitored by means of a prominent logon banner or some other frequent notification
  - This banner should state that by logging on to the system, the individual consents to electronic monitoring and is subject to a predefined punishment if the system is used for unlawful activities or if the user violates the organization's information security policy. It should also state that unauthorized access and use of the system is prohibited and subject to punishment.
- Ensure that monitoring is uniformly applied to all employees

- Explain what is considered acceptable use of the email system
- Explain who can read the email and how long it is backed up
- Not provide a guarantee of email privacy

In this context, it is useful to examine the difference between *enticement* and *entrapment*. Enticement occurs after an individual has gained unauthorized access to a system. The intruder is then lured to an attractive area or "honey pot" in order to provide time to determine the origin of the intrusion and eventually the identity of the intruder. For example, a student breaking into a professor's computer might be lured to a file entitled "Final Examination Questions." Entrapment, on the other hand, encourages the commission of a crime that the individual initially had no intention of committing.

Recent legislation has given the U.S. government additional license to monitor electronic communications and computer files. See the discussion on the Patriot Act in the section on Computer Security, Privacy, and Crime Laws.

The Platform for Privacy Preferences (P3P)

The Platform for Privacy Preferences (P3P) was developed by the World Wide Web Consortium (W3C) to implement privacy practices on Web sites. An excerpt of the W3C P3P Specification states, "P3P enables Web sites to express their privacy practices in a standard format that can be retrieved automatically and interpreted easily by user agents. P3P user agents will allow users to be informed of site practices (in both machine- and human-readable formats) and to automate decision-making based on these practices when appropriate. Thus users need not read the privacy policies at every site they visit."

The latest W3C working draft of P3P is P3P 1.0, January, 28, 2002, (www.w3.org/TR). With P3P, an organization can post its privacy policy in machine-readable form (XML) on its Web site. This policy statement includes:

- Who has access to collected information
- The type of information collected
- How the information is used
- The legal entity making the privacy statement

P3P also supports user agents that enable a user to configure a P3P-enabled Web browser with the user's privacy preferences. Then, when the user attempts to access a Web site, the user agent compares the user's stated preferences with the privacy policy in machine-readable form at the Web site. Access will be granted if the preferences match the policy. Otherwise, either access to the Web site will be blocked or a pop-up window will appear notifying the user that he or she must change the privacy preferences. Usually, this situation means that the user has to lower his or her privacy threshold. Microsoft Internet Explorer v6.0 incorporates P3P services.

Although P3P is a step in the right direction for privacy, it does not meet all the requirements of privacy. The *Electronic Privacy Information Center* (EPIC), www.epic.org, is critical of P3P for the following reasons:

- It essentially forces a user to accept privacy levels below that of the U.S. Code of Fair Information Practices to gain access to a Web site.

- Just as notification of "cookies" warnings, when requested, become overwhelming, the user might default to lower privacy levels just to be able to browse the Web, even for non-critical transactions.

- It is complex and confusing.

- P3P, with its standards below that of the Fair Information Practices and anticipated modes of operation, will actually provide less privacy protection to the user than might exist at the present time. This situation will occur because the user might accept lower privacy standards when requested by pop-up screens in order to gain access to a Web site.

- P3P was developed by W3C as a voluntary standard. W3C members include businesses that profit from acquiring information from individuals accessing Web sites, so P3P is not as rigorous relative to individual privacy as it could be.

Even the Center for Democracy & Technology (Washington, D.C.) and the Office of Information and Privacy Commissioner (Ontario, Canada), www.cdt.org/privacy/pet/p3pprivacy.shtml, members of W3C, and supporters of P3P cite the limitations of its use. An excerpt from their paper, P3P and Privacy: An Update for the Privacy Community, March 28, 2000, states, "In our opinion, P3P does not protect privacy, in and of itself. It does, however, help create a framework for informed choice on the part of consumers. Any efficacy that P3P has is dependent on the substantive privacy rules established through other processes—be they a result of regulatory, self-regulatory or public pressure. . . . Individuals and businesses hoping to protect privacy solely through the P3P specification would be wise to review the Fair Information Practice Principles. A quick read should convince even the most optimistic of P3P supporters that P3P is neither designed nor suited for addressing all critical elements of privacy protections."

Computer Security, Privacy, and Crime Laws

The following is a summary of laws, regulations, and directives that lists requirements pertaining to the protection of computer-related information:

1970 U.S. Fair Credit Reporting Act. Covers consumer reporting agencies

1970 U.S. Racketeer Influenced and Corrupt Organization (RICO) Act. Addresses both criminal and civil crimes involving racketeers influencing the operation of legitimate businesses; crimes cited in this act include mail fraud, securities fraud, and the use of a computer to perpetrate fraud

1973 U.S. Code of Fair Information Practices. Applies to personal record-keeping

1974 U.S. Privacy Act. Applies to federal agencies, provides for the protection of information about private individuals that is held in federal databases, and grants access by the individual to these databases

1980 Organization for Economic Cooperation and Development (OECD) Guidelines. Provides for data collection limitations, the quality of the data, specifications of the purpose for data collection, limitations on data use, information security safeguards, openness, participation by the individual on whom the data is being collected, and accountability of the data controller

1984 U.S. Medical Computer Crime Act. Addresses illegal access or alteration of computerized medical records through phone or data networks

1984 (strengthened in 1986 and 1994) First U.S. Federal Computer Crime Law Passed. Covered classified defense or foreign relations information, records of financial institutions or credit reporting agencies, and government computers. Unauthorized access or access in excess of authorization became a felony for classified information and a misdemeanor for financial information. This law made it a misdemeanor to knowingly access a U.S. Government computer without or beyond authorization if the U.S government's use of the computer would be affected.

1986 (amended in 1996) U.S. Computer Fraud and Abuse Act. Clarified the 1984 law and added three new crimes:

1. When use of a federal interest computer furthers an intended fraud

2. When altering, damaging, or destroying information in a federal interest computer or preventing the use of the computer or

information that causes a loss of $1,000 or more or could impair medical treatment

3. Trafficking in computer passwords if it affects interstate or foreign commerce or permits unauthorized access to government computers

1986 U.S. Electronic Communications Privacy Act. Prohibits eavesdropping or the interception of message contents without distinguishing between private or public systems

1987 U.S. Computer Security Act. Places requirements on federal government agencies to conduct security-related training, to identify sensitive systems, and to develop a security plan for those sensitive systems. A category of sensitive information called *Sensitive But Unclassified* (SBU) has to be considered. This category, formerly called Sensitive Unclassified Information (SUI), pertains to information below the government's classified level that is important enough to protect, such as medical information, financial information, and research and development knowledge. This act also partitioned the government's responsibility for security between the National Institute of Standards and Technology (NIST) and the National Security Agency (NSA). NIST was given responsibility for information security in general, primarily for the commercial and SBU arenas, and NSA retained the responsibility for cryptography for classified government and military applications.

1990 United Kingdom Computer Misuse Act. Defines computer-related criminal offenses

1991 U.S. Federal Sentencing Guidelines. Provides punishment guidelines for those found guilty of breaking federal law. These guidelines are as follows:

1. Treat the unauthorized possession of information without the intent to profit from the information as a crime.
2. Address both individuals and organizations.
3. Make the degree of punishment a function of the extent to which the organization has demonstrated *due diligence (due care or reasonable care)* in establishing a prevention and detection program.
4. Invoke the *prudent man rule* that requires senior officials to perform their duties with the care that ordinary, prudent people would exercise under similar circumstances.
5. Place responsibility on senior organizational management for the prevention and detection programs with fines of up to $290 million for nonperformance.

1992 OECD Guidelines to Serve as a Total Security Framework. The Framework includes laws, policies, technical and administrative measures, and education.

1994 U.S. Communications Assistance for Law Enforcement Act. Requires all communications carriers to make wiretaps possible

1994 U.S. Computer Abuse Amendments Act. This act accomplished the following:

1. Changed the federal interest computer to a computer used in interstate commerce or communications
2. Covers viruses and worms
3. Included intentional damage as well as damage done with "reckless disregard of substantial and unjustifiable risk"
4. Limited imprisonment for the unintentional damage to one year
5. Provides for civil action to obtain compensatory damages or other relief

1995 Council Directive (Law) on Data Protection for the European Union (EU). Declares that each EU nation is to enact protections similar to those of the OECD Guidelines

1996 U.S. Economic and Protection of Proprietary Information Act. Addresses industrial and corporate espionage and extends the definition of property to include proprietary economic information in order to cover the theft of this information

1996 U.S. Kennedy-Kassebaum Health Insurance and Portability Accountability Act (HIPAA), with the additional requirements added in December 2000. Addresses the issues of personal health care information privacy, security, transactions and code sets, unique identifiers, and health plan portability in the United States. An overview of HIPAA is given in Appendix F.

1996 U.S. National Information Infrastructure Protection Act. Enacted in October 1996 as part of Public Law 104-294, it amended the Computer Fraud and Abuse Act, which is codified at 18 U.S.C. § 1030. The amended Computer Fraud and Abuse Act is patterned after the OECD Guidelines for the Security of Information Systems and addresses the protection of the confidentiality, integrity, and availability of data and systems. This path is intended to encourage other countries to adopt a similar framework, thus creating a more uniform approach to addressing computer crime in the existing global information infrastructure.

1998 U.S. Digital Millennium Copyright Act (DMCA). The DMCA prohibits trading, manufacturing, or selling in any way that is intended to bypass copyright protection mechanisms. It also addresses ISPs that unknowingly support the posting of copyrighted material by subscribers. If the ISP is notified that the material is copyrighted, the ISP must remove the material. Additionally, if the posting party proves that the removed material was of "lawful use," the ISP must restore the material and notify the copyright owner within 14 business days. Two important rulings regarding the DMCA were made in 2001. The rulings involved DeCSS, which is a program that bypasses the Content Scrambling System (CSS) software used to prevent the viewing of DVD movie disks on unlicensed platforms. In a trade secrecy case (*DVD-CCA v. Banner*), the California appellate court overturned a lower court ruling that an individual who posted DeCSS on the Internet had revealed the trade secret of CSS. The appeals court has reversed an injunction on the posting of DeCSS, stating that the code is speech protected by the First Amendment.

The second case (*Universal City v. Reimerdes*) was the first constitutional challenge to DMCA anticircumvention rules. The case involved Eric Corley, the publisher of the hacker magazine *2600 Magazine*. Corley was covering the DeCSS situation, and as part of that coverage he posted DeCSS on his publication's Web site. The trial and appellate courts both ruled that the posting violated the DMCA and was, therefore, illegal. This ruling upheld the DMCA. It appears that there will be more challenges to DMCA in the future.

1999 U.S. Uniform Computers Information Transactions Act (UCITA). The National Commissioners on Uniform State Laws (NCCUSL) voted to approve the Uniform Computers Information Transactions Act (UCITA) on July 29, 1999. This legislation, which will have to be enacted state-by-state, will greatly affect libraries' access to and use of software packages. It also will keep in place the current licensing practices of software vendors. At present, shrink-wrap or click-wrap licenses limit rights that are normally granted under copyright law. Under Section 109 of the U.S. 1976 Copyright Act, the first sale provision permits "the owner of a particular copy without the authority of the copyright owner, to sell or otherwise dispose of the possession of that copy." The software manufacturers use the term "license" in their transactions, however. As opposed to the word "sale," the term "license" denotes that the software manufacturers are permitting users to use a copy of their software. Thus, the software vendor still owns the software. Until each state enacts the legislation, it is not clear whether shrink-wrap licenses that restrict users' rights under copyright law are legally enforceable. For clarification, shrink-wrap licenses physically accompany a disk while click-on and active click-wrap licenses are usually transmitted electronically. Sometimes, the term shrink-wrap is interpreted to mean both physical and electronic licenses to use software. The focus of the UCITA legislation is not on the physical media but on the information contained on the media.

2000 U.S. Congress Electronic Signatures in Global and National Commerce Act ("ESIGN"). Facilitates the use of electronic records and signatures in interstate and foreign commerce by ensuring the validity and legal effect of contracts entered into electronically. An important provision of the act requires that businesses obtain electronic consent or confirmation from consumers to receive information electronically that a law normally requires to be in writing.

The legislation is intent on preserving the consumers' rights under consumer protection laws and went to extraordinary measures to meet this goal. Thus, a business must receive confirmation from the consumer in electronic format that the consumer consents to receiving information electronically that used to be in written form. This provision ensures that the consumer has access to the Internet and is familiar with the basics of electronic communications.

2001 U.S. Provide Appropriate Tools Required to Intercept and Obstruct Terrorism (PATRIOT) Act. This act permits the:

- Subpoena of electronic records
- Monitoring of Internet communications
- Search and seizure of information on live systems (including routers and servers), backups, and archives

This act gives the U.S. government new powers to subpoena electronic records and to monitor Internet traffic. In monitoring information, the government can require the assistance of ISPs and network operators. This monitoring can even extend into individual organizations. In the Patriot Act, Congress permits investigators to gather information about email without having to show probable cause that the person to be monitored had committed a crime or was intending to commit a crime. Routers, servers, backups, and so on now fall under existing search and seizure laws. A new twist is delayed notification of a search warrant. Under the Patriot Act, if it suspected that notification of a search warrant would cause a suspect to flee, a search can be conducted before notification of a search warrant is given.

Generally Accepted Systems Security Principles (GASSP). These items are not laws but are accepted principles that have a foundation in the OECD Guidelines:

1. Computer security supports the mission of the organization.
2. Computer security is an integral element of sound management.
3. Computer security should be cost-effective.
4. Systems owners have security responsibilities outside their organizations.
5. Computer security responsibilities and accountability should be made explicit.
6. Computer security requires a comprehensive and integrated approach.
7. Computer security should be periodically reassessed.
8. Computer security is constrained by societal factors.

Investigation

The field of investigating computer crime is also known as *computer forensics*. Specifically, computer forensics is the collecting of information from and about computer systems that is admissible in a court of law.

Computer Investigation Issues

Because of the nature of information that is stored on the computer, investigating and prosecuting computer criminal cases have unique issues, such as the following:

- Investigators and prosecutors have a compressed time frame for the investigation.
- The information is intangible.
- The investigation might interfere with the normal conduct of the business of an organization.
- There might be difficulty in gathering the evidence.
- Data associated with the criminal investigation might be located on the same computer as data needed for the normal conduct of business (co-mingling of data).
- In many instances, an expert or specialist is required.
- Locations involved in the crime might be geographically separated by long distances in different jurisdictions. This separation might result in differences in laws, attitudes toward computer crimes, definitions of computer crimes, as well as difficulty in obtaining search warrants, lack of cooperation, and so forth.
- Many jurisdictions have expanded the definition of property to include electronic information.

Evidence

The gathering, control, storage, and preservation of evidence are extremely critical in any legal investigation. Because the evidence involved in a computer crime might be intangible and subject to easy modification without a trace, evidence must be carefully handled and controlled throughout its entire life cycle. Specifically, there is a *chain of evidence* that one must follow and protect. The following are the major components of this chain of evidence:

- Location of evidence when obtained
- Time evidence was obtained
- Identification of individual(s) who discovered evidence
- Identification of individual(s) who secured evidence
- Identification of individual(s) who controlled evidence and/or who maintained possession of that evidence

The *evidence life cycle* covers the evidence gathering and application process. This life cycle has the following components:

- Discovery and recognition
- Protection
- Recording
- Collection
  - Collect all relevant storage media.
  - Make an image of the hard disk before removing power.
  - Print out the screen.
  - Avoid degaussing equipment.
- Identification (tagging and marking)
- Preservation
  - Protect magnetic media from erasure.
  - Store in a proper environment.
- Transportation
- Presentation in a court of law
- Return of evidence to owner

Evidence Admissibility

To be admissible in a court of law, evidence must meet certain stringent requirements. The evidence must be *relevant, legally permissible, reliable,* properly *identified*, and properly *preserved*. The main points of these requirements are as follows:

Relevant. The evidence is related to the crime in that it shows that the crime has been committed, can provide information describing the crime, can provide information as to the perpetrator's motives, can verify what had occurred, and can fix the crime's time of occurrence.

Legally permissible. The evidence was obtained in a lawful manner.

Reliability. The evidence has not been tampered with or modified.

Identification. The evidence is properly identified without changing or damaging the evidence. In computer forensics, this process includes the following:

- Labeling printouts with permanent markers
- Identifying the operating system used, the hardware types, and so on
- Recording serial numbers
- Marking evidence without damaging it or by placing it in sealed containers that are marked

Preservation. The evidence is not subject to damage or destruction. The following are the recommended procedures for preservation:

- Do not prematurely remove power.
- Back up the hard disk image by using disk imaging hardware or software.
- Avoid placing magnetic media in the proximity of sources of magnetic fields.
- Store media in a dust- and smoke-free environment at a proper temperature and humidity.
- Write-protect media.
- Authenticate the file system by creating a digital signature based on the contents of a file or disk sector. One-way hash algorithms, such as the Secure Hash Algorithm (SHA) as described in Chapter 4, "Cryptography," can be used.

Types of Evidence

Legal evidence can be classified into the following types.

Best evidence. Original or primary evidence rather than a copy or duplicate of the evidence

Secondary evidence. A copy of evidence or oral description of its contents; not as reliable as best evidence

Direct evidence. Proves or disproves a specific act through oral testimony based on information gathered through the witness's five senses

Conclusive evidence. Incontrovertible; overrides all other evidence

Opinions. The following are the two types of opinions:

- *Expert.* Can offer an opinion based on personal expertise and facts
- *Nonexpert.* Can testify only as to facts

Circumstantial evidence. Inference of information from other, intermediate, relevant facts

Hearsay evidence (third party). Evidence that is not based on personal, firsthand knowledge of the witness but that was obtained from another source. Under the U.S. Federal Rules of Evidence (803), hearsay evidence is generally not admissible in court. Computer-generated records and other business records fall under the category of hearsay evidence because these records cannot be proven accurate and reliable. This inadmissibility is known as the hearsay rule. However, there are certain exceptions to the *hearsay rule* for records that are:

- Made during the regular conduct of business and authenticated by witnesses familiar with their use
- Relied upon in the regular course of business
- Made by a person with knowledge of the records
- Made by a person with information transmitted by a person with knowledge
- Made at or near the time of occurrence of the act being investigated
- In the custody of the witness on a regular basis

Searching and Seizing Computers

The U.S. Department of Justice (DOJ) Computer Crime and Intellectual Property Section (CCIPS) has issued the publication *Searching and Seizing Computers and Obtaining Evidence in Criminal Investigations* (January 2001). The document introduction states, "This publication provides a comprehensive guide to the legal issues that arise when federal law enforcement agents search and seize computers and obtain electronic evidence in criminal investigations. The topics covered include the application of the Fourth Amendment to computers and the Internet, the Electronic Communications and Privacy Act, workplace privacy, the law of electronic surveillance and evidentiary information system security uses." The document also cites the following U.S. Codes relating to searching and seizing computers:

18 U.S.C. § 12510. Definitions

18 U.S.C. § 2511. Interception and disclosure of wire, oral, or electronic communications prohibited

18 U.S.C. § 2701. Unlawful access to stored communications

18 U.S.C. § 2702. Disclosure of contents

18 U.S.C. § 2703. Requirements for governmental access

18 U.S.C. § 2705. Delayed notice

18 U.S.C. § 2711. Definitions

18 U.S.C. § 2000aa. Searches and seizures by government officers and employees in connection with the investigation or prosecution of criminal offenses

The headings of these codes illustrate the areas covered and, in general, the increased concern for the privacy of the individual.

Export Issues and Technology

In July 2000, the U.S. announced a relaxation of its encryption export policy to certain countries. To quote the President's Chief of Staff, John D. Podesta, "Under our new policy, American companies can export any encryption product to any end user in the European Union and eight other trading partners. We're also speeding up the time to market by eliminating the thirty-day waiting period when exporting encryption goods to these countries." Podesta also pointed out the effect that advancing technology has had on the *Electronic Communications and Privacy Act* (ECPA). He pointed out that "ECPA, like its predecessors, has, in many ways, become outdated by the new advances in computer technology and electronic communication. Since its passage in 1986, we've seen a communications revolution with the explosion of the cell phone and the development and use of the World Wide Web. Today, there more than 95 million cell phone users, and more than 50 million households on line in the United States. More than 1.4 billion e-mails [sic] change hands every day . . . ECPA was not devised to address many of the issues related to these newer, faster means of electronic communication. It doesn't extend the stringent Title III protections to the capture of email that you send to your friends or business partners." Podesta cited legislation, which is being proposed to amend existing statutes and outmoded language, which applies primarily to wiretapping and to define protections for hardware and software systems in general.

Conducting the Investigation

There are many issues involved in the conduct of an investigation of suspected computer crime. For example, in a corporate environment, an investigation should involve management, corporate security, human resources, the legal department, and other appropriate staff members. The act of investigating may also affect critical operations. For example, it may prompt a suspect to commit retaliatory acts that may compromise data or result in a DoS, generate negative publicity, or open individual privacy issues. Thus, it is important to prepare a plan beforehand on how to handle reports of suspected computer crimes. A committee of appropriate personnel should be set up beforehand to address the following issues:

- Establishing a prior liaison with law enforcement
- Deciding when and whether to bring in law enforcement (in the United States, the FBI and Secret Service have jurisdiction over computer crimes)
- Setting up means of reporting computer crimes
- Establishing procedures for handling and processing reports of computer crime
- Planning for and conducting investigations
- Involving senior management and the appropriate departments, such as legal, internal audit, information systems, and human resources
- Ensuring the proper collection of evidence, which includes identification and protection of the various storage media

If a computer crime is suspected, it is important not to alert the suspect. A preliminary investigation should be conducted to determine whether a crime has been committed by examining the audit records and system logs, interviewing witnesses, and assessing the damage incurred. It is critical to determine whether disclosure to legal authorities is required by law or regulation. U.S. Federal Sentencing Guidelines require organizations to report criminal acts. There are a number of pertinent issues to consider relative to outside disclosure. Negative publicity resulting in a lack of confidence in the business of the organization is an obvious concern. Once an outside entity such as law enforcement is involved, information dissemination is out of the hands of the organization. Law enforcement involvement necessarily involves support from the organization in terms of personnel time.

The timing of requesting outside assistance from law enforcement is another major issue. In the United States, law enforcement personnel are bound by the Fourth Amendment to the U.S. Constitution and must obtain a warrant to search for evidence. This amendment protects individuals from unlawful search and seizure. Search warrants are issued when there is probable cause for the search and provide legal authorization to search a location for specific evidence. Private citizens are not held to this strict requirement and, thus, in some cases, a private individual can conduct a search for possible evidence without a warrant. However, if a private individual were asked by a law enforcement officer to search for evidence, a warrant would be required because the private individual would be *acting as an agent of law enforcement*.

An exception to the search warrant requirement for law enforcement officers is the *Exigent Circumstances Doctrine*. Under this doctrine, if probable cause is present and destruction of the evidence is deemed imminent, the search can be conducted without the delay of having the warrant in-hand.

Thus, if law enforcement is called in too early when a computer crime is suspected, the law enforcement investigators will be held to a stricter standard than the organization's employees in regard to searching for and gathering evidence. However, there is a higher probability that any evidence acquired will be admissible in court because law enforcement personnel are trained in preserving the chain of evidence. As stated previously, the dissemination of information and the corresponding publicity will also be out of the organization's control when the investigation is turned over to law enforcement. Conversely, if law enforcement is called in too late to investigate a possible computer crime, improper handling of the investigation and evidence by untrained organization employees may reduce or eliminate the chances of a successful prosecution.

Good sources of evidence include telephone records, video cameras, audit trails, system logs, system backups, witnesses, results of surveillance, and emails.

A standard discriminator used to determine whether a subject may be the perpetrator of a crime is to evaluate whether the individual had a *Motive*, the *Opportunity*, and *Means* to commit the crime. This test is known as *MOM*.

If the investigation is undertaken internally, the suspect should be interviewed to acquire information and to determine who committed the offense. This interrogation should be planned in advance, and expert help should be obtained in the conduct of the interview. Obviously, the suspect is alerted when he or she is scheduled for interrogation and a common mistake in setting up and conducting the interview is providing the suspect with too much information. With this information, the suspect may try to alter additional evidence, leave the premises, or warn other co-conspirators. In the conduct of the interrogation, the pertinent information relative to the crime should be obtained and the questions should be scripted beforehand. Original documents should not be used in the conduct of the interview to avoid the possible destruction of critical information by the suspect.

Liability

In 1997, the Federal Sentencing Guidelines were extended to apply to computer crime. Recall that, under these guidelines, senior corporate officers can be personally subject to up to $290 million in fines if their organizations do not comply with the law. These guidelines also treat the possession of illegally acquired material without intent to resell as a crime.

Management has the obligation to protect the organization from losses due to natural disasters, malicious code, compromise of proprietary information, damage to reputation, violation of the law, employee privacy suits, and stockholder suits. Management must follow the *prudent man rule* that "requires officers to perform duties with diligence and care that ordinary, prudent people would exercise under similar circumstances." The officers must exercise *due care or reasonable care* to carry out their responsibilities to the organization. In exercising due care, corporate officers must institute the following protections:

- Means to prevent the organization's computer resources from being used as a source of attack on another organization's computer system (such as in Distributed DoS attacks)
    - Relates to the principle of *proximate causation* in which an action that was taken or not taken was part of a chain that resulted in negative consequences
- Backups
- Scans for malicious code
- Business continuity/disaster recovery plans
- Local and remote access control
- Elimination of unauthorized and unsecured modems
- Organizational security policies, procedures, and guidelines
- Personnel screening procedures
    - Ensuring the confidentiality, integrity, and availability of organizational databases
    - Addressing the organization's responsibilities to other entities such as customers and prime contractors
    - Establishing an organizational incident-handling capability

The criteria for evaluating the legal requirements for implementing safeguards is to evaluate the cost (C) of instituting the protection versus the estimated loss (L) resulting from exploitation of the corresponding vulnerability. If $C < L$, then a legal liability exists.

Incident handling noted in the prevention list is an important part of contingency planning that addresses handling malicious attacks, usually by technical means. Incident handling or an emergency response should be planned for prior to the occurrence of any incidents and should address the following:

- What is considered an incident?
- How should an incident be reported?
- To whom should the incident be reported?
- When should management be informed of the incident?
- What action should be taken if an incident is detected?
- Who should handle the response to the incident?
- How much damage was caused by the incident?
- What information was damaged or compromised by the incident?
- Are recovery procedures required to remediate damages caused by the incident?
- What type of follow-up and review should be conducted after the incident is handled?
- Should additional safeguards be instituted as a result of the incident?

Incident handling can be considered as the portion of contingency planning that responds to malicious technical threats and can be addressed by establishing a Computer Incident Response Team (CIRT.) A proper incident response is important to limit the resulting damage, to provide information for prevention of future incidents, and to serve as a means of increasing employee awareness. The majority of incidents do not occur from outside crackers and malicious code. Many incidents are the result of incompetent employees, malicious employees, other insiders, accidental actions, and natural disasters. The Carnegie Mellon University Computer Emergency Response Team Coordination Center (CERT®/CC) is an excellent source of information for establishing and maintaining organizational CIRTs.

Ethics

Ethical computing is a phrase that is often used but difficult to define. Certified professionals are morally and legally held to a higher standard of ethical conduct. In order to instill proper computing behavior, ethics should be incorporated into an organizational policy and further developed into an organizational ethical computing policy. A number of organizations have addressed the issue of ethical computing and have generated guidelines for ethical behavior. A few of these ethical codes are presented to provide a familiarization with the items addressed in such codes. Some of these lists are under revision, however, the versions illustrate the general areas that are important in ethical computing behavior.

(ISC)² Code of Ethics

Certified Information Systems Security Professionals (CISSPs) shall:

1. Conduct themselves in accordance with the highest standards of moral, ethical, and legal behavior

2. Not commit or be a party to any unlawful or unethical act that may negatively affect their professional reputation or the reputation of their profession

3. Appropriately report activity related to the profession that they believe to be unlawful and shall cooperate with resulting investigations

4. Support efforts to promote understanding and acceptance of prudent information security measures throughout the public, private, and academic sectors of our global information society

5. Provide competent service to their employers and clients, and shall avoid any conflicts of interest

6. Execute responsibilities in a manner consistent with the highest standards of their profession

7. Not misuse the information in which they come into contact during the course of their duties, and they shall maintain the confidentiality of all information in their possession that is so identified

The Computer Ethics Institute's Ten Commandments of Computer Ethics

In 1992, the Coalition for Computer Ethics incorporated as the Computer Ethics Institute (CEI) to focus on the interface of advances in information technologies, ethics and corporate and public policy. CEI addresses industrial, academic, and public policy organizations. The Institute's founding organizations are the Brookings Institution, IBM, the Washington Consulting Group and the Washington Theological Consortium. The Institute is concerned with the ethical issues associated with the advancement of information technologies in society and has generated the following ten commandments of computer ethics.

1. Thou shalt not use a computer to harm other people.

2. Thou shalt not interfere with other people's computer work.

3. Thou shalt not snoop around in other people's computer files.

4. Thou shalt not use a computer to steal.

5. Thou shalt not use a computer to bear false witness.

6. Thou shalt not copy or use proprietary software for which you have not paid.

7. Thou shalt not use other people's computer resources without authorization or the proper compensation.

8. Thou shalt not appropriate other people's intellectual output.
9. Thou shalt think about the social consequences of the program you are writing for the system you are designing.
10. Thou shalt use a computer in ways that ensure consideration and respect for your fellow humans.

The Internet Activities Board (IAB) Ethics and the Internet (RFC 1087)

"Access to and use of the Internet is a privilege and should be treated as such by all users of the system."

Any activity is defined as unacceptable and unethical that purposely:

1. Seeks to gain unauthorized access to the resources of the Internet
2. Destroys the integrity of computer-based information
3. Disrupts the intended use of the Internet
4. Wastes resources such as people, capacity, and computers through such actions
5. Compromises the privacy of users
6. Involves negligence in the conduct of Internet-wide experiments

The U.S. Department of Health, Education, and Welfare Code of Fair Information Practices

The United States Department of Health, Education, and Welfare has developed the following list of fair information practices that focuses on the privacy of individually, identifiable personal information:

1. There must not be personal data record-keeping systems whose very existence is secret.
2. There must be a way for a person to find out what information about them is in a record and how it is used.
3. There must be a way for a person to prevent information about them, which was obtained for one purpose, from being used or made available for another purposes without their consent.
4. Any organization creating, maintaining, using, or disseminating records of identifiable personal data must ensure the reliability of the data for their intended use and must take precautions to prevent misuses of that data.

Individual ethical behavior widely varies because a person's perception of ethics is a function of many variables in that person's background. Because one is not stealing physical property, the "borrowing" or "viewing" of information on an organization's computers is perceived by many as innocent behavior. Some crackers (malicious hackers) feel that any information available for access or subject to access by virtue of inadequate control measures is fair game. Others are of the opinion that hacking into an organization's information systems is performing a service by alerting the organization to weaknesses in their system safeguards. These naïve and incorrect perspectives trample on the rights of individual privacy and compromise critical and organizational proprietary information.

These breaches of security can result in million-dollar losses to an organization through the destruction or unavailability of critical data and resources or through stock devaluation. From the national perspective, destructive cracker behavior could seriously affect a nation's critical infrastructure, economic health, and national security. Clearly, these types of malicious hacking results cannot be explained away by claims of freedom of speech and freedom of expression rights.

The *Organization for Economic Cooperation and Development (OECD)*

The Organization for Economic Cooperation and Development (OECD) (www.oecd.org) has issued guidelines that are summarized as follows:

- Collection Limitation Principle:
    1. There should be limits to the collection of personal data and any such data should be obtained by lawful and fair means and, where appropriate, with the knowledge or consent of the data subject.
- Data Quality Principle:
    2. Personal data should be relevant to the purposes for which they are to be used, and, to the extent necessary for those purposes, should be accurate, complete and kept up-to-date.
- Purpose Specification Principle:
    3. The purposes for which personal data are collected should be specified not later than at the time of data collection and the subsequent use limited to the fulfillment of those purposes or such others as are not incompatible with those purposes and as are specified on each occasion of change of purpose.
- Use Limitation Principle:
    4. Personal data should not be disclosed, made available or otherwise used for purposes other than those specified in accordance with Paragraph 9 except:

a) With the consent of the data subject

b) By the authority of law

■ Security Safeguards Principle:

5. Personal data should be protected by reasonable security safeguards against such risks as loss or unauthorized access, destruction, use, modification or disclosure of data.

■ Openness Principle:

6. There should be a general policy of openness about developments, practices and policies with respect to personal data. Means should be readily available of establishing the existence and nature of personal data, and the main purposes of their use, as well as the identity and usual residence of the data controller.

■ Individual Participation Principle:

7. An individual should have the right:

a) To obtain from a data controller, or otherwise, confirmation of whether or not the data controller has data relating to him

b) To have communicated to him, data relating to him within a reasonable time at a charge, if any, that is not excessive

In a reasonable manner

In a form that is readily intelligible to him

c) To be given reasons if a request made under subparagraphs (a) and (b) is denied, and to be able to challenge such denial

d) To challenge data relating to him and, if the challenge is successful to have the data erased, rectified, completed or amended

■ Accountability Principle:

8. A data controller should be accountable for complying with measures that give effect to the principles stated above.

■ Transborder Issues:

9. A Member country should refrain from restricting transborder flows of personal data between itself and another Member country except where the latter does not yet substantially observe these Guidelines or where the re-export of such data would circumvent its domestic privacy legislation.

10. A Member country can also impose restrictions in respect of certain categories of personal data for which its domestic privacy legislation includes specific regulations in view of the nature of those data and for which the other Member country provides no equivalent protection.

Sample Questions

You can find answers to the following questions in Appendix H.

1. According to the Internet Activities Board (IAB), an activity that causes which of the following is considered a violation of ethical behavior on the Internet?

    a. Wasting resources

    b. Appropriating other people's intellectual output

    c. Using a computer to steal

    d. Using a computer to bear false witness

2. Which of the following best defines social engineering?

    a. Illegal copying of software

    b. Gathering information from discarded manuals and printouts

    c. Using people skills to obtain proprietary information

    d. Destruction or alteration of data

3. Because the development of new technology usually outpaces the law, law enforcement uses which traditional laws to prosecute computer criminals?

    a. Malicious mischief

    b. Embezzlement, fraud, and wiretapping

    c. Immigration

    d. Conspiracy and elimination of competition

4. Which of the following is NOT a category of law under the Common Law System?

    a. Criminal law

    b. Civil law

    c. Administrative/Regulatory law

    d. Derived law

5. A trade secret:

    a. Provides the owner with a legally enforceable right to exclude others from practicing the art covered for a specified time period

    b. Protects "original" works of authorship

    c. Secures and maintains the confidentiality of proprietary technical or business-related information that is adequately protected from disclosure by the owner

    d. Is a word, name, symbol, color, sound, product shape, or device used to identify goods and to distinguish them from those made or sold by others

6. Which of the following is NOT a European Union (EU) principle?

    a. Data should be collected in accordance with the law.

    b. Transmission of personal information to locations where "equivalent" personal data protection cannot be assured is permissible.

    c. Data should be used only for the purposes for which it was collected and should be used only for a reasonable period of time.

    d. Information collected about an individual cannot be disclosed to other organizations or individuals unless authorized by law or by consent of the individual.

7. The Federal Sentencing Guidelines:

    a. Hold senior corporate officers personally liable if their organizations do not comply with the law

    b. Prohibit altering, damaging, or destroying information in a federal interest computer

    c. Prohibit eavesdropping or the interception of message contents

    d. Established a category of sensitive information called Sensitive But Unclassified (SBU)

8. What does the prudent man rule require?

    a. Senior officials to post performance bonds for their actions

    b. Senior officials to perform their duties with the care that ordinary, prudent people would exercise under similar circumstances

    c. Senior officials to guarantee that all precautions have been taken and that no breaches of security can occur

    d. Senior officials to follow specified government standards

9. Information Warfare is:

    a. Attacking the information infrastructure of a nation to gain military and/or economic advantages

    b. Developing weapons systems based on artificial intelligence technology

    c. Generating and disseminating propaganda material

    d. Signal intelligence

10. The chain of evidence relates to:

    a. Securing laptops to desks during an investigation

    b. DNA testing

    c. Handling and controlling evidence

    d. Making a disk image

11. The Kennedy-Kassebaum Act is also known as:
    a. RICO
    b. OECD
    c. HIPAA
    d. EU Directive

12. Which of the following refers to a U.S. Government program that reduces or eliminates emanations from electronic equipment?
    a. CLIPPER
    b. ECHELON
    c. ECHO
    d. TEMPEST

13. Imprisonment is a possible sentence under:
    a. Civil (tort) law
    b. Criminal law
    c. Both civil and criminal law
    d. Neither civil nor criminal law

14. Which one of the following conditions must be met if legal electronic monitoring of employees is conducted by an organization?
    a. Employees must be unaware of the monitoring activity.
    b. All employees must agree with the monitoring policy.
    c. Results of the monitoring cannot be used against the employee.
    d. The organization must have a policy stating that all employees are regularly notified that monitoring is being conducted.

15. Which of the following is a key principle in the evolution of computer crime laws in many countries?
    a. All members of the United Nations have agreed to uniformly define and prosecute computer crime.
    b. Existing laws against embezzlement, fraud, and wiretapping cannot be applied to computer crime.
    c. The definition of property was extended to include electronic information.
    d. Unauthorized acquisition of computer-based information without the intent to resell is not a crime.

16. The concept of Due Care states that senior organizational management must ensure that:
    a. All risks to an information system are eliminated.
    b. Certain requirements must be fulfilled in carrying out their responsibilities to the organization.

    c. Other management personnel are delegated the responsibility for information system security.

    d. The cost of implementing safeguards is greater than the potential resultant losses resulting from information security breaches.

17. Liability of senior organizational officials relative to the protection of the organizations information systems is prosecutable under:

    a. Criminal law

    b. Civil law

    c. International law

    d. Financial law

18. Responsibility for handling computer crimes in the United States is assigned to:

    a. The Federal Bureau of Investigation (FBI) and the Secret Service

    b. The FBI only

    c. The National Security Agency (NSA)

    d. The Central Intelligence Agency (CIA)

19. In general, computer-based evidence is considered:

    a. Conclusive

    b. Circumstantial

    c. Secondary

    d. Hearsay

20. Investigating and prosecuting computer crimes is made more difficult because:

    a. Backups may be difficult to find.

    b. Evidence is mostly intangible.

    c. Evidence cannot be preserved.

    d. Evidence is hearsay and can never be introduced into a court of law.

21. Which of the following criteria are used to evaluate suspects in the commission of a crime?

    a. Motive, Intent, and Ability

    b. Means, Object, and Motive

    c. Means, Intent, and Motive

    d. Motive, Means, and Opportunity

22. 18 U.S.C. §2001 (1994) refers to:

    a. Article 18, U.S. Code, Section 2001, 1994 edition

    b. Title 18, University of Southern California, Article 2001, 1994 edition

    c. Title 18, Section 2001 of the U.S. Code, 1994 edition

    d. Title 2001 of the U.S. Code, Section 18, 1994 edition

23. What is enticement?

    a. Encouraging the commission of a crime when there was initially no intent to commit a crime

    b. Assisting in the commission of a crime

    c. Luring the perpetrator to an attractive area or presenting the perpetrator with a lucrative target after the crime has already been initiated

    d. Encouraging the commission of one crime over another

24. Which of the following is NOT a computer investigation issue?

    a. Evidence is easy to obtain.

    b. The time frame for investigation is compressed.

    c. An expert may be required to assist.

    d. The information is intangible.

25. Conducting a search without the delay of obtaining a warrant if destruction of evidence seems imminent is possible under:

    a. Federal Sentencing Guidelines

    b. Proximate Causation

    c. Exigent Circumstances

    d. Prudent Man Rule

Bonus Questions

You can find answers to the following questions in Appendix H.

1. The U.S. Government *Tempest* program was established to thwart which one of the following types of attacks?

    a. Denial of Service

    b. Emanation Eavesdropping

    c. Software Piracy

    d. Dumpster Diving

2. Which entity of the U.S. legal system makes "common laws?"

    a. Administrative agencies

    b. Legislative branch

    c. Executive branch

    d. Judicial branch

3. Which one of the following items is NOT TRUE concerning the Platform for Privacy Preferences (P3P) developed by the World Wide Web Consortium (W3C)?

    a. It allows Web sites to express their privacy practices in a standard format that can be retrieved automatically and interpreted easily by user agents.

    b. It allows users to be informed of site practices in human-readable format.

    c. It does not provide the site privacy practices to users in machine-readable format.

    d. It automates decision-making based on the site's privacy practices when appropriate.

4. Which one of the following is NOT a recommended practice regarding electronic monitoring of employees' email?

    a. Monitoring should be applied in a consistent fashion

    b. Provide individuals being monitored with a guarantee of email privacy

    c. Inform all that email is being monitored by means of a prominent log-in banner

    d. Explain who is authorized to read monitored email

5. Discovery, recording, collection, and preservation are part of what process related to the gathering of evidence?

    a. Admissibility of evidence

    b. The chain of evidence

   c. The evidence life cycle

   d. Relevance of evidence

6. Relative to legal evidence, which one of the following correctly describes the difference between an expert and a nonexpert in delivering an opinion?

   a. An expert can offer an opinion based on personal expertise and facts, but a nonexpert can testify only as to facts.

   b. A nonexpert can offer an opinion based on personal expertise and facts, but an expert can testify only as to facts.

   c. An expert can offer an opinion based on personal expertise and facts, but a nonexpert can testify only as to personal opinion.

   d. An expert can offer an opinion based on facts only, but a nonexpert can testify only as to personal opinion.

7. What principle requires corporate officers to institute appropriate protections regarding the corporate intellectual property?

   a. Need-to-know

   b. Due care

   c. Least privilege

   d. Separation of duties

8. If C represents the cost of instituting safeguards in an information system and L is the estimated loss resulting from exploitation of the corresponding vulnerability, a legal liability exists if the safeguards are not implemented when:

   a. C/L = a constant

   b. $C > L$

   c. $C < L$

   d. $C = 2L$

Advanced Sample Questions

You can find answers to the following questions in Appendix I.

The following questions are supplemental to and coordinated with Chapter 9 and are at a level commensurate with that of the CISSP Examination.

These questions include advanced material relative to computer law, investigation and ethics both in the U.S. and internationally. Questions address the recently passed U.S. Patriot Act, international copyright issues, computer forensics, changes in search and seizure laws, Internet monitoring, electronic signatures and the U.S. Health Information Portability and Accountability Act (HIPAA).

It is assumed that the reader has a basic knowledge of the material contained in Chapter 9. These questions and answers build upon the questions and answers covered in Chapter 9.

1. In the legal field, there is a term that is used to describe a computer system so that everyone can agree on a common definition. The term describes a computer for the purposes of computer security as "any assembly of electronic equipment, hardware, software and firmware configured to collect, create, communicate, disseminate, process, store and control data or information." This definition includes peripheral items such as keyboards, printers, and additional memory. The term that corresponds to this definition is:

   a. A central processing unit (CPU)

   b. A microprocessor

   c. An arithmetic logic unit (ALU)

   d. An automated information system (AIS)

2. In general, computer crimes fall into two major categories and two additional related categories. Which of the following categories is NOT one of these four?

   a. The computer as a target of the crime

   b. Crimes using the computer

   c. Malfeasance by computer

   d. Crimes associated with the prevalence of computers

3. Which of the following is NOT a valid legal issue associated with computer crime?

   a. Electronic Data Interchange (EDI) makes it easier to relate a crime to an individual.

   b. It may be difficult to prove criminal intent.

    c. It may be difficult to obtain a trail of evidence of activities performed on the computer.

    d. It may be difficult to show causation.

4. The Federal Intelligence Surveillance Act (FISA) of 1978, the Electronic Communications Privacy Act (ECPA) of 1986, and the Communications Assistance for Law Enforcement Act (CALEA) of 1994 are legislative acts passed by the United States Congress. These acts all address what major information security issue?

    a. Computer fraud

    b. Wiretapping

    c. Malicious code

    d. Unlawful use of and access to government computers and networks

5. A *pen register* is a:

    a. Device that identifies the cell in which a mobile phone is operating

    b. Device that records the URLs accessed by an individual

    c. Device that records the caller-ID of incoming calls

    d. Device that records all the numbers dialed from a specific telephone line

6. A device that is used to monitor Internet Service Provider (ISP) data traffic is called:

    a. Carnivore

    b. Echelon

    c. Escrowed encryption

    d. Key manager

7. In 1996, the World Intellectual Property Organization (WIPO) sponsored a treaty under which participating countries would standardize treatment of digital copyrights. One of the items of standardization was the prohibition of altering copyright management information (CMI) that is included with the copyrighted material. CMI is:

    a. An encryption algorithm

    b. Product description information

    c. A listing of Public keys

    d. Licensing and ownership information

8. The European Union (EU) has enacted a Conditional Access Directive (CAD) that addresses which of the following?

    a. Access to and use of copyrighted material

    b. Reverse engineering

    c. Unauthorized access to Internet subscription sites and pay TV services

    d. Use of copyrighted material by libraries

9. Which of the following actions by the U.S. government is NOT permitted or required by the U.S. Patriot Act, signed into law on October 26, 2001?

    a. Subpoena of electronic records

    b. Monitoring of Internet communications

    c. Search and seizure of information on live systems (including routers and servers), backups, and archives

    d. Reporting of cash and wire transfers of $5,000 or more

10. The U.S. Uniform Computer Information Transactions Act (UCITA) is a:

    a. Model act that is intended to apply uniform legislation to software licensing

    b. Model act that addresses digital signatures

    c. Model act that is intended to apply uniform legislation to electronic credit transactions

    d. Model act that addresses electronic transactions conducted by financial institutions

11. The European Union Electronic Signature Directive of January, 2000, defines an "advanced electronic signature." This signature must meet all of the following requirements except that:

    a. It must be uniquely linked to the signatory.

    b. It must be created using means that are generally accessible and available.

    c. It must be capable of identifying the signatory.

    d. It must be linked to the data to which it relates in such a manner that any subsequent change of the data is detectable.

12. On June 30, 2000, the U.S. Congress enacted the Electronic Signatures in Global and National Commerce Act (ESIGN) "to facilitate the use of electronic records and signatures in interstate and foreign commerce by ensuring the validity and legal effect of contracts entered into electronically." An important provision of the Act requires that:

    a. Businesses obtain electronic consent or confirmation from consumers to receive information electronically that a law normally requires to be in writing.

    b. The e-commerce businesses do not have to determine whether the consumer has the ability to receive an electronic notice before transmitting the legally required notices to the consumer.

c. Businesses have the ability to use product price to persuade consumers to accept electronic records instead of paper.

d. Specific technologies be used to ensure technical compatibility.

13. Under Civil Law, the victim is NOT entitled to which of the following types of damages?

a. Statutory

b. Punitive

c. Compensatory

d. Imprisonment of the offender

14. Which of the following is NOT one of the European Union (EU) privacy principles?

a. Individuals are entitled to receive a report on the information that is held about them.

b. Data transmission of personal information to locations where "equivalent" personal data protection cannot be assured is prohibited.

c. Information collected about an individual can be disclosed to other organizations or individuals unless specifically prohibited by the individual.

d. Individuals have the right to correct errors contained in their personal data.

15. Which of the following is NOT a goal of the Kennedy-Kassebaum Health Insurance Portability and Accountability Act (HIPAA) of 1996?

a. Provide for restricted access by the patient to personal healthcare information

b. Administrative simplification

c. Enable the portability of health insurance

d. Establish strong penalties for healthcare fraud

16. The proposed HIPAA Security Rule mandates the protection of the confidentiality, integrity, and availability of protected health information (PHI) through three of the following activities. Which of the activities is NOT included under the proposed HIPAA Security Rule?

a. Administrative procedures

b. Physical safeguards

c. Technical services and mechanisms

d. Appointment of a Privacy Officer

17. Individual privacy rights as defined in the HIPAA Privacy Rule include consent and authorization by the patient for the release of PHI. The difference between consent and authorization as used in the Privacy Rule is:

    a. Consent grants general permission to use or disclose PHI, and authorization limits permission to the purposes and the parties specified in the authorization.

    b. Authorization grants general permission to use or disclose PHI, and consent limits permission to the purposes and the parties specified in the consent.

    c. Consent grants general permission to use or disclose PHI, and authorization limits permission to the purposes specified in the authorization.

    d. Consent grants general permission to use or disclose PHI, and authorization limits permission to the parties specified in the authorization.

18. Because of the nature of information that is stored on the computer, the investigation and prosecution of computer criminal cases have specific characteristics, one of which is:

    a. Investigators and prosecutors have a longer time frame for the investigation.

    b. The information is intangible.

    c. The investigation does not usually interfere with the normal conduct of the business of an organization.

    d. Evidence is usually easy to gather.

19. In order for evidence to be admissible in a court of law, it must be relevant, legally permissible, reliable, properly identified, and properly preserved. Reliability of evidence means that:

    a. It must tend to prove a material fact; the evidence is related to the crime in that it shows that the crime has been committed, can provide information describing the crime, can provide information as to the perpetrator's motives, can verify what had occurred, and so on.

    b. The evidence is identified without changing or damaging the evidence.

    c. The evidence has not been tampered with or modified.

    d. The evidence is not subject to damage or destruction.

20. In the U.S. Federal Rules of Evidence, Rule 803 (6) permits an exception to the Hearsay Rule regarding business records and computer records. Which one of the following is NOT a requirement for business or computer records exception under Rule 803 (6)?

    a. Made during the regular conduct of business and authenticated by witnesses familiar with their use

    b. Relied upon in the regular course of business

    c. Made only by a person with knowledge of the records

    d. Made by a person with information transmitted by a person with knowledge

21. Law enforcement officials in the United States, up until passage of the Patriot Act (see Question 9), had extensive restrictions on search and seizure as established in the Fourth Amendment to the U.S. Constitution. These restrictions are still, essentially, more severe than those on private citizens, who are not agents of a government entity. Thus, internal investigators in an organization or private investigators are not subject to the same restrictions as government officials. Private individuals are not normally held to the same standards regarding search and seizure since they are not conducting an unconstitutional government search. However, there are certain exceptions where the Fourth Amendment applies to private citizens if they act as agents of the government/police. Which of the following is NOT one of these exceptions?

    a. The government is aware of the intent to search or is aware of a search conducted by the private individual and does not object to these actions.

    b. The private individual performs the search to aid the government.

    c. The private individual conducts a search that would require a search warrant if conducted by a government entity.

    d. The private individual conducts a warrantless search of company property for the company.

22. One important tool of computer forensics is the disk image backup. The disk image backup is:

    a. Copying the system files

    b. Conducting a bit-level copy, sector by sector

    c. Copying the disk directory

    d. Copying and authenticating the system files

23. In the context of legal proceedings and trial practice, *discovery* refers to:
    a. The process in which the prosecution presents information it has uncovered to the defense, including potential witnesses, reports resulting from the investigation, evidence, and so on
    b. The process undertaken by the investigators to acquire evidence needed for prosecution of a case
    c. A step in the computer forensic process
    d. The process of obtaining information on potential and existing employees using background checks

24. Which of the following alternatives should NOT be used by law enforcement to gain access to a password?
    a. Using password "cracker" software
    b. Compelling the suspect to provide the password
    c. Contacting the developer of the software for information to gain access to the computer or network through a back door
    d. Data manipulation and trial procedures applied to the original version of the system hard disk

25. During the investigation of a computer crime, audit trails can be very useful. To ensure that the audit information can be used as evidence, certain procedures must be followed. Which of the following is NOT one of these procedures?
    a. The audit trail information must be used during the normal course of business.
    b. There must be a valid organizational security policy in place and in use that defines the use of the audit information.
    c. Mechanisms should be in place to protect the integrity of the audit trail information.
    d. Audit trails should be viewed prior to the image backup.

26. The Internet Activities Board (IAB) considers which of the following behaviors relative to the Internet as unethical?
    a. Negligence in the conduct of Internet experiments
    b. Record-keeping whose very existence is secret
    c. Record-keeping in which an individual cannot find out what information concerning that individual is in the record
    d. Improper dissemination and use of identifiable personal data

27. Which of the following is NOT a form of computer/network surveillance?
    a. Keyboard monitoring
    b. Use of network sniffers

    c. Use of CCTV cameras

    d. Review of audit logs

28. Which of the following is NOT a definition or characteristic of "Due Care?"

    a. Just, proper, and sufficient care, so far as the circumstances demand it.

    b. That care which an ordinary prudent person would have exercised under the same or similar circumstances.

    c. Implies that a party has been guilty of a violation of the law in relation to the subject matter or transaction.

    d. It may and often does require extraordinary care.

29. The definition "A mark used in the sale or advertising of services to identify the services of one person and distinguish them from the services of others" refers to a:

    a. Trademark

    b. Service mark

    c. Trade name

    d. Copyright

30. It is estimated that the Asia/Pacific region accounts for about $4 billion worth of loss of income to software publishers due to software piracy. As with the Internet, cross-jurisdictional law enforcement issues make investigating and prosecuting such crime difficult. Which of the following items is NOT an issue in stopping overseas software piracy?

    a. Obtaining the cooperation of foreign law enforcement agencies and foreign governments.

    b. The quality of the illegal copies of the software is improving, making it more difficult for purchasers to differentiate between legal and illegal products.

    c. The producers of the illegal copies of software are dealing in larger and larger quantities, resulting in faster deliveries of illicit software.

    d. Lack of a central, nongovernmental organization to address the issue of software piracy.

CHAPTER

10

Physical Security

The Physical Security Domain of Information Systems Security is a fairly clear and concise domain. Simply put, the Physical Security Domain examines those elements of the surrounding physical environment and supporting infrastructure that affect the *confidentiality, integrity, and availability* (C.I.A.) of information systems. We are not talking about logical controls here, but you will notice that some of the physical controls described are duplicated in some of the other domains, such as Operations and Access Control (for example, Biometrics). Natural disasters are an example of physical threats to security. Facility controls to unauthorized entry or theft are elements of physical security. The area known as Industrial Security contains many of these concepts, such as Closed-Circuit Television (CCTV), guards, fencing, lighting, and so forth. To most engineers or security professionals, this domain is probably the least sexy of the 10 domains. Who cares how high perimeter fencing should be to protect critical buildings? But you need to know this stuff because 1) some of this information will be on the test, and 2) the best-configured firewall in the world will not stand up to a well-placed brick.

From the published (ISC)² goals for the CISSP candidate:

A CISSP professional should fully understand the following:

- *The elements involved in choosing a secure site and its design and configuration*
- *The methods for securing a facility against unauthorized access*
- *The methods for securing the equipment against theft of either the equipment or its contained information*
- *The environmental and safety measures needed to protect personnel, and the facility and its resources*

Our Goals

A security practitioner needs to be aware of the elements that threaten the physical security of an enterprise and those controls that can mitigate the risk incurred from those threats. In this chapter, we will examine threats to physical security and controls for physical security.

Domain Definition

The Physical Security domain addresses the threats, vulnerabilities, and countermeasures that can be utilized to physically protect an enterprise's resources and sensitive information. These resources include personnel, the facility in which they work, and the data, equipment, support systems, and media with which they work. Physical security often refers to the measures taken to protect systems, buildings, and their related supporting infrastructure against threats that are associated with the physical environment.

Physical computer security can also be defined as the process used to control personnel, the physical plant, equipment, and data involved in information processing. A CISSP candidate will be expected to understand the threats and controls that are related to physically protecting the enterprise's sensitive information assets.

Threats to Physical Security

Before we can begin an investigation into the various ways an enterprise can implement proper physical security, we obviously need to know what aspects of our environment constitute a threat to our computing infrastructure. When a risk analysis or business impact assessment is performed, a list of all possible threats must be compiled. It does not matter if the likelihood of any specific vulnerability is low or nonexistent (a tsunami in Ohio, for example), all possible threats must be compiled and examined. Many assessment methods (SSE-CMM or IAM) have the practitioner compile these complete lists before making a determination as to their likelihood.

The triad of Confidentiality, Availability, and Integrity is at risk in the physical environment and must be protected. Examples of risks to C.I.A. include the following:

- Interruptions in providing computer services—availability
- Physical damage—Availability
- Unauthorized disclosure of information—Confidentiality
- Loss of control over system—Integrity
- Physical theft—Confidentiality, Integrity, and Availability

Examples of threats to physical security are as follows:

- Emergencies
  - Fire and smoke contaminants
  - Building collapse or explosion
  - Utility loss (electrical power, air conditioning, heating)
  - Water damage (pipe breakage)
  - Toxic materials release
- Natural disasters
  - Earth movement (such as earthquakes and mudslides)
  - Storm damage (such as snow, ice, and floods)
- Human intervention
  - Sabotage
  - Vandalism
  - War
  - Strikes

Donn B. Parker, in his book, *Fighting Computer Crime* (Wiley, 1998), has compiled a very comprehensive list that he calls the seven major sources of physical loss with examples provided for each:

1. *Temperature.* Extreme variations of heat or cold, such as sunlight, fire, freezing, and heat
2. *Gases.* War gases, commercial vapors, humidity, dry air, and suspended particles are included. Examples of these would be Sarin nerve gas, PCP from exploding transformers, air conditioning failures, smoke, smog, cleaning fluid, fuel vapors, and paper particles from printers.

3. *Liquids.* Water and chemicals are included. Examples of these are floods, plumbing failures, precipitation, fuel leaks, spilled drinks, acid and base chemicals used for cleaning, and computer printer fluids.

4. *Organisms.* Viruses, bacteria, people, animals, and insects are included. Examples of these are sickness of key workers, molds, contamination from skin oils and hair, contamination and electrical shorting from defecation and release of body fluids, consumption of information media such as paper or cable insulation, and shorting of microcircuits from cobwebs.

5. *Projectiles.* Tangible objects in motion and powered objects are included. Examples of these are meteorites, falling objects, cars and trucks, bullets and rockets, explosions, and wind.

6. *Movement.* Collapse, shearing, shaking, vibration, liquefaction, flows, waves, separation, and slides are included. Examples of these are dropping or shaking of fragile equipment, earthquakes, Earth slides, lava flows, sea waves, and adhesive failures.

7. *Energy anomalies.* Types of electric anomalies are electric surges or failure, magnetism, static electricity, aging circuitry, radiation, sound, light, and radio, microwave, electromagnetic, and atomic waves. Examples of these include electric utility failures, proximity of magnets and electromagnets, carpet static, decomposition of circuit materials, decomposition of paper and magnetic disks, Electro-Magnetic Pulse (EMP) from nuclear explosions, lasers, loudspeakers, high-energy radio frequency (HERF) guns, radar systems, cosmic radiation, and explosions.

Controls for Physical Security

Under the heading of Physical Security Controls, there are several areas. In general, these controls should match up with the listed threats. In this chapter, we have grouped the controls into two areas: Administrative Controls, and Physical and Technical Controls.

Administrative Controls

Administrative controls, as opposed to physical or technical controls, can be thought of as the area of physical security protection that benefits from the proper administrative steps. These steps encompass proper emergency procedures, personnel control (in the area of Human Resources), proper planning, and policy implementation.

We will look at the following various elements of Administrative Controls:

■ Facility Requirements Planning

■ Facility Security Management

■ Administrative Personnel Controls

Facility Requirements Planning

Facility Requirements Planning describes the concept of the need for planning for physical security controls in the early stages of the construction of a data facility. There might be an occasion when security professionals are able to provide input at the construction phase of a building or data center. Some of the physical security elements involved at the construction stage include choosing and designing a secure site.

Choosing a Secure Site

The environmental placement of the facility is also a concern during initial planning. Security professionals need to consider such questions as:

Visibility. What kind of neighbors will the proposed site have? Will the site have any external markings that will identify it as a sensitive processing area? Low visibility is the rule here.

Local considerations. Is the proposed site near possible hazards (for example, a waste dump)? What is the local rate of crime (such as forced entry and burglary)?

Natural disasters. Is it likely this location will have more natural disasters than other locations? Natural disasters can include weather-related problems (wind, snow, flooding, and so forth) and the existence of an earthquake fault.

Transportation. Does the site have a problem due to excessive air, highway, or road traffic?

Joint tenancy. Are access to environmental and HVAC controls complicated by a shared responsibility? A data center might not have full access to the systems when an emergency occurs.

External services. Do you know the relative proximity of the local emergency services, such as police, fire, and hospitals or medical facilities?

Designing a Secure Site

Information Security processing areas are the main focus of physical control. Examples of areas that require attention during the construction planning stage are:

Walls. Entire walls, from the floor to the ceiling, must have an acceptable fire rating. Closets or rooms that store media must have a high fire rating.

Ceilings. Issues of concern regarding ceilings are the weight-bearing rating and the fire rating.

Floors. The following are the concerns about flooring:

- *Slab.* If the floor is a concrete slab, the concerns are the physical weight it can bear (known as loading, which is commonly 150 pounds per square foot) and its fire rating.

- *Raised.* The fire rating, its electrical conductivity (grounding against static buildup), and that it employs a non-conducting surface material are concerns of raised flooring in the data center.

Windows. Windows are normally not acceptable in the data center. If they do exist, however, they must be translucent and shatterproof.

Doors. Doors in the data center must resist forcible entry and have a fire rating equal to the walls. Emergency exits must be clearly marked and monitored or alarmed. Electric door locks on emergency exits should revert to a disabled state if power outages occur to enable safe evacuation. While this may be considered a security issue, personnel safety always takes precedence, and these doors should be manned in an emergency.

Sprinkler system. The location and type of fire suppression system must also be known.

Liquid or gas lines. Security professionals should know where the shut-off valves are to water, steam, or gas pipes entering the building. Also, water drains should be "positive," that is, they should flow outward, away from the building, so they do not carry contaminants into the facility.

Air conditioning. AC units should have dedicated power circuits. Security professionals should know where the Emergency Power Off (EPO) switch is. As with water drains, the AC system should provide outward, positive air pressure and have protected intake vents to prevent air-carried toxins from entering the facility.

Electrical requirements. The facility should have established backup and alternate power sources. Dedicated feeders and circuits are required in the data center. Security professionals should check for access controls to the electrical distribution panels and circuit breakers.

Facility Security Management

Under the grouping of Facility Security Management, we list audit trails and emergency procedures. These are elements of the Administrative Security Controls that are not related to the initial planning of the secure site, but are required to be implemented on an ongoing basis.

Audit Trails

An audit trail (or access log) is a record of events. A computer system might have several audit trails, each focused on a particular type of activity—such as detecting security violations, performance problems, and design and programming flaws in applications. In the domain of physical security, audit trails and access control logs are vital because management needs to know where access attempts existed and who attempted them.

The audit trails or access logs must record the following:

- The date and time of the access attempt
- Whether the attempt was successful or not
- Where the access was granted (which door, for example)
- Who attempted the access
- Who modified the access privileges at the supervisor level

Some audit trail systems can also send alarms or alerts to personnel if multiple access failure attempts have been made.

Remember that audit trails and access logs are detective, rather than preventative. They do not stop an intrusion—although knowing that an audit trail of the entry attempt is being compiled may influence the intruder to not attempt entry. Audit trails do help an administrator reconstruct the details of an intrusion post-event, however.

Emergency Procedures

The implementation of emergency procedures and the employee training and knowledge of these procedures is an important part of administrative physical controls. These procedures should be clearly documented, readily accessible (including copies stored off-site in the event of a disaster), and updated periodically.

Elements of emergency procedure administration should include the following:

- Emergency system shutdown procedures
- Evacuation procedures

- Employee training, awareness programs, and periodic drills
- Periodic equipment and systems tests

Administrative Personnel Controls

Administrative Personnel Controls encompass those administrative processes that are implemented commonly by the Human Resources department during employee hiring and firing. Examples of personnel controls implemented by HR often include the following:

- Pre-employment screening:
  - Employment, references, or educational history checks
  - Background investigation or credit rating checks for sensitive positions
- On-going employee checks:
  - Security clearances—generated only if the employee is to have access to classified documents
  - Ongoing employee ratings or reviews by their supervisor
- Post-employment procedures:
  - Exit interview
  - Removal of network access and change of passwords
  - Return of computer inventory or laptops

Environmental and Life Safety Controls

Environmental and Life Safety Controls are considered to be those elements of physical security controls that are required to sustain either the computer's operating environment or the personnel's operating environment. The following are the three main areas of environmental control:

1. Electrical power
2. Fire detection and suppression
3. Heating, Ventilation, and Air Conditioning (HVAC)

Electrical Power

Electrical systems are the lifeblood of computer operations. The continued supply of clean, steady power is required to maintain the proper personnel environment as well as to sustain data operations. Many elements can threaten power systems, the most common being noise, brownouts, and humidity.

Noise

Noise in power systems refers to the presence of electrical radiation in the system that is unintentional and interferes with the transmission of clean power. Some power issues have been covered in Chapter 3, "Telecommunications and Network Security," such as Uninterruptible Power Supplies (UPS) and backup power. In this section, we will go into more detail about these types of power problems and their recommended solutions.

There are several types of noise, the most common being Electromagnetic Interference (EMI) and Radio Frequency Interference (RFI).

EMI is noise that is caused by the generation of radiation due to the charge difference between the three electrical wires—the hot, neutral, and ground wires.

Two common types of EMI generated by electrical systems are:

Common-mode noise. Noise from the radiation generated by the difference between the hot and ground wires

Traverse-mode noise. Noise from the radiation generated by the difference between the hot and neutral wires

RFI is generated by the components of an electrical system, such as radiating electrical cables, fluorescent lighting, and electric space heaters. RFI can be so serious that it not only interferes with computer operations, but it also can permanently damage sensitive components.

Several protective measures for noise exist. Some of the ones that need to be noted are:

- Power line conditioning
- Proper grounding of the system to the earth
- Cable shielding
- Limiting exposure to magnets, fluorescent lights, electric motors, and space heaters

Table 10.1 lists various electrical power terms and descriptions.

Brownouts

Unlike a sag, a brownout is a prolonged drop in supplied usable voltage that can do serious physical damage to delicate electronic components. The American National Standards Institute (ANSI) standards permit an 8 percent drop between the power source and the building's meter, and permit a 3.5 percent drop between the meter and the wall. In New York City, 15 percent fluctuations

Table 10.1 Electrical Power Definitions

ELEMENT	DESCRIPTION
Fault	Momentary power loss
Blackout	Complete loss of power
Sag	Momentary low voltage
Brownout	Prolonged low voltage
Spike	Momentary high voltage
Surge	Prolonged high voltage
Inrush	Initial surge of power at the beginning
Noise	Steady interfering disturbance
Transient	Short duration of line noise disturbances
Clean	Non-fluctuating pure power
Ground	One wire in an electrical circuit must be grounded

are common, and a prolonged brownout can lower the supplied voltage more than 10 percent.

In addition, surges and spikes occurring when the power comes back up from either a brownout or an outage can also be damaging to the components. All computer equipment should be protected by surge suppressors, and critical equipment will need an Uninterruptible Power Supply (UPS).

Humidity

The ideal operating humidity range is defined as 40 percent to 60 percent. High humidity, which is defined as greater than 60 percent, can produce a problem by creating condensation on computer parts. High humidity also creates problems with the corrosion of electrical connections. A process similar to electroplating occurs, causing the silver particles to migrate from the connectors onto the copper circuits, thus impeding the electrical efficiency of the components.

Low humidity of less than 40 percent increases the static electricity damage potential. A static charge of 4000 volts is possible under normal humidity conditions on a hardwood or vinyl floor, and charges up to 20,000 volts or more are possible under conditions of very low humidity with non-static-free carpeting. Although you cannot control the weather, you certainly can control your relative humidity level in the computer room through your HVAC systems. Table 10.2 lists the damage various static electricity charges can do to computer hardware.

Table 10.2 Static Charge Damage

STATIC CHARGE IN VOLTS	WILL DAMAGE
40	Sensitive circuits and transistors
1,000	Scramble monitor display
1,500	Disk drive data loss
2,000	System shutdown
4,000	Printer jam
17,000	Permanent chip damage

CHECK YOUR CARPETS!

A major New York City legal client once brought me into an emergency situation. They were scheduled for a cut over to a major new computer system the next weekend and were having problems keeping their system online. They had been operating it successfully in parallel for a few weeks in the lab, but once the system was moved to the operations center, it would frequently abort and reset for no apparent reason. After examining every conceivable parameter of the configuration and scratching my head for a bit, I noticed that I could cause a very small static discharge when I touched the case, thereby resetting the unit. Evidently the building contractor had run out of static-free carpet in the operations center and had finished the job with regular carpeting. Once we relocated the system, everything ran fine.

Some precautions you can take to reduce static electricity damage are:

- Use anti-static sprays where possible.
- Operations or computer centers should have anti-static flooring.
- Building and computer rooms should be grounded properly.
- Anti-static table or floor mats can be used.
- HVAC should maintain the proper level of relative humidity in computer rooms.

Fire Detection and Suppression

The successful detection and suppression of fire is an absolute necessity for the safe, continued operation of information systems. A CISSP candidate will need to know the classes, combustibles, detectors, and suppression methods of fire safety.

Fire Classes and Combustibles

Table 10.3 lists the three main types of fires, what type of combustible gives the fire its class rating, and the recommended extinguishing agent.

For rapid oxidation to occur (a fire), three elements must be present: oxygen, heat, and fuel. Each suppression medium affects a different element and is therefore better suited for different types of fires.

Water. Suppresses the temperature required to sustain the fire.

Soda Acid. Suppresses the fuel supply of the fire.

CO_2. Suppresses the oxygen supply required to sustain the fire.

Halon. A little different, it suppresses combustion through a chemical reaction that kills the fire.

Anyone who has had the misfortune to throw water on a grease fire in a skillet and has suffered the resultant explosion will never need to be reminded that certain combustibles require very specific suppression methods.

Fire Detectors

Fire detectors respond to heat, flame, or smoke to detect thermal combustion or its by-products. Different types of detectors have various properties and use the different properties of a fire to raise an alarm.

Heat-sensing. Heat-actuated sensing devices usually detect one of the two conditions: 1) the temperature reaches a predetermined level, or 2) the temperature rises quickly regardless of the initial temperature. The first type, the fixed temperature device, has a much lower rate of false positives (false alarms) than the second, the rate-of-rise detector.

Flame-actuated. Flame-actuated sensing devices are fairly expensive, as they sense either the infrared energy of a flame or the pulsation of the flame, and have a very fast response time. They are usually used in specialized applications for the protection of valuable equipment.

Table 10.3 Fire Classes and Suppression Mediums

CLASS	DESCRIPTION	SUPPRESSION MEDIUMS
A	Common combustibles	Water or soda acid
B	Liquid	CO_2, soda acid, or Halon
C	Electrical	CO_2 or Halon

Smoke-actuated. Smoke-actuated fire sensing devices are used primarily in ventilation systems where an early-warning device would be useful. Photoelectric devices are triggered by the variation in the light hitting the photoelectric cell as a result of the smoke condition. Another type of smoke detector, the Radioactive Smoke Detection device, generates an alarm when the ionization current created by its radioactive material is disturbed by the smoke.

Automatic Dial-up Fire Alarm. This is a type of signal response mechanism that dials the local fire and/or police stations and plays a prerecorded message when a fire is detected. This alarm system is often used in conjunction with the previous fire detectors. These units are inexpensive, but can easily be intentionally subverted.

Fire Extinguishing Systems

Fire extinguishing systems come in two flavors: water sprinkler systems and gas discharge systems.

Water sprinkler systems come in four variations:

Wet Pipe. Wet pipe sprinkler systems always contain water in them, and are also called a closed head system. In the most common implementation: In the event of a heat rise to 165° F, the fusible link in the nozzle melts causing a gate valve to open, allowing water to flow. This is considered the most reliable sprinkler system; however, its main drawbacks are that nozzle or pipe failure can cause a water flood, and the pipe can freeze if exposed to cold weather.

Dry Pipe. In a dry pipe system, there is no water standing in the pipe—it is being held back by a clapper valve. Upon the previously described fire conditions arising, the valve opens, the air is blown out of the pipe, and the water flows. While this system is considered less efficient, it is commonly preferred over wet pipe systems for computer installations because a time delay may enable the computer systems to power down before the dry pipe system activates.

Deluge. A deluge system is a type of dry pipe, but the volume of water discharged is much larger. Unlike a sprinkler head, a deluge system is designed to deliver a large amount of water to an area quickly. It is not considered appropriate for computer equipment, however, due to the time required to get back on-line after an incident.

Preaction. This is currently the most recommended water system for a computer room. It combines both the dry and wet pipe systems, by first releasing the water into the pipes when heat is detected (dry pipe), then releasing the water flow when the link in the nozzle melts (wet pipe).

This feature enables manual intervention before a full discharge of water on the equipment occurs.

Gas discharge systems employ a pressurized inert gas and are usually installed under the computer room raised floor. The fire detection system typically activates the gas discharge system to quickly smother the fire either under the floor in the cable areas or throughout the room. Typical agents of a gas discharge system are carbon dioxide (CO_2) or Halon. Halon 1211 does not require the sophisticated pressurization system of Halon 1301 and is used in self-pressurized portable extinguishers. Of the various replacements for Halon, FM-200 is now the most common.

Suppression Mediums

Carbon Dioxide (CO_2). CO_2 is a colorless and odorless gas commonly used in gas discharge fire suppression systems. It is very effective in fire suppression due to the fact that it quickly removes any oxygen that can be used to sustain the fire. This oxygen removal also makes it very dangerous for personnel and it is potentially lethal. It is primarily recommended for use in unmanned computer facilities, or if used in manned operations centers, the fire detection and alarm system must enable personnel ample time to either exit the facility or to cancel the release of the CO_2.

Portable fire extinguishers commonly contain CO_2 or Soda Acid and should be:

■ Commonly located at exits

■ Clearly marked with their fire types

■ Checked regularly by licensed personnel

Halon. At one time, Halon was considered the perfect fire suppression method in computer operations centers, due to the fact that it is not harmful to the equipment, mixes thoroughly with the air, and spreads extremely fast. The benefits of using Halons are that they do not leave liquid or solid residues when discharged. Therefore, they are preferred for sensitive areas, such as computer rooms and data storage areas.

Several issues arose with its deployment, however, such as that it cannot be breathed safely in concentrations greater than 10 percent, and when deployed on fires with temperatures greater than 900°, it degrades into seriously toxic chemicals—hydrogen fluoride, hydrogen bromide, and bromine. Implementation of halogenated extinguishing agents in computer rooms must be extremely well designed to enable personnel to evacuate immediately when deployed, whether Halon is released under the flooring or overhead in the raised ceiling.

At the Montreal Protocol of 1987, Halon was designated an ozone-depleting substance due to its use of Chlorofluorocarbon Compounds (CFCs). Halon has an extremely high ozone-depleting potential (three to ten times more than CFCs), and its intended use results in its release into the environment.

No new Halon 1301 installations are allowed, and existing installations are encouraged to replace Halon with a non-toxic substitute, like the ones in the following list. Current federal regulations prohibit the production of Halons, and the import and export of recovered Halons except by permit. There are federal controls on the uses, releases, and mandatory removal of Halon prior to decommissioning equipment, and reporting Halon releases, accidental or not, is mandatory.

There are alternatives to Halon. Many large users of Halon are taking steps to remove Halon-containing equipment from all but the most critical areas. Most Halon 1211 in commercial and industrial applications is being replaced and recovered. Halon 1301 is being banked for future use.

The two types of Halon used are:

Halon 1211. A liquid steaming agent that is used in portable extinguishers

Halon 1301. A gaseous agent that is used in fixed total flooding systems

Some common EPA-acceptable Halon replacements are:

- FM-200 (HFC-227ea)
- CEA-410 or CEA-308
- NAF-S-III (HCFC Blend A)
- FE-13 (HFC-23)
- Argon (IG55) or Argonite (IG01)
- Inergen (IG541)
- Low-pressure water mists

Contamination and Damage

Environmental contamination resulting from the fire (or its suppression) can cause damage to the computer systems by depositing conductive particles on the components.

The following are some examples of fire contaminants:

- Smoke
- Heat
- Water
- Suppression medium contamination (Halon or CO_2)

Table 10.4 lists the temperatures required to damage various computer parts.

Heating, Ventilation, and Air Conditioning

HVAC is sometimes referred to as HVACR for the addition of refrigeration. HVAC systems can be quite complex in modern high-rise buildings, and are the focal point for environmental controls. An IT manager needs to know who is responsible for HVAC, and clear escalation steps need to be defined well in advance of an environment-threatening incident. The same department is often responsible for fire, water, and other disaster response, all of which impact the availability of the computer systems.

Physical and Technical Controls

Under this general grouping, we discuss those elements of physical security that are not considered specifically administrative solutions, although they obviously have administrative aspects. Here we have the areas of environmental controls, fire protection, electrical power, guards, and locks.

We will discuss the elements of control as they relate to the areas of:

- Facility Control Requirements
- Facility Access Control Devices
- Intrusion Detection and Alarms
- Computer Inventory Control
- Media Storage Requirements

Facility Control Requirements

Several elements are required to maintain physical site security for facility control:

Table 10.4 Heat Damage Temperatures

ITEM	TEMPERATURE
Computer hardware	175° F
Magnetic storage	100° F
Paper products	350° F

Guards

Guards are the oldest form of security surveillance. Guards still have a very important and primary function in the physical security process, particularly in perimeter control. A guard can make determinations that hardware or other automated security devices cannot make due to his ability to adjust to rapidly changing conditions, to learn and alter recognizable patterns, and to respond to various conditions in the environment. Guards provide deterrent capability, response, and control capabilities, in addition to receptionist and escort functions. Guards are also the best resource during periods of personnel safety risks (they maintain order, crowd control, and evacuation), and are better at making value decisions at times of incidents. They are appropriate whenever immediate, discriminating judgment is required by the security entity.

Guards have several drawbacks, however, such as the following:

Availability. They cannot exist in environments that do not support human intervention.

Reliability. The pre-employment screening and bonding of guards is not foolproof.

Training. Guards can be socially engineered, or may not always have up-to-date lists of access authorization.

Cost. Maintaining a guard function either internally or through an external service is expensive.

Dogs

Using guard dogs is almost as old a concept as using people to guard something. Dogs are loyal, reliable (they rarely have substance abuse issues), and have a keen sense of smell and hearing. However, a guard dog is primarily acceptable for perimeter physical control, and is not as useful as a human guard for making judgment calls. Some additional drawbacks include cost, maintenance, and insurance/liability issues.

Fencing

Fencing is the primary means of perimeter/boundary facility access control. The category of fencing includes fences, gates, turnstiles, and mantraps.

Fencing and other barriers provide crowd control and help deter casual trespassing by controlling access to entrances. Drawbacks to fencing include its cost, its appearance (it might be ugly), and its inability to stop a determined intruder. Table 10.5 is a very important table; a CISSP candidate should know these heights.

Table 10.5 Fencing Height Requirements

HEIGHT	PROTECTION
3' to 4' high	Deters casual trespassers
6' to 7' high	Too hard to climb easily
8' high with 3 strands of barbed wire	Deters intruders

Mantrap. A physical access control method where the entrance is routed through a set of double doors that might be monitored by a guard.

Lighting

Lighting is also one of the most common forms of perimeter or boundary protection. Extensive outside protective lighting of entrances or parking areas can discourage prowlers or casual intruders. Critical protected buildings should be illuminated up to 8 feet high with 2 feet candle power. Common types of lighting include floodlights, streetlights, fresnel lights, and searchlights.

Locks

After the use of guards, locks are probably one of the oldest access control methods ever used. Locks can be divided into two types: preset and programmable.

Preset locks. These are your typical door locks. The combinations to enter cannot be changed except by physically removing them and replacing the internal mechanisms. There are various types of preset locks, including key-in-knob, mortise, and rim locks. These all consist of variations of latches, cylinders, and dead bolts.

Programmable locks. These locks can be either mechanically or electronically based. A mechanical, programmable lock is often a typical dial combination lock, like the kind you would use on your gym locker. Another type of mechanical programmable lock is the common five-key pushbutton lock that requires the user to enter a combination of numbers. This is a very popular lock for IT operations centers. An electronic programmable lock requires the user to enter a pattern of digits on a numerical-style keypad, and it may display the digits in random order each time to prevent shoulder surfing for input patterns. It is also known as a cipher lock or keypad access control.

Closed-Circuit Television

Visual surveillance or recording devices such as closed circuit television are used in conjunction with guards in order to enhance their surveillance ability and to record events for future analysis or prosecution. These devices can either be photographic in nature (as in still or movie film cameras), or electronic in nature (the closed-circuit TV camera). CCTV can be used to monitor live events occurring in an area remote to the guard, or they can be used in conjunction with a VCR for a cost-effective method of recording these events.

Remember that the monitoring of live events is preventative, and the recording of events is considered detective in nature.

Facility Access Control Devices

This access includes personnel access control to the facility and general operations centers, in addition to specific data center access control.

Security Access Cards

Security access cards are a common method of physical access control. There are two common card types—photo-image and digitally encoded cards. These two groups are also described as dumb and smart cards. Dumb cards require a guard to make a decision as to its validity, while smart cards make the entry decision electronically.

Photo-Image Cards. Photo-image cards are simple identification cards with the photo of the bearer for identification. These are your standard photo ID cards, like a drivers license or employee ID badge. These cards are referred to as "dumb" cards because they have no intelligence imbedded in them, and they require an active decision to be made by the entry personnel as to their authenticity.

Digital-Coded Cards. Digitally encoded cards contain chips or magnetically encoded strips (possibly in addition to a photo of the bearer). The card reader may be programmed whether to accept an entry based upon an online access control computer that can also provide information about the date and time of entry. These cards may also be able to create multi-level access groupings. There are two common forms of digitally encoded cards, which are referred to as smart and smarter cards.

Smart entry cards can either have a magnetic stripe or a small Integrated Circuit (IC) chip imbedded in them. This card may require knowledge of a password or Personal Identification Number (PIN) to enable entry. A bank ATM card is an example of this card type. These cards may contain a processor encoded with the host system's authentication protocol, read-only memory storage of programs and data, and even some kind of user interface.

In some scenarios, a smart card can be coupled with an authenti-cation token that generates a one-time or challenge-response password or PIN. While two-actor (or dual-factor) authentication is most often used for logical access to network services, it can be combined with an intelligent card reader to provide extremely strong facility access control.

Wireless Proximity Readers. A proximity reader does not require the user to physically insert the access card. This card may also be referred to as a wireless security card. The card reader senses the card in possession of a user in the general area (proximity) and enables access. There are two general types of proximity readers—user activated and system sensing.

A user-activated proximity card transmits a sequence of keystrokes to a wireless keypad on the reader. The keypad on the reader contains either a fixed preset code or a programmable unique key pattern.

A system-sensing proximity card recognizes the presence of the coded device in the reader's general area. The following are the three common types of system-sensing cards, which are based upon the way the power is generated for these devices:

1. *Passive devices.* These cards contain no battery or power on the card, but sense the electromagnetic field transmitted by the reader and transmit at different frequencies using the power field of the reader.

2. *Field-powered devices.* They contain active electronics, a radio frequency transmitter, and a power supply circuit on the card.

3. *Transponders.* Both the card and reader each contain a receiver, transmitter, active electronics, and a battery. The reader transmits an interrogating signal to the card, which in turn causes it to transmit an access code. These systems are often used as portable devices for dynamically assigning access control.

Table 10.6 lists the various types of security access cards.

Biometric Devices

Biometric access control devices and techniques, such as fingerprinting or retinal scanning, are discussed thoroughly in Chapter 2, "Access Control Systems." Keep in mind that because they constitute a physical security control, biometric devices are also considered a physical access security control device.

WHAT ARE THOSE THREE THINGS AGAIN?

What are the three elements, which we learned, that are commonly used for authentication? 1) something you have (like a token card), 2) something you know (like your PIN or password), and 3) Something you are (biometrics).

Table 10.6 Dumb, Smart, and Smarter Cards

TYPE OF CARD	DESCRIPTION
Photo ID	Facial photograph
Optical-coded	Laser-burned lattice of digital dots
Electric circuit	Printed IC on the card
Magnetic stripe	Stripe of magnetic material
Magnetic strip	Rows of copper strips
Passive electronic	Electrically tuned circuitry read by RF
Active electronic	Badge transmitting encoded electronics

Intrusion Detectors and Alarms

Intrusion detection refers to the process of identifying attempts to penetrate a system or building to gain unauthorized access. While Chapter 3 details ID systems that detect logical breaches of the network infrastructure, here we are talking about devices that detect physical breaches of perimeter security, such as a burglar alarm.

Perimeter Intrusion Detectors

The two most common types of physical perimeter detectors are either based on photoelectric sensors or dry contact switches.

Photoelectric sensors. Photoelectric sensors receive a beam of light from a light-emitting device creating a grid of either visible, white light, or invisible, infrared light. An alarm is activated when the beams are broken. The beams can be physically avoided if seen; therefore, invisible infrared light is often used. Also, employing a substitute light system can defeat the sensor.

Dry contact switches. Dry contact switches and tape are probably the most common types of perimeter detection. This can consist of metallic foil tape on windows, or metal contact switches on door frames. This type of physical intrusion detection is the cheapest and easiest to maintain, and is very commonly used for shop front protection.

Motion Detectors

In addition to the two types of intrusion detectors previously mentioned, motion detectors are used to sense unusual movement within a predefined interior security area. They can be grouped into three categories: wave pattern motion detectors, capacitance detectors, and audio amplification devices.

Wave Pattern. Wave pattern motion detectors generate a frequency wave pattern and send an alarm if the pattern is disturbed as it is reflected back to its receiver. These frequencies can either be in the low, ultrasonic, or microwave range.

Capacitance. Capacitance detectors monitor an electrical field surrounding the object being monitored. They are used for spot protection within a few inches of the object, rather than for overall room security monitoring used by wave detectors. Penetration of this field changes the electrical capacitance of the field enough to generate an alarm.

Audio Detectors. Audio detectors are passive, in that they do not generate any fields or patterns like the previous two methods. Audio detectors simply monitor a room for any abnormal sound wave generation and trigger an alarm. This type of detection device generates a higher number of false alarms than the other two methods, and should only be used in areas that have controlled ambient sound.

Alarm Systems

The detection devices previously listed monitor and report on a specific change in the environment. These detectors can be grouped together to create alarm systems. There are four general types of alarm systems:

Local Alarm Systems. A local alarm system rings an audible alarm on the local premises that it protects. This alarm must be protected from tampering and be audible for at least 400 feet. It also requires guards to respond locally to the intrusion.

Central Station Systems. Private security firms operate these systems that are monitored around the clock. The central stations are signaled by detectors over leased lines. These stations typically offer many additional features, such as CCTV monitoring and printed reports, and the customers' premises are commonly less than 10 minutes travel time away from the central monitoring office.

Proprietary Systems. These systems are similar to the central station systems, except that the monitoring system is owned and operated by the customer. They are like local alarms, except that a sophisticated computer system provides many of the features in-house that a third-party firm would provide with a central station system.

Auxiliary Station Systems. Any of the previous three systems may have auxiliary alarms that ring at the local fire or police stations. Most central station systems include this feature, which requires permission from the local authorities before implementation.

Two other terms related to alarms are:

Line supervision. Line supervision is a process where an alarm-signaling transmission medium is monitored to detect any line tampering to subvert its effectiveness. The *Underwriters Laboratory* (UL) standard 611-1968 states, "the connecting line between the central station and the protection shall be supervised so as to automatically detect a compromise attempt by methods of resistance substitution, potential substitution, or any single compromise attempt." Secure detection and alarm systems require line supervision.

Power supplies. Alarm systems require separate circuitry and backup power with 24 hours minimum discharge time. These alarms help reduce the probability of an alarm system's failure due to a power failure.

Computer Inventory Control

Computer Inventory Control is the control of computers and computer equipment from physical theft and protection from damage. The two main areas of concern are computer physical control and laptop control.

PC Physical Control

Due to the proliferation of distributed computing and the proliferation of laptops, inventory control at the microcomputer level is a major headache. Some groups estimate that 40 percent of computer inventory shrinkage is due to microcomputer parts walking out the door. Several physical controls must be taken to minimize this loss:

Cable locks. A cable lock consists of a vinyl-covered steel cable anchoring the PC or peripherals to the desk. They often consist of screw kits, slot locks, and cable traps.

Port controls. Port controls are devices that secure data ports (such as a floppy drive or a serial or parallel port) and prevent their use.

Switch controls. A switch control is a cover for the on/off switch, which prevents a user from switching off the file server's power.

Peripheral switch controls. These types of controls are lockable switches that prevent a keyboard from being used.

Electronic security boards. These boards are inserted into an expansion slot in the PC and forces a user to enter a password when the unit is booted. This is also a standard part of the *Basic Input Output System* (BIOS) of many off-the-shelf PCs. They might also be called cryptographic locks.

Laptop Control

The proliferation of laptops and portables is the next evolution of distributed computing and constitutes a challenge to security practitioners. Now the computing resources can be strewn all over the globe, and physical inventory control is nearly impossible for an organization without a substantive dedication of IT resources. A laptop theft is a very serious issue because it creates a failure of all three elements of C.I.A.: Confidentiality, as the data can now be read by someone outside of a monitored environment; Availability, as the user has lost the unit's computing ability; and Integrity, as the data residing on the unit and any telecommunications from it are now suspect.

Media Storage Requirements

The ongoing storage of data media and the proper disposal of unneeded media and reports is a serious concern to security practitioners. Sometimes an organization will devote a large amount of resources to perimeter protection and network security, then will dispose of reports improperly. Or, they will reuse laptops or diskettes without fully and appropriately wiping the data.

Because laptop theft is rampant, encryption of any sensitive data on a portable is also an absolute necessity. An associate of mine was recently lent a laptop while working at a top brokerage firm, only to discover that the hard drive had not been reformatted, and contained dozens of sensitive emails pertaining to the 1996 presidential election (the previous owner had worked as an advisor to the GOP Bob Dole campaign).

The following types of media commonly require storage, destruction, or reuse:

■ Data backup tapes

■ CDs

■ Diskettes

■ Hard drives

■ Paper printouts and reports

The common storage areas for such media are:

On-site. Areas within the facility, such as operations centers, offices, desks, storage closets, cabinets, safes, and so on

Off-site. Areas outside of the facility, such as data backup vault services, partners and vendors, and disposal systems. Transportation to or from an external data vault services vendor is a security concern, and it should be examined for problems relating to theft, copying, alteration, or destruction of data.

We have the following resources and elements in our control to protect the media:

■ Physical access control to the storage areas

■ Environmental controls, such as fire and water protections

■ Diskette inventory controls and monitoring

■ Audits of media use

Data Destruction and Reuse

Data that is no longer needed or used must be destroyed. Information on magnetic media is typically "destroyed" by degaussing or overwriting. Formatting a disk once does not completely destroy all data, so the entire media must be overwritten or formatted seven times to conform to standards for object reuse.

Paper reports should be shredded by personnel with the proper level of security clearance. Some shredders cut in straight lines or strips, others cross-cut or disintegrate the material into pulp. Care must be taken to limit access to the reports prior to disposal and those stored for long periods. Reports should never be disposed of without shredding, such as when they are placed in a dumpster intact. Burning is also sometimes used to destroy paper reports, especially in the Department of Defense and military.

Object Reuse and Data Remanence

Object Reuse is the concept of reusing data storage media after its initial use. Data Remanence is the problem of residual information remaining on the media after erasure, which may be subject to restoration by another user, thereby resulting in a loss of confidentiality. Diskettes, hard drives, tapes, and any magnetic or writable media are susceptible to data remanence. Retrieving the bits and pieces of data that have not been thoroughly removed from storage media is a common method of computer forensics,

---

DISKETTE STORAGE TIPS

A few basic controls should be put in place to protect diskettes (or other magnetic media) from damage or loss, such as

1. Keep the disks in locked cases.
2. Don't bend the diskettes.
3. Maintain the proper temperature and humidity.
4. Avoid external magnetic fields (such as TVs or radios).
5. Don't write directly on the jacket or sleeve.

> ### THE JOY OF DUMPSTER DIVING
>
> New York is the capital of ticker-tape parades. New Yorkers never seem to tire of trying to find some reason to throw large volumes of paper out of high story office windows. Sometimes, however, the enthusiasm for the moment overrides the immediate availability of shredded reports, and some office workers will begin to toss out unshredded, full-page printed pages. Local reporters have begun to collect these reports before they are swept up by sanitation and have reported that the information contained is considerable (especially due to the fact that the parades are often down Broadway, past Wall Street). These pages often contain credit card account numbers, bank account numbers and balances, credit rating details, and so forth.

and is often used by law enforcement personnel to preserve evidence and to construct a trail of misuse. Anytime a storage medium is reused (and also when it is discarded), there is the potential for the media's information to be retrieved. Methods must be employed to properly destroy the existing data to ensure that no residual data is available to new users. The Orange Book standard recommends that magnetic media be formatted seven times before discard or reuse.

Terminology relative to the various stages of data erasure is as follows:

Clearing. This term refers to the overwriting of data media (primarily magnetic) intended to be reused in the same organization or monitored environment.

Purging. This term refers to degaussing or overwriting media intended to be removed from a monitored environment, such as during resale (laptops) or donations to charity.

Destruction. This term refers to completely destroying the media, and therefore the residual data. Paper reports, diskettes, and optical media (CD-ROMs) need to be physically destroyed before disposal.

The following are the common problems with magnetic media erasure that may cause data remanence:

1. Erasing the data through an operating system does not remove the data, it just changes the File Allocation Table and renames the first character of the file. This is the most common way computer forensics investigators can restore files.

2. Damaged sectors of the disk may not be overwritten by the format utility. Degaussing may need to be used, or formatting seven times is recommended.

WALK-THROUGH SECURITY LIST

The simplest way to get a handle on your office's state of physical security is to do a minimal "walk-about." This consists of an after-hours walk-through of your site, checking for these specific things:

1. Sensitive company information is not lying open on desks or in traffic areas.
2. Workstations are logged out and turned off.
3. Offices are locked and secured.
4. Stairwell exits are not propped open (I have seen them propped open with fire extinguishers, so folks wouldn't have to use the elevators!).
5. Files, cabinets, and desks are locked and secured.
6. Diskettes and data tapes are put away and secured.

---

3. Rewriting files on top of the old files may not overwrite all data areas on the disk, because the new file may not be as long as the older file, and data may be retrieved past the file end control character.

4. Degausser equipment failure or operator error may result in an inadequate erasure.

5. There may be an inadequate number of formats. Magnetic media containing sensitive information should be formatted seven times or more.

Sample Questions

You can find answers to the following questions in Appendix H.

1. The recommended optimal relative humidity range for computer operations is:

   a. 10%–30%

   b. 30%–40%

   c. 40%–60%

   d. 60%–80%

2. How many times should a diskette be formatted to comply with TCSEC Orange Book object reuse recommendations?

   a. Three

   b. Five

   c. Seven

   d. Nine

3. Which of the following more closely describes the combustibles in a Class B-rated fire?

   a. Paper

   b. Gas

   c. Liquid

   d. Electrical

4. Which of the following is NOT the proper suppression medium for a Class B fire?

   a. CO_2

   b. Soda Acid

   c. Halon

   d. Water

5. What does an audit trail or access log usually NOT record?

   a. How often a diskette was formatted

   b. Who attempted access

   c. The date and time of the access attempt

   d. Whether the attempt was successful

6. A Brownout can be defined as a:

   a. Prolonged power loss

   b. Momentary low voltage

   c. Prolonged low voltage

   d. Momentary high voltage

7. A surge can be defined as a(n):

   a. Prolonged high voltage

   b. Initial surge of power at start

   c. Momentary power loss

   d. Steady interfering disturbance

8. Which is NOT a type of fire detector?

   a. Heat-sensing

   b. Gas-discharge

   c. Flame-actuated

   d. Smoke-actuated

9. Which of the following is NOT considered an acceptable replacement for Halon discharge systems?

   a. FA200

   b. Inergen (IG541)

   c. Halon 1301

   d. Argon (IG55)

10. Which type of fire extinguishing method contains standing water in the pipe, and therefore generally does not enable a manual shutdown of systems before discharge?

   a. Dry Pipe

   b. Wet pipe

   c. Preaction

   d. Deluge

11. Which type of control below is NOT an example of a physical security access control?

   a. Retinal scanner

   b. Guard dog

   c. Five-key programmable lock

   d. Audit trail

12. Which is NOT a recommended way to dispose of unwanted used data media?

   a. Destroying CD-ROMs

   b. Formatting diskettes seven or more times

c. Shredding paper reports by cleared personnel

d. Copying new data over existing data on diskettes

13. Which of the following is an example of a "smart" card?

   a. A driver's license

   b. A bank ATM card

   c. An employee photo ID

   d. A library card

14. Which is NOT an element of two-factor authentication?

   a. Something you are

   b. Something you know

   c. Something you have

   d. Something you ate

15. The theft of a laptop poses a threat to which tenet of the C.I.A. triad?

   a. Confidentiality

   b. Integrity

   c. Availability

   d. All of the above

16. Which is a benefit of a guard over an automated control?

   a. Guards can use discriminating judgment.

   b. Guards are cheaper.

   c. Guards do not need training.

   d. Guards do not need pre-employment screening.

17. Which is NOT considered a preventative security measure?

   a. Fences

   b. Guards

   c. Audit trails

   d. Preset locks

18. Which is NOT a PC security control device?

   a. A cable lock

   b. A switch control

   c. A port control

   d. A file cabinet lock

19. What is the recommended height of perimeter fencing to keep out casual trespassers?

    a. 1' to 2' high

    b. 3' to 4' high

    c. 6' to 7' high

    d. 8' to 12' high

20. Why should extensive exterior perimeter lighting of entrances or parking areas be installed?

    a. To enable programmable locks to be used

    b. To create two-factor authentication

    c. To discourage prowlers or casual intruders

    d. To prevent data remanence

21. Which of the following is NOT a form of data erasure?

    a. Clearing

    b. Remanence

    c. Purging

    d. Destruction

22. Which is NOT considered a physical intrusion detection method?

    a. Audio motion detector

    b. Photoelectric sensor

    c. Wave pattern motion detector

    d. Line supervision

Bonus Questions

You can find answers to the following questions in Appendix H.

1. Which type of fire extinguisher below should be used on an electrical fire?

    a. Water

    b. Soda Acid

    c. CO_2

    d. Kerosene

2. Which type of fire detector sends an alarm when the temperature of the room rises dramatically?

    a. Heat-sensing

    b. Odor-sensing

    c. Smoke-actuated

    d. Flame-actuated

3. Which medium below is the most sensitive to damage from temperature?

    a. Computer hardware

    b. Floppy diskettes

    c. Paper products

    d. Sheet rock

4. Which choice below is the BEST description of a Central Station Alarm System?

    a. Rings an audible alarm on the local premises that it protects

    b. Rings an alarm in a central monitoring office of a third-party monitoring firm

    c. Rings an alarm in the office of the customer

    d. Also rings an alarm in the local fire or police station

5. Which choice below is NOT a type of motion detector?

    a. Wave pattern detection

    b. Capacitance detection

    c. Smoke detection

    d. Audio detection

6. Which choice below BEST describes the process of data purging?

  a. Overwriting of data media intended to be reused in the same organization or area

  b. Degaussing or thoroughly overwriting media intended to be removed from the control of the organization or area

  c. Complete physical destruction of the media

  d. Reusing data storage media after its initial use

7. Which choice below BEST describes a power sag?

  a. Complete loss of power

  b. Momentary high voltage

  c. Prolonged high voltage

  d. Momentary low voltage

8. Which choice below BEST describes a mantrap?

  a. A physical access control using at least 6' to 7' high fencing

  b. A physical access control using double doors and a guard

  c. A physical access control using flood lighting

  d. A physical access control using CCTV

9. Which choice below describes the reason for using cable locks on workstations?

  a. To prevent unauthorized access to the network from the unit

  b. To prevent the robbery of the unit

  c. To prevent unauthorized downloading of data to the unit's floppy drive

  d. To prevent the unit from being powered on

10. Which choice below is not a description or element of a raised floor?

  a. A platform with removable panels where equipment is installed

  b. Flooring with space between it and the main building floor housing cabling

  c. Raised area used to supply conditioned air to the data processing equipment and room

  d. Area used for storage of paper files

Advanced Sample Questions

You can find answers to the following questions in Appendix I.

The following questions are supplemental to and coordinated with Chapter 10 and are at a level commensurate with that of the CISSP Examination. These advanced questions and answers build upon the questions and answers covered in this chapter. While these questions may be more difficult than the actual questions on the exam, they are good preparation for the concepts covered, such as fire suppression, physical access control, and physical intrusion detection.

1. Which choice below is NOT a common biometric method?

   a. Retina pattern devices

   b. Fingerprint devices

   c. Handprint devices

   d. Phrenologic devices

2. According to the NFPA, which choice below is NOT a recommended risk factor to consider when determining the need for protecting the computing environment from fire?

   a. Life safety aspects of the computing function or process

   b. Fire threat of the installation to occupants or exposed property

   c. Distance of the computing facility from a fire station

   d. Economic loss of the equipment's value

3. Which choice below is NOT an example of a Halocarbon Agent?

   a. HFC-23

   b. FC-3-1-10

   c. IG-541

   d. HCFC-22

4. Which choice below is NOT an example of a combustible in a Class B fire?

   a. Grease

   b. Rubber

   c. Oil-base paints

   d. Flammable gases

5. Which statement below most accurately describes a "dry pipe" sprinkler system?

   a. Dry pipe is the most commonly used sprinkler system.

   b. Dry pipe contains air pressure.

c. Dry pipe sounds an alarm and delays water release.

d. Dry pipe may contain carbon dioxide.

6. Which choice below is NOT a recommendation for records and materials storage in the computer room, for fire safety?

a. Green bar printing paper for printers should be stored in the computer room.

b. Abandoned cables shall not be allowed to accumulate.

c. Space beneath the raised floor shall not be used for storage purposes.

d. Only minimum records shall be required for essential and efficient operation.

7. Which choice below is NOT considered an element of two-factor authentication?

a. Something you know

b. Something you do

c. Something you have

d. Something you are

8. Which choice below is NOT an example of a "clean" fire extinguishing agent?

a. CO_2

b. IG-55

c. IG-01

d. HCFC-22

9. Which choice below is NOT considered a requirement to install an automatic sprinkler system?

a. The building is required to be sprinklered.

b. The computer room is vented to outside offices.

c. The computer room contains a significant quantity of combustible materials.

d. A computer system's enclosure contains combustible materials.

10. Which choice below is NOT a type of motion detection system?

a. Ultrasonic detection system

b. Microwave detection system

c. Host-based intrusion detection system

d. Sonic detection system

11. Which fire extinguishant choice below does NOT create toxic HF levels?

a. Halon 1301

b. Halon 1211

    c. IG-01

    d. HCFC-22

12. Which choice below is NOT permitted under computer room raised flooring?

    a. Interconnecting DP cables enclosed in a raceway

    b. Underfloor ventilation for the computer room only

    c. Nonabrasive openings for cables

    d. Underfloor ventilation to the rest of the offices' ventilation system

13. Which choice below represents the BEST reason to control the humidity in computer operations areas?

    a. Computer operators do not perform at their peak if the humidity is too high.

    b. Electrostatic discharges can harm electronic equipment.

    c. Static electricity destroys the electrical efficiency of the circuits.

    d. If the air is too dry, electroplating of conductors may occur.

14. Which statement below is NOT accurate about smoke damage to electronic equipment?

    a. Smoke exposure during a fire for a relatively short period does little immediate damage.

    b. Continuing power to the smoke-exposed equipment can increase the damage.

    c. Moisture and oxygen corrosion constitute the main damage to the equipment.

    d. The primary damage done by smoke exposure is immediate.

15. Which choice below most accurately describes the prime benefit from using guards?

    a. Human guards are less expensive than guard dogs.

    b. Guards can exercise discretionary judgment in a way that automated systems can't.

    c. Automated systems have a greater reliability rate than guards.

    d. Guard dogs cannot discern an intruder's intent.

16. Which choice below is an accurate statement about EMI and RFI?

    a. EMI can contain RFI.

    b. EMI is generated naturally; RFI is man-made.

    c. RFI is generated naturally; EMI is man-made.

    d. Natural sources of EMI pose the greatest threat to electronic equipment.

17. In which proper order should the steps below be taken after electronic equipment or media has been exposed to water?

_____ a. Place all affected equipment or media in an air-conditioned area, if portable.

_____ b. Turn off all electrical power to the equipment.

_____ c. Open cabinet doors and remove panels and covers to allow water to run out.

_____ d. Wipe with alcohol or Freon-alcohol solutions or spray with water-displacement aerosol sprays.

18. Which choice below is NOT an example of using a social engineering technique to gain physical access to a secure facility?

    a. Asserting authority or pulling rank

    b. Intimidating or threatening

    c. Praising or flattering

    d. Employing the salami fraud

19. In which proper order should the steps below be taken after electronic equipment or media has been exposed to smoke contaminants?

_____ a. Turn off power to equipment.

_____ b. Spray corrosion-inhibiting aerosol to stabilize metal contact surfaces.

_____ c. Spray connectors, backplanes, and printed circuit boards with Freon or Freon-alcohol solvents.

_____ d. Move equipment into an air-conditioned and humidity-controlled environment.

20. Which fire suppression medium below is considered to be the MOST toxic to personnel?

    a. CO_2

    b. IG-01

    c. Halon 1301

    d. Halocarbon Agents

21. Which type of personnel control below helps prevent piggybacking?

    a. Man traps

    b. Back doors

    c. Brute force

    d. Maintenance hooks

22. Which type of physical access control method below is best suited for high-security areas?

    a. Deadbolts

    b. Access token

    c. Key locks

    d. Pushbutton locks

23. Which term below refers to a standard used in determining the fire safety of a computer room?

    a. Noncombustible

    b. Fire-resistant

    c. Fire-retardant

    d. Nonflammable

A Process Approach
to HIPAA Compliance
through a HIPAA-CMM

(Copyright, Corbett Technologies, Inc.)

Addressing the *Health Insurance Portability and Accountability Act* (HIPAA) health information standards in an effective manner requires a sound, structured approach. The method of compliance with the HIPAA privacy regulations and pending Security and Electronic Signature standards should provide proper and complete coverage of the requirements of the law and should support metrics for evaluating the effectiveness of the implementation.

The major issue relative to meeting HIPAA information security requirements at this time is that there is no standard process in place to determine HIPAA compliance. This situation becomes more complicated when institutions are evaluated according to different criteria and methodologies. What is needed is a standard methodology and evaluation model that is based on proven, valid techniques that are recognized by the information security community. This paper proposes a *HIPAA-Capability Maturity Model* (HIPAA-CMM) based on such techniques. The model is based on the proven and recognized CMM framework developed initially for measuring the quality and maturity level of an organization's software development process and has been extended to systems engineering and systems security engineering.

While the Security and Electronic Signature standards regulation portions of the HIPAA implementation are still in draft form and are subject to amendment, the privacy regulation already provides that "a covered entity must have in place appropriate administrative, technical and physical safeguards to protect the privacy of protected health information." A review of the current draft regulation regarding security standards reveals that it codifies information system security practices that are generally accepted as best in commercial government arenas. In order to comply with the act and with the privacy regulation's requirement for "appropriate administrative, technical and physical safeguards," covered entities will have to demonstrate due diligence in implementing generally accepted best information system security practices.

The HIPAA-CMM is proposed as the standard framework for evaluating and assuring HIPAA compliance. The *process areas* (PAs) selected for the HIPAA-CMM are based on the generally accepted best practices of systems security engineering. (A PA is a defined set of related security engineering process characteristics that, when performed collectively, can achieve a defined purpose.) Thus, the use of the HIPAA-CMM will not only measure compliance with current HIPAA requirements, but with the standards that are likely to be included in the final privacy, will also measure Security and Electronic Signature standards regulation when it is issued.

The HIPAA-CMM is based on the Systems Security Engineering Capability Maturity Model" (SSE-CMM), [SSE99]. The PAs of the SSE-CMM incorporate the technical, organizational, and best project practices of systems security engineering. As such, they provide a process-based common thread that encompasses most security-related evaluation criteria and security guidance documents. Corbett's HIPAA-CMM incorporates a specific subset of the 22 SSE-CMM PAs to address the privacy and information security portions of HIPAA. To provide the complete coverage and granularity required by the HIPAA regulations that are not addressed by the SSE-CMM, additional PAs have been developed. These PAs are HIPAA-Specific PAs (HPAs) and serve to customize the model for the HIPAA application. Because the HIPAA regulations have not been finalized as yet, the corresponding requirements have been developed based on the extant HIPAA documentation and generally accepted best security practices. The HIPAA-CMM is designed as the basis for providing the full evaluation coverage that is necessary to address all the HIPAA information security compliance requirements.

The catalyst for the HIPAA-CMM was an initial investigation of the relationship between the SSE-CMM and other federal information security compliance standards. The questions addressed were as follows:

- How can the SSE-CMM assist in supporting the use of federal security standards and guidelines?
- How can the SSE-CMM be used to gather evidence of compliance?

In the past, SSE-CMM PA mappings to federal security standards and guidelines have been shown to be feasible and valuable in providing evidence for the evaluation of assurance mechanisms. In all such mappings, the SSE-CMM is viewed as complementary to the associated evaluation criteria and provides a structured basis for evidence gathering and assurance. The HIPAA regulations, however, require an enterprise view of an organization's privacy and security processes and procedures that is not implemented by the IT/IS evaluation mechanisms or fully covered by the SSE-CMM. Thus, there is a need for supplemental PAs to meet the proposed HIPAA information security legislative requirements. These supplemental PAs and selected SSE-CMM PAs comprise Corbett's HIPAA-CMM.

The SSE-CMM mappings that have been investigated ([FER97] and [GAL97]) were to the Common Criteria Assurance Requirements [CCP96], Defense Information Technology Security Certification and Accreditation Process (DITSCAP [DOD97]), and the Trusted Computer System Evaluation Criteria (TCSEC [DOD85]). The mappings also apply to the *National Information Assurance Certification and Accreditation Process* (NIACAP, [NST00]) because the NIACAP is an extension of the DITSCAP for non-defense government organizations. They were developed for the independent evaluation of government IT/IS and are very effective in performing that function. Also, a version of the NIACAP, the *Commercial INFOSEC Analysis Process* (CIAP), is under development for the evaluation of critical commercial systems.

Other SSE-CMM mappings have been proposed [HOP99] to ISO/IEC 13335 Information Technology—Security Techniques—Guidelines for the Management of IT Security (GMITS)—Part 2 [ISO]; the NIST Handbook [NIS95]; BS 7799 [BSI98]; and the Canadian Handbook on Information Technology Security MG-9 [CSE98].

We discuss the SSE-CMM mappings in more detail in Appendix D of this report.

Background

The major issue relative to meeting HIPAA information security requirements at this time is that there is no standard process in place to determine HIPAA compliance. This situation becomes more complicated when institutions are evaluated according to different criteria and methodologies. What is needed is a standard methodology and evaluation model that is based on proven, valid techniques that are recognized by the information security community. The Corbett Technologies HIPAA-CMM was developed based on such techniques.

Reviews of HIPAA information security issues and *Capability Maturity Models* (CMMs) are presented in the following sections to provide a basis for developing the corresponding mappings.

HIPAA

The United States *Kennedy-Kassebaum Health Insurance Portability and Accountability Act* (HIPAA-Public Law 104-191), effective August 21, 1996, addresses the issues of health care privacy, security, transactions and code sets, unique identifiers, electronic signatures, and plan portability in the United States. With respect to privacy, the act stated, "Not later than the date that is 12 months after the date of the enactment of this Act, the Secretary of Health and Human Services shall submit . . . detailed recommendations on standards with respect to the privacy of individually identifiable health information." The act further stated, "The recommendations... shall address at least the following:

- The rights that an individual who is a subject of individually identifiable health information should have
- The procedures that should be established for the exercise of such rights
- The uses and disclosures of such information that should be authorized or required"

The act then provided that if the legislation governing standards with respect to the privacy of individually identifiable health information is not enacted by "the date that is 36 months after the enactment of this Act, the Secretary of Health and Human Services shall promulgate final regulations containing such standards not later than the date that is 42 months after the date of the enactment of this Act." Congress failed to act by that date, and therefore the Secretary of Health and Human Services was required to issue the privacy regulations no later than February 21, 2000. This date was not met, but the regulations were announced in December 2000 [HHS00] and included the following items:

- Coverage was extended to medical records of all forms, not only those in electronic form. This coverage includes oral and paper communications that did not exist in electronic form.
- Patient consent is required for routine disclosures of health records.
- Disclosure of full medical records for the purposes of treatment to providers is allowed.
- Protection was issued against the unauthorized use of medical records for employment purposes.

The privacy regulations were reopened for public comment for an additional period that closed on April 26, 2002. In August 2002, the Privacy Rule was modified to ensure that compliance with the regulations would not impede the delivery of health care to the patient. Also, the Security and Electronic Signature standards are still in draft form. The privacy regulations, however, state the following in reference to information system security requirements:

c) (1) Standard: safeguards. A covered entity must have in place appropriate administrative, technical, and physical safeguards to protect the privacy of protected health information.

(2) Implementation specification: safeguards. A covered entity must reasonably safeguard protected health information from any intentional or unintentional use or disclosure that is in violation of the standards, implementation specifications or other requirements of this subpart."

At the present state of the regulations, HIPAA provides the following penalties for violations:

- *General penalty for failure to comply*—Each violation is $100; maximum for all violations of an identical requirement cannot exceed $25,000
- *Wrongful disclosure of identifiable health information*—$50,000, imprisonment of not more than one year or both
- *Wrongful disclosure of identifiable health information under false pretenses*—$100,000, imprisonment of not more than five years or both
- *Offense with intent to sell information*—$250,000, imprisonment of not more than 10 years, or both

For a more detailed discussion of HIPAA, please see Appendix F.

Process Improvement

The basic premise of process improvement is that the quality of services produced is a direct function of the quality of the associated development and maintenance processes. The Carnegie Mellon *Software Engineering Institute* (SEI) has developed an approach to process improvement called the IDEAL model. IDEAL stands for Initiating, Diagnosing, Establishing, Acting, and Learning as defined in Table A.1.

The goal is to establish a continuous cycle of evaluating the current status of your organization, making improvements, and repeating this cycle. The high-level steps are shown in Table A.1.

Each of the five phases of the IDEAL approach is made up of several activities. These activities are summarized in Appendix C for application to security engineering.

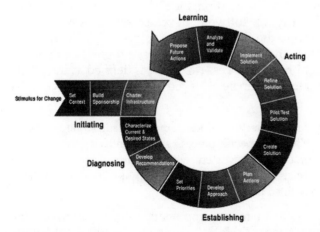

Figure A.1 The IDEAL Process Improvement Approach [SSE99].

Table A.1 The IDEAL Model [SSE99]

I	Initiating	Laying the groundwork for a successful improvement effort.
D	Diagnosing	Determining where you are relative to where you want to be.
E	Establishing	Planning the specifics of how you will reach your destination.
A	Acting	Doing the work according to the plan.
L	Learning	Learning from the experience and improving your ability.

The following basic principles of process change are necessary to implement a successful process improvement activity:

- Major changes must be sponsored by senior management.
- Focus on fixing the process, not assigning blame.
- Understand the current process first.
- Change is continuous.
- Improvement requires investment.
- Retaining improvement requires periodic reinforcement.

CMMs

In 1986, in collaboration with Mitre Corporation, the SEI developed a methodology for measuring the maturity of software development processes. This methodology was formalized into the CMM of Software [PAU95] [SEI95].

A CMM describes the stages through which processes progress as they are defined, implemented, and improved. Process capability is defined as the quantifiable range of expected results that can be achieved by following a process. To quote from the SSE-CMM:

> "The model provides a guide for selecting process improvement strategies by determining the current capabilities of specific processes and identifying the issues most critical to quality and process improvement within a particular domain. A CMM may take the form of a reference model to be used as a guide for developing and improving a mature and defined process."

The CMM has been applied to many environments as the framework for implementing process improvement. Table A.2 contrasts the SSE-CMM with other related efforts. Note that the SSE-CMM is the only approach that is focused on information system security engineering.

Table A.2 The SSE-CMM and Related Efforts [SSE99]

EFFORT	GOAL	APPROACH	SCOPE
SSE-CMM	Define, improve, and assess security engineering capability	Continuous security engineering maturity model and appraisal method	Security engineering organizations
SE-CMM	Improve system or product engineering process	Continuous maturity model of systems engineering practices and appraisal method	Systems engineering organizations
SEI CMM for Software	Improve the management of software development	Staged maturity model of software engineering and management practices	Software engineering organizations
Trusted CMM	Improve the process of high integrity software development and its environment	Staged maturity model of software engineering and management practices including security	High integrity software organizations
CMMI	Combine existing process improvement models into a single architectural framework	Sort, combine, and arrange process improvement building blocks to form tailored models	Engineering organizations
Systems Engineering CM (EIA731)	Define, improve, and assess systems engineering capability	Continuous systems engineering maturity model and appraisal method	Systems engineering organizations
Common Criteria	Improve security by enabling reusable protection profiles for classes of technology	Set of functional and assurance requirements for security, along with an evaluation process	Information technology
CISSP	Make security professional a recognized discipline	Security body of knowledge and certification tests for security profession	Security practitioners
Assurance Frameworks	Improve security assurance by enabling a broad range of evidence	Structured approach for creating assurance arguments and efficiently producing evidence	Security engineering organizations
ISO 9001	Improve organizational quality management	Specific requirements for quality management practices	Service organizations
ISO 15504	Software process improvement and assessment	Software process improvement model and appraisal methodology	Software engineering organizations
ISO 13335	Improvement of management of information technology security	Guidance on process used to achieve and maintain appropriate levels of security for information and services	Security engineering organizations

The HIPAA-CMM is based on the SE-CMM and SSE-CMM; therefore, the SE and SSE-CMMs are described briefly in the following sections.

The Systems Engineering CMM

The SSE-CMM is based on the *Systems Engineering CMM* (SE-CMM). The eleven Project and Organizational PAs of the SSE-CMM come directly from the SE-CMM. These areas are as follows:

PA12—Ensure Quality

PA13—Manage Configuration

PA14—Manage Project Risk

PA15—Monitor and Control Technical Effort

PA16—Plan Technical Effort

PA17—Define Organization's Systems Engineering Process

PA18—Improve Organization's Systems Engineering Process

PA19—Manage Product Line Evolution

PA20—Manage Systems Engineering Support Environment

PA21—Provide Ongoing Skills and Knowledge

PA22—Coordinate with Suppliers

The SE-CMM [BAT94] describes the essential elements of an organization's systems engineering process that must exist in order to ensure good systems engineering. It also provides a reference to compare existing systems engineering practices against the essential systems engineering elements described in the model. The definition of systems engineering on which the SE-CMM is based is defined as the selective application of scientific and engineering efforts to:

- Transform an operational need into a description of the system configuration that best satisfies the operational need according to the measures of effectiveness
- Integrate related technical parameters and ensure compatibility of all physical, functional, and technical program interfaces in a manner that optimizes the total system definition and design
- Integrate the efforts of all engineering disciplines and specialties into the total engineering effort

Similarly, a system is defined as follows:

- An integrated composite of people, products, and processes that provide a capability to satisfy a need or objective
- An assembly of things or parts forming a complex or unitary whole; a collection of components organized to accomplish a specific function or set of functions
- An interacting combination of elements that are viewed in relation to function

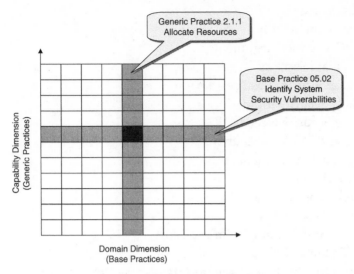

Figure A.2 The capability and domain dimensions of the SSE-CMM [SSE99].

The SSE-CMM

The SSE-CMM takes a process-based approach to information systems security and is based on the SE-CMM. The methodology and metrics of the SE-CMM are duplicated in the SSE-CMM in that they provide a reference for comparing the existing best systems security engineering practices against the essential systems security engineering elements described in the model. The SSE-CMM is the primary element of the proposed HIPAA-CMM.

The SSE-CMM defines two dimensions that are used to measure the capability of an organization to perform specific activities. These dimensions are *domain* and *capability*. The domain dimension consists of all of the practices that collectively define security engineering. These practices are called *base practices* (BPs). The capability dimension represents practices that indicate process management and institutionalization capability. These practices are called *generic practices* (GPs) because they apply across a wide range of domains. The GPs represent activities that should be performed as part of performing BPs. The relationship between BPs and GPs is given in Figure A.2, illustrating the evaluation of allocating resources in order to support the BP with identifying system security vulnerabilities.

For the domain dimension, the SSE-CMM specifies 11 security engineering PAs and 11 organizational and project-related PAs, each of which are comprised of BPs. BPs are mandatory characteristics that must exist within an implemented security engineering process before an organization can claim satisfaction in a given PA. The 22 PAs and their corresponding BPs incorporate the best practices of systems security engineering. The PAs are as follows:

- Technical
  - PA01—Administer Security Controls
  - PA02—Assess Impact
  - PA03—Assess Security Risk

- PA04—Assess Threat
- PA05—Assess Vulnerability
- PA06—Build Assurance Argument
- PA07—Coordinate Security
- PA08—Monitor Security Posture
- PA09—Provide Security Input
- PA10—Specify Security Needs
- PA11—Verify and Validate Security
- Project and Organizational Practices
  - PA12—Ensure Quality
  - PA13—Manage Configuration
  - PA14—Manage Project Risk
  - PA15—Monitor and Control Technical Effort
  - PA16—Plan Technical Effort
  - PA17—Define Organization's Systems Engineering Process
  - PA18—Improve Organization's Systems Engineering Process
  - PA19—Manage Product Line Evolution
  - PA20—Manage Systems Engineering Support Environment
  - PA21—Provide Ongoing Skills and Knowledge
  - PA22—Coordinate with Suppliers

The GPs are ordered in degrees of maturity and are grouped to form and distinguish among five levels of security engineering maturity. The attributes of these five levels are as follows [SSE99]:

- Level 1
  - BPs are Performed
- Level 2
  - 2.1—Planning Performance
  - 2.2—Disciplined Performance
  - 2.3—Verifying Performance
  - 2.4—Tracking Performance
- Level 3
  - 3.1—Defining a Standard Process
  - 3.2—Perform the Defined Process
  - 3.3—Coordinate the Process
- Level 4
  - 4.1—Establishing Measurable Quality Goals
  - 4.2—Objectively Managing Performance
- Level 5
  - 5.1—Improving Organizational Capability
  - 5.2—Improving Process Effectiveness

The corresponding descriptions of the five levels are given as follows [SSE99]:

Level 1, "Performed Informally." Focuses on whether an organization or project performs a process that incorporates the BPs. A statement characterizing this level would be, "You have to do it before you can manage it."

Level 2, "Planned and Tracked." Focuses on project-level definition, planning, and performance issues. A statement characterizing this level would be, "Understand what's happening with the project before defining organization-wide processes."

Level 3, "Well Defined." Focuses on disciplined tailoring from defined processes at the organization level. A statement characterizing this level would be, "Use the best of what you've learned from your projects to create organization-wide processes."

Level 4, "Quantitatively Controlled." Focuses on measurements being tied to the business goals of the organization. Although it is essential to begin collecting and using basic project measures early, the measurement and use of data is not expected organization-wide until the higher levels have been achieved. Statements characterizing this level would be, "You can't measure it until you know what 'it' is" and "Managing with measurement is only meaningful when you're measuring the right things."

Level 5, "Continuously Improving." Gains leverage from all of the management practice improvements seen in the earlier levels, then emphasizes the cultural shifts that will sustain the gains made. A statement characterizing this level would be, "A culture of continuous improvement requires a foundation of sound management practice, defined processes, and measurable goals."

The HIPAA-CMM uses the GPs, capability levels, and a major subset of the PAs of the SSE-CMM to evaluate HIPAA information security compliance. Remediation of the areas of weakness or noncompliance can then be addressed with confidence in a cost-effective manner.

HIPAA Security Requirements Mappings to PAs

Ideally, there would be a one-to-one mapping of all HIPAA information security requirements to the SSE-CMM PAs. There are, in fact, such mappings, but these mappings do not complete HIPAA compliance coverage based on the present state of the HIPAA regulations and the corresponding generally accepted best information security practices. Obviously, where the HIPAA requirements are process-oriented, there is a better mapping to the SSE-CMM PAs. The other HIPAA privacy regulations require more granularity and coverage of information security issues than the PAs of the SSE-CMM provide. These additional requirements are met by using the *HIPAA-specific PAs* (HPAs) as defined in this document.

In reviewing the HIPAA assurance requirements based on the extant privacy regulations, the draft Security and Electronic Signature standards, and the corresponding best information security practices, the following PAs from the SSE-CMM were selected. These PAs address a subset of the HIPAA requirements:

- Technical
  - PA01—Administer Security Controls
  - PA02—Assess Impact
  - PA03—Assess Security Risk
  - PA04—Assess Threat
  - PA05—Assess Vulnerability
  - PA06—Build Assurance Argument
  - PA07—Coordinate Security
  - PA08—Monitor Security Posture
  - PA09—Provide Security Input
  - PA10—Specify Security Needs
  - PA11—Verify and Validate Security
- Project and Organizational Practices
  - PA12—Ensure Quality
  - PA13—Manage Configuration
  - PA14—Manage Project Risk
  - PA15—Monitor and Control Technical Effort
  - PA17—Define Organization's Systems Engineering Process
  - PA21—Provide Ongoing Skills and Knowledge
  - PA22—Coordinate with Suppliers

The selected SSE-CMM PAs are detailed in Appendix A of this document.

To complete the coverage of evaluation of HIPAA Privacy and security compliance, newly defined PAs that are tailored to the remaining HIPAA requirements are needed. These HPAs are developed and described in the next section and are also included in Appendix A of this document. They are undergoing modification as of this writing to reflect the changes in the HIPAA Privacy Rule.

The capability dimension of the SSE-CMM with its GPs will be used for the HIPAA-CMM model and its PAs.

Figure A.3 illustrates the combining of complementary SSE-CMM and HPAs to develop the HIPAA-CMM and to implement continuous process improvement.

HPAs

Based on an analysis of the HIPAA privacy regulations and the draft Security and Electronic Signature standards, the following five categories of HIPAA

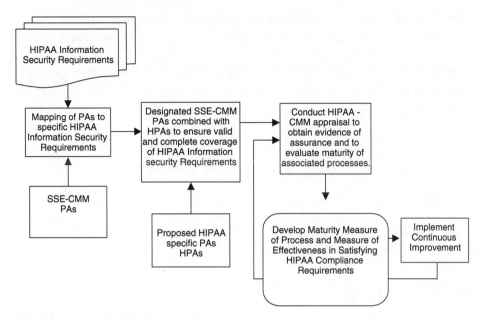

Figure A.3 The HIPAA-CMM structure and its use.

requirements based on best information security practices could not be directly matched to PAs of the SSE-CMM:

- Establishing and designating responsibility for ensuring that policies and procedures are followed relative to the release of individually identifiable patient healthcare information and establishing recourse for violations of these policies

- Development of disaster recovery and business continuity plans for all relevant networks and systems

- Establishing patient health care information protection, validation, and authentication through logical controls and protecting the confidentiality and data integrity of exchanged information with external entities

- Establishing personnel information security policies and procedures

- Addressing physical security requirements for information systems protection, including theft, fire, and other hazards

Therefore, in order to complete the required coverage of the HIPAA compliance requirements, five PAs with corresponding BPs are needed. These HPAs incorporate the generally accepted best security engineering practices and are focused on the five identified HIPAA categories that could not be met by PAs of the SSE-CMM. The goals of the HPAs map to the HIPAA requirements, and the BPs provide guidance on the specific actions to take in order to confirm that the goals are accomplished.

The HPAs are listed as follows and are detailed with their base practices in Appendix A, Section A.2 of this document:

- HPA 01   Administer Patient Health Care Information Controls
- HPA 02   Develop Disaster Recovery and Business Continuity Plans For All Relevant Networks And Systems
- HPA 03   Establish Patient Health Care Information Security Controls
- HPA 04   Evolve Personnel Information Security Policies and Procedures
- HPA 05   Administer Physical Security Controls

Defining and Using the HIPAA-CMM

The HIPAA information security requirements based on the extant HIPAA regulations and draft standards have been developed by using the generally accepted best information security practices. These requirements are best estimates at this time and are summarized in Tables A.3, A.4, and A.5.

HIPAA Mappings

The HIPAA security requirement mappings to SSE-CMM and the HPAs are also provided in Tables A.3, A.4, and A.5. The listed PAs ensure that the processes are in place to evaluate the application of the specific assurance mechanisms

Table A.3 Administrative Procedures

HIPAA INFORMATION SECURITY REQUIREMENTS	SSE-CMM MAPPING	HPAS
1. Adopt written policies and procedures for the receipt, storage, processing, and distribution of information.	PA 01, 17, 22	
2. Designate a Privacy Officer who is responsible for ensuring that the policies and procedures are followed and for the release of individually identifiable patient healthcare information.	PA 07, 10	HPA 01
3. Establish a security certification process that determines the degree to which the system, application, or network meets security requirements.	PA 11, 12	
4. Develop disaster recovery and business continuity plans for all relevant networks and systems.	PA 02, 03, 04, 05, 06, 14	HPA 02
5. Train employees to ensure that they understand the new privacy protection procedures.	PA 21	
6. Establish contracts with all business partners protecting confidentiality and data integrity of exchanged information.	PA 22	HPA 03

HIPAA INFORMATION SECURITY REQUIREMENTS	SSE-CMM MAPPING	HPAS
7. Implement personnel security, including clearance policies and procedures.	PA 01, 09	HPA 04
8. Develop and implement system auditing policies and procedures.	PA 01, 06, 08, 12, 13, 15	
9. Establish boundaries on use and release of individual medical records.	PA 01, 06, 10, 11	HPA 01
10. Ensure that patient consent is obtained prior to the release of medical information and that the consent is not coerced.	PA 01, 10	HPA 01
11. Provide patients with education on the privacy protection accorded to them.	PA 01, 10	HPA 01
12. Ensure patients access to their medical records.	PA 01, 10	HPA 01
13. Establish patient recourse and penalties for violations of security policies and procedures.	PA 01, 10, 11	HPA 01
14. Establish procedures for processing terminated personnel to prevent violation of information security policies and procedures.	PA 01, 21	HPA 04

Table A.4 Technological Security Safeguards

HIPAA INFORMATION SECURITY REQUIREMENTS	SSE-CMM MAPPING	HPAS
1. Implement encryption and/or access controls to prevent and detect unauthorized intrusions into the system and network.	PA 01, 10, 22	HPA 03
2. Implement identification and authentication mechanisms for access to the system and network.	PA 01, 11, 13	HPA 03
3. Ensure that sensitive information is altered or destroyed by authorized personnel only and that these activities are logged.	PA 01, 06, 11	HPA 03
4. Establish means for message non-repudiation and authentication.	PA 01, 06, 11	HPA 03
5. Establish means to preserve integrity of messages or means to detect modification of a message.	PA 01, 06, 11	HPA 03
6. Establish and implement log-on and log-off procedures to protect against unauthorized access to workstations and systems.	PA 01, 08, 11	HPA 03

Table A.5 Physical Security Measures

HIPAA INFORMATION SECURITY REQUIREMENTS	SSE-CMM MAPPING	HPAS
1. Develop policies and procedures for handling, storage, and disposal of magnetic media and for object reuse.	PA 01, 06	HPA 05
2. Protect computer systems and related buildings and equipment from fire and other hazards.	PA 01, 02, 03, 04, 05, 08, 11	HPA 05
3. Use physical controls to limit access to computer systems and facilities to authorized personnel.	PA 01, 03, 07, 11	HPA 05
4. Physically secure workstations and laptops.	PA 01, 03, 11	HPA 05

required by the HIPAA legislation. A complete listing of the HIPAA-CMM PAs is given in Appendix A.

Using the HIPAA-CMM

Conducting an appraisal by using the mappings defined in the tables provides the means to measure the quality of the processes in place to meet the HIPAA information security-related regulation requirements. To provide meaningful results, the question of, "What capability level ensures compliance?" has to be answered. The standard proposed in this approach is that *for all the HIPAA-CMM PAs, the Level 2 GPs as defined in the SSE-CMM have to be achieved for minimum HIPAA information security-related compliance. For the compliance to remain in place over the long term and be considered an element of continuous process improvement, the Level 3 GPs must be obtained as a minimum.*

As noted in Figure A.3, the appraisal results are used to implement continuous improvement of the information security processes.

Conclusion

A HIPAA-CMM and assessment methodology is being developed as a standard for evaluating HIPAA compliance. With appropriate guidance and use of the SSE-CMM PAs and the defined HPAs to achieve the additional granularity and coverage as required, the proposed HIPAA-CMM provides a formal, repeatable, and consistent methodology to assess an organization's HIPAA compliance. This approach will identify areas of strong compliance, marginal compliance, and lack of compliance and will provide a consistent basis for defining remediation means. Inherently, the HIPAA-CMM also serves as a tool for implementing continuous improvement and for evaluating the effectiveness of the improvement measures.

References

[BAT94] Bate, Roger, Garcia, Suzanne et al, "A Systems Engineering Capability Maturity Model Version 1.0," SEI, 1994.

[BSI98] British Standards Institute, United Kingdom, "Information Security Management, British Standard 7799," 1998.

[CCP96] Common Criteria Project; "Common Criteria for Information Technology Security Evaluation, v1.0," January 1996.

[CSE98] Communications Security Establishment, Government of Canada, "Canadian Handbook on Information Technology Security MG-9," 1998.

[CUR95] Curtis, Bill; Hefley, William; and Miller, Sally, "The People Capability Maturity Model," SEI, 1995.

[DOD85] Department of Defense, "Department of Defense Trusted Computer System Evaluation Criteria," DoD 5200.28-STD, December 1985.

[DOD97] Department of Defense; "Department of Defense Information Technology Security Certification and Accreditation Process," 1997.

[NST00] National Security Telecommunications and Information Systems Security Committee; "National Security Telecommunications and Information Systems Security Instruction (NSTISSI) No. 1000, National Information Assurance Certification and Accreditation Process (NIACAP)," April 2000.

[FER97] Ferraiolo, Karen; Gallagher, Lisa; Thompson, Victoria; "Final Report Contract Number 50-DKNB-7-90099, Process-Based Assurance Product Suite," December 1997.

[GAL97] Ferraiolo, Karen; Gallagher, Lisa; Thompson, Victoria; "Building a Case for Assurance from Process," December 1999.

[HHS00] HHS; "HHS Fact Sheet," December 2000.

[HOP99] Hopkinson, John; "The Relationship Between the SSE-CMM and IT Security Guidance Documentation," 1999.

[HUM89] Humphrey, Watts; "Managing the Software Process," 1989.

[ISO] ISO; "ISO/IEC 13335 Information Technology—Security Techniques—Guidelines for the Management of IT Security—Part 1: Concepts and Models, Part 2: Managing and Planning, Part 3: Management Techniques, Part 4: Baseline Control, and Part 5: Safeguards for External Connections."

[NIS95] National Institute of Standards and Technology, Technology Administration, U.S. Department of Commerce, "An Introduction to Computer Security"; The NIST Handbook, 1995.

[PAU95] SEI, "The Capability Maturity Model: Guidelines for Improving the Software Process," Addison Wesley, 1995.

[SEI95] SEI, "The Capability Maturity Model," 1995.

[SSE99] "The Systems Security Engineering Capability Maturity Model v2.0," 1999.

Appendix A: HIPAA-CMM PA Overview

(Comprised of PAs from the SSE-CMM v2.0 and the HPAs)

A.1 SSE-CMM

PA 01

ADMINISTER SECURITY CONTROLS	
Goal 1	Security controls are properly configured and used.
BP.01.01	Establish responsibilities and accountability for security controls and communicate them to everyone in the organization.
BP.01.02	Manage the configuration of system security controls.
BP.01.03	Manage security awareness, training, and education programs for all users and administrators.
BP.01.04	Manage periodic maintenance and administration of security services and control mechanisms.

PA 02

ASSESS IMPACT	
Goal 1	The security impacts of risks to the system are identified and characterized.
BP.02.01	Identify, analyze, and prioritize operational, business, or mission capabilities leveraged by the system.
BP.02.02	Identify and characterize the system assets that support the key operational capabilities or the security objectives of the system.
BP.02.03	Select the impact metric to be used for this assessment.
BP.02.04	Identify the relationship between the selected metrics for this assessment and metric conversion factors if required.
BP.02.05	Identify and characterize impacts.
BP.02.06	Monitor ongoing changes in the impacts.

PA 03

ASSESS SECURITY RISK	
Goal 1	An understanding of the security risk associated with operating the system within a defined environment is achieved.
Goal 2	Risks are prioritized according to a defined methodology.
BP.03.01	Select the methods, techniques, and criteria by which security risks for the system in a defined environment are analyzed, assessed, and compared.
BP.03.02	Identify threat/vulnerability/impact triples (exposures).
BP.03.03	Assess the risk associated with the occurrence of an exposure.
BP.03.04	Assess the total uncertainty associated with the risk for the exposure.
BP.03.05	Order the risks by priority.
BP.03.06	Monitor ongoing changes in the risk spectrum and changes to their characteristics.

PA 04

ASSESS THREAT	
Goal 1	Threats to the security of the system are identified and characterized.
BP.04.01	Identify applicable threats arising from a natural source.
BP.04.02	Identify applicable threats arising from man-made sources, either accidental or deliberate.
BP.04.03	Identify appropriate units of measure, and applicable ranges, in a specified environment.
BP.04.04	Assess capability and motivation of threat agent for threats arising from manmade sources.
BP.04.05	Assess the likelihood of an occurrence of a threat event.
BP.04.06	Monitor ongoing changes in the threat spectrum and changes to their characteristics.

PA 05

ASSESS VULNERABILITY	
Goal 1	An understanding of system security vulnerabilities within a defined environment is achieved.
BP.05.01	Select the methods, techniques, and criteria by which security system vulnerabilities in a defined environment are identified and characterized.
BP.05.02	Identify system security vulnerabilities.
BP.05.03	Gather data related to the properties of the vulnerabilities.
BP.05.04	Assess the system vulnerability and aggregate vulnerabilities that result from specific vulnerabilities and combinations of specific vulnerabilities.
BP.05.05	Monitor changes in applicable vulnerabilities and to their characteristics.

PA 06

BUILD ASSURANCE AGREEMENT	
Goal 1	The work products and processes clearly provide the evidence that the customer's security needs have been met.
BP.06.01	Identify the security assurance objectives.
BP.06.02	Define a security assurance strategy to address all assurance objectives.
BP.06.03	Identify and control security assurance evidence.
BP.06.04	Perform analysis of security assurance evidence.
BP.06.05	Provide a security assurance argument that demonstrates the customer's security needs are met.

PA 07

COORDINATE SECURITY

Goal 1	All members of the project team are aware of and involved with security engineering activities to the extent necessary to perform their functions.
Goal 2	Decisions and recommendations related to security are communicated and coordinated.
BP.07.01	Define security engineering coordination objectives and relationships.
BP.07.02	Identify coordination mechanisms for security engineering.
BP.07.03	Facilitate security engineering coordination.
BP.07.04	Use the identified mechanisms to coordinate decisions and recommendations related to security.

PA 08

MONITOR SECURITY POSTURE

Goal 1	Both internal and external security-related events are detected and tracked.
Goal 2	Incidents are responded to in accordance with policy.
Goal 3	Changes to the operational security posture are identified and handled in accordance with the security objectives.
BP.08.01	Analyze event records to determine the cause of an event, how it proceeded, and likely future events.
BP.08.02	Monitor changes in threats, vulnerabilities, impacts, risks, and environment.
BP.08.03	Identify security-relevant incidents.
BP.08.04	Monitor the performance and functional effectiveness of security safeguards.
BP.08.05	Review the security posture of the system to identify necessary changes.
BP.08.06	Manage the response to security-relevant incidents.
BP.08.07	Ensure that the artifacts related to security monitoring are suitably protected.

PA 09

PROVIDE SECURITY INPUT	
Goal 1	All system issues are reviewed for security implications and are resolved in accordance with security goals.
Goal 2	All members of the project team have an understanding of security so they can perform their functions.
Goal 3	The solution reflects the security input provided.
BP.09.01	Work with designers, developers, and users to ensure that appropriate parties have a common understanding of security input needs.
BP.09.02	Determine the security constraints and considerations needed to make informed engineering choices.
BP.09.03	Identify alternative solutions to security-related engineering problems.
BP.09.04	Analyze and prioritize engineering alternatives using security constraints and considerations.
BP.09.05	Provide security-related guidance to the other engineering groups.
BP.09.06	Provide security-related guidance to operational system users and administrators.

PA 10

SPECIFIC SECURITY NEEDS	
Goal 1	A common understanding of security needs is reached between all parties, including the customer.
BP.10.01	Gain an understanding of the customer's security needs.
BP.10.02	Identify the laws, policies, standards, external influences, and constraints that govern the system.
BP.10.03	Identify the purpose of the system in order to determine the security context.
BP.10.04	Capture a high-level security-oriented view of the system operation.
BP.10.05	Capture high-level goals that define the security of the system.
BP.10.06	Define a consistent set of statements that define the protection to be implemented in the system.
BP.10.07	Obtain agreement that the specified security meets the customer's needs.

PA 11

VERIFY AND VALIDATE SECURITY	
Goal 1	Solutions meet security requirements.
Goal 2	Solutions meet the customer's operational security needs.
BP.11.01	Identify the solution to be verified and validated.
BP.11.02	Define the approach and level of rigor for verifying and validating each solution.
BP.11.03	Verify that the solution implements the requirements associated with the previous level of abstraction.
BP.11.04	Validate the solution by showing that it satisfies the needs associated with the previous level of abstraction, ultimately meeting the customer's operational security needs.
BP.11.05	Capture the verification and validation results for the other engineering groups.

Project and Organizational PA Overview

The project and organizational PA category groups together those PAs that are primarily concerned with improving project and organizational capability.

PA 12

ENSURE QUALITY	
Goal 1	Process quality is defined and measured.
Goal 2	Expected work product quality is achieved.
BP.12.01	Monitor conformance to the defined process.
BP.12.02	Measure work product quality.
BP.12.03	Measure quality of the process.
BP.12.04	Analyze quality measurements.
BP.12.05	Obtain participation.
BP.12.06	Initiate quality improvement activities.
BP.12.07	Detect need for corrective actions.

PA 13

MANAGE CONFIGURATIONS	
Goal 1	Control over work product configurations is maintained.
BP.13.01	Establish configuration management methodology.
BP.13.02	Identify configuration units.
BP.13.03	Maintain work product baselines.
BP.13.04	Control changes.
BP.13.05	Communicate configuration status.

PA 14

MANAGE PROJECT RISK	
Goal 1	Risks to the program are identified, understood, and mitigated.
BP.14.01	Develop a risk-management approach.
BP.14.02	Identify risks.
BP.14.03	Assess risks.
BP.14.04	Review your risk assessment.
BP.14.05	Execute risk mitigation.
BP.14.06	Track risk mitigation.

PA 15

MONITOR AND CONTROL TECHNICAL EFFORT	
Goal 1	The technical effort is monitored and controlled.
BP.15.01	Direct the technical effort.
BP.15.02	Track project resources.
BP.15.03	Track technical parameters.
BP.15.04	Review project performance.
BP.15.05	Analyze project issues.
BP.15.06	Take corrective action.

PA 17

DEFINE ORGANIZATION'S SECURITY ENGINEERING PROCESS

Goal 1	A standard systems engineering process is defined for the organization.
BP.17.01	Establish process goals.
BP.17.02	Collect process assets.
BP.17.03	Develop the organization's security engineering process.
BP.17.04	Define tailoring guidelines.

PA 21

PROVIDE ONGOING SKILLS AND KNOWLEDGE

Goal 1	The organization has the skills necessary to achieve project and organizational objectives.
BP.21.01	Identify training needs.
BP.21.02	Select mode of knowledge or skill acquisition.
BP.21.03	Assure availability of skill and knowledge.
BP.21.04	Prepare training materials.
BP.21.05	Train personnel.
BP.21.06	Assess training effectiveness.
BP.21.07	Maintain training records.
BP.21.08	Maintain training materials.

PA 22

COORDINATE WITH SUPPLIERS

Goal 1	Effective suppliers are selected and used.
BP.22.01	Identify systems components or services.
BP.22.02	Identify competent suppliers or vendors.
BP.22.03	Choose suppliers or vendors.
BP.22.04	Provide expectations.
BP.22.05	Maintain communications.

A.2 HPAs

HPA 01

ADMINISTER PATIENT HEALTH CARE INFORMATION CONTROLS	
Goal 1	Privacy officer is designated with required authority and responsibility.
Goal 2	Limitations and guidance on the use and disclosure of individual medical information are established.
BP 01.01	Designate a privacy officer who is responsible for enforcing policies and procedures and for the release of individually identifiable patient healthcare information.
BP 01.02	Establish boundaries on individual medical records' use and release.
BP 01.03	Establish recourse for violations of policies on use and release of individual medical records.
BP 01.04	Provide patients with education on the privacy protection accorded to them.
BP 01.05	Establish patient recourse and penalties for violations of security policies and procedures.
BP 01.06	Ensure patient access to their individual medical records.

HPA 02

DEVELOP DISASTER RECOVERY AND BUSINESS CONTINUITY PLANS FOR ALL RELEVANT NETWORKS AND SYSTEMS	
Goal 1	Business Continuity Plan is developed and institutionalized.
Goal 2	Disaster Recovery Plan is developed and institutionalized.
BP 02.01	Establish Disaster Recovery Plan (Evaluate this process using supplementary information from SSE-CMM PAs 02, 03, 04 and 05).
BP 02.02	Establish Business Continuity Plan (Evaluate this process using supplementary information from SSE-CMM PAs 02, 03, 04, and 05).
BP 02.03	Institutionalize Disaster Recovery Plan.
BP 02.04	Institutionalize Business Continuity Plan.

HPA 03

ESTABLISH PATIENT HEALTH CARE INFORMATION SECURITY CONTROLS	
Goal 1	Individual patient health care information is protected from unauthorized disclosure and modification.
Goal 2	Authentication and non-repudiation are established for external and internal patient health care information exchange.
BP 03.01	Provide encryption to preserve privacy of transmitted or stored patient health care information.
BP 03.02	Provide identification and authentication mechanisms for access to the system and network.
BP 03.03	Manage the destruction or alteration of sensitive information, including logging of these activities.
BP 03.04	Provide means for message non-repudiation and authentication.
BP 03.05	Preserve the integrity of messages and provide means to detect modification of messages.
BP 03.06	Provide log-on and log-off procedures to protect against unauthorized access to workstations and systems.
BP 03.07	Protect the confidentiality and data integrity of exchanged information with partners through appropriate contracts (evaluate in conjunction with PA 22 of the SSE-CMM).

HPA 04

EVOLVE PERSONNEL INFORMATION SECURITY POLICIES AND PROCEDURES	
Goal 1	Personnel security controls are properly defined, administered, and used.
BP 04.01	Provide means and methods for processing terminated personnel to prevent violation of information security policies and procedures.
BP 04.02	Manage personnel security issues, including clearance policies and procedures.

HPA 05

ADMINISTER PHYSICAL SECURITY CONTROLS	
Goal 1	Physical security controls are properly administered and used.
BP 05.01	Establish policies and procedures for handling, storage, and disposal of magnetic media and for object reuse.
BP 05.02	Provide means and methods to protect computer systems and related buildings and equipment from fire and other hazards.
BP 05.03	Provide physical controls to limit access to computer systems and facilities to authorized personnel.
BP 05.04	Provide for physical security of workstations and laptops.

Appendix B: Glossary (SSE-CMM v2.0)

Accountability—The property that ensures that the actions of an entity can be traced uniquely to the entity [ISO 7498-2; 1988]

Accreditation—A formal declaration by a designated approving authority that a system is approved to operate in a particular security mode by using a prescribed set of safeguards

Assessment—An appraisal by a trained team of professionals to determine the state of an organization's current process, to determine the high-priority, process-related issues facing an organization, and to obtain the organizational support for process improvement

Asset—Anything that has value to the organization [ISO 13335-1: 1996]

Assurance—The degree of confidence that security needs are satisfied [NIST94]

Assurance Argument—A set of structured assurance claims supported by evidence and reasoning that demonstrate clearly how assurance needs have been satisfied

Assurance Claim—An assertion or supporting assertion that a system meets a security need. Claims address both direct threats (for example, system data are protected from attacks by outsiders) and indirect threats (for example, system code has minimal flaws)

Assurance Evidence—Data on which a judgment or conclusion about an assurance claim can be based. The evidence might consist of observations, test results, analysis results, and appraisals providing support for the associated claims.

Authenticity—The property that ensures that the identity of a subject or resource is the one claimed. Authenticity applies to entities such as users, processes, systems, and information [ISO 13335-1:1996].

Availability—The property of being accessible and useable upon demand by an authorized entity [ISO 7498-2: 1988]

Baseline—A specification or product that has been formally reviewed and agreed upon that thereafter serves as the basis for further development and that can be changed only through formal change control procedures [IEEE-STD-610]

Certification—Comprehensive evaluation of security features and other safeguards of an AIS to establish the extent to which the design and implementation meet a set of specified security requirements

Confidentiality—The property that information is not made available or disclosed to unauthorized individuals, entities, or processes [ISO 7498-2:1988]

Consistency—The degree of uniformity, standardization, and freedom from contradiction among the documents or parts of a system or component [IEEE-STD-610]

Correctness—A property of a representation of a system or product such that it accurately reflects the specified security requirements for that system or product

Customer—The individual or organization that is responsible for accepting the product and authorizing payment to the service/development organization

Data Integrity—The property that data has not been altered or destroyed in an unauthorized manner [ISO 7498-2:1988]

Effectiveness—A property of a system or product representing how well it provides security in the context of its proposed or actual operational use

Engineering Group—A collection of individuals (both managers and technical staff) who are responsible for project or organizational activities related to a particular engineering discipline (for example, hardware, software, software configuration management, software quality assurance, systems, system test, and system security)

Evidence—Directly measurable characteristics of a process and/or product that represent objective, demonstrable proof that a specific activity satisfies a specified requirement

Group—The collection of departments, managers, and individuals who have responsibility for a set of tasks or activities. The size can vary from a single individual assigned part-time, to several part-time individuals assigned from different departments, to several dedicated full-time individuals.

Integrity—See *data integrity* and *system integrity*.

Maintenance—The process of modifying a system or component after delivery in order to correct flaws, improve performance or other attributes, or to adapt to a changed environment [IEEE-STD-610]

Methodology—A collection of methods, procedures, and standards that define an integrated synthesis of engineering approaches to the development of a product or system

Objective—Non-biased

Penetration Profile—A delineation of the activities that are required to effect a penetration

Privacy—The right of an individual or entity to control the acquisition, storage, and dissemination of information about the individual or entity

Procedure—A written description of a course of action to be taken in order to perform a given task [IEEE-STD-610]

Process—A sequence of steps performed for a given purpose [IEEE-STD-620]

Reliability—The property of consistent behavior and results [IEEE 13335-1:1996]

Residual Risk—The risk that remains after safeguards have been implemented [IEEE 13335-1:1996]

Risk—The potential that a given threat will exploit vulnerabilities of an asset or group of assets to cause loss or damage to the assets [IEEE 13335-1:1996]

Risk Analysis—The process of identifying security risks, determining their magnitude, and identifying areas needing safeguards [IEEE 13335-1:1996]

Risk Management—The process of assessing and quantifying risk and establishing an acceptable level of risk for the organization [IEEE 13335-1:1996]

Security—The preservation of confidentiality, integrity, availability, and authenticity of information; protection from intrusion or compromise of information that will cause harm to the organization

Security Engineering—Security engineering is an evolving discipline. As such, a precise definition with community consensus does not exist today. Some generalizations are possible, however. Some goals of security engineering are to:

- Gain an understanding of the security risks associated with an enterprise
- Establish a balanced set of security needs in accordance with identified risks
- Transform security needs into security guidance to be integrated into the activities of other disciplines employed on a project and into descriptions of a system configuration or operation
- Establish confidence or assurance in the correctness and effectiveness of security mechanisms
- Determine that operational impacts due to residual security vulnerabilities in a system or its operation are tolerable (acceptable risks)
- Integrate the efforts of all engineering disciplines and specialties into a combined understanding of the trustworthiness of a system

Security Policy—Rules, directives, and practices that govern how assets, including sensitive information, are managed, protected, and distributed within an organization and its systems

Security-Related Requirements—Requirements that have a direct effect on the secure operation of a system or enforce conformance to a specified security policy

Signature Authority—Official with the authority to formally assume responsibility for operating a system at an acceptable level of risk

System—A collection of components organized to accomplish a specific function or set of functions [IEEE-STD-610]; a system can include many products; a product can be the system

Threat Capabilities—Intentions, and attack methods of adversaries to exploit, or any circumstance or event with the potential to cause harm to information or a system

Validation—The process of assessing a system to determine whether it satisfies the specified requirements

Verification—The process of assessing a system to determine whether the work products of a given development phase satisfy the conditions imposed at the start of that phase

Vulnerability—Includes a weakness of an asset or group of assets that can be exploited by a threat [IEEE 13335-1:1996]

Work Product—Output of a process

Appendix C: The Ideal Approach to Process Improvement

The Carnegie Mellon *Software Engineering Institute* (SEI) has developed an approach to process improvement called IDEAL, which stands for Initiating, Diagnosing, Establishing, Acting, and Learning.

The goal is to establish a continuous cycle of evaluating the current status of your organization, making improvements, and repeating this process. The high-level steps are described as follows and appear in Table A.1.

I	Initiating	Laying the groundwork for a successful improvement effort
D	Diagnosing	Determining where you are relative to where you want to be
E	Establishing	Planning the specifics of how you will reach your destination
A	Acting	Doing the work according to the plan
L	Learning	Learning from the experience and improving your ability

The Initiating Phase

Embarking upon a security engineering process improvement effort should be handled in the same manner in which all new projects within an organization are approached. One must become familiar with the project's objectives and means for their accomplishment, develop a business case for the implementation, gain the approval and confidence of management, and develop a method for the project's implementation.

Effective and continuous support of the effort throughout its lifetime is essential for successful process improvement. Sponsorship involves not only making available the financial resources necessary to continue the process but also requires personal attention from management to the project.

After the relationship between the proposed effort and business goals has been established and key sponsors have given their commitment, a mechanism for the project's implementation must be established.

The Diagnosing Phase

In order to perform process development/improvement activities, it is imperative that an understanding of the organization's current and desired future state of process maturity be established. These parameters form the basis of the organization's process improvement action plan.

Performing a gap analysis emphasizes the differences between the current and desired states of the organization's processes and reveals additional information or findings about the organization. Grouped according to area of interest, these findings form the basis of recommendations for how to improve the organization.

The Establishing Phase

In this phase, a detailed plan of action based on the goals of the effort and the recommendations developed during the diagnosing phase is developed. In addition, the plan must take into consideration any possible constraints, such as resource limitations, which might limit the scope of the improvement effort. Priorities along with specific outputs and responsibilities are also put forth in the plan.

Time constraints, available resources, organizational priorities, and other factors might not allow for all of the goals to be realized or recommendations implemented during a single instance of the process improvement lifecycle. Therefore, the organization must establish priorities for its improvement effort.

As a result of the organization characterization defined in the diagnosing phase and established priorities, the scope of the process improvement effort might be different from that developed in the initiating phase. The develop approach step requires that the redefined objectives and recommendations be mapped to potential strategies for accomplishing the desired outcomes.

At this point, all of the data, approaches, recommendations, and priorities are brought together in the form of a detailed action plan. Included in the plan are the allocation of responsibilities, resources, and specific tasks, tracking tools to be used, and established deadlines and milestones. The plan should also include contingency plans and coping strategies for any unforeseen problems.

The Acting Phase

This phase is the implementation phase and requires the greatest level of effort of all the phases both in terms of resources and time. Achieving the goals of the organization might require multiple parallel cycles within the acting phase in order to address all of the desired improvements and priorities.

Solutions, or improvement steps, for each problem area are developed based on available information on the issue and resources for implementation. At this stage, the solutions are 'best guess' efforts of a technical working group.

The first step in designing processes that will meet the business needs of an enterprise is to understand the business, product, and organizational context that will be present when the process is being implemented. Some questions that need to be answered before process design include the following:

- How is security engineering practiced within the organization?
- What life cycle will be used as a framework for this process?
- How is the organization structured to support projects?
- How are support functions handled (for example, by the project or by the organization)?
- What are the management and practitioner roles used in this organization?
- How critical are these processes to organizational success?

Because first attempts at generating solutions rarely succeed, all solutions must be tested before they are implemented across an organization. How an organization chooses to test its solutions is dependent upon the nature of the area of interest, the proposed solution, and the resources of the organization.

Using information collected during testing, potential solutions should be modified to reflect new knowledge about the solution. The importance of the processes under focus as well as the complexity of the proposed improvements will dictate the degree of testing and refinement proposed solutions must undergo before being considered acceptable for implementation throughout the organization.

Once a proposed improved process has been accepted, it must be implemented beyond the test group. Depending upon the nature and degree to which a process is being improved, the implementation stage might require significant time and resources. Implementation can occur in a variety of ways depending upon the organization's goals.

The Learning Phase

The learning phase is both the final stage of the initial process improvement cycle and the initial phase of the next process improvement effort. Here the entire process improvement effort is evaluated in terms of goal realization and how future improvements can be instituted more efficiently. This phase is only as constructive as the detail of records kept throughout the process and the ability of participants to make recommendations.

Determining the success of process improvement requires analyzing the final results in light of the established goals and objectives. It also requires evaluating the efficiency of the effort and determining where further enhancements to the process are required. These lessons learned are then collected, summarized, and documented.

Based on the analysis of the improvement effort itself, the lessons learned are translated into recommendations for improving subsequent improvement efforts. These recommendations should be promulgated outside those guiding the improvement effort for incorporation in this and other improvement efforts.

Appendix D: SSE-CMM MAPPINGS and General Considerations

This mapping of process-based mechanisms (SSE-CMM) to assurance-based mechanisms (Common Criteria, DITSCAP, TCSEC) has been addressed by [GAL97] and [FER97] and produced the following general conclusions:

- Although there is a significant overlap between the SSE-CMM PAs and the assurance-based activities, there is not always a complete one-to-one mapping.
- The SSE-CMM might not provide the level of granularity required to directly address all specific assurance requirements.
- The SSE-CMM can be used to develop assurance arguments and product assurance evidence if applied with appropriate guidance.
- In most cases, the PAs of the SSE-CMM correspond well with the processes of the traditional assurance methods.
- The processes defined in the SSE-CMM are considered to contribute to the development of assurance arguments by integrators, product developers, evaluators, and manufacturers.
- With the appropriate guidance, tailoring, and evidence gathering, it was demonstrated that the results of an SSE-CMM assessment could support important aspects of traditional assurance-based mechanisms.
- The SSE-CMM can be viewed as a common thread that logically links traditional assurance methods.

In a similar vein, Hopkinson [HOP99] has proposed mappings to ISO/IEC 13335 Information Technology—Security Techniques—*Guidelines for the Management of IT Security* (GMITS) —Part 2 [ISO]; the NIST Handbook [NIS95]; BS 7799 [BSI98]; and the Canadian Handbook on Information Technology Security MG-9 [CSE98].

In all of the referenced mappings and the HIPAA mappings developed in this paper, the SSE-CMM is complementary to the associated evaluation criteria and provides a structured basis for evidence gathering and assurance. For specific assurance areas in HIPAA requiring more granularity than provided by the SSE-CMM, however, additional BPs must be applied.

As stated in [GAL97], "For the evaluators and certifiers, the SSE-CMM can provide direct evidence regarding process claims, as well as a uniform method to evaluate claims and evidence, thus contributing to the normalization of the evaluation/certification process—making the process more defined and repeatable and less intuitive. Ultimately, this direct benefit can be measured in terms of cost/schedule savings to evaluation and certification efforts."

Therefore, for assurance-based security mechanisms such as required by HIPAA, the SSE-CMM can provide a basis to develop a structured framework for the following:

- Ensuring the appropriate processes corresponding to the required assurance mechanisms are in place
- Evidence gathering to support assurance claims
- Ensuring complete coverage of required regulations or standards
- Measuring the present information security posture
- Evaluating effectiveness of remediation efforts
- Ensuring repeatability of the appraisal process
- Continuous improvement of the security processes

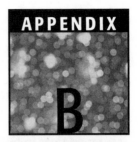

The NSA InfoSec Assessment Methodology

As a result of Presidential Decision Directive #63, forming the National Infrastructure Protection Center, the National Security Agency's *Information Systems Security Organization* (ISSO) instituted a program intended to improve the overall level of security protection of America's computing infrastructure. To help achieve this goal, the ISSO designed the *InfoSec Assessment Methodology* (IAM) and implemented a training course focused on private, commercial business security providers. Because the ISSO itself focuses solely on auditing those parts of the computing infrastructure that are considered critical to the government, it implemented a training and certification process for security practitioners in the private sector with the intention that those practitioners would incorporate the IAM into their repertoire of security auditing procedures. The IAM certification courses are conducted a few times each year. A security practitioner has to satisfy a fairly stringent experience requirement to be considered for the training.

History of the NIPC

Excerpted from www.nipc.gov:

February 26, 1998, the Department of Justice and *the Federal Bureau of Investigation* (FBI) created the *National Infrastructure Protection Center* (NIPC) at FBI Headquarters in Washington, D.C. The center is a joint government and private-sector partnership that includes representatives from the relevant agencies of federal, state, and local government. The concept for the NIPC grew out of recommendations of the President's Commission on Critical Infrastructure Protection and from the government's experiences in dealing with illegal intrusions into government and private-sector computer systems over the years.

May 22, 1998, President Clinton announced two new directives (see the following text) designed to strengthen the Nation's defenses against terrorism and other unconventional threats: *Presidential Decision Directives* (PDD) 62 and 63. PDD-62 highlights the growing range of unconventional threats that we face, including "cyber terrorism" and chemical, radiological, and biological weapons, and creates a new and more systematic approach to defending against these attacks. PDD-63 focuses specifically on protecting the Nation's critical infrastructures from both physical and cyber attacks.

These attacks might come from foreign governments, foreign and domestic terrorist organizations, or foreign and domestic criminal organizations. The NIPC is part of the broader framework of government efforts established by PDD-63. Under the PDD, the NIPC serves as the national focal point for threat assessment, warning, investigation, and responses to attacks on the critical infrastructures. A significant part of its mission involves establishing mechanisms to increase the sharing of vulnerability and threat information between the government and private industry.

About the ISSO

Excerpted in its entirety from the NSA INFOSEC Page—About the ISSO—Delivering IA Solutions for Cyber Systems, Revised November 2, 1999.

In order to enable our customers to protect and defend cyber systems, the NSA develops and supports a variety of products and services. We also conduct ongoing research to aid in the development of next generation solutions. Our IA solutions must encompass a wide range of voice, data, and video applications extending across networked, tactical, and satellite systems. IA solutions include the technologies, specifications and criteria, products, product configurations, tools, standards, and operational doctrine and support activities that are needed to implement the protect, detect and report, and respond elements of cyber defense.

The Information Assurance Framework Forum, developed in a collaborative effort by NSA solution architects, customers with requirements, component vendors, and commercial integrators, guides our solution development. It finds the right solution for environments ranging from outer space to the office or foxhole. Our framework provides top-level guidance in addition to the specification of essential security features and assurances for the security products. It brings producers and consumers together before products are built so that products that better meet our customers' needs will be built.

The internationally recognized *Common Criteria* (CC) employs standardized terms to describe the security functionality and assurance of consumers' requirements and manufacturers' products. CC-based Protection Profiles specify what consumers need at both the system and component level in order to fulfill their mission. CC-based Security Targets describe how specific products meet consumers' requirements.

These IA solutions take maximum advantage of commercial components, using NSA developed products and services to fill gaps in areas that are not satisfied by commercial offerings. *Commercial, off-the-shelf* (COTS) products include security products (for example, a firewall) or security-enabled or enhanced *information technology* (IT) products (for example, an e-mail application or secure cellular telephone). Our solutions include technologies and tools that are necessary for a layered defense, in-depth strategy, and tools for defensive information operations such as intrusion detection, automated data reduction, and modeling/simulation tools.

The NSA constantly works with its government and industry partners to facilitate emerging technology, taking the lead in problems not addressed by industry.

The InfoSec Assessment Methodology

Excerpted from NSA INFOSEC Page—INFOSEC Assessment Methodology (IAM); revised February 28, 2001. Information and registration materials can be found at www.nsa.gov/isso/iam/index.htm.

The National Security Agency, a national leader in Information Assurance, is offering a limited number of *Information Systems Security* (INFOSEC) *Assessment Methodology* (IAM) classes to facilitate the transfer of government-developed technology into the private sector. The IAM course was originally developed by NSA to train United States *Department of Defense* (DoD) organizations to perform their own INFOSEC assessments. NSA has developed specialized knowledge with regard to information systems security assessments through its completion of INFOSEC assessments for its U.S. Government customers over the past 15 years.

Description

The IAM is a two-day course for experienced Information Systems Security analysts who conduct, or are interested in conducting, INFOSEC assessments of U.S. Government information systems. The course teaches NSA's INFOSEC assessment process, a high-level, non-intrusive process for identifying and correcting security weaknesses in information systems and networks.

Prerequisites

a. U.S. citizenship
b. Five years of demonstrated experience in the field of INFOSEC, COMSEC, or computer security, with two of the five years of experience directly involved in analyzing computer system/network vulnerabilities and security risks

NSA Certificate of Course Completion: To qualify for an IAM certificate of completion, students must attend all of the two-day class; demonstrate an understanding of the IAM through group exercises and class discussions; and obtain a passing grade (at least 70 percent) on the IAM test.

Short Outline of the IAM Process

In brief, the IAM process is a high-level security assessment not unlike a subset of the Systems Security Engineering Capability Maturity Model (see Appendix D). More specifically, it is a Level I assessment—a non-intrusive, standardized baseline analysis of the InfoSec posture of an automated system. A Level II assessment commonly defines a more hands-on evaluation of the security systems (both Level I and Level II are considered "cooperative"). A Level III evaluation is a "red team" assessment (possibly non-cooperative).

The IAM process will also provide recommendations for the elimination or mitigation of the vulnerability. The IAM is considered a qualitative risk analysis process because it assigns ordinality to the risks that are identified (high/medium/low), rather than a hard cost/benefit ratio to the results.

The IAM is conducted in three phases:

1. *Pre-assessment phase*—The assessment team defines the customer's needs and begins to identify the system, its boundaries, and the criticality of the information and begins to write the assessment plan. This phase normally takes about two to four weeks.

2. *On-site phase*—Explore and confirm the conclusions made during phase I, gather data and documentation, conduct interviews, and provide an initial analysis. This phase takes about one to two weeks.

3. *Post-assessment phase*—Finalize the analysis and prepare and distribute the report and recommendations. This phase can take anywhere from two to eight weeks.

The heart of the IAM is the creation of the Organizational Criticality Matrix. In this chart, all relevant automated systems are assigned impact attributes (high, medium, or low) based on their estimated effect on Confidentiality, Integrity, and Availability, and criticality to the organization. Other elements can be added to the matrix, such as Non-repudiation or Authentication, but the basic three tenets of InfoSec (that we have been drilling into the reader throughout the book) must remain.

While this type of Level I assessment might be thought to be too high-level, (in other words, not relevant to day-to-day security issues), it is remarkable how many organizations really do not know or do not take the time to determine how critical one system is in relation to another (and more importantly, how critical the system is to the viability of the enterprise). A Level I assessment is fundamental to the design and implementation of a sound organization security architecture.

PDD#63

(Excerpts from the National Infrastructure Protection Center's (NIPC) white paper: "The Clinton Administration's Policy on Critical Infrastructure Protection: Presidential Decision Directive 63, May 22, 1998")

I. A Growing Potential Vulnerability

The United States possesses both the world's strongest military and its largest national economy. Those two aspects of our power are mutually reinforcing and dependent. They are also increasingly reliant upon certain critical infrastructures and upon cyber-based information systems.

Critical infrastructures are those physical and cyber-based systems essential to the minimum operations of the economy and government. They include, but are not limited to, telecommunications, energy, banking and finance, transportation, water systems, and emergency services, both governmental and private. Many of the nation's critical infrastructures have historically been physically and logically separate systems that had little interdependence. As a result of advances in information technology and the necessity of improved efficiency, however, these infrastructures have become increasingly automated and interlinked. These same advances have created new vulnerabilities to equipment failures, human error, weather and other natural causes, and physical and cyber attacks. Addressing these vulnerabilities will necessarily require flexible, evolutionary approaches that span both the public and private sectors and that protect both domestic and international security. Because of our military strength, future enemies, whether nations, groups or individuals, might seek to harm us in non-traditional ways, including attacks within the United States. Our economy is increasingly reliant upon interdependent and cyber-supported infrastructures and non-traditional attacks on our infrastructure, and information systems might be capable of significantly harming both our military power and our economy.

II. The President's Intent

It has long been the policy of the United States to assure the continuity and viability of critical infrastructures. President Clinton intends that the United States will take all necessary measures to swiftly eliminate any significant vulnerability to both physical and cyber attacks on our critical infrastructures, including especially our cyber systems.

III. A National Goal

No later than the year 2000, the United States shall have achieved an initial operating capability—and no later than five years from the day the President signed Presidential Decision Directive 63, the United States shall have achieved and shall maintain the capability to protect our nation's critical infrastructures from intentional acts that would significantly diminish the abilities of the following:

- The Federal Government to perform essential national security missions and to ensure the general public health and safety; state and local governments to maintain order and to deliver minimum essential public services

- The private sector to ensure the orderly functioning of the economy and the delivery of essential telecommunications, energy, financial and transportation services

- Any interruptions or manipulations of these critical functions must be brief, infrequent, manageable, geographically isolated, and minimally detrimental to the welfare of the United States.

IV. A Public-Private Partnership to Reduce Vulnerability

Because the targets of attacks on our critical infrastructure would likely include both facilities in the economy and those in the government, the elimination of our potential vulnerability requires a closely coordinated effort of both the public and the private sector. To succeed, this partnership must be genuine, mutual, and cooperative. In seeking to meet our national goal to eliminate the vulnerabilities of our critical infrastructure, therefore, the U.S. government should, to the extent feasible, seek to avoid outcomes that increase government regulation or expand unfunded government mandates to the private sector.

For each of the major sectors of our economy that are vulnerable to infrastructure attack, the Federal Government will appoint from a designated Lead Agency a senior officer of that agency as the Sector Liaison Official to work with the private sector. Sector Liaison Officials, after discussions and coordination with private sector entities of their infrastructure sector, will identify a private sector counterpart (Sector Coordinator) to represent their sector. Together, these two individuals and the departments and corporations they represent shall contribute to a sectoral National Infrastructure Assurance Plan by:

- Assessing the vulnerabilities of the sector to cyber or physical attacks

- Recommending a plan to eliminate significant vulnerabilities

- Proposing a system for identifying and preventing attempted major attacks

- Developing a plan for alerting, containing, and rebuffing an attack in progress and then, in coordination with the Federal Emergency

Management Agency (FEMA) as appropriate, rapidly reconstituting minimum essential capabilities in the aftermath of an attack

During the preparation of the sectoral plans, the National Coordinator (see section VI), in conjunction with the Lead Agency Sector Liaison Officials and a representative from the National Economic Council, shall ensure their overall coordination and the integration of the various sectoral plans with a particular focus on interdependencies.

V. Guidelines

In addressing this potential vulnerability and the means of eliminating it, President Clinton wants those involved to be mindful of the following general principles and concerns:

- We shall consult with, and seek input from, the Congress on approaches and programs to meet the objectives set forth in this directive.

- The protection of our critical infrastructures is necessarily a shared responsibility and partnership between owners, operators and the government. Furthermore, the Federal Government shall encourage international cooperation to help manage this increasingly global problem.

- Frequent assessments shall be made of our critical infrastructures' existing reliability, vulnerability and threat environment because, as technology and the nature of the threats to our critical infrastructures will continue to change rapidly, so must our protective measures and responses be robustly adaptive.

- The incentives that the market provides are the first choice for addressing the problem of critical infrastructure protection; regulation will be used only in the face of a material failure of the market to protect the health, safety, or well being of the American people. In such cases, agencies shall identify and assess available alternatives to direct regulation, including providing economic incentives to encourage the desired behavior, or providing information upon which choices can be made by the private sector. These incentives, along with other actions, shall be designed to help harness the latest technologies, bring about global solutions to international problems, and enable private sector owners and operators to achieve and maintain the maximum feasible security.

- The full authorities, capabilities and resources of the government, including law enforcement, regulation, foreign intelligence and defense preparedness shall be available, as appropriate, to ensure that critical infrastructure protection is achieved and maintained.

- Care must be taken to respect privacy rights. Consumers and operators must have confidence that information will be handled accurately, confidentially and reliably.

- The Federal Government shall, through its research, development and procurement, encourage the introduction of increasingly capable methods of infrastructure protection.

- The Federal Government shall serve as a model to the private sector on how infrastructure assurance is best achieved and shall, to the extent feasible, distribute the results of its endeavors. We must focus on preventative measures as well as threat and crisis management. To that end, private sector owners and operators should be encouraged to provide maximum feasible security for the infrastructures they control and to provide the government necessary information to assist them in that task. In order to engage the private sector fully, it is preferred that participation by owners and operators in a national infrastructure protection system be voluntary.

- Close cooperation and coordination with state and local governments and first responders is essential for a robust and flexible infrastructure protection program. All critical infrastructure protection plans and actions shall take into consideration the needs, activities and responsibilities of state and local governments and first responders.

VI. Structure and Organization

The Federal Government shall be organized for the purposes of this endeavor around four components:

Lead Agencies for Sector Liaison

For each infrastructure sector that could be a target for significant cyber or physical attacks, there will be a single U.S. Government department that will serve as the lead agency for liaison. Each Lead Agency will designate one individual of Assistant Secretary rank or higher to be the Sector Liaison Official for that area and to cooperate with the private sector representatives (Sector Coordinators) in addressing problems related to critical infrastructure protection (and, in particular, in recommending components of the National Infrastructure Assurance Plan). Together, the Lead Agency and the private sector counterparts will develop and implement a Vulnerability Awareness and Education Program for their sector.

Lead Agencies for Special Functions

There are, in addition, certain functions related to critical infrastructure protection that must be chiefly performed by the Federal Government (national defense, foreign affairs, intelligence, and law enforcement). For each of those special functions, there shall be a Lead Agency that will be responsible for coordinating all of the activities of the United States Government in that area. Each lead agency will appoint a senior officer of Assistant Secretary rank or higher to serve as the Functional Coordinator for that function for the Federal Government.

Interagency Coordination

The Sector Liaison Officials and Functional Coordinators of the Lead Agencies, as well as representatives from other relevant departments and agencies including the National Economic Council, will meet to coordinate the implementation of this directive under the auspices of a *Critical Infrastructure Coordination Group* (CICG) chaired by the National Coordinator for Security, Infrastructure Protection and Counter-Terrorism. The National Coordinator will be appointed by and report to the President through the Assistant to the President for National Security Affairs, who shall ensure appropriate coordination with the Assistant to the President for Economic Affairs. Agency representatives to the CICG should be at a senior policy level (Assistant Secretary or higher). Where appropriate, the CICG will be assisted by extant policy structures, such as the Security Policy Board, Security Policy Forum, and the National Security and Telecommunications and Information System Security Committee.

National Infrastructure Assurance Council

On the recommendation of the Lead Agencies, the National Economic Council, and the National Coordinator, the President will appoint a panel of major infrastructure providers and state and local government officials to serve as the National Infrastructure Assurance Council. The President will appoint the Chairman. The National Coordinator will serve as the Council's Executive Director. The National Infrastructure Assurance Council will meet periodically to enhance the partnership of the public and private sectors in protecting our critical infrastructures and will provide reports to the President as appropriate. Senior Federal Government officials will participate in the meetings of the National Infrastructure Assurance Council as appropriate.

VII. Protecting Federal Government Critical Infrastructures

Every department and agency of the Federal Government shall be responsible for protecting its own critical infrastructure, especially its cyber-based systems. Every department and agency Chief Information Officer (CIO) shall be responsible for information assurance. Every department and agency shall appoint a Chief Infrastructure Assurance Officer (CIAO) who shall be responsible for the protection of all of the other aspects of that department's critical infrastructure. The CIO might be double-hatted as the CIAO at the discretion of the individual department. These officials shall establish procedures for obtaining expedient and valid authorizations to allow vulnerability assessments to be performed on government computer and physical systems. The Department of Justice shall establish legal guidelines for providing for such authorizations.

No later than 180 days from issuance of this directive, every department and agency shall develop a plan for protecting its own critical infrastructure, including but not limited to its cyber-based systems. The National Coordinator shall be responsible for coordinating analyses required by the departments and agencies of inter-governmental dependencies and the mitigation of those dependencies. The Critical Infrastructure Coordination Group (CICG) shall sponsor an expert review process for those plans. No later than two years from today, those plans shall have been implemented and shall be updated every two years. In meeting this schedule, the Federal Government shall present a model to the private sector on how best to protect critical infrastructure.

VIII. Tasks

Within 180 days, the Principals Committee should submit to the President a schedule for completion of a National Infrastructure Assurance Plan with milestones for accomplishing the following subordinate and related tasks:

Vulnerability Analyses. For each sector of the economy and each sector of the government that might be a target of infrastructure attack intended to significantly damage the United States, there shall be an initial vulnerability assessment followed by periodic updates. As appropriate, these assessments shall also include the determination of the minimum essential infrastructure in each sector.

Remedial Plan. Based upon the vulnerability assessment, there shall be a recommended remedial plan. The plan shall identify timelines for implementation, responsibilities, and funding.

Warning. A national center to warn of significant infrastructure attacks will be established immediately. As soon thereafter as possible, we will put in place an enhanced system for detecting and analyzing such attacks, with maximum possible participation of the private sector.

Response. A system for responding to a significant infrastructure attack while it is underway will be established, with the goal of isolating and minimizing damage.

Reconstitution. For varying levels of successful infrastructure attacks, we shall have a system to rapidly reconstitute minimum required capabilities.

Education and Awareness. There shall be Vulnerability Awareness and Education Programs within both the government and the private sector in order to sensitize people regarding the importance of security and to train them in security standards, particularly regarding cyber systems.

Research and Development. Federally sponsored research and development in support of infrastructure protection shall be coordinated, be subject to multi-year planning, take into account private-sector research, and be adequately funded to minimize our vulnerabilities on a rapid but achievable timetable.

Intelligence. The Intelligence Community shall develop and implement a plan for enhancing collection and analysis of the foreign threat to our national infrastructure, to include (but not be limited to) the foreign cyber/information warfare threat.

International Cooperation. There shall be a plan to expand cooperation on critical infrastructure protection with like-minded and friendly nations, international organizations, and multi-national corporations.

Legislative and Budgetary Requirements. There shall be an evaluation of the executive branch's legislative authorities and budgetary priorities regarding critical infrastructure, and ameliorative recommendations shall be made to the President as necessary. The evaluations and recommendations, if any, shall be coordinated with the director of the *Office of Management and Budget* (OMB).

IX. Implementation

In addition to the 180-day report, the National Coordinator, working with the National Economic Council, shall provide an annual report on the implementation of this directive to the President and to the heads of departments and agencies through the Assistant to the President for National Security Affairs. The report should include an updated threat assessment, a status report on achieving the milestones identified for the National Plan, and additional policy, legislative, and budgetary recommendations. The evaluations and recommendations, if any, shall be coordinated with the Director of OMB. In addition, following the establishment of an initial operating capability in the year 2000, the National Coordinator shall conduct a zero-based review.

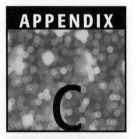
The Case for Ethical Hacking

The purpose of this appendix is to acquaint the security practitioner with the issues involved with the procedure known as "ethical hacking." The process of testing the network infrastructure by employing external penetration testing has been around for quite a while, but very recently the importance of this procedure has dramatically increased due to the global nature of the Internet and the fact that most corporations do not have a physically isolated network perimeter anymore.

External penetration testing is called many different things, including the following:

- Ethical hacking
- Penetration testing
- Vulnerability assessment (although external penetration testing is really only just a part of a full vulnerability assessment; see the BCP/DRP domain)
- Internet security testing
- Web site testing
- Red teaming

The majority of security professionals agree that external network perimeter testing is a vital part of implementing a fully balanced security process, and it is commonly used to augment the audit and security methodologies we have discussed in the book. What we will describe as follows is the proper way in which *Ethical Hacking* (EH) should be employed in the enterprise.

We will examine three fundamental concepts of EH:

Rationale. Why EH should be employed and its benefits

Roles and responsibilities. How to determine who should perform the testing and the reasons for the choice

Implementation. How to maximize the testing quality and minimize the risk by using best practices

Rationale

Today, organizations face global risks once their computing infrastructures are externally exposed. This situation is most commonly due to e-commerce and the Internet. EH can be a strong weapon in the information security professional's arsenal to help mitigate that risk. No matter how extensive and layered the security architecture is constructed, the organization does not know the real potential for external intrusion until the perimeter defenses are realistically tested.

To ensure security, systems should be ethically hacked. EH is important because of the risks that organizations face and the similarity of Internet systems to all other systems. Web sites and their underlying systems face an ongoing and increasing risk from external penetration. Security gaps can result from either simple system changes or advances in hacker technology. A successful attack is costly, resource- and time-consuming, and embarrassing to the credibility of the organization.

The only way to know whether the organization's Web sites, associated services, IP addresses, and underlying systems are secure is to test them. Web sites are similar to all other systems: when they are changed or when they are expected to handle external changes (in other words, advances in hacker technology), they should be tested. This situation is similar to the tenets of configuration and change control, which require a full testing process prior to and after implementation.

Roles and Responsibilities

Determining who should perform the testing is a critical step in the EH process. Points to consider when making the choice between internal and external hacking teams could include the following:

Maximizing cost effectiveness. Which choice will ensure the lowest cost for the greatest benefit?

Assuring thorough testing. How thorough will the testing need to be in order to guarantee the minimum risk?

Avoiding potential risks. What risk will the production systems incur as a direct result of the testing? Also, what legal or compliance liability will the organization be exposed to during the testing?

Assuring full reporting. How complete and non-partisan will the final report be?

To ensure this cost effectiveness, the efficient use of staff, a lack of corporate bias, and full and complete reporting, the EH should be performed by an independent outside firm that has proven integrity.

Using an external penetration service firm rather than internal corporate resources has quantitative and qualitative advantages:

Greater bang for the buck. Firms that specialize in EH can afford the ongoing research and development, systems development, and maintenance that is needed to operate state-of-the-art proprietary and open source testing tools and techniques. It is not cost-effective for a single firm, even a firm that has many subsidiaries and Web sites, to fund such an effort.

More effective use of staff. Internal system security departments have a limited amount of time and a limited budget. By outsourcing Web security testing, a firm's internal system security team increases the time it spends on closing and preventing security gaps (in other words, implementing remediation to the vulnerabilities that are found in the testing report).

Lack of corporate bias. External ethical hackers are more effective than internal penetration testers because the external penetration service firm is not influenced by any previous system security decisions, knowledge of the current system environment, or future system security plans.

Full reporting. An employee who is functioning as a penetration tester might be reluctant to fully report security gaps. This person might believe that presenting any bad news would be bad for his career by showing how poor the security was designed or implemented. Or, perhaps he might feel that he has created the vulnerabilities identified, inadvertently through ignorance or incompetence, or that there might be vulnerabilities intentionally created by people known to him (the worst scenario). Conversely, career advancement and professional recognition at external penetration service firms is dependent upon identifying security gaps.

Ex-Hackers or Not?

So you are convinced to begin looking for a firm to begin the EH. Before you start, let's add a cautionary note on selecting the right external firm. The same care and due diligence should take place when evaluating external ethical hackers as would take place when evaluating any other vendor (quality, cost, dependability, references, and so on). In addition, there are two points that are somewhat unique to ethical hacking that should also be considered: integrity and independence.

Integrity. Ethics matter. Do not use an ethical hacking firm that hires or subcontracts to ex-hackers or others who have criminal records. Some of the largest consulting firms, some of the "big five" auditing firms, and some system security boutiques hire hackers who have criminal records. Your firm might not want to invite them into your systems. Check on your potential vendors' hiring and subcontracting policies. By using a firm that does not employ ex-hackers, an entire subset of risks can be avoided. Also, many security certification organizations require the signing of ethical statements as a condition of receiving their certification (the CISSP program, for example).

Independence. Use ethical hackers who do not sell auditing, consulting, hardware, software, firewall, hosting, and/or networking services. A firm that conducts EH but that also provides security solutions or remediation has an inherent conflict of interest. It is unlikely that an EH firm will report a security vulnerability if its advice or products do not provide the needed protection or if some of its colleagues were responsible for previously securing the Web site. Full reporting of security gaps is dependent upon avoiding this conflict of interest.

Implementation

The following best practices should be utilized by the ethical hackers:

Test Remotely

By testing remotely, the ethical hacking firm emulates the hackers' approach more realistically. Also, the firm being tested avoids the security risks associated with having consultants on-site.

Testing remotely also releases the client organization from several responsibilities, including providing the following:

- Advance preparation by the staff
- Allotting staff or resource time to assist during the test
- Configuration changes required to production systems during any phase of the test
- Actual system down time
- Facilities space (as is required for an on-site auditing team)

Test Transparently

Security vulnerabilities (in other words, the ability to cause a denial of service, gain root access to key systems, alter Web pages, and so on) can be and should be identified without doing any alteration (or at worst, real damage) to the organization's systems. EH should not involve writing to or modifying the target systems or reducing the target's network response time.

An important component of testing transparently is the need to test for security gaps during network traffic peaks. Certain security gaps (in other words, those associated with the processing of fragmented packets) are more likely to appear during peak traffic, so the ethical hackers need to be able to test during these periods without reducing network response time.

Use the Right Testing Tools, and Use Them Correctly

Ethical hackers should use both open source and proprietary testing tools. There are currently more than 20 excellent open-source testing tools that each have different strengths; using every one has definite benefits.

The ethical hackers should modify and optimize each of the open source tools prior to each use. This optimization should be done at the operating system, configuration, and (if applicable) application level. Each tool's test results will vary depending upon which operating system it is run and how the machine is configured. Application-level modifications should include both adding code (enhancing testing) and disabling code (preventing damage). All of these modifications should take place prior to the ethical hacking attempt.

Open-Source Testing Tools

The following tools (with modification) are excellent for ethical hacking:

- authforce
- cgichk.pl
- cheops
- dnswalk
- ess (the Echo scanner)
- ftpcheck.pl
- fts-rvscan
- hunt
- nessus
- nlog
- nmap
- nperf
- nsat
- rascan
- relaychk.pl
- Saint
- SARA
- sbscan
- scanssh
- snmpscan
- snort
- whisker

Test Each Month, Not Once or Twice a Year

EH performed on an ongoing routine schedule is the only way to know whether new security gaps have appeared in your network. Any change to the computing infrastructure, no matter how insignificant, can create new vulnerabilities. Also, hacker technology continues to advance quickly, and hackers do not try to penetrate systems just once or twice a year. As a countermeasure, EH should be conducted each month.

Test at Varying and Random Times Each Month

Some security vulnerabilities are more likely to appear when network traffic is light (for example, predictable TCP sequence numbers), and some are more likely to appear when network traffic is heavy (for example, fragmented packet security gaps). In addition, system changes and enhancements occur at different times throughout any given month.

In order to test these varying conditions, EH should be conducted at all different times:

- Weekdays and weekends
- Days and nights
- Holidays and non-holidays

Summary

We have described the three main points of EH:

1. Its position of importance in the implementation of a well-rounded security policy
2. Why an ethical, external firm should be engaged for the task
3. Why best practices should be employed during the test to guarantee the greatest cost effectiveness and risk mitigation level

Whatever you choose to call it, ethical hacking is a cornerstone of the trusted, secure computing infrastructure. When properly executed, ethical hacking can provide the level of security required to conduct business securely and efficiently on the Internet and maintain the three main tenets of information systems security: confidentiality, integrity, and availability.

(Written by Ken Brandt with Russell Dean Vines. Ken Brandt (kbrandt@ tigertesting.com) is a managing director and co-founder of Tiger Testing, a firm that specializes exclusively in ethical hacking.)

The Common Criteria

The following excepts are reproduced with permission and without alteration from http://csrc.nist.gov/cc. It's important for the reader to note the link between the *Common Criteria* (CC) and its official ISO clone, the *International Standard* (IS) 15408. The CC is becoming a global standard, so the CISSP candidate might be required to know that IS15408 and CC are commonly applied synonymously.

Common Criteria: Launching the International Standard

The Common Criteria (CC) for *Information Technology* (IT) Security Evaluation is the new standard for specifying and evaluating the security features of computer products and systems. The CC is intended to replace previous security criteria used in North America and Europe with a standard that can be used everywhere in the world.

Developing the CC has been a five-year international project involving NIST and the *National Security Agency* (NSA), on behalf of the United States, and security organizations in Canada, France, Germany, the Netherlands, and the United

Kingdom. They have worked in close cooperation with the International Standards Organization (ISO).

In the United States, the new international standard CC has formed the basis for the *National Information Assurance Partnership* (NIAP), a joint activity of NIST and NSA to establish an IT product security evaluation program supported by a number of accredited, independent testing laboratories. The main goals of NIAP are to establish cost-effective evaluation of security-capable IT products and to promote the wide availability of tested products to federal agencies and others, thus playing a crucial role in helping to protect the U.S. information infrastructure.

NOTE A glossary at the end of this appendix defines key terms used throughout the document.

Purpose of CC

The CC will be used as the basis for evaluation of the security properties of IT products and systems. By using such a common criteria base, a wider audience may find the results of an IT security evaluation meaningful. The CC permits comparability among the results of independent security evaluations. It does so by providing a common set of requirements for the security functions of IT products and systems and the assurance measures applied to them during a security evaluation.

The evaluation process establishes a level of confidence that the security functions of such products and systems and the assurance measures applied to them must meet. The evaluation results may help consumers determine whether the IT product or system is secure enough for their intended application and whether the security risks implicit in its use are tolerable.

The CC supports the development of standardized sets of well-understood IT product security requirements by user communities in the form of *Protection Profiles* (PPs) for use in procurements and advice to manufacturers. Manufacturers can use similar sets of CC-based requirements to describe the security capabilities of their products. These are called *Security Targets* (STs), which can then be used as the basis for security evaluations of those products. Security evaluations are formalized testing and analytic processes that use the CC to determine whether IT products have been correctly developed to specification and whether they are effective in countering the security problems as claimed. Users can integrate evaluated IT products into their systems with increased confidence that their claimed security features will operate as intended.

Earlier Security Criteria Work

The CC represents the outcome of a long series of efforts to develop criteria for the security evaluation of IT products and systems that can be broadly useful within the international community. In the early 1980s, NSA developed the *Trusted Computer System Evaluation Criteria* (TCSEC or "Orange Book"). NSA has used the TCSEC extensively since then in its IT security product evaluation program.

In the succeeding decade, various countries initiated the development of evaluation criteria that built upon the concepts of the TCSEC but were more flexible and adaptable to the evolving nature of IT.

In Europe, the European Commission published the *Information Technology Security Evaluation Criteria* (ITSEC) in 1991 after joint development by France, Germany, the Netherlands, and the United Kingdom.

In Canada, the *Canadian Trusted Computer Product Evaluation Criteria* (CTCPEC) were published in early 1993 as a combination of the ITSEC and TCSEC approaches.

In the United States, NIST and NSA jointly developed the draft *Federal Criteria* for Information Technology Security (FC) version 1.0, which was also published in early 1993 as a second approach to combining North American and European concepts for evaluation criteria.

Work began in 1990 in ISO to develop an international standard evaluation criteria for general use. The new criteria were to be responsive to the need for mutual recognition of standardized security evaluation results in a global IT market. This task was assigned to the *Joint Technical Committee 1—Information Technology* (JTC1), subcommittee 27—Security Techniques (SC27), *Working Group 3—Security Criteria* (WG3).

Development of the Common Criteria

In June 1993, the seven organizations responsible for all the North American and European security criteria (listed at end of bulletin) pooled their efforts to align their separate criteria into a single set of widely useful international IT security criteria. This joint multi-national activity, named the CC Project, sought to resolve the conceptual and technical differences among the source criteria. The results were to be delivered to WG3 as a contribution to the international standard criteria under development.

The CC Project sponsoring organizations formed the *CC Editorial Board* (CCEB) to develop the CC. They established a formal cooperative liaison with WG3 and contributed several early versions of the CC to WG3's work, which were in turn influenced by WG3 experts' interaction. Beginning in 1994, WG3 adopted these versions as successive working drafts of the ISO criteria.

Version 1.0 of the CC was completed in January 1996 and distributed by ISO in April 1996 as a *Committee Draft* (CD). The CC Project used this version to perform a number of trial evaluations. A widespread public review of the document was also conducted.

The *CC Implementation Board* (CCIB) extensively revised the CC based on the results of trial use, public review, and interaction with ISO. Working closely with WG3, the CCIB completed CC version 2.0 in April 1998, and it was sent out by ISO for balloting as a Final Committee Draft. In October 1998, WG3 slightly revised the document and approved it as Final Draft International Standard 15408, for final balloting in the winter of 1998. The document is expected to become IS 15408 in early 1999 without further change. For historical and continuity purposes, ISO has accepted the continued use of the term *"Common Criteria"* (CC) within the document, while recognizing that the official ISO name for the new IS 15408 is "Evaluation Criteria for Information Technology Security."

CC Project Sponsoring Organizations

The seven European and North American governmental organizations provided nearly all of the effort that went into developing the CC from its inception to its completion. These organizations are also "evaluation authorities," managing product security evaluation programs for their respective national governments. They have committed themselves to replacing their respective evaluation criteria with the new IS 15408. Their goal is mutual recognition of each other's security product evaluation results, permitting a wider global market for good IT security products.

Interim Mutual Recognition

In April 1996, NIST in cooperation with NSA published a bulletin called "Guidance on the Selection of Low Level Assurance Evaluated Products." The bulletin recommended TCSEC Class C2—"Controlled Access Protection" as an acceptable minimum set of security criteria for general use in low-threat environments. The bulletin also publicly acknowledged that the Canadian CTCPEC and the European ITSEC contained similar requirements.

The NIST bulletin recognized that, while full equivalency among these three criteria was not easy to establish, enough similarities existed to recommend the use of low-level assurance products evaluated under any of them. The bulletin also noted that equivalency should cease to be an issue once the CC is adopted and implemented by the participating countries.

With the advent of CC version 2.0 and its ISO counterpart, IS 15408, supported by the CC-based Mutual Recognition Arrangement signed by these countries in October 1998 (see end of bulletin), equivalency is no longer an issue.

Three Parts of the CC

Part 1—Introduction and General Model

Part 1 introduces the CC. It defines general concepts and principles of IT security evaluation and presents a general model of evaluation. Part 1 also defines constructs for expressing IT security objectives, for selecting and defining IT security requirements, and for writing high-level specifications for products and systems. These constructs are called *Protection Profiles* (PPs), *Security Targets* (STs), and packages and are described in a later section. In addition, Part 1 describes the usefulness of each part of the CC in terms of each of the target audiences.

Part 2—Security Functional Requirements

Part 2 contains a catalog of well-defined and understood security functional requirements that are intended to be used as a standard way of expressing the security requirements for IT products and systems. The catalog is organized into classes, families, and components:

- Classes are high-level groupings of families of requirements, all sharing a common security focus (e.g., identification and authentication).
- Families are lower-level groupings of requirement components all sharing specific security objectives but differing in rigor or emphasis (e.g., user authentication).
- Components are the lowest selectable requirements that may be included in PPs, STs, or packages (e.g., unforgeable user authentication).

Part 2 also includes an extensive annex of application notes for applying the material that it contains. While it is possible to explicitly state functional requirements not included in the Part 2 catalog in building CC-based constructs (PPs, STs, and packages), that course is not advised unless it is clearly not practical to use Part 2 components. Using functional requirements not part of the catalog could jeopardize widespread acceptance of the result.

Part 3—Security Assurance Requirements

Part 3 contains a catalog that establishes a set of assurance components that can be used as a standard way of expressing the assurance requirements for IT products and systems. The Part 3 catalog is organized into the same class-family-component structure as Part 2. Part 3 also defines evaluation criteria for PPs and STs. Part 3 presents the seven *Evaluation Assurance Levels* (EALs), which are predefined packages of assurance components that make up the CC scale for rating confidence in the security of IT products and systems.

The EALs have been developed with the goal of preserving the concepts of assurance drawn from the source criteria (TCSEC, ITSEC, and CTCPEC) so that results of previous evaluations remain relevant. For example, EALs levels 2–7 are generally equivalent to the assurance portions of the TCSEC C2-A1 scale. Note, however, that this equivalency should be used with caution as the levels do not derive assurance in the same manner, and exact mappings do not exist.

As with Part 2, it is possible but not necessarily advisable to explicitly state assurance requirements not from Part 3 or to augment EAL packages with additional Part 3 components. Mutual recognition of product evaluation results is based largely on the EAL, so use of unique combinations of assurance requirements could jeopardize international acceptance of products evaluated against them.

Key Concepts

The CC defines three useful constructs for putting IT security requirements from Parts 2 and 3 together: the PP, the ST, and the Package. The CC has been developed around the central notion of using in these constructs, wherever possible, the security requirements in Parts 2 and 3 of the CC, which represent a well-known and understood domain.

Protection Profile

The PP is an implementation-independent statement of security needs for a set of IT security products that could be built. The PP contains a set of security requirements, preferably taken from the catalogs in Parts 2 and 3, which should include an EAL. A PP is intended to be a reusable definition of product security requirements that are known to be useful and effective.

A PP could be developed by user communities, IT product developers, or other parties interested in defining such a common set of requirements. A PP gives consumers a means of referring to a specific set of security needs and communicating them to manufacturers. The PP also helps future product evaluation against those needs.

The PP contains the following items:

- PP introduction—Identification and overview information, which allows users to identify PPs useful to them
- *Target of evaluation* (TOE) description—Description of the IT product and its purpose, not necessarily from a security perspective
- TOE security environment-description of the security aspects of the environment in which the product is intended to be used and the manner in which it is expected to be employed. This statement includes the following:
  - Assumptions about the security aspects of the product's expected usage and operating environment, such as value of assets and limitations of use. Assumptions also describe the environment's physical, personnel, and connectivity aspects.
  - Threats against which the product or its supporting environment must specifically provide protection.
  - Organizational security policies or rules with which the product must comply. These can be any explicit statements of IT security needs that the product must meet.
  - Security objectives—A high-level statement of what the product and its environment are intended to accomplish in covering the threats, policies, and assumptions.

- IT security requirements—The detailed statement of IT security functional and assurance requirements that the product and its operating environment must satisfy to meet the objectives.

- Application notes—Additional supporting information that may be useful for the construction, evaluation, or use of the product.

- Rationale—The evidence describing how the PP is complete and cohesive and how a product built against it would be effective in meeting the objectives.

Security Target

An ST is a statement of security claims for a particular IT security product or system. The ST parallels the structure of the PP, though it has additional elements that include product-specific detailed information. The ST contains a set of security requirements for the product or system, which may be made by reference to a PP, directly by reference to CC functional or assurance components, or stated explicitly. An ST is the basis for agreement among all parties as to what security the product or system offers, and therefore the basis for its security evaluation. The ST contains a summary specification, which defines the specific measures taken in the product or system to meet the security requirements.

Package

An intermediate combination of security requirement components is termed a package. The package permits the expression of a set of either functional or assurance requirements that meet some particular need, expressed as a set of security objectives. A package is intended to be reusable and to define requirements that are known to be useful and effective in meeting the identified objectives. A package may be used in the construction of more complex packages or PPs and STs. The seven *evaluation assurance levels* (EALs) contained in Part 3 are predefined assurance packages.

Target of Evaluation

The TOE is an IT product or system to be evaluated, the security characteristics of which are described in specific terms by a corresponding ST, or in more general terms by a PP. In CC philosophy, it is important that a product or system be evaluated against the specific set of criteria expressed in the ST. This evaluation consists of rigorous analysis and testing performed by an accredited, independent laboratory. The scope of a TOE evaluation is set by the EAL and other requirements specified in the ST. Part of this process is an evaluation of the ST itself, to ensure that it is correct, complete, and internally consistent and can be used as the baseline for the TOE evaluation.

Uses of the CC

The CC is used in two general ways:

- As a standardized way to describe security requirements, e.g., PPs and STs for IT products and systems
- As a sound technical basis for evaluating the security features of these products and systems

The following hypothetical scenarios describe these two uses.

Describing Security Requirements

In a typical PP development scenario, a community of users (e.g., a banking consortium) will determine that a standardized set of security capabilities should be used in software or hardware on their systems. They will begin to construct a PP to express those common requirements. They will first identify the type of product or products envisioned and the general IT features needed. They will then consider the environment in which it will operate - in particular identifying the security problems and challenges that must be addressed. That activity is, in essence, a risk analysis and leads to a statement of general needs or security objectives to be met both by the product and by its environment.

Security objectives are transformed by use of the CC Part 2 catalog into a set of coherent and mutually supportive IT security functional requirements statements. Based on the desired level of confidence in the security of products to be built, an EAL from Part 3 is assigned. (Note that the higher the EAL, the greater the burden on the product developer, and consequently the more time and money needed to bring the product to complete availability.)

The outcome of the process just described is a PP. It is desirable that the PP be submitted to an independent testing laboratory for evaluation, to ensure that it is correct, complete, and internally consistent. The PP may then be entered into a central registry for use by the community to communicate the product security needs to manufacturers, either informally or by incorporation into procurement documents.

The preceding scenario involving a user community is only one possible approach to developing a PP, although it is the most commonly expected approach. It is also possible for one or several manufacturers to develop a PP that incorporates the features of their products, as a means of communication with potential users, ensuring interoperability via standardization or for other purposes.

Evaluating Product Security

In a typical product evaluation scenario, a manufacturer identifies a market niche for an IT product with security capability. This niche may be represented by a PP incorporating the product desires of a group of users and potential customers. The manufacturer builds the product, following the PP-specified functional requirements from CC Part 2 and the developer assurance requirements in the EAL from Part 3. Once the product is built, the manufacturer prepares an ST, which in the simplest case makes a claim of compliance with a particular PP—thereby covering the functional and assurance requirements for the product. The manufacturer also develops as part of the ST a summary specification of the ways that the product's features meet these requirements. The manufacturer then submits the ST, the product, and accompanying documentation to an accredited, independent testing laboratory for evaluation.

The laboratory evaluates the ST, to determine that it is a sound baseline for evaluation of the product and that any claims of PP compliance are supportable. The laboratory then proceeds to evaluate the product and its documentation against the ST. If the product passes evaluation, it can be submitted to an evaluation authority for validation of the evaluation results.

While definitely preferable, it is not necessary for a product to claim compliance with a PP. In the absence of PP claims, the ST is prepared in a process similar to that described for the PP. The evaluation of the ST and then the corresponding product can proceed as before, but no PP compliance claims will be examined.

Validating The Results

An integral part of the CC-based process, as described in its Part 1, is the independent validation of evaluation results in order to ensure that a product's evaluation was conducted properly. An evaluation authority is a body that implements the CC for a specific community, responsible for setting the standards and monitoring the quality of evaluations conducted by testing laboratories within that community. Each of the CC partners is an evaluation authority for the government of its respective country. NIST and NSA work together as a single U.S. authority, as described below. The evaluation authority is responsible for overseeing all evaluations in its jurisdiction, qualitatively reviewing the results, and certifying or validating the findings.

The term "validation" is used in the U.S. for this process, while the other CC partners use "certification," but the process is the same. Upon validation of a successful product evaluation, the product is awarded a CC certificate and is added to an official validated products list available to the public.

Evaluating Installed Systems

Another way that the CC process can be used is to evaluate installed systems for such purposes as system certification and accreditation programs used in several federal agencies. The organization responsible for certifying a system's secure operation could develop an ST describing the system architecture, its functions and operational environment, and the security features it embodies. An independent entity, such as an accredited testing laboratory, could then perform an on-site evaluation of the system against the ST, providing a report to support a request for accreditation.

CC Evaluation Programs

Numerous organizations throughout the world are now implementing the CC, including all of the CC project partners (listed next), as well as other European Union nations, Australia, New Zealand, Japan, Korea, and parts of the former Soviet Union. It is expected that this number will grow significantly as soon as the CC is formally published as International Standard 15408 in early 1999.

In the U.S., NIST and NSA jointly operate *the National Information Assurance Partnership* (NIAP). NIAP is a broadly based program that operates principally as the CC-based evaluation authority for the federal government. NIAP is dedicated to demonstrating the value of independent testing and validation as a measure of security and trust in IT products. Through its efforts, NIAP fosters the establishment and accreditation of commercial IT product security testing laboratories in the U.S.

The Goal of Mutual Recognition

On October 5, 1998, six of the seven CC project partners officially signed a *Mutual Recognition Arrangement* (MRA). The purpose of the MRA is to bring about an international situation in which IT products and PPs that earn a CC certificate can be procured and used in different jurisdictions without the need for them to be evaluated and certified/validated more than once. By recognizing the results of each other's evaluations, products evaluated in one MRA member nation can be accepted in the other member nations. It is anticipated that, as other nations develop high quality IT product security evaluation programs, they too may seek to join the MRA. This path is open to other evaluation authorities upon demonstration that they can fulfill the stringent technical and procedural conditions for mutual recognition laid down in the MRA.

As product evaluations can be costly and time-consuming, both manufacturers and users have welcomed the MRA breakthrough. The anticipated outcome is a "level playing field" for multi-national IT product manufacturers, leading to a much wider availability of useful IT security products to secure the global information infrastructure.

These two factors have been the major goal of the CC project from its inception and have been the driving force and vision that empowered the ISO criteria activity as well. The joint development of the CC has created an environment of mutual respect among the partners, and the CC itself has formed the technical basis for mutual recognition, both of which were necessary for the inception of the MRA.

Glossary

The following key terms used in this appendix are adapted from CC definitions:

Assurance—grounds for confidence that an IT product or system meets its security objectives

Evaluation—assessment of an IT product or system against defined security functional and assurance criteria, performed by a combination of testing and analytic techniques

Evaluation Assurance Level (**EAL**)—one of seven increasingly rigorous packages of assurance requirements from CC Part 3. Each numbered package represents a point on the CCs predefined assurance scale. An EAL can be considered a level of confidence in the security functions of an IT product or system.

Package—a reusable set of either functional or assurance components (e.g., an EAL), combined together to satisfy a set of identified security objectives

Product—IT software, firmware and/or hardware, providing functions designed for use or incorporation within a multiplicity of systems

Protection Profile (**PP**)—an implementation-independent set of security functional and assurance requirements for a category of IT products that meet specific consumer needs

Security Functional Requirements—requirements, preferably from CC Part 2, that when taken together specify the security behavior of an IT product or system

Security Objective—A statement of intent to counter specified threats and/or satisfy specified organizational security policies and assumptions

Security Target (**ST**)—a set of security functional and assurance requirements and specifications to be used as the basis for evaluation of an identified product or system

System—a specific IT installation, with a particular purpose and operational environment

Target of Evaluation (**TOE**)—another name for an IT product or system described in a PP or ST. The TOE is the entity that is subject to security evaluation.

For More Information

REFERENCES:

NIST CSL Bulletin, April 1996
Common Criteria for IT Security v.2.0
ISO FDIS 15408, Parts 1-2-3
Common Criteria Mutual Recognition Arrangement, October 1998

WEB SITES:

Common Criteria Project: http://csrc.nist.gov/cc
NIAP: http://niap.nist.gov

CC PROJECT ORGANIZATIONS:

■ CANADA:

Communications Security Establishment
E-mail: criteria@cse-cst.gc.ca
WWW: www.cse-cst.gc.ca/cse/english/cc.html

■ FRANCE

Service Central de la Securité, des Systémes d'Information (SCSSI)
E-mail: ssi20@calva.net

■ GERMANY:

Bundesamt für Sicherheit in der Informationstechnik (BSI)
German Information Security Agency (GISA)
E-mail: cc@bsi.de
WWW: www.bsi.bund.de

■ NETHERLANDS:

Netherlands National Communications Security Agency
E-mail: criteria@nlncsa.minbuza.nl
WWW: www.tno.nl/instit/fel/refs/cc.html

■ UNITED KINGDOM:

Communications-Electronics Security Group
E-mail: criteria@cesg.gov.uk
WWW: www.cesg.gov.uk/cchtml

■ UNITED STATES—NIST:

National Institute of Standards and Technology
E-mail: criteria@nist.gov
WWW: http://csrc.nist.gov/cc

■ UNITED STATES—NSA:

National Security Agency
E-mail: common_criteria@radium.ncsc.mil
WWW: www.radium.ncsc.mil/tpep/

APPENDIX E

BS7799

Considered by some as the leading *Information Security Management System* (ISMS), the Code of Practice for Information Security Management (BS7799) has been developed by the British Standards Institute.

A group of leading companies joined, first, to develop the Code of Practice for Information Security Management, now known as BS7799 Part 1, *Code of Practice*, then, in 1998, to develop BS7799 Part 2, *Specification for Information Security Management Systems*. The United Kingdom Department of Trade and Industry commissioned the BS 7799 certification scheme in 1998.

BS7799 is geared to assuring integrity, availability, and confidentiality of information assets. Assurance is attained through controls that management creates and maintains within the organization. BS7799 requires that company management address 10 specific areas:

- Security policy
- Security organization
- Assets, classification, and control
- Personnel security
- Physical and environmental security
- Computer and network management

- System access control
- System development controls
- Business continuity planning
- Compliance and auditing

The scheme requires that participating certification bodies be accredited by recognized national accreditation bodies. The United Kingdom Accreditation Service has accredited six bodies under ISO Guide 62 (EN 45012) to perform certification to BS7799:

- BSI Quality Assurance
- Bureau Veritas Quality International Ltd.
- Det Norske Veritas Quality Assurance Ltd.
- Lloyd's Register Quality Assurance Ltd.
- National Quality Assurance Ltd.
- SGS Yarsley International Certification Service Ltd.

A drive to gain worldwide acceptance of BS7799 has been the primary thrust of the Joint Information Technology Committee of the ISO and the *International Electrotechnical Commission* (IEC). These organizations are transitioning BS7799 into an international standard known as ISO 17799.

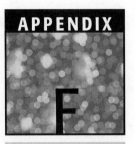
HIPAA Updates

Scope

HIPAA Public Law 104-191, the Kennedy-Kassebaum Health Insurance Portability and Accountability Act of 1996, is designed to:

- Provide for greater access to personal health care information
- Enable portability of health insurance
- Establish strong penalties for health care fraud
- Administrative simplification

Title II of HIPAA, Administrative Simplification, contains the Security and Privacy requirements and, therefore, the remainder of this discussion focuses on Administrative Simplification.

Title II Administrative Simplification

The goals of Title II are to:

- Improve the efficiency and effectiveness of the U.S. health care system by standardizing the exchange of administrative and financial data.

- Protect Security and Privacy of individually identifiable health information

Covered Entities under HIPAA are health plans, health care clearinghouses, insurers to include corporate employers' self-insured plans, and health care providers who transmit health information electronically in connection with standard transactions.

The principle areas addressed under Administrative Simplification are:

- Transaction Standards and Code Sets for claims, enrollment, premium payments and others as adopted by HHS

- Unique Health Identifiers for health care providers, health plans, employers and individuals

- Security and Electronic Signatures

- Privacy for individually identifiable health information

Dates

Publication dates of the proposed rules and final rules vary for the major areas addressed by Title II. Also, some of the rules have set compliance dates and, as of this writing, some do not. The important dates are summarized in the following sections.

Security

HHS published proposed Security standards on August 12, 1998 and as of this writing, the final security rule has not been published.

Privacy

The final Privacy rule was published on December 28, 2000 with a compliance date of April 14, 2003. Changes were proposed to the final Privacy rule by HHS and published in the Federal Register on March 28, 2002. The purpose of the proposed changes was to "maintain strong protections for Privacy of individually identifiable health information while clarifying misinterpretations, addressing the unintended negative affects of the Privacy rule on health care quality or access to health care, and relieving unintended administrative burden created by the Privacy rule." The changes were subject to a 30-day pubic comment period that ended on April 26, 2002. These proposed changes would not affect the April 14, 2003 deadline for compliance with the final Privacy rule. These changes were finalized by HHS and went into effect in August 2002.

Transactions and Code Sets

The final rule for electronic transactions and code sets was published on August 17, 2000, with a compliance date of October 16, 2002. On December 27, 2001, President Bush amended HIPAA with the Administrative Simplification Compliance Act, Public Law 107-105. This act gave organizations the option of applying for a one-year delay in implementing the transactions and code sets standards if the organization applied for an extension before October 16, 2002. Thus, the new deadline for an organization requesting a delay will be October 16, 2003.

Unique Health Identifiers

Proposed rules for a national provider identifier and national employer identifier were published in 1998. Proposed rules for a national health plan identifier have not been released as of this writing, and plans for a national individual identifier are on hold because of privacy concerns.

Summary of Administrative Simplification Rules

A description of the standards described in Title II will provide the reader with the requirements associated with achieving HIPAA compliance.

Security

The HIPAA Security rule mandates the protection of the confidentiality, integrity, and availability of *protected health information* (PHI) through:

- Administrative procedures such as awareness training, chain of trust agreements, policies and internal auditing.
- Physical safeguards to include physical protection of workstations and media, facility access control, and disposal of magnetic media.
- Technical services and mechanisms such as authentication and access controls.
- Electronic Signatures when an industry standard can be agreed upon. They are not currently required.
- Appointment of a security officer.

Privacy

The HIPAA Privacy rule covers PHI that is transmitted or stored in electronic, paper or oral form. The final Privacy rule of December 28, 2000, stated that PHI cannot be disclosed unless:

- Disclosure is approved by the individual
- Permitted by the legislation
- For treatment
- For payment
- For health care operations
- As required by law

When the practical day-to-day health care operations were considered, there were a number of concerns about the details of the Privacy rule that may affect the delivery of health care. As a result, changes were proposed to the Privacy rule, published on March 28, 2002, that severely relaxed the consent requirements of the December 28, 2002 version of the rule. Privacy advocates have expressed strong concerns about these and other proposed changes. The changes, which went into effect in August 2002, are summarized as follows:

Removal of the Mandatory HIPAA Consent Requirement

Concerns focused on the impracticality of providers' obtaining consent before the initial encounter with the patient. Pharmacies commented on the need to allow individuals other than the patient to pick up the patient's prescription, and so on.

The amendment removes the consent requirement and would permit covered entities to use and disclose a patient's PHI for their own treatment, payment or health care operations and for treatment, payment, and certain health care operations of other parties without prior written patient permission.

Use and Disclosure with an Authorization

Under the Privacy Rule, covered entities must obtain a written authorization for the use or disclosure of PHI for purposes other than treatment, payment or operations. The amendments consolidate the various essential elements for authorizations into a single set of criteria.

Accounting of Disclosures of PHI

The Privacy Rule provides individuals with the right to obtain an accounting of any disclosures of their PHI made by a covered entity pursuant to an authorization during the six years preceding the request for accounting. HHS exempts from the accounting requirement all disclosures made pursuant to an individual's authorization.

Minimum Necessary and Oral Communications

The Privacy Rule requires that covered entities disclose only that amount of PHI that is necessary to fulfill the purpose of the disclosure. HHS explicitly permits incidental use or disclosure of PHI.

Business Associates

The business associate (BA) provisions of the Privacy Rule require a covered entity to impose, through contracts, the Privacy standards of the Privacy Rule on parties who access and use PHI. HHS amended the transition provisions of the Privacy Rule to give covered entities (other than small health plans, which currently have a 2004 compliance date) at least another year, until April 14, 2004, in which to modify existing written (but not oral) agreements or amendments of their PHI if the BA does not have the PHI in a "designated record set," as defined by the Privacy Rule.

Marketing

The Privacy Rule defines marketing as the making of a communication "about a product or service a purpose of which is to encourage recipients of the communication to purchase or use the product or service." The amendments to the Privacy Rule require a patient authorization for any use or disclosure of PHI for marketing purposes, unless the marketing occurs in a face-to-face communication between the covered entity and the patient or the covered entity is merely providing a promotional gift of nominal value.

Parents/Minors

Under the Privacy Rule, a covered entity must treat a person with the authority to act on behalf of an unemancipated minor as that minor's personal representative for purposes of use and disclosure of the minor's PHI. The amendments permit a covered entity to disclose PHI to a parent if a specific provision of state or other law, including case law, permits such a disclosure. Conversely, if such law prohibits such a disclosure, the covered entity would not be permitted to make it. Finally, the amendments require a covered entity, consistent with state or other applicable law, to disclose the minor's PHI to a parent or other personal representative of the minor, to the minor, or to both.

Research

The amendment makes significant changes to research authorizations by simplifying and clarifying the requirements. HHS defines a single set of essential elements that apply generally to any authorization regardless of the purpose for the use or disclosure.

Uses and Disclosures for FDA-Regulated Products or Activities

Public health organizations have expressed concern that the Privacy Rule stifles current public health reporting activities. In addition, some covered entities have expressed fear of liability for disclosing PHI to a manufacturer's employee who is not a person subject to FDA jurisdiction. The amendment clarifies that a covered entity may disclose protected health information to representatives of manufacturers or other companies, who are subject to FDA jurisdiction.

Research Transition Provisions

The research community is also concerned that the Privacy Rule does not address transition for studies that will continue after the compliance date but for which patient consent or authorization had not been sought. The amendments eliminate the distinction between research involving treatment and other research for purposes of transition.

De-Identification of PHI

The Privacy Rule provides two ways by which a covered entity can ensure that PHI has been adequately de-identified: It may obtain an expert opinion that there is a statistically small risk that the released information could be used to identify the individual subject; or it may strip from all disclosed information the 18 identifiers that are enumerated in the Privacy Rule's safe harbor provision.

Hybrid Entities

The Privacy Rule defines covered entities that primarily engage in non-covered functions as "hybrid entities" and applies the Privacy standards only to their health care components. HHS eliminates the term "primary functions" from its definition of "hybrid entity" and effectively permits covered entities, such as many universities and insurance companies, that engage in both covered functions and non-covered functions to elect to be treated as either a hybrid entity or a single entity.

Transactions and Code Sets

This portion of Title II requires the adoption of ANSI (American National Standards Institute) ASC X12N (Accredited Standards Committee X12) version 4010 EDI (Electronic Data Interchange) Standard for transactions. This requirement specifies standards for the "enveloping" of data for successful message routing.

This rule also mandates the use of standard code sets for diagnoses and inpatient services, professional services, dental services (replaces 'D' codes), drugs (instead of 'J' codes) and eliminates "local" codes.

HIPAA EDI Transactions

The HIPAA EDI Transaction Standards specifically apply to:

- Health claims or similar encounter information
- Health care payment and remittance advice
- Coordination of benefits
- Health claim status
- Enrollment and dis-enrollment in a health plan
- Eligibility for a health plan
- Health plan premium payments
- Referral certification and authorization

The Transactions Standard defines data elements required or conditionally required, each data element, technical transaction formats for the transmission of the data, and code sets or values that can appear in selected data elements. The following standard "forms" are to be used:

- Health care claims or coordination of benefits
  - Retail drug NCPCP (National Council for Prescription Drug Programs) v. 32
  - Dental claim ASC X12N 837: dental
  - Professional claim ASC X12N 837: professional
  - Institutional claim ASC X12N 837: institutional
- Payment & remittance advice ASC X12N 835
- Health claim status ASC X12N 276/277
- Plan enrollment ASC X12 834
- Plan eligibility ASC X12 270/271
- Plan premium payments ASC X12 820
- Referral certification ASC X12 N 278

Code Sets

Code sets specifications are as follows:

For diseases, injuries, impairments, other health related problems, their manifestations, and causes of injury, disease, impairment: International Classification of Diseases, 9th Ed., Clinical Modification) ICD-9-CM (vol. 1 & 2)

For procedures or other actions taken to prevent, diagnose, treat, or manage diseases, injuries and impairments: (Current Procedural Terminology, 4th Ed.) CPT-4, (Code on Dental Procedures and Nomenclature, 2nd Ed.) CDT-2, or ICD -9-CM (vol. 3)

For drugs: (National Drug Codes) NDC

For other health related services, other substances, equipment, supplies, or other items used in health care services: (Health Care Financing Administration Common Procedure Coding System) HCPCS

Unique Health Identifiers

The Unique Health Identifier (UHI) is used to identify a health care provider, a health plan, an employer or an individual. Its purpose is to facilitate electronic transactions. The present formats for the different identifiers are as follows:

Provider. Ten-digit numeric with a check digit or an eight-character alphanumeric

Employer. Federal Employer Identification Number (EIN) that consists of nine digits separated by a hyphen in the format dd-ddddddd

Health Plan. No Notice of Proposed Rule Making (NPRM) has been released as of this writing; possibly will be a 10-digit number with a check digit

Individual. On hold at this time

Penalties

The penalties for violation of the HIPAA law are given in Table F.1.

Table F.1 Summary of HIPAA Violation Penalties

MONETARY PENALTY	TERM OF IMPRISONMENT	OFFENSE
$100	N/A	Single violation of a provision
Up to $25,000	N/A	Multiple violations of an identical requirement or prohibition made during a calendar year
Up to $50,000	Up to one year	Wrongful disclosure of individually identifiable health information
Up to $100,000	Up to five years	Wrongful disclosure of individually identifiable health information committed under false pretenses
Up to $250,000	Up to 10 years	Wrongful disclosure of individually identifiable health information committed under false pretenses with intent to sell, transfer, or use for commercial advantage, personal gain, or malicious harm

Conclusion

Compliance with HIPAA is a challenge for most organizations, but it offers the opportunity to streamline transaction processing and implement procedures that will make an organization more efficient and thus, a stronger competitor in the marketplace.

APPENDIX

G

References for Further Study

This appendix contains a listing of the references we used for the compilation of the book, some additional references that may be useful to you, and the URLs of Web sites that have good information for study or general security information. We used almost all of these publications when researching for this text, and many of them you should read to study for the exam. We have listed them in what we consider to be priority order, from the most relevant to the CISSP candidate to the least. In some cases, newer editions of the reference books are available.

Books

Krause, Micki and Tipton, Harold F., Eds. *Handbook of Information Security Management, 1999*. Boca Raton: CRC Press\Auerbach Publications, 1999.

Kaufman, Elizabeth and Newman, Andrew. *Implementing IPSec*. New York: John Wiley & Sons, 1999.

Russell, Deborah and Gangemi, G. T., CISSP. *Computer Security Basics*. New York: O'Reilly & Associates, 1992.

Horak, Ray. *Communication Systems and Networks (Second Edition)*. New York: John Wiley & Sons, Inc., 2000.

Garfinkel, Simson and Spafford, Gene. *Practical Unix & Internet Security.* New York: O'Reilly & Associates, 1996.

Schneier, Bruce. *Applied Cryptography (Second Edition).* New York: John Wiley & Sons, 1996.

Schneier, Bruce. *Secrets and Lies: Digital Security in a Networked World.* New York: John Wiley & Sons, 2000.

Smith, Marina. *Virtual LANs.* New York: McGraw-Hill, 1997.

Parker, Donn B. *Fighting Computer Crime.* New York: John Wiley & Sons, 1998.

Wood, Charles C. *Information Security Policies Made Easy.* Sausalito: Baseline Software, 1999.

Stallings, William. *Cryptography and Network Security (Second Edition).* Upper Saddle River: Prentice Hall Inc., 1999.

Kabay, Michel E. *The NCSA Guide to Enterprise Security.* New York: McGraw-Hill, 1996.

Hutt, Arthur E., Seymour Bosworth, and Douglas B. Hoyt. *Computer Security Handbook, Third Edition.* New York: John Wiley & Sons, 1995.

Denning, Dorothy. *Information Warfare and Security.* New York: Addison-Wesley, 1999.

Denning, Dorothy. *Internet Besieged.* New York: Addison-Wesley, 1998.

Gollmann, Dieter. *Computer Security.* New York: John Wiley & Sons, 1999.

Oaks, Scott. *Java Security.* Cambridge: O'Reilly and Associates, 1998.

Northcutt, Stephen. *Network Intrusion Detection.* Indianapolis: New Riders Publishing, 1999.

Nichols, Randall K., Ryan, Daniel J., and Ryan, Julie J. C. H. *Defending Your Digital Assets.* New York: McGraw-Hill, 1999.

Klarder, Lars. *Hacker Proof.* Las Vegas: Jamsa Press, 1997.

McClure, Stuart, Scambray, Joel, and Kurtz, George. *Hacking Exposed.* New York: Osborne/McGraw Hill, 1999.

Escamilla, Terry. *Intrusion Detection.* New York: John Wiley & Sons, 1998.

Kaeo, Merike. *Designing Network Security.* Indianapolis: Cisco Press, 1999.

Brenton, Chris. *Mastering Network Security.* San Francisco: SYBEX, 1999.

Anonymous. *Maximum Security (Second edition).* Indianapolis: SAMs/Macmillan, 1998.

Minoli, Daniel and Minoli, Emma. *Web Commerce Technology Handbook.* New York: McGraw-Hill, 1998.

Summers, Rita C. *Secure Computing: Threats and Safeguards.* New York: McGraw-Hill, 1997.

Norton, Peter and Stockman, Mike. *Network Security Fundamentals.* Indianapolis: SAMs/Macmillan, 2000.

Scott, Charlie, Wolfe, Paul, Erwin, Mike, and Oram, Andy (Ed.).*Virtual Private Networks (Second edition)*. Cambridge: O'Reilly and Associates, 1998.

Tiwana, Amrit. *Web Security*. Boston: Butterworth-Heinemann, 1999.

Garfinkel, Simson and Spafford, Gene. *Web Security and Commerce*. Cambridge: O'Reilly and Associates, 1997.

Rubin, Aviel D., Geer, Daniel, and Ranum, Marcus J. *Web Security Sourcebook*. New York: John Wiley & Sons, 1997.

CISSP Examination Textbooks, Volume 1: Theory. Schaumburg: SRV Professional Publications, 2000. www.srvbooks.com.

Shim, Jae K., Qureshi, Anique A., and Siegel, Joel G. *The International Handbook of Computer Security*. Chicago: Glenlake Publishing Company, 2000.

Andress, Mandy. *Surving Security*. Indianapolis: SAMS Publishing, 2002.

Web Sites

The Web sites are of interest to the CISSP candidate, either directly (as in the case of the (ISC²) or indirectly (as a resource for more info on InfoSec).

InfoSec and Government Information Sites

www.isc2.org	(This site is the headquarters of the CISSP program, your main contact for the CISSP certification process.)
www.intiss.com/intisslinks.html	(This site has a lot of great links for every domain of InfoSec.)

www.issa-intl.org
csrc.nist.gov/cc
www.nipc.gov
www.icsa.net
www.cerias.purdue.edu/coast/coast.html
www.alw.nih.gov/Security/security.html
www-cse.ucsd.edu/users/bsy/sec.html
www.cerberus-isc.com/resources.html
www.info-sec.com/ciao/63factsheet.html
www.fbi.gov/nipc/welcome.htm
www.gocsi.com
www.nsa.gov
www.nist.gov
www.nswc.navy.mil/ISSEC/CID
www.cerias.purdue.edu/

www.sans.org/giactc.htm
www.isalliance.org
www.securityportal.com
www.fedcirc.gov
www.cert.org
www.ciac.org/ciac
www.asisonline.org
www.bsa.org
www.eff.org
www.fbi.gov/scitech.htm
www.first.org
www.hert.org
www.htcia.org
www.usenix.org
www.ntbugtrak.com

www.nsi.org/compsec.html

www.boran.com/security

xforce.iss.net

www.itpolicy.gsa.gov

www.nswc.navy.mil/ISSEC

www.dda-ltd.co.uk/bs7799.html

Information Security Products, Services, and Training

www.checkpoint.com

www.cisco.com

www.corbett-tech.com

www.strozassociates.com

www.tigertesting.com

www.misti.com

www.securify.com

www.kroll-ogara.com

www.verisign.com

www.rsasecurity.com

www.securecomputing.com

www.atomictangerine.com

www.infosecnews.com

www.rdvgroup.com

Hacker Sites

Be careful of these sites—they might bite. Please take precautions before visiting them. Also, many of these sites come and go frequently; they might not be there by the time you read this book.

rootshell.com/beta/news.html

www.hackers.com

www.l0pht.com

www.thecodex.com

www.defcon.org

www.lordsomer.com

www.2600.com

www.phrack.com

www.cultdeadcow.com

www.hfactorx.org

www.digicrime.com

www.hideaway.net

www.hackernews.com

www.crimeonline.org

www.technotronic.com

www.happyhacker.org

www.webfringe.com/host/

APPENDIX

H

Answers to Sample and Bonus Questions

Chapter 1—Security Management Practices

Sample Questions

1. Which formula accurately represents an Annualized Loss Expectancy (ALE) calculation?

   a. SLE × ARO

   b. Asset Value (AV) × EF

   c. ARO × EF − SLE

   d. % of ARO × AV

   > *Answer:* a
   >
   > The correct answer is a. Answer b is the formula for an SLE, and answers c and d are nonsense.

2. What is an ARO?

   a. A dollar figure assigned to a single event

   b. The annual expected financial loss to an organization from a threat

   c. A number that represents the estimated frequency of an occurrence of an expected threat

   d. The percentage of loss that a realized threat event would have on a specific asset

   Answer: c

   The correct answer is c. Answer a is the definition of SLE, b is an ALE, and d is an EF.

3. Which choice MOST accurately describes the difference between the role of a data owner versus the role of a data custodian?

   a. The custodian implements the information classification scheme after the initial assignment by the owner.

   b. The data owner implements the information classification scheme after the initial assignment by the custodian.

   c. The custodian makes the initial information classification assignments, and the operations manager implements the scheme.

   d. The custodian implements the information classification scheme after the initial assignment by the operations manager.

   Answer: a

4. Which choice is NOT an accurate description of C.I.A.?

   a. C stands for confidentiality.

   b. I stands for integrity.

   c. A stands for availability.

   d. A stands for authorization.

   Answer: d

5. Which group represents the MOST likely source of an asset loss through inappropriate computer use?

   a. Crackers

   b. Hackers

   c. Employees

   d. Saboteurs

   Answer: c

   The correct answer is c. Internal personnel far and away constitute the largest amount of dollar loss due to unauthorized or inappropriate computer use.

6. Which choice is the BEST description of authentication as opposed to authorization?

   a. The means by which a user provides a claim of his or her identity to a system

   b. The testing or reconciliation of evidence of a user's identity

   c. A system's capability to determine the actions and behavior of a single individual within a system

   d. The rights and permissions granted to an individual to access a computer resource

   Answer: b

   The correct answer is b. Answer a is identification, c is accountability, and d is authorization.

7. What is a noncompulsory recommendation on how to achieve compliance with published standards called?

   a. Procedures

   b. Policies

   c. Guidelines

   d. Standards

   Answer: c

8. Place the following four information classification levels in their proper order, from the least sensitive classification to the most sensitive:

   _____ a. SBU

   _____ b. Top secret

   _____ c. Unclassified

   _____ d. Secret

   Answer: c, a, d, and b

9. How is an SLE derived?

   a. (Cost – benefit) $\times$ (% of Asset Value)

   b. AV $\times$ EF

   c. ARO $\times$ EF

   d. % of AV – implementation cost

   Answer: b

   The correct answer is b. A Single Loss Expectancy is derived by multiplying the Asset Value with its Exposure Factor. The other answers do not exist.

10. What are the detailed instructions on how to perform or implement a control called?

    a. Procedures

    b. Policies

    c. Guidelines

    d. Standards

    Answer: a

11. What is the BEST description of risk reduction?

    a. Altering elements of the enterprise in response to a risk analysis

    b. Removing all risk to the enterprise at any cost

    c. Assigning any costs associated with risk to a third party

    d. Assuming all costs associated with the risk internally

    Answer: a

    The correct answer is a. Answer b is not possible or desirable, c is risk transference, and d is risk acceptance.

12. Which choice MOST accurately describes the differences between standards, guidelines, and procedures?

    a. Standards are recommended policies, and guidelines are mandatory policies.

    b. Procedures are step-by-step recommendations for complying with mandatory guidelines.

    c. Procedures are the general recommendations for compliance with mandatory guidelines.

    d. Procedures are step-by-step instructions for compliance with mandatory standards.

    Answer: d

    The correct answer is d. The other answers are incorrect.

13. A purpose of a security awareness program is to improve:

    a. The security of vendor relations.

    b. The performance of a company's intranet.

    c. The possibility for career advancement of the IT staff.

    d. The company's attitude about safeguarding data.

    Answer: d

14. What is the MOST accurate definition of a safeguard?

    a. A guideline for policy recommendations

    b. A step-by-step instructional procedure

    c. A control designed to counteract a threat

    d. A control designed to counteract an asset

Answer: c

The correct answer is c. Answer a is a guideline, b is a procedure, and d is a distracter.

15. What does an Exposure Factor (EF) describe?

   a. A dollar figure that is assigned to a single event

   b. A number that represents the estimated frequency of the occurrence of an expected threat

   c. The percentage of loss that a realized threat event would have on a specific asset

   d. The annual expected financial loss to an organization from a threat

   Answer: c

   The correct answer is c. Answer a is an SLE, b is an ARO, and d is an ALE.

16. Which choice would be an example of a cost-effective way to enhance security awareness in an organization?

   a. Train every employee in advanced InfoSec.

   b. Create an award or recognition program for employees.

   c. Calculate the cost-benefit ratio of the asset valuations for a risk analysis.

   d. Train only managers in implementing InfoSec controls.

   Answer: b

17. What is the prime directive of Risk Management?

   a. Reduce the risk to a tolerable level.

   b. Reduce all risks regardless of cost.

   c. Transfer any risk to external third parties.

   d. Prosecute any employees that are violating published security policies.

   Answer: a

   The correct answer is a. Risk can never be eliminated, and Risk Management must find the level of risk the organization can tolerate and still function effectively.

18. Which choice MOST closely depicts the difference between qualitative and quantitative risk analysis?

   a. A quantitative RA does not use the hard costs of losses, and a qualitative RA does.

   b. A quantitative RA uses less guesswork than a qualitative RA.

   c. A qualitative RA uses many complex calculations.

   d. A quantitative RA cannot be automated.

   Answer: b

   The correct answer is b. The other answers are incorrect.

19. Which choice is NOT a good criterion for selecting a safeguard?

    a. The ability to recover from a reset with the permissions set to "allow all"

    b. Comparing the potential dollar loss of an asset to the cost of a safeguard

    c. The ability to recover from a reset without damaging the asset

    d. Accountability features for tracking and identifying operators

    Answer: a

    The correct answer is a. Permissions should be set to "deny all" during reset.

20. Which policy type is MOST likely to contain mandatory or compulsory standards?

    a. Guidelines

    b. Advisory

    c. Regulatory

    d. Informative

    Answer: c

    The correct answer is c. Answer b, advisory policies, might specify penalties for non-compliance, but regulatory policies are required to be followed by the organization. Answers a and d are informational or recommended policies only.

21. What are high-level policies?

    a. They are recommendations for procedural controls.

    b. They are the instructions on how to perform a Quantitative Risk Analysis.

    c. They are statements that indicate a senior management's intention to support InfoSec.

    d. They are step-by-step procedures to implement a safeguard.

    Answer: c

    The correct answer is c. High-level policies are senior management statements of recognition of the importance of InfoSec controls.

Bonus Questions

1. Place the general information classification procedures below in their proper order:

    _____ a. Classify the data.

    _____ b. Specify the controls.

_____ c. Specify the classification criteria.

_____ d. Publicize awareness of the classification controls.

>   *Answer:* c, a, b, d

2. Which choice below is NOT considered an information classification role?

   a. Data owner

   b. Data custodian

   c. Data alterer

   d. Data user

   >   *Answer:* c

   >   The correct answer is c. Data owners, custodians, and users all have defined roles in the process of information classification. Answer c is a distracter.

3. Which choice below is NOT an example of the appropriate external distribution of classified information?

   a. Compliance with a court order

   b. Upon senior-level approval after a confidentiality agreement

   c. IAW contract procurement agreements for a government project

   d. To influence the value of the company's stock price

   >   *Answer:* d

   >   The correct answer is d. Answers a, b, and c are all examples of the need for possible external distribution of internal classified information.

4. Which choice below is usually the number one used criterion to determine the classification of an information object?

   a. Value

   b. Useful life

   c. Age

   d. Personal association

   >   *Answer:* a

   >   The correct answer is a. Value of the information asset to the organization is usually the first and foremost criteria used in determining its classification. Answer b refers to declassification of an information object due to some change in situation.

5. Which choice below is the BEST description of a vulnerability?

   a. A weakness in a system that could be exploited

   b. A company resource that could be lost due to an incident

   c. The minimization of loss associated with an incident

   d. A potential incident that could cause harm

Answer: a

The correct answer is a. Answer b describes an asset, answer c describes risk management, and answer d describes a threat.

6. Which choice below is NOT a common result of a risk analysis?

   a. A detailed listing of relevant threats

   b. Valuations of critical assets

   c. Likelihood of a potential threat

   d. Definition of business recovery roles

   Answer: d

   The correct answer is d. The first three answers are common results of a risk analysis to determine the probability and effect of threats to company assets. Answer d is a distracter.

7. Which choice below is the BEST definition of advisory policies?

   a. Non-mandated policies, but strongly suggested

   b. Policies implemented for compliance reasons

   c. Policies implemented due to public regulation

   d. Mandatory policies implemented as a consequence of legal action

   Answer: a

   The correct answer is a. Advisory policies might have consequences of failure attached to them, but they are still considered non-mandatory. The other three answers are examples of mandatory, regulatory policies.

8. Which statement below BEST describes the primary purpose of risk analysis?

   a. To create a clear cost-to-value ratio for implementing security controls

   b. To influence the system design process

   c. To influence site selection decisions

   d. To quantify the impact of potential threats

   Answer: d

   The correct answer is d. The main purpose of performing a risk analysis is to put a hard cost or value onto the loss of a business function. The other answers are benefits of risk management but not its main purpose.

9. Put the following steps in the qualitative scenario procedure in order:

   _____ a. The team prepares its findings and presents them to management.

   _____ b. A scenario is written to address each identified threat.

   _____ c. Business unit managers review the scenario for a reality check.

   _____ d. The team works through each scenario by using a threat, asset, and safeguard.

   Answer: b, c, d, a

10. Which statement below is NOT correct about safeguard selection in the risk analysis process?

    a. Maintenance costs need to be included in determining the total cost of the safeguard.

    b. The best possible safeguard should always be implemented, regardless of cost.

    c. The most commonly considered criteria is the cost effectiveness of the safeguard.

    d. Many elements need to be considered in determining the total cost of the safeguard.

    Answer: b

    The correct answer is b. Performing a cost-benefit analysis of the proposed safeguard before implementation is vital. The level of security afforded could easily outweigh the value of a proposed safeguard. Other factors need to be considered in the safeguard selection process, such as accountability, auditability, and the level of manual operations needed to maintain or operate the safeguard.

Chapter 2—Access Control Systems and Methodology

Sample Questions

1. The goals of integrity do NOT include:

    a. Accountability of responsible individuals

    b. Prevention of the modification of information by unauthorized users

    c. Prevention of the unauthorized or unintentional modification of information by authorized users

    d. Preservation of internal and external consistency

    Answer: a

    The correct answer is a. Accountability is holding individuals responsible for their actions. Answers b, c, and d are the three goals of integrity.

2. Kerberos is an authentication scheme that can be used to implement:

    a. Public key cryptography.

    b. Digital signatures.

    c. Hash functions.

    d. Single Sign-On (SSO).

    Answer: d

    The correct answer is d. Kerberos is a third-party authentication protocol that can be used to implement SSO. Answer a is incorrect because public key cryptography is not used in the basic Kerberos protocol. Answer b is a public key-based capability, and answer c is a one-way transformation used to disguise passwords or to implement digital signatures.

3. The fundamental entity in a relational database is the:

   a. Domain.
   b. Relation.
   c. Pointer.
   d. Cost.

   Answer: b

   The correct answer is b. The fundamental entity in a relational database is the relation in the form of a table. Answer a is the set of allowable attribute values, and answers c and d are distracters.

4. In a relational database, security is provided to the access of data through:

   a. Candidate keys.
   b. Views.
   c. Joins.
   d. Attributes.

   Answer: b

   The correct answer is b. Candidate keys, (answer a) are the set of unique keys from which the primary key is selected. Answer c, joins, indicates operations that can be performed on the database, and the attributes (d) denote the columns in the relational table.

5. In biometrics, a "one-to-one" search to verify an individual's claim of an identity is called:

   a. Audit trail review.
   b. Authentication.
   c. Accountability.
   d. Aggregation.

   Answer: b

   The correct answer is b. Answer a is a review of audit system data, usually done after the fact. Answer c is holding individuals responsible for their actions, and answer d is obtaining higher-sensitivity information from a number of pieces of information of lower sensitivity.

6. Biometrics is used for identification in the physical controls and for authentication in the:

   a. Detective controls.
   b. Preventive controls.
   c. Logical controls.
   d. Corrective controls.

Answer: c

The correct answer is c. The other answers are different categories of controls where preventive controls attempt to eliminate or reduce vulnerabilities before an attack occurs; detective controls attempt to determine that an attack is taking place or has taken place; and corrective controls involve taking action to restore the system to normal operation after a successful attack.

7. Referential integrity requires that for any foreign key attribute, the referenced relation must have:

   a. A tuple with the same value for its primary key.
   b. A tuple with the same value for its secondary key.
   c. An attribute with the same value for its secondary key.
   d. An attribute with the same value for its other foreign key.

   Answer: a

   The correct answer is a. Answers b and c are incorrect because a secondary key is not a valid term. Answer d is a distracter, because referential integrity has a foreign key referring to a primary key in another relation.

8. A password that is the same for each logon is called a:

   a. Dynamic password.
   b. Static password.
   c. Passphrase.
   d. One-time pad.

   Answer: b

   The correct answer is b. In answer a, the password changes at each logon. For answer c, a passphrase is a long word or phrase that is converted by the system to a password. In answer d, a one-time pad refers to a using a random key only once when sending a cryptographic message.

9. The number of times a password should be changed is NOT a function of:

   a. The criticality of the information to be protected.
   b. The frequency of the password's use.
   c. The responsibilities and clearance of the user.
   d. The type of workstation used.

   Answer: d

   The correct answer is d. The type of workstation used as the platform is not the determining factor. Items a, b, and c are determining factors.

10. The description of a relational database is called the:

    a. Attribute
    b. Record

    c. Schema

    d. Domain

> *Answer:* c
>
> The correct answer is c. The other answers are portions of a relation or table.

11. A statistical anomaly-based intrusion detection system:

    a. Acquires data to establish a normal system operating profile.

    b. Refers to a database of known attack signatures.

    c. Will detect an attack that does not significantly change the system's operating characteristics.

    d. Does not report an event that caused a momentary anomaly in the system.

> *Answer:* a
>
> The correct answer is a. A statistical anomaly-based intrusion detection system acquires data to establish a normal system operating profile. Answer b is incorrect because it is used in signature-based intrusion detection. Answer c is incorrect because a statistical anomaly-based intrusion detection system will not detect an attack that does not significantly change the system operating characteristics. Similarly, answer d is incorrect because the statistical anomaly-based IDS is susceptible to reporting an event that caused a momentary anomaly in the system.

12. Intrusion detection systems can be all of the following types EXCEPT:

    a. Signature-based.

    b. Statistical anomaly-based.

    c. Network-based.

    d. Defined-based.

> *Answer:* d
>
> The correct answer is d. All the other answers are types of IDSs.

13. In a relational database system, a primary key is chosen from a set of:

    a. Foreign keys.

    b. Secondary keys.

    c. Candidate keys.

    d. Cryptographic keys.

> *Answer:* c
>
> The correct answer is c, candidate keys by definition. Answer a is incorrect because a foreign key in one table refers to a primary key in another. Answer b is a made-up distracter, and answer d refers to keys used in encipherment and decipherment.

14. A standard data manipulation and relational database definition language is:

    a. OOD

    b. SQL

    c. SLL

    d. Script

    Answer: b

    The correct answer is b. All other answers do not apply.

15. An attack that can be perpetrated against a remote user's callback access control is:

    a. Call forwarding.

    b. A Trojan horse.

    c. A maintenance hook.

    d. Redialing.

    Answer: a

    The correct answer is a. A cracker can have a person's call forwarded to another number to foil the callback system. Answer b is incorrect because it is an example of malicious code embedded in useful code. Answer c is incorrect because it might enable bypassing controls of a system through a means used for debugging or maintenance. Answer d is incorrect because it is a distracter.

16. The definition of CHAP is:

    a. Confidential Hash Authentication Protocol.

    b. Challenge Handshake Authentication Protocol.

    c. Challenge Handshake Approval Protocol.

    d. Confidential Handshake Approval Protocol.

    Answer: b

17. Using symmetric key cryptography, Kerberos authenticates clients to other entities on a network and facilitates communications through the assignment of:

    a. Public keys.

    b. Session keys.

    c. Passwords.

    d. Tokens.

    Answer: b

    The correct answer is b. Session keys are temporary keys assigned by the KDC and used for an allotted period of time as the secret key between two entities. Answer a is incorrect because it refers to asymmetric encryption that is not used in the basic Kerberos protocol. Answer c is incorrect because it is not a key, and answer d is incorrect because a token generates dynamic passwords.

18. Three things that must be considered for the planning and implementation of access control mechanisms are:

    a. Threats, assets, and objectives.

    b. Threats, vulnerabilities, and risks.

    c. Vulnerabilities, secret keys, and exposures.

    d. Exposures, threats, and countermeasures.

    Answer: b

    The correct answer is b. Threats define the possible source of security policy violations; vulnerabilities describe weaknesses in the system that might be exploited by the threats; and the risk determines the probability of threats being realized. All three items must be present to meaningfully apply access control. Therefore, the other answers are incorrect.

19. In mandatory access control, the authorization of a subject to have access to an object is dependent upon:

    a. Labels.

    b. Roles.

    c. Tasks.

    d. Identity.

    Answer: a

    The correct answer is a. Mandatory access controls use labels to determine whether subjects can have access to objects, depending on the subjects' clearances. Answer b, roles, is applied in non-discretionary access control as is answer c, tasks. Answer d, identity, is used in discretionary access control.

20. The type of access control that is used in local, dynamic situations where subjects have the ability to specify what resources certain users can access is called:

    a. Mandatory access control.

    b. Rule-based access control.

    c. Sensitivity-based access control.

    d. Discretionary access control.

    Answer: d

    The correct answer is d. Answers a and b require strict adherence to labels and clearances. Answer c is a made-up distracter.

21. Role-based access control is useful when:

    a. Access must be determined by the labels on the data.

    b. There are frequent personnel changes in an organization.

c. Rules are needed to determine clearances.

d. Security clearances must be used.

Answer: b

The correct answer is b. Role-based access control is part of non-discretionary access control. Answers a, c, and d relate to mandatory access control.

22. Clipping levels are used to:

a. Limit the number of letters in a password.

b. Set thresholds for voltage variations.

c. Reduce the amount of data to be evaluated in audit logs.

d. Limit errors in callback systems.

Answer: c

The correct answer is c—reducing the amount of data to be evaluated by definition. Answer a is incorrect because clipping levels do not relate to letters in a password. Answer b is incorrect because clipping levels in this context have nothing to do with controlling voltage levels. Answer d is incorrect because they are not used to limit callback errors.

23. Identification is:

a. A user being authenticated by the system.

b. A user providing a password to the system.

c. A user providing a shared secret to the system.

d. A user professing an identity to the system.

Answer: d

The correct answer is d. A user presents an ID to the system as identification. Answer a is incorrect because presenting an ID is not an authentication act. Answer b is incorrect because a password is an authentication mechanism. Answer c is incorrect because it refers to cryptography or authentication.

24. Authentication is:

a. The verification that the claimed identity is valid.

b. The presentation of a user's ID to the system.

c. Not accomplished through the use of a password.

d. Only applied to remote users.

Answer: a

The correct answer is a. Answer b is incorrect because it is an identification act. Answer c is incorrect because authentication can be accomplished through the use of a password. Answer d is incorrect because authentication is applied to local and remote users.

25. An example of two-factor authentication is:

    a. A password and an ID.

    b. An ID and a PIN.

    c. A PIN and an ATM card.

    d. A fingerprint.

    Answer: c

    The correct answer is c. These items are something you know and something you have. Answer a is incorrect because essentially, only one factor is being used: something you know (password.) Answer b is incorrect for the same reason. Answer d is incorrect because only one biometric factor is being used.

26. In biometrics, a good measure of performance of a system is the:

    a. False detection.

    b. Crossover Error Rate (CER).

    c. Positive acceptance rate.

    d. Sensitivity.

    Answer: b

    The correct answer is b. The other items are made-up distracters.

27. In finger scan technology,

    a. The full fingerprint is stored.

    b. Features extracted from the fingerprint are stored.

    c. More storage is required than in fingerprint technology.

    d. The technology is applicable to large, one-to-many database searches.

    Answer: b

    The correct answer is b. The features extracted from the fingerprint are stored. Answer a is incorrect because the equivalent of the full fingerprint is not stored in finger scan technology. Answers c and d are incorrect because the opposite is true of finger scan technology.

28. An acceptable biometric throughput rate is:

    a. One subject per two minutes.

    b. Two subjects per minute.

    c. Ten subjects per minute.

    d. Five subjects per minute.

    Answer: c

29. In a relational database, the *domain* of a relation is the set of allowable values:

    a. That an attribute can take.

    b. That tuples can take.

c. That a record can take.

d. Of the primary key.

Answer: a

30. Object-Oriented Database (OODB) systems:

a. Are ideally suited for text-only information.

b. Require minimal learning time for programmers.

c. Are useful in storing and manipulating complex data, such as images and graphics.

d. Consume minimal system resources.

Answer: c

The correct answer is c. The other answers are false, because for answer a relational databases are ideally suited to text-only information, b and d. OODB systems have a steep learning curve and consume a large amount of system resources.

Bonus Questions

1. An important element of database design that ensures that the attributes in a table depend only on the primary key is:

a. Database management.

b. Data normalization.

c. Data integrity.

d. Data reuse.

Answer: b

The correct answer is b. Normalization includes eliminating redundant data and eliminating attributes in a table that are not dependent on the primary key of that table. In answer a, a database management system (DBMS) provides access to the database and is used for maintaining the database. Answers c and d are distracters.

2. A database View operation implements the principle of:

a. Least privilege.

b. Separation of duties.

c. Entity integrity.

d. Referential integrity.

Answer: a

The correct answer is a. Least privilege, in the database context, requires that subjects be granted the most restricted set of access privileges to the data in the database that are consistent with the performance of their tasks. Answer b, separation of duties, assigns parts of security-sensitive tasks to several individuals. Entity integrity, answer c, requires that each row in the relation table must have a non-NULL attribute. Relational integrity, answer d, refers to the requirement that for any foreign key attribute, the referenced relation must have the same value for its primary key.

3. Which of the following is NOT a technical (logical) mechanism for protecting information from unauthorized disclosure?

   a. Smart cards

   b. Encryption

   c. Labeling (of sensitive materials)

   d. Protocols

   Answer: c

   The correct answer is c. Labeling is an administrative control mechanism.

4. A token that generates a unique password at fixed time intervals is called:

   a. An asynchronous dynamic password token.

   b. A time-sensitive token.

   c. A synchronous dynamic password token.

   d. A challenge-response token.

   Answer: c

   The correct answer is c. An asynchronous dynamic password token, answer a, generates a new password that does not have to fit into a fixed time window for authentication, as is the case for a synchronous dynamic password token. Answer b is a distracter. Answer d, a challenge-response token, generates a random challenge string as the owner enters the string into the token along with a PIN. Then, the token generates a response that the owner enters into the workstation for authentication.

5. In a biometric system, the time it takes to register with the system by providing samples of a biometric characteristic is called:

   a. Set-up time.

   b. Log-in time.

   c. Enrollment time.

   d. Throughput time.

   Answer: c

   The correct answer is c. Answers a and b are distracters. Answer d, throughput, refers to the rate at which individuals—once enrolled—can be processed and identified or authenticated by a biometric system.

6. Which of the following is NOT an assumption of the basic Kerberos paradigm?

   a. Client computers are not secured and are easily accessible.

   b. Cabling is not secure.

   c. Messages are not secure from interception.

   d. Specific servers and locations cannot be secured.

   > *Answer:* d
   >
   > The correct answer is d. Kerberos requires that centralized servers implementing the trusted authentication mechanism must be secured.

7. Which one of the following statements is TRUE concerning the Terminal Access Controller Access Control System (TACACS) and TACACS+?

   a. TACACS supports prompting for a password change.

   b. TACACS+ employs tokens for two-factor, dynamic password authentication.

   c. TACACS+ employs a user ID and static password.

   d. TACACS employs tokens for two-factor, dynamic password authentication.

   > *Answer:* b
   >
   > The correct answer is b. TACACS employs a user ID and static password and does not support prompting for password change or the use of dynamic password tokens.

8. Identity-based access control is a subset of which one of the following access control categories?

   a. Discretionary access control

   b. Mandatory access control

   c. Non-discretionary access control

   d. Lattice-based access control

   > *Answer:* a
   >
   > The correct answer is a. Identity-based access control is a type of discretionary access control that grants access privileges based on the user's identity. A related type of discretionary access control is user-directed access control that gives the user, with certain limitations, the right to alter the access control to certain objects.

9. Procedures that ensure that the access control mechanisms correctly implement the security policy for the entire life cycle of an information system are known as:

   a. Accountability procedures.

   b. Authentication procedures.

c. Assurance procedures.

d. Trustworthy procedures.

> *Answer:* c
>
> The correct answer is c. Accountability, answer a, refers to the ability to determine the actions and behaviors of a single individual within a system and to identify that individual. Answer b, authentication, involves testing or reconciling of evidence of a user's identity in order to establish that identity. Answer d is a distracter.

10. Which of the following is NOT a valid database model?

    a. Hierarchical

    b. Relational

    c. Object-relational

    d. Relational-rational

    > *Answer:* d
    >
    > The correct answer is d, a distracter. The other answers are valid database models. Additional valid models include network and object-oriented databases.

Chapter 3—Telecommunications and Network Security

Sample Questions

1. Which of the following is NOT a type of data network?

   a. LAN

   b. WAN

   c. MAN

   d. GAN

   > *Answer:* d
   >
   > The correct answer is d. GAN does not exist. LAN stands for Local Area Network, WAN stands for Wide Area Network, and MAN stands for Metropolitan Area Network.

2. Which of the following is NOT a network cabling type?

   a. Twisted Pair

   b. Token Ring

   c. Fiber Optic

   d. Coaxial

   > *Answer:* b
   >
   > The correct answer is b, Token Ring. Token Ring is a LAN media access method, not a cabling type.

3. Which of the following is NOT a property of a Packet Filtering Firewall?

   a. Considered a first-generation firewall

   b. Uses ACLs

   c. Operates at the Application Layer

   d. Examines the source and destination addresses of the incoming packet

   > *Answer:* c

   > The correct answer is c. A packet-filtering firewall can operate at the network or transport layers.

4. Which of the following is NOT a remote computing technology?

   a. PGP

   b. ISDN

   c. Wireless

   d. xDSL

   > *Answer:* a

   > The correct answer is a. PGP stands for Pretty Good Privacy, an email encryption technology.

5. A firewall that performs stateful inspection of the data packet across all layers is considered a:

   a. First-generation firewall.

   b. Second-generation firewall.

   c. Third-generation firewall.

   d. Fourth-generation firewall.

   > *Answer:* c

   > The correct answer is c. A stateful inspection firewall is considered a third-generation firewall.

6. RAID refers to the:

   a. Redundant Arrays of Intelligent Disks.

   b. Redundant And fault tolerant Internetworking Devices.

   c. Rapid And Inexpensive Digital tape backup.

   d. Remote Administration of Internet Domains.

   > *Answer:* a

   > The correct answer is a, Redundant Arrays of Intelligent Disks. The other acronyms do not exist.

7. Which of the following is NOT a true statement about Network Address Translation (NAT)?

   a. NAT is used when corporations want to use private addressing ranges for internal networks.

   b. NAT is designed to mask the true IP addresses of internal systems.

    c. Private addresses can easily be routed globally.

    d. NAT translates private IP addresses to registered "real" IP addresses.

      Answer: c

      The correct answer is c. Private addresses are not easily routable; hence the reason for using NAT.

8. What does LAN stand for?

    a. Local Arena News

    b. Local Area Network

    c. Layered Addressed Network

    d. Local Adaptive Network

      Answer: b

9. What does CSMA stand for?

    a. Carrier Station Multi-port Actuator

    b. Carrier Sense Multiple Access

    c. Common Systems Methodology Applications

    d. Carrier Sense Multiple Attenuation

      Answer: b

      The correct answer is b. The other acronyms do not exist.

10. Which is NOT a property of a packet-switched network?

    a. Packets are assigned sequence numbers

    b. Characterized by "bursty" traffic

    c. Connection-oriented network

    d. Connectionless network

      Answer: c

      The correct answer is c. Packet-switched networks are considered connectionless networks; circuit-switched networks are considered connection-oriented.

11. Which is NOT a layer in the OSI architecture model?

    a. Transport

    b. Internet

    c. Data Link

    d. Session

      Answer: b

      The correct answer is b. The Internet Layer is a TCP/IP architecture model layer.

12. Which is NOT a layer in the TCP/IP architecture model?

    a. Internet

    b. Application

    c. Host-to-host

    d. Session

       Answer: d

       The correct answer is d. The Session Layer is an OSI model layer.

13. Which is NOT a backup method type?

    a. Differential

    b. Full

    c. Reactive

    d. Incremental

       Answer: c

       The correct answer is c. Reactive is not a backup method.

14. What does TFTP stand for?

    a. Trivial File Transport Protocol

    b. Transport for TCP/IP

    c. Trivial File Transfer Protocol

    d. Transport File Transfer Protocol

       Answer: c

       The correct answer is c. The other acronyms do not exist.

15. What does the Data Encapsulation in the OSI model do?

    a. Creates seven distinct layers

    b. Wraps data from one layer around a data packet from an adjoining layer

    c. Provides "best effort" delivery of a data packet

    d. Makes the network transmission deterministic

       Answer: b

       The correct answer is b. Data Encapsulation attaches information from one layer to the packet as it travels from an adjoining layer. The OSI-layered architecture model creates seven layers. The TCP/IP protocol UDP provides "best effort" packet delivery, and a token-passing transmission scheme creates a deterministic network because it is possible to compute the maximum predictable delay.

16. What is NOT a feature of TACACS+?

    a. Enables two-factor authentication

    b. Replaces older Frame Relay-switched networks

    c. Enables a user to change passwords

    d. Resynchronizes security tokens

       Answer: b

       The correct answer is b. TACACS+ has nothing to do with Frame Relay networks.

17. What is NOT true of a star-wired topology?

    a. Cabling termination errors can crash the entire network.

    b. The network nodes are connected to a central LAN device.

    c. It has more resiliency than a BUS topology.

    d. 10BaseT Ethernet is star-wired.

    Answer: a

    The correct answer is a. Cabling termination errors are an inherent issue with bus topology networks.

18. FDDI uses what type of network topology?

    a. BUS

    b. RING

    c. STAR

    d. MESH

    Answer: b

    The correct answer is b. FDDI is a RING topology, like Token Ring.

19. What does the protocol ARP do?

    a. Takes a MAC address and finds an IP address to match

    b. Sends messages to the devices regarding the health of the network

    c. Takes an IP address and finds out the MAC address to which it belongs

    d. Facilitates file transfers

    Answer: c

    The correct answer is c. ARP starts with an IP address, then queries the network to find the MAC or hardware address of the workstation to which it belongs. ICMP performs b, RARP performs a, and FTP performs d.

20. What does the protocol RARP do?

    a. Takes a MAC address and finds an IP address to match

    b. Sends messages to the devices regarding the health of the network

    c. Takes an IP address and finds out the MAC address to which it belongs

    d. Facilitates file transfers

    Answer: a

    The correct answer is a, the reverse of ARP. The Reverse Address Resolution Protocol knows a MAC (Media Access Control) address and asks the RARP server to match it with an IP address.

21. What is the protocol that supports sending and receiving email?

    a. SNMP

    b. SMTP

c. ICMP

d. RARP

Answer: b

The correct answer is b, Simple Mail Transport Protocol. It queues and transfers email. SNMP stands for Simple Network Management Protocol. ICMP stands for Internet Control Message Protocol. RARP stands for Reverse Address Resolution Protocol

22. Which of the following is NOT a VPN remote computing protocol?

a. PPTP

b. L2F

c. L2TP

d. UTP

Answer: d

The correct answer is d. UTP stands for unshielded twisted pair wiring.

23. Which of the following is NOT a property of CSMA?

a. The workstation continuously monitors the line.

b. The workstation transmits the data packet when it thinks that the line is free.

c. Workstations are not permitted to transmit until they are given permission from the primary host.

d. It does not have a feature to avoid the problem of one workstation dominating the conversation.

Answer: c

The correct answer is c. The polling transmission type uses primary and secondary hosts, and the secondary must wait for permission from the primary before transmitting.

24. Which of the following is NOT a property of Token Ring networks?

a. Workstations cannot transmit until they receive a token.

b. These networks were originally designed to serve large, bandwidth-consuming applications.

c. These networks were originally designed to serve sporadic and only occasionally heavy traffic.

d. All end stations are attached to a MSAU.

Answer: c

The correct answer is c. Ethernet networks were originally designed to work with more sporadic traffic than Token Ring networks.

25. Which is NOT a property of Fiber Optic cabling?

a. Carries signals as light waves

b. Transmits at higher speeds than copper cable

   c. Easier to tap than copper cabling

   d. Very resistant to interference

     Answer: c

     The correct answer is c. Fiber Optic cable is much harder to tap than copper cable.

26. Which is NOT a property of a bridge?

   a. Forwards the data to all other segments if the destination is not on the local segment

   b. Operates at Layer 2, the Data Link Layer

   c. Operates at Layer 3, the Network Layer

   d. Can create a broadcast storm

     Answer: c

     The correct answer is c. A bridge operates at Layer 2 and therefore does not use IP addressing to make routing decisions.

27. Which is NOT a standard type of DSL?

   a. ADSL

   b. FDSL

   c. VDSL

   d. HDSL

     Answer: b

     The correct answer is b. FDSL does not exist.

28. Which is a property of a circuit-switched network as opposed to a packet-switched network?

   a. Physical, permanent connections exist from one point to another in a circuit-switched network.

   b. The data is broken up into packets.

   c. The data is sent to the next destination, which is based on the router's understanding of the best available route.

   d. Packets are reassembled according to their originally assigned sequence numbers.

     Answer: a

     The correct answer is a. Permanent connections are a feature of circuit-switched networks.

29. Which is NOT a packet-switched technology?

   a. SMDS

   b. T1

   c. Frame Relay

   d. X.25

Answer: b

The correct answer is b. A T1 line is a type of leased line, which uses a dedicated, point-to-point technology.

30. Which is NOT a remote security method?

   a. VoIP

   b. Callback

   c. Caller ID

   d. Restricted Address

   Answer: a

   The correct answer is a. VoIP stands for Voice-Over-IP, a digital telephony technology.

31. To what does covert channel eavesdropping refer?

   a. Using a hidden, unauthorized network connection to communicate unauthorized information

   b. Nonbusiness or personal use of the Internet

   c. Socially engineering passwords from an ISP

   d. The use of two-factor passwords

   Answer: a

   The correct answer is a. A Covert Channel is a connection intentionally created to transmit unauthorized information from inside a trusted network to a partner at an outside, untrusted node. Answer c is called masquerading.

32. To what does logon abuse refer?

   a. Breaking into a network primarily from an external source

   b. Legitimate users accessing networked services that would normally be restricted to them

   c. Nonbusiness or personal use of the Internet

   d. Intrusions via dial-up or asynchronous external network connections

   Answer: b

   The correct answer is b. Logon abuse entails an otherwise proper user attempting to access areas of the network that are deemed off-limits. Answer a is called network intrusion, and d refers to back-door remote access.

33. What is probing used for?

   a. To induce a user into taking an incorrect action

   b. To give an attacker a road map of the network

   c. To use up all of a target's resources

   d. To covertly listen to transmissions

   Answer: b

The correct answer is b. Probing is a procedure whereby the intruder runs programs that scan the network to create a network map for later intrusion. Answer a is spoofing, c is the objective of a DoS attack, and d is passive eavesdropping.

34. Which is NOT a property of or issue with tape backup?

   a. Slow data transfer during backups and restores

   b. Server disk space utilization expands

   c. The possibility that some data re-entry might need to be performed after a crash

   d. One large disk created by using several disks

   Answer: d

   The correct answer is d. RAID level 0 striping is the process of creating a large disk out of several smaller disks.

35. What is a server cluster?

   a. A primary server that mirrors its data to a secondary server

   b. A group of independent servers that are managed as a single system

   c. A tape array backup implementation

   d. A group of WORM optical jukeboxes

   Answer: b

   The correct answer is b. A server cluster is a group of servers that appears to be a single server to the user. Answer a refers to redundant servers.

36. In which OSI layer does the MIDI digital music protocol standard reside?

   a. Application Layer

   b. Presentation Layer

   c. Session Layer

   d. Transport Layer

   Answer: b

   The correct answer is b. MIDI is a Presentation layer protocol.

Bonus Questions

1. Which statement about a VPN tunnel below is incorrect?

   a. It can be created by implementing IPSec devices only.

   b. It can be created by installing software or hardware agents on the client or network.

   c. It can be created by implementing key and certificate exchange systems.

   d. It can be created by implementing node authentication systems.

Answer: a

The correct answer is a. IPSec-compatible and non-IPSec compatible devices are used to create VPNs. The other three answers are all ways in which VPNs can be created.

2. Which answer below is true about the difference between FTP and TFTP?

   a. FTP does not have a directory-browsing capability, whereas TFTP does.

   b. FTP enables print job spooling, whereas TFTP does not.

   c. TFTP is less secure because session authentication does not occur.

   d. FTP is less secure because session authentication does not occur.

   Answer: c

   The correct answer is c. The Trivial File Transfer Protocol (TFTP) is considered less secure than the File Transfer Protocol (FTP) because authentication does not occur during session establishment (although FTP is very insecure in its own right).

3. Which answer below is true about the difference between TCP and UDP?

   a. UDP is considered a connectionless protocol and TCP is connection-oriented.

   b. TCP is considered a connectionless protocol, and UDP is connection-oriented.

   c. UDP acknowledges the receipt of packets, and TCP does not.

   d. TCP is sometimes referred to as an unreliable protocol.

   Answer: a

   The correct answer is a. As opposed to the Transmission Control Protocol (TCP), the User Datagram Protocol (UDP) is a connectionless protocol. It does not sequence the packets, acknowledge the receipt of packets, and is referred to as an unreliable protocol.

4. Which TCP/IP protocol operates at the OSI Network layer?

   a. FTP

   b. IP

   c. TCP

   d. UDP

   Answer: b

   The correct answer is b. IP operates at the network layer of the OSI model and at the Internet layer of the TCP/IP model. FTP operates at the application layer of the TCP/IP model, which is roughly similar to the top three layers of the OSI model: the Application, Presentation, and Session layers. TCP and UDP both operate at the OSI Transport layer, which is similar to the TCP/IP Host-to-host layer.

5. Which IEEE standard defines wireless networking in the 5GHz band with speeds of up to 54 Mbps?

   a. 802.5

   b. 802.11a

   c. 802.11b

   d. 802.3

   Answer: b

   The correct answer is b. Answer a defines a token-passing ring access method. Answer c defines a wireless LAN in the 2.4 GHz band with speeds up to 11 Mbps. Answer d describes a bus topology using CSMA/CD at 10 Mbps.

6. Which UTP cable category is rated for 16 Mbps?

   a. Category 4

   b. Category 5

   c. Category 6

   d. Category 7

   Answer: a

   The correct answer is a. UTP Category 4 cabling is common in later Token Ring networks and is rated for up to 16 Mbps. Answer b, category 5, is rated for 100Mbps; answer c is rated for 155 Mbps; and answer d is rated for 1Gbps.

7. Which statement below about the difference between analog and digital signals is incorrect?

   a. An analog signal produces an infinite waveform.

   b. Analog signals cannot be used for data communications.

   c. An analog signal can be varied by amplification.

   d. A digital signal produces a saw-tooth wave form.

   Answer: b

   The correct answer is b. The other answers are all properties of analog or digital signals.

8. Which choice below BEST describes coaxial cable?

   a. Coax consists of two insulated wires wrapped around each other in a regular spiral pattern.

   b. Coax consists of a hollow outer cylindrical conductor surrounding a single, inner conductor.

   c. Coax does not require a fixed spacing between connections that UTP requires.

   d. Coax carries signals as light waves.

   Answer: b

The correct answer is b. Coax consists of a hollow outer cylindrical conductor surrounding a single, inner wire conductor. Answer a describes UTP. Coax requires fixed spacing between connections, and answer d describes fiber-optic cable.

9. Which LAN transmission method below describes a packet sent from a single source to multiple specific destinations?

    a. Unicast

    b. Multicast

    c. Broadcast

    d. Anycast

    Answer: b

    The correct answer is b, multicast. Unicast describes a packet sent from a single source to a single destination. Answer c, broadcast, describes a packet sent to all nodes on the network segment. Answer d, anycast, refers to communication between any sender and the nearest of a group of receivers in a network.

10. To what does 10Base-5 refer?

    a. 10 Mbps thinnet coax cabling rated to 185 meters maximum length

    b. 10 Mbps thicknet coax cabling rated to 500 meters maximum length

    c. 10 Mbps baseband optical fiber

    d. 100 Mbps unshielded twisted pair cabling

    Answer: b

    The correct answer is b. Answer a refers to 10Base-2; answer c refers to 10Base-F; and answer d refers to 100Base-T.

Chapter 4—Cryptography

Sample Questions

1. The Secure Hash Algorithm (SHA) is specified in the:

    a. Data Encryption Standard.

    b. Digital Signature Standard.

    c. Digital Encryption Standard.

    d. Advanced Encryption Standard.

    Answer: b

    The correct answer is b. Answer a refers to DES, a symmetric encryption algorithm; answer c is a distracter—there is no such term; answer d is the Advanced Encryption Standard, which has replaced DES and is now the Rijndael algorithm.

2. What does Secure Sockets Layer (SSL)/Transaction Security Layer (TSL) do?

   a. Implements confidentiality, authentication, and integrity above the TransportLayer

   b. Implements confidentiality, authentication, and integrity below the Transport Layer

   c. Implements only confidentiality above the Transport Layer

   d. Implements only confidentiality below the Transport Layer

   > *Answer:* a
   >
   > The correct answer is a by definition. Answer b is incorrect because SSL/TLS operates above the Transport Layer; answer c is incorrect because authentication and integrity are provided also, and answer d is incorrect because it cites only confidentiality and SSL/TLS operates above the Transport Layer.

3. What are MD4 and MD5?

   a. Symmetric encryption algorithms

   b. Asymmetric encryption algorithms

   c. Hashing algorithms

   d. Digital certificates

   > *Answer:* c
   >
   > The correct answer is c. Answers a and b are incorrect because they are general types of encryption systems, and answer d is incorrect because hashing algorithms are not digital certificates.

4. Elliptic curves, which are applied to public key cryptography, employ modular exponentiation that characterizes the:

   a. Elliptic curve discrete logarithm problem.

   b. Prime factors of very large numbers.

   c. Elliptic curve modular addition.

   d. Knapsack problem.

   > *Answer:* a
   >
   > The correct answer is a. Modular exponentiation in elliptic curves is the analog of the modular discreet logarithm problem. Answer b is incorrect because prime factors are involved with RSA public key systems; answer c is incorrect because modular addition in elliptic curves is the analog of modular multiplication; and answer d is incorrect because the knapsack problem is not an elliptic curve problem.

5. Which algorithm is used in the Clipper Chip?

   a. IDEA

   b. DES

   c. SKIPJACK

   d. 3 DES

Answer: c

The correct answer is c. Answers a, b, and d are other symmetric key algorithms.

6. The hashing algorithm in the Digital Signature Standard (DSS) generates a message digest of:

a. 120 bits

b. 160 bits

c. 56 bits

d. 130 bit

Answer: b

7. The protocol of the Wireless Application Protocol (WAP), which performs functions similar to SSL in the TCP/IP protocol, is called the:

a. Wireless Application Environment (WAE).

b. Wireless Session Protocol (WSP).

c. Wireless Transaction Protocol (WTP).

d. Wireless Transport Layer Security Protocol (WTLS).

Answer: d

The correct answer is d. SSL performs security functions in TCP/IP. The other answers refer to protocols in the WAP protocol stack also, but their primary functions are not security.

8. A Security Parameter Index (SPI) and the identity of the security protocol (AH or ESP) are the components of:

a. SSL

b. IPSec

c. S-HTTP

d. SSH-2

Answer: b

The correct answer is b. The SPI, AH and/or ESP and the destination IP address are components of an IPSec Security Association (SA.) The other answers describe protocols other than IPSec.

9. When two different keys encrypt a plaintext message into the same ciphertext, this situation is known as:

a. Public key cryptography.

b. Cryptanalysis.

c. Key clustering.

d. Hashing.

Answer: c

The correct answer is c. Answer a describes a type of cryptographic system using a public and a private key; answer b is the art/science of breaking ciphers; answer d is the conversion of a message of variable length into a fixed-length message digest.

10. What is the result of the Exclusive Or operation, 1XOR 0?
    a. 1
    b. 0
    c. Indeterminate
    d. 10

    Answer: a

    The correct answer is a. An XOR operation results in a 0 if the two input bits are identical and a 1 if one of the bits is a 1 and the other is a 0.

11. A block cipher:
    a. Encrypts by operating on a continuous data stream.
    b. Is an asymmetric key algorithm.
    c. Converts a variable-length of plaintext into a fixed length ciphertext.
    d. Breaks a message into fixed length units for encryption.

    Answer: d

    The correct answer is d. Answer a describes a stream cipher; answer b is incorrect because a block cipher applies to symmetric key algorithms; and answer c describes a hashing operation.

12. In most security protocols that support authentication, integrity and confidentiality,
    a. Public key cryptography is used to create digital signatures.
    b. Private key cryptography is used to create digital signatures.
    c. DES is used to create digital signatures.
    d. Digital signatures are not implemented.

    Answer: a

    The correct answer is a. Answer b is incorrect because private key cryptography does not create digital signatures; answer c is incorrect because DES is a private key system and, therefore, follows the same logic as in b; and answer d is incorrect because digital signatures are implemented to obtain authentication and integrity.

13. Which of the following is an example of a symmetric key algorithm?
    a. Rijndael
    b. RSA
    c. Diffie-Hellman
    d. Knapsack

    Answer: a

    The correct answer is a. The other answers are examples of asymmetric key systems.

14. Which of the following is a problem with symmetric key encryption?

    a. It is slower than asymmetric key encryption.

    b. Most algorithms are kept proprietary.

    c. Work factor is not a function of the key size.

    d. Secure distribution of the secret key.

    > *Answer:* d

    > The correct answer is d. Answer a is incorrect because the opposite is true; answer b is incorrect because most symmetric key algorithms are published; and answer c is incorrect because work factor is a function of key size. The larger the key is, the larger the work factor.

15. Which of the following is an example of an asymmetric key algorithm?

    a. IDEA

    b. DES

    c. 3 DES

    d. ELLIPTIC CURVE

    > *Answer:* d

    > The correct answer is d. All the other answers refer to symmetric key algorithms.

16. In public key cryptography,

    a. Only the private key can encrypt and only the public key can decrypt.

    b. Only the public key can encrypt and only the private key can decrypt.

    c. The public key is used to encrypt and decrypt.

    d. If the public key encrypts, then only the private key can decrypt.

    > *Answer:* d

    > The correct answer is d. Answers a and b are incorrect because if one key encrypts, the other can decrypt. Answer c is incorrect because if the public key encrypts, it cannot decrypt.

17. In a hybrid cryptographic system, usually:

    a. Public key cryptography is used for the encryption of the message.

    b. Private key cryptography is used for the encryption of the message.

    c. Neither public key nor private key cryptography is used.

    d. Digital certificates cannot be used.

    > *Answer:* b

    > The correct answer is b. Answer a is incorrect because public key cryptography is usually used for the encryption and transmission of the secret session key. Answer c is incorrect because both public and private key encryption are used, and answer d is incorrect because digital certificates can be used (and normally *are* used).

18. What is the block length of the Rijndael Cipher?

    a. 64 bits

    b. 128 bits

    c. Variable

    d. 256 bits

    Answer: c

    The correct answer is c. The other answers with fixed numbers are incorrect.

19. A polyalphabetic cipher is also known as:

    a. One-time pad.

    b. Vigenère cipher.

    c. Steganography.

    d. Vernam cipher.

    Answer: b

    The correct answer is b. Answer a is incorrect because a one-time pad uses a random key with length equal to the plaintext message and is used only once. Answer c is the process of sending a message with no indication that a message even exists. Answer d is incorrect because it applies to stream ciphers that are XORed with a random key string.

20. The classic Caesar cipher is a:

    a. Polyalphabetic cipher.

    b. Monoalphabetic cipher.

    c. Transposition cipher.

    d. Code group.

    Answer: b

    The correct answer is b. It uses one alphabet shifted three places. Answers a and c are incorrect because in answer a, multiple alphabets are used and in answer c, the letters of the message are transposed. Answer d is incorrect because code groups deal with words and phrases and ciphers deal with bits or letters.

21. In steganography,

    a. Private key algorithms are used.

    b. Public key algorithms are used.

    c. Both public and private key algorithms are used.

    d. The fact that the message exists is not known.

    Answer: d

    The correct answer is d. The other answers are incorrect because neither algorithm is used.

22. What is the key length of the Rijndael Block Cipher?

   a. 56 or 64 bits

   b. 512 bits

   c. 128, 192, or 256 bits

   d. 512 or 1024 bits

     Answer: c

23. In a block cipher, diffusion:

   a. Conceals the connection between the ciphertext and plaintext

   b. Spreads the influence of a plaintext character over many ciphertext characters

   c. Is usually implemented by non-linear S-boxes

   d. Cannot be accomplished

     Answer: b

     The correct answer is b. Answer a defines confusion; answer c defines how confusion is accomplished; and answer d is incorrect because it can be accomplished.

24. The NIST Advanced Encryption Standard uses the:

   a. 3 DES algorithm.

   b. Rijndael algorithm.

   c. DES algorithm.

   d. IDEA algorithm.

     Answer: b

     The correct answer is b. By definition, the others are incorrect.

25. The modes of DES do NOT include:

   a. Electronic Code Book.

   b. Cipher Block Chaining.

   c. Variable Block Feedback.

   d. Output Feedback.

     Answer: c

     The correct answer is c. There is no such encipherment mode.

26. Which of the following is true?

   a. The work factor of triple DES is the same as for double DES.

   b. The work factor of single DES is the same as for triple DES.

   c. The work factor of double DES is the same as for single DES.

   d. No successful attacks have been reported against double DES.

     Answer: c

     The correct answer is c. The Meet-in-the-Middle attack has been successfully applied to double DES, and the work factor is equivalent to that of single DES. Thus, answer d is incorrect. Answer a is false because the work factor of triple DES is greater than that for double DES. In triple DES, three levels of encryption and/or decryption are applied to the message. The work factor of double DES is equivalent to the work factor of single DES. Answer b is false because the work factor of single DES is less than for triple DES. In triple DES, three levels of encryption and/or decryption are applied to the message in triple DES.

27. The Rijndael Cipher employs a round transformation that is comprised of three *layers* of distinct, invertible transformations. These transformations are also defined as uniform, which means that every bit of the State is treated the same. Which of the following is NOT one of these layers?

   a. The non-linear layer, which is the parallel application of S-boxes that have the optimum worst-case non-linearity properties

   b. The linear mixing layer, which provides a guarantee of the high diffusion of multiple rounds

   c. The key addition layer, which is an Exclusive Or of the Round Key to the intermediate State

   d. The key inversion layer, which provides confusion through the multiple rounds

   Answer: d

   The correct answer is d. This answer is a distracter and does not exist.

28. The Escrowed Encryption Standard describes the:

   a. Rijndael Cipher.

   b. Clipper Chip.

   c. Fair Public Key Cryptosystem.

   d. Digital certificates.

   Answer: b

29. Enigma was:

   a. An English project created to break German ciphers.

   b. The Japanese rotor machine used in WWII.

   c. Probably the first programmable digital computer.

   d. The German rotor machine used in WWII.

   Answer: d

   The correct answer is d. Answer a describes the Ultra Project based in Bletchley Park, England; answer b describes the Japanese Purple Machine; and answer c refers to Collossus.

30. Which of the following characteristics does a one-time pad have if used properly?

   a. It can be used more than once.

   b. The key does not have to be random.

   c. It is unbreakable.

   d. The key has to be of greater length than the message to be encrypted.

Answer: c

The correct answer is c. If the one-time-pad is used only once and its corresponding key is truly random and does not have repeating characters, it is unbreakable. Answer a is incorrect because if used properly, the one-time-pad should be used only once. Answer b is incorrect because the key should be random. Answer d is incorrect because the key has to be of the same length as the message.

31. The DES key is:
    a. 128 bits.
    b. 64 bits.
    c. 56 bits.
    d. 512 bits.

    Answer: c

32. In a digitally-signed message transmission using a hash function,
    a. The message digest is encrypted in the private key of the sender.
    b. The message digest is encrypted in the public key of the sender.
    c. The message is encrypted in the private key of the sender.
    d. The message is encrypted in the public key of the sender.

    Answer: a

    The correct answer is a. The hash function generates a message digest. The message digest is encrypted with the private key of the sender. Thus, if the message can be opened with the sender's public key that is known to all, the message must have come from the sender. The message is not encrypted with the public key because the message is usually longer than the message digest and would take more computing resources to encrypt and decrypt. Because the message digest uniquely characterizes the message, it can be used to verify the identity of the sender.

    Answers b and d will not work because a message encrypted in the public key of the sender can only be read by using the private key of the sender. Because the sender is the only one who knows this key, no one else can read the message. Answer c is incorrect because the message is not encrypted, but the message digest is encrypted.

33. The strength of RSA public key encryption is based on the:
    a. Difficulty in finding logarithms in a finite field.
    b. Difficulty of multiplying two large prime numbers.
    c. Fact that only one key is used.
    d. Difficulty in finding the prime factors of very large numbers.

    Answer: d

    The correct answer is d. Answer a applies to public key algorithms such as Diffie-Hellman and Elliptic Curve. Answer b is incorrect because it is easy to multiply two large prime numbers. Answer c refers to symmetric key encryption.

34. Elliptic curve cryptosystems:
    a. Have a higher strength per bit than an RSA.
    b. Have a lower strength per bit than an RSA.
    c. Cannot be used to implement digital signatures.
    d. Cannot be used to implement encryption.

    Answer: a

    The correct answer is a. It is more difficult to compute Elliptic Curve discreet logarithms than conventional discreet logarithms or factoring. Smaller key sizes in the elliptic curve implementation can yield higher levels of security. Therefore, answer b is incorrect. Answers c and d are incorrect because elliptic curve cryptosystems can be used for digital signatures and encryption.

35. Which of the following is NOT a key management issue?
    a. Key recovery
    b. Key storage
    c. Key change
    d. Key exchange

    Answer: d

    The correct answer is d. The other answers are key management issues, but key exchange is a function of the encryption system.

Bonus Questions

1. A cryptographic attack in which portions of the ciphertext are selected for trial decryption while having access to the corresponding decrypted plaintext is known as what type of attack?
   a. Known plaintext
   b. Chosen ciphertext
   c. Chosen plaintext
   d. Adaptive chosen plaintext

   Answer: b

   The correct answer is b. In answer a, the attacker has a copy of the plaintext corresponding to the ciphertext. Answer c describes the situation where selected plaintext is encrypted and the output ciphertext is obtained. The adaptive chosen plaintext attack, answer d, is a form of chosen plaintext attack where the selection of the plaintext is altered according to previous results.

2. For a given hash function H, to prevent substitution of a message M1 for a message M2, it is necessary that:

   a. $H(M1) \neq H(M2)$

   b. $H(M1) = H(M2)$

   c. $H(M1) > H(M2)$

   d. $H(M1) < H(M2)$

   Answer: a

   The correct answer is a. If $H(M1) = H(M2)$, answer b, then the message digests of both M1 and M2 would be equal, and one would not know that one message was substituted for the other. The other answers are distracters.

3. The Secure Hash Algorithm (SHA-1) of the Secure Hash Standard (NIST FIPS PUB 180) processes data in block lengths of:

   a. 128 bits.

   b. 256 bits.

   c. 512 bits.

   d. 1024 bits.

   Answer: c

   The correct answer is c. If a block length is fewer than 512 bits, padding bits are added to make the block length equal to 512 bits. The other answers are distracters.

4. The technique of confusion, proposed by Claude Shannon, is used in block ciphers to:

   a. Spread the influence of a plaintext character over many ciphertext characters.

   b. Limit the influence of a plaintext character across ciphertext characters.

   c. Implement transposition to obtain the ciphertext.

   d. Conceal the statistical connection between ciphertext and plaintext.

   Answer: d

   The correct answer is d. Answer a defines the goal of diffusion. Answers b and c are distracters.

5. The Advanced Encryption Standard, the Rijndael cipher, can be described as:

   a. A recursive, sequential cipher

   b. A Feistel network

   c. A streaming block cipher

   d. An iterated block cipher

   Answer: d

The correct answer is d. Answers a, b, and c are distracters; however, answer b characterizes the Data Encryption Standard (DES) cipher.

6. The Rijndael cipher employs a round transformation that is itself comprised of three layers of transformations. Which of the following is NOT one of these layers?

   a. Key addition layer

   b. Linear mixing layer

   c. Non-linear mixing layer

   d. Non-linear layer

   Answer: c

   The correct answer is c, a distracter.

7. A secret mechanism that enables the implementation of the reverse function in a one-way function is called a:

   a. Trap door.

   b. View.

   c. Open door.

   d. Data diode.

   Answer: a

   The correct answer is a. Answer b, view, refers to a mechanism in a database system that restricts access to certain information within the database. The view implements the principle of least privilege. Answer c is a distracter, and answer d refers to a mechanism—usually in multilevel security systems—that limits the flow of classified information to one direction.

8. Which of the following is NOT a symmetric key algorithm?

   a. Advanced Encryption Standard (AES)

   b. Data Encryption Standard (DES)

   c. International Data Encryption Algorithm (IDEA)

   d. MD5

   Answer: d

   The correct answer is d. MD5 is a message digest algorithm.

9. The following elements comprise a portion of what services?

   ■ Digital certification

   ■ Certification authority

   ■ Timestamping

   ■ Lightweight Directory Access Protocol (LDAP)

   ■ Non-repudiation support

   a. IPSec

   b. Public Key Infrastructure (PKI)

    c. Transaction Layer Security (TLS)

    d. Wireless Application Protocol (WAP)

> *Answer:* b
>
> The correct answer is b, PKI, which describes the integration of digital certificates, digital signatures, and other services necessary to support e-commerce. The other answers are distracters.

10. The vulnerability associated with the requirement to change security protocols at a carriers' Wireless Application Protocol (WAP) gateway from the Wireless Transport Layer Security Protocol (WTLS) to SSL or TLS over the wired network is called:

    a. Wireless Transaction Protocol (WTP) Gap.

    b. Wired Equivalency Privacy (WEP) Gap.

    c. Wireless Application Protocol (WAP) Gap.

    d. Wireless Transport Layer Security Protocol (WTLS) Gap.

> *Answer:* c
>
> The correct answer is c, the WAP Gap. The other answers are distracters.

Chapter 5—Security Architecture and Models

Sample Questions

1. What does the Bell-LaPadula model NOT allow?

    a. Subjects to read from a higher level of security relative to their level of security

    b. Subjects to read from a lower level of security relative to their level of security

    c. Subjects to write to a higher level of security relative to their level of security

    d. Subjects to read at their same level of security

> *Answer:* a
>
> The correct answer is a. The other options are not prohibited by the model.

2. In the * (star) property of the Bell-LaPadula model,

    a. Subjects cannot read from a higher level of security relative to their level of security.

    b. Subjects cannot read from a lower level of security relative to their level of security.

    c. Subjects cannot write to a lower level of security relative to their level of security.

    d. Subjects cannot read from their same level of security.

       Answer: c

       The correct answer is c by definition of the star property.

3. The Clark-Wilson model focuses on data's:

    a. Integrity.

    b. Confidentiality.

    c. Availability.

    d. Format.

       Answer: a

       The correct answer is a. The Clark-Wilson model is an integrity model.

4. The * (star) property of the Biba model states that:

    a. Subjects cannot write to a lower level of integrity relative to their level of integrity.

    b. Subjects cannot write to a higher level of integrity relative to their level of integrity.

    c. Subjects cannot read from a lower level of integrity relative to their level of integrity.

    d. Subjects cannot read from a higher level of integrity relative to their level of integrity.

       Answer: b

5. Which of the following does the Clark-Wilson model NOT involve?

    a. Constrained data items

    b. Transformational procedures

    c. Confidentiality items

    d. Well-formed transactions

       Answer: c

       The correct answer is c. Answers a, b, and d are parts of the Clark-Wilson model.

6. The Take-Grant model:

    a. Focuses on confidentiality.

    b. Specifies the rights that a subject can transfer to an object.

    c. Specifies the levels of integrity.

    d. Specifies the levels of availability.

       Answer: b

7. The Biba model addresses:

    a. Data disclosure.

    b. Transformation procedures.

   c. Constrained data items.

   d. Unauthorized modification of data.

     Answer: d

     The correct answer is d. The Biba model is an integrity model. Answer a is associated with confidentiality. Answers b and c are specific to the Clark-Wilson model.

8. Mandatory access controls first appear in the Trusted Computer System Evaluation Criteria (TCSEC) at the rating of:

   a. D

   b. C

   c. B

   d. A

     Answer: c

9. In the access control matrix, the rows are:

   a. Access Control Lists (ACLs).

   b. Tuples.

   c. Domains.

   d. Capability lists.

     Answer: d

     The correct answer is d. Answer a is incorrect because the access control list is not a row in the access control matrix. Answer b is incorrect because a tuple is a row in the table of a relational database. Answer c is incorrect because a domain is the set of allowable values a column or attribute can take in a relational database.

10. Superscalar computer architecture is characterized by a:

   a. Computer using instructions that perform many operations per instruction.

   b. Computer using instructions that are simpler and require less clock cycles to execute.

   c. Processor that executes one instruction at a time.

   d. Processor that enables concurrent execution of multiple instructions in the same pipeline stage.

     Answer: d

     The correct answer is d. Answer a is the definition of a complex instruction set computer. Answer b is the definition of a reduced instruction set computer. Answer c is the definition of a scalar processor.

11. A Trusted Computing Base (TCB) is defined as:

   a. The total combination of protection mechanisms within a computer system that are trusted to enforce a security policy.

   b. The boundary separating the trusted mechanisms from the remainder of the system.

c. A trusted path that permits a user to access resources.

d. A system that employs the necessary hardware and software assurance measures to enable processing multiple levels of classified or sensitive information to occur.

> *Answer:* a
>
> The correct answer is a. Answer b is the security perimeter. Answer c is the definition of a trusted path. Answer d is the definition of a trusted computer system.

12. Memory space insulated from other running processes in a multiprocessing system is part of a:

a. Protection domain.

b. Security perimeter.

c. Least upper bound.

d. Constrained data item.

> *Answer:* a

13. The boundary separating the TCB from the remainder of the system is called the:

a. Star property.

b. Simple security property.

c. Discretionary control boundary.

d. Security perimeter.

> *Answer:* d
>
> The correct answer is d. Answers a and b deal with security models and answer c is a distracter.

14. The system component that enforces access controls on an object is the:

a. Security perimeter.

b. Trusted domain.

c. Reference monitor.

d. Access control matrix.

> *Answer:* c

15. In the discretionary portion of the Bell-LaPadula mode that is based on the access matrix, how the access rights are defined and evaluated is called:

a. Authentication.

b. Authorization.

c. Identification.

d. Validation.

> *Answer:* b
>
> The correct answer is b, since authorization is concerned with how access rights are defined and how they are evaluated.

16. A computer system that employs the necessary hardware and software assurance measures to enable it to process multiple levels of classified or sensitive information is called a:

    a. Closed system.

    b. Open system.

    c. Trusted system.

    d. Safe system.

    Answer: c

    The correct answer is c, by definition of a trusted system. Answers a and b refer to open, standard information on a product as opposed to a closed or proprietary product. Answer d is a distracter.

17. For fault-tolerance to operate, a system must be:

    a. Capable of detecting and correcting the fault.

    b. Capable of only detecting the fault.

    c. Capable of terminating operations in a safe mode.

    d. Capable of a cold start.

    Answer: a

    The correct answer is a. The two conditions required for a fault-tolerant system. Answer b is a distracter. Answer c is the definition of fail safe and answer d refers to starting after a system shutdown.

18. Which of the following choices describes the four phases of the National Information Assurance Certification and Accreditation Process (NIA-CAP)?

    a. Definition, Verification, Validation, and Confirmation

    b. Definition, Verification, Validation, and Post Accreditation

    c. Verification, Validation, Authentication, and Post Accreditation

    d. Definition, Authentication, Verification, and Post Accreditation

    Answer: b

19. What is a programmable logic device (PLD)?

    a. A volatile device

    b. Random Access Memory (RAM) that contains the software to perform specific tasks

    c. An integrated circuit with connections or internal logic gates that can be changed through a programming process

    d. A program resident on disk memory that executes a specific function

    Answer: c

    The correct answer is c. Answer a is incorrect because a PLD is non-volatile. Answer b is incorrect because random access memory is volatile memory that is not a non-volatile logic device. Answer d is a distracter.

20. The termination of selected, non-critical processing when a hardware or software failure occurs and is detected is referred to as:

    a. Fail safe.

    b. Fault tolerant.

    c. Fail soft.

    d. An exception.

    Answer: c

21. Which of the following are the three types of NIACAP accreditation?

    a. Site, type, and location

    b. Site, type, and system

    c. Type, system, and location

    d. Site, type, and general

    Answer: b

22. Content-dependent control makes access decisions based on:

    a. The object's data.

    b. The object's environment.

    c. The object's owner.

    d. The object's view.

    Answer: a

    The correct answer is a. Answer b is context-dependent control. Answers c and d are distracters.

23. The term failover refers to:

    a. Switching to a duplicate, "hot" backup component.

    b. Terminating processing in a controlled fashion.

    c. Resiliency.

    d. A fail-soft system.

    Answer: a

    The correct answer is a. Failover means switching to a "hot" backup system that maintains duplicate states with the primary system. Answer b refers to fail safe, and answers c and d refer to fail soft.

24. Primary storage is the:

    a. Memory directly addressable by the CPU, which is for the storage of instructions and data that are associated with the program being executed.

    b. Memory, such as magnetic disks, that provide non-volatile storage.

    c. Memory used in conjunction with real memory to present a CPU with a larger, apparent address space.

    d. Memory where information must be obtained by sequentially searching from the beginning of the memory space.

Answer: a

The correct answer is a. Answer b refers to secondary storage. Answer c refers to virtual memory, and answer d refers to sequential memory.

25. In the Common Criteria, a Protection Profile:

    a. Specifies the mandatory protection in the product to be evaluated.

    b. Is also known as the Target of Evaluation (TOE).

    c. Is also known as the Orange Book.

    d. Specifies the security requirements and protections of the products to be evaluated.

    Answer: d

    The correct answer is d. Answer a is a distracter. Answer b is the product to be evaluated. Answer c refers to TCSEC.

26. Context-dependent control uses which of the following to make decisions?

    a. Subject or object attributes or environmental characteristics

    b. Data

    c. Formal models

    d. Operating system characteristics

    Answer: a

    The correct answer is a. Answer b refers to content-dependent characteristics, and answers c and d are distracters.

27. What is a computer bus?

    a. A message sent around a Token Ring network

    b. Secondary storage

    c. A group of conductors for the addressing of data and control

    d. A message in object-oriented programming

    Answer: c

    The correct answer is c. Answer a is a token. Answer b refers to disk storage. Answer d is a distracter.

28. In a ring protection system, where is the security kernel usually located?

    a. Highest ring number

    b. Arbitrarily placed

    c. Lowest ring number

    d. Middle ring number

    Answer: c

29. Increasing performance in a computer by overlapping the steps of different instructions is called:

    a. A reduced instruction set computer.

    b. A complex instruction set computer.

   c. Vector processing.

   d. Pipelining.

     Answer: d

30. Random access memory is:

   a. Non-volatile.

   b. Sequentially addressable.

   c. Programmed by using fusible links.

   d. Volatile.

     Answer: d

     The correct answer is d. RAM is volatile. The other answers are incorrect because RAM is volatile, randomly accessible, and not programmed by fusible links.

31. The addressing mode in which an instruction accesses a memory location whose contents are the address of the desired data is called:

   a. Implied addressing.

   b. Indexed addressing.

   c. Direct addressing.

   d. Indirect addressing.

     Answer: d

32. Processes are placed in a ring structure according to:

   a. Least privilege.

   b. Separation of duty.

   c. Owner classification.

   d. First in, first out.

     Answer: a

     The correct answer is a. A process is placed in the ring that gives it the minimum privileges necessary to perform its functions.

33. The MULTICS operating system is a classic example of:

   a. An open system.

   b. Object orientation.

   c. Database security.

   d. Ring protection system.

     Answer: d

     The correct answer is d. Multics is based on the ring protection architecture.

34. What are the hardware, firmware, and software elements of a Trusted Computing Base (TCB) that implement the reference monitor concept called?

   a. The trusted path

   b. A security kernel

   c. An Operating System (OS)

   d. A trusted computing system

   Answer: b.

Bonus Questions

1. The memory hierarchy in a typical digital computer, in order, is:

   a. CPU, secondary memory, cache, primary memory.

   b. CPU, primary memory, secondary memory, cache.

   c. CPU, cache, primary memory, secondary memory.

   d. CPU, cache, secondary memory, primary memory.

   Answer: c

   The correct answer is c. In this architecture, the CPU "sees" the high-speed cache, which holds the instructions and data from primary memory that have a high probability of being executed by the program. In order of speed of access, the order in answer c goes from the fastest to the slowest access time.

2. Which one of the following is NOT a typical bus designation in a digital computer?

   a. Secondary

   b. Address

   c. Data

   d. Control

   Answer: a

   The correct answer is a, a distracter.

3. The addressing mode in a digital computer in which the address location that is specified in the program instructions contains the address of the final desired location is called:

   a. Indexed addressing.

   b. Implied addressing.

   c. Indirect addressing.

   d. Absolute addressing.

   Answer: c

   The correct answer is c. Answer a, indexed addressing, determines the desired memory address by adding the contents of the address defined in the program's instruction to that of an index register. Implied addressing, answer b, refers to registers usually contained inside the CPU. Answer d, absolute addressing, addresses the entire primary memory space.

4. A processor in which a single instruction specifies more than one CON-CURRENT operation is called:

   a. Pipelined processor.

   b. Superscalar processor.

   c. Very Long Instruction Word processor.

   d. Scalar processor.

   > *Answer:* c

   > The correct answer is c. A pipelined processor, answer a, overlaps the steps of different instructions. Answer b, a superscalar processor, performs a concurrent execution of multiple instructions in the same pipeline stage. A scalar processor, answer d, executes one instruction at a time.

5. Which one of the following is NOT a security mode of operation in an information system?

   a. System high

   b. Dedicated

   c. Multilevel

   d. Contained

   > *Answer:* d

   > The correct answer is d, a distracter. In the system high mode, answer a, the information system operates at the highest level of information classification. In this mode, all users must have security clearances for the highest level of classified information. Answer b, the dedicated mode, requires that all users must have a clearance or an authorization and a need-to-know for all information that is produced by the information system. The multi-level mode of operation, answer c, supports users with different clearances and data at multiple classification levels.

6. The standard process to certify and accredit U.S. defense critical information systems is called:

   a. DITSCAP

   b. NIACAP

   c. CIAP

   d. DIACAP

   > *Answer:* a

   > The correct answer is a, the Defense Information Technology Security Certification and Accreditation Process. Answer b refers to the U.S. government's non-defense *Certification and Accreditation* (C&A) process—the National Information Assurance Certification and Accreditation Process. CIAP, answer c, refers to the Commercial Information Security Analysis Process that is currently under development for application to commercial systems. Answer d is a distracter.

7. What information security model formalizes the U.S. Department of Defense multi-level security policy?

   a. Clark-Wilson

   b. Stark-Wilson

   c. Biba

   d. Bell-LaPadula

   Answer: d

   The correct answer is d. The Bell-LaPadula model addresses the confidentiality of classified material. Answers a and c are integrity models, and answer b is a distracter.

8. The Biba model axiom "An object at one level of integrity is not permitted to modify (write to) an object of a higher level of integrity (no write up)" is called:

   a. The Constrained Integrity Axiom

   b. The * (star) Integrity Axiom

   c. The Simple Integrity Axiom

   d. The Discretionary Integrity Axiom

   Answer: b

   The correct answer is b. Answers a and d are distracters. Answer c, the Simple Integrity Axiom, states, "A subject at one level of integrity is not permitted to observe (read) an object of lower integrity (no read down)."

9. The property that states, "Reading or writing is permitted at a particular level of sensitivity, but not to either higher or lower levels of sensitivity" is called the:

   a. Strong * (star) Property.

   b. Discretionary Security Property.

   c. Simple * (star) Property.

   d. * (star) Security Property.

   Answer: a

   The correct answer is a. Answer b, the Discretionary Security Property, specifies discretionary access control in the Bell-LaPadula model by the use of an access matrix. Answer c is distracter. Answer d, in the Bell-LaPadula model, states, "The writing of information by a subject at a higher level of sensitivity to an object at a lower level of sensitively is not permitted (no write down)."

10. Which one the following is NOT one of the three major parts of the Common Criteria (CC)?

    a. Introduction and General Model

    b. Security Evaluation Requirements

c. Security Functional Requirements

d. Security Assurance Requirements

> *Answer:* b
>
> The correct answer is b, a distracter. Answer a is Part 1 of the CC. It defines general concepts and principles of information security and defines the contents of the Protection Profile (PP), Security Target (ST), and the Package. The Security Functional Requirements, answer c, are Part 2 of the CC, which contains a catalog of well-defined standard means of expressing security requirements of IT products and systems. Answer d is Part 3 of the CC and comprises a catalog of a set of standard assurance components.

11. In the Common Criteria, an implementation-independent statement of security needs for a set of IT security products that *could be built* is called a:

    a. Security Target (ST).

    b. Package.

    c. Protection Profile (PP).

    d. Target of Evaluation (TOE).

    > *Answer:* c
    >
    > The correct answer is c. Answer a, ST, is a statement of security claims for a particular IT product or system. A Package, answer b, is defined in the CC as "an intermediate combination of security requirement components." A TOE, answer d, is "an IT product or system to be evaluated."

12. In Part 3 of the Common Criteria, *Security Assurance Requirements*, seven predefined Packages of assurance components "that make up the CC scale for rating confidence in the security of IT products and systems" are called:

    a. Evaluation Assurance Levels (EALs).

    b. Protection Assurance Levels (PALs).

    c. Assurance Levels (ALs).

    d. Security Target Assurance Levels (STALs).

    > *Answer:* a
    >
    > The correct answer is a. The other answers are distracters.

13. Which one of the following is NOT a component of a CC Protection Profile?

    a. Target of Evaluation (TOE) description

    b. Threats against the product that must be addressed

    c. Product-specific security requirements

    d. Security objectives

    > *Answer:* c

The correct answer is c. Product-specific security requirements for the product or system are contained in the Security Target (ST). Additional items in the PP are:

- TOE security environment description
- Assumptions about the security aspects of the product's expected use
- Organizational security policies or rules
- Application notes
- Rationale

Chapter 6: Operations Security

Sample Questions

1. What does IPL stand for?
   a. Initial Program Life Cycle
   b. Initial Program Load
   c. Initial Post-Transaction Logging
   d. Internet Police League

   Answer: b

   The correct answer is b. The IPL is a task performed by the operator to boot up the system. The other terms do not exist.

2. Which of the following is NOT a use of an audit trail?
   a. Provides information about additions, deletions, or modifications to the data
   b. Collects information such as passwords or infrastructure configurations
   c. Assists the monitoring function by helping to recognize patterns of abnormal user behavior
   d. Enables the security practitioner to trace a transaction's history

   Answer: b

   The correct answer is b. Auditing should not be used to collect user's passwords. It is used for the other three examples, however.

3. Why is security an issue when a system is booted into "single-user mode"?
   a. The operating system is started without the security front-end loaded.
   b. The users cannot log in to the system, and they will complain.
   c. Proper forensics cannot be executed while in single-user mode.
   d. Backup tapes cannot be restored while in single-user mode.

Answer: a

The correct answer is a. When the operator boots the system in "single-user mode," the user front-end security controls are not loaded. This mode should be used for recovery and maintenance procedures only, and all operations should be logged and audited.

4. Which of the following examples is the best definition of Fail Secure?

   a. Access personnel have security clearance, but they do not have a "need-to-know."

   b. The operating system is started without the security front-end loaded.

   c. The system fails to preserve a secure state during and after a system crash.

   d. The system preserves a secure state during and after a system crash.

   Answer: d

   The correct answer is d. Based on the Common Criteria, a system can be evaluated as fail secure if it "preserves a secure state during and after identified failures occur."

5. Which of the following would NOT be an example of compensating controls being implemented?

   a. Sensitive information requiring two authorized signatures to release

   b. A safety deposit box needing two keys to open

   c. Modifying the timing of a system resource in some measurable way to covertly transmit information

   d. Signing in or out of a traffic log and using a magnetic card to access to an operations center

   Answer: c

   The correct answer is c. This is the definition for a covert timing channel. The other three are examples of compensating controls, which are a combination of technical, administrative, or physical controls to enhance security.

6. "Separation of duties" embodies what principle?

   a. An operator does not know more about the system than the minimum required to do the job.

   b. Two operators are required to work in tandem to perform a task.

   c. The operators' duties are frequently rotated.

   d. The operators have different duties to prevent one person from compromising the system.

   Answer: d

   The correct answer is d. "Separation of duties" means that the operators are prevented from generating and verifying transactions alone, for example. A task might be divided into different smaller tasks to accomplish this, or in the case of an operator with multiple duties, the operator makes a logical, functional job change when performing such conflicting duties. Answer a is "need-to-know," answer b is "dual-control," and c is "job rotation."

7. Which is NOT true about Covert Channel Analysis?

   a. It is an operational assurance requirement that is specified in the Orange Book.

   b. It is required for B2 class systems in order to protect against covert storage channels.

   c. It is required for B2 class systems to protect against covert timing channels.

   d. It is required for B3 class systems to protect against both covert storage and covert timing channels.

   Answer: c

   The correct answer is c. Orange Book B2 class systems do not need to be protected from covert timing channels. Covert channel analysis must be performed for B2-level class systems to protect against covert storage channels only. B3 class systems need to be protected against both covert storage channels and covert timing channels.

8. An audit trail is an example of what type of control?

   a. Deterrent control

   b. Preventative control

   c. Detective control

   d. Application control

   Answer: c

   The correct answer is c. An audit trail is a record of events to piece together what has happened and allow enforcement of individual accountability by creating a reconstruction of events. They can be used to assist in the proper implementation of the other controls, however.

9. Using pre-numbered forms to initiate a transaction is an example of what type of control?

   a. Deterrent control

   b. Preventative control

   c. Detective control

   d. Application control

   Answer: b

   The correct answer is b. Pre-numbered forms are an example of preventative controls. They can also be considered a transaction control and input control.

10. Which of the following is a reason to institute output controls?

    a. To preserve the integrity of the data in the system while changes are being made to the configuration

    b. To protect the output's confidentiality

    c. To detect irregularities in the software's operation

    d. To recover damage after an identified system failure

    Answer: b

    The correct answer is b. In addition to being used as a transaction control verification mechanism, output controls are used to ensure that output, such as printed reports, is distributed securely. Answer a, is an example of Configuration or Change control, c is an example of Application controls, and d is an example of Recovery controls.

11. Convert Channel Analysis, Trusted Facility Management, and Trusted Recovery are parts of which book in the TCSEC Rainbow Series?

    a. Red Book

    b. Orange Book

    c. Green Book

    d. Dark Green Book

    Answer: b

    The correct answer is b. Answer a, the Red Book, is the Trusted Network Interpretation (TNI) summary of network requirements (described in the Telecommunications and Network Security domain); c, the Green Book, is the Department of Defense (DoD) *Password Management Guideline*; and d, the Dark Green Book, is *The Guide to Understanding Data Remanence in Automated Information Systems*.

12. How do covert timing channels convey information?

    a. By changing a system's stored data characteristics

    b. By generating noise and traffic with the data

    c. By performing a covert channel analysis

    d. By modifying the timing of a system resource in some measurable way

    Answer: d

    The correct answer is d. A covert timing channel alters the timing of parts of the system to enable it to be used to communicate information covertly (outside the normal security function). Answer a is the description of the use of a covert storage channel, b is a technique to combat the use of covert channels, and c is the Orange Book requirement for B3, B2, and A1 evaluated systems.

13. Which of the following is the best example of "need-to-know"?

    a. An operator does not know more about the system than the minimum required to do the job.

    b. Two operators are required to work together to perform a task.

   c. The operators' duties are frequently rotated.

   d. An operator cannot generate and verify transactions alone.

     Answer: a

     The correct answer is a. "Need-to-know" means the operators are working in an environment that limits their knowledge of the system, applications, or data to the minimum elements that they require to perform their job. Answer b is "dual-control," c is "job rotation," and answer d is "separation of duties."

14. Which of the following is an example of "least privilege"?

   a. An operator does not know more about the system than the minimum required to do the job.

   b. An operator does not have more system rights than the minimum required to do the job.

   c. The operators' duties are frequently rotated.

   d. An operator cannot generate and verify transactions alone.

     Answer: b

     The correct answer is b. "Least Privilege" embodies the concept that users or operators should be granted the lowest level of system access or system rights that allows them to perform their job. Answer a is "need-to-know," c is "job rotation," and d is "separation of duties."

15. Which of the following would be the BEST description of clipping levels?

   a. A baseline of user errors above which violations will be recorded

   b. A listing of every error made by users to initiate violation processing

   c. Variance detection of too many people with unrestricted access

   d. Changes a system's stored data characteristics

     Answer: a

     The correct answer is a. This description of a clipping level is the best. It is not b, because the reason for creating a clipping level is to prevent auditors from having to examine every error. The answer c is a common use for clipping levels but is not a definition. Answer d is a distracter.

16. Which of the following is NOT a proper media control?

   a. The data media should be logged to provide a physical inventory control.

   b. All data storage media should be accurately marked.

   c. A proper storage environment should be provided for the media.

   d. The media that is reused in a sensitive environment does not need sanitization.

     Answer: d

The correct answer is d. Sanitization is the process of removing information from used data media to prevent data remanence. Different media require different types of sanitation. All the others are examples of proper media controls.

17. Configuration management control best refers to:

a. The concept of "least control" in operations.

b. Ensuring that changes to the system do not unintentionally diminish security.

c. The use of privileged-entity controls for system administrator functions.

d. Implementing resource protection schemes for hardware control.

Answer: b

The correct answer is b. Configuration Management Control (and Change Control) are processes to ensure that any changes to the system are managed properly and do not inordinately affect either the availability or security of the system.

18. Which of the following would NOT be considered a penetration testing technique?

a. War dialing

b. Sniffing

c. Data manipulation

d. Scanning

Answer: c

The correct answer is c. Data manipulation describes the corruption of data integrity to perform fraud for personal gain or other reasons. External penetration testing should not alter the data in any way. The other three are common penetration techniques.

19. Inappropriate computer activities could be described as:

a. Computer behavior that might be grounds for a job action or dismissal.

b. Loss incurred unintentionally though the lack of operator training.

c. Theft of information or trade secrets for profit or unauthorized disclosure.

d. Data scavenging through the resources available to normal system users.

Answer: a

The correct answer is a. While all of the activities described are considered in the broad category of inappropriate activities, this description is used to define a narrower category of inappropriate activities. Answer b is defined as accidental loss. Answer c is considered intentionally illegal computer activity. Answer d is a "keyboard attack," a type of data scavenging attack using common tools or utilities available to the user.

20. Why are maintenance accounts a threat to operations controls?

   a. Maintenance personnel could slip and fall and sue the organization.

   b. Maintenance accounts are commonly used by hackers to access network devices.

   c. Maintenance account information could be compromised if printed reports are left out in the open.

   d. Maintenance might require physical access to the system by vendors or service providers.

   Answer: b

   The correct answer is b. Maintenance accounts are login accounts to systems resources, primarily networked devices. They often have the factory-set passwords that are frequently distributed through the hacker community.

Bonus Questions

1. Which choice below is NOT an example of intentionally inappropriate operator activity?

   a. Making errors when manually inputting transactions

   b. Using the company's system to store pornography

   c. Conducting private business on the company system

   d. Using unauthorized access levels to violate information confidentiality

   Answer: a

   The correct answer is a. While choice a is most certainly an example of a threat to a system's integrity, it is considered unintentional loss, not an intentional activity.

2. Which choice below would NOT be a common element of a transaction trail?

   a. The date and time of the transaction

   b. Who processed the transaction

   c. Why the transaction was processed

   d. At which terminal the transaction was processed

   Answer: c

   The correct answer is c. Why the transaction was processed is not initially a concern of the audit log, but we will investigate it later. The other three elements are all important information that the audit log of the transaction should record.

3. Which choice below is NOT an element of proper media control?

    a. Accurately and promptly marking all data storage media
    b. Assuring the accuracy of the backup data
    c. The safe and clean handling of the media
    d. The proper environmental storage of the media

    Answer: b

    The correct answer is b. Answer b is an example of a software integrity control, although the other three elements of media control listed apply to the backup tapes themselves.

4. Which choice below best describes the function of change control?

    a. To ensure that system changes are implemented in an orderly manner
    b. To guarantee that an operator is only given the privileges needed for the task
    c. To guarantee that transaction records are retained IAW compliance requirements
    d. To assign parts of security-sensitive tasks to more than one individual

    Answer: a

    The correct answer is a. Answer b describes "least privilege," answer c describes "record retention," and answer d describes "separation on duties."

5. Which task below would normally be a function of the security administrator, not the system administrator?

    a. Installing system software
    b. Adding and removing system users
    c. Reviewing audit data
    d. Managing print queues

    Answer: c

    The correct answer is c. Reviewing audit data should be a function separate from the day-to-day administration of the system.

6. Which choice below BEST describes the type of control that a firewall exerts on a network infrastructure?

    a. Corrective control
    b. Preventative control
    c. Detective control
    d. Application control

    Answer: b

    The correct answer is b. A firewall is primarily intended to prevent unauthorized access.

7. Which choice below BEST describes a threat as defined in the Operations Security domain?

   a. A potential incident that could cause harm

   b. A weakness in a system that could be exploited

   c. A company resource that could be lost due to an incident

   d. The minimization of loss associated with an incident

   Answer: a

   The correct answer is a. Answer b describes a vulnerability, answer c describes an asset, and answer d describes risk management.

8. Which choice below is considered the HIGHEST level of operator privilege?

   a. Read/Write

   b. Read Only

   c. Access Change

   d. Write Only

   Answer: c

   The correct answer is c. The three common levels of operator privileges, based on the concept of "least privilege," are:

   ■ Read Only—Lowest level, view data only

   ■ Read/Write—View and modify data

   ■ Access Change—Highest level, right to change data/operator permissions

   Answer d is a distracter.

9. Which choice below is NOT a common example of exercising due care or due diligence in security practices?

   a. Implementing security awareness and training programs

   b. Implementing employee compliance statements

   c. Implementing controls on printed documentation

   d. Implementing employee casual Friday

   Answer: d

   The correct answer is d. The concepts of due care and due diligence require that an organization engage in good security practices relative to industry standards.

10. Which choice below is NOT an example of a software control?

    a. Controlling diagnostic ports on networked equipment

    b. Employing anti-virus management and tools

    c. Implementing a formal application upgrade process

    d. Routinely testing the backup data for accuracy

Answer: a

The correct answer is a. Answer a is an example of a hardware control. The other three are examples of software controls.

Chapter 7—Applications and Systems Development

Sample Questions

1. What is a data warehouse?
   a. A remote facility used for storing backup tapes
   b. A repository of information from heterogeneous databases
   c. A table in a relational database system
   d. A hot backup building

   Answer: b

   The correct answer is b, a repository of information from heterogeneous databases. Answers a and d describe physical facilities for backup and recovery of information systems, and answer c describes a relation in a relational database.

2. What does normalizing data in a data warehouse mean?
   a. Redundant data is removed.
   b. Numerical data is divided by a common factor.
   c. Data is converted to a symbolic representation.
   d. Data is restricted to a range of values.

   Answer: a

   The correct answer is a, removing redundant data.

3. What is a neural network?
   a. A hardware or software system that emulates the reasoning of a human expert
   b. A collection of computers that are focused on medical applications
   c. A series of networked PCs performing artificial intelligence tasks
   d. A hardware or software system that emulates the functioning of biological neurons

   Answer: d

   The correct answer is d. A neural network is a hardware or software system that emulates the functioning of biological neurons. Answer a refers to an expert system, and answers b and c are distracters.

4. A neural network learns by using various algorithms to:
   a. Adjust the weights applied to the data.
   b. Fire the rules in knowledge base.

c. Emulate an inference engine.

d. Emulate the thinking of an expert.

Answer: a

The correct answer is "A neural network learns by using various algorithms to adjust the weights applied to the data." Answers b, c, and d are terminology referenced in expert systems.

5. The SEI Software Capability Maturity Model is based on the premise that:

a. Good software development is a function of the number of expert programmers in the organization.

b. The maturity of an organization's software processes cannot be measured.

c. The quality of a software product is a direct function of the quality of its associated software development and maintenance processes.

d. Software development is an art that cannot be measured by conventional means.

Answer: c

The correct answer is c. The quality of a software product is a direct function of the quality of its associated software development and maintenance processes. Answer a is false because the SEI Software CMM relates the production of good software to having the proper processes in place in an organization and not to expert programs or heroes. Answer b is false because the Software CMM provides means to measure the maturity of an organization's software processes. Answer d is false for the same reason as answer b.

6. In configuration management, a configuration item is:

a. The version of the operating system that is operating on the workstation that provides information security services.

b. A component whose state is to be recorded and against which changes are to be progressed.

c. The network architecture used by the organization.

d. A series of files that contains sensitive information.

Answer: b

The correct answer is b. A component whose state is to be recorded and against which changes are to be progressed. Answers a, c, and d are incorrect by the definition of a configuration item.

7. In an object-oriented system, polymorphism denotes:

a. Objects of many different classes that are related by some common superclass; thus, any object denoted by this name can respond to some common set of operations in a different way.

b. Objects of many different classes that are related by some common superclass; thus, all objects denoted by this name can respond to some common set of operations in identical fashion.

c. Objects of the same class; thus, any object denoted by this name can respond to some common set of operations in the same way.

d. Objects of many different classes that are unrelated but respond to some common set of operations in the same way.

Answer: a

The correct answer is a, objects of many different classes that are related by some common superclass that are able to respond to some common set of operations in a different way. Answers b, c, and d are incorrect by the definition of polymorphism.

8. The simplistic model of software life cycle development assumes that:

a. Iteration will be required among the steps in the process.

b. Each step can be completed and finalized without any effect from the later stages that might require rework.

c. Each phase is identical to a completed milestone.

d. Software development requires reworking and repeating some of the phases.

Answer: b

The correct answer is b. Each step can be completed and finalized without any effect from the later stages that might require rework. Answer a is incorrect because no iteration is allowed for in the model. Answer c is incorrect because it applies to the modified Waterfall model. Answer d is incorrect because no iteration or reworking is considered in the model.

9. What is a method in an object-oriented system?

a. The means of communication among objects

b. A guide to the programming of objects

c. The code defining the actions that the object performs in response to a message

d. The situation where a class inherits the behavioral characteristics of more that one parent class

Answer: c

The correct answer is c. A method in an object-oriented system is the code that defines the actions that the object performs in response to a message. Answer a is incorrect because it defines a message. Answer b is a distracter, and answer d refers to multiple inheritance.

10. What does the Spiral Model depict?

a. A spiral that incorporates various phases of software development

b. A spiral that models the behavior of biological neurons

c. The operation of expert systems

d. Information security checklists

Answer: a

The correct answer is a—a spiral that incorporates various phases of software development. The other answers are distracters.

11. In the software life cycle, verification:
    a. Evaluates the product in development against real-world requirements.
    b. Evaluates the product in development against similar products.
    c. Evaluates the product in development against general baselines.
    d. Evaluates the product in development against the specification.

    Answer: d

    The correct answer is d. In the software life cycle, verification evaluates the product in development against the specification. Answer a defines validation. Answers b and c are distracters.

12. In the software life cycle, validation:
    a. Refers to the work product satisfying the real-world requirements and concepts.
    b. Refers to the work product satisfying derived specifications.
    c. Refers to the work product satisfying software maturity levels.
    d. Refers to the work product satisfying generally accepted principles.

    Answer: a

    The correct answer is a. In the software life cycle, validation is the work product satisfying the real-world requirements and concepts. The other answers are distracters.

13. In the modified Waterfall Model:
    a. Unlimited backward iteration is permitted.
    b. The model was reinterpreted to have phases end at project milestones.
    c. The model was reinterpreted to have phases begin at project milestones.
    d. Product verification and validation are not included.

    Answer: b

    The correct answer is b. The modified Waterfall model was reinterpreted to have phases end at project milestones. Answer a is false because unlimited backward iteration is not permitted in the modified Waterfall model. Answer c is a distracter, and answer d is false because verification and validation are included.

14. Cyclic redundancy checks, structured walkthroughs, and hash totals are examples of what type of application controls?
    a. Preventive security controls
    b. Preventive consistency controls
    c. Detective accuracy controls
    d. Corrective consistency controls

Answer: c

The correct answer is c. Cyclic redundancy checks, structured walkthroughs, and hash totals are examples of detective accuracy controls. The other answers do not apply by the definition of the types of controls.

15. In a system life cycle, information security controls should be:

    a. Designed during the product implementation phase.

    b. Implemented prior to validation.

    c. Part of the feasibility phase.

    d. Specified after the coding phase.

    Answer: c

    The correct answer is c. In the system life cycle, information security controls should be part of the feasibility phase. The other answers are incorrect because the basic premise of information system security is that controls should be included in the earliest phases of the software life cycle and not added later in the cycle or as an afterthought.

16. The software maintenance phase controls consist of:

    a. Request control, change control, and release control.

    b. Request control, configuration control, and change control.

    c. Change control, security control, and access control.

    d. Request control, release control, and access control.

    Answer: a

    The correct answer is a. The software maintenance phase controls consist of request control, change control, and release control by definition. The other answers are, therefore, incorrect.

17. In configuration management, what is a software library?

    a. A set of versions of the component configuration items

    b. A controlled area accessible only to approved users who are restricted to the use of an approved procedure

    c. A repository of backup tapes

    d. A collection of software build lists

    Answer: b

    The correct answer is b. In configuration management, a software library is a controlled area accessible only to approved users who are restricted to the use of approved procedure. Answer a is incorrect because it defines a build list. Answer c is incorrect because it defines a backup storage facility. Answer d is a distracter.

18. What is configuration control?

    a. Identifying and documenting the functional and physical characteristics of each configuration item

    b. Controlling changes to the configuration items and issuing versions of configuration items from the software library

    c. Recording the processing of changes

    d. Controlling the quality of the configuration management procedures

    Answer: b

    The correct answer is b. Configuration control is controlling changes to the configuration items and issuing versions of configuration items from the software library. Answer a is the definition of configuration identification. Answer c is the definition of configuration status accounting, and answer d is the definition of configuration audit.

19. What is searching for data correlations in the data warehouse called?

    a. Data warehousing

    b. Data mining

    c. A data dictionary

    d. Configuration management

    Answer: b

    The correct answer is b. Searching for data correlations in the data warehouse is called data mining. Answer a is incorrect because data warehousing is creating a repository of information from heterogeneous databases that is available to users for making queries. Answer c is incorrect because a data dictionary is a database for system developers. Answer d is incorrect because configuration management is the discipline of identifying the components of a continually evolving system for the purposes of controlling changes to those components and maintaining integrity and traceability throughout the life cycle.

20. The security term that is concerned with the same primary key existing at different classification levels in the same database is:

    a. Polymorphism.

    b. Normalization.

    c. Inheritance.

    d. Polyinstantiation.

    Answer: d

    The correct answer is d. The security term that is concerned with the same primary key existing at different classification levels in the same database is polyinstantiation. Answer a is incorrect because polymorphism is defined as objects of many different classes that are related by some common superclass; thus, any object denoted by this name is able to respond to some common set of operations in a different way. Answer b is incorrect because normalization refers to removing redundant or incorrect data from a database. Answer c is incorrect because inheritance refers to methods from a class inherited by another subclass.

21. What is a data dictionary?

    a. A database for system developers

    b. A database of security terms

    c. A library of objects

    d. A validation reference source

    Answer: a

    The correct answer is a. A data dictionary is a database for system developers. Answers b, c, and d are distracters.

22. Which of the following is an example of mobile code?

    a. Embedded code in control systems

    b. Embedded code in PCs

    c. Java and ActiveX code downloaded into a Web browser from the World Wide Web (WWW)

    d. Code derived following the spiral model

    Answer: c

    The correct answer is c. An example of mobile code is Java and ActiveX code downloaded into a Web browser from the World Wide Web. Answers a, b, and d are incorrect because they are types of code that are not related to mobile code.

23. Which of the following is NOT true regarding software unit testing?

    a. The test data is part of the specifications.

    b. Correct test output results should be developed and known beforehand.

    c. Live or actual field data is recommended for use in the testing procedures.

    d. Testing should check for out-of-range values and other bounds conditions.

    Answer: c

    The correct answer is c. Live or actual field data are NOT recommended for use in testing because they do not thoroughly test all normal and abnormal situations—and the test results are not known beforehand. Answers a, b, and d, are true of testing.

Bonus Questions

1. Which of the following is NOT a component of configuration management?

    a. Configuration control

    b. Configuration review

    c. Configuration status accounting

    d. Configuration audit

    Answer: b

    The correct answer is b, a distracter. Answer a, configuration control, involves controlling changes to configuration items and issuing versions of configuration items from the software library. Configuration status accounting, answer c, is the processing of changes, and answer d is the process of controlling the quality of configuration management procedures.

2. Which one of the following is NOT one of the maturity levels of the Software Capability Maturity Model (CMM)?

    a. Fundamental

    b. Repeatable

    c. Defined

    d. Managed

    Answer: a

    The correct answer is a, a distracter. The first level of the Software CMM is the Initiating level. At this level, processes are performed on an ad hoc basis. Answer b, the Repeatable level, is the second maturity level in the model. In the third level, Defined, of answer c management practices are institutionalized and technical procedures are integrated into the organizational structure. The Managed level of answer d has both product and processes quantitatively controlled. The fifth level of the Software CMM is the Optimized level, where continuous process improvement is institutionalized.

3. The communication to an object to carry out an operation in an object-oriented system is called a:

    a. Note.

    b. Method.

    c. Behavior.

    d. Message.

    Answer: d

    The correct answer is d. Answer a is a distracter. A method, answer b, is the code that defines the actions an object performs in response to a message. Answer c, behavior, is the result exhibited by an object upon receipt of a message.

4. In an object-oriented system, the situation wherein objects with a common name respond differently to a common set of operations is called:

   a. Delegation.
   b. Polyresponse.
   c. Polymorphism.
   d. Polyinstantiation.

   Answer: c

   The correct answer is c. Delegation, answer a, is the forwarding of a request by one object to another object. Answer b is a distracter. Polyinstantiation, answer d, is the development of a detailed version of an object from another object. The new object uses values that are different from those in the original object.

5. What phase of the object-oriented software development life cycle is described as emphasizing the employment of objects and methods rather than types or transformations as in other software approaches?

   a. Object-oriented requirements analysis
   b. Object-oriented programming
   c. Object-oriented analysis
   d. Object-oriented design

   Answer: b

   The correct answer is b. Answer a defines classes of objects and their interactions. Answer c, object-oriented analysis, is the process of understanding and modeling of a specific problem within a problem domain. Object-oriented design, answer d, is design in which the object is the basic unit of modularity and objects are instantiations of a class.

6. A system that exhibits reasoning similar to that of humans knowledgeable in a particular field to solve a problem in that field is called:

   a. A "smart" system.
   b. A data warehouse.
   c. A neural network.
   d. An expert system.

   Answer: d

   The correct answer is d. Answer a, smart system, is a distracter. A data warehouse, answer b, is a repository of information from heterogeneous databases that is available to users for making queries. Answer c, a neural network, is a "self-learning" system that bases its operation on the model of the functioning of biological neurons.

7. What type of security controls operate on the input to a computing system, on the data being processed, and the output of the system?

   a. Numerical controls
   b. Data controls

    c. Application controls

    d. Normative controls

       Answer: c

       The correct answer is c. The other answers are distracters.

8. The Common Object Model (COM) that supports the exchange of objects among programs was formerly known as:

    a. The Distributed Common Object Model (DCOM).

    b. Object Linking and Embedding (OLE).

    c. Object Rationalization and Linking (ORL).

    d. An Object Request Broker (ORB).

       Answer: b

       The correct answer is b. Answer a defines the standard for sharing objects in a networked environment. Answer c is a distracter. An ORB, answer d, is a locator and distributor of objects across networks.

9. In a distributed environment, a surrogate program that performs services in one environment on behalf of a principal in another environment is called:

    a. A proxy.

    b. A slave.

    c. A virtual processor.

    d. An agent.

       Answer: d

       The correct answer is d. Answer a, proxy, is similar in nature but might hide the characteristics of the principal it is representing. Answers b and c are distracters.

Chapter 8—Business Continuity Planning—Disaster Recovery Planning

Sample Questions

1. Which of the following is NOT one of the five disaster recovery plan testing types?

    a. Simulation

    b. Checklist

    c. Mobile

    d. Full Interruption

       Answer: c

The correct answer is c, mobile. The other three are proper examples of elements of the five disaster recovery plan testing types.

2. Why is it so important to test disaster recovery plans frequently?

   a. The businesses that provide subscription services might have changed ownership.

   b. A plan is not considered viable until a test has been performed.

   c. Employees might get bored with the planning process.

   d. Natural disasters can change frequently.

      Answer: b

      The correct answer is b. A plan is not considered functioning and viable until a test has been performed. An untested plan sitting on a shelf is useless and might even have the reverse effect of creating a false sense of security. While the other answers, especially a, are good reasons to test, b is the primary reason.

3. What is the purpose of the Business Impact Assessment (BIA)?

   a. To create a document to be used to help understand what impact a disruptive event would have on the business

   b. To define a strategy to minimize the effect of disturbances and to allow for the resumption of business processes

   c. To emphasize the organization's commitment to its employees and vendors

   d. To work with executive management to establish a DRP policy

      Answer: a

      The correct answer is a: to create a document to be used to help understand what impact a disruptive event would have on the business. Answer b is the definition of business continuity planning.

4. Which of the following is NOT considered an element of a backup alternative?

   a. Electronic vaulting

   b. Remote journaling

   c. Warm site

   d. Checklist

      Answer: d

      The correct answer is d. A checklist is a type of disaster recovery plan test. Electronic vaulting is the batch transfer of backup data to an off-site location. Remote journaling is the parallel processing of transactions to an alternate site. A warm site is a backup processing alternative.

5. Which type of backup subscription service will allow a business to recover quickest?

   a. A hot site

   b. A mobile or rolling backup service

    c. A cold site

    d. A warm site

       Answer: a

       The correct answer is a. Warm and cold sites require more work after the event occurs to get them to full operating functionality. A "mobile" backup site might be useful for specific types of minor outages, but a hot site is still the main choice of backup processing site.

6. Which of the following would best describe a "cold" backup site?

    a. A computer facility with electrical power and HVAC, all needed applications installed and configured on the file/print servers, and enough workstations present to begin processing

    b. A computer facility with electrical power and HVAC but with no workstations or servers on-site prior to the event and no applications installed

    c. A computer facility with no electrical power or HVAC

    d. A computer facility available with electrical power and HVAC and some file/print servers, although the applications are not installed or configured and all of the needed workstations may not be on site or ready to begin processing

       Answer: b

       The correct answer is b. A computer facility with electrical power and HVAC, with workstations and servers available to be brought on-site when the event begins and no applications installed, is a cold site. Answer a is a hot site, and d is a warm site. Answer c is just an empty room.

7. Which of the following is NOT considered a natural disaster?

    a. Earthquake

    b. Sabotage

    c. Tsunami

    d. Flood

       Answer: b

8. What could be a major disadvantage to a "mutual aid" or "reciprocal" type of backup service agreement?

    a. It is free or at a low cost to the organization.

    b. The use of prefabricated buildings makes recovery easier.

    c. In a major emergency, the site might not have the capacity to handle the operations required.

    d. Annual testing by the Info Tech department is required to maintain the site.

       Answer: c

       The correct answer is c. The site might not have the capacity to handle the operations required during a major disruptive event.

While mutual aid might be a good system for sharing resources during a small or isolated outage, a major natural or other type of disaster can create serious resource contention between the two organizations.

9. What is considered the major disadvantage to employing a "hot" site for disaster recovery?

    a. Exclusivity is assured for processing at the site.

    b. Maintaining the site is expensive.

    c. The site is immediately available for recovery.

    d. Annual testing is required to maintain the site.

    Answer: b

    The correct answer is b, the expense of maintaining the site. A hot site is commonly used for those extremely time-critical functions that the business must have up and running to continue operating, but the expense of duplicating and maintaining all of the hardware, software, and application elements is a serious resource drain to most organizations.

10. When is the disaster considered to be officially over?

    a. When the danger has passed and the disaster has been contained

    b. When the organization has processing up and running at the alternate site

    c. When all of the elements of the business have returned to normal functioning at the original site

    d. When all employees have been financially reimbursed for their expenses

    Answer: c

    The correct answer is c: when all of the elements of the business have returned to normal functioning at the original site. It's important to remember that a threat to continuity exists when processing is being returned to its original site after salvage and cleanup has been done.

11. What is the number one priority of disaster response?

    a. Transaction processing

    b. Personnel safety

    c. Protecting the hardware

    d. Protecting the software

    Answer: b

    The correct answer is b. The number one function of all disaster response and recovery is the protection of the safety of people; all other concerns are vital to business continuity but are secondary to personnel safety.

12. Put the five disaster recovery testing types in their proper order, from the least extensive to the most:

    a. Full-interruption

    b. Checklist

    c. Structured walk-through

    d. Parallel

    e. Simulation

    Answer: b, c, e, d, a

13. What is the difference between a "parallel" disaster recovery plan test and a "full interruption" disaster recovery plan test?

    a. There is no difference; both terms mean the same thing.

    b. While a full-interruption test tests the processing functionality of the alternate site, the parallel test actually replicates a disaster by halting production.

    c. While a parallel test tests the processing functionality of the alternate site, the full-interruption test actually replicates a disaster by halting production.

    d. Functional business unit representatives meet to review the plan to ensure it accurately reflects the organization's recovery strategy.

    Answer: c

    The correct answer is c. A parallel test tests the processing functionality of the alternate site, whereas the full-interruption test actually replicates a disaster by halting production. Answer d is the definition of a checklist test type.

14. Which of the following is NOT one of the primary goals of a BIA?

    a. Resource requirements

    b. Personnel safety

    c. Criticality prioritization

    d. Downtime estimation

    Answer: b

    The correct answer is b. Personnel safety is the primary priority of BCP and DRP, not BIA.

Bonus Questions

1. Which choice below is the BEST description of the criticality prioritization goal of the Business Impact Assessment (BIA) process?

    a. The identification and prioritization of every critical business unit process

    b. The identification of the resource requirements of the critical business unit processes

c. The estimation of the maximum down time the business can tolerate

d. The presentation of the documentation of the results of the BIA

Answer: a

The correct answer is a. The three primary goals of a BIA are criticality prioritization, maximum down time estimation, and identification of critical resource requirements. Answer d is a distracter.

2. Which choice below is most accurate regarding the information needed to define the continuity strategy?

a. A strategy needs to be defined to preserve computing elements, such as hardware, software, and networking elements.

b. The strategy needs to address facility use during a disruptive event.

c. The strategy needs to define personnel roles in implementing continuity.

d. All of the above.

Answer: d

The correct answer is d. All of the answers are correct.

3. Which choice below is NOT an element of BCP plan approval and implementation?

a. Creating an awareness of the plan

b. Executing a disaster scenario and documenting the results

c. Obtaining senior management approval of the results

d. Updating the plan regularly and as needed

Answer: b

The correct answer is b. Answer b is a distracter, although it could be considered a loose description of disaster recovery plan testing. The other three choices are primary elements of BCP approval, implementation, and maintenance.

4. Which choice below would NOT be a good reason to test the disaster recovery plan?

a. Testing verifies the processing capability of the alternate backup site.

b. Testing allows processing to continue at the database shadowing facility.

c. Testing prepares and trains the personnel to execute their emergency duties.

d. Testing identifies deficiencies in the recovery procedures.

Answer: b

The correct answer is b. Answer b is a distracter. The other three answers are good reasons to test the disaster recovery plan.

5. Which statement below is the most accurate about the results of the disaster recovery plan test?

   a. If no deficiencies were found during the test, then the plan is probably perfect.

   b. The results of the test should be kept secret.

   c. If no deficiencies were found during the test, then the test was probably flawed.

   d. The plan should not be changed no matter what the results of the test.

      Answer: c

      The correct answer is c. The purpose of the test is to find weaknesses in the plan. Every plan has weaknesses. After the test, all parties should be advised of the results and the plan updated to reflect the new information.

6. Which statement is true regarding company/employee relations during and after a disaster?

   a. The organization has a responsibility to continue salaries or other funding to the employees and/or families affected by the disaster.

   b. The organization's responsibility to the employee's families ends when the disaster stops the business from functioning.

   c. Employees should seek any means of obtaining compensation after a disaster, including fraudulent ones.

   d. Senior-level executives are the only employees who should receive continuing salaries during the disruptive event.

      Answer: a

      The correct answer is a. The organization has an inherent responsibility to its employees and their families during and after a disaster or other disruptive event. The company must be insured to the extent it can properly compensate its employees and families. Alternatively, employees do not have the right to obtain compensatory damages fraudulently if the organization cannot compensate.

7. Which statement below is NOT true regarding the relationship of the organization with the media during and after a disaster?

   a. The organization should establish a unified organizational response to the media during and after the disruptive event.

   b. The organization must avoid dealing with the media at all costs during and after the disruptive event.

   c. The company's response should be delivered by a credible, informed spokesperson.

   d. The company should be honest and accurate about what they know about the event and its effects.

Answer: b

The correct answer is b.

8. Which statement is true regarding the disbursement of funds during and after a disruptive event?

   a. Because access to funds is rarely an issue during a disaster, no special arrangements need to be made.

   b. No one but the finance department should ever disburse funds during or after a disruptive event.

   c. In the event senior-level or financial management is unable to disburse funds normally, the company will need to file for bankruptcy.

   d. Authorized, signed checks should be stored securely off-site for access by lower-level managers in the event senior-level or financial management is unable to disburse funds normally.

   Answer: d

   The correct answer is d.

9. Which statement below is NOT true about the post-disaster salvage team?

   a. The salvage team must return to the site as soon as possible regardless of the residual physical danger.

   b. The salvage team manages the cleaning of equipment after smoke damage.

   c. The salvage team identifies sources of expertise to employ in the recovery of equipment or supplies.

   d. The salvage team may be given the authority to declare when operations can resume at the disaster site.

   Answer: a

   The correct answer is a. Salvage cannot begin until all physical danger has been removed or mitigated and emergency personnel have returned control of the site to the organization.

10. Which statement below is NOT correct regarding the role of the recovery team during the disaster?

    a. The recovery team must be the same as the salvage team as they perform the same function.

    b. The recovery team is often separate from the salvage team as they perform different duties.

    c. The recovery team's primary task is to get predefined critical business functions operating at the alternate processing site.

    d. The recovery team will need full access to all backup media.

    Answer: a

    The correct answer is a. The recovery team performs different functions from the salvage team. The recovery team's primary mandate is to get critical processing re-established at an alternate site. The salvage team's primary mandate is to return the original processing site to normal processing environmental conditions.

Chapter 9—Law, Investigation, and Ethics

Sample Questions

1. According to the Internet Activities Board (IAB), an activity that causes which of the following is considered a violation of ethical behavior on the Internet?

   a. Wasting resources

   b. Appropriating other people's intellectual output

   c. Using a computer to steal

   d. Using a computer to bear false witness

   > *Answer:* a

   > The correct answer is a. Answers b, c, and d are ethical considerations of other organizations.

2. Which of the following best defines social engineering?

   a. Illegal copying of software

   b. Gathering information from discarded manuals and printouts

   c. Using people skills to obtain proprietary information

   d. Destruction or alteration of data

   > *Answer:* c

   > The correct answer is c. Using people skills to obtain proprietary information. Answer a is software piracy; answer b is dumpster diving; and answer d is a violation of integrity.

3. Because the development of new technology usually outpaces the law, law enforcement uses which traditional laws to prosecute computer criminals?

   a. Malicious mischief

   b. Embezzlement, fraud, and wiretapping

   c. Immigration

   d. Conspiracy and elimination of competition

   > *Answer:* b

   > The correct answer is b. Answer a is not a law; answer c is not applicable because it applies to obtaining visas and so on; and answer d is not correct because the crimes in answer b are more commonly used to prosecute computer crimes.

4. Which of the following is NOT a category of law under the Common Law System?

    a. Criminal law

    b. Civil law

    c. Administrative/Regulatory law

    d. Derived law

      Answer: d

      The correct answer is d. It is a distracter, and all of the other answers are categories under common law.

5. A trade secret:

    a. Provides the owner with a legally enforceable right to exclude others from practicing the art covered for a specified time period.

    b. Protects "original" works of authorship.

    c. Secures and maintains the confidentiality of proprietary technical or business-related information that is adequately protected from disclosure by the owner.

    d. Is a word, name, symbol, color, sound, product shape, or device used to identify goods and to distinguish them from those made or sold by others.

      Answer: c

      The correct answer is c. It defines a trade secret. Answer a refers to a patent. Answer b refers to a copyright. Answer d refers to a trademark.

6. Which of the following is NOT a European Union (EU) principle?

    a. Data should be collected in accordance with the law.

    b. Transmission of personal information to locations where "equivalent" personal data protection cannot be assured is permissible.

    c. Data should be used only for the purposes for which it was collected and should be used only for reasonable period of time.

    d. Information collected about an individual cannot be disclosed to other organizations or individuals unless authorized by law or by consent of the individual.

      Answer: b

      The correct answer is b. The transmission of data to locations where "equivalent" personal data protection cannot be assured is NOT permissible. The other answers are EU principles.

7. The Federal Sentencing Guidelines:

    a. Hold senior corporate officers personally liable if their organizations do not comply with the law.

    b. Prohibit altering, damaging, or destroying information in a federal interest computer.

   c. Prohibit eavesdropping or the interception of message contents.

   d. Established a category of sensitive information called Sensitive But Unclassified (SBU).

> *Answer:* a
>
> The correct answer is a. Answer b is part of the U.S. Computer Fraud and Abuse Act. Answer c is part of the U.S. Electronic Communications Privacy Act. Answer d is part of the U.S. Computer Security Act.

8. What does the prudent man rule require?

   a. Senior officials to post performance bonds for their actions

   b. Senior officials to perform their duties with the care that ordinary, prudent people would exercise under similar circumstances

   c. Senior officials to guarantee that all precautions have been taken and that no breaches of security can occur

   d. Senior officials to follow specified government standards

> *Answer:* b
>
> The correct answer is b. Answer a is a distracter and is not part of the prudent man rule. Answer c is incorrect because it is not possible to guarantee that breaches of security can never occur. Answer d is incorrect because the prudent man rule does not refer to a specific government standard but relates to what other prudent persons would do.

9. Information Warfare is:

   a. Attacking the information infrastructure of a nation to gain military and/or economic advantages.

   b. Developing weapons systems based on artificial intelligence technology.

   c. Generating and disseminating propaganda material.

   d. Signal intelligence.

> *Answer:* a
>
> The correct answer is a. Answer b is a distracter and has to do with weapon systems development. Answer c is not applicable. Answer d is the conventional acquisition of information from radio signals.

10. The chain of evidence relates to:

   a. Securing laptops to desks during an investigation.

   b. DNA testing.

   c. Handling and controlling evidence.

   d. Making a disk image.

> *Answer:* c
>
> The correct answer is c. Answer a relates to physical security; answer b is a type of biological testing; and answer d is part of the act of gathering evidence.

11. The Kennedy-Kassebaum Act is also known as:

    a. RICO

    b. OECD

    c. HIPAA

    d. EU Directive

    Answer: c

    The correct answer is c. The others refer to other laws or guidelines.

12. Which of the following refers to a U.S. Government program that reduces or eliminates emanations from electronic equipment?

    a. CLIPPER

    b. ECHELON

    c. ECHO

    d. TEMPEST

    Answer: d

    The correct answer is d. Answer a refers to the U.S. government Escrowed Encryption Standard. Answer b refers to the large-scale monitoring of RF transmissions. Answer c is a distracter.

13. Imprisonment is a possible sentence under:

    a. Civil (tort) law

    b. Criminal law

    c. Both civil and criminal law

    d. Neither civil nor criminal law

    Answer: b

    The correct answer is b. It is the only one of the choices where imprisonment is possible.

14. Which one of the following conditions must be met if legal electronic monitoring of employees is conducted by an organization?

    a. Employees must be unaware of the monitoring activity.

    b. All employees must agree with the monitoring policy.

    c. Results of the monitoring cannot be used against the employee.

    d. The organization must have a policy stating that all employees are regularly notified that monitoring is being conducted.

    Answer: d

    The correct answer is d. Answer a is incorrect because employees must be made aware of the monitoring if it is to be legal; answer b is incorrect because employees do not have to agree with the policy; and answer c is incorrect because the results of monitoring might be used against the employee if the corporate policy is violated.

15. Which of the following is a key principle in the evolution of computer crime laws in many countries?

    a. All members of the United Nations have agreed to uniformly define and prosecute computer crime.

    b. Existing laws against embezzlement, fraud, and wiretapping cannot be applied to computer crime.

    c. The definition of property was extended to include electronic information.

    d. Unauthorized acquisition of computer-based information without the intent to resell is not a crime.

    Answer: c

    The correct answer is c. Answer a is incorrect because all nations do not agree on the definition of computer crime and corresponding punishments. Answer b is incorrect because the existing laws can be applied against computer crime. Answer d is incorrect because in some countries, possession without intent to sell is considered a crime.

16. The concept of Due Care states that senior organizational management must ensure that:

    a. All risks to an information system are eliminated.

    b. Certain requirements must be fulfilled in carrying out their responsibilities to the organization.

    c. Other management personnel are delegated the responsibility for information system security.

    d. The cost of implementing safeguards is greater than the potential resultant losses resulting from information security breaches.

    Answer: b

    The correct answer is b. Answer a is incorrect because all risks to information systems cannot be eliminated; answer c is incorrect because senior management cannot delegate its responsibility for information system security under due care; and answer d is incorrect because the cost of implementing safeguards should be less than or equal to the potential resulting losses relative to the exercise of due care.

17. Liability of senior organizational officials relative to the protection of the organizations information systems is prosecutable under:

    a. Criminal law.

    b. Civil law.

    c. International law.

    d. Financial law.

    Answer: b

18. Responsibility for handling computer crimes in the United States is assigned to:

    a. The Federal Bureau of Investigation (FBI) and the Secret Service.

    b. The FBI only.

    c. The National Security Agency (NSA).

    d. The Central Intelligence Agency (CIA).

       Answer: a

       The correct answer is a, making the other answers incorrect.

19. In general, computer-based evidence is considered:

    a. Conclusive.

    b. Circumstantial.

    c. Secondary.

    d. Hearsay.

       Answer: d

       The correct answer is d. Answer a refers to incontrovertible evidence; answer b refers to inference from other, intermediate facts; and answer c refers to a copy of evidence or oral description of its content.

20. Investigating and prosecuting computer crimes is made more difficult because:

    a. Backups may be difficult to find.

    b. Evidence is mostly intangible.

    c. Evidence cannot be preserved.

    d. Evidence is hearsay and can never be introduced into a court of law.

       Answer: b

       The correct answer is b. Answer a is incorrect because if backups are done, they usually can be located. Answer c is incorrect because evidence can be preserved using the proper procedures. Answer d is incorrect because there are exceptions to the hearsay rule.

21. Which of the following criteria are used to evaluate suspects in the commission of a crime?

    a. Motive, Intent, and Ability

    b. Means, Object, and Motive

    c. Means, Intent, and Motive

    d. Motive, Means, and Opportunity

       Answer: d

22. 18 U.S.C. §2001 (1994) refers to:

    a. Article 18, U.S. Code, Section 2001, 1994 edition.

    b. Title 18, University of Southern California, Article 2001, 1994 edition.

   c. Title 18, Section 2001 of the U.S. Code, 1994 edition.

   d. Title 2001 of the U.S. Code, Section 18, 1994 edition.

     Answer: c

23. What is enticement?

   a. Encouraging the commission of a crime when there was initially no intent to commit a crime

   b. Assisting in the commission of a crime

   c. Luring the perpetrator to an attractive area or presenting the perpetrator with a lucrative target after the crime has already been initiated

   d. Encouraging the commission of one crime over another

     Answer: c

     The correct answer is c, the definition of enticement. Answer a is the definition of entrapment. Answers b and d are distracters.

24. Which of the following is NOT a computer investigation issue?

   a. Evidence is easy to obtain.

   b. The time frame for investigation is compressed.

   c. An expert may be required to assist.

   d. The information is intangible.

     Answer: a

     The correct answer is a. In many instances, evidence is difficult to obtain in computer crime investigations. Answers b, c, and d are computer investigation issues.

25. Conducting a search without the delay of obtaining a warrant if destruction of evidence seems imminent is possible under:

   a. Federal Sentencing Guidelines.

   b. Proximate Causation.

   c. Exigent Circumstances.

   d. Prudent Man Rule.

     Answer: c

     The correct answer is c. The other answers refer to other principles, guidelines, or rules.

Bonus Questions

1. The U.S. Government Tempest program was established to thwart which one of the following types of attacks?

   a. Denial of Service

   b. Emanation Eavesdropping

    c. Software Piracy

    d. Dumpster Diving

        Answer: b

        The correct answer is b. The Tempest program required shielding and other emanation reducing safeguards to be employed on computers processing classified data. The other answers are types of attacks against computers, but are not the focus of the Tempest program.

2. Which entity of the U.S. legal system makes "common laws?"

    a. Administrative agencies

    b. Legislative branch

    c. Executive branch

    d. Judicial branch

        Answer: d

        The correct answer is d. The judicial decisions made in the courts generate common law. Answer a, administrative agencies, create administrative laws and the legislative branch, answer b, generates statutory laws. The executive branch, answer c, does not make laws.

3. Which one of the following items is NOT TRUE concerning the Platform for Privacy Preferences (P3P) developed by the World Wide Web Consortium (W3C)?

    a. It allows Web sites to express their privacy practices in a standard format that can be retrieved automatically and interpreted easily by user agents.

    b. It allows users to be informed of site practices in human-readable format.

    c. It does not provide the site privacy practices to users in machine-readable format.

    d. It automates decision-making based on the site's privacy practices when appropriate.

        Answer: c

        The correct answer is c. In addition to the capabilities in answers a, b, and d, P3P does provide the site privacy practices to users in machine-readable format.

4. Which one of the following is NOT a recommended practice regarding electronic monitoring of employees' email?

    a. Apply monitoring in a consistent fashion.

    b. Provide individuals being monitored with a guarantee of email privacy.

    c. Inform all that e-mail is being monitored by means of a prominent log-in banner.

    d. Explain who is authorized to read monitored email.

Answer: b

The correct answer is b. No guarantee of e-mail privacy should be provided or implied by the employer.

5. Discovery, recording, collection, and preservation are part of what process related to the gathering of evidence?

   a. Admissibility of evidence

   b. The chain of evidence

   c. The evidence life cycle

   d. Relevance of evidence

   Answer: c

   The correct answer is c. The evidence life cycle covers the evidence gathering and application process. Answer a refers to certain requirements that evidence must meet to be admissible in court. Answer b, the chain of evidence, is comprised of steps that must be followed to protect the evidence. Relevance of evidence, answer d, is one of the requirements of evidence admissibility.

6. Relative to legal evidence, which one of the following correctly describes the difference between an expert and a nonexpert in delivering an opinion?

   a. An expert can offer an opinion based on personal expertise and facts, but a nonexpert can testify only as to facts.

   b. A nonexpert can offer an opinion based on personal expertise and facts, but an expert can testify only as to facts.

   c. An expert can offer an opinion based on personal expertise and facts, but a nonexpert can testify only as to personal opinion.

   d. An expert can offer an opinion based on facts only, but a nonexpert can testify only as to personal opinion.

   Answer: a

   The correct answer is a. The other answers are distracters.

7. What principle requires corporate officers to institute appropriate protections regarding the corporate intellectual property?

   a. Need-to-know

   b. Due care

   c. Least privilege

   d. Separation of duties

   Answer: b

   The correct answer is b. The Federal Sentencing Guidelines state, "The officers must exercise due care or reasonable care to carry out their responsibilities to the organization." The other answers are information security principles but are distracters in this instance.

8. If C represents the cost of instituting safeguards in an information system and L is the estimated loss resulting from exploitation of the corresponding vulnerability, a legal liability exists if the safeguards are not implemented when:

   a. C/L = a constant

   b. $C > L$

   c. $C < L$

   d. $C = 2L$

   > *Answer:* c
   >
   > The correct answer is c. If the cost to implement the safeguards is less than the estimated loss that would occur if the corresponding vulnerability were successfully exploited, then a legal liability exists. The other answers are distracters.

Chapter 10—Physical Security

Sample Questions

1. The recommended optimal relative humidity range for computer operations is:

   a. 10%–30%

   b. 30%–40%

   c. 40%–60%

   d. 60%–80%

   > *Answer:* c
   >
   > The correct answer is c. 40% to 60% relative humidity is recommended for safe computer operations. Too low humidity can create static discharge problems, and too high humidity can create condensation and electrical contact problems.

2. How many times should a diskette be formatted to comply with TCSEC Orange Book object reuse recommendations?

   a. Three

   b. Five

   c. Seven

   d. Nine

   > *Answer:* c
   >
   > The correct answer is c. Most computer certification and accreditation standards recommend that diskettes be formatted seven times to prevent any possibility of data remanence.

3. Which of the following more closely describes the combustibles in a Class B-rated fire?

   a. Paper

   b. Gas

   c. Liquid

   d. Electrical

   > *Answer:* c
   >
   > The correct answer is c. Paper is described as a common combustible and is therefore rated a class A fire. An electrical fire is rated Class C. Gas is not defined as a combustible.

4. Which of the following is NOT the proper suppression medium for a Class B fire?

   a. CO_2

   b. Soda Acid

   c. Halon

   d. Water

   > *Answer:* d
   >
   > The correct answer is d. Water is not a proper suppression medium for a class B fire. The other three are commonly used.

5. What does an audit trail or access log usually NOT record?

   a. How often a diskette was formatted

   b. Who attempted access

   c. The date and time of the access attempt

   d. Whether the attempt was successful

   > *Answer:* a
   >
   > The correct answer is a, how often a diskette was formatted. The other three answers are common elements of an access log or audit trail.

6. A brownout can be defined as a:

   a. Prolonged power loss.

   b. Momentary low voltage.

   c. Prolonged low voltage.

   d. Momentary high voltage.

   > *Answer:* c
   >
   > The correct answer is c. Answer a, prolonged power loss, is a blackout; answer b, momentary low voltage, is a sag; and d, momentary high voltage, is a spike.

7. A surge can be defined as a(n):

   a. Prolonged high voltage

   b. Initial surge of power at start

    c. Momentary power loss

    d. Steady interfering disturbance

       Answer: a

       The correct answer is a. Answer b, initial surge of power at start or power on, is called an inrush; c, momentary power loss, is a fault; and d, a steady interfering disturbance, is called noise.

8. Which is NOT a type of a fire detector?

    a. Heat-sensing

    b. Gas-discharge

    c. Flame-actuated

    d. Smoke-actuated

       Answer: b

       The correct answer is b. Gas-discharge is a type of fire extinguishing system, not a fire detection system.

9. Which of the following is NOT considered an acceptable replacement for Halon discharge systems?

    a. FA200

    b. Inergen (IG541)

    c. Halon 1301

    d. Argon (IG55)

       Answer: c

       The correct answer is c. Existing installations are encouraged to replace Halon 1301 with one of the substitutes listed.

10. Which type of fire extinguishing method contains standing water in the pipe, and therefore generally does not enable a manual shutdown of systems before discharge?

    a. Dry Pipe

    b. Wet pipe

    c. Preaction

    d. Deluge

       Answer: b

       The correct answer is b. The other three are variations on a dry pipe discharge method with the water not standing in the pipe until a fire is detected.

11. Which type of control below is NOT an example of a physical security access control?

    a. Retinal scanner

    b. Guard dog

    c. Five-key programmable lock

    d. Audit trail

      Answer: d

12. Which is NOT a recommended way to dispose of unwanted used data media?

    a. Destroying CD-ROMs

    b. Formatting diskettes seven or more times

    c. Shredding paper reports by cleared personnel

    d. Copying new data over existing data on diskettes

      Answer: d

      The correct answer is d, copying new data over existing data on diskettes. While this method might overwrite the older files, if the new data file is smaller than the older data file, recoverable data might exist past the file end marker of the new file.

13. Which of the following is an example of a "smart" card?

    a. A driver's license

    b. A bank ATM card

    c. An employee photo ID

    d. A library card

      Answer: b

      The correct answer is b. The other three cards are "dumb" cards because it is assumed that they contain no electronics, magnetic stripes, or integrated circuits.

14. Which is NOT an element of two-factor authentication?

    a. Something you are

    b. Something you know

    c. Something you have

    d. Something you ate

      Answer: d

15. The theft of a laptop poses a threat to which tenet of the C.I.A. triad?

    a. Confidentiality

    b. Integrity

    c. Availability

    d. All of the above

      Answer: d

      The correct answer is d, confidentiality, because the data can now be read by someone outside of a monitored environment; availability, because the user has lost the computing ability provided by the unit; and integrity, because the data residing on and any telecommunications from the portable are now suspect.

16. Which is a benefit of a guard over an automated control?

    a. Guards can use discriminating judgment.

    b. Guards are cheaper.

    c. Guards do not need training.

    d. Guards do not need pre-employment screening.

    Answer: a

    The correct answer is a. Guards can use discriminating judgment. Guards are typically more expensive than automated controls, need training as to the protection requirements of the specific site, and need to be screened and bonded.

17. Which is NOT considered a preventative security measure?

    a. Fences

    b. Guards

    c. Audit trails

    d. Preset locks

    Answer: c

    The correct answer is c. Audit trails are detective, rather than preventative, because they are used to piece together the information of an intrusion or intrusion attempt after the fact.

18. Which is NOT a PC security control device?

    a. A cable lock

    b. A switch control

    c. A port control

    d. A file cabinet lock

    Answer: d

    The correct answer is d. A cable lock is used to attach the PC to a desk; a switch control is used to prevent powering off of a unit; and a port control (such as a diskette drive lock) is used to prevent data from being downloaded from the PC.

19. What is the recommended height of perimeter fencing to keep out casual trespassers?

    a. 1′ to 2′ high

    b. 3′ to 4′ high

    c. 6′ to 7′ high

    d. 8′ to 12′ high

    Answer: b

The correct answer is b. 3' to 4' high fencing is considered minimal protection, only for restricting casual trespassers. Answers c and d are better protection against intentional intruders.

20. Why should extensive exterior perimeter lighting of entrances or parking areas be installed?

    a. To enable programmable locks to be used

    b. To create two-factor authentication

    c. To discourage prowlers or casual intruders

    d. To prevent data remanence

      Answer: c

      The correct answer is c. The other answers have nothing to do with lighting.

21. Which of the following is NOT a form of data erasure?

    a. Clearing

    b. Remanence

    c. Purging

    d. Destruction

      Answer: b

      The correct answer is b. Clearing refers to the overwriting of data media intended to be reused in same organization. Purging refers to degaussing or overwriting media intended to be removed from the organization. Destruction refers to completely destroying the media.

22. Which is NOT considered a physical intrusion detection method?

    a. Audio motion detector

    b. Photoelectric sensor

    c. Wave pattern motion detector

    d. Line supervision

      Answer: d

      The correct answer is d. Line supervision is the monitoring of the alarm signaling transmission medium to detect tampering. Audio detectors monitor a room for any abnormal sound wave generation. Photoelectric sensors receive a beam of light from a light-emitting device. Wave pattern motion detectors generate a wave pattern and send an alarm if the pattern is disturbed.

Bonus Questions

1. Which type of fire extinguisher below should be used on an electrical fire?

    a. Water

    b. Soda Acid

   c. CO_2

   d. Kerosene

     Answer: c

     The correct answer is c. The most common electrical fire suppression mediums for an electrical or electronic fire are CO_2, Halon, and its substitutes, including several inert gas agents.

2. Which type of fire detectors sends an alarm when the temperature of the room rises dramatically?

   a. Heat-sensing

   b. Odor-sensing

   c. Smoke-actuated

   d. Flame-actuated

     Answer: a

     The correct answer is a. A "rate-of-rise" detector triggers an alarm when the ambient temperature of a room increases rapidly. Another type of heat-sensing detector, a fixed temperature device, sends an alarm when the temperature passes a predetermined level.

3. Which medium below is the most sensitive to damage from temperature?

   a. Computer hardware

   b. Floppy diskettes

   c. Paper products

   d. Sheet rock

     Answer: b

     The correct answer is b. Of the four choices, magnetic media is the most sensitive to damage from heat, smoke, water, and humidity.

4. Which choice below is the BEST description of a Central Station Alarm System?

   a. Rings an audible alarm on the local premises that it protects

   b. Rings an alarm in a central monitoring office of a third-party monitoring firm

   c. Rings an alarm in the office of the customer

   d. Also rings an alarm in the local fire or police station

     Answer: b

     The correct answer is b. Answer a describes a Local Alarm System. Answer c describes a Proprietary System, and answer d describes an Auxiliary Station System.

5. Which choice below is NOT a type of motion detector?

   a. Wave pattern detection

   b. Capacitance detection

   c. Smoke detection

   d. Audio detection

     Answer: c

     The correct answer is c. The other three are examples of intrusion detectors designed to sense unusual movement within a defined interior security area.

6. Which choice below BEST describes the process of data purging?

   a. Overwriting of data media intended to be reused in the same organization or area

   b. Degaussing or thoroughly overwriting media intended to be removed the control of the organization or area

   c. Complete physical destruction of the media

   d. Reusing data storage media after its initial use

     Answer: b

     The correct answer is b. Answer a refers to data clearing. Answer c describes data destruction, and answer d describes object reuse.

7. Which choice below BEST describes a power sag?

   a. Complete loss of power

   b. Momentary high voltage

   c. Prolonged high voltage

   d. Momentary low voltage

     Answer: d

     The correct answer is d. Answer a is a blackout, answer b is a spike, and answer c is a surge.

8. Which choice below BEST describes a mantrap?

   a. A physical access control using at least 6′ to 7′ high fencing

   b. A physical access control using double doors and a guard

   c. A physical access control using flood lighting

   d. A physical access control using CCTV

     Answer: b

     The correct answer is b.

9. Which choice below describes the reason for using cable locks on workstations?

   a. To prevent unauthorized access to the network from the unit

   b. To prevent the robbery of the unit

   c. To prevent unauthorized downloading of data to the unit's floppy drive

   d. To prevent the unit from being powered on

     Answer: b

The correct answer is b. Answer a is a distracter. Answer c describes port locks or controls. Answer d describes switch controls.

10. Which choice below is not a description or element of a raised floor?
    a. A platform with removable panels where equipment is installed
    b. Flooring with space between it and the main building floor housing cabling
    c. Raised area used to supply conditioned air to the data processing equipment and room
    d. Area used for storage of paper files

    Answer: d

    The correct answer is d. The other three are all legitimate uses/elements of raised flooring (NFPA 75 1999 Edition).

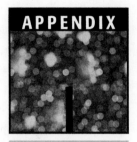

Answers to Advanced Sample Questions

Chapter 1—Security Management Practices

1. Which choice below most accurately reflects the goals of risk mitigation?
   a. Defining the acceptable level of risk the organization can tolerate, and reducing risk to that level
   b. Analyzing and removing all vulnerabilities and threats to security within the organization
   c. Defining the acceptable level of risk the organization can tolerate, and assigning any costs associated with loss or disruption to a third party, such as an insurance carrier
   d. Analyzing the effects of a business disruption and preparing the company's response

   Answer: a

   The correct answer is a. The goal of risk mitigation is to reduce risk to a level acceptable to the organization. Therefore risk needs to be defined for the organization through risk analysis, business impact assessment, and/or vulnerability assessment.

Answer b is not possible. Answer c is called risk transference. Answer d is a distracter.

2. Which answer below is the BEST description of a Single Loss Expectancy (SLE)?

a. An algorithm that represents the magnitude of a loss to an asset from a threat

b. An algorithm that expresses the annual frequency with which a threat is expected to occur

c. An algorithm used to determine the monetary impact of each occurrence of a threat

d. An algorithm that determines the expected annual loss to an organization from a threat

Answer: c

The correct answer is c. The Single Loss Expectancy (or Exposure) figure may be created as a result of a Business Impact Assessment (BIA). The SLE represents only the estimated monetary loss of a single occurrence of a specified threat event. The SLE is determined by multiplying the value of the asset by its exposure factor. This gives the expected loss the threat will cause for one occurrence.

Answer a describes the Exposure Factor (EF). The EF is expressed as a percentile of the expected value or functionality of the asset to be lost due to the realized threat event. This figure is used to calculate the SLE, above.

Answer b describes the Annualized Rate of Occurrence (ARO). This is an estimate of how often a given threat event may occur annually. For example, a threat expected to occur weekly would have an ARO of 52. A threat expected to occur once every five years has an ARO of 1/5 or .2. This figure is used to determine the ALE.

Answer d describes the Annualized Loss Expectancy (ALE). The ALE is derived by multiplying the SLE by its ARO. This value represents the expected risk factor of an annual threat event. This figure is then integrated into the risk management process.

3. Which choice below is the BEST description of an Annualized Loss Expectancy (ALE)?

a. The expected risk factor of an annual threat event, derived by multiplying the SLE by its ARO

b. An estimate of how often a given threat event may occur annually

    c. The percentile of the value of the asset expected to be lost, used to calculate the SLE

    d. A value determined by multiplying the value of the asset by its exposure factor

> *Answer:* a
>
> Answer b describes the Annualized Rate of Occurrence (ARO).
>
> Answer c describes the Exposure Factor (EF).
>
> Answer d describes the algorithm to determine the Single Loss Expectancy (SLE) of a threat.

4. Which choice below is NOT an example of appropriate security management practice?

    a. Reviewing access logs for unauthorized behavior

    b. Monitoring employee performance in the workplace

    c. Researching information on new intrusion exploits

    d. Promoting and implementing security awareness programs

> *Answer:* b
>
> Monitoring employee performance is not an example of security management, or a job function of the Information Security Officer. Employee performance issues are the domain of human resources and the employee's manager. The other three choices are appropriate practice for the information security area.

5. Which choice below is an accurate statement about standards?

    a. Standards are the high-level statements made by senior management in support of information systems security.

    b. Standards are the first element created in an effective security policy program.

    c. Standards are used to describe how policies will be implemented within an organization.

    d. Standards are senior management's directives to create a computer security program.

> *Answer:* c
>
> Answers a, b, and d describe policies. Guidelines, standards, and procedures often accompany policy, but always follow the senior level management's statement of policy. Procedures, standards, and guidelines are used to describe how these policies will be implemented within an organization. Simply put, the three break down as follows:
>
> ■ Standards specify the use of specific technologies in a uniform way (for example, the standardization of operating procedures).

- Guidelines are similar to standards but are recommended actions.
- Procedures are the detailed steps that must be performed for any task.

6. Which choice below is a role of the Information Systems Security Officer?

   a. The ISO establishes the overall goals of the organization's computer security program.

   b. The ISO is responsible for day-to-day security administration.

   c. The ISO is responsible for examining systems to see whether they are meeting stated security requirements.

   d. The ISO is responsible for following security procedures and reporting security problems.

   Answer: b

   Answer a is a responsibility of senior management. Answer c is a description of the role of auditing. Answer d is the role of the user, or consumer, of security in an organization.

7. Which statement below is NOT true about security awareness, training, and educational programs?

   a. Awareness and training help users become more accountable for their actions.

   b. Security education assists management in determining who should be promoted.

   c. Security improves the users' awareness of the need to protect information resources.

   d. Security education assists management in developing the in-house expertise to manage security programs.

   Answer: b

   The purpose of computer security awareness, training, and education is to enhance security by:

   - Improving awareness of the need to protect system resources
   - Developing skills and knowledge so computer users can perform their jobs more securely
   - Building in-depth knowledge, as needed, to design, implement, or operate security programs for organizations and systems

   Making computer system users aware of their security responsibilities and teaching them correct practices helps users change their behavior. It also supports individual accountability because without the knowledge of the necessary security measures and to how to use them, users cannot be truly accountable for their actions. Source: *National Institute of Standards and Technology, An Introduction to Computer Security: The NIST Handbook Special Publication 800-12.*

8. Which choice below is NOT an accurate description of an information policy?

   a. Information policy is senior management's directive to create a computer security program.

   b. An information policy could be a decision pertaining to use of the organization's fax.

   c. Information policy is a documentation of computer security decisions.

   d. Information policies are created after the system's infrastructure has been designed and built.

   Answer: d

   Computer security policy is often defined as the "documentation of computer security decisions." The term "policy" has more than one meaning. Policy is senior management's directives to create a computer security program, establish its goals, and assign responsibilities. The term "policy" is also used to refer to the specific security rules for particular systems. Additionally, policy may refer to entirely different matters, such as the specific managerial decisions setting an organization's e-mail privacy policy or fax security policy.

   A security policy is an important document to develop while designing an information system, early in the System Development Life Cycle (SDLC). The security policy begins with the organization's basic commitment to information security formulated as a general policy statement. The policy is then applied to all aspects of the system design or security solution. Source: *NIST Special Publication 800-27, Engineering Principles for Information Technology Security (A Baseline for Achieving Security).*

9. Which choice below MOST accurately describes the organization's responsibilities during an unfriendly termination?

   a. System access should be removed as quickly as possible after termination.

   b. The employee should be given time to remove whatever files he needs from the network.

   c. Cryptographic keys can remain the employee's property.

   d. Physical removal from the offices would never be necessary.

   Answer: a

Friendly terminations should be accomplished by implementing a standard set of procedures for outgoing or transferring employees. This normally includes:

- Removal of access privileges, computer accounts, authentication tokens.
- The control of keys.
- The briefing on the continuing responsibilities for confidentiality and privacy.
- Return of property.
- Continued availability of data. In both the manual and the electronic worlds this may involve documenting procedures or filing schemes, such as how documents are stored on the hard disk, and how they are backed up. Employees should be instructed whether or not to "clean up" their PC before leaving.
- If cryptography is used to protect data, the availability of cryptographic keys to management personnel must be ensured.

Given the potential for adverse consequences during an unfriendly termination, organizations should do the following:

- System access should be terminated as quickly as possible when an employee is leaving a position under less-than-friendly terms. If employees are to be fired, system access should be removed at the same time (or just before) the employees are notified of their dismissal.
- When an employee notifies an organization of the resignation and it can be reasonably expected that it is on unfriendly terms, system access should be immediately terminated.
- During the "notice of termination" period, it may be necessary to assign the individual to a restricted area and function. This may be particularly true for employees capable of changing programs or modifying the system or applications.
- In some cases, physical removal from the offices may be necessary.

Source: *NIST Special Publication 800-14 Generally Accepted Principles and Practices for Securing Information Technology Systems.*

10. Which choice below is NOT an example of an issue-specific policy?
    a. E-mail privacy policy
    b. Virus-checking disk policy

c. Defined router ACLs

d. Unfriendly employee termination policy

Answer: c

Answer c is an example of a system-specific policy, in this case the router's access control lists. The other three answers are examples of issue-specific policy, as defined by NIST. Issue-specific policies are similar to program policies, in that they are not technically focused. While program policy is traditionally more general and strategic (the organization's computer security program, for example), issue-specific policy is a nontechnical policy addressing a single or specific issue of concern to the organization, such as the procedural guidelines for checking disks brought to work or e-mail privacy concerns. System-specific policy is technically focused and addresses only one computer system or device type. Source: *National Institute of Standards and Technology, An Introduction to Computer Security: The NIST Handbook Special Publication 800-12.*

11. Who has the final responsibility for the preservation of the organization's information?

a. Technology providers

b. Senior management

c. Users

d. Application owners

Answer: b

Various officials and organizational offices are typically involved with computer security. They include the following groups:

■ Senior management

■ Program/functional managers/application owners

■ Computer security management

■ Technology providers

■ Supporting organizations

■ Users

Senior management has the final responsibility through due care and due diligence to preserve the capital of the organization and further its business model through the implementation of a security program. While senior management does not have the functional role of managing security procedures, it has the ultimate responsibility to see that business continuity is preserved.

12. Which choice below is NOT a generally accepted benefit of security awareness, training, and education?

    a. A security awareness program can help operators understand the value of the information.

    b. A security education program can help system administrators recognize unauthorized intrusion attempts.

    c. A security awareness and training program will help prevent natural disasters from occurring.

    d. A security awareness and training program can help an organization reduce the number and severity of errors and omissions.

    Answer: c

    An effective computer security awareness and training program requires proper planning, implementation, maintenance, and periodic evaluation.

    In general, a computer security awareness and training program should encompass the following seven steps:

    1. Identify program scope, goals, and objectives.

    2 Identify training staff.

    3. Identify target audiences.

    4. Motivate management and employees.

    5. Administer the program.

    6. Maintain the program.

    7. Evaluate the program.

    Source: *NIST Special Publication 800-14, Generally Accepted Principles and Practices for Securing Information Technology Systems.*

13. Which choice below is NOT a common information-gathering technique when performing a risk analysis?

    a. Distributing a questionnaire

    b. Employing automated risk assessment tools

    c. Reviewing existing policy documents

    d. Interviewing terminated employees

    Answer: d

    Any combination of the following techniques can be used in gathering information relevant to the IT system within its operational boundary:

    Questionnaire. The questionnaire should be distributed to the applicable technical and nontechnical management personnel who are designing or supporting the IT system.

On-site Interviews. On-site visits also allow risk assessment personnel to observe and gather information about the physical, environmental, and operational security of the IT system.

Document Review. Policy documents, system documentation, and security-related documentation can provide good information about the security controls used by and planned for the IT system.

Use of Automated Scanning Tools. Proactive technical methods can be used to collect system information efficiently.

Source: *NIST Special Publication 800-30, Risk Management Guide for Information Technology Systems.*

14. Which choice below is an incorrect description of a control?

a. Detective controls discover attacks and trigger preventative or corrective controls.

b. Corrective controls reduce the likelihood of a deliberate attack.

c. Corrective controls reduce the effect of an attack.

d. Controls are the countermeasures for vulnerabilities.

Answer: b

Controls are the countermeasures for vulnerabilities. There are many kinds, but generally they are categorized into four types:

■ Deterrent controls reduce the likelihood of a deliberate attack.

■ Preventative controls protect vulnerabilities and make an attack unsuccessful or reduce its impact. Preventative controls inhibit attempts to violate security policy.

■ Corrective controls reduce the effect of an attack.

■ Detective controls discover attacks and trigger preventative or corrective controls. Detective controls warn of violations or attempted violations of security policy and include such controls as audit trails, intrusion detection methods, and checksums.

Source: *Introduction to Risk Analysis, C & A Security Risk Analysis Group* and *NIST Special Publication 800-30, Risk Management Guide for Information Technology Systems.*

15. Which statement below is accurate about the reasons to implement a layered security architecture?

a. A layered security approach is not necessary when using COTS products.

b. A good packet-filtering router will eliminate the need to implement a layered security architecture.

c. A layered security approach is intended to increase the work-factor for an attacker.

d. A layered approach doesn't really improve the security posture of the organization.

Answer: c

Security designs should consider a layered approach to address or protect against a specific threat or to reduce a vulnerability. For example, the use of a packet-filtering router in conjunction with an application gateway and an intrusion detection system combine to increase the work-factor an attacker must expend to successfully attack the system. The need for layered protections is important when commercial-off-the-shelf (COTS) products are used. The current state-of-the-art for security quality in COTS products do not provide a high degree of protection against sophisticated attacks. It is possible to help mitigate this situation by placing several controls in levels, requiring additional work by attackers to accomplish their goals.

Source: *NIST Special Publication 800-27, Engineering Principles for Information Technology Security (A Baseline for Achieving Security).*

16. Which choice below represents an application or system demonstrating a need for a high level of confidentiality protection and controls?

a. Unavailability of the system could result in inability to meet payroll obligations and could cause work stoppage and failure of user organizations to meet critical mission requirements. The system requires 24-hour access.

b. The application contains proprietary business information and other financial information, which if disclosed to unauthorized sources, could cause an unfair advantage for vendors, contractors, or individuals and could result in financial loss or adverse legal action to user organizations.

c. Destruction of the information would require significant expenditures of time and effort to replace. Although corrupted information would present an inconvenience to the staff, most information, and all vital information, is backed up by either paper documentation or on disk.

d. The mission of this system is to produce local weather forecast information that is made available to the news media forecasters and the general public at all times. None of the information requires protection against disclosure.

Answer: b

Although elements of all of the systems described could require specific controls for confidentiality, given the descriptions above, system b fits the definition most closely of a system requiring a very high level of confidentiality. Answer a is an example of a system requiring high availability. Answer c is an example of a system that requires medium integrity controls. Answer d is a system that requires only a low level of confidentiality.

A system may need protection for one or more of the following reasons:

Confidentiality. The system contains information that requires protection from unauthorized disclosure.

Integrity. The system contains information that must be protected from unauthorized, unanticipated, or unintentional modification.

Availability. The system contains information or provides services which must be available on a timely basis to meet mission requirements or to avoid substantial losses.

Source: *NIST Special Publication 800-18, Guide for Developing Security Plans for Information Technology Systems*

17. Which choice below is an accurate statement about the difference between monitoring and auditing?

   a. Monitoring is a one-time event to evaluate security.

   b. A system audit is an ongoing "real-time" activity that examines a system.

   c. A system audit cannot be automated.

   d. Monitoring is an ongoing activity that examines either the system or the users.

   Answer: d

   System audits and monitoring are the two methods organizations use to maintain operational assurance. Although the terms are used loosely within the computer security community, a system audit is a one-time or periodic event to evaluate security, whereas monitoring refers to an ongoing activity that examines either the system or the users. In general, the more "real-time" an activity is, the more it falls into the category of monitoring. Source: *NIST Special Publication 800-14, Generally Accepted Principles and Practices for Securing Information Technology Systems.*

18. Which statement below is accurate about the difference between issue-specific and system-specific policies?

    a. Issue-specific policy is much more technically focused.

    b. System-specific policy is much more technically focused.

    c. System-specific policy is similar to program policy.

    d. Issue-specific policy commonly addresses only one system.

    Answer: b

    Often, managerial computer system security policies are categorized into three basic types:

    ■ Program policy—used to create an organization's computer security program

    ■ Issue-specific policies—used to address specific issues of concern to the organization

    ■ System-specific policies—technical directives taken by management to protect a particular system

    Program policy and issue-specific policy both address policy from a broad level, usually encompassing the entire organization. However, they do not provide sufficient information or direction, for example, to be used in establishing an access control list or in training users on what actions are permitted. System-specific policy fills this need. System-specific policy is much more focused, since it addresses only one system.

    Table A.1 helps illustrate the difference between these three types of policies. Source: *National Institute of Standards and Technology, An Introduction to Computer Security: The NIST Handbook Special Publication 800-12.*

Table A.1   Security Policy Types

POLICY TYPE	DESCRIPTION	EXAMPLE
Program policy	High-level program policy	Senior-level Management Statement
Issue-specific policy	Addresses single issue	Email privacy policy
System-specific policy	Single-system directives	Router Access Control Lists

19. Which statement below most accurately describes the difference between security awareness, security training, and security education?

    a. Security training teaches the skills that will help employees to perform their jobs more securely.

    b. Security education is required for all system operators.

    c. Security awareness is not necessary for high-level senior executives.

    d. Security training is more in depth than security education.

    Answer: a

    Awareness is used to reinforce the fact that security supports the mission of the organization by protecting valuable resources. The purpose of training is to teach people the skills that will enable them to perform their jobs more securely. Security education is more in depth than security training and is targeted for security professionals and those whose jobs require expertise in security. Management commitment is necessary because of the resources used in developing and implementing the program and also because the program affects their staff. Source: *National Institute of Standards and Technology, An Introduction to Computer Security: The NIST Handbook Special Publication 800-12.*

20. Which choice below BEST describes the difference between the System Owner and the Information Owner?

    a. There is a one-to-one relationship between system owners and information owners.

    b. One system could have multiple information owners.

    c. The Information Owner is responsible for defining the system's operating parameters.

    d. The System Owner is responsible for establishing the rules for appropriate use of the information.

    Answer: b

    The System Owner is responsible for ensuring that the security plan is prepared and for implementing the plan and monitoring its effectiveness. The System Owner is responsible for defining the system's operating parameters, authorized functions, and security requirements. The information owner for information stored within, processed by, or transmitted by a system may or may not be the same as the System Owner. Also, a single system may utilize information from multiple Information Owners.

    The Information Owner is responsible for establishing the rules for appropriate use and protection of the subject data/information (rules of behavior). The Information Owner retains that responsibility even when the data/information are shared with other organizations. Source: *NIST Special Publication 800-18, Guide for Developing Security Plans for Information Technology Systems.*

21. Which choice below is NOT an accurate statement about an organization's incident-handling capability?

    a. The organization's incident-handling capability should be used to detect and punish senior-level executive wrong-doing.

    b. It should be used to prevent future damage from incidents.

    c. It should be used to provide the ability to respond quickly and effectively to an incident.

    d. The organization's incident-handling capability should be used to contain and repair damage done from incidents.

    Answer: a

    An organization should address computer security incidents by developing an incident-handling capability. The incident-handling capability should be used to:

    ■ Provide the ability to respond quickly and effectively.

    ■ Contain and repair the damage from incidents. When left unchecked, malicious software can significantly harm an organization's computing, depending on the technology and its connectivity. Containing the incident should include an assessment of whether the incident is part of a targeted attack on the organization or an isolated incident.

    ■ Prevent future damage. An incident-handling capability should assist an organization in preventing (or at least minimizing) damage from future incidents. Incidents can be studied internally to gain a better understanding of the organization's threats and vulnerabilities.

    Source: *NIST Special Publication 800-14, Generally Accepted Principles and Practices for Securing Information Technology Systems.*

22. Place the data classification scheme in order, from the least secure to the most:

    a. Sensitive

    b. Public

    c. Private

    d. Confidential

    Answer: b, c, a, and d

    Various formats for categorizing the sensitivity of data exist. Although originally implemented in government systems, data classification is

Table A.2   A Sample H/M/L Data Classification

CATEGORY	DESCRIPTION
High	Could cause loss of life, imprisonment, major financial loss, or require legal action for correction if the information is compromised.
Medium	Could cause significant financial loss or require legal action for correction if the information is compromised.
Low	Would cause only minor financial loss or require only administrative action for correction if the information is compromised.

very useful in determining the sensitivity of business information to threats to confidentiality, integrity, or availability. Often an organization would use the high, medium, or low categories. This simple classification scheme rates each system by its need for protection based upon its C.I.A. needs, and whether it requires high, medium, or low protective controls. For example, a system and its information may require a high degree of integrity and availability, yet have no need for confidentiality.

Or organizations may categorize data into four sensitivity classifications with separate handling requirements, such as Sensitive, Confidential, Private, and Public.

This system would define the categories as follows:

Sensitive. This classification applies to information that requires special precautions to assure the integrity of the information, by protecting it from unauthorized modification or deletion. It is information that requires a higher-than-normal assurance of accuracy and completeness.

Confidential. This classification applies to the most sensitive business information that is intended strictly for use within the organization. Its unauthorized disclosure could seriously and adversely impact the organization, its stockholders, its business partners, and/or its customers. This information is exempt from disclosure under the provisions of the Freedom of Information Act or other applicable federal laws or regulations.

Private. This classification applies to personal information that is intended for use within the organization. Its unauthorized disclosure could seriously and adversely impact the organization and/or its employees.

Public. This classification applies to all other information that does not clearly fit into any of the preceding three classifications. While its unauthorized disclosure is against policy, it is not expected to impact seriously or adversely the organization, its employees, and/or its customers.

The designated owners of information are responsible for determining data classification levels, subject to executive management review. Table A.2 shows a sample H/M/L data classification for sensitive information. Source: *NIST Special Publication 800-26, Security Self-Assessment Guide for Information Technology Systems.*

23. Place the five system security life-cycle phases in order:

_____ a. Implementation phase

_____ b. Development/acquisition phase

_____ c. Disposal phase

_____ d. Operation/maintenance phase

_____ e. Initiation phase

    Answer: e, b, a, d, c

Security, like other aspects of an IT system, is best managed if planned for throughout the IT system life cycle. There are many models for the IT system life cycle, but most contain five basic phases: initiation, development/acquisition, implementation, operation, and disposal.

The order of these phases is:

a. Initiation phase—During the initiation phase, the need for a system is expressed and the purpose of the system is documented.

b. Development/acquisition phase—During this phase, the system is designed, purchased, programmed, developed, or otherwise constructed.

c. Implementation phase—During implementation, the system is tested and installed or fielded.

d. Operation/maintenance phase—During this phase, the system performs its work. The system is almost always being continuously modified by the addition of hardware and software and by numerous other events.

e. Disposal phase—The disposal phase of the IT system life cycle involves the disposition of information, hardware, and software.

Source: *NIST Special Publication 800-14, Generally Accepted Principles and Practices for Securing Information Technology Systems.*

24. How often should an independent review of the security controls be performed, according to OMB Circular A-130?

a. Every year

b. Every three years

c. Every five years

d. Never

Answer: b

The correct answer is b. OMB Circular A-130 requires that a review of the security controls for each major government application be performed at least every three years. For general support systems, OMB Circular A-130 requires that the security controls be reviewed either by an independent audit or self review. Audits can be self-administered or independent (either internal or external). The essential difference between a self-audit and an independent audit is objectivity; however, some systems may require a fully independent review. Source: Office of Management and Budget Circular A-130, revised November 30, 2000.

25. Which choice below is NOT one of NIST's 33 IT security principles?

a. Implement least privilege.

b. Assume that external systems are insecure.

c. Totally eliminate any level of risk.

d. Minimize the system elements to be trusted.

Answer: c

Risk can never be totally eliminated. NIST IT security principle #4 states: "Reduce risk to an acceptable level." The National Institute of Standards and Technology's (NIST) Information Technology Laboratory (ITL) released NIST Special Publication (SP) 800-27, "Engineering Principles for Information Technology Security (EP-ITS)" in June 2001 to assist in the secure design, development, deployment, and life-cycle of information systems. It presents 33 security principles which start at the design phase of the information system or application and continue until the system's retirement and secure disposal. Some of the other 33 principles are:

Principle 1. Establish a sound security policy as the "foundation" for design.

Principle 2. Treat security as an integral part of the overall system design.

Principle 5. Assume that external systems are insecure.

Principle 6. Identify potential trade-offs between reducing risk and increased costs and decrease in other aspects of operational effectiveness.

Principle 7. Implement layered security (ensure no single point of vulnerability).

Principle 11. Minimize the system elements to be trusted.

Principle 16. Isolate public access systems from mission critical resources (e.g., data, processes, etc.).

Principle 17. Use boundary mechanisms to separate computing systems and network infrastructures.

Principle 22. Authenticate users and processes to ensure appropriate access control decisions both within and across domains.

Principle 23. Use unique identities to ensure accountability.

Principle 24. Implement least privilege.

Source: *NIST Special Publication 800-27, Engineering Principles for Information Technology Security (A Baseline for Achieving Security)*, and "Federal Systems Level Guidance for Securing Information Systems," James Corrie, August 16, 2001.

26. Which choice below would NOT be considered an element of proper user account management?

a. Users should never be rotated out of their current duties.

b. The users' accounts should be reviewed periodically.

c. A process for tracking access authorizations should be implemented.

d. Periodically re-screen personnel in sensitive positions.

Answer: a

Organizations should ensure effective administration of users' computer access to maintain system security, including user account management, auditing, and the timely modification or removal of access. This includes:

User Account Management. Organizations should have a process for requesting, establishing, issuing, and closing user accounts, tracking users and their respective access authorizations, and managing these functions.

Management Reviews. It is necessary to periodically review user accounts. Reviews should examine the levels of access each individual has, conformity with the concept of least privilege, whether all accounts are still active, whether management authorizations are up-to-date, and whether required training has been completed.

Detecting Unauthorized/Illegal Activities. Mechanisms besides auditing and analysis of audit trails should be used to detect unauthorized and illegal acts, such as rotating employees in sensitive positions, which could expose a scam that required an employee's presence, or periodic re-screening of personnel.

Source: *NIST Special Publication 800-14, Generally Accepted Principles and Practices for Securing Information Technology Systems.*

27. Which question below is NOT accurate regarding the process of risk assessment?
    a. The likelihood of a threat must be determined as an element of the risk assessment.
    b. The level of impact of a threat must be determined as an element of the risk assessment.
    c. Risk assessment is the first process in the risk management methodology
    d. Risk assessment is the final result of the risk management methodology.

    Answer: d

    Risk is a function of the likelihood of a given threat-source's exercising a particular potential vulnerability, and the resulting impact of that adverse event on the organization. Risk assessment is the first process in the risk management methodology. The risk assessment process helps organizations identify appropriate controls for reducing or eliminating risk during the risk mitigation process.

    To determine the likelihood of a future adverse event, threats to an IT system must be analyzed in conjunction with the potential vulnerabilities and the controls in place for the IT system. The likelihood that a potential vulnerability could be exercised by a given threat-source can be described as high, medium, or low. Impact refers to the magnitude of harm that could be caused by a threat's exploitation of a vulnerability. The determination of the level of impact produces a relative value for the IT assets and resources affected. Source: *NIST Special Publication 800-30, Risk Management Guide for Information Technology Systems.*

28. Which choice below is NOT an accurate statement about the visibility of IT security policy?
    a. The IT security policy should not be afforded high visibility.
    b. The IT security policy could be visible through panel discussions with guest speakers.
    c. The IT security policy should be afforded high visibility.
    d. Include the IT security policy as a regular topic at staff meetings at all levels of the organization.

    Answer: a

    Especially high visibility should be afforded the formal issuance of IT security policy. This is because nearly all employees at all levels will in some way be affected, major organizational resources are being addressed, and many new terms, procedures, and activities will be introduced.

Including IT security as a regular topic at staff meetings at all levels of the organization can be helpful. Also, providing visibility through such avenues as management presentations, panel discussions, guest speakers, question/answer forums, and newsletters can be beneficial.

29. According to NIST, which choice below is not an accepted security self-testing technique?

    a. War Dialing

    b. Virus Distribution

    c. Password Cracking

    d. Virus Detection

    Answer: b

    Common types of self-testing techniques include:

    ■ Network Mapping

    ■ Vulnerability Scanning

    ■ Penetration Testing

    ■ Password Cracking

    ■ Log Review

    ■ Virus Detection

    ■ War Dialing

    Some testing techniques are predominantly human-initiated and conducted, while other tests are highly automated and require less human involvement. The staff that initiates and implements in-house security testing should have significant security and networking knowledge. These testing techniques are often combined to gain a more comprehensive assessment of the overall network security posture. For example, penetration testing almost always includes network mapping and vulnerability scanning to identify vulnerable hosts and services that may be targeted for later penetration. None of these tests by themselves will provide a complete picture of the network or its security posture. Source: *NIST Special Publication 800-42, DRAFT Guideline on Network Security Testing.*

30. Which choice below is NOT a concern of policy development at the high level?

    a. Identifying the key business resources

    b. Identifying the type of firewalls to be used for perimeter security

    c. Defining roles in the organization

    d. Determining the capability and functionality of each role

    Answer: b

Answers a, c, and d are elements of policy development at the highest level. Key business resources would have been identified during the risk assessment process. The various roles are then defined to determine the various levels of access to those resources. Answer d is the final step in the policy creation process and combines steps a and c. It determines which group gets access to each resource and what access privileges its members are assigned. Access to resources should be based on roles, not on individual identity. Source: *Surviving Security: How to Integrate People, Process, and Technology* by Mandy Andress (Sams Publishing, 2001).

Chapter 2—Access Control Systems and Methodology

1. The concept of limiting the routes that can be taken between a workstation and a computer resource on a network is called:

   a. Path limitation

   b. An enforced path

   c. A security perimeter

   d. A trusted path

   > *Answer:* b

   > Individuals are authorized access to resources on a network through specific paths and the *enforced path* prohibits the user from accessing a resource through a different route than is authorized to that particular user. This prevents the individual from having unauthorized access to sensitive information in areas off limits to that individual. Examples of controls to implement an enforced path include establishing virtual private networks (VPNs) for specific groups within an organization, using firewalls with access control lists, restricting user menu options, and providing specific phone numbers or dedicated lines for remote access. Answer a is a distracter. Answer c, *security perimeter*, refers to the boundary where security controls are in effect to protect assets. This is a general definition and can apply to physical and technical (logical) access controls. In physical security, a fence may define the security perimeter. In technical access control, a security perimeter can be defined in terms of a *Trusted Computing Base (TCB)*. A TCB is the total combination of protection mechanisms within a computer system. These mechanisms include the firmware, hardware, and software that enforce the system security policy. The *security perimeter* is the boundary that separates the TCB from the remainder of the system. In answer d, a *trusted path* is a path that exists to permit the user to access the TCB without being compromised by other processes or users.

2. An important control that should be in place for external connections to a network that uses call-back schemes is:

   a. Breaking of a dial-up connection at the remote user's side of the line

   b. Call forwarding

   c. Call enhancement

   d. Breaking of a dial-up connection at the organization's computing resource side of the line

   > *Answer:* d

One attack that can be applied when call back is used for remote, dial-up connections is that the caller may not hang up. If the caller had been previously authenticated and has completed his/her session, a "live" connection into the remote network will still be maintained. Also, an unauthenticated remote user may hold the line open, acting as if call-back authentication has taken place. Thus, an active disconnect should be effected at the computing resource's side of the line. Answer a is not correct since it involves the caller hanging up. Answer b, call forwarding, is a feature that should be disabled, if possible, when used with call-back schemes. With call back, a cracker can have a call forwarded from a valid phone number to an invalid phone number during the call-back process. Answer c is a distracter.

3. When logging on to a workstation, the log-on process should:

   a. Validate the log-on only after all input data has been supplied.

   b. Provide a Help mechanism that provides log-on assistance.

   c. Place no limits on the time allotted for log-on or on the number of unsuccessful log-on attempts.

   d. Not provide information on the previous successful log-on and on previous unsuccessful log-on attempts.

   Answer: a

   This approach is necessary to ensure that all the information required for a log-on has been submitted and to avoid providing information that would aid a cracker in trying to gain unauthorized access to the workstation or network. If a log-on attempt fails, information as to which part of the requested log-on information was incorrect should not be supplied to the user. Answer b is incorrect since a Help utility would provide help to a cracker trying to gain unauthorized access to the network. For answer c, maximum and minimum time limits should be placed on the log-on process. Also, the log-on process should limit the number of unsuccessful log-on attempts and temporarily suspend the log-on capability if that number is exceeded. One approach is to progressively increase the time interval allowed between unsuccessful log-on attempts. Answer d is incorrect since providing such information will alert an authorized user if someone has been attempting to gain unauthorized access to the network from the user's workstation.

4. A group of processes that share access to the same resources is called:

   a. An access control list

   b. An access control triple

   c. A protection domain

   d. A Trusted Computing Base (TCB)

Answer: c

In answer a, an *access control list (ACL)* is a list denoting which users have what privileges to a particular resource. Table A.3 illustrates an ACL. The table shows the *subjects* or users that have access to the *object*, FILE X and what privileges they have with respect to that file.

For answer b, an *access control triple* consists of the user, program, and file with the corresponding access privileges noted for each user. The TCB, of answer d, is defined in the answers to Question 1 as the total combination of protection mechanisms within a computer system. These mechanisms include the firmware, hardware, and software that enforce the system security policy.

5. What part of an access control matrix shows capabilities that one user has to multiple resources?

   a. Columns

   b. Rows

   c. Rows and columns

   d. Access control list

   Answer: b

   The rows of an access control matrix indicate the capabilities that users have to a number of resources. An example of a row in the access control matrix showing the capabilities of user JIM is given in Table A.4.

   Answer a, columns in the access control matrix, define the access control list described in question 4. Answer c is incorrect since capabilities involve only the rows of the access control matrix. Answer d

Table A.3   Access Control List

USER	FILE X
JIM	READ
PROGRAM Y	READ/WRITE
GAIL	READ/WRITE

Table A.4   Capabilities

USER	PROGRAM X	FILE X	FILE Y
JIM	EXECUTE	READ	READ/ WRITE

is incorrect since an ACL, again, is a column in the access control matrix.

6. A type of preventive/physical access control is:

   a. Biometrics for authentication

   b. Motion detectors

   c. Biometrics for identification

   d. An intrusion detection system

   Answer: c

   Biometrics applied to identification of an individual is a "one-to-many" search where an individual's physiological or behavioral characteristics are compared to a database of stored information. An example would be trying to match a person's fingerprints to a set in a national database of fingerprints. This search differs from the biometrics search for authentication in answer a. That search would be a "one-to-one" comparison of a person's physiological or behavioral characteristics with their corresponding entry in an authentication database. Answer b, motion detectors, is a type of detective physical control and answer d is a detective/technical control.

7. In addition to accuracy, a biometric system has additional factors that determine its effectiveness. Which one of the following listed items is NOT one of these additional factors?

   a. Throughput rate

   b. Acceptability

   c. Corpus

   d. Enrollment time

   Answer: c

   A *corpus* is a biometric term that refers to collected biometric images. The corpus is stored in a database of images. Potential sources of error are the corruption of images during collection and mislabeling or other transcription problems associated with the database. Therefore, the image collection, process and storage must be performed carefully with constant checking. These images are collected during the enrollment process and thus, are critical to the correct operation of the biometric device. In *enrollment*, images are collected and features are extracted, but no comparison occurs. The information is stored for use in future comparison steps. Answer a, the *throughput rate*, refers to the rate at which individuals, once enrolled, can be processed by a biometric system. If an individual is being authenticated, the biometric system will take a sample of the individual's characteristic to be evaluated and compare it to a template. A metric called *distance* is used to determine if the sample matches the template. Distance is the difference between the quantitative measure of the sample and the template. If the distance falls within a threshold value, a match is declared. If not, there is no match. Answer b, *acceptability*, is determined by privacy issues, invasiveness, and psychological and physical comfort when using the biometric system. *Enrollment time*, answer d, is the time it takes to initially "register" with a system by providing samples of the biometric characteristic to be evaluated.

8. Access control that is a function of factors such as location, time of day, and previous access history is called:

   a. Positive

   b. Content-dependent

   c. Context-dependent

   d. Information flow

   > *Answer:* c
   >
   > In answer c, access is determined by the context of the decision as opposed to the information contained in the item being accessed. The latter is referred to as *content-dependent* access control. (Answer b) In content-dependent access control, for example, the manager of a department may be authorized to access employment records of a department employee, but may not be permitted to view the health records of the employee. In answer a, the term "positive" in access control refers to positive access rights, such as read or write. Denial rights, such as denial to write to a file, can also be conferred upon a subject. Information flow, cited in answer d, describes a class of access control models. An *information flow model* is described by the set consisting of object, flow policy, states, and rules describing the transitions among states.

9. A persistent collection of data items that form relations among each other is called a:

   a. Database management system (DBMS)

   b. Data description language (DDL)

   c. Schema

   d. Database

   > *Answer:* d
   >
   > For a database to be viable, the data items must be stored on nonvolatile media and be protected from unauthorized modification. For answer a, a DBMS provides access to the items in the database and main-

tains the information in the database. The Data description language (DDL) in answer b provides the means to define the database and answer c, schema, is the description of the database.

10. A relational database can provide security through *view* relations. Views enforce what information security principle?

a. Aggregation

b. Least privilege

c. Separation of duties

d. Inference

Answer: b

The principle of *least privilege* states that a subject is permitted to have access to the minimum amount of information required to perform an authorized task. When related to government security clearances, it is referred to as "need-to-know." Answer a, *aggregation*, is defined as assembling or compiling units of information at one sensitivity level and having the resultant totality of data being of a higher sensitivity level than the individual components. *Separation of duties*, answer c, requires that two or more subjects are necessary to authorize an activity or task. Answer d, *inference*, refers to the ability of a subject to deduce information that is not authorized to be accessed by that subject from information that is authorized to that subject.

11. A software interface to the operating system that implements access control by limiting the system commands that are available to a user is called a(n):

a. Restricted shell

b. Interrupt

c. Physically constrained user interface

d. View

Answer: a

Answer b refers to a software or hardware interrupt to a processor that causes the program to jump to another program to handle the interrupt request. Before leaving the program that was being executed at the time of the interrupt, the CPU must save the state of the computer so that the original program can continue after the interrupt has been serviced. A physically constrained user interface, answer c, is one in which a user's operations are limited by the physical characteristics of the interface device. An example would be a keypad with the choices limited to the operations permitted by each key. Answer d refers to database *views*, which restrict access to information contained in a database through content-dependent access control.

12. Controlling access to information systems and associated networks is necessary for the preservation of their confidentiality, integrity, and availability. Which of the following is NOT a goal of integrity?

a. Prevention of the modification of information by unauthorized users

b. Prevention of the unauthorized or unintentional modification of information by authorized users

c. Prevention of authorized modifications by unauthorized users

d. Preservation of the internal and external consistency of the information

> *Answer:* c
>
> Answers a, b, and d are the three principles of integrity. Answer c is a distracter and does not make sense. In answer d, internal consistency ensures that internal data correlate. For example, the total number of a particular data item in the database should be the sum of all the individual, non-identical occurrences of that data item in the database. External consistency requires that the database content be consistent with the real world items that it represents.

13. In a Kerberos exchange involving a message with an authenticator, the authenticator contains the client ID and which of the following?

a. Ticket Granting Ticket (TGT)

b. Timestamp

c. Client/TGS session key

d. Client network address

> *Answer:* b
>
> A *timestamp*, t, is used to check the validity of the accompanying request since a Kerberos ticket is valid for some time window, v, after it is issued. The timestamp indicates when the ticket was issued. Answer a, the TGT, is comprised of the client ID, the client network address, the starting and ending time the ticket is valid (v), and the client/TGS session key. This ticket is used by the client to request the service of a resource on the network from the TGS. In answer c, the client/TGS session key, $K_{c, tgs}$, is the symmetric key used for encrypted communication between the client and TGS for this particular session. For answer d, the client network address is included in the TGT and not in the authenticator.

14. Which one of the following security areas is directly addressed by Kerberos?

    a. Confidentiality

    b. Frequency analysis

    c. Availability

    d. Physical attacks

    Answer: a

    Kerberos directly addresses the confidentiality and also the integrity of information. For answer b, attacks such as frequency analysis are not considered in the basic Kerberos implementation. In addition, the Kerberos protocol does not directly address availability issues. (Answer c.) For answer d, since the Kerberos TGS and the authentication servers hold all the secret keys, these servers are vulnerable to both physical attacks and attacks from malicious code. In the Kerberos exchange, the client workstation temporarily holds the client's secret key, and this key is vulnerable to compromise at the workstation.

15. The Secure European System for Applications in a Multivendor Environment (SESAME) implements a Kerberos-like distribution of secret keys. Which of the following is NOT a characteristic of SESAME?

    a. Uses a trusted authentication server at each host

    b. Uses secret key cryptography for the distribution of secret keys

    c. Incorporates two certificates or tickets, one for authentication and one defining access privileges

    d. Uses public key cryptography for the distribution of secret keys

    Answer: b

    SESAME uses public key cryptography for the distribution of secret keys. In addition, SESAME employs the MD5 and crc32 one-way hash functions. A weakness in SESAME is that, similar to Kerberos, it is subject to password guessing.

16. Windows 2000 uses which of the following as the primary mechanism for authenticating users requesting access to a network?

    a. Hash functions

    b. Kerberos

    c. SESAME

    d. Public key certificates

    Answer: b

While Kerberos is the primary mechanism, system administrators may also use alternative authentication services running under the Security Support Provider Interface (SSPI). Answer a, hash functions, are used for digital signature implementations. Answer c, SESAME, is incorrect. It is the Secure European System for Applications in a Multivendor Environment. SESAME performs similar functions to Kerberos, but uses public key cryptography to distribute the secret keys. Answer d is incorrect, since public key certificates are not used in the Windows 2000 primary authentication approach.

17. A protection mechanism to limit inferencing of information in statistical database queries is:

    a. Specifying a maximum query set size

    b. Specifying a minimum query set size

    c. Specifying a minimum query set size, but prohibiting the querying of all but one of the records in the database

    d. Specifying a maximum query set size, but prohibiting the querying of all but one of the records in the database

    Answer: c

    When querying a database for statistical information, individually identifiable information should be protected. Thus, requiring a minimum size for the query set (greater than one) offers protection against gathering information on one individual. However, an attack may consist of gathering statistics on a query set size M, equal to or greater than the minimum query set size, and then requesting the same statistics on a query set size of M + 1. The second query set would be designed to include the individual whose information is being sought surreptitiously. Thus with answer c, this type of attack could not take place. Answer b is, therefore, incorrect since it leaves open the loophole of the M+1 set size query. Answers a and d are incorrect since the critical metric is the minimum query set size and not the maximum size. Obviously, the maximum query set size cannot be set to a value less than the minimum set size.

18. In SQL, a relation that is actually existent in the database is called a(n):

    a. Base relation

    b. View

    c. Attribute

    d. Domain

    Answer: a

A *base relation* exists in the database while a view, answer b, is a virtual relation that is not stored in the database. A view is derived by the SQL definition and is developed from base relations or, possibly, other views. Answer c, an *attribute*, is a column in a relation table and answer d, a *domain*, is the set of permissible values of an attribute.

19. A type of access control that supports the management of access rights for groups of subjects is:

   a. Role-based

   b. Discretionary

   c. Mandatory

   d. Rule-based

   Answer: a

   Role-based access control assigns identical privileges to groups of users. This approach simplifies the management of access rights, particularly when members of the group change. Thus, access rights are assigned to a role, not to an individual. Individuals are entered as members of specific groups and are assigned the access privileges of that group. In answer b, the access rights to an object are assigned by the owner at the owner's discretion. For large numbers of people whose duties and participation may change frequently, this type of access control can become unwieldy. *Mandatory access control*, answer c, uses security labels or classifications assigned to data items and clearances assigned to users. A user has access rights to data items with a classification equal to or less than the user's clearance. Another restriction is that the user has to have a "need-to-know" the information; this requirement is identical to the principle of least privilege. Answer d, *rule-based* access control, assigns access rights based on stated rules. An example of a rule is "Access to trade-secret data is restricted to corporate officers, the data owner and the legal department."

20. The Simple Security Property and the Star Property are key principles in which type of access control?

   a. Role-based

   b. Rule-based

   c. Discretionary

   d. Mandatory

   Answer: d

   Two properties define fundamental principles of mandatory access control. These properties are:

   Simple Security Property.   A user at one clearance level cannot read data from a higher classification level.

Star Property. A user at one clearance level cannot write data to a lower classification level

Answers a, b, and c are discussed in Question 19.

21. Which of the following items is NOT used to determine the types of access controls to be applied in an organization?

a. Least privilege

b. Separation of duties

c. Relational categories

d. Organizational policies

Answer: c

The item, relational categories, is a distracter. Answers a, b, and d are important determinants of access control implementations in an organization.

22. Kerberos provides an integrity check service for messages between two entities through the use of:

a. A checksum

b. Credentials

c. Tickets

d. A trusted, third-party authentication server

Answer: a

A checksum that is derived from a Kerberos message is used to verify the integrity of the message. This checksum may be a message digest resulting from the application of a hash function to the message. At the receiving end of the transmission, the receiving party can calculate the message digest of the received message using the identical hash algorithm as the sender. Then the message digest calculated by the receiver can be compared with the message digest appended to the message by the sender. If the two message digests match, the message has not been modified en route, and its integrity has been preserved. For answers b and c, credentials and tickets are authenticators used in the process of granting user access to services on the network. Answer d is the AS or authentication server that conducts the ticket-granting process.

23. The Open Group has defined functional objectives in support of a user single sign-on (SSO) interface. Which of the following is NOT one of those objectives and would possibly represent a vulnerability?

a. The interface shall be independent of the type of authentication information handled.

b. Provision for user-initiated change of nonuser-configured authentication information.

c. It shall not predefine the timing of secondary sign-on operations.

d. Support shall be provided for a subject to establish a default user profile.

Answer: b

User configuration of nonuser-configured authentication mechanisms is not supported by the Open Group SSO interface objectives. Authentication mechanisms include items such as smart cards and magnetic badges. Strict controls must be placed to prevent a user from changing configurations that are set by another authority. Objective a supports the incorporation of a variety of authentication schemes and technologies. Answer c states that the interface functional objectives do not require that all sign-on operations be performed at the same time as the primary sign on. This prevents the creation of user sessions with all the available services even though these services are not needed by the user. For answer d, the creation of a default user profile will make the sign-on more efficient and less time-consuming.

In summary, the scope of the Open Group Single Sign-On Standards is to define services in support of:

- "The development of applications to provide a common, single end-user sign-on interface for an enterprise.

- The development of applications for the coordinated management of multiple user account management information bases maintained by an enterprise."

24. There are some correlations between relational data base terminology and object-oriented database terminology. Which of the following relational model terms, respectively, correspond to the object model terms of class, attribute and instance object?

a. Domain, relation, and column

b. Relation, domain, and column

c. Relation, tuple, and column

d. Relation, column, and tuple

Answer: d

Table A.5 shows the correspondence between the two models.

In comparing the two models, a class is similar to a relation; however, a relation does not have the inheritance property of a class. An attribute in the object model is similar to the column of a relational table. The column has limitations on the data types it can hold while an attribute in the object model can use all data types that are supported by the Java and C++ languages. An instance object in the object model corresponds to a tuple in the relational model. Again

Table A.5 Object and Relational Model Correspondence

OBJECT MODEL	RELATIONAL MODEL
CLASS	RELATION
ATTRIBUTE	COLUMN
INSTANCE OBJECT	TUPLE

the data structures of the tuple are limited while those of the instance object can use data structures of Java and C++.

25. A *reference monitor* is a system component that enforces access controls on an object. Specifically, the *reference monitor concept* is an abstract machine that mediates all access of subjects to objects. The hardware, firmware, and software elements of a trusted computing base that implement the reference monitor concept are called:

   a. The authorization database

   b. Identification and authentication (I & A) mechanisms

   c. The auditing subsystem

   d. The security kernel

   Answer: d

   The *security kernel* implements the reference model concept. The reference model must have the following characteristics:

   ■ It must mediate all accesses.

   ■ It must be protected from modification.

   ■ It must be verifiable as correct.

   Answer a, the authorization database, is used by the reference monitor to mediate accesses by subjects to objects. When a request for access is received, the reference monitor refers to entries in the authorization database to verify that the operation requested by a subject for application to an object is permitted. The authorization database has entries or *authorizations* of the form subject, object, access mode. In answer b, the I & A operation is separate from the reference monitor. The user enters his/her identification to the I & A function. Then the user must be authenticated. *Authentication* is verification that the user's claimed identity is valid. Authentication is based on the following three factor types:

   Type 1. Something you know, such as a PIN or password

   Type 2. Something you have, such as an ATM card or smart card

   Type 3. Something you are (physically), such as a fingerprint or retina scan

Answer c, the auditing subsystem, is a key complement to the reference monitor. The auditing subsystem is used by the reference monitor to keep track of the reference monitor's activities. Examples of such activities include the date and time of an access request, identification of the subject and objects involved, the access privileges requested and the result of the request.

26. Authentication in which a random value is presented to a user, who then returns a calculated number based on that random value is called:

   a. Man-in-the-middle

   b. Challenge-response

   c. One-time password

   d. Personal identification number (PIN) protocol

   Answer: b

   In *challenge-response authentication,* the user enters a random value (challenge) sent by the authentication server into a token device. The token device shares knowledge of a cryptographic secret key with the authentication server and calculates a response based on the challenge value and the secret key. This response is entered into the authentication server, which uses the response to authenticate the identity of the user by performing the same calculation and comparing results. Answer a, *man-in-the-middle,* is a type of attack in which a cracker is interposed between the user and authentication server and attempts to gain access to packets for replay in order to impersonate a valid user. A *one-time password,* answer c, is a password that is used only once to gain access to a network or computer system. A typical implementation is through the use of a token that generates a number based on the time of day. The user reads this number and enters it into the authenticating device. The authenticating device calculates the same number based on the time of day and uses the same algorithm used by the token. If the token's number matches that of the authentication server, the identity of the user is validated. Obviously, the token and the authentication server must be time-synchronized for this approach to work. Also, there is allowance for small values of time skew between the authorization device and the token. Answer d refers to a PIN number that is something you know used with something you have, such as an ATM card.

27. Which of the following is NOT a criterion for access control?

   a. Identity

   b. Role

c. Keystroke monitoring

d. Transactions

Answer: c

Keystroke monitoring is associated with the auditing function and not access control. For answer a, the identity of the user is a criterion for access control. The identity must be authenticated as part of the I & A process. Answer b refers to role-based access control where access to information is determined by the user's job function or role in the organization. Transactions, answer d, refer to access control through entering an account number or a transaction number, as may be required for bill payments by telephone, for example.

28. Which of the following is typically NOT a consideration in the design of passwords?

a. Lifetime

b. Composition

c. Authentication period

d. Electronic monitoring

Answer: d

Electronic monitoring is the eavesdropping on passwords that are being transmitted to the authenticating device. This issue is a technical one and is not a consideration in designing passwords. The other answers relate to very important password characteristics that must be taken into account when developing passwords. Password lifetime, in answer a, refers to the maximum period of time that a password is valid. Ideally, a password should be used only once. This approach can be implemented by token password generators and challenge response schemes. However, as a practical matter, passwords on most PC's and workstations are used repeatedly. The time period after which passwords should be changed is a function of the level of protection required for the information being accessed. In typical organizations, passwords may be changed every three to six months. Obviously, passwords should be changed when employees leave an organization or in a situation where a password may have been compromised. Answer b, the composition of a password, defines the characters that can be used in the password. The characters may be letters, numbers, or special symbols. The authentication period in answer c defines the maximum acceptable period between the initial authentication of a user and any subsequent reauthorization process. For example, users may be asked to authenticate themselves again after a specified period of time of being logged on to a server containing critical information.

29. A distributed system using passwords as the authentication means can use a number of techniques to make the password system stronger. Which of the following is NOT one of these techniques?

    a. Password generators

    b. Regular password reuse

    c. Password file protection

    d. Limiting the number or frequency of log-on attempts

    Answer: b

    Passwords should never be reused after the time limit on their use has expired. Answer a, password generators, supply passwords upon request. These passwords are usually comprised of numbers, characters, and sometimes symbols. Passwords provided by password generators are, usually, not easy to remember. For answer c, password file protection may consist of encrypting the password with a one-way hash function and storing it in a password file. A typical brute force attack against this type of protection is to encrypt trial password guesses using the same hash function and to compare the encrypted results with the encrypted passwords stored in the password file. Answer d provides protection in that, after a specified number of unsuccessful log-on attempts, a user may be locked out of trying to log on for a period of time. An alternative is to progressively increase the time between permitted log-on tries after each unsuccessful log-on attempt.

30. Enterprise Access Management (EAM) provides access control management services to Web-based enterprise systems. Which of the following functions is NOT normally provided by extant EAM approaches?

    a. Single sign-on

    b. Accommodation of a variety of authentication mechanisms

    c. Role-based access control

    d. Interoperability among EAM implementations

    Answer: d

    In general, security credentials produced by one EAM solution are not recognized by another implementation. Thus, reauthentication is required when linking from one Web site to another related Web site if the sites have different EAM implementations.   Single sign-on

(SSO), answer a, is approached in a number of ways. For example, SSO can be implemented on Web applications in the same domain residing on different servers by using nonpersistent, encrypted cookies on the client interface. This is accomplished by providing a cookie to each application that the user wishes to access. Another solution is to build a secure credential for each user on a reverse proxy that is situated in front of the Web server. The credential is, then, presented at each instance of a user attempting to access protected Web applications. For answer b, most EAM solutions accommodate a variety of authentication technologies, including tokens, ID/passwords and digital certificates. Similarly, for answer c, EAM solutions support role-based access controls, albeit they may be implemented in different fashions. Enterprise-level roles should be defined in terms that are universally accepted across most e-commerce applications.

31. The main approach to obtaining the true biometric information from a collected sample of an individual's physiological or behavioral characteristics is:

   a. Feature extraction

   b. Enrollment

   c. False rejection

   d. Digraphs

   Answer: a

   Feature extraction algorithms are a subset of signal/image processing and are used to extract the key biometric information from a sample that has been taken from an individual. Usually, the sample is taken in an environment that may have "noise" and other conditions that may affect the raw sample image. Neural networks are an example of a feature extraction approach. Answer b, *enrollment*, refers to the process of collecting samples that are averaged and then stored to use as a reference base against which future samples are compared. False rejection, answer c, refers to the false rejection in biometrics. *False rejection* is the rejection of an authorized user because of a mismatch between the sample and the reference template. Conversely, *false acceptance* is the acceptance of an unauthorized user because of an incorrect match to the template of an authorized user. The corresponding measures in percentage are the False Rejection Rate (FRR) and False Acceptance Rate (FAR). For answer d, diagraphs refer to sets of average values compiled in the biometrics area of keystroke dynamics. *Keystroke dynamics* involves analyzing the characteristics of a user typing on a keyboard. Keystroke duration samples as well as measures of the latency between keystrokes are taken and averaged. These averages for all pairs of keys are called *diagraphs. Trigraphs,* sample sets for all key triples, can also be used as biometric samples.

32. In a wireless General Packet Radio Services (GPRS) Virtual Private Network (VPN) application, which of the following security protocols is commonly used?

   a. SSL

   b. IPSEC

   c. TLS

   d. WTP

   Answer: b

   An example is the use of a GPRS-enabled laptop that connects to a corporate intranet via a VPN. The laptop is given an IP address and a RADIUS server authenticates the user. IPSEC is used to create the VPN. As background, GPRS is a second-generation (2G) packet data technology that is overlaid on existing Global System for Mobile communications (GSM). GSM is the wireless analog of the ISDN landline system. The key features of GPRS are that it is always on line (no dial-up needed), existing GSM networks can be upgraded with GPRS, and it can serve as the packet data core of third generation (3G) systems. Answers a and c, SSL and TLS, are similar security protocols that are used on the Internet side of the Wireless Application Protocol (WAP) Gateway. For answer d, WTP is the Wireless Transaction Protocol that is part of the WAP suite of protocols. WTP is a lightweight, message-oriented, transaction protocol that provides more reliable connections than UDP, but does not have the robustness of TCP.

33. How is authentication implemented in GSM?

   a. Using public key cryptography

   b. It is not implemented in GSM

   c. Using secret key cryptography

   d. Out-of-band verification

   Answer: c

   Authentication is effected in GSM through the use of a common secret key, K_s, that is stored in the network operator's Authentication Center (AuC) and in the subscriber's SIM card. The SIM card may be in the subscriber's laptop, and the subscriber is not privy to K_s. To begin the authentication exchange, the home location of the subscriber's mobile station, (MS), generates a 128-bit random number (RAND) and sends it to the MS. Using an algorithm that is known to both the AuC and MS, the RAND is encrypted by both parties using the secret key, K_s. The ciphertext generated at the MS is then sent to the AuC and compared with the ciphertext generated by the AuC. If the two results match, the MS is authenticated and the access request is granted. If they do not match, the access request is denied. Answers a, b, and d are, therefore, incorrect.

Chapter 3—Telecommunications and Network Security

1. Which of the choices below is NOT an OSI reference model Session Layer protocol, standard, or interface?

   a. SQL

   b. RPC

   c. MIDI

   d. ASP

   e. DNA SCP

   > *Answer:* c
   >
   > The Musical Instrument Digital Interface (MIDI) standard is a Presentation Layer standard for digitized music. The other answers are all Session layer protocols or standards. Answer a, SQL, refers to the Structured Query Language database standard originally developed by IBM. Answer b, RPC, refers to the Remote Procedure Call redirection mechanism for remote clients. Answer d, ASP, is the AppleTalk Session Protocol; and answer e, DNA SCP, refers to DECnet's Digital Network Architecture Session Control Protocol. Source: *Introduction to Cisco Router Configuration* edited by Laura Chappell (Cisco Press, 1999).

2. Which part of the 48-bit, 12-digit hexadecimal number known as the Media Access Control (MAC) address identifies the manufacturer of the network device?

   a. The first three bytes

   b. The first two bytes

   c. The second half of the MAC address

   d. The last three bytes

   > *Answer:* a
   >
   > The first three bytes (or first half) of the six-byte MAC address is the manufacturer's identifier (see Table A.6). This can be a good troubleshooting aid if a network device is acting up, as it will isolate the brand of the failing device. The other answers are distracters. Source: *Mastering Network Security* by Chris Brenton (Sybex, 1999).

3. Which IEEE protocol defines the Spanning Tree protocol?

   a. IEEE 802.5

   b. IEEE 802.3

Table A.6   Common Vendors' MAC Addresses

FIRST THREE BYTES	VENDOR
00000C	Cisco
0000A2	Bay Networks
0080D3	Shiva
00AA00	Intel
02608C	3COM
080007	Apple
080009	Hewlett-Packard
080020	Sun
08005A	IBM

   c. IEEE 802.11

   d. IEEE 802.1D

     Answer: d

The 802.1D spanning tree protocol is an Ethernet link-management protocol that provides link redundancy while preventing routing loops. Since only one active path can exist for an Ethernet network to route properly, the STP algorithm calculates and manages the best loop-free path through the network. Answer a, IEEE 802.5, specifies a token-passing ring access method for LANs. Answer b, IEEE 802.3, specifies an Ethernet bus topology using Carrier Sense Multiple Access Control/Carrier Detect (CSMA/CD). Answer c, IEEE 802.11, is the IEEE standard that specifies 1 Mbps and 2 Mbps wireless connectivity in the 2.4 MHz ISM (Industrial, Scientific, Medical) band. Source: *Designing Network Security* by Merike Kaeo (Cisco Press, 1999).

4. Which choice below is NOT one of the legal IP address ranges specified by RFC1976 and reserved by the Internet Assigned Numbers Authority (IANA) for nonroutable private addresses?

   a. 10.0.0.0 - 10.255.255.255

   b. 127.0.0.0 - 127.0.255.255

   c. 172.16.0.0 - 172.31.255.255

   d. 192.168.0.0 - 192.168.255.255

     Answer: b

The other three address ranges can be used for Network Address Translation (NAT). While NAT is, in itself, not a very effective security measure, a large network can benefit from using NAT with Dynamic Host Configuration Protocol (DHCP) to help prevent certain internal routing information from being exposed. The address 127.0.0.1 is called the "loopback" address. Source: *Designing Network Security* by Merike Kaeo (Cisco Press, 1999).

5. Which statement is correct about ISDN Basic Rate Interface?

   a. It offers 23 B channels and 1 D channel.

   b. It offers 2 B channels and 1 D channel.

   c. It offers 30 B channels and 1 D channel.

   d. It offers 1 B channel and 2 D channels.

     Answer: b

     Integrated Services Digital Network (ISDN) Basic Rate Interface (BRI) offers two B channels which carry user data at 64 Kbps each, and one control and signaling D channel operating at 16 Kbps. Answer a describes ISDN Primary Rate Interface (PRI) for North America and Japan, with 23 B channels at 64 Kbps and one 64 Kbps D channel, for a total throughput of 1.544 Mbps. Answer c describes ISDN PRI for Europe, Australia, and other parts of the world, with 30 64 Kbps B channels and one D channel, for a total throughput of 2.048 Mbps. Answer d is a distracter. Source: *Internetworking Technologies Handbook, Second Edition* (Cisco Press, 1998).

6. In the DoD reference model, which layer conforms to the OSI transport layer?

   a. Process/Application Layer

   b. Host-to-Host Layer

   c. Internet Layer

   d. Network Access Layer

     Answer: b

     In the DoD reference model, the Host-to-Host layer parallels the function of the OSI's transport layer. This layer contains the Transmission Control Protocol (TCP), and the User Datagram Protocol (UDP). Answer a, the DoD Process/Application layer, corresponds to the OSI's top three layers, the Application, Presentation, and Session layers. Answer c, the DoD Internet layer, corresponds to the OSI's Network layer, and answer d, the DoD Network Access Layer, is the equivalent of the Data Link and Physical layers of the OSI model. Source: *MCSE:TCP/IP Study Guide* by Todd Lammle, Monica Lammle, and John

Chellis (Sybex, 1997) and *Handbook of Information Security Management 1999* by Micki Krause and Harold F. Tipton (Auerbach, 1999).

7. What is the Network Layer of the OSI reference model primarily responsible for?

   a. Internetwork packet routing

   b. LAN bridging

   c. SMTP Gateway services

   d. Signal regeneration and repeating

   Answer: a

   Although many routers can perform most of the functions above, the OSI Network layer is primarily responsible for routing. Answer b, bridging, is a Data Link Layer function. Answer c, gateways, most commonly function at the higher layers. Answer d, signal regeneration and repeating, is primarily a Physical layer function. Source: *CCNA Study Guide* by Todd Lammle, Donald Porter, and James Chellis (Sybex, 1999).

8. Which IEEE protocol defines wireless transmission in the 5 GHz band with data rates up to 54 Mbps?

   a. IEEE 802.11a

   b. IEEE 802.11b

   c. IEEE 802.11g

   d. IEEE 802.15

   Answer: a

   IEEE 802.11a specifies high-speed wireless connectivity in the 5 GHz band using Orthogonal Frequency Division Multiplexing with data rates up to 54 Mbps. Answer b, IEEE 802.11b, specifies high-speed wireless connectivity in the 2.4 GHz ISM band up to 11 Mbps. Answer c, IEEE 802.11g, is a proposed standard that offers wireless transmission over relatively short distances at speeds from 20 Mbps up to 54 Mbps and operates in the 2.4 GHz range (and is therefore expected to be backward-compatible with existing 802.11b-based networks). Answer d, IEEE 802.15, defines Wireless Personal Area Networks (WPAN), such as Bluetooth, in the 2.4-2.5 GHz band. Source: IEEE Wireless Working Groups (grouper.ieee.org).

9. Which category of UTP wiring is rated for 100BaseT Ethernet networks?

   a. Category 1

   b. Category 2

   c. Category 3

   d. Category 4

   e. Category 5

Answer: e

Category 5 unshielded twisted-pair (UTP) wire is rated for transmissions of up to 100 Mbps and can be used in 100BaseT Ethernet networks. It is the most commonly installed type of UTP at this time. See Table A.7. Answer a, category 1 twisted-pair wire was used for early analog telephone communications and is not suitable for data. Answer b, category 2 twisted-pair wire, was used in AS/400 and IBM 3270 networks. Derived from IBM Type 3 cable specification. Answer c, category 3 twisted-pair wire, is rated for 10 Mbps and was used in 802.3 10Base-T Ethernet networks, and 4 Mbps Token Ring networks. Answer d, category 4 twisted-pair wire, is rated for 16 Mbps and is used in 4/16 Mbps Token Ring LANs. Source: The Electrical Industry Alliance (EIA/TIA-568).

10. Which choice below is the earliest and the most commonly found Interior Gateway Protocol?

   a. RIP

   b. OSPF

   c. IGRP

   d. EAP

Answer: a

The Routing Information Protocol (RIP) bases its routing path on the distance (number of hops) to the destination. RIP maintains optimum routing paths by sending out routing update messages if the network topology changes. For example, if a router finds that a particular link is faulty, it will update its routing table, then send a copy of the modified table to each of its neighbors. Answer b, the Open Shortest Path First (OSPF) is a link-state hierarchical routing algorithm intended as a successor to RIP. It features least-cost routing, multipath routing, and load balancing. Answer c, the Internet Gateway Routing Protocol (IGRP) is a Cisco protocol that uses a composite metric as its

Table A.7 UTP Categories of Performance

UTP CAT	RATED PERFORMANCE IN MHZ	COMMON APPLICATIONS
Cat1	Under 1 MHz	Analog voice, ISDN BRI
Cat2	1 MHz	IBM 3270, AS/400, Apple LocalTalk
Cat3	16 MHz	10BaseT, 4 Mbps Token Ring
Cat4	20 MHz	16 Mbps Token Ring
Cat5	100 MHz	10/100BaseT

routing metric, including bandwidth, delay, reliability, loading, and maximum transmission unit. Answer d, the Extensible Authentication Protocol (EAP), is a general protocol for PPP authentication that supports multiple remote authentication mechanisms. Source: *Introduction to Cisco Router Configuration* edited by Laura Chappell (Cisco Press, 1999).

11. The data transmission method in which data is sent continuously and doesn't use either an internal clocking source or start/stop bits for timing is known as:

   a. Asynchronous

   b. Synchronous

   c. Isochronous

   d. Pleisiochronous

   Answer: c

   Isochronous data is synchronous data transmitting without a clocking source, with the bits sent continuously and no start or stop bits. All bits are of equal importance and are anticipated to occur at regular time intervals. Answer a, asynchronous, is a data transmission method using a start bit at the beginning of the data value, and a stop bit at the end of the value. Answer b, synchronous, is a message-framed transmission method that uses clocking pulses to match the speed of the data transmission. Answer d, pleisiochronous, is a transmission method that uses more than one timing source, sometimes running at different speeds. This method may require master and slave clock devices. Source: *Communications Systems and Networks* by Ray Horak (M&T Books, 2000).

12. Which level of RAID is commonly referred to as "disk mirroring"?

   a. RAID 0

   b. RAID 1

   c. RAID 3

   d. RAID 5

   Answer: b

   Redundant Array of Inexpensive Disks (RAID) is a method of enhancing hard disk fault tolerance, which can improve performance (see Table A.8). RAID 1 maintains a complete copy of all data by duplicating each hard drive. Performance can suffer in some implementations of RAID 1, and twice as many drives are required. Novell developed a type of disk mirroring called disk duplexing, which uses

Table A.8   Commonly Used RAID Types

RAID LEVEL	DESCRIPTION
RAID 0	Multiple Drive Striping
RAID 1	Disk Mirroring
RAID 3	Single Parity Drive
RAID 5	Distributed Parity Information

multiple disk controller cards increasing both performance and reliability. Answer a, RAID 0, gives some performance gains by striping the data across multiple drives, but reduces fault tolerance, as the failure of any single drive disables the whole volume. Answer c, RAID 3, uses a dedicated error-correction disk called a parity drive, and stripes the data across the other data drives. Answer RAID 5, uses all disks in the array for both data and error correction, increasing both storage capacity and performance.

13. Which network attack below would NOT be considered a Denial of Service attack?

    a. Ping of Death

    b. SMURF

    c. Brute Force

    d. TCP SYN

    Answer: c

    A brute force attack is an attempt to use all combinations of key patterns to decipher a message. The other three attacks are commonly used to create a Denial of Service (DoS). Answer a, Ping of Death, exploits ICMP by sending an illegal ECHO packet of >65K octets of data, which can cause an overflow of system variables and lead to a system crash. Answer b, SMURF, is a type of attack using spoofed ICMP ECHO requests to broadcast addresses, which the routers attempt to propagate, congesting the network. Three participants are required for a SMURF attack: the attacker, the amplifying network, and the victim. Answer d, a TCP SYN flood attack, generates phony TCP SYN packets from random IP addresses at a rapid rate to fill up the connection queue and stop the system from accepting legitimate users. Source: *Hacking Exposed* by Stuart McClure, Joel Scambray, and George Kurtz (Osborne, 1999).

14. Which choice below is NOT an element of IPSec?

    a. Authentication Header

    b. Layer Two Tunneling Protocol

    c. Security Association

    d. Encapsulating Security Payload

    Answer: b

    The Layer Two Tunneling Protocol (L2TP) is a layer two tunneling protocol that allows a host to establish a virtual connection. Although L2TP, an enhancement to Layer Two Forwarding Protocol (L2F) and supporting some features of Point to Point Tunneling Protocol (PPTP), may coexist with IPSec, it is not natively an IPSec component. Answer a, the Authentication Header (AH), is an authenticating protocol that uses a hash signature in the packet header to validate the integrity of the packet data and the authenticity of the sender. Answer c, the Security Association (SA), is a component of the IPSec architecture that contains the information the IPSec device needs to process incoming and outbound IPSec packets. IPSec devices embed a value called the Security Parameter Index (SPI) in the header to associate a datagram with its SA, and store SAs in a Security Association Database (SAD). Answer d, the Encapsulating Security Payload (ESP), is an authenticating and encrypting protocol that provides integrity, source authentication, and confidentiality services. Source: *Implementing IPSec* by Elizabeth Kaufman and Andrew Newman (Wiley, 1999).

15. Which statement below is NOT true about the difference between cut-through and store-and-forward switching?

    a. A store-and-forward switch reads the whole packet and checks its validity before sending it to the next destination.

    b. Both methods operate at layer two of the OSI reference model.

    c. A cut-through switch reads only the header on the incoming data packet.

    d. A cut-through switch introduces more latency than a store-and-forward switch.

    Answer: d

    A cut-through switch provides less latency than a store-and-forward switch, as it forwards the frame before it has received the complete frame. However, cut-through switches may also forward defective or empty packets. Source: *Virtual LANs* by Mariana Smith (McGraw-Hill, 1998).

16. Which statement is NOT true about the SOCKS protocol?

    a. It is sometimes referred to as an application-level proxy.

    b. It uses an ESP for authentication and encryption.

    c. It operates in the transport layer of the OSI model.

    d. Network applications need to be SOCKS-ified to operate.

      The correct answer is b. The Encapsulating Security Payload, (ESP) is a component of IPSec. Socket Security (SOCKS) is a transport layer, secure networking proxy protocol. SOCKS replaces the standard network systems calls with its own calls. These calls open connections to a SOCKS proxy server for client authentication, transparently to the user. Common network utilities, like TELNET or FTP, need to be SOCKS-ified, or have their network calls altered to recognize SOCKS proxy calls. Source: *Designing Network Security* by Merike Kaeo (Cisco Press, 1999).

17. Which choice below does NOT relate to analog dial-up hacking?

    a. War Dialing

    b. War Walking

    c. Demon Dialing

    d. ToneLoc

      Answer: b

      War Walking (or War Driving) refers to scanning for 802.11-based wireless network information, by either driving or walking with a laptop, a wireless adapter in promiscuous mode, some type of scanning software such as NetStumbler or AiroPeek, and a Global Positioning System (GPS). Answer a, War Dialing, is a method used to hack into computers by using a software program to automatically call a large pool of telephone numbers to search for those that have a modem attached. Answer c, Demon Dialing, similar to War Dialing, is a tool used to attack one modem using brute force to guess the password and gain access. Answer d, ToneLoc, was one of the first war-dialing tools used by "phone phreakers." Sources: *Hacking Exposed* by Stuart McClure, Joel Scambray, and George Kurtz (Osborne, 1999) and "War Driving by the Bay" by Kevin Poulsen, The Register, April 13, 2001.

18. Which choice below is NOT a way to get Windows NT passwords?

    a. Obtain the backup SAM from the repair directory.

    b. Boot the NT server with a floppy containing an alternate operating system.

c. Obtain root access to the /etc/passwd file.

d. Use pwdump2 to dump the password hashes directly from the registry.

Answer: c

The /etc/passwd file is a Unix system file. The NT Security Accounts Manager, SAM, contains the usernames and encrypted passwords of all local (and domain, if the server is a domain controller) users. The SAM uses an older, weaker LanManager hash that can be broken easily by tools like L0phtcrack. Physical access to the NT server and the rdisks must be controlled. The "Sam._" file in the repair directory must be deleted after creation of an rdisk. Pwdump and pwdump2 are utilities that allow someone with Administrator rights to target the Local Security Authority Subsystem, isass.exe, from a remote system. Source: *Hacking Exposed* by Stuart McClure, Joel Scambray, and George Kurtz (Osborne, 1999).

19. A "back door" into a network refers to what?

a. Socially engineering passwords from a subject

b. Mechanisms created by hackers to gain network access at a later time

c. Undocumented instructions used by programmers to debug applications

d. Monitoring programs implemented on dummy applications to lure intruders

Answer: b

Back doors are very hard to trace, as an intruder will often create several avenues into a network to be exploited later. The only real way to be sure these avenues are closed after an attack is to restore the operating system from the original media, apply the patches, and restore all data and applications. Answer a, social engineering, is a technique used to manipulate users into revealing information like passwords. Answer c refers to a "trap door," which are undocumented hooks into an application to assist programmers with debugging. Although intended innocently, these can be exploited by intruders. Answer d is a "honey pot" or "padded cell." A honey pot uses a dummy server with bogus applications as a decoy for intruders. Source: *Fighting Computer Crime* by Donn B. Parker (Wiley, 1998).

20. Which protocol below does NOT pertain to e-mail?

a. SMTP

b. POP

c. CHAP

d. IMAP

Answer: c

The Challenge Handshake Authentication Protocol (CHAP) is used at the startup of a remote link to verify the identity of a remote node. Answer a, the Simple Mail Transfer Protocol (RFCs 821 and 1869), is used by a server to deliver e-mail over the Internet. Answer b, the Post Office Protocol (RFC 1939), enables users to read their email by downloading it from a remote server on to their local computer. Answer d, the Internet Message Access Protocol (RFC 2060), allows users to read their e-mail on a remote server, without downloading the mail locally. Source: *Handbook of Computer Crime Investigation* Edited by Eoghan Casey (Academic Press, 2002).

21. The IP address, 178.22.90.1, is considered to be in which class of address?

    a. Class A

    b. Class B

    c. Class C

    d. Class D

    Answer: b

    The class A address range is 1.0.0.0 to 126.255.255.255. The class B address range is 128.0.0.0 to 191.255.255.255. The class C address range is from 192.0.0.0 to 223.255.255.255. The class D address range is 244.0.0.0 to 239.255.255.255, and is used for multicast packets. Sources: *Designing Network Security* by Merike Kaeo (Cisco Press, 1999) and *CCNA Study Guide* by Todd Lammle, Donald Porter, and James Chellis (Sybex, 1999).

22. What type of firewall architecture employs two network cards and a single screening router?

    a. A screened-host firewall

    b. A dual-homed host firewall

    c. A screened-subnet firewall

    d. An application-level proxy server

    Answer: a

    Like a dual-homed host, a screened-host firewall uses two network cards to connect to the trusted and untrusted networks, but adds a screening router between the host and the untrusted network. Answer b, dual-homed host, has two NICs but not necessarily a screening router. Answer c, screened-subnet firewall, uses two NICs also, but has two screening routers with the host

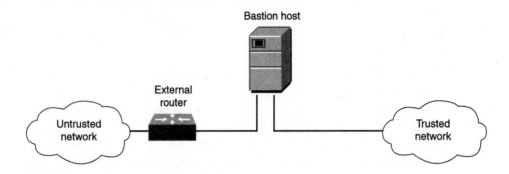

Figure A.1 Screened-host firewall.

acting as a proxy server on its own network segment. One screening router controls traffic local to the network while the second monitors and controls incoming and outgoing Internet traffic, Answer d, application-level proxy, is unrelated to this question. Source: *Hacker Proof* by Lars Klander (Jamsa Press, 1997).

Figure A.1 shows a Screened-host firewall.

23. What is one of the most common drawbacks to using a dual-homed host firewall?

   a. The examination of the packet at the Network layer introduces latency.

   b. The examination of the packet at the Application layer introduces latency.

   c. The ACLs must be manually maintained on the host.

   d. Internal routing may accidentally become enabled.

   Answer: d

   A dual-homed host uses two NICs to attach to two separate networks, commonly a trusted network and an untrusted network. It's important that the internal routing function of the host be disabled to create an application-layer chokepoint and filter packets. Many systems come with routing enabled by default, such as IP forwarding, which makes the firewall useless. The other answers are distracters. Source: *Hacker Proof* by Lars Klander (Jamsa Press, 1997).

24. Which firewall type below uses a dynamic state table to inspect the content of packets?

   a. A packet-filtering firewall

   b. An application-level firewall

c. A circuit-level firewall

d. A stateful-inspection firewall

Answer: d

A stateful-inspection firewall intercepts incoming packets at the Network level, then uses an Inspection Engine to extract state-related information from upper layers. It maintains the information in a dynamic state table and evaluates subsequent connection attempts. Answer a, packet-filtering firewall, is the simplest type of firewall commonly implemented on routers. It operates at the Network layer and offers good performance but is the least secure. Answer b, application-level firewall or application-layer gateway, is more secure because it examines the packet at the application layer, but at the expense of performance. Answer c, circuit-level firewall, is similar to the application-level firewall in that it functions as a proxy server, but differs in that special proxy application software is not needed. Sources: *Hacker Proof* by Lars Klander (Jamsa Press, 1997) and Checkpoint Firewall-1 Stateful Inspection Technology (www.checkpoint.com).

25. Which attack type below does NOT exploit TCP vulnerabilities?

a. Sequence Number attack

b. SYN attack

c. Ping of Death

d. land.c attack

Answer: c

The Ping of Death exploits the fragmentation vulnerability of large ICMP ECHO request packets by sending an illegal packet with more than 65K of data, creating a buffer overflow. Answer a is a TCP sequence number attack, which exploits the nonrandom predictable pattern of TCP connection sequence numbers to spoof a session. Answer b, a TCP SYN attack, is a DoS attack that exploits the TCP three-way handshake. The attacker rapidly generates randomly sourced SYN packets filling the target's connection queue before the connection can timeout. Answer d, land.c attack, is also a DoS attack that exploits TCP SYN packets. The attacker sends a packet that gives both the source and destination as the target's address, and uses the same source and destination port. Sources: *Designing Network Security* by Merike Kaeo (Cisco Press, 1999) and *Mastering Network Security* by Chris Brenton (Sybex, 1999).

26. Which utility below can create a server-spoofing attack?

a. DNS poisoning

b. C2MYAZZ

c. Snort

d. BO2K

> *Answer:* b
>
> C2MYAZZ is a utility that enables server spoofing to implement a session highjacking or man-in-the-middle exploit. It intercepts a client LANMAN authentication logon and obtains the session's logon credentials and password combination, transparently to the user. Answer a, DNS poisoning, is also known as cache poisoning. It is the process of distributing incorrect IP address information for a specific host with the intent to divert traffic from its true destination. Answer c, Snort, is a utility used for network sniffing. Network sniffing is the process of gathering traffic from a network by capturing the data as it passes and storing it to analyze later. Answer d, Back Orifice 2000 (BO2K), is an application-level Trojan Horse used to give an attacker backdoor network access. Source: *Security Complete,* edited by Mark Lierley (Sybex, 2001).

27. Which LAN topology below is MOST vulnerable to a single point of failure?

a. Ethernet Bus

b. Physical Star

c. FDDI

d. Logical Ring

> *Answer:* a
>
> Ethernet bus topology was the first commercially viable network topology, and consists of all workstations connected to a single coaxial cable. Since the cable must be properly terminated on both ends, a break in the cable stops all communications on the bus. Answer b, the physical star topology acts like a logical bus, but provides better fault tolerance, as a cable break only disconnects the workstation or hub directly affected. Answer d, logical ring topology, is used by Token Ring and FDDI and is highly resilient. Token Ring employs a beacon frame, which, in case of a cable break, initiates auto reconfiguration and attempts to reroute the network around the failed mode. Also, the Token Ring active monitor station performs ring maintenance functions, like removing continuously circulating frames from the ring. FDDI employs a second ring to provide redundancy. Sources: *Virtual LANs* by Mariana Smith (McGraw-Hill, 1998) and *Internetworking Technologies Handbook, Second Edition* (Cisco Press, 1998).

28. Which choice below does NOT accurately describe the difference between multi-mode and single-mode fiber optic cabling?

    a. Multi-mode fiber propagates light waves through many paths, single-mode fiber propagates a single light ray only.

    b. Multi-mode fiber has a longer allowable maximum transmission distance than single-mode fiber.

    c. Single-mode fiber has a longer allowable maximum transmission distance than multi-mode fiber.

    d. Both types have a longer allowable maximum transmission distance than UTP Cat 5.

    Answer: b

    Multi-mode fiber has a shorter allowable maximum transmission distance than single-mode fiber (2km vs. 10km). Multi-mode transmits the light through several different paths in the cable, whereas single-mode uses one light path, making single mode perform better. However, multi-mode is less expensive to install and is used more often in short-to-medium haul networks. Category 5 unshielded twisted pair (UTP) has a maximum transmission distance of 100 meters. Sources: *Catalyst 5000 Series Installation Guide* (Cisco Systems, 1996) and *Gigabit Ethernet* by Jayant Kadambi, Ian Crayford, and Mohan Kalkunte (Prentice Hall PTR, 1998).

29. Which statement below is correct regarding VLANs?

    a. A VLAN restricts flooding to only those ports included in the VLAN.

    b. A VLAN is a network segmented physically, not logically.

    c. A VLAN is less secure when implemented in conjunction with private port switching.

    d. A "closed" VLAN configuration is the least secure VLAN configuration.

    Answer: a

    A virtual local area network (VLAN) allows ports on the same or different switches to be grouped so that traffic is confined to members of that group only, and restricts broadcast, unicast, and multicast traffic. Answer b is incorrect, because a VLAN is segmented logically, rather than physically. Answer c is incorrect. When a VLAN is implemented with private port, or single-user, switching, it provides fairly stringent security because broadcast vulnerabilities are minimized. Answer d is incorrect, as a "closed" VLAN authenticates a user to an access control list on a central authentication server, where they are assigned authorization parameters to determine their level of network access. Sources: "Catalyst 5000 Series Installation Guide" (Cisco Systems) and *Virtual LANs* by Mariana Smith (McGraw-Hill, 1998).

30. Which choice below denotes a packet-switched connectionless wide area network (WAN) technology?

    a. X.25

    b. Frame Relay

    c. SMDS

    d. ATM

    > *Answer:* c
    >
    > Switched Multimegabit Data Service (SMDS) is a high-speed, connectionless, packet-switching public network service that extends LAN-like performance to a metropolitan area network (MAN) or a wide area network (WAN). It's generally delivered over a SONET ring with a maximum effective service radius of around 30 miles. Answer a, X.25, defines an interface to the first commercially successful connection-oriented packet-switching network, in which the packets travel over virtual circuits. Answer b, Frame Relay, was a successor to X.25, and offers a connection-oriented packet-switching network. Answer d, Asynchronous Transfer Mode (ATM), was developed from an outgrowth of ISDN standards, and is fast-packet, connection-oriented, cell-switching technology. Source: *Communications Systems and Networks* by Ray Horak (M&T Books, 2000).

31. Which statement below is accurate about the difference between Ethernet II and 802.3 frame formats?

    a. 802.3 uses a "Length" field, whereas Ethernet II uses a "Type" field.

    b. 802.3 uses a "Type" field, whereas Ethernet II uses a "Length" field.

    c. Ethernet II uses a 4-byte FCS field, whereas 802.3 uses an 8-byte Preamble field.

    d. Ethernet II uses an 8-byte Preamble field, whereas 802.3 uses a 4-byte FCS field.

    > *Answer:* a
    >
    > 802.3 uses a "Length" field which indicates the number of data bytes that are in the data field. Ethernet II uses a "Type" field in the same 2 bytes to identify the message protocol type. Both frame formats use a 8-byte Preamble field at the start of the packet, and a 4-byte Frame Check Sequence (FCS) field at the end of the packet, so

Ethernet_II

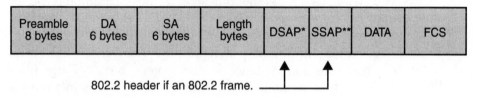

Preamble 8 bytes	DA 6 bytes	SA 6 bytes	Type 2 bytes	Data	FCS 4 bytes

802.3_Ethernet

Preamble 8 bytes	DA 6 bytes	SA 6 bytes	Length bytes	DSAP*	SSAP**	DATA	FCS

802.2 header if an 802.2 frame.

Figure A.2 Ethernet II versus 802.3 frame format.

those choices would be incorrect as to a difference in the frame formats. Sources: *Gigabit Ethernet* by Jayant Kadambi, Ian Crayford, and Mohan Kalkunte (Prentice Hall PTR, 1998) and *CCNA Study Guide* by Todd Lammle, Donald Porter, and James Chellis (Sybex, 1999).

Figure A.2 shows the differences between the Ethernet II and the 802.3 frame formats.

32. Which standard below does NOT specify fiber optic cabling as its physical media?

    a. 100BaseFX

    b. 1000BaseCX

    c. 1000BaseLX

    d. 1000BaseSX

    Answer: b

    1000BaseCX refers to 1000Mbps baseband copper cable, using two pairs of 150 ohm balanced cable for CSMA/CD LANs. Answer a, 100BaseFX, specifies a 100 Mbps baseband fiber optic CSMA/CD LAN. Answer c, 1000BaseLX, specifies a 1000Mbps CSMA/CD LAN over long wavelength fiber optics. Answer d, 1000BaseSX, specifies a 1000Mbps CSMA/CD LAN over short wavelength fiber optics. Answers b, c, and d are defined in IEEE 802.3z. Source: *Gigabit Ethernet* by Jayant Kadambi, Ian Crayford, and Mohan Kalkunte (Prentice Hall PTR, 1998).

33. Which type of routing below commonly broadcasts its routing table information to all other routers every minute?

    a. Static Routing

    b. Distance Vector Routing

    c. Link State Routing

    d. Dynamic Control Protocol Routing

    Answer: b

    Distance vector routing uses the routing information protocol (RIP) to maintain a dynamic table of routing information that is updated regularly. It is the oldest and most common type of dynamic routing. Answer a, static routing, defines a specific route in a configuration file on the router and does not require the routers to exchange route information dynamically. Answer c, link state routers, functions like distance vector routers, but only use first-hand information when building routing tables by maintaining a copy of every other router's Link State Protocol (LSP) frame. This helps to eliminate routing errors and considerably lessens convergence time. Answer d is a distracter. Source: *Mastering Network Security* by Chris Brenton (Sybex, 1999).

34. Which protocol is used to resolve a known IP address to an unknown MAC address?

    a. ARP

    b. RARP

    c. ICMP

    d. TFTP

    Answer: a

    The Address Resolution Protocol (ARP) sends a broadcast asking for the host with a specified IP address to reply with its MAC, or hardware address. This information is kept in the ARP Cache. Answer b, the Reverse Address Resolution Protocol (RARP) is commonly used on diskless machines, when the MAC is known, but not the IP address. It asks a RARP server to provide a valid IP address, which is somewhat the reverse of ARP. Answer c, the Internet Control Message Protocol (ICMP) is a management protocol for IP. Answer d, the Trivial File Transfer Protocol (TFTP), is a stripped-down version of the File Transfer Protocol (FTP). Source: *CCNA Study Guide* by Todd Lammle, Donald Porter, and James Chellis (Sybex, 1999).

35. Which statement accurately describes the difference between 802.11b WLAN ad hoc and infrastructure modes?

    a. The ad hoc mode requires an Access Point to communicate to the wired network.

    b. Wireless nodes can communicate peer-to-peer in the infrastructure mode.

    c. Wireless nodes can communicate peer-to-peer in the ad hoc mode.

    d. Access points are rarely used in 802.11b WLANs.

    Answer: c

    Nodes on an IEEE 802.11b wireless LANs can communicate in one of two modes: ad hoc or infrastructure. In ad hoc mode, the wireless nodes communicate directly with each other, without establishing a connection to an access point on a wired LAN. In infrastructure mode, the wireless nodes communicate to an access point, which operates similarly to a bridge or router and manages traffic between the wireless network and the wired network. Source: *Wireless Security Essentials* by Russell Dean Vines (Wiley, 2002).

    Figure A.3 shows access points attached to a wired LAN to create an Infrastructure Mode 802.11b WLAN.

36. Which type of cabling below is the most common type for recent Ethernet installations?

    a. ThickNet

    b. ThinNet

    c. Twinax

    d. Twisted Pair

    Answer: d

    Category 5 Unshielded Twisted Pair (UTP) is rated for very high data throughput (100 Mbps) at short distances (up to 100 meters), and is the standard cable type for Ethernet installations. Answer a, ThickNet, also known as 10Base5, uses traditional thick coaxial (coax) cable at data rates of up to 10 Mbps. Answer b, ThinNet, uses a thinner gauge coax, and is known as 10Base2. It has a shorter maximum segment distance than ThickNet, but is less expensive to install (also known as CheaperNet). Answer c, Twinax, is like ThinNet, but has two conductors, and was used in IBM Systems 36 and earlier AS/400 installations. Source: *Communications Systems and Networks* by Ray Horak (M&T Books, 2000).

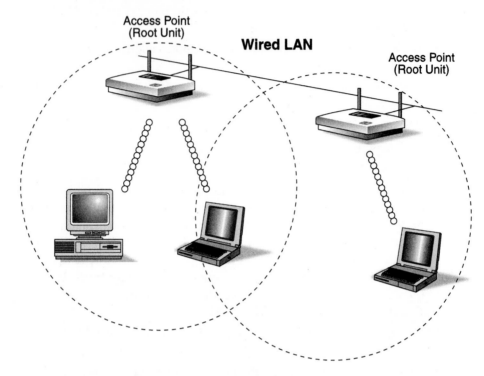

Figure A.3   802.11b infrastructure mode WLAN.

37. Which choice below most accurately describes SSL?

    a. It's a widely used standard of securing e-mail at the Application level.

    b. It gives a user remote access to a command prompt across a secure, encrypted session.

    c. It uses two protocols, the Authentication Header and the Encapsulating Security Payload.

    d. It allows an application to have authenticated, encrypted communications across a network.

    Answer: d

    The Secure Socket Layer (SSL) sits between higher-level application functions and the TCP/IP stack and provides security to applications. It includes a variety of encryption algorithms to secure transmitted data, but the functionality must be integrated into the application. Answer a refers to the Secure/Multipurpose Internet Mail Extension (S/MIME). Most major e-mail clients support

S/MIME today. Answer b describes Secure Shell (SSH). Answer c refers to IPSec. IPSec enables security to be built directly into the TCP/IP stack, without requiring application modification. Source: *Counter Hack* by Ed Skoudis (Prentice Hall PTR, 2002).

38. Which backup method listed below will probably require the backup operator to use the most number of tapes for a complete system restoration, if a different tape is used every night in a five-day rotation?

    a. Full Backup Method

    b. Differential Backup Method

    c. Incremental Backup Method

    d. Ad Hoc Backup Method

    Answer: c

    Most backup methods use the Archive file attribute to determine whether the file should be backed up or not. The backup software determines which files need to be backed up by checking to see if the Archive file attribute has been set, and then resets the Archive bit value to null after the backup procedure. The Incremental Backup Method backs up only files that have been created or modified since the last backup was made, because the Archive file attribute is reset. This can result in the backup operator needing several tapes to do a complete restoration, as every tape with changed files as well as the last full backup tape will need to be restored.

    Answer a, a Full or Complete backup backs up all files in all directories stored on the server regardless of when the last backup was made and whether the files have already been backed up. The Archive file attribute is changed to mark that the files have been backed up, and the tapes or tapes will have all data and applications on it. It's an incorrect answer for this question, however, as it's assumed answers b and c will additionally require differential or incremental tapes.

    Answer b, the Differential Backup Method, backs up only files that have been created or modified since the last backup was made, like an incremental backup. However, the difference between an incremental backup and a differential backup is that the Archive file attribute is not reset after the differential backup is completed, therefore the changed file is backed up every time the differential backup is run. The backup set grows in size until the next full backup as these files continue to be backed up during each subsequent differential backup, until the next complete backup occurs. The advantage of this backup method is that the backup operator should only need the full backup and the one differential backup to restore the system.

Table A.9 shows these three backup methods.

Answer d is a distracter.

Source: http://compreviews.about.com/library/weekly/aa042599.htm and http://www.nwconnection.com/sep.98/techsp98/jobs.html.

39. Which choice below is NOT an element of a fiber optic cable?

a. Core

b. BNC

c. Jacket

d. Cladding

Answer: b

A BNC refers to a Bayonet Neil Concelman RG58 connector for 10Base2. Fiber optic cable has three basic physical elements, the core, the cladding, and the jacket. The core is the innermost transmission medium, which can be glass or plastic. The next outer layer, the cladding is also made of glass or plastic, but has different properties, and helps to reflect the light back into the core. The outermost layer, the jacket, provides protection from heat, moisture, and other environmental elements. Source: *Gigabit Ethernet* by Jayant Kadambi, Ian Crayford, and Mohan Kalkunte (Prentice Hall PTR, 1998).

Figure A.4 shows a cross-section of a fiber optic cable.

40. Given an IP address of 172.16.0.0, which subnet mask below would allow us to divide the network into the maximum number of subnets with at least 600 host addresses per subnet?

a. 255.255.224.0

b. 255.255.240.0

c. 255.255.248.0

d. 255.255.252.0

Answer: d

The last two octets of this class B address, 252.0, gives us binary: 11111100.00000000. The six subnet bits give us 62 (2^6 -2) subnets, each with 1022 (2^{10} -2) hosts, which allows us to have the maximum number of subnets with almost double the required host addresses. Answer a, 224.0, is 11100000.00000000 binary, which gives us six (2^3 -2) subnets with 8190 (2^{13} -2) hosts each. Answer b, 240.0, is 11110000.00000000 binary, and gives us 14 (2^4 -2) subnets each with 4094 (2^{12} -2) hosts. Answer c, 248.0, is 11111000.00000000 binary, which creates 30 (2^5 -2) subnets with 2046 (2^{11} -2) hosts. Many books give detailed descriptions of IP subnetting.

Table A.9 Differential versus Incremental Backup Tape Contents

BACKUP METHOD	MONDAY	TUESDAY	WEDNESDAY	THURSDAY	FRIDAY
Differential	Changed File A	Changed Files A & B	Files A, B, & C	Files A, B, C, & D	
Incremental	Changed File A	Changed File B	Changed File C	Changed File D	
Full Backup					All Files

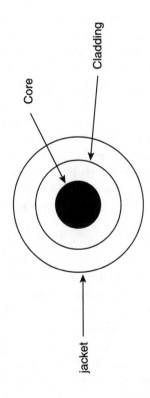

Core

Cladding

jacket

Figure A.4 Fiber optic cable layers.

Chapter 4—Cryptography

1. A cryptographic algorithm is also known as:

   a. A cryptosystem

   b. Cryptanalysis

   c. A cipher

   d. A key

   Answer: c

   A cipher is a cryptographic transformation that operates on characters or bits. In different words, a cipher is defined as a cryptographic algorithm or mathematical function that operates on characters or bits and implements encryption or decryption. In contrast, a code operates with words, phrases and sentences. In a code, a word may be the encipherment of a sentence or phrase. For example, the word SCARF may be the code for the term BEWARE OF DUTCH TRAITOR IN YOUR MIDST.

   In answer a, a cryptosystem is a set of transformations from a message space to a ciphertext space. This system includes all cryptovariables (keys), plaintexts and ciphertexts associated with the transformation algorithm. The difference between answers a and c is that answer c, the correct answer, refers to the algorithm alone and answer a refers to the algorithm and all plaintexts, ciphertexts and cryptovariables associated with this algorithm.

   Answer b, cryptanalysis, refers to being able to "break" the cipher so that the encrypted message can be read. Cryptanalysis may be accomplished by exploiting weaknesses in the cipher or, in some fashion, determining the key. This act of obtaining the plaintext or key from the ciphertext can be used to recover sensitive or classified information and, perhaps, to pass on altered or fake messages in order to deceive the original intended recipient.

   Answer d, the key or cryptovariable, is used with a particular algorithm to encipher or decipher the plaintext message. By using the key, the algorithm can be publicly known and evaluated for its strength against attack. The key associated with a particular transformation or algorithm can take on many values and the range of all of these possible values is called the *keyspace*. Ideally, an enciphered plaintext message using a specific algorithm will produce a unique ciphertext message for each different key that is used with that algorithm. The situation in which a plaintext message generates identical ciphertext messages using the same transformation algorithm, but with different cryptovariables, is called *key clustering*. Obviously, this is not a desirable situation, since it effectively reduces the number of keys that have to be tried by an attacker in order to recover the plaintext.

2. Which of the following is NOT an issue with secret key cryptography?

   a. Security of the certification authority.

   b. A networked group of m users with separate keys for each pair of users will require m (m-1)/2 keys.

   c. Secure distribution of the keys.

   d. Compromise of the keys can enable the attacker to impersonate the key owners and, therefore, read and send false messages.

   Answer: a

   The CA is used in public key cryptography, not secret key cryptography. A CA will certify that a public key actually belongs to a specific individual and that the information associated with the individual's key is valid and correct. The CA accomplishes this certification by digitally signing the individual's public key and associated information. The certification professes to another person who wants to send a message to this individual using public key encryption that the public key actually belongs to the intended individual. The Consultation Committee, International Telephone and Telegraph, International Telecommunications Union (CCITT-ITU)/ International Organization for Standardization (ISO) X.509 Authentication framework defines a format for public key certificates. This structure is outlined in Figure A.5.

   Answer b is an important issue in secret key cryptography; therefore it is not the correct answer. If, among a network of m users, each user wants to have secure communications with every other user on the network, then there must be a secret key for each pair of potential users. This concept can be illustrated with five users as shown in Figure A.6. Thus, with five users, the number of independent keys is equal to (5 x 4)/2 or 10 as depicted by the ten connecting lines in Figure A.6.

   The answer c is incorrect since securely distributing the keys to all users is, obviously, a very important requirement.

   Answer d is incorrect since a compromise of the keys can, indeed, enable the attacker to impersonate the key owners and, therefore, read and send false messages.

3. Which of the following is NOT a characteristic of the ElGamal public key cryptosystem?

   a. It can perform encryption.

   b. It can be used to generate digital signatures.

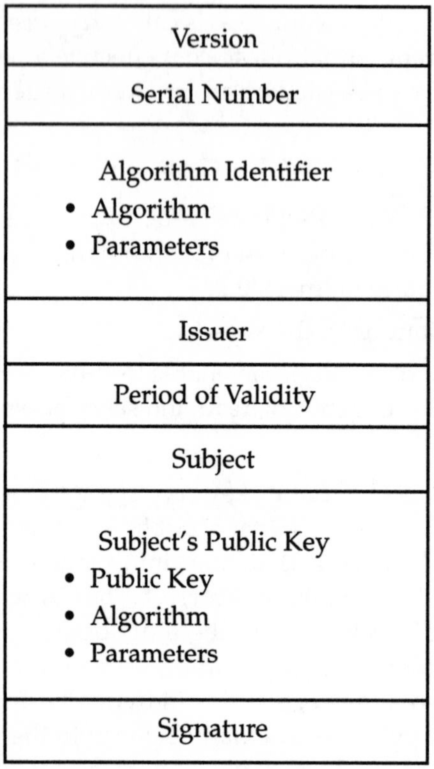

Version
Serial Number
Algorithm Identifier • Algorithm • Parameters
Issuer
Period of Validity
Subject
Subject's Public Key • Public Key • Algorithm • Parameters
Signature

Figure A.5 CCITT-ITU/ ISO X.509 certificate format.

c. It is based on the discrete logarithm problem.

d. It can perform encryption, but not digital signatures.

Answer: d

The ElGamal public key cryptosystem can perform both encryption and digital signatures based on the discrete logarithm problem. These three characteristics are shown in the examples that follow.

To generate a key pair in the ElGamal system:

a. Choose a prime number, p.

b. Choose two random numbers, g and x (g and x must both be less than p).

c. Calculate $y = g^x \bmod p$.

d. The private key is x and the public key is y, g, and p.

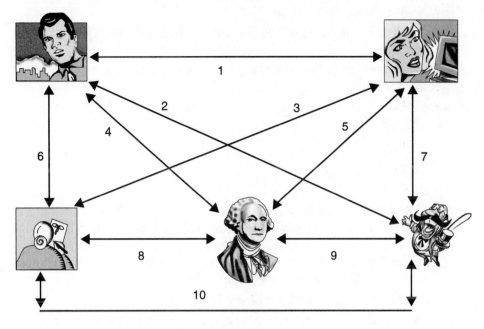

Figure A.6   Networked users requiring independent keys.

To encrypt a message, M, in the ElGamal system:

a. Select a random number, j, such that j is relatively prime to p-1. Recall that two numbers are relatively prime if they have no common factors other than 1.

b. Generate $w = g^j \bmod p$ and $z = y^j M \bmod p$.

c. w and z comprise the ciphertext.

To decrypt the message, M, in the ElGamal system, calculate $M = z/w^x \bmod p$. This can be shown by substituting the values of z and w in the equation as follows:

$M = y^j M \bmod p / g^{jx} \bmod p$

Since $y^j = g^{xj} \bmod p$

$M = (g^{xj} M / g^{jx}) \bmod p$

To sign a message, M, in the ElGamal system:

a. Select a random number, j, such that j is relatively prime to p-1. The value of j must not be disclosed. Generate $w = g^j \bmod p$.

b. Solve for z in the equation $M = (xw + jz) \bmod (p-1)$. The solution to this equation is beyond the scope of this coverage. Suffice to say that an algorithm exists to solve for the variable z.

c. w and z comprise the signature.

d. Verification of the signature is accomplished if $g^M \bmod p = y^w w^z \bmod p$.

4. The Transport Layer Security (TLS) 1.0 protocol is based on which Protocol Specification?

a. SSH-2

b. SSL-3.0

c. IPSEC

d. TCP/IP

Answer: b

The differences between TLS and SSL are not great, but there is enough of a difference such that TLS 1.0 and SSL 3.0 are not operationally compatible. If interoperability is desired, there is a capability in TLS that allows it to function as SSL. Question 5 provides additional discussion of the TLS protocol.

5. The primary goal of the TLS Protocol is to provide:

a. Privacy and authentication between two communicating applications

b. Privacy and data integrity between two communicating applications

c. Authentication and data integrity between two communicating applications

d. Privacy, authentication and data integrity between two communicating applications

Answer: b

The TLS Protocol is comprised of the TLS *Record* and *Handshake* Protocols. The TLS Record Protocol is layered on top of a transport protocol such as TCP and provides privacy and reliability to the communications. The privacy is implemented by encryption using symmetric key cryptography such as DES or RC4. The secret key is generated anew for each connection; however, the Record Protocol can be used without encryption. Integrity is provided through the use of a *keyed Message Authentication Code (MAC)* using hash algorithms such as SHA or MD5.

The TLS Record Protocol is also used to encapsulate a higher-level protocol such as the TLS Handshake Protocol. This Handshake Protocol is used by the server and client to authenticate each other. The authentication can be accomplished using asymmetric key cryptography such as RSA or DSS. The Handshake Protocol also sets up the encryption algorithm and cryptographic keys to enable the application protocol to transmit and receive information.

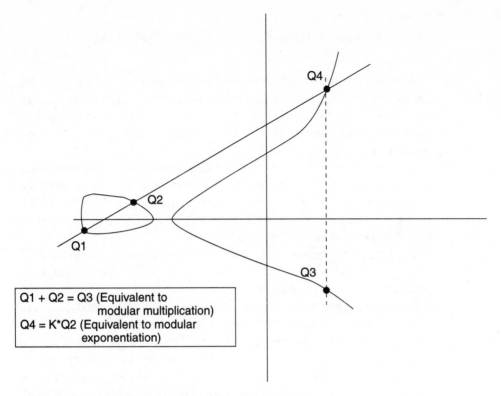

Figure A.7 Graph of the function $y^2 = x^3 + ax + b$.

6. The graph in Figure A.7, which depicts the equation $y^2 = x^3 + ax + b$, denotes the:

   a. Elliptic curve and the elliptic curve discrete logarithm problem
   b. RSA Factoring problem
   c. ElGamal discrete logarithm problem
   d. Knapsack problem

   Answer: a

   The elliptic curve is defined over a finite field comprised of real, complex or rational numbers. The points on an elliptic curve form a Group under addition as shown in Figure A.7. Multiplication (or multiple additions) in an elliptic curve system is equivalent to modular exponentiation; thus, defining a discreet logarithm problem.

7. In communications between two parties, encrypting the hash function of a message with a symmetric key algorithm is equivalent to:

   a. Generating a digital signature
   b. Providing for secrecy of the message

c. Generating a one-way function

d. Generating a keyed Message Authentication Code (MAC)

Answer: d

A MAC is used to authenticate files between users. If the sender and receiver both have the secret key, they are the only ones that can verify the hash function. If a symmetric key algorithm is used to encrypt the one-way hash function, then the one-way hash function becomes a keyed MAC.

Answer a is incorrect because a digital signature between two parties uses an asymmetric key algorithm. If a message is encrypted with the sender's private key, then only the sender's public key can decrypt the message. This proves that the message was sent by the sender since only the sender knows the private key.

In practice, asymmetric key encryption is very slow, especially for long messages. Therefore, a one-way hash of the message is encrypted with the sender's private key instead of encrypting the complete message. Then, the message and the encrypted hash are sent to a second party. The receiver takes the encrypted hash and decrypts it with the sender's public key. Then, the receiver takes the hash of the message, using the same one-way hash algorithm as the sender. The hash generated by the receiver is compared with the decrypted hash sent with the message. If the two hashes are identical, the digital signature is validated. Note that his method also will reveal if the message was changed en route, since the hash calculated by the receiver will, then, be different from the encrypted hash sent along with the message.

Answer b is incorrect since encrypting the hash of the message and sending the message in the clear does nothing to protect the confidentiality of the message. Since the hash function is a one-way function, the message cannot be recovered from its hash.

Answer c is incorrect since encrypting a hash of a message is not a one-way function. If it were, it would be of no use since no one would be able to reverse the process and decrypt it.

8. Which of the following is NOT a characteristic of a cryptographic hash function, H (m), where m denotes the message being hashed by the function H?

a. H (m) is collision free.

b. H (m) is difficult to compute for any given m.

c. The output is of fixed length.

d. H (m) is a one-way function.

Answer: b

For a cryptographic hash function, H (m) is relatively easy to compute for a given m. Answer a is a characteristic of a good cryptographic hash function, in that collision free means that for a given message, M, that produces H (M) = Z, it is computationally infeasible to find another message, M1, such that H (M1) = Z. Answer c is part of the definition of a hash function since it generates a fixed-length result that is independent of the length of the input message. This characteristic is useful for generating digital signatures since the signature can be applied to the fixed-length hash that is uniquely characteristic of the message instead of to the entire message, which is usually much longer than the hash. Answer d relates to answer b in that a one-way function is difficult or impossible to invert. This means that for a hash function H (M) = Z, it is computationally infeasible to reverse the process and find M given the hash Z and the function H.

9. Which one of the following statements BEST describes the operation of the Digital Signature Algorithm (DSA) (National Institute of Standards and Technology, NIST FIPS PUB 186, "Digital Signature Standard," U.S. Department of Commerce, May 1994) at the transmitting end of a communication between two parties?

   a. A message of < 2^{64} bits is input to the DSA, and the resultant message digest of 160 bits is fed into the Secure Hash Algorithm (SHA), which generates the digital signature of the message.

   b. A message of < 2^{64} bits is input to the Secure Hash Algorithm (SHA), and the resultant message digest of 128 bits is fed into the DSA, which generates the digital signature of the message.

   c. A message of < 2^{64} bits is input to the Secure Hash Algorithm (SHA), and the resultant message digest of 160 bits is used as the digital signature of the message.

   d. A message of < 2^{64} bits is input to the Secure Hash Algorithm (SHA), and the resultant message digest of 160 bits is fed into the DSA, which generates the digital signature of the message.

   Answer: d

   Answer d describes the proper sequence of operating on the message and has the correct value of 160 bits for the SHA message digest. At the receiving end, the message is fed into the SHA, and the result is compared to the received message digest to verify the signature. Answer a is incorrect since the order of the DSA and SHA are in reverse sequence from the correct order of their application. Answer b is incorrect since it has the incorrect value of 128 bits for the message digest produced by the SHA. Answer c is incorrect since the message digest has to be fed into the DSA to generate the digital signature of the message.

10. If the application of a hash function results in an m-bit fixed length output, an attack on the hash function that attempts to achieve a collision after 2 m/2 possible trial input values is called a(n):

   a. Adaptive-chosen-plaintext attack

   b. Chosen-ciphertext attack

   c. Birthday attack

   d. Meet-in-the-middle attack

   Answer: c

   This problem is analogous to asking the question "How many people must be in a room for the probability of two people having the same birthday to be equal to 50%?" The answer is 23. Thus, trying $2^{m/2}$ possible trial inputs to a hash function gives a 50% chance of finding two inputs that have the same hash value. Answer a, describes an attack in which the attacker can choose the plaintext to be encrypted and can modify his/her choice based on the results of a previous encryption. Answer b, the chosen-cipher text attack, is where the attacker can select different ciphertexts to be decrypted and has the decrypted plaintext available. This attack is used to determine the key or keys being used. Answer d is an attack against double encryption. This approach shows that for a key length of k bits, a chosen-plaintext attack could find the key after 2^{k+1} trials instead of 2^{2k} attempts. In this attack on double encryption, one encrypts from one end, decrypts from the other and compares the results "in-the-middle."

11. The minimum information necessary on a digital certificate is:

   a. Name, expiration date, digital signature of the certifier

   b. Name, expiration date, public key

   c. Name, serial number, private key

   d. Name, public key, digital signature of the certifier

   Answer: d

   The correct answer is d, where the name of the individual is certified and bound to his/her public key. This certification is validated by the digital signature of the certifying agent. In answer a, the public key is not present to be bound to the person's name. In answer b, the public key and name are present, but there is no digital signature verifying that the public key belongs to the name. Answer c is incorrect on a number of counts. First, the private key is never disclosed to the public and secondly, there is no digital signature.

12. What do the message digest algorithms MD2, MD4 and MD5 have in common?

   a. They all take a message of arbitrary length and produce a message digest of 160-bits.

   b. They all take a message of arbitrary length and produce a message digest of 128-bits.

   c. They are all optimized for 32-bit machines.

   d. They are all used in the Secure Hash Algorithm (SHA).

   Answer: b

   Answer a is obviously, then, incorrect. Answer c is incorrect since MD2 (B.S. Kaliski, "The MD2 Message Digest Algorithm," RFC 1319, April 1992) is targeted for 8-bit machines. It is used in Privacy Enhanced Mail (PEM). MD4 (R.L. Rivest, "The MD4 Message Digest Algorithm," RFC 1186, Oct 1990) and MD5 (R.L. Rivest, "The MD5 Message Digest Algorithm," RFC 1321, April 1992) are designed for 32-bit machines. MD5 is considered more secure than MD4, and MD5 is also used in PEM. Answer d is incorrect since the SHA is a separate algorithm from MD2, MD4, and MD5, but is modeled after MD4. SHA produces a 160-bit message digest.

13. What is the correct sequence which enables an authorized agency to use the Law Enforcement Access Field (LEAF) to decrypt a message sent by using the Clipper Chip? The following designations are used for the respective keys involved—K_f, the family key; K_s, the session key; U, a unique identifier for each Clipper Chip and K_u, the unit key that is unique to each Clipper Chip.

   a. Obtain a court order to acquire the two halves of K_u, the unit key. Recover K_u. Decrypt the LEAF with K_u and then recover Ks, the session key. Use the session key to decrypt the message.

   b. Decrypt the LEAF with the family key, K_f; recover U; obtain a court order to obtain the two halves of K_u; recover K_u; and then recover K_s, the session key. Use the session key to decrypt the message.

   c. Decrypt the LEAF with the family key, K_f; recover U; obtain a court order to obtain K_s, the session key. Use the session key to decrypt the message.

   d. Obtain a court order to acquire the family key, K_f; recover U and K_u; then recover K_s, the session key. Use the session key to decrypt the message.

LEAF FIELD Encrypted with Family Key

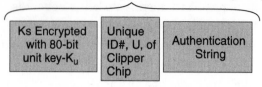

Ks Encrypted with 80-bit unit key-K_u	Unique ID#, U, of Clipper Chip	Authentication String

Figure A.8   Leaf field.

Answer: b

The explanation is based on the LEAF as shown in Figure A.8. The message is encrypted with the symmetric session key, K_s. In order to decrypt the message, then, K_s must be recovered. The LEAF contains the session key, but the LEAF is encrypted with the family key, K_f, that is common to all Clipper Chips. The authorized agency has access to K_f and decrypts the LEAF. However, the session key is still encrypted by the 80-bit unit key, K_u, that is unique to each Clipper Chip and is identified by the unique identifier, U. K_u is divided into two halves, and each half is deposited with an escrow agency. The law enforcement agency obtains the two halves of K_u by presenting the escrow agencies with a court order for the key identified by U. The two halves of the key obtained by the court order are XORed together to obtain K_u. Then, K_u is used to recover the session key, K_s, and K_s is used to decrypt the message.

The decryption sequence to obtain K_s can be summarized as:

$$K_f \rightarrow U \rightarrow [1/2K_u \text{ XOR } 1/2 K_u] \rightarrow K_u \rightarrow K_s$$

This is the sequence described in answer b. The sequences described in the other answers are incorrect.

14. What BEST describes the National Security Agency-developed Capstone?

  a. A device for intercepting electromagnetic emissions

  b. The PC Card implementation of the Clipper Chip system

  c. A chip that implements the U.S. Escrowed Encryption Standard

  d. A one-way function for implementation of public key encryption

  Answer: c

  Capstone is a Very Large Scale Integration (VLSI) chip that employs the Escrowed Encryption Standard and incorporates the

Skipjack algorithm, similar to the Clipper Chip. As such, it has a LEAF. Capstone also supports public key exchange and digital signatures. At this time, Capstone products have their LEAF function suppressed and a Certifying Authority provides for key recovery. Answer a is then, obviously, incorrect. For information purposes, though, the U.S. Government program to study and control the interception of electromagnetic emissions that may compromise classified information is called TEMPEST. Answer b is also, obviously, incorrect. However, Capstone was first implemented on a PC card called Fortezza. Answer d is incorrect since Capstone is not a mathematical function, but it incorporates mathematical functions for key exchange, authentication and encryption.

15. Which of the following BEST describes a block cipher?

    a. A symmetric key algorithm that operates on a variable-length block of plaintext and transforms it into a fixed-length block of ciphertext

    b. A symmetric key algorithm that operates on a fixed-length block of plaintext and transforms it into a fixed-length block of ciphertext

    c. An asymmetric key algorithm that operates on a variable-length block of plaintext and transforms it into a fixed-length block of ciphertext

    d. An asymmetric key algorithm that operates on a fixed-length block of plaintext and transforms it into a fixed-length block of ciphertext

    Answer: b

    A block cipher breaks the plaintext into fixed-length blocks, commonly 64-bits, and encrypts the blocks into fixed-length blocks of ciphertext. Another characteristic of the block cipher is that, if the same key is used, a particular plaintext block will be transformed into the same ciphertext block. Examples of block ciphers are DES, Skipjack, IDEA, RC5 and AES. An example of a block cipher in a symmetric key cryptosystem is the Electronic Code Book (ECB) mode of operation. In the ECB mode, a plaintext block is transformed into a ciphertext block as shown in Figure A.9. If the same key is used for each transformation, then a "Code Book" can be compiled for each plaintext block and corresponding ciphertext block.

    Answer a is incorrect since it refers to a variable-length block of plaintext being transformed into a fixed-length block of ciphertext. Recall that this operation has some similarity to a hash function, which takes a message of arbitrary length and converts it into a fixed-length message digest. Answers c and d are incorrect because they involve asymmetric key algorithms, and the block cipher is used with symmetric key algorithms.

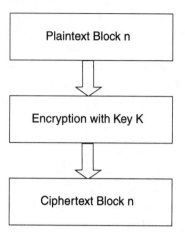

Figure A.9 A ciphertext block.

In other cryptographic modes of operation, such as Cipher Block Chaining (CBC), the result of the encryption of the plaintext block, Pn, is fed into the encryption process of plaintext block Pn+1. Thus, the result of the encryption of one block affects the result of the encryption of the next block in the sequence.

16. An iterated block cipher encrypts by breaking the plaintext block into two halves and, with a subkey, applying a "round" transformation to one of the halves. Then, the output of this transformation is XORed with the remaining half. The round is completed by swapping the two halves. This type of cipher is known as:

    a. RC4

    b. Diffie-Hellman

    c. RC6

    d. Feistel

    Answer: d

    The question stem describes one round of a Feistel cipher. This algorithm was developed by an IBM team led by Horst Feistel. (H. Feistel, "Cryptography and Computer Privacy," *Scientific American*, v.228, n.5, May 1973) The algorithm was called Lucifer and was the basis for the Data Encryption Standard (DES). In answer a, RC4 is a variable key-size stream cipher developed by Ronald Rivest. In this type of cipher, a sequence of bits that are the key is bit-wise XORed with the plaintext. In answer b, Diffie-Hellman describes the first public key algorithm and is based on the difficulty of calculating discrete logarithms in a finite field. (W. Diffie and M.E. Hellman, "New Directions in Cryptography," "*IEEE Transactions on Information Theory*," v. IT-22, n. 6, Nov 1976). It is used for exchanging keys. RC6, in answer c, is a fast block cipher designed by Rivest, Sidney and Yin. In RC6, the block size, the key size and the number of rounds are variable. The key size can be no larger than 2040 bits. RC6 was one of the five finalists in the Advanced Encryption Standard (AES) competition.

17. A key schedule is:

    a. A list of cryptographic keys to be used at specified dates and times

    b. A method of generating keys by the use of random numbers

    c. A set of subkeys derived from a secret key

    d. Using distributed computing resources to conduct a brute force attack on a symmetric algorithm

    Answer: c

    The subkeys are typically used in iterated block ciphers. In this type of cipher, the plaintext is broken into fixed-length blocks and enciphered in "rounds." In a round, the same transformation is applied using one of the subkeys of the key schedule. (See the answer to question 16.)

18. The Wireless Transport Layer Security (WTLS) Protocol in the Wireless Application Protocol (WAP) stack is based on which Internet Security Protocol?

    a. S-HTTP

    b. TLS

    c. SET

    d. IPSEC

    Answer: b

    TLS is discussed in the answer to question 5. WTLS has to incorporate functionality that is provided for in TLS by TCP in the TCP/IP Protocol suite in that WTLS can operate over UDP. WTLS supports data privacy, authentication and integrity. Because WTLS has to incorporate a large number of handshakes when security is implemented, significant delays may occur. During a WTLS handshake session, WTLS can set up the following security classes:

    Class 1. No certificates

    Class 2. The client does not have a certificate; the server has a certificate

    Class 3. The client and server have certificates

19. The Advanced Encryption Standard (Rijndael) block cipher requirements regarding keys and block sizes have now evolved to which configuration?

    a. Both the key and block sizes can be 128, 192, and 256 bits each.

    b. The key size is 128 bits, and the block size can be 128, 192, or 256 bits.

    c. The block size is 128 bits, and the key can be 128, 192, or 256 bits.

    d. The block size is 128 bits, and the key size is 128 bits.

    Answer: c

    AES is comprised of the three key sizes, 128, 192, and 256 bits with a fixed block size of 128 bits. The Advanced Encryption Standard (AES) was announced on November 26, 2001, as Federal Information Processing Standard Publication (FIPS PUB 197). FIPS PUB 197 states that "This standard may be used by Federal departments and agencies when an agency determines that sensitive (unclassified) information (as defined in P.L. 100-235) requires cryptographic protection. Other FIPS-approved cryptographic algorithms may be used in addition to, or in lieu of, this standard." Depending upon which of the three keys is used, the standard may be referred to as "AES-128," "AES-192" or "AES-256."

    The number of rounds used in the Rijndael cipher is a function of the key size as follows:

    256-bit key → 14 rounds

    192-bit key → 12 rounds

    128-bit key → 10 rounds

    Rijndael has a symmetric and parallel structure that provides for flexibility of implementation and resistance to cryptanalytic attacks. Attacks on Rijndael would involve the use of differential and linear cryptanalysis.

20. The Wireless Transport Layer Security Protocol (WTLS) in the Wireless Application Protocol (WAP) stack provides for security:

    a. Between the WAP gateway and the content server

    b. Between the WAP client and the gateway

    c. Between the Internet and the content server

    d. Between the WAP content server and the WAP client

    Answer: b

    Transport Layer Security (TLS) provides for security between the content server on the Internet and the WAP gateway. (Answer a is,

Figure A.10 WAP to WAP gateway to Internet block diagram.

thus, incorrect.) Similarly, WTLS provides security between the WAP mobile device (client software) and the WAP gateway. Since WAP cannot interface directly with the Internet, all WAP information has to be converted to HTTP in the WAP gateway to enable it to exchange information with the Internet content servers. The simple block diagram of Figure A.10 illustrates these concepts.

A vulnerability occurs since data encrypted with wireless protocols has to be decrypted in the WAP gateway and then re-encrypted with the Internet protocols. This process is reversed when data flows from the Internet content servers to the WAP client. Thus, the information is vulnerable while it is in the decrypted state on the WAP gateway. This condition is known as the WAP Gap. In order to address this issue, the WAP Forum has put forth specifications that will reduce this vulnerability and, thus, support e-commerce applications. These specifications are defined in WAP 1.2 as WMLScript Crypto Library and the WAP Identity Module (WIM). The WMLScript Crypto Library supports end-to-end security by providing for cryptographic functions to be initiated on the WAP client from the Internet content server. These functions include digital signatures originating with the WAP client and encryption and decryption of data. The WIM is a tamper-resistant device, such as a smart card, that cooperates with WTLS and provides cryptographic operations during the handshake phase.

The WAP Forum is also considering another alternative to providing the end-to-end encryption for WAP. This alternative, described in WAP specification 1.3, is the use of a client proxy server that communicates authentication and authorization information to the wireless network server.

Answer c is incorrect since the content server is on the Internet side of the communication and answer d assumes a direct interface between the content server and the client without going through the necessary Internet and wireless protocols.

21. What is a protocol that adds digital signatures and encryption to Internet MIME (Multipurpose Internet Mail Extensions)?

    a. IPSEC

    b. PGP

    c. S/MIME

    d. SET/MIME

    Answer: c

    The MIME protocol specifies a structure for the body of an email message. MIME supports a number of formats in the email body, including graphic, enhanced text and audio, but does not provide security services for these messages. S/MIME defines such services for MIME as digital signatures and encryption based on a standard syntax. Answer a is incorrect since IPSEC is not an email protocol but is a standard that provides encryption, access control, nonrepudiation, and authentication of messages over IP. It is designed to be functionally compatible with IPv6. Answer b is incorrect because PGP, Pretty Good Privacy, brings security to email through the use of a symmetric cipher, such as IDEA, to encipher the message. RSA is used for symmetric key exchange and for digital signatures. PGP is not an augmentation of MIME. RFC 2440 permits other algorithms to be used in PGP. In order of preference, they are ElGamal and RSA for key distribution; triple DES, IDEA and CAST5 for encryption of messages; DSA and RSA for digital signatures and SHA-1 or MD5 for generating hashes of the messages. Answer d is incorrect because there is no such protocol. There is a protocol called SET for Secure Electronic Transaction. It was developed by Visa and MasterCard to secure electronic bankcard transactions. SET requests authorization for payment and requires certificates binding a person's public key to their identity.

22. Digital cash refers to the electronic transfer of funds from one party to another. When digital cash is referred to as anonymous or identified, it means that:

    a. Anonymous—the identity of the cash holder is not known; Identified—the identity of the cash holder is known

    b. Anonymous—the identity of merchant is withheld; Identified—the identity of the merchant is not withheld

    c. Anonymous—the identity of the bank is withheld; Identified—the identity of the bank is not withheld

    d. Anonymous—the identity of the cash holder is not known; Identified—the identity of the merchant is known

Answer: a

Anonymous implementations of digital cash do not identify the cash holder and use blind signature schemes; identified implementations use conventional digital signatures to identify the cash holder. In looking at these two approaches, anonymous schemes are analogous to cash since cash does not allow tracing of the person who made the cash payment while identified approaches are the analog of credit or debit card transactions.

23. Which of the following is NOT a key recovery method?

   a. A message is encrypted with a session key and the session key is, in turn, encrypted with the public key of a trustee agent. The encrypted session key is sent along with the encrypted message. The trustee, when authorized, can then decrypt the message by recovering the session key with the trustee's private key.

   b. A message is encrypted with a session key. The session key, in turn, is broken into parts and each part is encrypted with the public key of a different trustee agent. The encrypted parts of the session key are sent along with the encrypted message. The trustees, when authorized, can then decrypt their portion of the session key and provide their respective parts of the session key to a central agent. The central agent can then decrypt the message by reconstructing the session key from the individual components.

   c. A secret key or a private key is broken into a number of parts and each part is deposited with a trustee agent. The agents can then provide their parts of the key to a central authority, when presented with appropriate authorization. The key can then be reconstructed and used to decrypt messages encrypted with that key.

   d. A message is encrypted with a session key and the session key is, in turn, encrypted with the private key of a trustee agent. The encrypted session key is sent along with the encrypted message. The trustee, when authorized, can then decrypt the message by recovering the session key with the trustee's public key.

   Answer: d

   Encrypting parts of the session key with the private keys of the trustee agents provides no security for the message since the message can be decrypted by recovering the key components of the session key using the public keys of the respective agents. These public keys are available to anyone. Answers a, b, and c are valid means of recovering keys, since key recovery refers to permitting access to encrypted messages under predefined circumstances. Answers a and b are also called *key encapsulation* since the session key is encapsulated in the public keys of the trustee agents and, therefore, can be decrypted only by these trustee agents with their private keys.

24. Theoretically, quantum computing offers the possibility of factoring the products of large prime numbers and calculating discreet logarithms in polynomial time. These calculations can be accomplished in such a compressed time frame because:

a. Information can be transformed into quantum light waves that travel through fiber optic channels. Computations can be performed on the associated data by passing the light waves through various types of optical filters and solid-state materials with varying indices of refraction, thus drastically increasing the throughput over conventional computations.

b. A quantum bit in a quantum computer is actually a linear superposition of both the one and zero states and, therefore, can theoretically represent both values in parallel. This phenomenon allows computation that usually takes exponential time to be accomplished in polynomial time since different values of the binary pattern of the solution can be calculated simultaneously.

c. A quantum computer takes advantage of quantum tunneling in molecular scale transistors. This mode permits ultra high-speed switching to take place, thus, exponentially increasing the speed of computations.

d. A quantum computer exploits the time-space relationship that changes as particles approach the speed of light. At that interface, the resistance of conducting materials effectively is zero and exponential speed computations are possible.

Answer: b

In digital computers, a bit is in either a one or zero state. In a quantum computer, through linear superposition, a quantum bit can be in both states, essentially simultaneously. Thus, computations consisting of trail evaluations of binary patterns can take place simultaneously in exponential time. The probability of obtaining a correct result is increased through a phenomenon called constructive interference of light while the probability of obtaining an incorrect result is decreased through destructive interference. Answer a describes optical computing that is effective in applying Fourier and other transformations to data to perform high-speed computations. Light representing large volumes of data passing through properly shaped physical objects can be subjected to mathematical transformations and recombined to provide the appropriate results. However, this mode of computation is not defined as quantum computing. Answers c and d are diversionary answers that do not describe quantum computing.

25. Which of the following statements BEST describes the Public Key Cryptography Standards (PKCS)?

a. A set of public-key cryptography standards that support algorithms such as Diffie-Hellman and RSA as well as algorithm independent standards

b. A set of public-key cryptography standards that support only "standard" algorithms such as Diffie-Hellman and RSA

c. A set of public-key cryptography standards that support only algorithm-independent implementations

d. A set of public-key cryptography standards that support encryption algorithms such as Diffie-Hellman and RSA, but does not address digital signatures

Answer: a

PKCS supports algorithm-independent and algorithm-specific implementations as well as digital signatures and certificates. It was developed by a consortium including RSA Laboratories, Apple, DEC, Lotus, Sun, Microsoft and MIT. At this writing, there are 15 PKCS standards. Examples of these standards are:

PKCS #1. Defines mechanisms for encrypting and signing data using the RSA public-key system

PKCS #3. Defines the Diffie-Hellman key agreement protocol

PKCS #10. Describes a syntax for certification requests

PKCS #15. Defines a standard format for cryptographic credentials stored on cryptographic tokens

26. An interface to a library of software functions that provide security and cryptography services is called:

a. A security application programming interface (SAPI)

b. An assurance application programming interface (AAPI)

c. A cryptographic application programming interface (CAPI)

d. A confidentiality, integrity and availability application programming interface (CIAAPI)

Answer: c

CAPI is designed for software developers to call functions from the library and, thus, make it easier to implement security services. An example of a CAPI is the Generic Security Service API (GSS-API.) The GSS-API provides data confidentiality, authentication, and data integrity services and supports the use of both public and secret key mechanisms. The GSS-API is described in the Internet Proposed Standard RFC 2078. The other answers are made-up distracters.

27. The British Standard 7799/ISO Standard 17799 discusses cryptographic policies. It states, "An organization should develop a policy on its use of cryptographic controls for protection of its information . . . . When developing a policy, the following should be considered:" (Which of the following items would most likely NOT be listed?)

    a. The management approach toward the use of cryptographic controls across the organization

    b. The approach to key management, including methods to deal with the recovery of encrypted information in the case of lost, compromised or damaged keys

    c. Roles and responsibilities

    d. The encryption schemes to be used

    Answer: d

    A policy is a general statement of management's intent, and therefore, a policy would not specify the encryption scheme to be used. Answers a, b, and c are appropriate for a cryptographic policy. The general standards document is BSI ISO/IEC 17799:2000,BS 7799-I: 2000, *Information technology-Code of practice for information security management,* British Standards Institution, London, UK. The standard is intended to "provide a comprehensive set of controls comprising best practices in information security." ISO refers to the International Organization for Standardization and IEC is the International Electrotechnical Commission. These two entities form the system for worldwide standardization.

    The main chapter headings of the standard are:

    ■ Security Policy

    ■ Organizational Security

    ■ Asset Classification and Control

    ■ Personnel Security

    ■ Physical and Environmental Security

    ■ Communications and Operations Management

    ■ Access Control

    ■ Systems Development and Maintenance

    ■ Business Continuity Management

    ■ Compliance

28. The Number Field Sieve (NFS) is a:

    a. General purpose factoring algorithm that can be used to factor large numbers

    b. General purpose algorithm to calculate discreet logarithms

    c. General purpose algorithm used for brute force attacks on secret key cryptosystems

    d. General purpose hash algorithm

    Answer: a

    The NFS has been successful in efficiently factoring numbers larger than 115 digits and a version of NFS has successfully factored a 155-digit number. Clearly, factoring is an attack that can be used against the RSA cryptosystem in which the public and private keys are calculated based on the product of two large prime numbers. Answers b, c, and d are distracters.

29. DESX is a variant of DES in which:

    a. Input plaintext is bitwise XORed with 64 bits of additional key material before encryption with DES.

    b. Input plaintext is bitwise XORed with 64 bits of additional key material before encryption with DES, and the output of DES is also bitwise XORed with another 64 bits of key material.

    c. The output of DES is bitwise XORed with 64 bits of key material.

    d. The input plaintext is encrypted X times with the DES algorithm using different keys for each encryption.

    Answer: b

    DESX was developed by Ron Rivest to increase the resistance of DES to brute force key search attacks; however, the resistance of DESX to differential and linear attacks is equivalent to that of DES with independent subkeys.

30. The ANSI X9.52 standard defines a variant of DES encryption with keys k1, k2, and k3 as:

    $$C = E_{k3} [D_{k2} [E_{k1} [M]]]$$

    What is this DES variant?

    a. DESX

    b. Triple DES in the EEE mode

    c. Double DES with an encryption and decryption with different keys

    d. Triple DES in the EDE mode

Answer: d

This version of triple DES performs an encryption (E) of plaintext message M with key k_1, a decryption (D) with key k_2 (essentially, another encryption), and a third encryption with key k_3. Another implementation of DES EDE is accomplished with keys k1 and k2 being independent, but with keys k1 and k3 being identical. This implementation of triple DES is written as:

$$C = E_{k1} [D_{k2} [E_{k1} [M]]]$$

Answer a is incorrect since, in DESX, input plaintext is bitwise XORed with 64 bits of additional key material before encryption with DES, and the output of DES is also bitwise XORed with another 64 bits of key material. Answer b, DES in the EEE, mode is written as:

$$C = E_{k3} [E_{k2} [E_{k1} [M]]]$$

where three consecutive encryptions are performed on plaintext message, M, with three independent keys, k1, k2, k3.

Answer c is incorrect since the question contains three encryptions. Implementing two DES encryptions does not provide the additional security anticipated over a single DES encryption because of the meet-in-the-middle attack. Consider a DES cipher with a key size of p. A double encryption will result in an effective key size of 2p and yield the final result R. Thus, one would anticipate that one would have to search a key space of 2^{2p} in an exhaustive search of the keys. However, it can be shown that a search of the key space on the order of 2p is all that is necessary. This search is the same size as required for a single DES encryption. This situation is illustrated as follows:

The sequences shown illustrate the first DES encryption of a plaintext message M with all keys k1 through k2p yielding the intermediate encrypted results C1 through C2p.

$$E_{k1} [M] \rightarrow C1$$

$$E_{k2} [M] \rightarrow C2$$

.

.

$$E_{k2p} [M] \rightarrow C2p$$

If we have available ciphertext R where $R = E_{k2} [E_{k1} [M]]$ for a pair of secret keys k1 and k2, for each key m there is only one key k such that $D_m[R] = E_k[M]$ where D is the decipherment of R back from the second DES encipherment. In other words, there are 2^p possible keys that will result in the pair [M,R] and, thus, can be found in a search of order 2^p.

31. Using a modulo 26 substitution cipher where the letters A to Z of the alphabet are given a value of 0 to 25, respectively, encrypt the message "OVERLORD BEGINS." Use the key K =NEW and D =3 where D is the number of repeating letters representing the key. The encrypted message is:

    a. BFAEQKEH XRKFAW

    b. BFAEPKEH XRKFAW

    c. BFAEPKEH XRKEAW

    d. BFAERKEH XRKEAW

    Answer: c

    The solution is as follows:

    OVERLORD becomes 14 21 4 17 11 14 17 3

    BEGINS becomes 1 4 6 8 13 18

    The key NEW becomes 13 4 22

    Adding the key repetitively to OVERLORD BEGINS modulo 26 yields 1 5 0 4 15 10 4 7 23 17 10 4 0 22, which translates to BFAEPKEH XRKEAW

32. The algorithm of the 802.11 Wireless LAN Standard that is used to protect transmitted information from disclosure is called:

    a. Wireless Application Environment (WAE)

    b. Wired Equivalency Privacy (WEP)

    c. Wireless Transaction Protocol (WTP)

    d. Wireless Transport Layer Security Protocol (WTLS)

    Answer: b

    WEP is designed to prevent the violation of the confidentiality of data transmitted over the wireless LAN. Another feature of WEP is to prevent unauthorized access to the network. The other answers are protocols in the Wireless Application Protocol, the security of which is discussed in Question 21.

33. The Wired Equivalency Privacy algorithm (WEP) of the 802.11 Wireless LAN Standard uses which of the following to protect the confidentiality of information being transmitted on the LAN?

    a. A secret key that is shared between a mobile station (e.g., a laptop with a wireless Ethernet card) and a base station access point

    b. A public/private key pair that is shared between a mobile station (e.g., a laptop with a wireless Ethernet card) and a base station access point

c. Frequency shift keying (FSK) of the message that is sent between a mobile station (e.g., a laptop with a wireless Ethernet card) and a base station access point

d. A digital signature that is sent between a mobile station (e.g., a laptop with a wireless Ethernet card) and a base station access point

Answer: a

The transmitted packets are encrypted with a secret key and an Integrity Check (IC) field comprised of a CRC-32 check sum that is attached to the message. WEP uses the RC4 variable key-size stream cipher encryption algorithm. RC4 was developed in 1987 by Ron Rivest and operates in output feedback mode. Researchers at the University of California at Berkely (wep@isaac.cs.berkeley.edu) have found that the security of the WEP algorithm can be compromised, particularly with the following attacks:

■ Passive attacks to decrypt traffic based on statistical analysis

■ Active attack to inject new traffic from unauthorized mobile stations, based on known plaintext

■ Active attacks to decrypt traffic, based on tricking the access point

■ Dictionary-building attack that, after analysis of about a day's worth of traffic, allows real-time automated decryption of all traffic

The Berkeley researchers have found that these attacks are effective against both the 40-bit and the so-called 128-bit versions of WEP using inexpensive off-the-shelf equipment. These attacks can also be used against networks that use the 802.11b Standard, which is the extension to 802.11 to support higher data rates, but does not change the WEP algorithm.

The weaknesses in WEP and 802.11 are being addressed by the IEEE 802.11i Working Group. WEP will be upgraded to WEP2 with the following proposed changes:

■ Modifying the method of creating the initialization vector (IV)

■ Modifying the method of creating the encryption key

■ Protection against replays

■ Protection against IV collision attacks

■ Protection against forged packets

In the longer term, it is expected that the Advanced Encryption Standard (AES) will replace the RC4 encryption algorithm currently used in WEP.

34. In a block cipher, diffusion can be accomplished through:
    a. Substitution
    b. XORing
    c. Nonlinear S-boxes
    d. Permutation

    Answer: d

    Diffusion is aimed at obscuring redundancy in the plaintext by spreading the effect of the transformation over the ciphertext. Permutation is also known as *transposition* and operates by rearranging the letters of the plaintext. Answer a, substitution, is used to implement *confusion* in a block cipher. Confusion tries to hide the relationship between the plaintext and the ciphertext. The Caesar cipher is an example of a substitution cipher. Answer b is incorrect since XORing, for example, as used in a stream cipher, implements confusion and not diffusion. Similarly, nonlinear S-boxes implement substitution. In DES, for example, there are eight different S-boxes that each has an input of 6 bits and an output of 4 bits. Thus, nonlinear substitution is effected.

35. The National Computer Security Center (NCSC) is:
    a. A division of the National Institute of Standards and Technology (NIST) that issues standards for cryptographic functions and publishes them as Federal Information Processing Standards (FIPS)
    b. A branch of the National Security Agency (NSA) that initiates research and develops and publishes standards and criteria for trusted information systems
    c. A joint enterprise between the NSA and NIST for developing cryptographic algorithms and standards
    d. An activity within the U.S. Department of Commerce that provides information security awareness training and develops standards for protecting sensitive but unclassified information

    Answer: b

    The NCSC promotes information systems security awareness and technology transfer through many channels, including the annual National Information Systems Security Conference. It was founded in 1981 as the Department of Defense Computer Security Center, and its name was change in 1985 to NCSC. It developed the Trusted Computer Evaluation Program Rainbow series for evaluating commercial products against information system security criteria. All the other answers are, therefore incorrect since they refer to NIST, which is under the U.S. Department of Commerce.

36. A portion of a Vigenère cipher square is given below using five (1, 2, 14, 16, 22) of the possible 26 alphabets. Using the key word bow, which of the following is the encryption of the word "advance" using the Vigenère cipher in Table A.10?

   a. b r r b b y h

   b. b r r b j y f

   c. b r r b b y f

   d. b r r b c y f

   Answer: c

   The Vigenère cipher is a *polyalphabetic* substitution cipher. The key word *bow* indicates which alphabets to use. The letter b indicates the alphabet of row 1, the letter o indicates the alphabet of row 14, and the letter w indicates the alphabet of row 22. To encrypt, arrange the key word, repetitively over the plaintext as shown in Table A.11. Thus, the letter a of the plaintext is transformed into b of alphabet in row 1, the letter d is transformed into r of row 14, the letter v is transformed into r of row 22 and so on.

37. There are two fundamental security protocols in IPSEC. These are the Authentication Header (AH) and the Encapsulating Security Payload (ESP). Which of the following correctly describes the functions of each?

   a. ESP-data encrypting protocol that also validates the integrity of the transmitted data; AH-source authenticating protocol that also validates the integrity of the transmitted data

   b. ESP-data encrypting and source authenticating protocol; AH-source authenticating protocol that also validates the integrity of the transmitted data

   c. ESP-data encrypting and source authenticating protocol that also validates the integrity of the transmitted data; AH-source authenticating protocol

   d. ESP-data encrypting and source authenticating protocol that also validates the integrity of the transmitted data; AH-source authenticating protocol that also validates the integrity of the transmitted data

   Answer: d

   ESP does have a source authentication and integrity capability through the use of a hash algorithm and a secret key. It provides confidentiality by means of secret key cryptography. DES and triple DES secret key block ciphers are supported by IPSEC and other algorithms will also be supported in the future. AH uses a hash algorithm in the packet header to authenticate the sender and validate the integrity of the transmitted data.

Table A.10 Vigenère Cipher

PLAINTEXT	A	B	C	D	E	F	G	H	I	J	K	L	M	N	O	P	Q	R	S	T	U	V	W	X	Y	Z
1	b	c	d	e	f	g	h	i	j	k	l	m	n	o	p	q	r	s	t	u	v	w	x	y	z	a
2	c	d	e	f	g	h	i	j	k	l	m	n	o	p	q	r	s	t	u	v	w	x	y	z	a	b
14	o	p	q	r	s	t	u	v	w	x	y	z	a	b	c	d	e	f	g	h	i	j	k	l	m	n
16	q	r	s	t	u	v	w	x	y	z	a	b	c	d	e	f	g	h	i	j	k	l	m	n	o	p
22	w	x	y	z	a	b	c	d	e	f	g	h	i	j	k	l	m	n	o	p	q	r	s	t	u	v

Table A.11 Encryption of Key Word *bow*

Key word	b	o	w	b	o	w	b
Plaintext	a	d	v	a	n	c	e
Ciphertext	b	r	r	b	b	y	f

38. Which of the following is NOT an advantage of a stream cipher?

    a. The same equipment can be used for encryption and decryption.

    b. It is amenable to hardware implementations that result in higher speeds.

    c. Since encryption takes place bit by bit, there is no error propagation.

    d. The receiver and transmitter must be synchronized.

    Answer: d

    The transmitter and receiver must be synchronized since they must use the same keystream bits for the same bits of the text that are to be enciphered and deciphered. Usually, synchronizing frames must be sent to effect the synchronization and, thus, additional overhead is required for the transmissions. Answer a describes an advantage since stream ciphers commonly use Linear Feedback Shift Registers (LFSRs) to generate the keystream and use XORs to operate on the plaintext input stream. Because of the characteristics of the XOR, the same XOR gates and LFSRs can also decrypt the message. Since LFSRs and XORs are used in a stream cipher to encrypt and decrypt, these components are amenable to hardware implementation, which means higher speeds of operation. Thus, answer b describes an advantage. For answer c, stream ciphers encrypt individual bits with no feedback of the generated ciphertext bits and, therefore, errors do not propagate.

39. Which of the following is NOT a property of a public key cryptosystem? (Let P represent the private key, Q represent the public key and M the plaintext message.)

    a. Q[P(M)] = M

    b. P[Q(M)] = M

    c. It is computationally infeasible to derive P from Q.

    d. P and Q are difficult to generate from a particular key value.

    Answer: d

    Answer d refers to the initial computation wherein the private and public keys are computed. The computation in this direction is relatively straightforward. Answers a and b state the true property of public key cryptography which is that a plaintext message encrypted with the private key can be decrypted by the public key and vice versa. Answer c states that it is computationally infeasible to derive the private key from the public key. Obviously, this is a critical property of public key cryptography.

40. A form of digital signature where the signer is not privy to the content of the message is called a:

    a. Zero knowledge proof

    b. Blind signature

    c. Masked signature

    d. Encrypted signature

    Answer: b

    A blind signature algorithm for the message M uses a blinding factor, f; a modulus m; the private key, s, of the signer and the public key, q, of the signer. The sender, who generates f and knows q, presents the message to the signer in the form:

    $Mf^q \pmod{m}$

    Thus, the message is not in a form readable by the signer since the signer does not know f. The signer signs $Mf^q \pmod m$ with his/her private key, returning

    $(Mf^q)^s \pmod m$

    This factor can be reduced to $fM^s \pmod m$ since s and q are inverses of each other. The sender then divides $fM^s \pmod m$ by the blinding factor, f, to obtain

    $M^s \pmod m$

    $M^s \pmod m$ is, therefore, the message, M, signed with the private key, s, of the signer.

    Answer a refers to a zero knowledge proof. In general, a zero knowledge proof involves a person, A, trying to prove that he/she knows something, S, to another person, B, without revealing S or anything about S. Answers c and d are distracters.

41. The following compilation represents what facet of cryptanalysis?

A 8.2	J 0.2	S 6.3
B 1.5	K 0.8	T 9.1
C 2.8	L 4.0	U 2.8
D 4.3	M 2.4	V 1.0
E 12.7	N 6.7	W 2.4
F 2.2	O 7.5	X 0.2
G 2.0	P 1.9	Y 2.0
H 6.1	Q 0.1	Z 0.1
I 7.0	R 6.0	

a. Period analysis

b. Frequency analysis

c. Cilly analysis

d. Cartouche analysis

Answer: b

The compilation is from a study by H. Becker and F. Piper that was originally published in *Cipher Systems: The Protection of Communication.* The listing shows the relative frequency in percent of the appearance of the letters of the English alphabet in large numbers of passages taken from newspapers and novels. Thus, in a substitution cipher, an analysis of the frequency of appearance of certain letters may give clues to the actual letter before transformation. Note that the letters E, A, and T have relatively high percentages of appearance in English text.

Answer a refers to a cryptanalysis that is looking for sequences that repeat themselves and for the spacing between repetitions. This approach is used to break the Vigenère cipher. Answer c is a reference to a cilly, which was a three-character message key used in the German Enigma machine.

In answer d, a cartouche is a set of hieroglyphs surrounded by a loop. A cartouche referring to King Ptolemy was found on the Rosetta Stone.

Chapter 5—Security Architecture and Models

1. When microcomputers were first developed, the instruction fetch time was much longer than the instruction execution time because of the relatively slow speed of memory accesses. This situation led to the design of the:

   a. Reduced Instruction Set Computer (RISC)

   b. Complex Instruction Set Computer (CISC)

   c. Superscalar processor

   d. Very-Long-Instruction-Word (VLIW) processor

   Answer: b

   The logic was that since it took a long time to fetch an instruction from memory relative to the time required to execute that instruction in the CPU, then the number of instructions required to implement a program should be reduced. This reasoning naturally resulted in densely coded instructions with more decode and execution cycles in the processor. This situation was ameliorated by *pipelining* the instructions wherein the decode and execution cycles of one instruction would be overlapped in time with the fetch cycle of the next instruction. Answer a, *RISC*, evolved when packaging and memory technology advanced to the point where there was not much difference in memory access times and processor execution times. Thus, the objective of the RISC architecture was to reduce the number of cycles required to execute an instruction. Accordingly, this increased the number of instructions in the average program by approximately 30%, but it reduced the number of cycles per instruction on the average by a factor of four. Essentially, the RISC architecture uses simpler instructions but makes use of other features such as optimizing compilers to reduce the number of instructions required and large numbers of general purpose registers in the processor and data caches. The *superscalar processor*, answer c, allows concurrent execution of instructions in the same pipelined stage. A *scalar processor* is defined as a processor that executes one instruction at a time. The term superscalar denotes multiple, concurrent operations performed on scalar values as opposed to *vectors* or *arrays* that are used as objects of computation in *array processors*. For answer d, the *very-long-instruction-word (VLIW)* processor, multiple, concurrent operations are performed in a single instruction. Because multiple operations are performed in one instruction rather than using multiple instructions, the number of instructions is reduced relative to those in a scalar processor. However, for this approach to be feasible, the operations in each VLIW instruction must be independent of each other.

2. The main objective of the Java Security Model (JSM) is to:

   a. Protect the user from hostile, network mobile code

   b. Protect a web server from hostile, client code

   c. Protect the local client from user-input hostile code

   d. Provide accountability for events

   Answer: a

   When a user accesses a Web page through a browser, class files for an applet are downloaded automatically, even from untrusted sources. To counter this possible threat, Java provides a customizable *sandbox* to which the applets' execution is confined. This sandbox provides such protections as preventing reading and writing to a local disk, prohibiting the creation of a new process, prevention of making a network connection to a new host and preventing the loading of a new dynamic library and directly calling a native method. The sandbox security features are designed into the *Java Virtual Machine (JVM)*. These features are implemented through array bounds checking, structured memory access, type-safe reference cast checking to ensure that casting to an object of a different type is valid, and checking for null references and automatic garbage collection. These checks are designed to limit memory accesses to safe, structured operations. Answers b, c, and d are distracters.

3. Which of the following would NOT be a component of a general enterprise security architecture model for an organization?

   a. Information and resources to ensure the appropriate level of risk management

   b. Consideration of all the items that comprise information security, including distributed systems, software, hardware, communications systems, and networks

   c. A systematic and unified approach for evaluating the organization's information systems security infrastructure and defining approaches to implementation and deployment of information security controls

   d. IT system auditing

   Answer: d

   The auditing component of the IT system should be independent and distinct from the information system security architecture for a system. In answer a, the resources to support intelligent risk management decisions include technical expertise, applicable evaluation processes, refinement of business objectives, and delivery plans. Answer b promotes an enterprise-wide view of information system security issues. For answer c, the intent is to show that a comprehensive security architecture model includes all phases involved in information system security including planning, design, integrating, testing, and production.

4. In a multilevel security system (MLS), the Pump is:

   a. A two-way information flow device

   b. A one-way information flow device

   c. Compartmented Mode Workstation (CMW)

   d. A device that implements role-based access control

   Answer: b

   The *Pump* (M.H. Kang, I.S. Moskowitz, "A Pump for Rapid, Reliable, Secure Communications," *The 1st ACM Conference on Computer and Communications Security*, Fairfax, VA, 1993) was developed at the U.S. Naval Research Laboratory (NRL). It permits information flow in one direction only, from a lower level of security classification or sensitivity to a higher level. It is a convenient approach to multilevel security in that it can be used to put together systems with different security levels. Answer a is a distracter. Answer c, the *CMW*, refers to windows-based workstations that require users to work with information at different classification levels. Thus, users may work with multiple windows with different classification levels on their workstations. When data is attempted to be moved from one window to another, mandatory access control policies are enforced. This prevents information of a higher classification from being deposited to a location of lower classification. Answer d, *role-based access control*, is an access control mechanism and is now being considered for mandatory access control based on users' roles in their organizations.

5. The Bell-LaPadula model addresses which one of the following items?

   a. Covert channels

   b. The creation and destruction of subjects and objects

   c. Information flow from high to low

   d. Definition of a secure state transition

   Answer: c

   Information flow from high to low is addressed by the *-property* of the Bell–LaPadula model, which states that a subject cannot write data from a higher level of classification to a lower level of classification. This property is also known as the *confinement property* or the *no write down* property. In answer a, *covert channels* are not addressed by the model. The Bell-LaPadula model deals with information flow through normal channels and does not address the covert passing of information through unintended paths. The creation and destruction of subjects and objects, answer b, is not addressed by the model. Answer d refers to the fact that the model discusses a secure transition from one secure state to another, but it never provides a definition of a secure transition.

6. In order to recognize the practical aspects of multilevel security in which, for example, an unclassified paragraph in a Secret document has to be moved to an Unclassified document, the Bell-LaPadula model introduces the concept of a:

 a. Simple security property

 b. Secure exchange

 c. Data flow

 d. Trusted subject

> *Answer:* d
>
> The model permits a *trusted subject* to violate the *-property but to comply with the intent of the *-property. Thus, a person who is a trusted subject could move unclassified data from a classified document to an unclassified document without violating the intent of the *-property. Another example would be for a trusted subject to downgrade the classification of material when it has been determined that the downgrade would not harm national or organizational security and would not violate the intent of the *-property. The *simple security property (ss-property)*, answer a, *states* that a subject cleared for one classification cannot read data from a higher classification. This property is also known as the *no read up* property. Answers b and c are distracters.

7. In a refinement of the Bell–LaPadula model, the *strong tranquility property* states that:

 a. Objects never change their security level.

 b. Objects never change their security level in a way that would violate the system security policy.

 c. Objects can change their security level in an unconstrained fashion.

 d. Subjects can read up.

> *Answer:* a

Answer b is known as the *weak tranquility property*. Answers c and d are distracters.

8. As an analog of confidentiality labels, integrity labels in the Biba model are assigned according to which of the following rules?

   a. Objects are assigned integrity labels identical to the corresponding confidentiality labels.

   b. Objects are assigned integrity labels according to their trustworthiness; subjects are assigned classes according to the harm that would be done if the data were modified improperly.

   c. Subjects are assigned classes according to their trustworthiness; objects are assigned integrity labels according to the harm that would be done if the data were modified improperly.

   d. Integrity labels are assigned according to the harm that would occur from unauthorized disclosure of the information.

   Answer: c

   As subjects in the world of confidentiality are assigned clearances related to their trustworthiness, subjects in the Biba model are assigned to integrity classes that are indicative of their trustworthiness. Also, in the context of confidentiality, objects are assigned classifications related to the amount of harm that would be caused by unauthorized disclosure of the object. Similarly, in the integrity model, objects are assigned to classes related to the amount of harm that would be caused by the improper modification of the object. Answer a is incorrect since integrity properties and confidentiality properties are opposites. For example, in the Bell-LaPadula model, there is no prohibition against a subject at one classification reading information from a lower level of confidentiality. However, when maintenance of the integrity of data is the objective, reading of information from a lower level of integrity by a subject at a higher level of integrity risks contaminating data at the higher level of integrity. Thus, the simple and * -properties in the Biba model are complements of the corresponding properties in the Bell-LaPadula model. Recall that the *Simple Integrity Property* states that a subject at one level of integrity is not permitted to observe (read) an object of a lower integrity (*no read down*). Also, the **- Integrity Property* states that an object at one level of integrity is not permitted to modify (write to) an object of a higher level of integrity (*no write up*). Answer b is incorrect since the words "object" and "subject" are interchanged. In answer d, unauthorized disclosure refers to confidentiality and not to integrity.

9. The Clark-Wilson Integrity Model (D. Clark, D. Wilson, "A Comparison of Commercial and Military Computer Security Policies," *Proceedings of the 1987 IEEE Computer Society Symposium on Research in Security and Privacy, Los Alamitos, CA, IEEE Computer Society Press, 1987*) focuses on what two concepts?

   a. Separation of duty and well-formed transactions

   b. Least privilege and well-formed transactions

   c. Capability lists and domains

   d. Well-formed transactions and denial of service

   > *Answer:* a
   >
   > The Clark-Wilson Model is a model focused on the needs of the commercial world and is based on the theory that integrity is more important than confidentiality for commercial organizations. Further, the model incorporates the commercial concepts of separation of duty and well-formed transactions. The *well-formed transaction* of the model is implemented by the *transformation procedure (TP.)* A TP is defined in the model as the mechanism for transforming the set of *constrained data items (CDIs)* from one valid state of integrity to another valid state of integrity. The Clark-Wilson Model defines rules for separation of duty that denote the relations between a user, TPs, and the CDIs that can be operated upon by those TPs. The model talks about the *access triple* that is the user, the program that is permitted to operate on the data, and the data. Answers b, c, and d are distracters.

10. The model that addresses the situation wherein one group is not affected by another group using specific commands is called the:

    a. Information flow model

    b. Non-interference model

    c. Composition model

    d. Clark-Wilson model

    > *Answer:* b
    >
    > In the *non-interference model,* security policy assertions are defined in the abstract. The process of moving from the abstract to developing conditions that can be applied to the transition functions that operate on the objects is called *unwinding.* Answer a refers to the *information flow model* in which information is categorized into classes, and rules define how information can flow between the classes. The model can be defined as [O, P, S, T] where O is the set of objects, P is the flow policy, S represents the valid states, and T repre-

sents the state transitions. The flow policy is usually implemented as a lattice structure. The *composition model*, answer c, investigates the resultant security properties when subsystems are combined. Answer d, the Clark-Wilson model, is discussed in question 9.

11. The secure path between a user and the Trusted Computing Base (TCB) is called:

    a. Trusted distribution

    b. Trusted path

    c. Trusted facility management

    d. The security perimeter

    > *Answer:* b

    > Answer a, *trusted distribution*, ensures that valid and secure versions of software have been received correctly. *Trusted facility management*, answer c, is concerned with the proper operation of trusted facilities as well as system administration and configuration. Answer d, the *security perimeter*, is the boundary that separates the TCB from the remainder of the system. Recall that the *TCB* is the totality of protection mechanisms within a computer system that are trusted to enforce a security policy.

12. The Common Criteria terminology for the degree of examination of the product to be tested is:

    a. Target of Evaluation (TOE)

    b. Protection Profile (PP)

    c. Functionality (F)

    d. Evaluation Assurance Level (EAL)

    > *Answer:* d

    > The *Evaluation Assurance Levels* range from EA1 (functional testing) to EA7 (detailed testing and formal design verification). The *Target of Evaluation (TOE)*, answer a, refers to the product to be tested. Answer b, *Protection Profile (PP)*, is an implementation-independent specification of the security requirements and protections of a product that could be built. A *Security Target (ST)* is a listing of the security claims for a particular IT security product. Also, the Common Criteria describes an intermediate grouping of security requirement components as a *package. Functionality*, answer c, refers to Part 2 of the Common Criteria that contains standard and well-understood functional security requirements for IT systems.

13. A difference between the Information Technology Security Evaluation Criteria (ITSEC) and the Trusted Computer System Evaluation Criteria (TCSEC) is:

    a. TCSEC addresses availability as well as confidentiality

    b. ITSEC addresses confidentiality only

    c. ITSEC addresses integrity and availability as well as confidentiality

    d. TCSEC separates functionality and assurance

    Answer: c

    TCSEC addresses confidentiality only and bundles functionality and assurance. Thus, answers a, b, and d are incorrect. By separating functionality and assurance as in ITSEC, one could specify fewer security functions that have a high level of assurance. This separation carried over into the Common Criteria.

14. Which of the following items BEST describes the standards addressed by Title II, Administrative Simplification, of the Health Insurance Portability and Accountability Act (*U.S. Kennedy-Kassebaum Health Insurance and Portability Accountability Act -HIPAA-Public Law 104-19*)?

    a. Transaction Standards, to include Code Sets; Unique Health Identifiers; Security and Electronic Signatures and Privacy

    b. Transaction Standards, to include Code Sets; Security and Electronic Signatures and Privacy

    c. Unique Health Identifiers; Security and Electronic Signatures and Privacy

    d. Security and Electronic Signatures and Privacy

    Answer: a

    HIPAA was designed to provide for greater access to personal health care information, enable portability of health care insurance, establish strong penalties for health care fraud, and streamline the health care claims process through administrative simplification. To accomplish the latter, Title II of the HIPAA law, Administrative Simplification, requires standardizing the formats for the electronic transmission of health care information. The *transactions and code sets* portion includes standards for submitting claims, enrollment information, premium payments, and others as adopted by HHS. The standard for transactions is the ANSI ASC X12N version 4010 EDI Standard. Standard code sets are required for diagnoses and inpatient services, professional services, dental services (replaces 'D' codes), and drugs (instead of 'J' codes). Also, local codes are not to be used. *Unique health identifiers* are required to identify health care providers, health plans, employers, and individuals. *Security and electronic signatures* are specified to protect health care information. *Pri-*

vacy protections are required to ensure that there is no unauthorized disclosure of individually identifiable health care information. Answers b, c, and d are incorrect since they do not include all four major standards. Additional information can be found at http:// aspe.hhs.gov/adminsimp.

15. Which one of the following is generally NOT considered a covered entity under Title II, Administrative Simplification, of the HIPAA law?

    a. Health care providers who transmit health information electronically in connection with standard transactions

    b. Health plans

    c. Employers

    d. Health care clearinghouses

    Answer: c

    Employers are not specifically covered under HIPAA. HIPAA applies to health care providers that transmit health care information in electronic form, health care clearinghouses, and health plans. However, some employers may be covered under the Gramm-Leach-Bliley Act. The *Gramm-Leach-Bliley (GLB) Act* was enacted on November 12, 1999, to remove Depression era restrictions on banks that limited certain business activities, mergers, and affiliations. It repeals the restrictions on banks affiliating with securities firms contained in sections 20 and 32 of the Glass-Steagall Act. GLB became effective on November 13, 2001. GLB also requires health plans and insurers to protect member and subscriber data in electronic and other formats. These health plans and insurers will fall under new state laws and regulations that are being passed to implement GLB, since GLB explicitly assigns enforcement of the health plan and insurer regulations to state insurance authorities (15 U.S.C. §6805). Some of the privacy and security requirements of Gramm-Leach-Bliley are similar to those of HIPAA. Most states required that health plans and insurers comply with the GLB requirements by July 1, 2001, and financial institutions were required to be in full compliance with Gramm-Leach-Bliley by this date. Answers a, b, and d are incorrect since they are covered by the HIPAA regulations.

16. The principles of Notice, Choice, Access, Security, and Enforcement refer to which of the following?

    a. Authorization

    b. Privacy

    c. Nonrepudiaton

    d. Authentication

    Answer: b

These items are *privacy* principles. *Notice* refers to the collection, use, and disclosure of *personally identifiable information (PII)*. *Choice* is the choice to opt out or opt in regarding the disclosure of PII to third parties; *Access* is access by consumers to their PII to permit review and correction of information. *Security* is the obligation to protect PII from unauthorized disclosure. *Enforcement* is the enforcement of applicable privacy policies and obligations. The other answers are distracters.

17. What is the simple security property of which one of the following models is described as:

"A user has access to a client company's information, c, if and only if for all other information, o, that the user can read, either $x(c) \neq z(o)$ or $x(c) = x(o)$, where $x(c)$ is the client's company and $z(o)$ is the competitors of $x(c)$."

  a. Biba

  b. Lattice

  c. Bell-LaPadula

  d. Chinese wall

    Answer: d

    This model, (D.C. Brewer and M.J. Nash, "Chinese Wall Model," *Proceedings of the 1989 IEEE Computer Society Symposium on Security and Privacy*, 1989), defines rules that prevent conflicts of interest in organizations that may have access to information from companies that are competitors of each other. Essentially, the model states that a user working on one account cannot work on a competitor's account for a designated period of time. Answer a, the *Biba model*, is an integrity model that is an analog of the *Bell-LaPadula confidentiality model* of answer c. Answer b, the *lattice*, refers to the general information flow model where security levels are represented by a lattice structure. The model defines a transitive ordering relation, $\leq$, on security classes. Thus, for security classes X, Y, and Z, the ordering relation $X \leq Y \leq Z$ describes the situation where Z is the highest security class and X is the lowest security class, and there is an ordering among the three classes.

18. The two categories of the policy of *separation of duty* are:

  a. Span of control and functional separation

  b. Inference control and functional separation

  c. Dual control and functional separation

  d. Dual control and aggregation control

    Answer: c

Dual control requires that two or more subjects act together simultaneously to authorize an operation. A common example is the requirement that two individuals turn their keys simultaneously in two physically separated areas to arm a weapon. Functional separation implies a sequential approval process such as requiring the approval of a manager to send a check generated by a subordinate. Answer a is incorrect. Span of control refers to the number of subordinates that can be optimally managed by a superior. Answer b is incorrect. Inference control is implementing protections that prevent the inference of information not authorized to a user from information that is authorized to be accessed by a user. Answer d is incorrect, but aggregation refers to the acquisition of large numbers of data items to obtain information that would not be available by analyzing a small number of the data items.

19. In the National Information Assurance Certification and Accreditation Process (NIACAP), a *type accreditation* performs which one of the following functions?

   a. Evaluates a major application or general support system

   b. Verifies the evolving or modified system's compliance with the information agreed on in the System Security Authorization Agreement (SSAA)

   c. Evaluates an application or system that is distributed to a number of different locations

   d. Evaluates the applications and systems at a specific, self-contained location

     Answer: c

     Answer a is the NIACAP *system accreditation*. Answer b is the Phase 2 or *Verification phase* of the Defense Information Technology Security Certification and Accreditation Process (DITSCAP). The objective is to use the SSAA to establish an evolving yet binding agreement on the level of security required before the system development begins or changes to a system are made. After accreditation, the SSAA becomes the baseline security configuration document. Answer d is the NIACAP *site accreditation*.

20. Which of the following processes establish the minimum national standards for certifying and accrediting national security systems?

   a. CIAP

   b. DITSCAP

   c. NIACAP

   d. Defense audit

Answer: c

The NIACAP provides a standard set of activities, general tasks, and a management structure to certify and accredit systems that will maintain the information assurance and security posture of a system or site. The NIACAP is designed to certify that the information system meets documented accreditation requirements and will continue to maintain the accredited security posture throughout the system life cycle. Answer a, CIAP, is being developed for the evaluation of critical commercial systems and uses the NIACAP methodology. DITSCAP, answer b, establishes for the defense entities a standard process, set of activities, general task descriptions, and a management structure to certify and accredit IT systems that will maintain the required security posture. The process is designed to certify that the IT system meets the accreditation requirements and that the system will maintain the accredited security posture throughout the system life cycle. The four phases to the DITSCAP are Definition, Verification, Validation, and Post Accreditation. Answer d is a distracter.

21. Which of the following terms is NOT associated with a Read Only Memory (ROM)?

    a. Flash memory

    b. Field Programmable Gate Array (FPGA)

    c. Static RAM (SRAM)

    d. Firmware

    Answer: c

    Static Random Access Memory (SRAM) is *volatile* and, therefore, loses its data if power is removed from the system. Conversely, a ROM is *nonvolatile* in that it does not lose its content when power is removed. *Flash memories,* answer a, are a type of electrically programmable ROM. Answer b, *FPGA,* is a type of Programmable Logic Device (PLD) that is programmed by blowing fuse connections on the chip or using an antifuse that makes a connection when a high voltage is applied to the junction. For answer d, *firmware* is a program that is stored on ROMs.

22. Serial data transmission in which information can be transmitted in two directions, but only one direction at a time, is called:

    a. Simplex

    b. Half-duplex

    c. Synchronized

    d. Full-duplex

    Answer: b

The time required to switch transmission directions in a half-duplex line is called the *turnaround time*. Answer a, *simplex*, refers to communication that takes place in one direction only. Answer c is a distracter. Full-duplex, answer d, can transmit and receive information in both directions simultaneously. The transmissions can be asynchronous or synchronous. In asynchronous transmission, a start bit is used to indicate the beginning of transmission. The start bit is followed by data bits and, then, by one or two stop bits to indicate the end of the transmission. Since start and stop bits are sent with every unit of data, the actual data transmission rate is lower since these "overhead" bits are used for synchronization and do not carry information. In this mode, data is sent only when it is available and the data is not transmitted continuously. In synchronous transmission, the transmitter and receiver have synchronized clocks and the data is sent in a continuous stream. The clocks are synchronized by using transitions in the data and, therefore, start and stop bits are not required for each unit of data sent.

23. The ANSI ASC X12 (American National Standards Institute Accredited Standards Committee X12) Standard version 4010 applies to which one of the following HIPAA categories?

    a. Privacy
    b. Code sets
    c. Transactions
    d. Security

    Answer: c

    The transactions addressed by HIPAA are:

    - Health claims or similar encounter information
    - Health care payment and remittance advice
    - Coordination of Benefits
    - Health claim status
    - Enrollment and disenrollment in a health plan
    - Eligibility for a health plan
    - Health plan premium payments
    - Referral certification and authorization

    The HIPAA EDI transaction standards to address these HIPAA transactions include the following:

    - Health care claims or coordination of benefits
    - Retail drug NCPCP (National Council for Prescription Drug Programs) v. 32
    - Dental claim ASC X12N 837: dental

- Professional claim ASC X12N 837: professional
- Institutional claim ASC X12N 837: institutional
- Payment and remittance advice ASC X12N 835
- Health claim status ASC X12N 276/277
- Plan enrollment ASC X12 834
- Plan eligibility ASC X12 270/271
- Plan premium payments ASC X12 820
- Referral certification ASC X12 N 278

The American National Standards Institute was founded in 1917 and is the only source of American Standards. The ANSI Accredited Standards Committee X12 was chartered in 1979 and is responsible for cross-industry standards for electronic documents. The HIPAA privacy standards, answer a, were finalized in April, 2001, and implementation must be accomplished by April 14, 2003. The privacy rule covers individually identifiable health care information transmitted, stored in electronic or paper form, or communicated orally. Protected health information (PHI) may not be disclosed unless disclosure is approved by the individual, permitted by the legislation, required for treatment, part of health care operations, required by law, or necessary for payment. PHI is defined as individually identifiable health information that is transmitted by electronic media, maintained in any medium described in the definition of electronic media under HIPAA, or is transmitted or maintained in any other form or medium. Answer b, code sets, refers to the codes that are used to fill in the data elements of the HIPAA transaction standards. Examples of these codes are:

- ICD-9-CM (vols. 1 and 2) International Classification of Diseases, 9th Ed., Clinical Modification—Diseases, injuries, impairments, other health related problems, their manifestations, and causes of injury, disease, impairment, or other health-related problems
- CPT (Current Procedural Terminology, 4th Ed. [CPT-4]), CDT (Code on Dental Procedures and Nomenclature, 2nd Ed. [CDT-2]) or ICD-9-CM (vol. 3)—Procedures or other actions taken to prevent, diagnose, treat, or manage diseases, injuries, and impairments
- NDC (National Drug Codes)—drugs
- HCPCS (Health Care Financing Administration Common Procedure Coding System)
- Other health-related services, other substances, equipment, supplies, or other items used in health care services

The proposed HIPAA Security Rule, answer d, mandates the protection of the confidentiality, integrity, and availability of protected health information (PHI) through:

- Administrative procedures
- Physical safeguards
- Technical services and mechanisms

The rule also addresses electronic signatures, but the final rule will depend on industry progress on reaching a standard. In addition, the proposed security rule requires the appointment of a security officer.

24. A 1999 law that addresses privacy issues related to health care, insurance and finance and that will be implemented by the states is:
    a. Gramm-Leach-Bliley (GLB)
    b. Kennedy-Kassebaum
    c. Medical Action Bill
    d. Insurance Reform Act

    Answer: a

    See the answers to Question 15 for a discussion of GLB. Answer b refers to the HIPAA legislation (*U.S. Kennedy-Kassebaum Health Insurance and Portability Accountability Act—HIPAA-Public Law 104-19).* Answers c and d are distracters.

25. The Platform for Privacy Preferences (P3P) was developed by the World Wide Web Consortium (W3C) for what purpose?
    a. To implement public key cryptography for transactions
    b. To evaluate a client's privacy practices
    c. To monitor users
    d. To implement privacy practices on Web sites

    Answer: d

    As of this writing, the latest W3C working draft of P3P is *P3P 1.0, 28 January, 2002* (www.w3.org/TR). An excerpt of the W3C P3P Specification states "P3P enables Web sites to express their privacy practices in a standard format that can be retrieved automatically and interpreted easily by user agents. P3P user agents will allow users to be informed of site practices (in both machine- and human-readable formats) and to automate decision-making based on these practices when appropriate. Thus users need not read the privacy policies at every site they visit."

    With P3, an organization can post its privacy policy in machine-readable form (XML) on its Web site. This policy statement includes:

    - Who has access to collected information
    - The type of information collected
    - How the information is used
    - The legal entity making the privacy statement

P3P also supports user agents that allow a user to configure a P3P-enabled Web browser with the user's privacy preferences. Then, when the user attempts to access a Web site, the user agent compares the user's stated preferences with the privacy policy in machine-readable form at the Web site. Access will be granted if the preferences match the policy. Otherwise, either access to the Web site will be blocked or a pop-up window will appear notifying the user that he/she must change their privacy preferences. Usually, this means that the user has to lower his/her privacy threshold. Answers a, b, and c are distracters.

26. What process is used to accomplish high-speed data transfer between a peripheral device and computer memory, bypassing the Central Processing Unit (CPU)?

    a. Direct memory access

    b. Interrupt processing

    c. Transfer under program control

    d. Direct access control

    Answer: a

    With DMA, a DMA controller essentially takes control of the memory busses and manages the data transfer directly. Answer b, interrupt processing, involves an external signal interrupting the "normal" CPU program flow. This interrupt causes the CPU to halt processing and "jump" to another program that services the interrupt. When the interrupt has been serviced, the CPU returns to continue executing the original program. Program control transfer, answer c, is accomplished by the processor executing input/output (I/O) instructions. Answer d is a distracter.

27. An associative memory operates in which one of the following ways?

    a. Uses indirect addressing only

    b. Searches for values in memory exceeding a specified value

    c. Searches for a specific data value in memory

    d. Returns values stored in a memory address location specified in the CPU address register

    Answer: c

    Answer a refers to an addressing mode used in computers where the address location that is specified in the program instruction contains the address of the final desired location. Answer b is a distracter and answer d is the description of the direct or absolute addressing mode.

28. The following concerns usually apply to what type of architecture?
    - Desktop systems can contain sensitive information that may be at risk of being exposed.
    - Users may generally lack security awareness.
    - Modems present a vulnerability to dial-in attacks.
    - Lack of proper backup may exist.
    a. Distributed
    b. Centralized
    c. Open system
    d. Symmetric

    Answer: a

    Additional concerns associated with distributed systems include:

    - A desktop PC or workstation can provide an avenue of access into critical information systems of an organization.
    - Downloading data from the Internet increases the risk of infecting corporate systems with a malicious code or an unintentional modification of the databases.
    - A desktop system and its associated disks may not be protected from physical intrusion or theft.

    For answer b, a *centralized* system, all the characteristics cited do not apply to a central host with no PCs or workstations with large amounts of memory attached. Also, the vulnerability presented by a modem attached to a PC or workstation would not exist. An *open system* or architecture, answer c, is comprised of vendor-independent subsystems that have published specifications and interfaces in order to permit operations with the products of other suppliers. One advantage of an open system is that it is subject to review and evaluation by independent parties. Answer d is a distracter.

29. The definition "A relatively small amount (when compared to primary memory) of very high speed RAM, which holds the instructions and data from primary memory, that has a high probability of being accessed during the currently executing portion of a program" refers to what category of computer memory?
    a. Secondary
    b. Real
    c. Cache
    d. Virtual

Answer: c

Cache logic attempts to predict which instructions and data in main (primary) memory will be used by a currently executing program. It then moves these items to the higher speed cache in anticipation of the CPU requiring these programs and data. Properly designed caches can significantly reduce the apparent main memory access time and thus increase the speed of program execution. Answer a, *secondary memory*, is a slower memory (such as a magnetic disk) that provides non-volatile storage. *Real or primary memory*, answer b, is directly addressable by the CPU and is used for the storage of instructions and data associated with the program that is being executed. This memory is usually high-speed, Random Access Memory (RAM). Answer d, *virtual memory*, uses secondary memory in conjunction with primary memory to present the CPU with a larger, apparent address space of the real memory locations.

30. The organization that "establishes a collaborative partnership of computer incident response, security and law enforcement professionals who work together to handle computer security incidents and to provide both proactive and reactive security services for the U.S. Federal government" is called:

    a. CERT®/CC

    b. Center for Infrastructure Protection

    c. Federal CIO Council

    d. Federal Computer Incident Response Center

    Answer: d

    To again quote the FedCIRC charter, "FedCIRC provides assistance and guidance in incident response and provides a centralized approach to incident handling across agency boundaries." Specifically, the mission of FedCIRC is to:

    - Provide civil agencies with technical information, tools, methods, assistance, and guidance
    - Be proactive and provide liaison activities and analytical support
    - Encourage the development of quality products and services through collaborative relationships with Federal civil agencies, the Department of Defense, academia, and private industry
    - Promote the highest security profile for government information technology (IT) resources
    - Promote incident response and handling procedural awareness with the federal government

    Answer a, the CERT Coordination Center (CERT/CC), is a unit of the Carnegie Mellon University Software Engineering Institute (SEI).

SEI is a Federally funded R&D Center. CERT's mission is to alert the Internet community to vulnerabilities and attacks and to conduct research and training in the areas of computer security, including incident response. Answer b is a distracter and answer c, the Federal Chief Information Officers' Council, is the sponsor of FedCIRC.

Chapter 6—Operations Security

1. Which book of the Rainbow series addresses the Trusted Network Interpretation (TNI)?

   a. Red Book

   b. Orange Book

   c. Green Book

   d. Purple Book

   Answer: a

   The Red Book is one book of the Rainbow Series, a six-foot-tall stack of books on evaluating "Trusted Computer Systems" according to the National Security Agency. The term "Rainbow Series" comes from the fact that each book is a different color. The Trusted Network Interpretation (TNI) extends the evaluation classes of the Trusted Systems Evaluation Criteria (DOD 5200.28-STD) to trusted network systems and components.

   Answer b, the Orange Book, is the main book of the Rainbow Series and most of the other books elaborate on the information contained in this book. The Orange Book is the DoD Trusted Computer System Evaluation Criteria [DOD 5200.28][1]. Answer c, the Green Book, is CSC-STD-002-85, the DoD Password Management Guidelines. Answer d, the Purple Book, is NCSC-TG-014, Guidelines for Formal Verification Systems. Source: NCSC-TG-005 Trusted Network Interpretation [Red Book] and DoD Trusted Computer System Evaluation Criteria [DOD 5200.28-Orange Book.]

2. Which choice describes the Forest Green Book?

   a. It is a tool that assists vendors in data gathering for certifiers.

   b. It is a Rainbow series book that defines the secure handling of storage media.

   c. It is a Rainbow series book that defines guidelines for implementing access control lists.

   d. It does not exist; there is no "Forest Green Book."

   Answer: b

   The Forest Green book is a Rainbow series book that defines the secure handling of sensitive or classified automated information system memory and secondary storage media, such as degaussers, magnetic tapes, hard disks, floppy disks, and cards. The Forest Green book details procedures for clearing, purging, declassifying, or destroying automated information system (AIS) storage media to prevent data remanence. Data remanence is the residual physical representation of data that has been erased in some way. After storage media is erased there may be some physical characteristics that allow data to be reconstructed.

Answer a is the Blue Book, NCSC-TG-019 Trusted Product Evaluation Questionnaire Version-2. The Blue book is a tool to assist system developers and vendors in gathering data to assist evaluators and certifiers assessing trusted computer systems.

Answer c is the Grey/Silver Book, NCSC-TG-020A, the Trusted UNIX Working Group (TRUSIX) Rationale for Selecting Access Control. The Grey/Silver book defines guidelines for implementing access control lists (ACLs) in the UNIX system. Source: NCSC-TG-025 A Guide to Understanding Data Remanence in Automated Information Systems, NCSC-TG-020A Trusted UNIX Working Group (TRUSIX) Rationale for Selecting Access Control, and NCSC-TG-019 Trusted Product Evaluation Questionnaire Version-2.

3. Which term below BEST describes the concept of "least privilege"?

a. Each user is granted the lowest clearance required for their tasks.

b. A formal separation of command, program, and interface functions.

c. A combination of classification and categories that represents the sensitivity of information.

d. Active monitoring of facility entry access points.

Answer: a

The "least privilege" principle requires that each subject in a system be granted the most restrictive set of privileges (or lowest clearance) needed for the performance of authorized tasks. The application of this principle limits the damage that can result from accident, error, or unauthorized use. Applying this principle may limit the damage resulting from accidents, errors, or unauthorized use of system resources.

Answer b describes "separation of privilege," which is the separation of functions, namely between the commands, programs, and interfaces implementing those functions, such that malicious or erroneous code in one function is prevented from affecting the code or data of another function.

Answer c is a security level. A security level is the combination of hierarchical classification and a set of non-hierarchical categories that represents the sensitivity of information.

Answer d is a distracter. Source: DoD 5200.28-STD—Department of Defense Trusted Computer System Evaluation Criteria.

4. Which general TCSEC security class category describes that mandatory access policies be enforced in the TCB?

   a. A

   b. B

   c. C

   d. D

   > *Answer:* b

   > The Trusted Computer System Evaluation Criteria [Orange Book] defines major hierarchical classes of security by the letters D (least secure) through A (most secure):

   > **D.** Minimal protection

   > **C.** Discretionary protection (C1&C2)

   > **B.** Mandatory protection (B1, B2, B3)

   > **A.** Verified protection; formal methods (A1)

   > Source: DoD 5200.28-STD—Department of Defense Trusted Computer System Evaluation Criteria.

   > Table A.12 shows these TCSEC Security Evaluation Categories.

5. Which statement below is the BEST definition of "need-to-know"?

   a. Need-to-know ensures that no single individual (acting alone) can compromise security controls.

   b. Need-to-know grants each user the lowest clearance required for their tasks.

Table A.12   TCSEC Security Evaluation Categories

CLASS	DESCRIPTION
D:	minimal protection
C:	discretionary protection
C1:	discretionary security protection
C2:	controlled access protection
B:	mandatory protection
B1:	labeled security protection
B2:	structured protection
B3:	security domains
A1:	verified protection

c. Need-to-know limits the time an operator performs a task.

d. Need-to-know requires that the operator have the minimum knowledge of the system necessary to perform his task.

Answer: d

The concept of "need-to-know" means that, in addition to whatever specific object or role rights a user may have on the system, the user has also the minimum amount of information necessary to perform his job function. Answer a is "separation of duties," assigning parts of tasks to different personnel. Answer b is "least privilege," the user has the minimum security level required to perform his job function. Answer c is "rotation of duties," wherein the amount of time an operator is assigned a security-sensitive task is limited before being moved to a different task with a different security classification.

6. Place the four systems security modes of operation in order, from the most secure to the least:

_____ a. Dedicated Mode

_____ b. Multilevel Mode

_____ c. Compartmented Mode

_____ d. System High Mode

Answer: a, d, c, and b

The "mode of operation" is a description of the conditions under which an AIS functions, based on the sensitivity of data processed and the clearance levels and authorizations of the users. Four modes of operation are defined:

Dedicated Mode. An AIS is operating in the dedicated mode when each user with direct or indirect individual access to the AIS, its peripherals, remote terminals, or remote hosts has all of the following:

a. A valid personnel clearance for all information on the system

b. Formal access approval for, and has signed nondisclosure agreements for all the information stored and/or processed (including all compartments, subcompartments, and/or special access programs)

c. A valid need-to-know for all information contained within the system

System-High Mode. An AIS is operating in the system-high mode when each user with direct or indirect access to the AIS, its peripherals, remote terminals, or remote hosts has all of the following:

    a. A valid personnel clearance for all information on the AIS

    b. Formal access approval for, and has signed nondisclosure agreements for all the information stored and/or processed (including all compartments, subcompartments, and/or special access programs)

    c. A valid need-to-know for some of the information contained within the AIS

Compartmented Mode. An AIS is operating in the compartmented mode when each user with direct or indirect access to the AIS, its peripherals, remote terminals, or remote hosts has all of the following:

    a. A valid personnel clearance for the most restricted information processed in the AIS

    b. Formal access approval for, and has signed nondisclosure agreements for that information to which he/she is to have access

    c. A valid need-to-know for that information to which he/she is to have access

Multilevel Mode. An AIS is operating in the multilevel mode when all the following statements are satisfied concerning the users with direct or indirect access to the AIS, its peripherals, remote terminals, or remote hosts:

    a. Some do not have a valid personnel clearance for all the information processed in the AIS.

    b. All have the proper clearance and have the appropriate formal access approval for that information to which he/she is to have access.

    c. All have a valid need-to-know for that information to which they are to have access.

Source: DoD 5200.28-STD—Department of Defense Trusted Computer System Evaluation Criteria.

7. Which media control below is the BEST choice to prevent data remanence on magnetic tapes or floppy disks?

    a. Overwriting the media with new application data

    b. Degaussing the media

    c. Applying a concentration of hydriodic acid (55% to 58% solution) to the gamma ferric oxide disk surface

    d. Making sure the disk is re-circulated as quickly as possible to prevent object reuse

Answer: b

Degaussing is recommended as the best method for purging most magnetic media. Degaussing is a process whereby the magnetic media is erased, i.e., returned to its initial virgin state. Erasure via degaussing may be accomplished in two ways:

- In AC erasure, the media is degaussed by applying an alternating field that is reduced in amplitude over time from an initial high value (i.e., AC-powered)

- In DC erasure, the media is saturated by applying a unidirectional field (i.e., DC-powered or by employing a permanent magnet)

Another point about degaussing: Degaussed magnetic hard drives will generally require restoration of factory-installed timing tracks, so data purging is recommended. Also, physical destruction of CDROM or WORM media is required.

Answer a is not recommended because the application may not completely overwrite the old data properly, and strict configuration controls must be in place on both the operating system and the software itself. Also, bad sectors on the media may not permit the software to overwrite old data properly. To satisfy the DoD clearing requirement, it is sufficient to write any character to all data locations in question (purging).

To purge the media, the DoD requires overwriting with a pattern, then its complement, and finally with another pattern; e.g., overwrite first with 0011 0101, followed by 1100 1010, then 1001 0111. The number of times an overwrite must be accomplished depends on the storage media, sometimes on its sensitivity, and sometimes on differing DoD component requirements, but seven times is often recommended.

Answer c is a rarely used method of media destruction, and acid solutions should be used in a well-ventilated area only by qualified personnel.

Answer d is wrong. Source: NCSC-TG-025 A Guide to Understanding Data Remanence in Automated Information Systems.

8. Which choice below is the BEST description of an audit trail?

   a. Audit trails are used to detect penetration of a computer system and to reveal usage that identifies misuse.

   b. An audit trail is a device that permits simultaneous data processing of two or more security levels without risk of compromise.

   c. An audit trail mediates all access to objects within the network by subjects within the network.

   d. Audit trails are used to prevent access to sensitive systems by unauthorized personnel.

   Answer: a

An audit trail is a set of records that collectively provide documentary evidence of processing used to aid in tracing from original transactions forward to related records and reports, and/or backward from records and reports to their component source transactions. Audit trails may be limited to specific events or may encompass all of the activities on a system.

User audit trails can usually log:

■ All commands directly initiated by the user

■ All identification and authentication attempts

■ Files and resources accessed

It is most useful if options and parameters are also recorded from commands. It is much more useful to know that a user tried to delete a log file (e.g., to hide unauthorized actions) than to know the user merely issued the delete command, possibly for a personal data file.

Answer b is a description of a multilevel device. A multilevel device is a device that is used in a manner that permits it to process data of two or more security levels simultaneously without risk of compromise. To accomplish this, sensitivity labels are normally stored on the same physical medium and in the same form (i.e., machine-readable or human-readable) as the data being processed.

Answer c refers to a network reference monitor, an access control concept that refers to an abstract machine that mediates all access to objects within the network by subjects within the network.

Answer d is incorrect, because audit trails are detective, and answer d describes a preventative process, access control. Source: NCSC-TG-001 A Guide to Understanding Audit in Trusted Systems and DoD 5200.28-STD—Department of Defense Trusted Computer System Evaluation Criteria.

9. Which TCSEC security class category below specifies "trusted recovery" controls?

a. C2

b. B1

c. B2

d. B3

Answer: d

TCSEC security categories B3 and A1 require the implementation of trusted recovery. Trusted recovery is the procedures and/or mechanisms provided to assure that, after an ADP system failure or other discontinuity, recovery without a protection compromise is obtained. A system failure represents a serious security risk because security controls may be bypassed when the system is not functioning normally. Trusted recovery has two primary activities: preparing for a system failure (backup) and recovering the system.

Source: DoD 5200.28-STD—Department of Defense Trusted Computer System Evaluation Criteria.

10. Which choice does NOT describe an element of configuration management?

   a. Configuration management involves information capture and version control.

   b. Configuration management reports the status of change processing.

   c. Configuration management is the decomposition process of a verification system into Configuration Items (CIs).

   d. Configuration management documents the functional and physical characteristics of each configuration item.

   Answer: c

   Configuration management is a discipline applying technical and administrative direction to:

   ■ Identify and document the functional and physical characteristics of each configuration item for the system

   ■ Manage all changes to these characteristics

   ■ Record and report the status of change processing and implementation

   Configuration management involves process monitoring, version control, information capture, quality control, bookkeeping, and an organizational framework to support these activities. The configuration being managed is the verification system plus all tools and documentation related to the configuration process.

   Answer c is the description of an element of Configuration Identification.

   Source: *NCSC-TG-014-89, Guidelines for Formal Verification Systems* [Purple Book].

11. Which choice below does NOT accurately describe a task of the Configuration Control Board?

   a. The CCB should meet periodically to discuss configuration status accounting reports.

   b. The CCB is responsible for documenting the status of configuration control activities.

c. The CCB is responsible for assuring that changes made do not jeopardize the soundness of the verification system.

d. The CCB assures that the changes made are approved, tested, documented, and implemented correctly.

Answer: b

All analytical and design tasks are conducted under the direction of the vendor's corporate entity called the Configuration Control Board (CCB). The CCB is headed by a chairperson who is responsible for assuring that changes made do not jeopardize the soundness of the verification system and assures that the changes made are approved, tested, documented, and implemented correctly.

The members of the CCB should interact periodically, either through formal meetings or other available means, to discuss configuration management topics such as proposed changes, configuration status accounting reports, and other topics that may be of interest to the different areas of the system development. These interactions should be held to keep the entire system team updated on all advancements or alterations in the verification system.

Answer b describes configuration accounting. Configuration accounting documents the status of configuration control activities and, in general, provides the information needed to manage a configuration effectively. The configuration accounting reports are reviewed by the CCB. Source: *NCSC-TG-014-89, Guidelines for Formal Verification Systems.*

12. Which choice below is NOT a security goal of an audit mechanism?

a. Deter perpetrators' attempts to bypass the system protection mechanisms

b. Review employee production output records

c. Review patterns of access to individual objects

d. Discover when a user assumes a functionality with privileges greater than his own

Answer: b

The audit mechanism of a computer system has five important security goals:

1. The audit mechanism must "allow the review of patterns of access to individual objects, access histories of specific processes

and individuals, and the use of the various protection mechanisms supported by the system and their effectiveness.[2]"

2. Allow discovery of both users' and outsiders' repeated attempts to bypass the protection mechanisms.

3. Allow discovery of any use of privileges that may occur when a user assumes a functionality with privileges greater than his or her own, i.e., programmer to administrator. In this case, there may be no bypass of security controls, but nevertheless, a violation is made possible.

4. Act as a deterrent against perpetrators' habitual attempts to bypass the system protection mechanisms. However, to act as a deterrent, the perpetrator must be aware of the audit mechanism's existence and its active use to detect any attempts to bypass system protection mechanisms.

5. Supply "an additional form of user assurance that attempts to bypass the protection mechanisms that are recorded and discovered."[3] Even if the attempt to bypass the protection mechanism is successful, the audit trail will still provide assurance by its ability to aid in assessing the damage done by the violation, thus improving the system's ability to control the damage.

Answer b is a distracter.

Source: NCSC-TG-001 A Guide to Understanding Audit in Trusted Systems [Tan Book], and Gligor, Virgil D., "Guidelines for Trusted Facility Management and Audit," University of Maryland, 1985.

13. Which choice below is NOT a common element of user account administration?

    a. Periodically verifying the legitimacy of current accounts and access authorizations

    b. Authorizing the request for a user's system account

    c. Tracking users and their respective access authorizations

    d. Establishing, issuing, and closing user accounts

    Answer: b

    For proper separation of duties, the function of user account establishment and maintenance should be separated from the function of initiating and authorizing the creation of the account. User account management focuses on identification, authentication, and access authorizations. This is augmented by the process of auditing and otherwise periodically verifying the legitimacy of current accounts and access authorizations. Also, there are considerations involved in the timely modification or removal of access and associated issues for employees who are reassigned, promoted, or terminated, or who retire.

Source: *National Institute of Standards and Technology, An Introduction to Computer Security: The NIST Handbook Special Publication 800-12.*

14. Which element of Configuration Management listed below involves the use of Configuration Items (CIs)?

 a. Configuration Accounting

 b. Configuration Audit

 c. Configuration Control

 d. Configuration Identification

   Answer: d

   Configuration management entails decomposing the verification system into identifiable, understandable, manageable, trackable units known as Configuration Items (CIs). A CI is a uniquely identifiable subset of the system that represents the smallest portion to be subject to independent configuration control procedures. The decomposition process of a verification system into CIs is called configuration identification. CIs can vary widely in size, type, and complexity. Although there are no hard-and-fast rules for decomposition, the granularity of CIs can have great practical importance. A favorable strategy is to designate relatively large CIs for elements that are not expected to change over the life of the system, and small CIs for elements likely to change more frequently.

   Answer a, configuration accounting, documents the status of configuration control activities and in general provides the information needed to manage a configuration effectively. It allows managers to trace system changes and establish the history of any developmental problems and associated fixes.

   Answer b, configuration audit, is the quality assurance component of configuration management. It involves periodic checks to determine the consistency and completeness of accounting information and to verify that all configuration management policies are being followed.

   Answer c, configuration control, is a means of assuring that system changes are approved before being implemented, only the proposed and approved changes are implemented, and the implementation is complete and accurate.

Source: *NCSC-TG-014-89, Guidelines for Formal Verification Systems.*

15. Which standard defines the International Standard for the Common Criteria?

    a. IS15408

    b. BS7799

    c. DoD 5200.28-STD

    d. CSC-STD-002-85

    Answer: a

    ISO/IEC 15408-1 is the International Standards version of the Common Criteria. The ISO approved and published the CC text as the new International Standard (IS) 15408 on December 1, 1999[4]. As of this writing the Common Criteria version is 2.1.

    Answer b is the Code of Practice for Information Security Management (BS7799) developed by the British Standards Institute. The BS7799 standard effectively comes in two parts:

    - ISO/IEC 17799:2000 (Part 1) is the standard code of practice and can be regarded as a comprehensive catalogue of recommended security policy.

    - BS7799-2:1999 (Part 2) is a standard specification for an Information Security Management System (ISMS). An ISMS is the means by which Senior Management monitors and controls their security, minimizing the residual business risk and ensuring that security continues to fulfill corporate, customer, and legal requirements.[5]

    Answer c is the Orange Book, the DoD Trusted Computer System Evaluation Criteria.

    Answer d is the Green Book, the DoD Password Management Guidelines.

    Source: The Common Criteria Project.

16. Which statement below is NOT correct about reviewing user accounts?

    a. User account reviews cannot be conducted by outside auditors.

    b. User account reviews can examine conformity with the concept of least privilege.

    c. User account reviews may be conducted on a system-wide basis.

    d. User account reviews may be conducted on an application-by-application basis.

    Answer: a

    It is necessary to regularly review user accounts on a system. Such reviews may examine the levels of access each individual has, conformity with the concept of least privilege, whether all accounts are still active, whether management authorizations are up-to-date, or whether required training has been completed, for example. These reviews can be conducted on at least two levels: on an application-by-application basis or on a systemwide basis. Both kinds of reviews can be conducted by, among others, in-house systems personnel (a self-audit), the organization's internal audit staff, or external auditors.

Source: *National Institute of Standards and Technology, An Introduction to Computer Security: The NIST Handbook Special Publication 800-12.*

17. Which statement below MOST accurately describes configuration control?

   a. The decomposition process of a verification system into CIs

   b. Assuring that only the proposed and approved system changes are implemented

   c. Tracking the status of current changes as they move through the configuration control process

   d. Verifying that all configuration management policies are being followed

   Answer: b

   Configuration control is a means of assuring that system changes are approved before being implemented, only the proposed and approved changes are implemented, and the implementation is complete and accurate. This involves strict procedures for proposing, monitoring, and approving system changes and their implementation. Configuration control entails central direction of the change process by personnel who coordinate analytical tasks, approve system changes, review the implementation of changes, and supervise other tasks such as documentation.

   Answer a is configuration identification. The decomposition process of a verification system into Configuration Items (CIs) is called configuration identification. A CI is a uniquely identifiable subset of the system that represents the smallest portion to be subject to independent configuration control procedures.

   Answer c is configuration accounting. Configuration accounting documents the status of configuration control activities and, in general, provides the information needed to manage a configuration effectively. It allows managers to trace system changes and establish the history of any developmental problems and associated fixes. Configuration accounting also tracks the status of current changes as they move through the configuration control process. Configuration accounting establishes the granularity of recorded information and thus shapes the accuracy and usefulness of the audit function.

Answer d is configuration audit. Configuration audit is the quality assurance component of configuration management. It involves periodic checks to determine the consistency and completeness of accounting information and to verify that all configuration management policies are being followed. A vendor's configuration management program must be able to sustain a complete configuration audit by an NCSC review team.

Source: NCSC-TG-014, Guidelines for Formal Verification Systems.

18. Which term below MOST accurately describes the Trusted Computing Base (TCB)?

   a. A computer that controls all access to objects by subjects

   b. A piece of information that represents the security level of an object

   c. Formal proofs used to demonstrate the consistency between a system's specification and a security model

   d. The totality of protection mechanisms within a computer system

   Answer: d

   The Trusted Computing Base (TCB)—The totality of protection mechanisms within a computer system, including hardware, firmware, and software, the combination of which is responsible for enforcing a security policy. A TCB consists of one or more components that together enforce a unified security policy over a product or system. The ability of a trusted computing base to correctly enforce a security policy depends solely on the mechanisms within the TCB and on the correct input by system administrative personnel of parameters (e.g., a user's clearance) related to the security policy.

   Answer a describes the reference monitor concept. The reference monitor is an access control concept that refers to an abstract machine that mediates all accesses to objects by subjects. The Security Kernel consists of the hardware, firmware, and software elements of a Trusted Computing Base (or Network Trusted Computing Base partition) that implement the reference monitor concept. It must mediate all accesses, be protected from modification, and be verifiable as correct.

   Answer b refers to a sensitivity label. A sensitivity label is a piece of information that represents the extra security level of an object and describes the sensitivity (e.g., classification) of the data in the object. Sensitivity labels are used by the TCB as the basis for mandatory access control decisions.

   Answer c describes formal verification. This is the process of using formal proofs to demonstrate the consistency (design verification) between a formal specification of a system and a formal security policy model or (implementation verification) between the formal specification and its program implementation. Source: DoD 5200.28-STD—Department of Defense Trusted Computer System Evaluation Criteria

19. Which choice below would NOT be considered a benefit of employing incident-handling capability?

    a. An individual acting alone would not be able to subvert a security process or control.

    b. It enhances internal communications and the readiness of the organization to respond to incidents.

    c. It assists an organization in preventing damage from future incidents.

    d. Security training personnel would have a better understanding of users' knowledge of security issues.

     Answer: a

    The primary benefits of employing an incident-handling capability are containing and repairing damage from incidents and preventing future damage. Additional benefits related to establishing an incident-handling capability are:

    Enhancement of the risk assessment process. An incident-handling capability will allow organizations to collect threat data that may be useful in their risk assessment and safeguard selection processes (e.g., in designing new systems). Statistics on the numbers and types of incidents in the organization can be used in the risk-assessment process as an indication of vulnerabilities and threats.

    Enhancement of internal communications and the readiness of the organization to respond to any type of incident, not just computer security incidents. Internal communications will be improved, management will be better organized to receive communications, and contacts within public affairs, legal staff, law enforcement, and other groups will have been pre-established.

    Security training personnel will have a better understanding of users' knowledge of security issues. Trainers can use actual incidents to vividly illustrate the importance of computer security. Training that is based on current threats and controls recommended by incident-handling staff provides users with information more specifically directed to their current needs, thereby reducing the risks to the organization from incidents.

Answer a is a benefit of employing "separation of duties" controls.

Source: *National Institute of Standards and Technology, An Introduction to Computer Security: The NIST Handbook Special Publication 800-12.*

20. Which statement below is accurate about Evaluation Assurance Levels (EALs) in the Common Criteria (CC)?

    a. A security level equal to the security level of the objects to which the subject has both read and write access

    b. A statement of intent to counter specified threats

    c. Requirements that specify the security behavior of an IT product or system

    d. Predefined packages of assurance components that make up security confidence rating scale

    Answer: d

    An Evaluation Assurance Level (EAL) is one of seven increasingly rigorous packages of assurance requirements from CC Part 3. Each numbered package represents a point on the CC's predefined assurance scale. An EAL can be considered a level of confidence in the security functions of an IT product or system. The EALs have been developed with the goal of preserving the concepts of assurance drawn from the source criteria, such as the Trusted Computer System Evaluation Criteria (TCSEC), Information Technology Security Evaluation Criteria (ITSEC), or Canadian Trusted Computer Evaluation Criteria (CTCPEC), so that results of previous evaluations remain relevant. EAL levels 2–7 are generally equivalent to the assurance portions of the TCSEC C2-A1 scale, although exact TCSEC mappings do not exist.

    Answer a is the definition of Subject Security Level. A subject's security level is equal to the security level of the objects to which it has both read and write access. A subject's security level must always be dominated by the clearance of the user with which the subject is associated.

    Answer b describes a Security Objective, which is a statement of intent to counter specified threats and/or satisfy specified organizational security policies and assumptions.

    Answer c describes Security Functional Requirements. These are requirements, preferably from CC Part 2, that when taken together specify the security behavior of an IT product or system.

    Source: CC Project and DoD 5200.28-STD.

21. Which choice below is the BEST description of operational assurance?

    a. Operational assurance is the process of examining audit logs to reveal usage that identifies misuse.

    b. Operational assurance has the benefit of containing and repairing damage from incidents.

c. Operational assurance is the process of reviewing an operational system to see that security controls are functioning correctly.

d. Operational assurance is the process of performing pre-employment background screening.

Answer: c

Operational assurance is the process of reviewing an operational system to see that security controls, both automated and manual, are functioning correctly and effectively. Operational assurance addresses whether the system's technical features are being bypassed or have vulnerabilities and whether required procedures are being followed.

To maintain operational assurance, organizations use two basic methods: system audits and monitoring. A system audit is a one-time or periodic event to evaluate security. Monitoring refers to an ongoing activity that examines either the system or the users.

Answer a is a description of an audit trail review. Answer b is a description of a benefit of incident handling. The main benefits of proper incident handling are containing and repairing damage from incidents, and preventing future damage. Answer d describes a personnel control.

Source: *National Institute of Standards and Technology, An Introduction to Computer Security: The NIST Handbook Special Publication 800-12.*

22. Which choice below MOST accurately describes a Covert Storage Channel?

a. A process that manipulates observable system resources in a way that affects response time

b. An information transfer path within a system

c. A communication channel that allows a process to transfer information in a manner that violates the system's security policy

d. An information transfer that involves the direct or indirect writing of a storage location by one process and the direct or indirect reading of the storage location by another process

Answer: d

A covert storage channel typically involves a finite resource (e.g., sectors on a disk) that is shared by two subjects at different security levels. One way to think of the difference between covert timing channels and covert storage channels is that covert timing channels are essentially memoryless, whereas covert storage channels are not. With a timing channel, the information transmitted from the sender must be sensed by the receiver immediately, or it will be lost. However, an error code indicating a full disk which is exploited to create a storage channel may stay constant for an indefinite amount of time, so a receiving process is not as constrained by time.

Answer a is a partial description of a covert timing channel. A covert timing channel is a covert channel in which one process signals information to another by modulating its own use of system resources (e.g., CPU time) in such a way that this manipulation affects the real response time observed by the second process.

Answer b is a generic definition of a channel. A channel may also refer to the mechanism by which the path is effected.

Answer c is a higher-level definition of a covert channel. While a covert storage channel fits this definition generically, answer d is the proper specific definition.

Source: DoD 5200.28-STD—Department of Defense Trusted Computer System Evaluation Criteria and NCSC-TG-030, A Guide To Understanding Covert Channel Analysis of Trusted Systems [Light Pink Book].

23. Which choice below is the BEST description of a Protection Profile (PP), as defined by the Common Criteria (CC)?

a. A statement of security claims for a particular IT security product

b. A reusable definition of product security requirements

c. An intermediate combination of security requirement components

d. The IT product or system to be evaluated

Answer: b

The Common Criteria (CC) is used in two ways:

- As a standardized way to describe security requirements for IT products and systems

- As a sound technical basis for evaluating the security features of these products and systems

The CC defines three useful constructs for building IT security requirements: the Protection Profile (PP), the Security Target (ST), and the Package. The PP is an implementation-independent statement of security needs for a set of IT security products. The PP contains a set of security requirements and is intended to be a reusable definition of product security requirements that are known to be useful and effective. A PP gives consumers a means of referring to a specific set of security needs and communicating them to manufacturers and helps future product evaluation against those needs.

Answer a defines the Security Target (ST). The ST is a statement of security claims for a particular IT security product or system. The ST parallels the structure of the PP, though it has additional elements that include product-specific detailed information. An ST is the basis for agreement among all parties as to what security the product or system offers, and therefore the basis for its security evaluation.

Answer c describes the Package. The Package is an intermediate combination of security requirements components. The package permits the expression of a set of either functional or assurance requirements that meet some particular need, expressed as a set of security objectives.

Answer d describes the Target of Evaluation (TOE). The TOE is an IT product or system to be evaluated, the security characteristics of which are described in specific terms by a corresponding ST, or in more general terms by a PP. This evaluation consists of rigorous analysis and testing performed by an accredited, independent laboratory. The scope of a TOE evaluation is set by the Evaluation Assurance Level (EAL) and other requirements specified in the ST. Part of this process is an evaluation of the ST itself, to ensure that it is correct, complete, and internally consistent and can be used as the baseline for the TOE evaluation.

Source: Common Criteria Project.

24. Which choice below is NOT one of the four major aspects of configuration management?
    a. Configuration status accounting
    b. Configuration product evaluation
    c. Configuration auditing
    d. Configuration identification

    Answer: b

    The four major aspects of configuration management are:

    ■ Configuration identification
    ■ Configuration control
    ■ Configuration status accounting
    ■ Configuration auditing

    These aspects are described earlier in this chapter. Answer b is a distracter. Source: *NCSC-TG-014-89, Guidelines for Formal Verification Systems* [Purple Book].

25. Which choice below MOST accurately describes "partitioned security mode"?
    a. All personnel have the clearance and formal access approval.
    b. All personnel have the clearance but not necessarily formal access approval.

c. The only state in which certain privileged instructions may be executed.

d. A system containing information accessed by personnel with different security clearances.

Answer: b

A partitioned security mode is a mode of operation wherein all personnel have the clearance but not necessarily formal access approval and need-to-know for all information contained in the system.

Answer a is a compartmented security mode. A compartmented security mode is a mode of operation wherein all personnel have a valid personnel clearance, formal access approval and signed nondisclosure agreements, and valid need-to-know for that information to which he/she is to have access.

Answer c is executive state. Executive state is one of several states in which a system may operate and the only one in which certain privileged instructions may be executed. Such instructions cannot be executed when the system is operating in other (e.g., user) states. Synonymous with supervisor state.

Answer d is multilevel secure. Multilevel secure is a class of system containing information with different sensitivities that simultaneously permits access by users with different security clearances and needs-to-know, but prevents users from obtaining access to information for which they lack authorization.

Source: DoD 5200.28-STD—Department of Defense Trusted Computer System Evaluation Criteria.

26. Which choice below is NOT an example of a media control?

a. Sanitizing the media before disposition

b. Printing to a printer in a secured room

c. Physically protecting copies of backup media

d. Conducting background checks on individuals

Answer: d

Answer d is a personnel control. Most support and operations staff have special access to the system. Some organizations conduct background checks on individuals filling these positions to screen out possibly untrustworthy individuals.

Answer a: The process of removing information from media before disposition is called sanitization. Three techniques are commonly used for media sanitization: overwriting, degaussing, and destruction.

Answer b: It may be necessary to actually output data to the media in a secure location, such as printing to a printer in a locked room instead of to a general-purpose printer in a common area.

Answer c: Physical protection of copies of backup media stored offsite should be accorded a level of protection equivalent to media containing the same information stored onsite.

Source: *National Institute of Standards and Technology, An Introduction to Computer Security: The NIST Handbook Special Publication 800-12.*

27. Which statement below is the BEST example of "separation of duties"?

a. An activity that checks on the system, its users, or the environment.

b. Getting users to divulge their passwords.

c. One person initiates a request for a payment and another authorizes that same payment.

d. A data entry clerk may not have access to run database analysis reports.

Answer: c

Separation of duties refers to dividing roles and responsibilities so that a single individual cannot subvert a critical process. In financial systems, no single individual should normally be given the authority to issue checks. Checks and balances need to be designed into both the process as well as the specific, individual positions of personnel who will implement the process.

Answer a describes system monitoring.

Answer b is "social engineering," a method of subverting system controls by getting users or administrators to divulge information about systems, including their passwords.

Answer d describes "least privilege." Least privilege refers to the security objective of granting users only those accesses they need to perform their official duties. Least privilege does not mean that all users will have extremely little functional access; some employees will have significant access if it is required for their position. It is important to make certain that the implementation of least privilege does not interfere with the ability to have personnel substitute for each other without undue delay. Without careful planning, access control can interfere with contingency plans.

Source: *National Institute of Standards and Technology, An Introduction to Computer Security: The NIST Handbook Special Publication 800-12.*

28. Which minimum TCSEC security class category specifies "trusted distribution" controls?

a. C2

b. B2

c. B3

d. A1

Answer: d

Trusted distribution is defined by the Orange Book as a requirement of A1 TCB assurance. Trusted distribution includes procedures to ensure that all of the TCB configuration items, such as the TCB software, firmware, hardware, and updates, distributed to a customer site arrive exactly as intended by the vendor without any alterations.

Any alteration to the TCB at any time during the system life cycle could result in a violation of the system security policy. Assurance that the system security policy is correctly implemented and operational throughout the system life cycle is provided by different TCSEC requirements. At TCSEC class A1, trusted distribution, in conjunction with configuration management, provides assurance that the TCB software, firmware, and hardware, both original and updates, are received by a customer site exactly as specified by the vendor's master copy. Trusted distribution also ensures that TCB copies sent from other than legitimate parties are detected. Source: NCSC-TG-008 A Guide to Understanding Trusted Distribution in Trusted Systems [Lavender Book].

29. Which statement is accurate about "trusted facility management"?

   a. The role of a security administrator shall be identified and auditable in C2 systems and above.

   b. The role of a security administrator shall be identified and auditable in B2 systems and above.

   c. The TCB shall support separate operator and administrator functions for C2 systems and above.

   d. The TCB shall support separate operator and administrator functions for B2 systems and above.

   Answer: d

   Trusted Facility Management has two different requirements, one for B2 systems and another for B3 systems. The B2 requirements state: the TCB shall support separate operator and administrator functions. The B3 requirements are as follows: The functions performed in the role of a security administrator shall be identified. System administrative personnel shall only be able to perform security administrator functions after taking a distinct auditable action to assume the security administrator role on the system. Non-security functions that can be performed in the security administration role shall be limited strictly to those essential to performing the security role effectively.[6]

Source: NCSC-TG-015, Guide To Understanding Trusted Facility Management [Brown Book].

30. Which statement below is accurate about the concept of Object Reuse?

    a. Object reuse protects against physical attacks on the storage medium.

    b. Object reuse ensures that users do not obtain residual information from system resources.

    c. Object reuse applies to removable media only.

    d. Object reuse controls the granting of access rights to objects.

    Answer: b

    Object reuse mechanisms ensure system resources are allocated and reassigned among authorized users in a way that prevents the leak of sensitive information, and ensure that the authorized user of the system does not obtain residual information from system resources. Object reuse is defined as "The reassignment to some subject of a storage medium (e.g., page frame, disk sector, magnetic tape) that contained one or more objects. To be securely reassigned, no residual data can be available to the new subject through standard system mechanisms."[7] The object reuse requirement of the TCSEC is intended to assure that system resources, in particular storage media, are allocated and reassigned among system users in a manner which prevents the disclosure of sensitive information.

    Answer a is incorrect. Object reuse does not necessarily protect against physical attacks on the storage medium. Answer c is also incorrect, as object reuse applies to all primary and secondary storage media, such as removable media, fixed media, real and virtual main memory (including registers), and cache memory. Answer d refers to authorization, the granting of access rights to a user, program, or process. Source: NCSC-TG-018, A Guide To Understanding Object Reuse in Trusted Systems [Light Blue Book].

Chapter 7—Applications and Systems Development

1. The definition "the science and art of specifying, designing, implementing and evolving programs, documentation and operating procedures whereby computers can be made useful to man" is that of:

   a. Structured analysis/structured design (SA/SD)

   b. Software engineering

   c. An object-oriented system

   d. Functional programming

   Answer: b

   This definition of software engineering is a combination of popular definitions of engineering and software. One definition of engineering is "the application of science and mathematics to the design and construction of artifacts which are useful to man." A definition of software is that it "consists of the programs, documentation and operating procedures by which computers can be made useful to man." Answer a, SA/SD, deals with developing specifications that are abstractions of the problem to be solved and not tied to any specific programming languages. Thus, SA/SD, through *data flow diagrams (DFDs)*, shows the main processing entities and the data flow between them without any connection to a specific programming language implementation. An *object-oriented system*, answer c, is a group of independent *objects* that can be requested to perform certain operations or exhibit specific behaviors. These objects cooperate to provide the system's required functionality. The objects have an *identity* and can be created as the program executes (*dynamic lifetime*). To provide the desired characteristics of object-oriented systems, the objects are *encapsulated*, i.e., they can only be accessed through messages sent to them to request performance of their defined operations. The object can be viewed as a "black box" whose internal details are hidden from outside observation and cannot normally be modified. Objects also exhibit the *substitution* property, which means that objects providing compatible operations can be substituted for each other. In summary, an object-oriented system contains objects that exhibit the following properties:

   - Identity—each object has a name that is used to designate that object.

   - Encapsulation—an object can only be accessed through messages to perform its defined operations.

■ Substitution—objects that perform compatible operations can be substituted for each other.

■ Dynamic lifetimes—objects can be created as the program executes.

Answer d, functional programming, uses only mathematical functions to perform computations and solve problems. This approach is based on the assumption that any algorithm can be described as a mathematical function. Functional languages have the characteristics that:

■ They support functions and allow them to be manipulated by being passed as arguments and stored in data structures.

■ Functional abstraction is the only method of procedural abstraction.

2. In software engineering, the term *verification* is defined as:

   a. To establish the truth of correspondence between a software product and its specification

   b. A complete, validated specification of the required functions, interfaces, and performance for the software product

   c. To establish the fitness or worth of a software product for its operational mission

   d. A complete, verified specification of the overall hardware-software architecture, control structure, and data structure for the product

   Answer: a

   In the Waterfall model (W.W. Royce, "Managing the Development of Large Software Systems: Concepts and Techniques," *Proceedings, WESCON*, August 1970), answer b defines the term *requirements*. Similarly, answer c, defines the term *validation*, and answer d is the definition of *product design*. In summary, the steps of the Waterfall model are:

   ■ System feasibility

   ■ Software plans and requirements

   ■ Product design

   ■ Detailed design

   ■ Code

   ■ Integration

   ■ Implementation

   ■ Operations and maintenance

   In this model, each phase finishes with a verification and validation (V&V) task that is designed to eliminate as many problems as possible in the results of that phase.

3. The discipline of identifying the components of a continually evolving system for the purposes of controlling changes to those components and maintaining integrity and traceability throughout the life cycle is called:

   a. Change control

   b. Request control

   c. Release control

   d. Configuration management

   Answer: d

   This is demonstrated in *Configuration management of computer-based systems*, British Standards Institution, 1984. Answers a, b, and c are components of the maintenance activity of software life cycle models. In general, one can look at the maintenance phase as the progression from request control, to change control, to release control. Answer b, *request control*, is involved with the users' requests for changes to the software. *Change control*, answer a, involves the analysis and understanding of the existing code, and the design of changes, and corresponding test procedures. Answer c, *release control*, involves deciding which requests are to be implemented in the new release, performing the changes and conducting testing.

4. The basic version of the Construction Cost Model (COCOMO), which proposes quantitative, life-cycle relationships, performs what function?

   a. Estimates software development effort based on user function categories

   b. Estimates software development effort and cost as a function of the size of the software product in source instructions

   c. Estimates software development effort and cost as a function of the size of the software product in source instructions modified by manpower buildup and productivity factors

   d. Estimates software development effort and cost as a function of the size of the software product in source instructions modified by hardware and input functions

   Answer: b

   The Basic COCOMO Model (B.W. Boehm, *Software Engineering Economics*, Prentice-Hall, Englewood Cliffs, New Jersey, 1981) proposes the following equations:

   "The number of man-months (MM) required to develop the most common type of software product, in terms of the number of thousands of delivered source instructions (KDSI) in the software product"

   $MM = 2.4 (KDSI)^{1.05}$

"The development schedule (TDEV) in months"

TDEV = 2.5(MM)$^{0.38}$

In addition, Boehm has developed an intermediate COCOMO Model that also takes into account hardware constraints, personnel quality, use of modern tools, and other attributes and their aggregate impact on overall project costs. A detailed COCOMO Model, by Boehm, accounts for the effects of the additional factors used in the intermediate model on the costs of individual project phases.

Answer b describes a *function point measurement model* that does not require the user to estimate the number of delivered source instructions. The software development effort is determined using the following five user functions:

- External input types
- External output types
- Logical internal file types
- External interface file types
- External inquiry types

These functions are tallied and weighted according to complexity and used to determine the software development effort.

Answer c describes the Rayleigh curve applied to software development cost and effort estimation. A prominent model using this approach is the Software Life Cycle Model (SLIM) estimating method. In this method, estimates based on the number of lines of source code are modified by the following two factors:

- The manpower buildup index (MBI), which estimates the rate of buildup of staff on the project
- A productivity factor (PF), which is based on the technology used

Answer d is a distracter.

5. A refinement to the basic Waterfall Model that states that software should be developed in increments of functional capability is called:

    a. Functional refinement
    b. Functional development
    c. Incremental refinement
    d. Incremental development

    Answer: d

    The advantages of *incremental development* include the ease of testing increments of functional capability and the opportunity to incorporate user experience into a successively refined product. Answers a, b, and c are distracters.

6. The Spiral Model of the software development process (B.W. Boehm, "A Spiral Model of Software Development and Enhancement," *IEEE Computer*, May, 1988) uses the following metric relative to the spiral:

   a. The radial dimension represents the cost of each phase

   b. The radial dimension represents progress made in completing each cycle

   c. The angular dimension represents cumulative cost

   d. The radial dimension represents cumulative cost

   > *Answer:* d
   >
   > The radial dimension represents cumulative cost and the angular dimension represents progress made in completing each cycle of the spiral. The spiral model is actually a meta-model for software development processes. A summary of the stages in the spiral is as follows:
   >
   > - The spiral begins in the top, left-hand quadrant by determining the objectives of the portion of the product being developed, the alternative means of implementing this portion of the product, and the constraints imposed on the application of the alternatives.
   >
   > - Next, the risks of the alternatives are evaluated based on the objectives and constraints. Following this step, the relative balances of the perceived risks are determined.
   >
   > - The spiral then proceeds to the lower right-hand quadrant where the development phases of the projects begin. A major review completes each cycle and then the process begins anew for succeeding phases of the project. Typical succeeding phases are software product design, integration and test plan development, additional risk analyses, operational prototype, detailed design, code, unit test, acceptance test, and implementation.
   >
   > Answers a, b, and c are distracters.

7. In the Capability Maturity Model (CMM) for software, the definition "describes the range of expected results that can be achieved by following a software process" is that of:

   a. Structured analysis/structured design (SA/SD)

   b. Software process capability

   c. Software process performance

   d. Software process maturity

   > *Answer:* b
   >
   > A *software process* is a set of activities, methods, and practices that are used to develop and maintain software and associated products. *Software process capability* is a means of predicting the outcome of the next

software project conducted by an organization. Answer c, *software process performance*, is the result achieved by following a software process. Thus, software capability is aimed at expected results while software performance is focused on results that have been achieved. *Software process maturity*, answer d, is the extent to which a software process is:

- Defined
- Managed
- Measured
- Controlled
- Effective

Software process maturity, then, provides for the potential for growth in capability of an organization. An immature organization develops software in a crisis mode, usually exceeds budgets and time schedules, and software processes are developed in an ad hoc fashion during the project. In a mature organization, the software process is effectively communicated to staff, the required processes are documented and consistent, software quality is evaluated, and roles and responsibilities are understood for the project.

Answer a is a distracter, but is discussed in question 1.

8. Which of the following is NOT a Software CMM maturity level?

a. Initial

b. Repeatable

c. Behavioral

d. Managed

Answer: c

The word behavioral is a distracter. The five software process maturity levels are:

- Initial—the software process is ad hoc and most processes are undefined.
- Repeatable—fundamental project management processes are in place.
- Defined—the software process for both management and engineering functions is documented, standardized, and integrated into the organization.
- Managed—the software process and product quality are measured, understood, and controlled.
- Optimizing—continuous process improvement is being performed.

9. The main differences between a *software process assessment* and a *software capability evaluation* are:

a. Software process assessments determine the state of an organization's current software process and are used to gain support from within the organization for a software process improvement program; software capability evaluations are used to identify contractors who are qualified to develop software or to monitor the state of the software process in a current software project.

b. Software capability evaluations determine the state of an organization's current software process and are used to gain support from within the organization for a software process improvement program; software process assessments are used to identify contractors who are qualified to develop software or to monitor the state of the software process in a current software project.

c. Software process assessments are used to develop a risk profile for source selection; software capability evaluations are used to develop an action plan for continuous process improvement.

d. Software process assessments and software capability evaluations are essentially identical, and there are no major differences between the two.

Answer: a

The correct answer is a. Answers b, c, and d are distracters. If, in answer c, the terms "software process assessments" and "software capability evaluations" were interchanged, that result would also be correct. It would then read, "Software capability evaluations are used to develop a risk profile for source selection; software process assessments are used to develop an action plan for continuous process improvement."

10. Which of the following is NOT a common term in object-oriented systems?

a. Behavior

b. Message

c. Method

d. Function

Answer: d

Answer a, *behavior*, is a characteristic of an object. The object is defined as a collection of operations that, when selected, reveal or manipulate the state of the object. Thus, consecutive invocations of an object may result in different behaviors, based on the last operations selected. Answer b, *message*, is a request sent to an object to carry out a particular operation. A *method*, answer c, is the code that describes what the object will do when sent a message.

11. In object-oriented programming, when all the methods of one class are passed on to a subclass, this is called:

    a. Forward chaining

    b. Inheritance

    c. Multiple Inheritance

    d. Delegation

    Answer: b

    In *inheritance*, all the methods of one class, called a superclass, are inherited by a subclass. Thus, all messages understood by the superclass are understood by the subclass. In other words, the subclass inherits the behavior of the superclass. Answer a is a distracter and describes data-driven reasoning used in expert systems. *Multiple inheritance,* answer c, describes the situation where a subclass inherits the behavior of multiple superclasses. Answer d, delegation, is an alternative to inheritance in an object-oriented system. With *delegation,* if an object does not have a method to satisfy a request it has received, it can delegate the request to another object.

12. Which of the following languages is NOT an object-oriented language?

    a. Smalltalk

    b. Simula 67

    c. Lisp

    d. C++

    Answer: c

    Lisp, for list processing, is a functional language that processes symbolic expressions rather than numbers. It is used in the artificial intelligence field. The languages cited in answers a, b, and d are object-oriented languages.

13. Which of the following items is NOT a component of a knowledge-based system (KBS)?

    a. Knowledge base

    b. Procedural code

    c. Inference Engine

    d. Interface between the user and the system

    Answer: b

    Procedural code in a *procedural language* implies sequential execution of instructions based on the von Neumann architecture of a CPU, Memory, and Input/Output device. Variables are part of the sets of instructions used to solve a particular problem and, thus, the data are not separate from the statements. Such languages have control statements such as *goto, if...then...else* and so on. The program execution is iterative and corresponds to a sequence of state changes in a state machine. Answer a, *knowledge base*, refers to the rules and facts of the particular problem domain. *The inference engine*, answer c, takes the inputs to the KBS and uses the knowledge base to infer new facts and to solve the problem. Answer d refers to the interface between the user and the system through which the data are entered, displayed, and output.

14. In an expert system, the process of beginning with a possible solution and using the knowledge in the knowledge base to justify the solution based on the raw input data is called:

a. Dynamic reasoning

b. Forward chaining

c. Backward chaining

d. A blackboard solution

   Answer: c

   Backward chaining is generally used when there are a large number of possible solutions relative to the number of inputs. Answer a is a distracter. Answer b, *forward chaining*, is the reasoning approach that can be used when there is a small number of solutions relative to the number of inputs. The input data is used to reason "forward" to prove that one of the possible solutions in a small solution set is the correct one. The *blackboard*, answer d, is an expert system reasoning methodology in which a solution is generated by the use of a virtual "blackboard" wherein information or potential solutions are placed on the blackboard by a plurality of individuals or expert knowledge sources. As more information is placed on the blackboard in an iterative process, a solution is generated.

15. An off-the-shelf software package that implements an inference engine, a mechanism for entering knowledge, a user interface, and a system to provide explanations of the reasoning used to generate a solution is called:

a. An expert system shell

b. A knowledge base

c. A neural network

d. A knowledge acquisition system

   Answer: a

An *expert system shell* provides the fundamental building blocks of an expert system and supports the entering of domain knowledge. Thus, for an application that is not complex and does not require the custom development of the components of an expert system, an expert system shell is a useful tool that will save development time. A knowledge base, answer b, is a component of an expert system and is described in Question 13. A *neural network* is another type of artificial intelligence system that uses the neurons of the brain as a model and solves problems using nonlinear pattern-matching techniques and "learning" approaches. A *knowledge acquisition system*, answer d, refers to the means of identifying and acquiring the knowledge to be entered into the knowledge base. In simple terms, it is trying to determine how an expert thinks when developing a solution to a problem.

16. What key professional or professionals are required to develop an expert system?

    a. Knowledge engineer and object designer

    b. Knowledge engineer and domain expert

    c. Domain expert

    d. Domain expert and object designer

    Answer: b

    The *knowledge engineer* usually has a computer-related and expert system background, but does not have the knowledge of the specific discipline or domain being addressed by the expert system. For example, the expert system being developed may be a medical diagnostic system requiring input from diagnostic specialists and other types of physicians. These individuals are the *domain experts*. It is the job of the knowledge engineer to elicit the critical knowledge from the domain expert and incorporate it into the expert system knowledge base. The term "object designer" in the answers is a distracter.

17. An expert system that has rules of the form "If w is low and x is high then y is intermediate," where w and x are input variables and y is the output variable, is called a:

    a. Neural network

    b. Realistic expert system

    c. Boolean expert system

    d. Fuzzy expert system

    Answer: d

    A fuzzy expert system is an expert system that uses fuzzy membership functions and rules, instead of Boolean logic, to reason about data. Thus, fuzzy variables can have an approximate range of values instead of the binary True or False used in conventional expert systems. When it is desired to convert the fuzzy output to a single value, *defuzzification* is used. One approach to defuzzification is the CENTROID method. With this method, a value of the output variable is computed by finding the variable value of the center of gravity of the membership function for the fuzzy output value. Answers a and b are distracters, and answer c is incorrect since it refers to Boolean values of one or zero.

18. What is a "subject-oriented, integrated, time-variant, non-volatile collection of data in support of management's decision-making process"?

   a. Data mart

   b. Data warehouse

   c. Data model

   d. Data architecture

   Answer: b

   This definition of a data warehouse is that of Bill Inmon, a pioneer in the field. To create a *data warehouse*, data is taken from an operational database, redundancies are removed, and the data is "cleaned up" in general. This activity is referred to as *normalizing* the data. Then the data is placed into a relational database and can be analyzed using On-Line Analytical Processing (OLAP) and statistical modeling tools. The data warehouse can be used as a *Decision Support System (DSS)*, for example, by performing a time series analysis of the data. The data in the data warehouse must be maintained to ensure that it is timely and valid. The term *data scrubbing* refers to maintenance of the data warehouse by deleting information that is unreliable or no longer relevant. A *data mart*, answer a, is a database that is comprised of data or relations that have been extracted from the data warehouse. Information in the data mart is usually of interest to a particular group of people. For example, a data mart may be developed for all health care-related data. Answers c and d are distracters, although a *data model*, in this context, sometimes refers to the result of analyzing relationships among enterprise-wide data items. Another perspective on data models is discussed in the answers to Question 21.

19. The process of analyzing large data sets in a data warehouse to find non-obvious patterns is called:

   a. Data mining

   b. Data scanning

   c. Data administration

   d. Derived data

Answer: a

For example, mining of consumer-related data may show a correlation between the number of children under four years old in a household and the fathers' preferences in aftershave lotion. Answer b is a distracter. *Data administration,* answer c, describes the degree of management's dedication to the data warehouse concept. Answer d, *derived data,* is data that is obtained through the processing of raw data.

20. The equation $Z = f\,[\sum w_n i_n\,]$, where Z is the output, w_n are weighting functions, and i_n is a set of inputs describes:

    a. An expert system
    b. A knowledge-based system
    c. An artificial neural network (ANN)
    d. A knowledge acquisition system

    Answer: c

    The equation defines a *single layer ANN* as shown in Figure A.11. Each input, i_n, is multiplied by a weight, w_n, and these products are fed into a summation transfer function, $\sum$, that generates an output, Z. Most neural networks have multiple layers of summation and weighting functions, whose interconnections can also be changed.

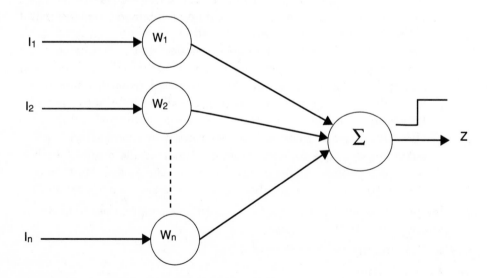

Figure A.11 A single layer artificial neural network.

There are a number of different learning paradigms for neural networks, including *reinforcement* learning and *back propagation*. In reinforcement learning a training set of inputs is provided to the ANN along with a measure of how close the network is coming to a solution. Then, the weights and connections are readjusted. In back propagation, information is fed back inside the neural network from the output and is used by the ANN to make weight and connection adjustments. Answers a and b are distracters that describe systems that use knowledge-based rules of experts to solve problems using an inferencing mechanism. A *knowledge acquisition system*, answer d, refers to the means of identifying and acquiring the knowledge to be entered into the knowledge base of an expert system.

21. A database that comprises tools to support the analysis, design, and development of software and support good software engineering practices is called a:

    a. Data model

    b. Database management system (DBMS)

    c. Data dictionary

    d. Data type dictionary

       Answer: c

       Computer Aided Software Engineering (CASE) tools and an *Integrated Project Support Environment (IPSE)* are terms used to describe similar software engineering support environments. Answer a, *data model*, "is a basic system of constructs used in describing reality," (Kent, W., *Data and Reality*, North Holland, 1978). A *DBMS*, answer b, is a system that supports the creation, use, and administration of a database system. Answer d, a *data type dictionary*, refers to a collection of items on which certain operations, such as insert, delete, and search, are to be performed. This arrangement of items is in contrast to a *priority queue*, in which the collection of items is arranged in order of priority and the relevant operations to be performed are insert, find-max, and delete-max.

22. Another type of artificial intelligence technology involves genetic algorithms. Genetic algorithms are part of the general class known as:

    a. Neural networks

    b. Suboptimal computing

    c. Evolutionary computing

    d. Biological computing

       Answer: c

Evolutionary computing uses the Darwinian principles of survival of the fittest, mutation, and the adaptation of successive generations of populations to their environment. The *genetic algorithm* implements this process through iteration of generations of a constant-size population of items or individuals. Each individual is characterized by a finite string of symbols called *genomes*. The genomes are used to represent possible solutions to a problem in a fixed search space. For example, if the fixed population of the first generation of individuals consists of random binary numbers, and the problem is to find the minimum binary number that can be represented by an individual, each binary number is assigned a *fitness value* based on the individual's binary number value. The smaller the binary number represented by a *parent* individual, the higher level of fitness that is assigned to it. Through cross breeding among the numbers (known as *crossover*), mutations of the numbers, and pairing of numbers with high fitness ratings, the smallest value that can be represented by the number of bits in the binary number will emerge in later generations. Answer a, neural networks, is incorrect and has been discussed extensively in previous questions in this chapter. Answer b is a distracter and answer d, biological computing, refers to computation performed by using certain characteristics of living organisms.

23. The Object Request Architecture (ORA) is a high-level framework for a distributed environment. It consists of four components. Which of the following items is NOT one of those components?

    a. Object Request Brokers (ORBs)

    b. Object Services

    c. Application Objects

    d. Application Services

    Answer: d

    Answers a, b, and c plus *Common Facilities* comprise the ORA. The ORA is a product of the *Object Management Group (OMG)*, which is a nonprofit consortium in Framingham, Massachusetts that was put together in 1989 to promote the use of object technology in distributed computing systems (www.omg.org). In answer a, the *ORB* is the fundamental building block of ORA and manages the communications between the ORA entities. The purpose of the ORB is to support the interaction of objects in heterogeneous, distributed environments. The objects may be on different types of computing platforms. Answer b, *Object Services*, supports the ORB in creating and tracking objects as well as performing access control functions. *Application Objects*, answer c, and *Common Facilities* support the end user and use the system services to perform their functions.

24. A standard that uses the Object Request Broker (ORB) to implement exchanges among objects in a heterogeneous, distributed environment is called:

    a. The Object Management Group (OMG) Object Model

    b. A Common Object Request Broker Architecture (CORBA)

    c. Open Architecture

    d. An Interface Definition Language (IDL)

    Answer: b

    In answer a, the *OMG Object Model* provides standard means for describing the externally visible characteristics of objects. Answer c is a distracter. *IDL*, answer d, is a standard interface language that is used by clients to request services from objects.

25. Another model that allows two software components to communicate with each other independent of their platforms' operating systems and languages of implementation is:

    a. Common Object Model (COM)

    b. Sandbox

    c. Basic Object Model (BOM)

    d. Spiral Model

    Answer: a

    As in the object-oriented paradigm, COM works with encapsulated objects. Communications with a COM object are through an *interface contract* between an object and its clients that defines the functions that are available in the object and the behavior of the object when the functions are called. Answer b, a *sandbox*, is an access control-based protection mechanism. It is commonly applied to restrict the access rights of mobile code that is downloaded from a Web site as an applet. The code is set up to run in a "sandbox" that blocks its access to the local workstation's hard disk, thus preventing the code from malicious activity. The sandbox is usually interpreted by a virtual machine such as the Java Virtual Machine. Answer c is a distracter and answer d refers to the software development life cycle model as discussed in Question 6.

26. A distributed object model that has similarities to the Common Object Request Broker Architecture (CORBA) is:

    a. Distributed Component Object Model (DCOM)

    b. The Chinese Wall Model

    c. Inference Model

    d. Distributed Data Model

Answer: a

DCOM is the distributed version of COM that supports remote objects as if the objects reside in the client's address space. A COM client can access a COM object through the use of a pointer to one of the object's interfaces and, then, invoking methods through that pointer. As discussed in Question 24, CORBA is a distributed object framework developed by the Object Management Group. Answer b, the *Chinese Wall Model* (D.C. Brewer & M.J. Nash, "Chinese Wall Model," *Proceedings of the 1989 IEEE Computer Society Symposium on Security and Privacy*, pp. 215-228, 1989), uses internal rules to "compartmentalize" areas in which individuals may work to prevent disclosure of proprietary information and to avoid conflicts of interest. The Chinese Wall model also incorporates the principle of separation of duty. Answers c and d are distracters.

27. Which of the following is NOT a characteristic of a client in the client/server model?

    a. Extensive user interface

    b. May be diskless

    c. Data entry screens

    d. Systems backup and database protection

    Answer: d

    In the client/server model, the server is the data storage resource and is responsible for data backups and protection/maintenance of the database. Answer b refers to a diskless workstation or PC at the client side. By not providing local data storage capabilities at the client side, security is increased since the data is less vulnerable at a protected server location. Also, because the client is the user's path into the network, the client must have extensive, user friendly interfaces such as described in answers a and c.

28. A client/server implementation approach in which any platform may act as a client or server or both is called:

    a. Simple file transfer

    b. Peer-to-peer

    c. Application Programming Interface (API)

    d. Graphical User Interface (GUI)

    Answer: b

    In answer a, a workstation or PC uses terminal emulation software and a client application program to receive data from a host machine. For answer c, an API defines how the client and server appear to each other and supports the exchange of information without either entity knowing the details of a particular resource that is accessed using the API. One example is the Generalized Security Application Programming Interface (GSAPI) that applications can use to access security services. Answer d, the GUI approach, is similar to the API implementation and employs a user interface such as SQL to access a server database.

29. Which of the following is NOT a characteristic of a distributed data processing (DDP) approach?

    a. Consists of multiple processing locations that can provide alternatives for computing in the event of a site becoming inoperative.

    b. Distances from user to processing resource are transparent to the user.

    c. Security is enhanced because of networked systems.

    d. Data stored at multiple, geographically separate locations is easily available to the user.

    Answer: c

    Security is more of a concern in distributed systems since there are vulnerabilities associated with the network and the many locations from which unauthorized access to the computing resources can occur. Answers a, b, and d are characteristics of a DDP architecture.

30. A database management system (DBMS) is useful in situations where:

    a. Rapid development of applications is required and preprogrammed functions can be used to provide those applications along with other support features such as security, error recovery, and access control.

    b. Data are processed infrequently and results are not urgently needed.

    c. Large amounts of data are to be processed in time-critical situations.

    d. The operations to be performed on the data are modified infrequently and the operations are relatively straightforward.

    Answer: a

    A DBMS is called for when the required skilled programming resources are not available, information to be stored and accessed is common to many organizational business units, the processing requirements change frequently and timely responses are required for queries on the data.

Chapter 8—Business Continuity Planning— Disaster Recovery Planning

1. Which choice below is the MOST accurate description of a warm site?

   a. A backup processing facility with adequate electrical wiring and air conditioning, but no hardware or software installed

   b. A backup processing facility with most hardware and software installed, which can be operational within a matter of days

   c. A backup processing facility with all hardware and software installed and 100% compatible with the original site, operational within hours

   d. A mobile trailer with portable generators and air conditioning

   Answer: b

   The three most common types of remote off-site backup processing facilities are hot sites, warm sites, and cold sites. They are primarily differentiated by how much preparation is devoted to the site, and therefore how quickly the site can be used as an alternate processing site. Answer c is an example of a "cold" site, which is a designated computer operations room with HVAC, that may have few or no computing systems installed and therefore would require a substantial effort to install the hardware and software required to begin alternate processing. This type of site is rarely useful in an actual emergency.

   Answer b, a "warm" site, is a backup processing facility with most hardware and software installed, which would need a minor effort to be up and running as an alternate processing center. It may use cheaper or older equipment and create a degradation in processing performance, but would be able to handle the most important processing tasks. A "hot" site, answer c, has all the required hardware and software installed to begin alternate processing either immediately or within an acceptably short time frame. This site would be 100% compatible with the original site and would only need an upgrade of the most current data to duplicate operations. Source: *The International Handbook of Computer Security* by Jae K. Shim, Anique A. Qureshi, and Joel G. Siegel (The Glenlake Publishing Co. Ltd, 2000), and "NFPA 1600 Standard on Disaster/Emergency Management and Business Continuity," National Fire Protection Association, 2000 edition.

   Table A.13 shows a common scheme to classify the recovery time frame needs of each business function.

Table A.13 Recovery Time Frame Classification Scheme

RATING CLASS	RECOVERY TIMEFRAME NEEDED
AAA	Immediate recovery needed; no downtime allowed.
AA	Full functional recovery required within four hours.
A	Same business day recovery required.
B	Up to 24 hours downtime acceptable.
C	24 to 72 hours downtime acceptable.
D	Greater than 72 hours downtime acceptable.

2. Which choice below is NOT an accurate description or element of remote sensing technology?

   a. Photographic, radar, infrared, or multi-spectral imagery from manned or unmanned aircraft

   b. Photographic, radar, infrared, or multi-spectral imagery from land-based tracking stations

   c. Photographic, radar, infrared, or multi-spectral imagery from geostationary or orbiting satellites

   d. RS intelligence may be integrated into geographic information systems (GIS) to produce map-based products

   Answer: b

   Remote sensing is the acquisition of information via aerial or satellite sensors. The most critical category of information to capture immediately following a disaster is accurate and timely intelligence about the scope, extent, and impact of the event. Intelligent and effective decisions hinge on the credible characterization of the situation. If the disaster is extensive enough, it may cause serious damage to the telephone or wireless infrastructure and ground communications may be unusable to accurately assess the situation. Remote sensing systems can provide a highly effective alternative means of gathering intelligence about the event. Answer a describes remote sensing using aerial-derived information. Answer c describes satellite-derived remote sensing. Answer d describes a common use of the remote sensing data. Source: "Remote Sensing in Federal Disaster Areas, Standard Operating Procedures," FEMA 9321.1-PR, June 1999

3. Which disaster recovery/emergency management plan testing type below is considered the most cost-effective and efficient way to identify areas of overlap in the plan before conducting more demanding training exercises?

   a. Full-scale exercise

   b. Walk-through drill

   c. Table-top exercise test

   d. Evacuation drill

   Answer: c

   In a table-top exercise, members of the emergency management group meet in a conference room setting to discuss their responsibilities and how they would react to emergency scenarios. Disaster recovery/emergency management plan testing scenarios have several levels, and can be called different things. The primary hierarchy of disaster/emergency testing plan types is shown below.

   Checklist review. Plan is distributed and reviewed by business units for its thoroughness and effectiveness.

   Table-top exercise or structured walk-through test. Members of the emergency management group meet in a conference room setting to discuss their responsibilities and how they would react to emergency scenarios by stepping through the plan.

   Walk-through drill or simulation test. The emergency management group and response teams actually perform their emergency response functions by walking through the test, without actually initiating recovery procedures. More thorough than the table-top exercise.

   Functional drills. Test specific functions such as medical response, emergency notifications, warning and communications procedures, and equipment, although not necessarily all at once. Also includes evacuation drills, where personnel walk the evacuation route to a designated area where procedures for accounting for the personnel are tested.

   Parallel test or full-scale exercise. A real-life emergency situation is simulated as closely as possible. Involves all of the participants that would be responding to the real emergency, including community and external organizations. The test may involve ceasing some real production processing.

   Source: "Emergency Management Guide for Business and Industry," Federal Emergency Management Agency, August 1998 and *Computer Security Basics*, by Deborah Russell and G.T. Gangemi, Sr. (O'Reilly, 1992).

4. Which task below would normally be considered a BCP task, rather than a DRP task?

   a. Life safety processes

   b. Project scoping

   c. Restoration procedures

   d. Recovery procedures

   Answer: b

   Although many processes in making business continuity plans are similar to processes in creating disaster recovery plans, several differences exist. Business continuity planning processes that are unique to BCP could include:

   ■ Project scoping and assigning roles

   ■ Creating business impact and vulnerability assessments

   ■ Choosing alternate processing sites

   whereas unique disaster recovery/emergency management processes could include:

   ■ Implementing relocation procedures to the alternate site

   ■ Plan testing and training

   ■ Recovering data

   ■ Salvaging damaged equipment

   Source: "CISSP Examination Textbooks, Volume One: Theory," by S. Rao Vallabhaneni, SRV Professional Publications first edition 2000 and "Handbook of Information Security Management," by Micki Krause and Harold F. Tipton, Auerback, 1999 edition.

5. Which choice below is NOT a role or responsibility of the person designated to manage the contingency planning process?

   a. Providing direction to senior management

   b. Providing stress reduction programs to employees after an event

   c. Ensuring the identification of all critical business functions

   d. Integrating the planning process across business units

   Answer: b

   Contingency planners have many roles and responsibilities when planning business continuity, disaster recovery, emergency management, or business resumption processes. In addition to answers a, c, and d, above, some of these roles and responsibilities can include:

   ■ Ensuring executive management compliance with the contingency plan program

- Providing periodic management reports and status
- Coordinating and integrating the activation of emergency response organizations

Answer b, providing stress reduction programs to employees after an event, is a responsibility of the human resources area. Source: *Contingency Planning and Management*, "Contingency Planning 101," by Kelley Goggins, March 1999.

6. Which choice below is NOT an emergency management procedure directly related to financial decision making?

   a. Establishing accounting procedures to track the costs of emergencies
   b. Establishing procedures for the continuance of payroll
   c. Establishing critical incident stress procedures
   d. Establishing program procurement procedures

   Answer: c

   Answers a, b, and d are all examples of emergency management procedures which must be established by the financial department to ensure that fiscal decisions are executed in accordance with authority levels and accounting practices. Answer c is an example of a procedure that should be developed by the human resources department. The quality of employee morale and well-being can include psychological needs as well as physical needs, and the role of the human resources department is critical in monitoring and managing immediate, short-term, and long-term employee stress. Source: "NFPA 1600 Standard on Disaster/Emergency Management and Business Continuity," National Fire Protection Association, 2000 edition.

7. Which choice below is NOT considered an appropriate role for senior management in the business continuity and disaster recovery process?

   a. Delegate recovery roles
   b. Publicly praise successes
   c. Closely control media and analyst communications
   d. Assess the adequacy of information security during the disaster recovery

   Answer: d

   The tactical assessment of information security is a role of information management or technology management, not senior management. In addition to the elements of answers a, b, and c above, senior management has many very important roles in the process of disaster recovery, including:

- Remaining visible to employees and stakeholders
- Directing, managing, and monitoring the recovery
- Rationally amending business plans and projections
- Clearly communicating new roles and responsibilities

Senior management must resist the temptation to participate hands-on in the recovery effort, as these efforts should be delegated. Information or technology management has more tactical roles to play, such as:

- Identifying and prioritizing mission-critical applications
- Continuously reassessing the recovery site's stability
- Recovering and constructing all critical data

Source: "Business Recovery Checklist," KPMG LLP 2001.

8. Which choice below is NOT considered a potential hazard resulting from natural events?

   a. Earthquake/land shift
   b. Forest fire
   c. Arson
   d. Urban fire

   Answer: c

   According to the NFPA, arson is an example of a potential hazard caused by a human event. Fires, in themselves, are considered natural events, like forest fires, range fires, urban or city fires, unless arson is thought to be the source of the blaze. Of the three categories of potential hazards (natural, technological, and human), human events could include:

   - General strikes
   - Terrorism
   - Sabotage
   - Mass hysteria
   - Civil unrest

   Source: "NFPA 1600 Standard on Disaster/Emergency Management and Business Continuity," National Fire Protection Association, 2000 edition.

9. Which choice below represents the most important first step in creating a business resumption plan?

   a. Performing a risk analysis
   b. Obtaining senior management support

c. Analyzing the business impact

d. Planning recovery strategies

Answer: b

The business resumption, or business continuity plan, must have total, highly visible senior management support. Senior management must agree on the scope of the project, delegate resources for the success of the project, and support the timeline and training efforts. Source: *Contingency Planning and Management,* "Contingency Planning 101," by Kelley Goggins, March 1999.

10. Which choice below would NOT be a valid reason for testing the disaster recovery plan?

a. Testing provides the contingency planner with recent documentation.

b. Testing verifies the accuracy of the recovery procedures.

c. Testing prepares the personnel to properly execute their emergency duties.

d. Testing identifies deficiencies within the recovery procedures.

Answer: a

Answers b, c, and d are all excellent reasons for testing a disaster recovery plan. Until a disaster recovery plan has been tested thoroughly, no plan can be considered complete. Since the functionality of the plan directly determines the ability of an organization to survive a business interrupting event, testing is the only way to have some degree of confidence that the plan will work. Answer a is a distracter. Source: *The International Handbook of Computer Security,* by Jae K. Shim, Anique A. Qureshi, and Joel G. Siegel (The Glenlake Publishing Co. Ltd, 2000).

11. Which choice below is NOT a commonly accepted definition for a disaster?

a. An occurrence that is outside the normal computing function

b. An occurrence or imminent threat to the entity of widespread or severe damage, injury, loss of life, or loss of property

c. An emergency that is beyond the normal response resources of the entity

d. A suddenly occurring event that has a long-term negative impact on social life

Answer: a

The disaster/emergency management and business continuity community consists of many different types of entities, such as governmental (federal, state, and local), nongovernmental (business and industry), and individuals. Each entity has its own focus and its own definition of a disaster. Answers b, c, and d are examples of these various definitions of disasters.

- A very common definition of a disaster is "a suddenly occurring or unstoppable developing event that":
- Claims loss of life, suffering, loss of valuables, or damage to the environment.
- Overwhelms local resources or efforts.
- Has a long-term impact on social or natural life that is always negative in the beginning.

Source: "NFPA 1600 Standard on Disaster/Emergency Management and Business Continuity," National Fire Protection Association, 2000 edition.

12. Which choice below is NOT considered an appropriate role for Financial Management in the business continuity and disaster recovery process?
    a. Tracking the recovery costs
    b. Monitoring employee morale and guarding against employee burnout
    c. Formally notifying insurers of claims
    d. Reassessing cash flow projections

    Answer: b

    Monitoring employee morale and guarding against employee burnout during a disaster recovery event is the proper role of human resources. Other emergency recovery tasks associated with human resources could include:

- Providing appropriate retraining
- Monitoring productivity of personnel
- Providing employees and family with counseling and support

    In addition to answers a, c, and d above, during an emergency, the financial area is responsible for:

- Re-establishing accounting processes, such as payroll, benefits, and accounts payable
- Re-establishing transaction controls and approval limits

Source: "Business Recovery Checklist," KPMG LLP 2001, and *Contingency Planning and Management*, "Contingency Planning 101," by Kelley Goggins, March 1999.

13. Which choice below most accurately describes a business continuity program?

   a. Ongoing process to ensure that the necessary steps are taken to identify the impact of potential losses and maintain viable recovery

   b. A program that implements the mission, vision, and strategic goals of the organization

   c. A determination of the effects of a disaster on human, physical, economic, and natural resources

   d. A standard that allows for rapid recovery during system interruption and data loss

   Answer: a

   A business continuity program is an ongoing process supported by senior management and funded to ensure that the necessary steps are taken to identify the impact of potential losses, maintain viable recovery strategies and recovery plans, and ensure continuity of services through personnel training, plan testing, and maintenance. Answer b describes a disaster/emergency management program. A disaster/emergency management program, like a disaster recovery program, is a program that implements the mission, vision, and strategic goals and objectives as well as the management framework of the program and organization. Answer c describes a damage assessment. A damage assessment is an appraisal or determination of the effects of a disaster on human, physical, economic, and natural resources. Answer d is a distracter. Source: "NFPA 1600 Standard on Disaster/Emergency Management and Business Continuity," National Fire Protection Association, 2000 edition.

14. What is the responsibility of the contingency planner regarding LAN backup and recovery if the LAN is part of a building server environment?

   a. Getting a copy of the recovery procedures from the building server administrator

   b. Recovering client/server systems owned and supported by internal staff

   c. Classifying the recovery time frame of the business unit LAN

   d. Identifying essential business functions

   Answer: a

   When any part of the LAN is not hosted internally, and is part of a building server environment, it is the responsibility of the contingency planner to identify the building server administrator, identify for him the recovery time frame required for your business applications, obtain a copy of the recovery procedures, and participate in the validation of the building's server testing. If all or part of the business is not in the building server environment, then the other three choices are also the responsibility of the contingency planner. Source: *Contingency Planning and Management,* "Contingency Planning 101," by Kelley Goggins, March 1999.

15. Which choice below is the correct definition of a Mutual Aid Agreement?

    a. A management-level analysis that identifies the impact of losing an entity's resources

    b. An appraisal or determination of the effects of a disaster on human, physical, economic, and natural resources

    c. A prearranged agreement to render assistance to the parties of the agreement

    d. Activities taken to eliminate or reduce the degree of risk to life and property

    Answer: c

    A mutual aid agreement is used by two or more parties to provide for assistance if one of the parties experiences an emergency. It is expected that the other parties will assist the affected party in various ways, perhaps by making office space available, or computing time or resources, or supplying manpower if needed. While mutual aid agreements may be a very cost-effective solution for disaster recovery, it does not provide for full operations redundancy. An example of a problem with a total reliance on mutual aid would be the event that affects all parties to the agreement, thereby rendering the agreement useless. While they are an effective means to provide some resources to the organization in an emergency, they in themselves are not a replacement for a full disaster recovery plan, including alternate computer processing sites.

    Answer a describes a business continuity plan. Answer b describes a damage assessment, and answer d describes risk mitigation. Source: "NFPA 1600 Standard on Disaster/Emergency Management and Business Continuity," National Fire Protection Association, 2000 edition, and "Emergency Management Guide for Business and Industry," Federal Emergency Management Agency, August 1998.

16. In which order should the following steps be taken to create an emergency management plan?

    ——— a. Implement the plan

    _____ b. Form a planning team

_____ c. Develop a plan

_____ d. Conduct a vulnerability assessment

> *Answer:* b, d, c, and a
>
> The proper order of steps in the emergency management planning process is:
>
> - Establish a planning team
> - Analyze capabilities and hazards
> - Develop the plan
> - Implement the plan
>
> Source: "Emergency Management Guide for Business and Industry," Federal Emergency Management Agency, August 1998.

17. Place the BRP groups below in their properly tiered organizational structure, from highest to lowest:

———— a. Policy group

———— b. Senior executives

———— c. Emergency response team

———— d. Disaster management team

> *Answer:* b, a, d, and c
>
> Some organizations with mature business resumption plans (BRPs) employ a tiered structure that mirrors the organization's hierarchy. Senior management is always the highest level of decision-makers in the BRP process, although the policy group also consists of upper-level executives. The policy group approves emergency management decisions involving expenditures, liabilities, and service impacts. The next group, the disaster management team, often consists of department and business unit representatives and makes decisions regarding life safety and disaster recovery efforts. The next group, the emergency response team, supplies tactical response to the disaster, and may consist of members of data processing, user support, or persons with first aid and evacuation responsibilities. Source: *Contingency Planning and Management*, "Business Contingency Planning 201," by Paul H. Rosenthal May, 2000.

18. Which choice below most accurately describes a business impact analysis (BIA)?

    a. A program that implements the strategic goals of the organization

    b. A management-level analysis that identifies the impact of losing an entity's resources

c. A prearranged agreement between two or more entities to provide assistance

d. Activities designed to return an organization to an acceptable operating condition

Answer: b

A business impact analysis (BIA) measures the effect of resource loss and escalating losses over time in order to provide the entity with reliable data upon which to base decisions on hazard mitigation and continuity planning. A BIA is performed as one step during the creation of a Business Continuity Plan (BCP). A common five-step approach to a BCP could consist of:

■ BCP project scope creation

■ Business impact assessment

■ Recovery strategy development

■ Recovery plan development

■ Implementation, testing, and maintenance.

Answer a is a definition of a disaster/emergency management program. Answer c describes a mutual aid agreement. Answer d is the definition of a recovery program. Source: "NFPA 1600 Standard on Disaster/Emergency Management and Business Continuity," National Fire Protection Association, 2000 edition and "Handbook of Information Security Management," by Micki Krause and Harold F. Tipton, Auerback, 1999 edition.

19. In which order should the following steps be taken to perform a vulnerability assessment?

____ a. List potential emergencies

____ b. Estimate probability

____ c. Assess external and internal resources

____ d. Assess potential impact

Answer: a, b, d, and c

Common steps to performing a vulnerability assessment could be:

1. List potential emergencies, both internally to your facility and externally to the community. Natural, man-made, technological, and human error are all categories of potential emergencies and errors.

2. Estimate the likelihood that each emergency could occur, in a subjective analysis.

TYPE OF EMERGENCY	Probability	Human Impact	Property Impact	Business Impact	Internal Resources	External Resources	Total
	High 5 ←→ Low 1	High Impact 5 ←→ 1 Low Impact			Weak Resources 5 ←→ 1 Strong Resources		

Figure A.12 Sample vulnerability assessment matrix.

3. Assess the potential impact of the emergency on the organization in the areas of human impact (death or injury), property impact (loss or damage), and business impact (market share or credibility).

4. Assess external and internal resources required to deal with the emergency, and determine if they are located internally or if external capabilities or procedures are required.

Source: "Emergency Management Guide for Business and Industry," Federal Emergency Management Agency, August 1998.

Figure A.12 shows a sample vulnerability matrix. This can be used to create a subjective impact analysis for each type of emergency and its probability. The lower the final number the better, as a high number means a high probability, impact, or lack of remediation resources.

20. According to FEMA, which choice below is NOT a recommended way to purify water after a disaster?

a. Adding 16 drops per gallon of household liquid bleach to the water

b. Boiling from 3 to 5 minutes

    c. Adding water treatment tablets to the water

    d. Distilling the water for twenty minutes

       Answer: c

       FEMA recommends that water treatment products sold in camping or surplus stores should not be used, unless the only active ingredient is 5.25 percent hypochlorite. When adding liquid bleach, it should contain 5.25 percent hypochlorite and no other added cleaners or scents. Distilling the water is the most highly recommended method, as it also removes other chemicals and heavy metals, as well as most microbes. Source: *Emergency Water and Food Procedures,* Federal Emergency Management Agency, April, 1997.

21. Which choice below is NOT a recommended step to take when resuming normal operations after an emergency?

    a. Re-occupy the damaged building as soon as possible.

    b. Account for all damage-related costs.

    c. Protect undamaged property.

    d. Conduct an investigation.

       Answer: a

       Re-occupying the site of a disaster or emergency should not be undertaken until a full safety inspection has been done, an investigation into the cause of the emergency has been completed, and all damaged property has been salvaged and restored. During and after an emergency, the safety of personnel must be monitored, any remaining hazards must be assessed, and security must be maintained at the scene. After all safety precautions have been taken, an inventory of damaged and undamaged property must be done to begin salvage and restoration tasks. Also, the site must not be re-occupied until all investigative processes have been completed. Detailed records must be kept of all disaster-related costs and valuations must be made of the effect of the business interruption. Source: "Emergency Management Guide for Business and Industry," Federal Emergency Management Agency, August 1998.

22. In developing an emergency or recovery plan, which choice below would NOT be considered a short-term objective?

    a. Priorities for restoration

    b. Acceptable downtime before restoration

    c. Minimum resources needed to accomplish the restoration

    d. The organization's strategic plan

Answer: d

The organization's strategic plan is considered a long-term goal. In developing plans, consideration should be given to both short-term and long-term goals and objectives. Short-term goals can include:

- Vital personnel, systems, operations, and equipment
- Priorities for restoration and mitigation
- Acceptable downtime before restoration to a minimum level of operations
- Minimum resources needed to accomplish the restoration

   Long-term goals and objectives can include:
- The organization's strategic plan
- Management and coordination of activities
- Funding and fiscal management
- Management of volunteer, contractual, and entity resources

Source: "NFPA 1600 Standard on Disaster/Emergency Management and Business Continuity," National Fire Protection Association, 2000 edition.

23. When should security isolation of the incident scene start?
    a. Immediately after the emergency is discovered
    b. As soon as the disaster plan is implemented
    c. After all personnel have been evacuated
    d. When hazardous materials have been discovered at the site

    Answer: a

    Isolation of the incident scene should begin as soon as the emergency has been discovered. Authorized personnel should attempt to secure the scene and control access; however, no one should be placed in physical danger to perform these functions. It's important for life safety that access be controlled immediately at the scene, and only by trained personnel directly involved in the disaster response. Additional injury or exposure to recovery personnel after the initial incident must be tightly controlled. Source: "Emergency Management Guide for Business and Industry," Federal Emergency Management Agency, August, 1998.

24. Place the following backup processing alternatives in order, from the most expensive solution to the least expensive:
    _____ a. Warm site
    _____ b. Hot site
    _____ c. Cold site
    _____ d. Mutual aid agreement

Answer: b, a, c, and d

A mutual aid agreement is likely to be the least expensive of the four, as it doesn't necessarily entail any resource investment. As far as the ability of the alternatives to actually provide redundancy and processing in the event of a business-interrupting incident, the order is exactly the opposite, with mutual aid and cold sites providing the least, and hot sites providing the highest level of processing redundancy assurance. Source: *The International Handbook of Computer Security*, by Jae K. Shim, Anique A. Qureshi, and Joel G. Siegel (The Glenlake Publishing Co. Ltd, 2000).

25. Which choice below is incorrect regarding when a BCP, DRP, or emergency management plan should be evaluated and modified?

   a. Never; once it has been tested it should not be changed.

   b. Annually, in a scheduled review.

   c. After training drills, tests, or exercises.

   d. After an emergency or disaster response.

   Answer: a

   Emergency management plans, business continuity plans, and disaster recovery plans should be regularly reviewed, evaluated, modified, and updated. At a minimum, the plan should be reviewed at an annual audit. It should also be re-evaluated:

   ■ After tests or training exercises, to adjust any discrepancies between the test results and the plan

   ■ After a disaster response or an emergency recovery, as this is an excellent time to amend the parts of the plan that were not effective

   ■ When personnel, their responsibilities, their resources, or organizational structures change, to familiarize new or reorganized personnel with procedures

   ■ When polices, procedures, or infrastructures change

   Source: "Emergency Management Guide for Business and Industry" Federal Emergency Management Agency, August, 1998 and "NFPA 1600 Standard on Disaster/Emergency Management and Business Continuity" National Fire Protection Association, 2000 edition.

26. Which choice below refers to a business asset?

   a. Events or situations that could cause a financial or operational impact to the organization

   b. Protection devices or procedures in place that reduce the effects of threats

c. Competitive advantage, credibility, or good will

d. Personnel compensation and retirement programs

Answer: c

Assets are considered the physical and financial assets that are owned by the company. Examples of business assets that could be lost or damaged during a disaster are:

■ Revenues lost during the incident

■ On-going recovery costs

■ Fines and penalties incurred by the event.

■ Competitive advantage, credibility, or good will damaged by the incident

Answer a is a definition for a threat. Answer b is a description of mitigating factors that reduce the effect of a threat, such as a UPS, sprinkler systems, or generators. Answer d is a distracter. Source: Contingency Planning and Management, "Contingency Planning 101" by Kelley Goggins, March, 1999.

27. Which choice below is an example of a potential hazard due to a technological event, rather than a human event?

a. Sabotage

b. Financial collapse

c. Mass hysteria

d. Enemy attack

Answer: b

A financial collapse is considered a technological potential hazard, the other three are human events. Of the three categories of potential hazards (natural, technological, and human), technological events could include:

■ Hazard material release (HazMat)

■ Explosion or fire (non-arson)

■ Fuel shortage

■ Structure collapse

■ Utility failure

■ Severe air pollution

Source: "NFPA 1600 Standard on Disaster/Emergency Management and Business Continuity," National Fire Protection Association, 2000 edition.

28. When should the public and media be informed about a disaster?

a. Whenever site emergencies extend beyond the facility

b. When any emergency occurs at the facility, internally or externally

c. When the public's health or safety is in danger

d. When the disaster has been contained

Answer: a

When an emergency occurs that could potentially have an impact outside the facility, the public must be informed, regardless of whether there is any immediate threat to public safety. The disaster recovery plan should include determinations of the audiences that may be affected by an emergency, and procedures to communicate with them. Information the public will want to know could include public safety or health concerns, the nature of the incident, the remediation effort, and future prevention steps. Common audiences for information could include:

- The media
- Unions and contractors
- Shareholders
- Neighbors
- Employees' families and retirees

Since the media is such an important link to the public, disaster plans and tests must contain procedures for addressing the media and communicating important information. A trained spokesperson should be designated, and established communications procedures should be prepared. Accurate and approved information should be released in a timely manner, without speculation, blame, or obfuscation. Source: "Emergency Management Guide for Business and Industry," Federal Emergency Management Agency, August, 1998.

29. Which choice below is the first priority in an emergency?

a. Communicating with employees' families the status of the emergency

b. Notifying external support resources for recovery and restoration

c. Protecting the health and safety of everyone in the facility

d. Warning customers and contractors of a potential interruption of service

Answer: c

Life safety, or protecting the health and safety of everyone in the facility is the first priority in an emergency or disaster. Evacuation routes, assembly areas, and accounting for personnel (head counts and last-known locations) are the most important function of emergency procedures, before anything else. Once all personnel have been accounted for and emergency teams have arrived to prevent further damage or hazard, family members should be notified of the status of the event. Providing restoration and recovery, and implementing alternative production methods also comes later. Source: "Emergency Management Guide for Business and Industry," Federal Emergency Management Agency, August, 1998.

Chapter 9—Law, Investigation, and Ethics

1. In the legal field, there is a term that is used to describe a computer system so that everyone can agree on a common definition. The term describes a computer for the purposes of computer security as "any assembly of electronic equipment, hardware, software and firmware configured to collect, create, communicate, disseminate, process, store and control data or information." This definition includes peripheral items such as keyboards, printers, and additional memory. The term that corresponds to this definition is:

   a. A central processing unit (CPU)

   b. A microprocessor

   c. An arithmetic logic unit (ALU)

   d. An automated information system (AIS)

   > *Answer:* d
   >
   > In some ways, this terminology harkens back to the days of large mainframe computers, but the term AIS is used in the legal community to refer to a computer system. Answer a, CPU, refers to the portion of a computer that performs arithmetic and logical operations on data. To support these operations, the CPU incorporates a hardware arithmetic logic unit or ALU (answer c). The CPU is synonymous with the word *"processor."* If the CPU is integrated onto a silicon chip, it is called a *microprocessor* (answer b). If the CPU is connected with memory and Input/Output (I/O) through a set of wires called a *bus*, the resulting combination is called a computer. This concept is shown in Figure A.13.

2. In general, computer crimes fall into two major categories and two additional related categories. Which of the following categories is NOT one of these four?

   a. The computer as a target of the crime

   b. Crimes using the computer

   c. Malfeasance by computer

   d. Crimes associated with the prevalence of computers

   > *Answer:* c
   >
   > Malfeasance by computer is an act involving a computer that is technically and ethically improper, but may or may not be illegal. Some of these activities may not be considered illegal by the user and may be unintentional. Examples of such behavior are:
   >
   > ■ Using a password that you have been given by someone else to have access to their computer and using that password to view files that were not intended for your perusal

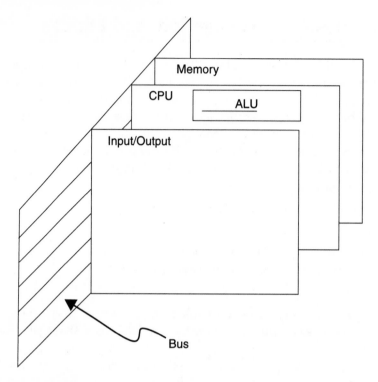

Figure A.13 A computer.

- Giving a copy of a software package that you purchased to a member of your family for personal use (In most instances, this is illegal based on software licenses.)
- Using the computer at your place of employment to store some information related to an outside business activity

Answers a, b, and d are valid categories of computer crime. The fourth category is a crime where the computer is incidental to other crimes. Examples in these four categories are:

The computer is a target of the crime. Sabotage or theft of intellectual property, disruption of business operations, illegal access to government and personal information, and falsifying or changing records.

Crimes using the computer. Theft of money from financial accounts, credit card fraud, fraud involving stock transfers, billing charges illegally to another party, and telecommunications fraud.

Crimes associated with the prevalence of computers. Violation of copyright restrictions on commercial software packages, software piracy and software counterfeiting.

The computer is incidental to other crimes. (In this category, the crime could be committed without the computer, but the computer permits the crime to be committed more efficiently and in higher volume.) Money laundering, keeping records and books of illegal activity and illegal gambling.

3. Which of the following is NOT a valid legal issue associated with computer crime?

   a. Electronic Data Interchange (EDI) makes it easier to relate a crime to an individual.

   b. It may be difficult to prove criminal intent.

   c. It may be difficult to obtain a trail of evidence of activities performed on the computer.

   d. It may be difficult to show causation.

   Answer: a

   EDI makes it more difficult to tie an individual to transactions since EDI involves computer-to-computer data interchanges and this makes it more difficult to trace the originator of some transactions. Answer b is a valid legal issue since it may be very difficult to prove criminal intent by a person perusing computer files and then causing damage to the files. The damage may have not been intentional. Answer c describes the situation of trying to track activities on a computer where the information is volatile and may have been destroyed. In answer d, common law refers to *causation* of the criminal act. Causation is particularly difficult to show in instances where a virus or other malicious code erases itself after causing damage to vital information.

4. The Federal Intelligence Surveillance Act (FISA) of 1978, the Electronic Communications Privacy Act (ECPA) of 1986, and the Communications Assistance for Law Enforcement Act (CALEA) of 1994 are legislative acts passed by the United States Congress. These acts all address what major information security issue?

   a. Computer fraud

   b. Wiretapping

   c. Malicious code

   d. Unlawful use of and access to government computers and networks

   Answer: b

These laws reflected different views concerning wiretapping as technology progressed. The Federal Intelligence Surveillance Act (FISA) of 1978 limited wiretapping for national security purposes as a result of the record of the Nixon Administration in using illegal wiretaps. The Electronic Communications Privacy Act (ECPA) of 1986 prohibited eavesdropping or the interception of message contents without distinguishing between private or public systems. The Communications Assistance for Law Enforcement Act (CALEA) of 1994 required all communications carriers to make wiretaps possible in ways approved by the FBI.

5. A *pen register* is a:

   a. Device that identifies the cell in which a mobile phone is operating

   b. Device that records the URLs accessed by an individual

   c. Device that records the caller-ID of incoming calls

   d. Device that records all the numbers dialed from a specific telephone line

   Answer: d

   (Electronic Privacy Information Center, "Approvals for Federal Pen Registers and Trap and Trace Devices 1987-1998," www.epic. org). Gathering information as to which numbers are dialed from a specific telephone line is less costly and time-consuming than installing a wiretap and recording the information. There is also equipment that can record the information listed in answers a and b. The device referred to in answer c is called a *trap-and-trace* device. All of the answers in this question are a subset of the category of *traffic analysis* wherein patterns and frequency associated with communications are studied instead of the content of the communications.

6. A device that is used to monitor Internet Service Provider (ISP) data traffic is called:

   a. Carnivore

   b. Echelon

   c. Escrowed encryption

   d. Key manager

   Answer: a

   Carnivore is a device used by the U.S. FBI to monitor ISP traffic. (S.P. Smith, et. al., *Independent Technical Review of the Carnivore System—Draft report*, U.S. Department of Justice Contract # 00-C-328 IITRI, CR-022-216, Nov 17, 2000). Answer b, *Echelon*, refers to a cooperative, worldwide signal intelligence system that is run by the NSA of the United States, the Government Communications Head Quarters (GCHQ) of

England, the Communications Security Establishment (CSE) of Canada, the Australian Defense Security Directorate (DSD), and the General Communications Security Bureau (GCSB) of New Zealand. These organizations are bound together under a secret 1948 agreement, UKUSA, [European Parliament, "Development of Surveillance Technology and the Risk of Abuse of Economic Information," Luxembourg (April 1999), PE 166.184/Part 3 /4]. Answer c is a distracter and is discussed in the questions and answers of Chapter 4, "Cryptography." Answer d is a distracter.

7. In 1996, the World Intellectual Property Organization (WIPO) sponsored a treaty under which participating countries would standardize treatment of digital copyrights. One of the items of standardization was the prohibition of altering copyright management information (CMI) that is included with the copyrighted material. CMI is:

a. An encryption algorithm

b. Product description information

c. A listing of Public keys

d. Licensing and ownership information

Answer: d

The other answers are distracters. The WIPO digital copyright legislation that resulted in the U.S. was the 1998 Digital Millennium Copyright Act (DMCA). In addition to addressing answer d, the DMCA prohibits trading, manufacturing, or selling in any way that is intended to bypass copyright protection mechanisms. It also addresses Internet Service Providers (ISPs) that unknowingly support the posting of copyrighted material by subscribers. If the ISP is notified that the material is copyrighted, the ISP must remove the material. Additionally, if the posting party proves that the removed material was of "lawful use," the ISP must restore the material and notify the copyright owner within 14 business days.

Two important rulings regarding the DMCA were made in 2001. The rulings involved DeCSS, which is a program that bypasses the Content Scrambling System (CSS) software used to prevent viewing of DVD movie disks on unlicensed platforms. In a trade secrecy case [DVD-CCA v. Banner], the California Appellate Court overturned a lower court ruling that an individual who posted DeCSS on the Internet had revealed the trade secret of CSS. The appeals court has reversed an injunction on the posting of DeCSS, stating that the code is speech-protected by the First Amendment.

The second case [Universal City v. Reimerdes] was the first constitutional challenge to DMCA anti-circumvention rules. The case involved Eric Corley, the publisher of the hacker magazine *2600 Magazine*. Corley was covering the DeCSS situation and, as part of that coverage, posted DeCSS on his publication's Web site. The trial and appellate courts both ruled that the posting violated the DMCA and was, therefore, illegal. This ruling upheld the DMCA. It appears that there will be more challenges to DMCA in the future.

8. The European Union (EU) has enacted a Conditional Access Directive (CAD) that addresses which of the following?

a. Access to and use of copyrighted material

b. Reverse engineering

c. Unauthorized access to Internet subscription sites and pay TV services

d. Use of copyrighted material by libraries

Answer: c

The focus of the CAD is on access to services as opposed to access to works. As of this writing, the EU is discussing a directive focusing on copyrights, but it has not been finalized. It is anticipated that this directive will be similar to the U.S. DMCA (Question 7). Answers a, b, and d are copyright issues that will be addressed by the EU Copyright Directive or by other related directives.

9. Which of the following actions by the U.S. government are NOT permitted or required by the U.S. Patriot Act, signed into law on October 26, 2001?

a. Subpoena of electronic records

b. Monitoring of Internet communications

c. Search and seizure of information on live systems (including routers and servers), backups, and archives

d. Reporting of cash and wire transfers of $5,000 or more

Answer: d

Wire and cash transfers of $10,000 or more in a single transaction must be reported to government officials. Actions in answers a, b, and c are permitted under the Patriot Act. In answers a and b, the government has new powers to subpoena electronic records and to monitor Internet traffic. In monitoring information, the government can require the assistance of ISPs and network operators. This monitoring can even extend into individual organizations. In the Patriot Act, Congress permits investigators to gather information about electronic mail without having to show probable cause that the person to be monitored had committed a crime or was intending to commit a crime. In answer c, the items cited now fall under existing search and seizure laws. A new twist is delayed notification of a search warrant. Under the Patriot Act, if it suspected that notification of a search warrant would cause a suspect to flee, a search can be conducted before notification of a search warrant is given.

In a related matter, the U.S. and numerous other nations have signed the Council of Europe's "Cybercrime Convention." In the U.S., participation in the Convention has to be ratified by the Senate. In essence, the Convention requires the signatory nations to spy on their own residents, even if the action being monitored is illegal in the country in which the monitoring is taking place.

10. The U.S. Uniform Computer Information Transactions Act (UCITA) is a:

   a. Model act that is intended to apply uniform legislation to software licensing

   b. Model act that addresses digital signatures

   c. Model act that is intended to apply uniform legislation to electronic credit transactions

   d. Model act that addresses electronic transactions conducted by financial institutions

   Answer: a

   The National Commissioners on Uniform State Laws (NCUSL) voted to approve the Uniform Computers Information Transactions Act (UCITA) on July 29, 1999. This legislation, which will have to be enacted state-by-state, will greatly affect libraries' access to and use of software packages. It also will keep in place the current licensing practices of software vendors. At the present time, shrink-wrap or click-wrap licenses limit rights that are normally granted under copyright law. Under Section 109 of the U.S. 1976 Copyright Act, the first sale provision permits "the owner of a particular copy without the authority of the copyright owner, to sell or otherwise dispose of the possession of that copy." However, the software manufacturers use the term license in their transactions. As opposed to the word "sale," the term license denotes that the software manufacturers are permitting users to use a copy of their software. Thus, the software vendor still owns the software. Until each state enacts the legislation, it is not clear if shrink-wrap licenses that restrict users' rights under copyright law are legally enforceable. For clarification, shrink-wrap licenses physically accompany a disk while click-on and active click-wrap licenses are usually transmitted electronically. Sometimes, the term shrink-wrap is interpreted to mean both physical and electronic licenses to use software. The focus of the UCITA legislation is not on the physical media, but on the information contained on the media.

11. The European Union Electronic Signature Directive of January, 2000, defines an "advanced electronic signature." This signature must meet all of the following requirements except that:

    a. It must be uniquely linked to the signatory.

    b. It must be created using means that are generally accessible and available.

    c. It must be capable of identifying the signatory.

    d. It must be linked to the data to which it relates in such a manner that any subsequent change of the data is detectable.

    Answer: b

    The Directive requires that the means be maintained under the sole control of the signatory. This requirement is a particularly difficult one to achieve. One approach is to use different tokens or smart cards for the different transactions involved. The other answers are typical characteristics of digital signatures that can be implemented with public key cryptography.

12. On June 30, 2000, the U.S. Congress enacted the Electronic Signatures in Global and National Commerce Act (ESIGN) "to facilitate the use of electronic records and signatures in interstate and foreign commerce by ensuring the validity and legal effect of contracts entered into electronically." An important provision of the Act requires that:

    a. Businesses obtain electronic consent or confirmation from consumers to receive information electronically that a law normally requires to be in writing.

    b. The e-commerce businesses do not have to determine whether the consumer has the ability to receive an electronic notice before transmitting the legally required notices to the consumer.

    c. Businesses have the ability to use product price to persuade consumers to accept electronic records instead of paper.

    d. Specific technologies be used to ensure technical compatibility.

    Answer: a

    The legislation is intent on preserving the consumers' rights under consumer protection laws and went to extraordinary measures to meet this goal. Thus, a business must receive confirmation from the consumer in electronic format that the consumer consents to receiving information electronically that used to be in written form. This provision ensures that the consumer has access to the Internet and is familiar with the basics of electronic communications. Answer b is, therefore, incorrect. Answer c is also incorrect since the legislation reduces the ability of businesses to use product price unfairly to persuade consumers to accept electronic records. Answer d is incorrect since the legislation is specifically technology-neutral to permit the use of the best technology for the application.

13. Under Civil Law, the victim is NOT entitled to which of the following types of damages?

 a. Statutory

 b. Punitive

 c. Compensatory

 d. Imprisonment of the offender

  Answer: d

  Imprisonment or probation is not a type of punishment available for conviction of a civil crime. Answer a refers to awards set by law. Answer b, punitive damages, are usually determined by the jury and are intended to punish the offender. Compensatory awards are used to provide restitution and compensate the victim for such items as costs of investigations and attorneys' fees.

14. Which of the following is NOT one of the European Union (EU) privacy principles?

 a. Individuals are entitled to receive a report on the information that is held about them.

 b. Data transmission of personal information to locations where "equivalent" personal data protection cannot be assured is prohibited.

 c. Information collected about an individual can be disclosed to other organizations or individuals unless specifically prohibited by the individual.

 d. Individuals have the right to correct errors contained in their personal data.

  Answer: c

  This principle is stated as an "opt-out" principle in which the individual has to take action to prevent information from being circulated to other organizations. The correct corresponding European Union principle states that "information collected about an individual cannot be disclosed to other organizations or individuals unless authorized by law or by consent of the individual." Thus, the individual would have to take an active role or "opt-in" to authorize the disclosure of information to other organizations. The other principles are valid EU privacy principles.

15. Which of the following is NOT a goal of the Kennedy-Kassebaum Health Insurance Portability and Accountability Act (HIPAA) of 1996?

    a. Provide for restricted access by the patient to personal healthcare information

    b. Administrative simplification

    c. Enable the portability of health insurance

    d. Establish strong penalties for healthcare fraud

    Answer: a

    HIPAA is designed to provide for greater access by the patient to personal healthcare information. In answer b, administrative simplification, the goal is to improve the efficiency and effectiveness of the healthcare system by:

    ■ Standardizing the exchange of administrative and financial data

    ■ Protecting the security and privacy of individually identifiable health information

    Answers c and d are self-explanatory.

16. The proposed HIPAA Security Rule mandates the protection of the confidentiality, integrity, and availability of protected health information (PHI) through three of the following activities. Which of the activities is NOT included under the proposed HIPAA Security Rule?

    a. Administrative procedures

    b. Physical safeguards

    c. Technical services and mechanisms

    d. Appointment of a Privacy Officer

    Answer: d

    HIPAA separates the activities of Security and Privacy. HIPAA Security is mandated under the main categories listed in answers a, b, and c. The proposed HIPAA Security Rule mandates the appointment of a Security Officer. The HIPAA Privacy Rule mandates the appointment of a Privacy Officer. HIPAA Privacy covers individually identifiable health care information transmitted, stored in electronic or paper or oral form. PHI may not be disclosed except for the following reasons:

    ■ Disclosure is approved by the individual

    ■ Permitted by the legislation

    ■ For treatment

    ■ Payment

    ■ Health care operations

■ As required by law

Protected Health Information (PHI) is individually identifiable health information that is:

■ Transmitted by electronic media

■ Maintained in any medium described in the definition of electronic media …[under HIPAA]

■ Transmitted or maintained in any other form or medium

17. Individual privacy rights as defined in the HIPAA Privacy Rule include consent and authorization by the patient for the release of PHI. The difference between consent and authorization as used in the Privacy Rule is:

a. Consent grants general permission to use or disclose PHI, and authorization limits permission to the purposes and the parties specified in the authorization.

b. Authorization grants general permission to use or disclose PHI, and consent limits permission to the purposes and the parties specified in the consent.

c. Consent grants general permission to use or disclose PHI, and authorization limits permission to the purposes specified in the authorization.

d. Consent grants general permission to use or disclose PHI, and authorization limits permission to the parties specified in the authorization.

Answer: a

Answer b is therefore incorrect. Answer c is incorrect since the limits to authorization do not include the parties concerned. Answer d is incorrect since the limits to authorization do not include the specified purposes. The other individual privacy rights listed in the HIPAA Privacy Rule are:

■ Notice (of the covered entities' privacy practices)

■ Right to request restriction

■ Right of access

■ Right to amend

■ Right to an accounting

In August of 2002, the U.S. Department of Health and Human Services (HHS) modified the Privacy Rule to ease the requirements of consent and allow the covered entities to use notice. The changes are summarized as follows:

■ Covered entities must provide patients with notice of the patient's privacy rights and the privacy practices of the covered entity.

- Direct treatment providers must make a good faith effort to obtain patient's written acknowledgement of the notice of privacy rights and practices. (The Rule does not prescribe a form of written acknowledgement; the patient may sign a separate sheet or initial a cover sheet of the notice.)

- Mandatory consent requirements are removed that would inhibit patient access to health care while providing covered entities with the option of developing a consent process that works for that entity. If the provider cannot obtain a written acknowledgement, it must document its good faith efforts to obtain one and the reason for its inability to obtain the acknowledgement.

- Consent requirements already in place may continue.

18. Because of the nature of information that is stored on the computer, the investigation and prosecution of computer criminal cases have specific characteristics, one of which is:

   a. Investigators and prosecutors have a longer time frame for the investigation.

   b. The information is intangible.

   c. The investigation does not usually interfere with the normal conduct of the business of an organization.

   d. Evidence is usually easy to gather.

   Answer: b

   The information is stored in memory on the computer and is intangible as opposed to a physical object. Answer a is incorrect since investigators and prosecutors are under time pressure to gather evidence and proceed to prosecution. If the suspect is alerted, he or she may do damage to the system or destroy important evidence. Search warrants may have to be obtained by law enforcement to search the suspect's home and workplace and seize computers and disks. Answer c is incorrect since an investigation will interfere with the normal conduct of business. Some of the ways in which an investigation may affect an organization are:

   - The organization will have to provide experts to work with law enforcement.

   - Information key to the criminal investigation may be co-resident on the same computer system as information critical to the day-to-day operation of the organization.

   - Proprietary data may be subject to disclosure.

- Management may be exposed if they have not exercised "Due Care" to protect information resources.
- There may be negative publicity that will be harmful to the organization.

Answer d is incorrect. Evidence is difficult to gather since it is intangible and easily subject to modification or destruction.

19. In order for evidence to be admissible in a court of law, it must be relevant, legally permissible, reliable, properly identified, and properly preserved. Reliability of evidence means that:

  a. It must tend to prove a material fact; the evidence is related to the crime in that it shows that the crime has been committed, can provide information describing the crime, can provide information as to the perpetrator's motives, can verify what had occurred, and so on.

  b. The evidence is identified without changing or damaging the evidence.

  c. The evidence has not been tampered with or modified.

  d. The evidence is not subject to damage or destruction.

  Answer: c

  This requirement is a critical issue with computer evidence since computer data may be easily modified without having an indication that a change has taken place. Answer a defines the *relevancy* of evidence, answer b describes the *identification* of evidence, and answer d describes the *preservation* of evidence.

20. In the U.S. Federal Rules of Evidence, Rule 803 (6) permits an exception to the Hearsay Rule regarding business records and computer records. Which one of the following is NOT a requirement for business or computer records exception under Rule 803 (6)?

  a. Made during the regular conduct of business and authenticated by witnesses familiar with their use

  b. Relied upon in the regular course of business

  c. Made only by a person with knowledge of the records

  d. Made by a person with information transmitted by a person with knowledge

  Answer: c

  The business or computer records may be made by a person with information transmitted by a person with knowledge, also. The other answers are requirements for exceptions to the Hearsay Rule.

21. Law enforcement officials in the United States, up until passage of the Patriot Act (see Question 9), had extensive restrictions on search and seizure as established in the Fourth Amendment to the U.S. Constitution. These restrictions are still, essentially, more severe than those on private citizens, who are not agents of a government entity. Thus, internal investigators in an organization or private investigators are not subject to the same restrictions as government officials. Private individuals are not normally held to the same standards regarding search and seizure since they are not conducting an unconstitutional government search. However, there are certain exceptions where the Fourth Amendment applies to private citizens if they act as agents of the government/police. Which of the following is NOT one of these exceptions?

    a. The government is aware of the intent to search or is aware of a search conducted by the private individual and does not object to these actions.

    b. The private individual performs the search to aid the government.

    c. The private individual conducts a search that would require a search warrant if conducted by a government entity.

    d. The private individual conducts a warrantless search of company property for the company.

    Answer: d

    Since the private individual, say an employee of the company, conducts a search for evidence on property that is owned by the company and is not acting as an agent of the government, a warrantless search is permitted. The Fourth Amendment does not apply. For review, the Fourth Amendment guarantees:

    The right of the people to be secure in their persons, houses, papers, and effects, against unreasonable searches and seizures, shall not be violated, and no Warrants shall issue, but upon probable cause, supported by oath or affirmation, and particularly describing the place to be searched, and the persons or things to be seized.

    The *exigent circumstances doctrine* provides an exception to these guarantees if destruction of evidence is imminent. Then, a warrantless search and seizure of evidence can be conducted if there is probable cause to suspect criminal activity. Answers a, b, and c describe exceptions where the private individual is subject to the Fourth Amendment guarantees.

22. One important tool of computer forensics is the disk image backup. The disk image backup is:

   a. Copying the system files

   b. Conducting a bit-level copy, sector by sector

   c. Copying the disk directory

   d. Copying and authenticating the system files

   Answer: b

   Copying sector by sector at the bit level provides the capability to examine slack space, undeleted clusters and possibly, deleted files. With answer a, only the system files are copied and the other information recovered in answer b would not be captured. Answer c does not capture the data on the disk, and answer d has the same problem as answer a. Actually, authenticating the system files is another step in the computer forensics process wherein a message digest is generated for all system directories and files to be able to validate the integrity of the information at a later time. This authentication should be conducted using a backup copy of the disk and not the original to avoid modifying information on the original.

   For review purposes, *computer forensics* is the collecting of information from and about computer systems that is admissible in a court of law.

23. In the context of legal proceedings and trial practice, *discovery* refers to:

   a. The process in which the prosecution presents information it has uncovered to the defense, including potential witnesses, reports resulting from the investigation, evidence, and so on

   b. The process undertaken by the investigators to acquire evidence needed for prosecution of a case

   c. A step in the computer forensic process

   d. The process of obtaining information on potential and existing employees using background checks

   Answer: a

   The key words are legal proceedings and trial practice. Information and property obtained in the investigation by law enforcement officials must be turned over to the defense. For some information that is proprietary to an organization, restrictions can be placed on who has access to the data. Answers b, c, and d are forms of the investigative process. During an investigation, answers b and c are appropriate definitions of discovery.

24. Which of the following alternatives should NOT be used by law enforcement to gain access to a password?

    a. Using password "cracker" software

    b. Compelling the suspect to provide the password

    c. Contacting the developer of the software for information to gain access to the computer or network through a back door

    d. Data manipulation and trial procedures applied to the original version of the system hard disk

    Answer: d

    The original disk of a computer involved in a criminal investigation should not be used for any experimental purposes since data may be modified or destroyed. Any operations should be conducted on a copy of the system disk. However, the answers in a, b, and c are the preferred methods of gaining access to a password-protected system. Interestingly, in answer b, there is legal precedent to order a suspect to provide the password of a computer that is in the custody of law enforcement.

25. During the investigation of a computer crime, audit trails can be very useful. To ensure that the audit information can be used as evidence, certain procedures must be followed. Which of the following is NOT one of these procedures?

    a. The audit trail information must be used during the normal course of business.

    b. There must be a valid organizational security policy in place and in use that defines the use of the audit information.

    c. Mechanisms should be in place to protect the integrity of the audit trail information.

    d. Audit trails should be viewed prior to the image backup.

    Answer: d

    The image backup should be done first in order not to modify any information on the hard disk. For example, the authentication process applied to a hard disk can change the time of last access information on files. Thus, authentication should be applied to a disk image copy.

26. The Internet Activities Board (IAB) considers which of the following behaviors relative to the Internet as unethical?

    a. Negligence in the conduct of Internet experiments

    b. Recordkeeping whose very existence is secret

   c. Recordkeeping in which an individual cannot find out what information concerning that individual is in the record

   d. Improper dissemination and use of identifiable personal data

   Answer: a

   The IAB document, *Ethics and the Internet* (RFC 1087) listed behaviors as unethical that:

   ■ Seek to gain unauthorized access to the resources of the Internet

   ■ Destroy the integrity of computer-based information

   ■ Disrupt the intended use of the Internet

   ■ Waste resources such as people, capacity and computers through such actions

   ■ Compromise the privacy of users

   ■ Involve negligence in the conduct of Internetwide experiments

   Answers b, c, and d are taken from the Code of Fair Information Practices of the U.S. Department of Health, Education of Welfare.

27. Which of the following is NOT a form of computer/network surveillance?

   a. Keyboard monitoring

   b. Use of network sniffers

   c. Use of CCTV cameras

   d. Review of audit logs

   Answer: c

   CCTV cameras fall under the category of physical surveillance. Answers a and b are forms of active surveillance. These types of surveillance require an organizational policy informing the employees that the surveillance is being conducted. Additionally, warning banners describing the surveillance at log-on to a computer or network should be prominently displayed. These banners usually state that by logging on, the user acknowledges the warning and agrees to the monitoring. Answer d is a passive form of computer/network surveillance.

28. Which of the following is NOT a definition or characteristic of "Due Care?"

   a. Just, proper, and sufficient care, so far as the circumstances demand it.

   b. That care which an ordinary prudent person would have exercised under the same or similar circumstances.

   c. Implies that a party has been guilty of a violation of the law in relation to the subject-matter or transaction.

   d. It may and often does require extraordinary care.

      Answer: c

      Due Care implies that not only has a party not been negligent or careless, but also that he/she has been guilty of no violation of law in relation to the subject mater or transaction which constitutes the cause of action. "Due Care" and "Reasonable Care" are used interchangeably. The definitions of Due Care given in answers a, b, and c are from Black's Law Dictionary, Abridged Fifth Edition, West Publishing Company, St. Paul Minnesota, 1983.

29. The definition "A mark used in the sale or advertising of services to identify the services of one person and distinguish them from the services of others" refers to a:

   a. Trademark

   b. Service mark

   c. Trade name

   d. Copyright

      Answer: b

      For answer a, a trademark is a "distinctive mark of authenticity, through which the products of particular manufacturers or the vendible commodities of particular merchants may be distinguished from those of others." Answer c, a trade name is "any designation which is adopted and used by a person to denominate goods which he markets, or services which he renders or business which he conducts. A trade name is descriptive of a manufacturer or dealer and applies to business and goodwill. A trademark is applicable only to vendible commodities. In answer d, a copyright is "an intangible, incorporeal right granted by statute to the author or originator of certain literary or artistic productions, whereby he is invested, for a statutorily prescribed period, with the sole and exclusive privilege of multiplying copies of the same and publishing and selling them. (These definitions were also taken from Black's Law Dictionary, Abridged Fifth Edition, West Publishing Company, St. Paul Minnesota, 1983.)

30. It is estimated that the Asia/Pacific region accounts for about $4 billion worth of loss of income to software publishers due to software piracy.

As with the Internet, cross-jurisdictional law enforcement issues make investigating and prosecuting such crime difficult. Which of the following items is NOT an issue in stopping overseas software piracy?

a. Obtaining the cooperation of foreign law enforcement agencies and foreign governments.

b. The quality of the illegal copies of the software is improving, making it more difficult for purchasers to differentiate between legal and illegal products.

c. The producers of the illegal copies of software are dealing in larger and larger quantities, resulting in faster deliveries of illicit software.

d. Lack of a central, nongovernmental organization to address the issue of software piracy.

Answer: d

The Business Software Alliance (BSA) is a nongovernmental anti-software piracy organization (www.bsa.org). The mission statement of the BSA is:

The Business Software Alliance is an international organization representing leading software and e-commerce developers in 65 countries around the world. Established in 1988, BSA has offices in the United States, Europe, and Asia . . . . Our efforts include educating computer users about software copyrights; advocating public policy that fosters innovation and expands trade opportunities; and fighting software piracy.

Chapter 10—Physical Security

1. Which choice below is NOT a common biometric method?

    a. Retina pattern devices

    b. Fingerprint devices

    c. Handprint devices

    d. Phrenologic devices

    Answer: d

    Biometrics are commonly used to verify the authenticity of someone attempting to gain access to a secure facility. Biometrics examine each person's unique physiological characteristics to provide positive personal identification. Fingerprints and handwritten signatures have been used in the past for identification, but modern biometric devices use many other physical traits to allow entrance to a facility or access to a system. Several types of biometric devices are common, such as retina pattern devices, fingerprint devices, handprint devices, and voice pattern devices. The effectiveness of these procedures and the impact of false positive and false negative error rates is covered in the Access Control domain.

    Phrenology was a pseudo-science developed in the late 18th century to assign behavior attributes based upon the examination, the shape, and unevenness of a head or skull. It was believed that one could discover the development of the particular cerebral "organs" responsible for different intellectual aptitudes and character traits. For example, a prominent protuberance in the forehead at the position attributed to the organ of "benevolence" was meant to indicate that the individual had a "well developed" organ of benevolence and would therefore be expected to exhibit benevolent behavior. It was thought this could predict criminal or anti-social behavior. Source: *Computer Security Basics* by Deborah Russell and G.T. Gangemi Sr. (O'Reilly, 1992) and John van Wyhe, *The History of Phrenology on the Web* (http://pages.britishlibrary.net/phrenology/), February 8, 2002.

2. According to the NFPA, which choice below is NOT a recommended risk factor to consider when determining the need for protecting the computing environment from fire?

    a. Life safety aspects of the computing function or process

    b. Fire threat of the installation to occupants or exposed property

    c. Distance of the computing facility from a fire station

    d. Economic loss of the equipment's value

    Answer: c

While the distance of the computing facility from a fire station should be considered when initially determining the physical location of a computing facility (as should police and hospital proximity), it is not considered a primary factor in determining the need for internal fire suppression systems. The National Fire Protection Association (NFPA) defines risk factors to consider when designing fire and safety protection for computing environments. The factors to be used when assessing the impact of damage and interruption resulting from a fire, in priority order, are:

- The life safety aspects of the function, such as air traffic controls or safety processing controls
- The fire threat of the installation to the occupants or property of the computing area
- The economic loss incurred from the loss of computing function or loss of stored records
- The economic loss incurred from the loss of the value of the equipment

As in all evaluations of risk, not only fire risk, life safety is always the number one priority. Source: "NFPA 75 Standard for the Protection of Electronic Computer/Data Processing Equipment" National Fire Protection Association, 1999 Edition.

3. Which choice below is NOT an example of a Halocarbon Agent?

   a. HFC-23

   b. FC-3-1-10

   c. IG-541

   d. HCFC-22

   Answer: c

   IG-541 is an inert gas agent, not a halocarbon agent. Halocarbon agents or inert gas agents can be replacements for Halon 1301 and Halon 1211 in gas-discharge fire extinguishing systems. Halocarbon agents contain one or more organic compounds as primary components, such as the elements fluorine, chlorine, bromine, or iodine. Inert gas agents contain as primary components one or more of the gases helium, neon, argon, or nitrogen. Some inert gas agents also contain carbon dioxide as a secondary component. Halocarbon agents are hydrofluorocarbons (HFCs), hydrochloroflurocarbons (HCFCs), perfluorocarbons (PFCs or FCs), or fluoroiodocarbons (FICs). Common inert gas agents for fire extinguishing systems are IG-01, IG-100, IG -55, and IG-541. Source: "NFPA 2001 Standard on

Table A.14 Combustible Materials Fire Class Ratings

FIRE CLASS	COMBUSTIBLE MATERIALS
A	Wood, cloth, paper, rubber, most plastics, ordinary combustibles
B	Flammable liquids and gases, oils, greases, tars, oil-base paints and lacquers
C	Energized electrical equipment
D	Flammable chemicals such as magnesium and sodium

Clean Agent Fire Extinguishing Systems" National Fire Protection Association, 2000 Edition.

4. Which choice below is NOT an example of a combustible in a Class B fire?

   a. Grease

   b. Rubber

   c. Oil-base paints

   d. Flammable gases

   Answer: b

   Fire combustibles are rated as either Class A, B, C, or D based upon their material composition, and this determines which type of extinguishing system or agent is used. Rubber is considered an ordinary Class A combustible. Table A.14 shows the different combustibles and their related classes. Source: "NFPA 2001 Standard on Clean Agent Fire Extinguishing Systems" National Fire Protection Association, 2000 Edition.

5. Which statement below most accurately describes a "dry pipe" sprinkler system?

   a. Dry pipe is the most commonly used sprinkler system.

   b. Dry pipe contains air pressure.

   c. Dry pipe sounds an alarm and delays water release.

   d. Dry pipe may contain carbon dioxide.

   Answer: b

   In a dry pipe system, air pressure is maintained until the sprinkler head seal is ruptured. The air then escapes, and the water is brought into the room. One advantage of the dry pipe system is that the wet pipe system is vulnerable to broken pipes due to freezing. Answer a is incorrect; wet pipe is the most commonly used sprinkler system, dry pipe is second. In a wet pipe system, water is standing in the pipe and is released when heat breaks the sprinkler head seal. Answer c describes a preaction pipe, which sounds an alarm and delays the water release. This allows computer operations to shut down before the release of water. A preaction pipe may or may not be a dry pipe, but not all dry pipes are preaction. Answer d is incorrect, because a dry pipe is a water release system. Source: "NFPA 75 Standard for the Protection of Electronic Computer/Data Processing Equipment" National Fire Protection Association, 1999 Edition and "NFPA 13 Standard for the Installation of Sprinkler Systems."

6. Which choice below is NOT a recommendation for records and materials storage in the computer room, for fire safety?

   a. Green bar printing paper for printers should be stored in the computer room.

   b. Abandoned cables shall not be allowed to accumulate.

   c. Space beneath the raised floor shall not be used for storage purposes.

   d. Only minimum records required for essential and efficient operation.

   Answer: a

   The NFPA recommends that only the absolute minimum essential records, paper stock, inks, unused recording media, or other combustibles be housed in the computer room. Because of the threat of fire, these combustibles should not be stored in the computer room or under raised flooring, including old, unused cabling. Underfloor abandoned cables can interfere with airflow and extinguishing systems. Cables that are not intended to be used should be removed from the room. It also recommends that tape libraries and record storage rooms be protected by an extinguishing system and separated from the computer room by wall construction fire-resistant rated for not less than one hour. Source: "NFPA 75 Standard for the Protection of Electronic Computer/Data Processing Equipment" National Fire Protection Association, 1999 Edition.

7. Which choice below is NOT considered an element of two-factor authentication?

   a. Something you know

   b. Something you do

   c. Something you have

   d. Something you are

> *Answer:* b
>
> Something you do, is an element of role-based access authentication, but is not an element of two-factor authentication. The most common implementation of two-factor authentication are "smart cards." Some smart cards employ two-factor authentication because they are an example of "something you have," the encoded card, with "something you know," like a PIN or password. "Something you are" describes biometric authentication. Source: *Computer Security Basics* by Deborah Russell and G.T. Gangemi Sr. (O'Reilly, 1992).

8. Which choice below is NOT an example of a "clean" fire extinguishing agent?

   a. CO_2

   b. IG-55

   c. IG-01

   d. HCFC-22

> *Answer:* a
>
> Since Halon was banned for use in fire suppression systems, many different chemical agents have been used. Some of these agents are called "clean" agents, because they do not leave a residue on electronic parts after evaporation. CO_2, carbon dioxide, does leave a corrosive residue, and is therefore not recommended for computer facility fire suppression systems. A "clean agent" is defined as an electrically nonconducting, nonvolatile fire extinguishant that does not leave a residue upon evaporation. Answers b and c, IG-55, and IG-01, are inert gas agents that do not decompose measurably or leave corrosive decomposition products and are, therefore, considered clean agents. Answer d, HCFC-22, is a halocarbon agent, which also is considered a clean agent. Source: "NFPA 2001 Standard on Clean Agent Fire Extinguishing Systems" National Fire Protection Association, 2000 Edition.

9. Which choice below is NOT considered a requirement to install an automatic sprinkler system?

   a. The building is required to be sprinklered.

   b. The computer room is vented to outside offices.

c. The computer room contains a significant quantity of combustible materials.

d. A computer system's enclosure contains combustible materials.

Answer: b

Computer room venting is an element of smoke detection and protection. The room should not be vented to the outside unless damping elements are installed to prevent smoke from the computer room from entering other offices. An automatic sprinkler system must be provided to protect the computer room or computer areas when either:

■ The enclosure of a computer system is built entirely or in part of a significant quantity of combustible materials.

■ The operation of the computer room or area involves a significant quantity of combustible materials.

■ The building is otherwise required to be sprinklered.

Source: "NFPA 75 Standard for the Protection of Electronic Computer/Data Processing Equipment" National Fire Protection Association, 1999 Edition and "NFPA 13 Standard for the Installation of Sprinkler Systems."

10. Which choice below is NOT a type of motion-detection system?

a. Ultrasonic-detection system

b. Microwave-detection system

c. Host-based intrusion-detection system

d. Sonic-detection system

Answer: c

Host-based intrusion-detection systems are used to detect unauthorized logical access to network resources, not the physical presence of an intruder. There are four basic technologies for detecting the physical presence of an intruder:

■ Photometric systems, which detect changes in the level of light

■ Motion-detection systems, which detect Doppler-type changes in the frequency of energy waves

■ Acoustical seismic-detection systems, which detect changes in the ambient noise level or vibrations

■ Proximity-detection systems, which detect the approach of an individual into an electrical field

Of the motion detection types, three kinds exist: sonic, ultrasonic, and microwave, depending upon the wavelength of the transmitters and receivers. Motion detectors sense the motion of a body by the

Table A.15   Common Motion Detection System Frequencies

DETECTOR TYPE	FREQUENCY
Sonic	1500-2000 hertz
Ultrasonic	19,000-20,000 hertz
Microwave	400-10,000 megahertz

change in frequency from the source transmission. Sonic detection systems operate in the audible range, ultrasonic detection systems operate in the high frequency, and microwave detection systems utilize radio frequencies. Table A.15 shows the common frequencies of motion detectors. Source: *CISSP Examination Textbooks, Volume one: Theory* by S. Rao Vallabhaneni (SRV Professional Publications, first edition 2000).

11. Which fire extinguishant choice below does NOT create toxic HF levels?

    a. Halon 1301

    b. Halon 1211

    c. IG-01

    d. HCFC-22

        Answer: c

        HF stands for Hydrogen fluoride, a toxic by-product of hydrocarbon agents after discharge. Answer c, IG-01, is an inert gas, which doesn't contain HFs. Inert gas does, however, create a danger to personnel by removing most of the breathable oxygen in a room when flooded, and precautions must be taken before its use. The inert gas agent IG-541 contains CO_2 as an additive, which appears to allow for more breathable time in the computer facility to allow for evacuation, however CO_2 lessens the agent's use as a "clean" agent. CO_2 and Halon are both toxic. Source: "NFPA 2001 Standard on Clean Agent Fire Extinguishing Systems" National Fire Protection Association, 2000 Edition.

12. Which choice below is NOT permitted under computer room raised flooring?

    a. Interconnecting DP cables enclosed in a raceway

    b. Underfloor ventilation for the computer room only

    c. Nonabrasive openings for cables

    d. Underfloor ventilation to the rest of the offices' ventilation system

        Answer: d

        Underfloor ventilation, as is true of all computer room ventilation, should not vent to any other office or area. HVAC air ducts serving other rooms should not pass through the computer room unless an automatic damping system is provided. A damper is activated by fire and smoke detectors and prevents the spread of computer room smoke or toxins through the building HVAC. Raised flooring, also called a false floor or a secondary floor, has very strict requirements as to its construction and use. Electrical cables must be enclosed in metal conduit, and data cables must be enclosed in raceways, with all abandoned cable removed. Openings in the raised floor must be smooth and nonabrasive, and should be protected to minimize the entrance of debris or other combustibles. Obviously, the raised flooring and decking must be constructed from noncombustible materials. Source: "NFPA 75 Standard for the Protection of Electronic Computer/Data Processing Equipment" National Fire Protection Association, 1999 Edition.

13. Which choice below represents the BEST reason to control the humidity in computer operations areas?

   a. Computer operators do not perform at their peak if the humidity is too high.

   b. Electrostatic discharges can harm electronic equipment.

   c. Static electricity destroys the electrical efficiency of the circuits.

   d. If the air is too dry, electroplating of conductors may occur.

     Answer: b

     Electrostatic discharges from static electricity can damage sensitive electronic equipment, even in small amounts. Even though a static charge of several thousand volts may be too low to harm humans, computer equipment is sensitive to static charges. Dry air, below 40 percent relative humidity, increases the chance of static electricity being generated. When the relative humidity is too high, say more than 80 percent, electrical connections become inefficient. The electrical contacts start to corrode and a form of electroplating begins. The recommended optimal relative humidity level is 40 percent to 60 percent for computer operations. Source: *The International Handbook of Computer Security* by Jae K. Shim, Anique A. Qureshi, and Joel G. Siegel (The Glenlake Publishing Co. Ltd, 2000).

14. Which statement below is NOT accurate about smoke damage to electronic equipment?

   a. Smoke exposure during a fire for a relatively short period does little immediate damage.

   b. Continuing power to the smoke-exposed equipment can increase the damage.

c. Moisture and oxygen corrosion constitute the main damage to the equipment.

d. The primary damage done by smoke exposure is immediate.

Answer: d

Immediate smoke exposure to electronic equipment does little damage. However, the particulate residue left after the smoke has dissipated contains active by-products that corrode metal contact surfaces in the presence of moisture and oxygen. Removal of the contaminant from the electrical contacts, such as printed circuits boards and backplanes, should be implemented as soon as possible, as much of the damage is done during this corrosion period. Also, power should be immediately disconnected to the affected equipment, as continuing voltage can plate the contaminants into the circuitry permanently. Source: "NFPA 75 Standard for the Protection of Electronic Computer/Data Processing Equipment" National Fire Protection Association, 1999 edition and "NFPA 2001 Standard on Clean Agent Fire Extinguishing Systems" 2000 edition.

15. Which choice below most accurately describes the prime benefit of using guards?

a. Human guards are less expensive than guard dogs.

b. Guards can exercise discretionary judgment in a way that automated systems can't.

c. Automated systems have a greater reliability rate than guards.

d. Guard dogs cannot discern an intruder's intent.

Answer: b

The prime advantage to using human guards is that they can exercise discretionary judgment when the need arises. For example, during an emergency guards can switch roles from access control to evacuation support, something guard dogs or automated systems cannot. While guard dogs are relatively expensive to keep, guards are generally the most expensive option for access control. Answers c and d are distracters. An issue with guards, however, is that they can be socially engineered, and must be thoroughly vetted and trained. Source: *The NCSA Guide to Enterprise Security* by Michel E. Kabay (McGraw-Hill, 1996).

16. Which choice below is an accurate statement about EMI and RFI?

a. EMI can contain RFI.

b. EMI is generated naturally; RFI is man-made.

c. RFI is generated naturally; EMI is man-made.

d. Natural sources of EMI pose the greatest threat to electronic equipment.

Answer: a

Electromagnetic interference (EMI) and radio-frequency interference (RFI) are terms used to describe disruption or noise generated by electromagnetic waves. RFI refers to noise generated from radio waves, and EMI is the general term for all electromagnetic interference, including radio waves. EMI and RFI are often generated naturally, for example solar sunspots or the earth's magnetic field. Man-made sources of EMI and RFI pose the largest threat to electronic equipment from sources like cell phones, laptops, and other computers. Guidelines to prevent EMI and RFI interference in the computer room should be adopted, such as limiting the use and placement of magnets or cell phones around sensitive equipment. The United States government created the TEMPEST (Transient ElectroMagnetic Pulse Emanations Standard) standard to prevent EMI eavesdropping by employing heavy metal shielding. Source: *The NCSA Guide to Enterprise Security* by Michel E. Kabay (McGraw-Hill, 1996).

17. In which proper order should the steps below be taken after electronic equipment or media has been exposed to water?

_____ a. Place all affected equipment or media in an air-conditioned area, if portable.

_____ b. Turn off all electrical power to the equipment.

_____ c. Open cabinet doors and remove panels and covers to allow water to run out.

_____ d. Wipe with alcohol or Freon-alcohol solutions or spray with water-displacement aerosol sprays.

Answer: b, c, a, and d.

Water-based emergencies could include pipe breakage, or damage to sensitive electronic equipment due to the proper use of water fire sprinklers. The first order of business is shutting down the power to the effected equipment, to prevent shock hazards, shorting, or further damage. Any visible standing water should be removed and allowed to drain from around and the inside the unit. As the room may still be extremely humid, move the equipment, if possible, to a humidity-controlled environment, then wipe the parts and use water displacement sprays. If corrective action is initiated immediately, the damage done to the computer equipment can be greatly reduced and the chances of recovering the data are increased. Source: "NFPA 75 Standard for the Protection of Electronic Computer/Data Processing Equipment" National Fire Protection Association, 1999 Edition and "Electronics and Magnetic Media Recovery" Blackmon-Mooring-Steamatic Catastrophe Inc.

18. Which choice below is NOT an example of using a social engineering technique to gain physical access to a secure facility?

    a. Asserting authority or pulling rank

    b. Intimidating or threatening

    c. Praising or flattering

    d. Employing the salami fraud

    Answer: d

    The "salami fraud" is an automated fraud technique. In the salami fraud, a programmer will create or alter a program to move small amounts of money into his personal bank account. The amounts are intended to be so small as to be unnoticed, such as rounding in foreign currency exchange transactions. Hence the reference to slicing a salami.

    The other three choices are common techniques used by an intruder to gain either physical access or system access:

    Asserting authority or pulling rank.   Professing to have the authority, perhaps supported with altered identification, to enter the facility or system.

    Intimidating or threatening.   Browbeating the access control subjects with harsh language or threatening behavior to permit access or release information.

    Praising, flattering, or sympathizing.   Using positive reinforcement to coerce the subjects into giving access or information for system access.

    Source: *Fighting Computer Crime* by Donn B. Parker (Wiley, 1998).

19. In which proper order should the steps below be taken after electronic equipment or media has been exposed to smoke contaminants?

    _____ a. Turn off power to equipment.

    _____ b. Spray corrosion-inhibiting aerosol to stabilize metal contact surfaces.

    _____ c. Spray connectors, backplanes, and printed circuit boards with Freon or Freon-alcohol solvents.

    _____ d. Move equipment into an air-conditioned and humidity-controlled environment.

    Answer: a, d, c, and b.

    As with water damage, smoke damage can be mitigated with a quick response. Immediately cut power to the equipment to lessen the chance of contaminant plating, and move the equipment to an air-conditioned area free of smoke exposure. Smoke contaminant particles are invisible, so the effected area will contain these articles for a long time. Freon or alcohol-based solvents can remove the initial layer of contaminant particles, then use corrosion-inhibiting aerosols to stabilize the contact surfaces from further corrosion. Like with water damage, if the recovery is prompt and successful, data may be able to be removed from the system after stabilization. Also, like water or other types of damage, the treated systems should never be used again once all usable data has been recovered.

Source: "NFPA 75 Standard for the Protection of Electronic Computer/ Data Processing Equipment" National Fire Protection Association, 1999 edition and "Electronics and Magnetic Media Recovery" Blackmon-Mooring-Steamatic Catastrophe Inc.

20. Which fire suppression medium below is considered to be the MOST toxic to personnel?

    a. CO_2

    b. IG-01

    c. Halon 1301

    d. Halocarbon Agents

    Answer: a

    Carbon dioxide (CO_2) is fatal to personnel when used in large concentrations, like the level required to flood a computer room during a fire. CO_2 is generally used for direct fire suppression at the source. The other three choices can be toxic in that they remove the oxygen from a room to end the fire, but they also remove the breathable air accessible to personnel. Halon 1301 has been banned by the 1987 Montreal Protocol as it contributes to the depletion of the ozone layer. Source: "NFPA 2001 Standard on Clean Agent Fire Extinguishing Systems" National Fire Protection Association, 2000 Edition.

21. Which type of personnel control below helps prevent piggybacking?

    a. Man traps

    b. Back doors

    c. Brute force

    d. Maintenance hooks

    Answer: a

    "Piggybacking" describes an unauthorized person entering a facility through a carded or controlled door by following an authorized person who has opened the door. A man trap is a set of double doors, often with a guard, that is intended to control physical personnel entrance to the facility. Of course, the best protection from this type of intrusion is through security awareness training, to prevent employees from holding the door open or allowing unauthorized intruders from entering.

The other three answers are not personnel or physical controls, but are technical threats or vulnerabilities. Answer b, back doors, commonly refers to Trojan Horses used to give an attacker backdoor network access covertly. Back doors are installed by hackers to gain network access at a later time. Answer c, brute force, is a cryptographic attack attempting to use all combinations of key patterns to decipher a message. Answer d, maintenance hooks, are undocumented openings into an application to assist programmers with debugging. Although intended innocently, these can be exploited by intruders. They are also called "trap doors." Source: *The International Handbook of Computer Security* by Jae K. Shim, Anique A. Qureshi, and Joel G. Siegel (The Glenlake Publishing Co. Ltd, 2000).

22. Which type of physical access control method below is best suited for high-security areas?

    a. Deadbolts

    b. Access token

    c. Key locks

    d. Pushbutton locks

    Answer: b

    Answers a, c, and d are examples of mechanical locks, whereas choice b is an element of an electronic system. An electronic system can be very sophisticated perhaps using smart cards, random keypads, auditing features, and time-operation limits. Deadbolts, keyed locks, and five-button pushbutton locks cannot provide the control and detection features necessary for high-security facilities. Source: *Computer Security Basics* by Deborah Russell and G.T. Gangemi Sr. (O'Reilly, 1992) and *The NCSA Guide to Enterprise Security* by Michel E. Kabay (McGraw-Hill, 1996).

23. Which term below refers to a standard used in determining the fire safety of a computer room?

    a. Noncombustible

    b. Fire-resistant

    c. Fire retardant

    d. Nonflammable

    Answer: b

    The fire-resistant rating of construction materials is a major factor in determining the fire safety of a computer operations room. The term fire-resistant refers to materials or construction that has a fire resistance rating of not less than the specified standard. For example, the computer room must be separated from other occupancy areas by construction with a fire-resistant rating of not less than one hour. Answer a, noncombustible, means material that will not aid or add appreciable heat to an ambient fire. Answer c, fire retardant, describes material that lessens or prevents the spread of a fire. Fire retardant coatings are designed to protect materials from fire exposure damage. Answer d, nonflammable, describes material that will not burn. Source: "NFPA 2001 Standard on Clean Agent Fire Extinguishing Systems" National Fire Protection Association, 2000 Edition.

Notes

1. CSC-STD-001-83

2. Gligor, Virgil D., "Guidelines for Trusted Facility Management and Audit," University of Maryland, 1985.

3. Ibid.

4. The ISO/IEC's web site is at http://isotc.iso.ch/livelink/livelink/fetch/2000/2489/Ittf_Home/ITTF.htm.

5. For more information about BS7799, visit:www.gammassl.co.uk/bs7799/works.html.

6. NCSC-TG-O15, Guide To Understanding Trusted Facility Management [Brown Book].

7. A Guide to Understanding Data Remanence in Automated Information Systems, NCSC-TG-025, National Computer Security Center, September 1991.

What's on the CD-ROM

This appendix provides you with information on the contents of the CD that accompanies this book. For the latest and greatest information, please refer to the ReadMe file located at the root of the CD. Here is what you will find:

- System Requirements
- Using the CD with Windows
- What's on the CD
- Troubleshooting

System Requirements

Make sure that your computer meets the minimum system requirements listed in this section. If your computer doesn't match up to most of these requirements, you may have a problem using the contents of the CD.

For Windows 9x, Windows 2000, Windows NT4 (with SP 4 or later), Windows Me, or Windows XP:

- PC with a Pentium processor running at 120 Mhz or faster

■ At least 32 MB of total RAM installed on your computer; for best performance, we recommend at least 64 MB

■ A CD-ROM drive

Using the CD with Windows

To install the items from the CD to your hard drive, follow these steps:

1. Insert the CD into your computer's CD-ROM drive.

2. A window will appear with the following options: Install, Explore, and Exit.

   Install: Gives you the option to install the supplied software and/or the author-created samples on the CD-ROM.

   Explore: Allows you to view the contents of the CD-ROM in its directory structure.

   Exit: Closes the autorun window.

If you do not have autorun enabled or if the autorun window does not appear, follow the steps below to access the CD.

1. Click Start @@> Run.

2. In the dialog box that appears, type d:\setup.exe, where d is the letter of your CD-ROM drive. This will bring up the autorun window described above.

3. Choose the Install, Explore, eBook, Links, or Exit option from the menu. (See Step 2 in the preceding list for a description of these options.)

What's on the CD

Included on the CD-ROM is a testing engine that is powered by Boson Software. This program resembles the testing engine that will be used by the testing center where you will be taking your exam. The goal of the testing engine is to make you comfortable with the testing interface so that taking your exam will not be the first time you see that style of exam.

The questions used in the testing engine are those presented in the book, and covers all 10 domains of the exam. When installed and run, the test engine presents you with a multiple-choice, question-and-answer format. Each question deals directly with exam-related material.

There are two tests available, one covers the standard questions from *The CISSP Prep Guide: Gold Edition* and the other contains the advanced questions from *Advanced CISSP Prep Guide: Exam Q&A*.

Once you select what you believe to be the correct answer for each question, the test engine not only notes whether you are correct or not, but also provides information as to why the right answer is right and the wrong answers are wrong, pro-viding you with valuable information for further review. Thus, the test engine gives not only valuable simulated exam experience, but useful tutorial direction as well.

Troubleshooting

If you have difficulty installing or using any of the materials on the companion CD, try the following solutions:

Turn off any anti-virus software that you may have running. Installers sometimes mimic virus activity and can make your computer incorrectly believe that it is being infected by a virus. (Be sure to turn the anti-virus software back on later.)

Close all running programs. The more programs you're running, the less memory is available to other programs. Installers also typically update files and programs; if you keep other programs running, installation may not work properly.

Reference the ReadMe: Please refer to the ReadMe file located at the root of the CD-ROM for the latest product information at the time of publication.

If you still have trouble with the CD, please call the Wiley Customer Care phone number: (800) 762-2974. Outside the United States, call 1 (317) 572-3994. You can also contact Wiley Customer Service by email at techsupdum@wiley.com. Wiley will provide technical support only for installation and other general quality control items; for technical support on the applications themselves, consult the program's vendor or author.

Glossary of Terms and Acronyms

* property (or star property)   A Bell-LaPadula security model rule enabling a subject write access to an object only if the security level of the object dominates the security level of the subject. Also called confinement property.

1000BaseT   1000 Mbps (1Gbps) baseband Ethernet using twisted-pair wire.

100BaseT   100 Mbps baseband Ethernet using twisted-pair wire.

10Base2   802.3 IEEE Ethernet standard for 10 Mbps Ethernet using coaxial cable (thinnet) rated to 185 meters.

10Base5   10 Mbps Ethernet using coaxial cable (thicknet) rated to 500 meters.

10BaseF   10 Mbps baseband Ethernet using optical fiber.

10BaseT   10 Mbps UTP Ethernet rated to 100 meters.

10Broad36   10 Mbps broadband Ethernet rated to 3,600 meters.

3DES   Triple Data Encryption Standard.

802.10   IEEE standard that specifies security and privacy access methods for LANs.

802.11   IEEE standard that specifies 1 Mbps and 2 Mbps wireless connectivity. Defines aspects of frequency hopping and direct sequence spread spectrum systems for use in the 2.4 MHz ISM (industrial, scientific, medical) band. Also refers to the IEEE Committee responsible for setting wireless LAN standards.

802.11a   Specifies high-speed wireless connectivity in the 5 GHz band using orthogonal frequency division multi-plexing (OFDM) with data rates up to 54 Mbps.

802.11b   Specifies high-speed wireless connectivity in the 2.4 GHz ISM band up to 11 Mbps.

802.15   Specification for Bluetooth LANs in the 2.4-2.5 GHz band.

802.2   Standard that specifies the logical link control (LLC).

802.3   Ethernet bus topology using carrier sense medium access control/carrier detect (CSMA/CD) for 10 Mbps wired LANs. Currently the most popular LAN topology.

802.4   Specifies a token-passing bus access method for LANs.

802.5   Specifies a token-passing ring access method for LANs.

acceptance inspection   The final inspection to determine whether or not a facility or system meets the specified technical and performance standards. Note: This inspection is held immediately after facility and software testing and is the basis for commissioning or accepting the information system.

acceptance testing   Type of testing used to determine whether the network is acceptable to the actual users.

access   A specific type of interaction between a subject and an object that results in the flow of information from one to the other.

access control   The process of limiting access to the resources of a system only to authorized programs, processes, or other systems (on a network). This term is synonymous with controlled access and limited access.

access control mechanism   Hardware or software features, operating procedures, management procedures, and various combinations of these that are designed to detect and prevent unauthorized access and to permit authorized access in an automated system.

access level   The hierarchical portion of the security level that is used to identify the sensitivity of data and the clearance or authorization of users. Note: The access level, in conjunction with the non-hierarchical categories, forms the sensitivity label of an object. See category, security level, and sensitivity label.

access list   A list of users, programs, and/or processes and the specifications of access categories to which each is assigned; a list denoting which users have what privileges to a particular resource.

access period   A segment of time, generally expressed on a daily or weekly basis, during which access rights prevail.

access point (AP)   A wireless LAN transceiver interface between the wireless network and a wired network. Access points forward frames between wireless devices and hosts on the LAN.

access port   A logical or physical identifier that a computer uses to distinguish different terminal input/output data streams.

access type   The nature of an access right to a particular device, program, or file (for example, read, write, execute, append, modify, delete, or create).

accountability   The property that enables activities on a system to be traced to individuals who might then be held responsible for their actions.

accreditation   A formal declaration by the DAA that the AIS is approved to operate in a particular security mode by using a prescribed set of safeguards. Accreditation is the official management authorization for operation of an AIS and is based on the certification process as well as on other management considerations. The accreditation statement affixes security responsibility with the DAA and shows that due care has been taken for security.

accreditation authority   Synonymous with Designated Approving Authority.

ACK   Acknowledgment; a short-return indication of the successful receipt of a message.

acknowledged connectionless service   A datagram-style service that includes error-control and flow-control mechanisms.

ACO   Authenticated ciphering offset.

adaptive routing   A form of network routing whereby the path data packets traverse from a source to a destination node that depends on the current state of the network; calculates the best path through the network.

add-on security   The retrofitting of protection mechanisms implemented by hardware or software.

Address Resolution Protocol (ARP)   A TCP/IP protocol that binds logical (IP) addresses to physical addresses.

administrative security   The management constraints and supplemental controls established to provide an acceptable level of protection for data. Synonymous with procedural security.

Advanced Encryption Standard (AES) (Rijndael)   A symmetric block cipher with a block size of 128 bits and in which the key can be 128, 192 or 256 bits. The Advanced Encryption Standard replaces the Date Encryption Standard (DES) and was announced on November 26, 2001 as Federal Information Processing Standard Publication (FIPS PUB 197).

AIS   Automated Information System

analog signal   An electrical signal with an amplitude that varies continuously.

application layer   The top layer of the OSI model concerned with application programs. It provides services such as file transfer and e-mail to the end users of the network.

application process   An entity, either human or software, that uses the services offered by the application layer of the OSI reference model.

application program interface   A software interface provided between a specialized communications program and an end-user application.

application software   Software that accomplishes functions such as database access, electronic mail, and menu prompts.

architecture   As refers to a computer system, an architecture describes the type of components, interfaces, and protocols the system uses and how they fit together.

assurance   A measure of confidence that the security features and architecture of an AIS accurately mediate and enforce the security policy. Grounds for confidence that an IT product or system meets its security objectives. See DITSCAP.

asymmetric (public) key encryption   Cryptographic system which employs two keys, a public key and a private key. The public key is made available to anyone wishing to send an encrypted message to an individual holding the corresponding private key of the public-private key pair. Any message encrypted with one of these keys can be decrypted with the other. The private key is always kept private. The private key should not be able to be derived from the public key.

asynchronous transfer mode A cell-based connection-oriented data service offering high-speed data communications. ATM integrates circuit and packet switching to handle both constant and burst information at rates up to 2.488 Gbps. Also called cell relay.

asynchronous transmission Type of communications data synchronization with no defined time relationship between transmission of data frames. See Synchronous transmission.

Attachment Unit Interface (AUI) A 15-pin interface between an Ethernet network interface card and a transceiver.

attack The act of trying to bypass security controls on a system. An attack can be active, resulting in the alteration of data, or passive, resulting in the release of data. Note: The fact that an attack is made does not necessarily mean that it will succeed. The degree of success depends on the vulnerability of the system or activity and the effectiveness of existing countermeasures.

audit trail A chronological record of system activities that is sufficient to enable the reconstruction, reviewing, and examination of the sequence of environments and activities surrounding or leading to an operation, a procedure, or an event in a transaction from its inception to its final results.

authenticate (1) To verify the identity of a user, device, or other entity in a computer system, often as a prerequisite to allowing access to resources in a system. (2) To verify the integrity of data that have been stored, transmitted, or otherwise exposed to possible unauthorized modification.

authentication device A device whose identity has been verified during the lifetime of the current link based on the authentication procedure.

authentication Generically, the process of verifying who is at the other end of a transmission.

authenticator The means used to confirm the identity or to verify the eligibility of a station, originator, or individual.

authorization The granting of access rights to a user, program, or process.

automated data processing security Synonymous with automated information systems security.

automated information system (AIS) An assembly of computer hardware, software, and/or firmware that is configured to collect, create, communicate, compute, disseminate, process, store, and/or control data or information.

automated information system security Measures and controls that protect an AIS against denial of service and unauthorized (accidental or intentional) disclosure, modification, or destruction of AISs and data. AIS security includes consideration of all hardware and/or software functions, characteristics and/or features; operational procedures, accountability procedures, and access controls at the central computer facility, remote computers, and terminal facilities; management constraints; physical structures and devices; and personnel and communication controls that are needed to provide an acceptable level of risk for the AIS and for the data and information contained in the AIS. It includes the totality of security safeguards needed to provide an acceptable protection level for an AIS and for data handled by an AIS.

automated security monitoring   The use of automated procedures to ensure that security controls are not circumvented.

availability of data   The state in which data are in the place needed by the user, at the time the user needs them, and in the form needed by the user.

backbone network   A network that interconnects other networks.

back door   Synonymous with trapdoor.

backup plan   Synonymous with contingency plan.

backward chaining   In an expert system, the process of beginning with a possible solution and using the knowledge in the knowledge base to justify the solution based on the raw input data. Backward chaining is generally used when there are a large number of possible solutions relative to the number of inputs.

bandwidth   Specifies the amount of the frequency spectrum that is usable for data transfer. In other words, it identifies the maximum data rate a signal can attain on the medium without encountering significant attenuation (loss of power). Also, the amount of information one can send through a connection.

baud rate   The number of pulses of a signal that occur in one second. Thus, baud rate is the speed at which the digital signal pulses travel. Also, the rate at which data are transferred.

Bell-LaPadula model   A formal state transition model of computer security policy that describes a set of access control rules. In this formal model, the entities in a computer system are divided into abstract sets of subjects and objects. The notion of a secure state is defined, and it is proven that each state transition preserves security by moving from secure state to secure state, thereby inductively proving that the system is secure. A system state is defined to be secure if the only permitted access modes of subjects to objects are in accordance with a specific security policy. In order to determine whether or not a specific access mode is allowed, the clearance of a subject is compared to the classification of the object, and a determination is made as to whether the subject is authorized for the specific access mode. See star property (* property) and simple security property.

benign environment   A non-hostile environment that might be protected from external hostile elements by physical, personnel, and procedural security countermeasures.

between-the-lines entry   Unauthorized access obtained by tapping the temporarily inactive terminal of a legitimate user. See piggyback.

beyond A1   A level of trust defined by the DoD Trusted Computer System Evaluation Criteria (TCSEC) that is beyond the state-of-the-art technology available at the time the criteria were developed. It includes all of the A1-level features plus additional ones that are not required at the A1 level.

biometrics   Access control method in which an individual's physiological or behavioral characteristics are used to determine access of that individual to a particular resource.

BIOS   Basic Input/Output System.

bit   Short for binary digit. A single digit number in binary, 0 or 1. Bit is short for binary digit.

bit rate   The transmission rate of binary symbols 0s and 1s. Bit rate is equal to the total number of bits transmitted in one second.

blackboard   An expert system reasoning methodology in which a solution is generated by the use of a virtual "blackboard" wherein information or potential solutions are placed on the blackboard by a plurality of individuals or expert knowledge sources. As more information is placed on the blackboard in an iterative process, a solution is generated.

blind signature   A form of digital signature where the signer is not privy to the content of the message.

block cipher   A symmetric key algorithm that operates on a fixed-length block of plaintext and transforms it into a fixed-length block of ciphertext. A block cipher is obtained by segregating plaintext into blocks of n characters or bits and applying the identical encryption algorithm and key to each block.

Bluetooth   An open specification for wireless communication of data and voice, based on a low-cost short-range radio link facilitating protected ad hoc connections for stationary and mobile communication environments.

bridge   A network device that provides internetworking functionality by connecting networks. Bridges can provide segmentation of data frames and can be used to connect LANs by forwarding packets across connections at the media access control (MAC) sublayer of the data-link layer of the OSI model.

broadband   A transmission system in which signals are encoded and modulated into different frequencies and then transmitted simultaneously with other signals, that is, having undergone a shift in frequency. A LAN broadband signal is commonly analog.

browsing   The act of searching through storage to locate or acquire information without necessarily knowing the existence or the format of the information being sought.

BSI ISO/IEC 17799:2000,BS 7799-I: 2000, Information technology—Code of practice for information security management, British Standards Institution, London, UK   A standard intended to "provide a comprehensive set of controls comprising best practices in information security." ISO refers to the International Organization for Standardization and IEC is the International Electrotechnical Commission.

bus topology   A type of network topology wherein all nodes are connected to a single length of cabling with a terminator at each end.

Business Software Alliance   An international organization representing leading software and e-commerce developers in 65 countries around the world. BSA efforts include educating computer users about software copyrights; advocating public policy that fosters innovation and expands trade opportunities; and fighting software piracy.

byte   A set of bits, usually eight, that represent a single character.

call back   A procedure for identifying a remote terminal. In a call back, the host system disconnects the caller and then dials the authorized telephone number of the remote terminal in order to re-establish the connection. Synonymous with dial back.

capability   A protected identifier that both identifies the object and specifies the access rights to be allowed to the accessor who possesses the capability. In a capability-based system, access to protected objects (such as files) is granted if the would-be accessor possesses a capability for the object.

Capstone   A Very Large Scale Integration (VLSI) chip that employs the Escrowed Encryption Standard and incorporates the Skipjack algorithm, similar to the Clipper Chip. As such, it has a Law Enforcement Access Field (LEAF). Capstone also supports public key exchange and digital signatures. At this time, Capstone products have their LEAF function suppressed and a Certifying Authority provides for key recovery.

Carnivore   A device used by the U.S. FBI to monitor ISP traffic. (S.P. Smith, et. al., Independent Technical Review of the Carnivore System – Draft report, U.S. Department of Justice Contract # 00-C-328 IITRI, CR-022-216, November 17, 2000)

carrier current LAN   A LAN that uses power lines within the facility as a medium for the transport of data.

Carrier Sense Multiple Access (CSMA)   The technique used to reduce transmission contention by listening for contention before transmitting.

Carrier Sense Multiple Access with Collision Detection (CSMA/CD) Most common Ethernet cable access method.

category   A restrictive label that has been applied to classified or unclassified data as a means of increasing the protection of the data and further restricting access to the data.

Category 1 twisted-pair wire   Used for early analog telephone communications; not suitable for data.

Category 2 twisted-pair wire   Rated for 4 Mbps, and used in 802.5 token ring networks.

Category 3 twisted-pair wire   Rated for 10 Mbps, and used in 802.3 10Base-T Ethernet networks.

Category 4 twisted-pair wire   Rated for 16 Mbps, and used in 802.5 token ring networks.

Category 5 twisted-pair wire   Rated for 100 Mbps, and used in 100BaseT Ethernet networks.

CBC   Cipher block chaining.

CC   Common Criteria

Centronics   A de facto standard 36-pin parallel 200 Kbps asynchronous interface for connecting printers and other devices to a computer.

CERT Coordination Center (CERT©/CC)   A unit of the Carnegie Mellon University Software Engineering Institute (SEI). SEI is a federally funded R&D Center. CERT's mission is to alert the Internet community to vulnerabilities and attacks and to conduct research and training in the areas of computer security, including incident response.

certification   The comprehensive evaluation of the technical and non-technical security features of an AIS and other safeguards, made in support of the accreditation process, that establishes the extent to which a particular design and implementation meets a specified set of security requirements.

Chinese Wall model   Uses internal rules to "compartmentalize" areas in which individuals may work to prevent disclosure of proprietary information and to avoid conflicts of interest. The Chinese Wall model also incorporates the principle of separation of duty.

cipher   A cryptographic transformation that operates on characters or bits.

ciphertext or cryptogram   An unintelligible encrypted message.

circuit-switched   The application of a network wherein which a dedicated line is used to transmit information, as opposed to packet-switched.

client   A computer that accesses the resources of a server.

client/server architecture   A network system design in which a processor or computer designated as a file server or database server provides services to other client processors or computers. Applications are distributed between a host server and a remote client.

closed security environment   An environment in which both of the following conditions hold true: 1) Application developers (including maintainers) have sufficient clearances and authorizations to provide an acceptable presumption that they have not introduced malicious logic, and 2) Configuration control provides sufficient assurance that applications and the equipment are protected against the introduction of malicious logic prior to and during the operation of system applications.

closed shop   Data processing area using physical access controls to limit access to authorized personnel.

clustering   Situation in which a plaintext message generates identical ciphertext messages using the same transformation algorithm, but with different cryptovariables or keys.

coaxial cable (coax)   Type of transmission cable consisting of a hollow outer cylindrical conductor that surrounds a single inner wire conductor for current flow. Because the shielding reduces the amount of electrical noise interference, coax can extend to much greater lengths than twisted-pair wiring.

Code Division Multiple Access (CDMA)   A spread-spectrum digital cellular radio system that uses different codes to distinguish users.

codes   Cryptographic transformation that operates at the level of words or phrases.

collision detection   The detection of simultaneous transmission on the communications medium.

Common Object Model (COM)   A model that allows two software components to communicate with each other independent of their platforms' operating systems and languages of implementation. As in the object-oriented paradigm, COM works with encapsulated objects.

Common Object Request Broker Architecture (CORBA)   A standard that uses the Object Request Broker (ORB) to implement exchanges among objects in a heterogeneous, distributed environment.

Communications Assistance for Law Enforcement Act (CALEA) of 1994
This act required all communications carriers to make wiretaps possible in ways approved by the FBI.

communications security (COMSEC)   Measures taken to deny unauthorized persons information derived from telecommunications of the U.S. government concerning national security and to ensure the authenticity of such telecommunications. Communications security includes cryptosecurity, transmission security, emission security, and physical security of communications security material and information.

compartment   A class of information that has need-to-know access controls beyond those normally provided for access to confidential, secret, or top secret information.

compartmented security mode   See modes of operation.

compensating controls   A combination of controls such as physical and technical or technical and administrative (or all three).

composition model   An information security model that investigates the resultant security properties when subsystems are combined.

compromise   A violation of the security policy of a system such that unauthorized disclosure of sensitive information might have occurred.

compromising emanations   Unintentional data-related or intelligence-bearing signals that, if intercepted and analyzed, disclose the information transmission that is received, handled, or otherwise processed by any information processing equipment. See TEMPEST.

COMPUSEC   Computer security.

computer abuse   The misuse, alteration, disruption, or destruction of data-processing resources. The key aspect is that it is intentional and improper.

computer cryptography   The use of a crypto-algorithm in a computer, microprocessor, or microcomputer to perform encryption or decryption in order to protect information or to authenticate users, sources, or information.

computer facility   Physical structure housing data processing operations.

computer forensics   The collecting of information from and about computer systems that is admissible in a court of law.

computer fraud   Computer-related crimes involving deliberate misrepresentation, alteration, or disclosure of data in order to obtain something of value (usually for monetary gain). A computer system must have been involved in the perpetration or cover-up of the act or series of acts. A computer system might have been involved through improper manipulation of input data, output or results, applications programs, data files, computer operations, communications, or computer hardware, systems software, or firmware.

computer security (COMPUSEC)   Synonymous with automated information systems security.

computer security subsystem   A device that is designed to provide limited computer security features in a larger system environment.

Computer Security Technical Vulnerability Reporting Program (CSTVRP)   A program that focuses on technical vulnerabilities in commercially available hardware, firmware, and software products acquired by DoD. CSTVRP provides for the reporting, cataloging, and discreet dissemination of technical vulnerability and corrective measure information to DoD components on a need-to-know basis.

COMSEC   Communications security.

concealment system   A method of achieving confidentiality in which sensitive information is hidden by embedding it inside irrelevant data.

confidentiality   The concept of holding sensitive data in confidence, limited to an appropriate set of individuals or organizations.

configuration control   The process of controlling modifications to the system's hardware, firmware, software, and documentation that provides sufficient assurance that the system is protected against the introduction of improper modifications prior to, during, and after system implementation. Compare with configuration management.

configuration management   The management of security features and assurances through control of changes made to a system's hardware, software, firmware, documentation, test, test fixtures, and test documentation throughout the development and operational life of the system. Compare with configuration control.

confinement   The prevention of the leaking of sensitive data from a program.

confinement channel   Synonymous with covert channel.

confinement property   Synonymous with star property (* property).

confusion   A method of hiding the relationship between the plaintext and the ciphertext.

connection-oriented service   Service that establishes a logical connection that provides flow control and error control between two stations needing to exchange data.

connectivity   A path through which communications signals can flow.

connectivity software   A software component that provides an interface between the networked appliance and the database or application software located on the network.

Construction Cost Model (COCOMO), basic version   Estimates software development effort and cost as a function of the size of the software product in source instructions.

containment strategy   A strategy for containment (in other words, stopping the spread) of the disaster and the identification of the provisions and processes required to contain the disaster.

contamination   The intermixing of data at different sensitivity and need-to-know levels. The lower-level data is said to be contaminated by the higher-level data; thus, the contaminating (higher-level) data might not receive the required level of protection.

contingency management   Establishing actions to be taken before, during, and after a threatening incident.

contingency plan   A plan for emergency response, backup operations, and post-disaster recovery maintained by an activity as a part of its security program that will ensure the availability of critical resources and facilitate the continuity of operations in an emergency situation. Synonymous with disaster plan and emergency plan.

continuity of operations Maintenance of essential IP services after a major outage.

control zone The space, expressed in feet of radius, surrounding equipment processing sensitive information that is under sufficient physical and technical control to preclude an unauthorized entry or compromise.

controlled access See access control.

controlled sharing The condition that exists when access control is applied to all users and components of a system.

Copper Data Distributed Interface (CDDI) A version of FDDI specifying the use of unshielded twisted-pair wiring.

cost-risk analysis The assessment of the costs of providing data protection for a system versus the cost of losing or compromising the data.

countermeasure Any action, device, procedure, technique, or other measure that reduces the vulnerability of or threat to a system.

countermeasures/safeguards An entity that mitigates the potential risk.

covert channel A communications channel that enables two cooperating processes to transfer information in a manner that violates the system's security policy. Synonymous with confinement channel.

covert storage channel A covert channel that involves the direct or indirect writing of a storage location by one process and the direct or indirect reading of the storage location by another process. Covert storage channels typically involve a finite resource (for example, sectors on a disk) that is shared by two subjects at different security levels.

covert timing channel A covert channel in which one process signals information to another by modulating its own use of system resources (for example, CPU time) in such a way that this manipulation affects the real response time observed by the second process.

CPU The central processing unit of a computer.

Criteria See DoD Trusted Computer System Evaluation Criteria.

CRL Certificate Revocation List

cryptanalysis Refers to being able to "break" the cipher so that the encrypted message can be read. Cryptanalysis can be accomplished by exploiting weaknesses in the cipher or in some fashion determining the key.

crypto-algorithm A well-defined procedure or sequence of rules or steps used to produce a key stream or cipher text from plain text and vice-versa. Step-by-step procedure that is used to encipher plaintext and decipher ciphertext. Also called cryptographic algorithm.

cryptographic application programming interface (CAPI) An interface to a library of software functions that provide security and cryptography services. CAPI is designed for software developers to call functions from the library and, thus, make it easier to implement security services.

cryptography The principles, means, and methods for rendering information unintelligible and for restoring encrypted information to intelligible form. The word "cryptography" comes from the Greek word *kryptos*, meaning hidden, and *graphein*, meaning to write.

cryptosecurity   The security or protection resulting from the proper use of technically sound cryptosystems.

cryptosystem   A set of transformations from a message space to a ciphertext space. This system includes all cryptovariables (keys), plaintexts and ciphertexts associated with the transformation algorithm.

CSMA/CA   Carrier sense multiple access with collision avoidance, commonly used in 802.11 Ethernet and LocalTalk.

CSMA/CD   Carrier Sense multiple access with collision detection, used in 802.3 Ethernet.

CSTVRP   Computer Security Technical Vulnerability Reporting Program.

Cyclic redundancy check (CRC)   A common error-detection process. A mathematical operation is applied to the data when transmitted. The result is appended to the core packet. Upon receipt, the same mathematical operation is performed and checked against the CRC. A mismatch indicates a very high probability that an error has occurred during transmission.

DAA   Designated Approving Authority.

DAC   Discretionary Access Control.

data dictionary   A database that comprises tools to support the analysis, design, and development of software and support good software engineering practices.

Data Encryption Standard (DES)   A cryptographic algorithm for the protection of unclassified data, published in Federal Information Processing Standard (FIPS) 46. The DES, which was approved by the National Institute of Standards and Technology (NIST), is intended for public and government use.

data flow control   Synonymous with information flow control.

data integrity   The property that data meet a prior expectation of quality.

data link layer   The OSI level that performs the assembly and transmission of data packets, including error control.

data mart   A database that is comprised of data or relations that have been extracted from the data warehouse. Information in the data mart is usually of interest to a particular group of people.

data mining   The process of analyzing large data sets in a data warehouse to find non-obvious patterns.

data scrubbing   Maintenance of a data warehouse by deleting information that is unreliable or no longer relevant.

data security   The protection of data from unauthorized (accidental or intentional) modification, destruction, or disclosure.

Data service unit/channel service unit (DSU/CSU)   A set of network components that reshape data signals into a form that can be effectively transmitted over a digital transmission medium, typically a leased 56 Kbps or T1 line.

data warehouse   A subject-oriented, integrated, time-variant, non-volatile collection of data in support of management's decision-making process.

database   A persistent collection of data items that form relations among each other.

database shadowing   Database shadowing uses the live processing of remote journaling but creates even more redundancy by duplicating the database sets to multiple servers. See server redundancy in the Telecommunications section.

datagram service   A connectionless form of packet switching whereby the source does not need to establish a connection with the destination before sending data packets.

DB-15   A standard 15-pin connector commonly used with RS-232 serial interfaces, Ethernet transceivers, and computer monitors.

DB-25   A standard 25-pin connector commonly used with RS-232 serial interfaces. The DB-25 connector will support all RS-232 functions.

DB-9   A standard 9-pin connector commonly used with RS-232 serial interfaces on portable computers. The DB-9 connector will not support all RS-232 functions.

de facto standard   A standard based on broad usage and support but not directly specified by the IEEE.

decipher   To unscramble the encipherment process to make the message human-readable.

declassification of AIS storage media   An administrative decision or procedure to remove or reduce the security classification of the subject media.

DeCSS   A program that bypasses the Content Scrambling System (CSS) software used to prevent the viewing of DVD movie disks on unlicensed platforms.

dedicated security mode   See modes of operation.

default   A value or option that is automatically chosen when no other value is specified.

default classification   A temporary classification reflecting the highest classification being processed in a system. The default classification is included in the caution statement that is affixed to the object.

Defense Information Technology Systems Certification and Accreditation Process (DITSCAP)   Establishes for the defense entities a standard process, set of activities, general task descriptions, and a management structure to certify and accredit IT systems that will maintain the required security posture. The process is designed to certify that the IT system meets the accreditation requirements and that the system will maintain the accredited security posture throughout the system life cycle. The four phases to the DITSCAP are Definition, Verification, Validation, and Post Accreditation.

degauss   The purpose of degaussing magnetic storage media.

Degausser Products List (DPL)   A list of commercially produced degaussers that meet National Security Agency specifications. This list is included in the NSA Information Systems Security Products and Services Catalogue and is available through the Government Printing Office.

degraded fault tolerance   Specifies which capabilities the TOE will still provide after a failure of the system. Examples of general failures are flooding of the computer room, short-term power interruption, breakdown of a CPU or host, software failure, or buffer overflow. Only functions specified must be available.

denial of service (DoS)   Any action (or series of actions) that prevents any part of a system from functioning in accordance with its intended purpose. This action includes any action that causes unauthorized destruction, modification, or delay of service. Synonymous with interdiction.

DES   Data Encryption Standard.

Descriptive Top-Level Specification (DTLS)   A top-level specification that is written in a natural language (for example, English), an informal design notation, or a combination of the two.

Designated Approving Authority (DAA)   The official who has the authority to decide on accepting the security safeguards prescribed for an AIS or that official who might be responsible for issuing an accreditation statement that records the decision to accept those safeguards.

dial back   Synonymous with call back.

dial-up   The service whereby a computer terminal can use the telephone to initiate and effect communication with a computer.

diffusion   A method of obscuring redundancy in plaintext by spreading the effect of the transformation over the ciphertext.

Digital Millennium Copyright Act (DMCA) of 1998   In addition to addressing licensing and ownership information, the DMCA prohibits trading, manufacturing, or selling in any way that is intended to bypass copyright protection mechanisms.

direct sequence spread spectrum (DSSS)   A method used in 802.11b to split the frequency into 14 channels, each with a frequency range, by combining a data signal with a chipping sequence. Data rates of 1, 2, 5.5, 11 Mbps are obtainable. DSSS spreads its signal continuously over this wide-frequency band.

disaster   A sudden, unplanned, calamitous event that brings about great damage or loss; any event that creates an inability on the organization's part to provide critical business functions for some undetermined period of time.

disaster plan   Synonymous with contingency plan.

disaster recovery plan   Procedure for emergency response, extended backup operations, and post-disaster recovery when an organization suffers a loss of computer resources and physical facilities.

discovery (in the context of legal proceedings and trial practice)   The process in which the prosecution presents information it has uncovered to the defense, including potential witnesses, reports resulting from the investigation, evidence, and so on. During an investigation, discovery refers to:

- The process undertaken by the investigators to acquire evidence needed for prosecution of a case
- A step in the computer forensic process

discretionary access control (DAC) A means of restricting access to objects based on the identity and need-to-know of the user, process, and/or groups to which they belong. The controls are discretionary in the sense that a subject that has certain access permission is capable of passing that permission (perhaps indirectly) along to any other subject. Compare with mandatory access control.

disk image backup Conducting a bit-level copy, sector by sector of a disk, which provides the capability to examine slack space, undeleted clusters, and possibly, deleted files.

Distributed Component Object Model (DCOM) A distributed object model that has similarities to the Common Object Request Broker Architecture (CORBA). DCOM is the distributed version of COM that supports remote objects as if the objects reside in the client's address space. A COM client can access a COM object through the use of a pointer to one of the object's interfaces and, then, invoking methods through that pointer.

Distributed Queue Dual Bus (DQDB) The IEEE 802.6 standard that provides full-duplex 155 Mbps operation between nodes in a metropolitan area network.

distributed routing A form of routing wherein each router on the network periodically identifies neighboring nodes, updates its routing table, and, with this information, then sends its routing table to all of its neighbors. Because each node follows the same process, complete network topology information propagates through the network and eventually reaches each node.

DITSCAP See Defense Information Technology Systems Certification and Accreditation Process.

DoD U.S. Department of Defense.

DoD Trusted Computer System Evaluation Criteria (TCSEC) A document published by the National Computer Security Center containing a uniform set of basic requirements and evaluation classes for assessing degrees of assurance in the effectiveness of hardware and software security controls built into systems. These criteria are intended for use in the design and evaluation of systems that will process and/or store sensitive or classified data. This document is Government Standard DoD 5200.28-STD and is frequently referred to as "The Criteria" or "The Orange Book."

DOJ U.S. Department of Justice.

domain The unique context (for example, access control parameters) in which a program is operating; in effect, the set of objects that a subject has the ability to access. See process and subject.

dominate Security level S1 is said to dominate security level S2 if the hierarchical classification of S1 is greater than or equal to that of S2 and if the non-hierarchical categories of S1 include all those of S2 as a subset.

DoS Denial of Service attack.

DPL Degausser Products List.

DT Data Terminal.

DTLS Descriptive Top-Level Specification.

due care   That care which an ordinary prudent person would have exercised under the same or similar circumstances. "Due Care" and "Reasonable Care" are used interchangeably.

Dynamic Host Configuration Protocol (DHCP)   A protocol that issues IP addresses automatically within a specified range to devices such as PCs when they are first powered on. The device retains the use of the IP address for a specific license period that the system administrator can define.

EAP   Extensible Authentication Protocol. Cisco proprietary protocol for enhanced user authentication and wireless security management.

EBCDIC   Extended Binary-Coded Decimal Interchange Code. An 8-bit character representation developed by IBM in the early 1960s.

ECC   Elliptic Curve Cryptography.

ECDSA   Elliptic Curve Digital Signature Algorithm.

Echelon   A cooperative, worldwide signal intelligence system that is run by the NSA of the United States, the Government Communications Head Quarters (GCHQ) of England, the Communications Security Establishment (CSE) of Canada, the Australian Defense Security Directorate (DSD), and the General Communications Security Bureau (GCSB) of New Zealand.

Electronic Communications Privacy Act (ECPA) of 1986   This act prohibited eavesdropping or the interception of message contents without distinguishing between private or public systems.

Electronic Data Interchange (EDI)   A service that provides communications for business transactions. ANSI standard X.12 defines the data format for EDI.

electronic vaulting   Electronic vaulting refers to the transfer of backup data to an off-site location. This process is primarily a batch process of dumping the data through communications lines to a server at an alternate location.

Electronics Industry Association (EIA)   A U.S. standards organization that represents a large number of electronics firms.

emanations   See compromising emanations.

embedded system   A system that performs or controls a function, either in whole or in part, as an integral element of a larger system or subsystem.

emergency plan   Synonymous with contingency plan.

emission security   The protection resulting from all measures that are taken to deny unauthorized persons information of value that might be derived from intercept and from an analysis of compromising emanations from systems.

encipher   To make the message unintelligible to all but the intended recipients.

Endorsed Tools List (ETL)   The list of formal verification tools endorsed by the NCSC for the development of systems that have high levels of trust.

end-to-end encryption   The protection of information passed in a telecommunications system by cryptographic means from the point of origin to the point of destination.

end-to-end encryption   Encrypted information sent from the point of origin to the final destination. In symmetric key encryption, this process requires the sender and receiver to have the identical key for the session.

Enhanced Hierarchical Development Methodology   An integrated set of tools designed to aid in creating, analyzing, modifying, managing, and documenting program specifications and proofs. This methodology includes a specification parser and typechecker, a theorem prover, and a multi-level security checker. Note: This methodology is not based upon the Hierarchical Development Methodology.

entrapment   The deliberate planting of apparent flaws in a system for the purpose of detecting attempted penetrations.

environment   The aggregate of external procedures, conditions, and objects that affect the development, operation, and maintenance of a system.

EPL   Evaluated Products List.

erasure   A process by which a signal recorded on magnetic media is removed. Erasure is accomplished in two ways: 1) By alternating current erasure, by which the information is destroyed by applying an alternating high and low magnetic field to the media; or 2) By direct current erasure in which the media are saturated by applying a unidirectional magnetic field.

Ethernet   An industry-standard local area network media access method that uses a bus topology and CSMA/CD. IEEE 802.3 is a standard that specifies Ethernet.

Ethernet repeater   A component that provides Ethernet connections among multiple stations sharing a common collision domain. Also referred to as a shared Ethernet hub.

Ethernet switch   More intelligent than a hub, having the capability to connect the sending station directly to the receiving station.

ETL   Endorsed Tools List.

ETSI   European Telecommunications Standards Institute.

Evaluated Products List (EPL)   A list of equipment, hardware, software, and/or firmware that have been evaluated against, and found to be technically compliant, at a particular level of trust with the DoD TCSEC by the NCSC. The EPL is included in the National Security Agency Information Systems Security Products and Services Catalogue, which is available through the Government Printing Office (GPO).

evaluation   Assessment of an IT product or system against defined security functional and assurance criteria performed by a combination of testing and analytic techniques.

Evaluation Assurance Level (EAL)   In the Common Criteria, the degree of examination of the product to be tested. EALs range from EA1 (functional testing) to EA7 (detailed testing and formal design verification). Each numbered package represents a point on the CCs predefined assurance scale. An EAL can be considered a level of confidence in the security functions of an IT product or system.

executive state   One of several states in which a system can operate and the only one in which certain privileged instructions can be executed. Such instructions cannot be executed when the system is operating in other (for example, user) states. Synonymous with supervisor state.

exigent circumstances doctrine   Specifies that a warrantless search and seizure of evidence can be conducted if there is probable cause to suspect criminal activity or destruction of evidence.

expert system shell   An off-the-shelf software package that implements an inference engine, a mechanism for entering knowledge, a user-interface, and a system to provide explanations of the reasoning used to generate a solution. It provides the fundamental building blocks of an expert system and supports the entering of domain knowledge.

exploitable channel   Any information channel that is usable or detectable by subjects that are external to the trusted computing base whose purpose is to violate the security policy of the system. See covert channel.

exposure   An instance of being exposed to losses from a threat.

fail over   When one system/application fails, operations will automatically switch to the backup system.

fail safe   Pertaining to the automatic protection of programs and/or processing systems to maintain safety when a hardware or software failure is detected in a system.

fail secure   The system preserves a secure state during and after identified failures occur.

fail soft   Pertaining to the selective termination of affected non-essential processing when a hardware or software failure is detected in a system.

failure access   An unauthorized and usually inadvertent access to data resulting from a hardware or software failure in the system.

failure control   The methodology that is used to detect and provide fail-safe or fail-soft recovery from hardware and software failures in a system.

fault   A condition that causes a device or system component to fail to perform in a required manner.

fault-resilient systems   Systems designed without redundancy; in the event of failure, they result in a slightly longer down time.

FCC   Federal Communications Commission

FDMA   Frequency division multiple access. A spectrum-sharing technique whereby the available spectrum is divided into a number of individual radio channels.

FDX   Full Duplex.

Federal Intelligence Surveillance Act (FISA) of 1978   This act limited wiretapping for national security purposes as a result of the record of the Nixon Administration in using illegal wiretaps.

fetch protection   A system-provided restriction to prevent a program from accessing data in another user's segment of storage.

Fiber-Distributed Data Interface (FDDI)   An ANSI standard for token-passing networks. FDDI uses optical fiber and operates at 100 Mbps in dual counter-rotating rings.

Fiestel cipher   An iterated block cipher that encrypts by breaking a plaintext block into two halves and, with a subkey, applying a "round" transformation to one of the halves. Then, the output of this transformation is XORed with the remaining half. The round is completed by swapping the two halves.

FIFO   Acronym for first in, first out.

file server   A computer that provides network stations with controlled access to sharable resources. The network operating system (NOS) is loaded on the file server, and most sharable devices, including disk subsystems and printers, are attached to it.

file protection   The aggregate of all processes and procedures in a system designed to inhibit unauthorized access, contamination, or elimination of a file.

file security   The means by which access to computer files is limited to authorized users only.

File Transfer Protocol (FTP)   A TCP/IP protocol for file transfer.

FIPS   Federal Information Processing Standard

firewall   A network device that shields the trusted network from unauthorized users in the untrusted network by blocking certain specific types of traffic. Many type of firewalls exist, including packet filtering and stateful inspection.

firmware   Executable programs stored in non-volatile memory.

flaw hypothesis methodology   A systems analysis and penetration technique in which specifications and documentation for the system are analyzed and then flaws in the system are hypothesized. The list of hypothesized flaws is then prioritized on the basis of the estimated probability that a flaw exists, and assuming that a flaw does exist, on the ease of exploiting it, and on the extent of control or compromise that it would provide. The prioritized list is used to direct a penetration attack against the system.

flow control   See information flow control.

FM   Frequency modulation; a method of transmitting information over a radio wave by changing frequencies.

formal access approval   Documented approval by a data owner to allow access to a particular category of information.

Formal Development Methodology   A collection of languages and tools that enforces a rigorous method of verification. This methodology uses the Ina Jo specification language for successive stages of system development, including identification and modeling of requirements, high-level design, and program design.

formal proof   A complete and convincing mathematical argument presenting the full logical justification for each proof step for the truth of a theorem or set of theorems.

formal security policy model   A mathematically precise statement of a security policy. To be adequately precise, such a model must represent the initial state of a system, the way in which the system progresses from one state to another, and a definition of a secure state of the system. To be acceptable as a basis for a TCB, the model must be supported by a formal proof that if the initial state of the system satisfies the definition of a secure state and if all assumptions required by the model hold, then all future states of the system will be secure. Some formal modeling techniques include state transition models, denotational semantics models, and algebraic specification models. See the Bell-LaPadula model and security policy model.

Formal Top-Level Specification (FTLS)   A top-level specification that is written in a formal mathematical language to enable theorems showing the correspondence of the system specification to its formal requirements to be hypothesized and formally proven.

formal verification   The process of using formal proofs to demonstrate the consistency between a formal specification of a system and a formal security policy model (design verification) or between the formal specification and its high-level program implementation (implementation verification).

forward chaining   The reasoning approach that can be used when there are a small number of solutions relative to the number of inputs. The input data is used to reason "forward" to prove that one of the possible solutions in a small solution set is the correct one.

Fractional T-1   A 64Kbps increment of a T1 frame.

Frame Relay   A packet-switching interface that operates at data rates of 56 Kbps to 2 Mbps. Frame relay is minus the error control overhead of X.25, and assumes that a higher-layer protocol will check for transmission errors.

Frequency Division Multiple Access (FDMA)   A digital radio technology that divides the available spectrum into separate radio channels. Generally used in conjunction with time division multiple access (TDMA) or code division multiple access (CDMA).

Frequency Hopping Multiple Access (FHMA)   A system using frequency-hopping spread spectrum (FHSS) to permit multiple, simultaneous conversations or data sessions by assigning different hopping patterns to each.

Frequency Hopping Spread Spectrum (FHSS)   A method used to share the available bandwidth in 802.11b WLANs. FHSS takes the data signal and modulates it with a carrier signal that hops from frequency to frequency on a cyclical basis over a wide band of frequencies. FHSS in the 2.4 GHz frequency band will hop between 2.4 GHz and 2.483 GHz. The receiver must be set to the same hopping code.

Frequency Shift Keying (FSK)   A modulation scheme for data communications using a limited number of discrete frequencies to convey binary information.

front-end security filter   A security filter that could be implemented in hardware or software that is logically separated from the remainder of the system in order to protect the system's integrity.

FTLS   Formal Top-Level Specification.

functional programming   A programming method that uses only mathematical functions to perform computations and solve problems.

functional testing   The segment of security testing in which the advertised security mechanisms of the system are tested, under operational conditions, for correct operation.

gateway   A network component that provides interconnectivity at higher network layers.

genetic algorithms   Part of the general class known as evolutionary computing, which uses the Darwinian principles of survival of the fittest, mutation, and the adaptation of successive generations of populations to their environment. The genetic algorithm implements this process through iteration of generations of a constant-size population of items or individuals.

gigabyte (GB, GByte)   A unit of measure for memory or disk storage capacity; 1,073,741,824 bytes.

gigahertz (GHz)   A measure of frequency; one billion hertz.

Global System for Mobile (GSM) communications   The wireless analog of the ISDN landline system.

Gramm-Leach-Bliley (GLB) Act of November 1999   This act removes Depression era restrictions on banks that limited certain business activities, mergers, and affiliations. It repeals the restrictions on banks affiliating with securities firms contained in sections 20 and 32 of the Glass-Steagall Act. GLB became effective on November 13, 2001. GLB also requires health plans and insurers to protect member and subscriber data in electronic and other formats. These health plans and insurers will fall under new state laws and regulations that are being passed to implement GLB, since GLB explicitly assigns enforcement of the health plan and insurer regulations to state insurance authorities (15 U.S.C. §6805). Some of the privacy and security requirements of Gramm-Leach-Bliley are similar to those of HIPAA.

granularity   An expression of the relative size of a data object; for example, protection at the file level is considered coarse granularity, whereas protection at field level is considered to be of a finer granularity.

guard   A processor that provides a filter between two disparate systems operating at different security levels or between a user terminal and a database in order to filter out data that the user is not authorized to access.

Gypsy Verification Environment   An integrated set of tools for specifying, coding, and verifying programs written in the Gypsy language—a language similar to Pascal that has both specification and programming features. This methodology includes an editor, a specification processor, a verification condition generator, a user-directed theorem prover, and an information flow tool.

handshaking procedure   A dialogue between two entities (for example, a user and a computer, a computer and another computer, or a program and another program) for the purpose of identifying and authenticating the entities to one another.

HDX   Half Duplex.

hertz (Hz)   Unit of frequency measurement; one cycle of a periodic event per second. Used to measure frequency.

Hierarchical Development Methodology   A methodology for specifying and verifying the design programs written in the Special specification language. The tools for this methodology include the Special specification processor, the Boyer-Moore theorem prover, and the Feiertag information flow tool.

high-level data link control   An ISO protocol for link synchronization and error control.

HIPAA   See Kennedy-Kassebaum Act of 1996.

host to front-end protocol   A set of conventions governing the format and control of data that are passed from a host to a front-end machine.

host   A time-sharing computer accessed via terminals or terminal emulation; a computer to which an expansion device attaches.

HTTP   Hypertext Transfer Protocol.

Hypertext Markup Language (HTML)   A standard used on the Internet for defining hypertext links between documents.

I&A   Identification and Authentication

IAC   Inquiry access code; used in inquiry procedures. The IAC can be one of two types: a dedicated IAC for specific devices or a generic IAC for all devices.

IAW   Acronym for "in accordance with."

ICV   Integrity check value. In WEP encryption, the frame is run through an integrity algorithm, and the ICV generated is placed at the end of the encrypted data in the frame. Then the receiving station runs the data through its integrity algorithm and compares it to the ICV received in the frame. If it matches, the unencrypted frame is passed to the higher layers. If it does not match, the frame is discarded.

ID   Common abbreviation of identifier or identity.

identification   The process that enables recognition of an entity by a system, generally by the use of unique machine-readable usernames.

IDS   Intrusion Detection System.

IETF   Internet Engineering Task Force.

IKE   Internet Key Exchange.

impersonating   Synonymous with spoofing.

incomplete parameter checking   A system design flaw that results when all parameters have not been fully anticipated for accuracy and consistency, thus making the system vulnerable to penetration.

individual accountability   The ability to associate positively the identity of a user with the time, method, and degree of access to a system.

Industrial, scientific, and medicine (ISM) bands   Radio frequency bands authorized by the Federal Communications Commission (FCC) for wireless LANs. The ISM bands are located at 902 MHz, 2.400 GHz, and 5.7 GHz. The transmitted power is commonly less than 600mw; therefore no FCC license is required.

inference engine   Takes the inputs to a knowledge-based-system and uses the knowledge base to infer new facts and to solve the problem.

information flow control   A procedure to ensure that information transfers within a system are not made from a higher security level object to an object of a lower security level. See covert channel, simple security property, and star property (* property). Synonymous with data flow control and flow control.

information flow model   Information security model in which information is categorized into classes and rules define how information can flow between the classes.

Information System Security Officer (ISSO)   The person who is responsible to the DAA for ensuring that security is provided for and implemented throughout the life cycle of an AIS from the beginning of the concept development plan through its design, development, operation, maintenance, and secure disposal.

Information Systems Security Products and Services Catalogue   A catalogue that is issued quarterly by the National Security Agency that incorporates the DPL, EPL, ETL, PPL, and other security product and service lists. This catalogue is available through the U.S. Government Printing Office, Washington, D.C., 20402, (202) 783-3238.

infrared (IR) light   Light waves having wavelengths ranging from about 0.75 to 1,000 microns, which is lower in frequency than the spectral colors but higher in frequency than radio waves.

inheritance (in object-oriented programming)   When all the methods of one class are passed on to a subclass. In inheritance, all the methods of one class, called a superclass, are inherited by a subclass. Thus, all messages understood by the superclass are understood by the subclass.

Institute of Electrical and Electronic Engineers (IEEE)   A United States-based standards organization participating in the development of standards for data transmission systems. The IEEE has made significant progress in the establishment of standards for LANs, namely the IEEE 802 series of standards.

Integrated Services Digital Network (ISDN)   A collection of CCITT standards specifying WAN digital transmission services. The overall goal of ISDN is to provide a single physical network outlet and transport mechanism for the transmission of all types of information, including data, video, and voice.

integration testing   Testing process used to verify the interface between network components as the components are installed. The installation crew should integrate components into the network one-by-one and perform integration testing when necessary to ensure proper gradual integration of components.

integrity   Sound, unimpaired, or perfect condition.

interdiction   See denial of service.

Interface Definition Language (IDL)   A standard interface language that is used by clients to request services from objects.

internal security controls   Hardware, firmware, and software features within a system that restrict access to resources (hardware, software, and data) to authorized subjects only (persons, programs, or devices).

International Standards Organization (ISO)   A non-treaty standards organization active in the development of international standards such as the Open System Interconnection (OSI) network architecture.

International Telecommunications Union (ITU)   An intergovernmental agency of the United States responsible for making recommendations and standardization regarding telephone and data communications systems for public and private telecommunication organizations and providing coordination for the development of international standards.

International Telegraph and Telephone Consultative Committee (CCITT)   An international standards organization that is part of the ITU and dedicated to establishing effective and compatible telecommunications among members of the United Nations. CCITT develops the widely used V-series and X-series standards and protocols.

Internet Protocol (IP)   The Internet standard protocol that defines the Internet datagram as the unit of information passed across the Internet. IP provides the basis of a best-effort packet delivery service. The Internet protocol suite is often referred to as TCP/IP because IP is one of the two fundamental protocols, the other being the Transfer Control Protocol.

Internet   The largest network in the world. Successor to ARPANET, the Internet includes other large internetworks. The Internet uses the TCP/IP protocol suite and connects universities, government agencies, and individuals around the world.

Internetwork Packet Exchange (IPX)   NetWare protocol for the exchange of message packets on an internetwork. IPX passes application requests for network services to the network drives and then to other workstations, servers, or devices on the internetwork.

IPSec   Secure Internet Protocol

isochronous transmission   Type of synchronization whereby information frames are sent at specific times.

isolation   The containment of subjects and objects in a system in such a way that they are separated from one another as well as from the protection controls of the operating system.

ISP   Internet Service Provider.

ISSO   Information System Security Officer.

ITA   Industrial Telecommunications Association.

IV   Initialization vector; for WEP encryption.

Joint application design (JAD)   A parallel team design process simultaneously defining requirements composed of users, sales people, marketing staff, project managers, analysts, and engineers. Members of this team are used to simultaneously define requirements.

Kennedy-Kassebaum Health Insurance Portability and Accountability Act (HIPAA) of 1996   A set of regulations that mandate the use of standards in health care record keeping and electronic transactions. The act requires that health care plans, providers, insurers, and clearinghouses:

- Provide for restricted access by the patient to personal healthcare information

- Implement administrative simplification standards

- Enable the portability of health insurance

- Establish strong penalties for healthcare fraud

Kerberos   A trusted, third party authentication protocol that was developed under Project Athena at MIT. In Greek mythology, Kerberos is a three–headed dog that guards the entrance to the underworld. Using symmetric key cryptography, Kerberos authenticates clients to other entities on a network of which a client requires services.

key clustering   The situation in which a plaintext message generates identical ciphertext messages by using the same transformation algorithm but with different cryptovariables.

key or cryptovariable   Information or sequence that controls the enciphering and deciphering of messages. Also known as cryptovariable. Used with a particular algorithm to encipher or decipher the plaintext message.

key schedule   A set of subkeys derived from a secret key.

kilobyte (KB, Kbyte)   A unit of measurement, of memory or disk storage capacity; a data unit of- 2 10 (1,024) bytes.

kilohertz (kHz)   A unit of frequency measurement equivalent to 1,000 hertz.

knowledge acquisition system   The means of identifying and acquiring the knowledge to be entered into the knowledge base of an expert system.

knowledge base   Refers to the rules and facts of the particular problem domain in an expert system.

least privilege   The principle that requires each subject to be granted the most restrictive set of privileges needed for the performance of authorized tasks. The application of this principle limits the damage that can result from accident, error, or unauthorized use.

light-emitting diode (LED)   Used in conjunction with optical fiber, an LED emits incoherent light when current is passed through it. Its advantages to LEDs include low cost and long lifetime, and are capable of operating in the Mbps range.

limited access   Synonymous with access control.

limited fault tolerance   Specifies against what type of failures the TOE must be resistant. Examples of general failures are flooding of the computer room, short-term power interruption, breakdown of a CPU or host, software failure, or overflow of buffer. Requires all functions to be available if specified failure occurs.

Link Access Procedure   An ITU error-correction protocol derived from the HDLC standard.

link encryption   Each entity has keys in common with its two neighboring nodes in the chain of transmission. Thus, a node receives the encrypted message from its predecessor neighboring node, decrypts it, then re-encrypts it with another key that is common to the successor node. Then, the encrypted message is sent on to the successor node where the process is repeated until the final destination is reached. Obviously, this mode provides no protection if the nodes along the transmission path are subject to compromise.

list-oriented   A computer protection system in which each protected object has a list of all subjects that are authorized to access it. Compare with ticket-oriented.

LLC   Logical Link Control; the IEEE layer 2 protocol.

Local Area Network (LAN)   A network that interconnects devices in the same office, floor, or building, or close buildings.

lock-and-key protection system   A protection system that involves matching a key or password with a specific access requirement.

logic bomb   A resident computer program that triggers the perpetration of an unauthorized act when particular states of the system are realized.

logical link control layer   The highest layer of the IEEE 802 Reference Model; provides similar functions to those of a traditional data link control protocol.

loophole   An error of omission or oversight in software or hardware that permits circumventing the system security policy.

LSB   Least-significant bit.

MAC   Mandatory Access Control.

magnetic remanence   A measure of the magnetic flux density remaining after removal of the applied magnetic force. Refers to any data remaining on magnetic storage media after removal of the power.

mail gateway   A type of gateway that interconnects dissimilar e-mail systems.

maintenance hook   Special instructions in software to enable easy maintenance and additional feature development. These are not clearly defined during access for design specification. Hooks frequently enable entry into the code at unusual points or without the usual checks, so they are a serious security risk if they are not removed prior to live implementation. Maintenance hooks are special types of trap doors.

malicious logic   Hardware, software, or firmware that is intentionally included in a system for an unauthorized purpose (for example, a Trojan horse).

MAN   Acronym for metropolitan area network.

management information base (MIB)   A collection of managed objects residing in a virtual information store.

mandatory access control (MAC)   A means of restricting access to objects based on the sensitivity (as represented by a label) of the information contained in the objects and the formal authorization (in other words, clearance) of subjects to access information of such sensitivity. Compare discretionary access control.

MAPI   Microsoft's mail application programming interface.

masquerading   Synonymous with spoofing.

media access control (MAC)   IEEE 802 standards sublayer used to control access to a network medium, such as a wireless LAN. Also deals with collision detection. Each computer has its own unique MAC address.

medium access   The data-link layer function that controls how devices access a shared medium. IEEE 802.11 uses either CSMA/CA or contention-free access modes. Also, a data-link function that controls the use of a common network medium.

megabits per second (Mbps)   One million bits per second.

megabyte (MB, Mbyte)   A unit of measurement for memory or disk storage capacity. 220 (usually 1,048,576) bytes; sometimes interpreted as 1 million bytes.

megahertz (MHz)   A measure of frequency equivalent to one million cycles per second.

middleware   An intermediate software component located on the wired network between the wireless appliance and the application or data residing on the wired network. Middleware provides appropriate interfaces between the appliance and the host application or server database.

mimicking   Synonymous with spoofing.

Mobile IP   A protocol developed by the IETF to enable users to roam to parts of the network associated with a different IP address than the one loaded in the user's appliance. Also refers to any mobile device that contains the IEEE 802.11 MAC and physical layers.

modes of operation   A description of the conditions under which an AIS functions, based on the sensitivity of data processed and the clearance levels and authorizations of the users. Four modes of operation are authorized:

(1) *Dedicated Mode*

An AIS is operating in the dedicated mode when each user who has direct or indirect individual access to the AIS, its peripherals, remote terminals, or remote hosts has all of the following:

a. A valid personnel clearance for all information on the system

b. Formal access approval and has signed non-disclosure agreements for all the information stored and/or processed (including all compartments, subcompartments, and/or special access programs)

c. A valid need-to-know for all information contained within the system

(2) *System-High Mode*

An AIS is operating in the system-high mode when each user who has direct or indirect access to the AIS, its peripherals, remote terminals, or remote hosts has all of the following:

a. A valid personnel clearance for all information on the AIS

b. Formal access approval for, and signed non-disclosure agreements for all the information stored and/or processed (including all compartments, subcompartments, and/or special access programs)

c. A valid need-to-know for some of the information contained within the AIS

(3) *Compartmented Mode*

An AIS is operating in the compartmented mode when each user who has direct or indirect access to the AIS, its peripherals, remote terminals, or remote hosts has all of the following:

a. A valid personnel clearance for the most restricted information processed in the AIS

b. Formal access approval for, and signed non-disclosure agreements for that information to which he or she is to have access

c. A valid need-to-know for that information to which he or she is to have access

(4) *Multilevel Mode*

An AIS is operating in the multi-level mode when all of the following statements are satisfied concerning the users who have direct or indirect access to the AIS, its peripherals, remote terminals, or remote hosts:

a. Some do not have a valid personnel clearance for all the information processed in the AIS.

b. All have the proper clearance and have the appropriate formal access approval for that information to which they are to have access.

c. All have a valid need-to-know for that information to which they are to have access.

modulation   The process of translating the baseband digital signal to a suitable analog form. Any of several techniques for combining user information with a transmitter's carrier signal.

MSB   Most Significant Bit.

multilevel device   A device that is used in a manner that permits it to simultaneously process data of two or more security levels without risk of compromise. To accomplish this, sensitivity labels are normally stored on the same physical medium and in the same form (for example, machine-readable or human-readable) as the data being processed.

multilevel secure   A class of system containing information with different sensitivities that simultaneously permits access by users with different security clearances and needs-to-know but that prevents users from obtaining access to information for which they lack authorization.

multilevel security mode   See modes of operation.

multipath   The signal variation caused when radio signals take multiple paths from transmitter to receiver.

multipath fading   A type of fading caused by signals taking different paths from the transmitter to the receiver and consequently interfering with each other.

multiple access rights terminal   A terminal that can be used by more than one class of users; for example, users who have different access rights to data.

multiple inheritance (in object-oriented programming)   The situation where a subclass inherits the behavior of multiple superclasses.

multiplexer   A network component that combines multiple signals into one composite signal in a form suitable for transmission over a long-haul connection, such as leased 56-Kbps or T1 circuits.

Multi-station Access Unit (MAU)   A multi-port wiring hub for token-ring networks.

multiuser mode of operation   A mode of operation designed for systems that process sensitive, unclassified information in which users might not have a need-to-know for all information processed in the system. This mode is also for microcomputers that are processing sensitive unclassified information that cannot meet the requirements of the stand-alone mode of operation.

Musical Instrument Digital Interface (MIDI)   A standard protocol for the interchange of musical information between musical instruments and computers.

mutually suspicious   The state that exists between interacting processes (subsystems or programs) in which neither process can expect the other process to function securely with respect to some property.

MUX   Multiplexing sublayer; a sublayer of the L2CAP layer.

NACK or NAK   Negative acknowledgement. This can be a deliberate signal that the message was received in error or can be inferred by a time out.

National Computer Security Assessment Program   A program that is designed to evaluate the interrelationship of empirical data of computer security infractions and critical systems profiles while comprehensively incorporating information from the CSTVRP. The assessment will build threat and vulnerability scenarios that are based on a collection of facts from relevant reported cases. Such scenarios are a powerful, dramatic, and concise form of representing the value of loss experience analysis.

National Computer Security Center (NCSC)   Originally named the DoD Computer Security Center, the NCSC is responsible for encouraging the widespread availability of trusted computer systems throughout the federal government. It is a branch of the National Security Agency (NSA) that also initiates research and develops and publishes standards and criteria for trusted information systems.

National Information Assurance Certification and Accreditation Process (NIACAP)   Provides a standard set of activities, general tasks, and a management structure to certify and accredit systems that will maintain the information assurance and security posture of a system or site. The NIACAP is designed to certify that the information system meets documented accreditation requirements and will continue to maintain the accredited security posture throughout the system life cycle.

National Security Decision Directive 145 (NSDD 145)   Signed by President Ronald Reagan on September 17, 1984, this directive is entitled "National Policy on Telecommunications and Automated Information Systems Security." This directive provides initial objectives, policies, and an organizational structure to guide the conduct of national activities toward safeguarding systems that process, store, or communicate sensitive information; establishes a mechanism for policy development, and assigns implementation responsibilities.

National Telecommunications and Information System Security Directives (NTISSD) NTISS directives establish national-level decisions relating to NTISS policies, plans, programs, systems, or organizational delegations of authority. NTISSDs are promulgated by the executive agent of the government for telecommunications and information systems security or by the chairman of the NTISSC when so delegated by the executive agent. NTISSDs are binding upon all federal departments and agencies.

National Telecommunications and Information Systems Security Advisory Memoranda/Instructions (NTISSAM, NTISSI) NTISS Advisory Memoranda and Instructions provide advice, assistance, or information that is of general interest on telecommunications and systems security to all applicable federal departments and agencies. NTISSAMs/NTISSIs are promulgated by the National Manager for Telecommunications and Automated Information Systems Security and are recommendatory.

NCSC National Computer Security Center.

need-to-know The necessity for access to, knowledge of, or possession of specific information that is required to carry out official duties.

Network Basic Input/Output System (NetBIOS) A standard interface between networks and PCs that allows applications on different computers to communicate within a LAN. NetBIOS was created by IBM for its early PC network, was adopted by Microsoft, and has since become a de facto industry standard. It is not routable across a WAN.

network file system (NFS) A distributed file system enabling a set of dissimilar computers to access each other's files in a transparent manner.

network front end A device that implements the necessary network protocols, including security-related protocols, to enable a computer system to be attached to a network.

network interface card (NIC) A network adapter inserted into a computer to enable the computer to be connected to a network.

network monitoring A form of operational support enabling network management to view the inner-workings of the network. Most network monitoring equipment is non-obtrusive and can be used to determine the network's utilization and to locate faults.

network re-engineering A structured process that can help an organization proactively control the evolution of its network. Network re-engineering consists of continually identifying factors influencing network changes, analyzing network modification feasibility, and performing network modifications as necessary.

network service access point (NSAP) A point in the network where OSI network services are available to a transport entity.

NIST National Institute of Standards and Technology.

node Any network-addressable device on the network, such as a router or network interface card. Any network station.

non-interference model The information security model that addresses the situation wherein one group is not affected by another group using specific commands.

NSA   National Security Agency.

NSDD 145   See National Security Decision Directive 145.

NTISSC   National Telecommunications and Information Systems Security.

Number Field Sieve (NFS)   General-purpose factoring algorithm that can be used to factor large numbers.

object   A passive entity that contains or receives information. Access to an object potentially implies access to the information that it contains. Examples of objects include the following: records, blocks, pages, segments, files, directories, directory trees, and programs as well as bits, bytes, words, fields, processors, video displays, keyboards, clocks, printers, and network nodes.

Object Request Broker (ORB)   The fundamental building block of the Object Request Architecture (ORA); manages the communications between the ORA entities. The purpose of the ORB is to support the interaction of objects in heterogeneous, distributed environments. The objects may be on different types of computing platforms.

object reuse   The reassignment and reuse of a storage medium (for example, page frame, disk sector, and magnetic tape) that once contained one or more objects. To be securely reused and assigned to a new subject, storage media must contain no residual data (data remanence) from the object(s) that were previously contained in the media.

Object Services   Support the ORB in creating and tracking objects as well as performing access control functions.

OFDM   Orthogonal frequency division multi-plexing; a set of frequency-hopping codes that never use the same frequency at the same time. Used in IEEE 802.11a for high-speed data transfer.

one-time pad   Encipherment operation performed using each component k_i of the key, K, only once to encipher a single character of the plaintext. Therefore, the key has the same length as the message. The popular interpretation of one-time pad is that the key is used only once and never used again. Ideally, the components of the key are truly random and have no periodicity or predictability, making the ciphertext unbreakable.

Open Database Connectivity (ODBC)   A standard database interface enabling interoperability between application software and multi-vendor ODBC-compliant databases.

Open Data-Link Interface (ODI)   Novell's specification for network interface card device drivers, allowing simultaneous operation of multiple protocol stacks.

open security environment   An environment that includes those systems in which at least one of the following conditions holds true: 1) Application developers (including maintainers) do not have sufficient clearance or authorization to provide an acceptable presumption that they have not introduced malicious logic, and 2) Configuration control does not provide sufficient assurance that applications are protected against the introduction of malicious logic prior to and during the operation of system applications.

Open Shortest Path First (OSPF)   Routing protocol for TCP/IP routers that bases routing decisions on the least number of hops from source to destination.

open system authentication   The IEEE 802.11 default authentication method, which is a very simple, two-step process. First the station wanting to authenticate with another station sends an authentication management frame containing the sending station's identify. The receiving station then sends back a frame alerting whether it recognizes the identity of the authenticating station.

Open System Interconnection (OSI)   An ISO standard specifying an open system capable of enabling the communications between diverse systems. OSI has the following seven layers of distinction: physical, data link, network, transport, session, presentation, and application. These layers provide the functions necessary to allow standardized communications between two application processes.

operations security   Controls over hardware and media and operators who have access, protects against asset threats, baseline or selective mechanisms.

Operations Security (OPSEC)   An analytical process by which the United States government and its supporting contractors can deny to potential adversaries information about capabilities and intentions by identifying, controlling, and protecting evidence of the planning and execution of sensitive activities and operations.

operator   Supports system operations from the operator's console: monitors execution of the system, controls the flow of jobs, and mounts input/output volumes (be alert for shoulder surfing).

OPSEC   Operations Security.

Orange Book   Alternate name for DoD Trusted Computer Security Evaluation Criteria.

original equipment manufacturer (OEM)   A manufacturer of products for integration in other products or systems.

OS   Commonly used abbreviation for operating system.

overt channel   A path within a computer system or network that is designed for the authorized transfer of data. Compare with covert channel.

overwrite procedure   A stimulation to change the state of a bit followed by a known pattern. See magnetic remanence.

packet   A basic message unit for communication across a network. A packet usually includes routing information, data, and (sometimes) error-detection information.

packet-switched   A network that routes data packets based on an address contained in the data packet is said to be a packet-switched network. Multiple data packets can share the same network resources. A communications network that uses shared facilities to route data packets from and to different users. Unlike a circuit-switched network, a packet-switched network does not set up dedicated circuits for each session.

PAD   Acronym for packet assembly/disassembly.

partitioned security mode   A mode of operation wherein all personnel have the clearance but not necessarily formal access approval and need-to-know for all information contained in the system. Not to be confused with compartmented security mode.

password A protected/private character string that is used to authenticate an identity.

PCMCIA Personal Computer Memory Card International Association. The industry group that defines standards for PC cards (and the name applied to the cards themselves). These roughly credit card-sized adapters for memory and modem cards come in three thicknesses: 3.3, 5, and 10.5 mm.

PDN Public Data Network.

PED Personal Electronic Device.

peer-to-peer network A network in which a group of devices can communicate between a group of equal devices. A peer-to-peer LAN does not depend upon a dedicated server, but allows any node to be installed as a non-dedicated server and share its files and peripherals across the network.

pen register A device that records all the numbers dialed from a specific telephone line.

penetration The successful act of bypassing the security mechanisms of a system.

penetration signature The characteristics or identifying marks that might be produced by a penetration.

penetration study A study to determine the feasibility and methods for defeating the controls of a system.

penetration testing The portion of security testing in which the evaluators attempt to circumvent the security features of a system. The evaluators might be assumed to use all system design and implementation documentation, which can include listings of system source code, manuals, and circuit diagrams. The evaluators work under the same constraints that are applied to ordinary users.

performance modeling The use of simulation software to predict network behavior, allowing developers to perform capacity planning. Simulation makes it possible to model the network and impose varying levels of utilization to observe the effects.

performance monitoring Tracks performance of a network during normal operations. Performance monitoring includes real-time monitoring, during which metrics are collected and compared against thresholds; recent-past monitoring, where metrics are collected and analyzed for trends that may lead to performance problems; and historical data analysis, where metrics are collected and stored for later analysis.

periods processing The processing of various levels of sensitive information at distinctly different times. Under periods processing, the system must be purged of all information from one processing period before transitioning to the next when there are different users who have differing authorizations.

permissions A description of the type of authorized interactions that a subject can have with an object. Examples include read, write, execute, add, modify, and delete.

permutation Also known as transposition and operates by rearranging the letters of the plaintext.

personnel security   The procedures that are established to ensure that all personnel who have access to sensitive information have the required authority as well as appropriate clearances. Procedures to ensure a person's background; provides assurance of necessary trustworthiness.

PGP   Pretty Good Privacy, a form of encryption.

physical layer (PHY)   The layer of the OSI model that provides the transmission of bits through a communication channel by defining electrical, mechanical, and procedural specifications, and establishes protocols for voltage and data transmission timing and rules for "handshaking."

physical security   The application of physical barriers and control procedures as preventive measures or countermeasures against threats to resources and sensitive information.

piconet   A collection of devices connected via Bluetooth technology in an ad hoc fashion. A piconet starts with two connected devices, such as a portable PC and cellular phone, and can grow to eight connected devices.

piggyback   Gaining unauthorized access to a system via another user's legitimate connection. See between-the-lines entry.

pipelining   In computer architecture, a design in which the decode and execution cycles of one instruction are overlapped in time with the fetch cycle of the next instruction.

PKI   Public Key Infrastructure.

plain old telephone system (POTS)   The original common analog telephone system, which is still in wide use today.

plaintext   Message text in cleartext, human-readable form.

Platform for Privacy Preferences (P3P)   Proposed standards developed by the World Wide Web Consortium (W3C) to implement privacy practices on Web sites.

Point-to-Point Protocol   A protocol that provides router-to-router and host-to-network connections over both synchronous and asynchronous circuits. PPP is the successor to SLIP.

portability   Defines network connectivity that can be easily established, used, then dismantled.

PPL   Preferred Products List.

PRBS   Pseudorandom Bit Sequence.

Preferred Products List (PPL)   A list of commercially produced equipment that meets TEMPEST and other requirements prescribed by the National Security Agency. This list is included in the NSA Information Systems Security Products and Services Catalogue, issued quarterly and available through the Government Printing Office.

presentation layer   Layer of the OSI model that negotiates data transfer syntax for the application layer and performs translations between different data types, if necessary.

print suppression   Eliminating the displaying of characters in order to preserve their secrecy; for example, not displaying the characters of a password as it is keyed at the input terminal.

private key encryption   See symmetric key encryption.

privileged instructions   A set of instructions (for example, interrupt handling or special computer instructions) to control features (such as storage protection features) that are generally executable only when the automated system is operating in the executive state.

PRNG   Pseudo-Random Number Generator.

procedural language   Implies sequential execution of instructions based on the von Neumann architecture of a CPU, memory, and input/output device. Variables are part of the sets of instructions used to solve a particular problem and, thus, the data is not separate from the statements.

procedural security   Synonymous with administrative security.

process   A program in execution. See domain and subject.

Protected Health Information (PHI)   Individually identifiable health information that is:

- Transmitted by electronic media

- Maintained in any medium described in the definition of electronic media (under HIPAA)

- Transmitted or maintained in any other form or medium

protection philosophy   An informal description of the overall design of a system that delineates each of the protection mechanisms employed. A combination, appropriate to the evaluation class, of formal and informal techniques is used to show that the mechanisms are adequate enough to enforce the security policy.

Protection Profile (PP)   In the Common Criteria, an implementation-independent specification of the security requirements and protections of a product that could be built.

protection ring   One of a hierarchy of privileged modes of a system that gives certain access rights to user programs and processes authorized to operate in a given mode.

protection-critical portions of the TCB   Those portions of the TCB whose normal function is to deal with the control of access between subjects and objects. Their correct operation is essential to the protection of the data on the system.

protocols   A set of rules and formats, semantic and syntactic, that permits entities to exchange information.

prototyping   A method of determining or verifying requirements and design specifications. The prototype normally consists of network hardware and software that support a proposed solution. The approach to prototyping is typically a trial-and-error experimental process.

pseudo-flaw   An apparent loophole deliberately implanted in an operating system program as a trap for intruders.

PSTN   Public-switched telephone network; the general phone network.

public key cryptography   See asymmetric key encryption.

Public Key Cryptography Standards (PKCS)   A set of public-key cryptography standards that support algorithms such as Diffie-Hellman and RSA as well as algorithm-independent standards.

Public Law 100-235 (P.L. 100-235)   Also known as the Computer Security Act of 1987, this law creates a means for establishing minimum acceptable security practices for improving the security and privacy of sensitive information in federal computer systems. This law assigns to the National Institute of Standards and Technology responsibility for developing standards and guidelines for federal computer systems processing unclassified data. The law also requires establishment of security plans by all operators of federal computer systems that contain sensitive information.

pump (in a multi-level security system, or MLS)   A one-way information flow device or data diode. It permits information flow in one direction only, from a lower level of security classification or sensitivity to a higher level. It is a convenient approach to multi-level security in that it can be used to put together systems with different security levels.

purge   The removal of sensitive data from an AIS, AIS storage device, or peripheral device with storage capacity at the end of a processing period. This action is performed in such a way that there is assurance proportional to the sensitivity of the data that the data cannot be reconstructed. An AIS must be disconnected from any external network before a purge. After a purge, the medium can be declassified by observing the review procedures of the respective agency.

RADIUS   Remote Authentication Dial-In User Service.

RC4   RSA cipher algorithm 4.

read   A fundamental operation that results only in the flow of information from an object to a subject.

read access   Permission to read information.

recovery planning   The advance planning and preparations that are necessary to minimize loss and to ensure the availability of the critical information systems of an organization.

recovery procedures   The actions that are necessary to restore a system's computational capability and data files after a system failure or outage/disruption.

Red Book   A document of the United States National Security Agency (NSA) defining criteria for secure networks.

Reduced Instruction Set Computer (RISC)   A computer architecture designed to reduce the number of cycles required to execute an instruction. An RISC architecture uses simpler instructions, but makes use of other features such as optimizing compilers to reduce the number of instructions required, large numbers of general purpose registers in the processor and data caches.

reference monitor concept   An access-control concept that refers to an abstract machine that mediates all accesses to objects by subjects.

reference validation mechanism   An implementation of the reference monitor concept. A security kernel is a type of reference-validation mechanism.

reliability   The probability of a given system performing its mission adequately for a specified period of time under the expected operating conditions.

remote bridge   A bridge connecting networks separated by longer distances. Organizations use leased 56Kbps circuits, T1 digital circuits, and radio waves to provide long-distance connections between remote bridges.

remote journaling   Remote journaling refers to the parallel processing of transactions to an alternate site, as opposed to a batch dump process like electronic vaulting. A communications line is used to transmit live data as it occurs, which enables the alternate site to be fully operational at all times and introduces a very high level of fault tolerance.

repeater   A network component that provides internetworking functionality at the physical layer of a network's architecture. A repeater amplifies network signals, extending the distance they can travel.

residual risk   The portion of risk that remains after security measures have been applied.

residue   Data left in storage after processing operations are complete but before degaussing or rewriting has taken place.

resource encapsulation   The process of ensuring that a resource not be directly accessible by a subject but that it be protected so that the reference monitor can properly mediate access to it.

restricted area   Any area to which access is subject to special restrictions or controls for reasons of security or safeguarding of property or material.

RFC   Acronym for request for comment.

RFP   Acronym for request for proposal.

ring topology   A topology where a set of nodes are joined in a closed loop.

risk   The probability that a particular threat will exploit a particular vulnerability of the system.

risk analysis   The process of identifying security risks, determining their magnitude, and identifying areas needing safeguards. Risk analysis is a part of risk management. Synonymous with risk assessment.

risk assessment   Synonymous with risk analysis.

risk index   The disparity between the minimum clearance or authorization of system users and the maximum sensitivity (for example, classification and categories) of data processed by a system. See CSC-STD-003-85 and CSC-STD-004-85 for a complete explanation of this term.

risk management   The total process of identifying, controlling, and eliminating or minimizing uncertain events that might affect system resources. It includes risk analysis, a cost-benefit analysis, selection, implementation and tests, a security evaluation of safeguards, and an overall security review.

ROM   Read-Only Memory.

router   A network component that provides internetworking at the network layer of a network's architecture by allowing individual networks to become part of a WAN. A router works by using logical and physical addresses to connect two or more separate networks. It determines the best path by which to send a packet of information.

Routing Information Protocol (RIP)   A common type of routing protocol. RIP bases its routing path on the distance (number of hops) to the destination. RIP maintains optimum routing paths by sending out routing update messages if the network topology changes.

RS-232 A serial communications interface. Serial communication standards are defined by the Electronic Industries Association (EIA). The ARS-232n EIA standard that specifies up to 20-Kbps, 50-foot, serial transmission between computers and peripheral devices.

RS-422 An EIA standard specifying electrical characteristics for balanced circuits (in other words, both transmit and return wires are at the same voltage above ground). RS-422 is used in conjunction with RS-449.

RS-423 An EIA standard specifying electrical characteristics for unbalanced circuits (in other words, the return wire is tied to ground). RS-423 is used in conjunction with RS-449.

RS-449 An EIA standard specifying a 37-pin connector for high-speed transmission.

RS-485 An EIA standard for multi-point communications lines.

S/MIME A protocol that adds digital signatures and encryption to Internet MIME (Multipurpose Internet Mail Extensions).

safeguards See security safeguards.

SAISS Subcommittee on Automated Information Systems Security of NTISSC

sandbox An access control-based protection mechanism. It is commonly applied to restrict the access rights of mobile code that is downloaded from a Web site as an applet. The code is set up to run in a "sandbox" that blocks its access to the local workstation's hard disk, thus preventing the code from malicious activity. The sandbox is usually interpreted by a virtual machine such as the Java Virtual Machine (JVM).

SBU Abbreviation for sensitive but unclassified; an information designation.

scalar processor A processor that executes one instruction at a time.

scavenging Searching through object residue to acquire unauthorized data.

SDLC Synchronous Data Link Control.

secure configuration management The set of procedures that are appropriate for controlling changes to a system's hardware and software structure for the purpose of ensuring that changes will not lead to violations of the system's security policy.

secure state A condition in which no subject can access any object in an unauthorized manner.

secure subsystem A subsystem that contains its own implementation of the reference monitor concept for those resources it controls. The secure subsystem, however, must depend on other controls and the base operating system for the control of subjects and the more primitive system objects.

security critical mechanisms Those security mechanisms whose correct operation is necessary to ensure that the security policy is enforced.

security evaluation An evaluation that is done in order to assess the degree of trust that can be placed in systems for the secure handling of sensitive information. One type, a product evaluation, is an evaluation performed on the hardware and software features and assurances of a computer product from a perspective that excludes the application environment. The other type, a system evaluation, is done for the purpose of assessing a system's security safeguards with respect to a specific operational mission and is a major step in the certification and accreditation process.

security fault analysis   A security analysis, usually performed on hardware at the gate level, to determine the security properties of a device when a hardware fault is encountered.

security features   The security-relevant functions, mechanisms, and characteristics of system hardware and software. Security features are a subset of system security safeguards.

security filter   A trusted subsystem that enforces a security policy on the data that pass through it.

security flaw   An error of commission or omission in a system that might enable protection mechanisms to be bypassed.

security flow analysis   A security analysis performed on a formal system specification that locates the potential flows of information within the system.

security functional requirements   Requirements, preferably from the Common Criteria, Part 2, that when taken together specify the security behavior of an IT product or system.

security kernel   The hardware, firmware, and software elements of a Trusted Computer Base (TCB) that implement the reference monitor concept. It must mediate all accesses, be protected from modification and be verifiable as correct.

security label   A piece of information that represents the security level of an object.

security level   The combination of a hierarchical classification and a set of non-hierarchical categories that represents the sensitivity of information.

security measures   Elements of software, firmware, hardware, or procedures that are included in a system for the satisfaction of security specifications.

security objective   A statement of intent to counter specified threats and/or satisfy specified organizational security policies and assumptions.

security perimeter   The boundary where security controls are in effect to protect assets.

security policy   The set of laws, rules, and practices that regulates how an organization manages, protects, and distributes sensitive information.

security policy model   A formal presentation of the security policy enforced by the system. It must identify the set of rules and practices that regulate how a system manages, protects, and distributes sensitive information. See the Bell-LaPadula model and formal security policy model.

security range   The highest and lowest security levels that are permitted in or on a system, system component, subsystem, or network.

security requirements   The types and levels of protection that are necessary for equipment, data, information, applications, and facilities to meet security policy.

security requirements baseline A description of minimum requirements necessary for a system to maintain an acceptable level of security.

security safeguards The protective measures and controls that are prescribed to meet the security requirements specified for a system. Those safeguards can include (but are not necessarily limited to) the following: hardware and software security features, operating procedures, accountability procedures, access and distribution controls, management constraints, personnel security, and physical structures, areas, and devices. Also called safeguards.

security specifications A detailed description of the safeguards required to protect a system.

Security Target (ST) In the Common Criteria, a listing of the security claims for a particular IT security product. A set of security functional and assurance requirements and specifications to be used as the basis for evaluation of an identified product or system.

security test and evaluation An examination and analysis of the security safeguards of a system as they have been applied in an operational environment to determine the security posture of the system.

security testing A process that is used to determine that the security features of a system are implemented as designed. This process includes hands-on functional testing, penetration testing, and verification.

sensitive information Any information, the loss, misuse, modification of, or unauthorized access to, could affect the national interest or the conduct of federal programs or the privacy to which individuals are entitled under Section 552a of Title 5, U.S. Code, but that has not been specifically authorized under criteria established by an executive order or an act of Congress to be kept classified in the interest of national defense or foreign policy.

sensitivity label A piece of information that represents the security level of an object. Sensitivity labels are used by the TCB as the basis for mandatory access control decisions.

serial interface An interface to provide serial communications service.

Serial Line Internet Protocol (SLIP) An Internet protocol used to run IP over serial lines and dial-up connections.

session layer One of the seven OSI model layers. Establishes, manages, and terminates sessions between applications.

shared key authentication A type of authentication that assumes each station has received a secret shared key through a secure channel, independent from an 802.11 network. Stations authenticate through shared knowledge of the secret key. Use of shared key authentication requires implementation of the 802.11 Wireless Equivalent Privacy (WEP) algorithm.

Simple Mail Transfer Protocol (SMTP) The Internet e-mail protocol.

Simple Network Management Protocol (SNMP) The network management protocol of choice for TCP/IP-based Internets. Widely implemented with 10BASE-T Ethernet. A network management protocol that defines the transfer of information between management information bases (MIBs).

simple security condition See simple security property.

simple security property A Bell-LaPadula security model rule enabling a subject read access to an object only if the security level of the subject dominates the security level of the object. Synonymous with simple security condition.

Single User Mode OS loaded without Security Front End.

single-level device An automated information systems device that is used to process data of a single security level at any one time.

SMS Short (or small) Message Service

SNR Signal-to-Noise Ratio

Software Development Methodologies Methodologies for specifying and verifying design programs for system development. Each methodology is written for a specific computer language. See Enhanced Hierarchical Development Methodology, Formal Development Methodology, Gypsy Verification Environment, and Hierarchical Development Methodology.

software engineering The science and art of specifying, designing, implementing and evolving programs, documentation, and operating procedures whereby computers can be made useful to man.

software process A set of activities, methods, and practices that are used to develop and maintain software and associated products.

software process capability Describes the range of expected results that can be achieved by following a software process.

software process maturity The extent to which a software process is defined, managed, measured, controlled, and effective.

software process performance The result achieved by following a software process.

software security General purpose (executive, utility, or software development tools) and applications programs or routines that protect data that are handled by a system.

software system test and evaluation process A process that plans, develops, and documents the quantitative demonstration of the fulfillment of all baseline functional performance and operational and interface requirements.

spoofing An attempt to gain access to a system by posing as an authorized user. Synonymous with impersonating, masquerading, or mimicking.

SSL Secure Sockets Layer.

SSO System Security Officer.

Subcommittee on Automated Information Systems Security The SAISS is composed of one voting member from each organization that is represented on the NTISSC.

ST connector An optical fiber connector that uses a bayonet plug and socket.

standalone, shared system A system that is physically and electrically isolated from all other systems and is intended to be used by more than one person, either simultaneously (for example, a system that has multiple terminals) or serially, with data belonging to one user remaining available to the system while another user is using the system (for example, a personal computer that has non-removable storage media, such as a hard disk).

standalone, single-user system A system that is physically and electrically isolated from all other systems and that is intended to be used by one person at a time, with no data belonging to other users remaining in the system (for example, a personal computer that has removable storage media, such as a floppy disk).

star property See * property.

star topology A topology wherein each node is connected to a common central switch or hub.

State Delta Verification System A system that is designed to give high confidence regarding microcode performance by using formulae that represent isolated states of a computation to check proofs concerning the course of that computation.

state variable A variable that represents either the state of the system or the state of some system resource.

storage object An object that supports both read and write access.

Structured Query Language (SQL) An international standard for defining and accessing relational databases.

STS Subcommittee on Telecommunications Security of NTISSC

Subcommittee on Automated Information Systems Security (SAISS) NSDD-145 authorizes and directs the establishment, under the NTISSC, of a permanent subcommittee on Automated Information Systems Security. The SAISS is composed of one voting member from each organization that is represented on the NTISSC.

Subcommittee on Telecommunications Security (STS) NSDD-145 authorizes and directs the establishment, under the NTISSC, of a permanent subcommittee on Telecommunications Security. The STS is composed of one voting member from each organization that is represented on the NTISSC.

subject An active entity, generally in the form of a person, process, or device, that causes information to flow among objects or that changes the system state. Technically, a process/domain pair.

subject security level A subject's security level is equal to the security level of the objects to which it has both read and write access. A subject's security level must always be dominated by the clearance of the user with which the subject is associated.

superscalar processor A processor that allows concurrent execution of instructions in the same pipelined stage. The term superscalar denotes multiple, concurrent operations performed on scalar values as opposed to vectors or arrays that are used as objects of computation in array processors.

supervisor state Synonymous with executive state.

Switched multi-megabit Digital Service (SMDS) A packet switching connectionless data service for WANs.

symmetric (private) key encryption Cryptographic system in which the sender and receiver both know a secret key, and it is used to encrypt and decrypt the message.

Synchronous Optical NETwork (SONET) A fiber optic transmission system for high-speed digital traffic. SONET is part of the B-ISDN standard.

synchronous transmission   Type of communications data synchronization whereby with frames are sent within defined time periods. It uses a clock to control the timing of bits being sent. See asynchronous transmission.

system   Data processing facility.

System Development Methodologies   Methodologies developed through software engineering to manage the complexity of system development. Development methodologies include software engineering aids and high-level design analysis tools.

system high security mode   System and all peripherals protected in accordance with (IAW) requirements for highest security level of material in system; personnel with access have security clearance but not need-to-know. See also modes of operation.

system integrity   The quality that a system has when it performs its intended function in an unimpaired manner, free from deliberate or inadvertent unauthorized manipulation of the system.

system low   The lowest security level supported by a system at a particular time or in a particular environment.

System Security Officer (SSO)   See Information System Security Officer.

system testing   Type of testing that verifies the installation of the entire network. Testers normally complete system testing in a simulated production environment, simulating actual users in order to ensure that the network meets all stated requirements.

Systems Network Architecture (SNA)   IBM's proprietary network architecture.

Systems Security Steering Group   The senior government body established by NSDD-145 to provide top-level review and policy guidance for the telecommunications security and automated information systems security activities of the United States government. This group is chaired by the assistant to the President for National Security Affairs and consists of the Secretary of State, Secretary of Treasury, the Secretary of Defense, the Attorney General, the Director of the Office of Management and Budget, and the Director of Central Intelligence.

T1   A standard specifying a time division multi-plexing scheme for point-to-point transmission of digital signals at 1.544 Mbps.

tampering   An unauthorized modification that alters the proper functioning of an equipment or system in a manner that degrades the security or functionality that it provides.

Target of Evaluation (TOE)   In the Common Criteria, TOE refers to the product to be tested.

TCB   Trusted Computing Base

TCSEC   DoD Trusted Computer System Evaluation Criteria

TDD   Time Division Duplex

technical attack   An attack that can be perpetrated by circumventing or nullifying hardware and software protection mechanisms, rather than by subverting system personnel or other users.

technical vulnerability   A hardware, firmware, communication, or software flaw that leaves a computer processing system open for potential exploitation, either externally or internally—thereby resulting in a risk for the owner, user, or manager of the system.

Telnet   A virtual terminal protocol used in the Internet, enabling users to log in to a remote host. A terminal emulation defined as part of the TCP/IP protocol suite.

TEMPEST   The study and control of spurious electronic signals emitted by electrical equipment.

terminal identification   The means used to uniquely identify a terminal to a system.

test case   An executable test with a specific set of input values and a corresponding expected result.

threat   Any circumstance or event that has the potential to cause harm to a system in the form of destruction, disclosure, modification of data, and/or denial of service.

threat agent   A method that is used to exploit a vulnerability in a system, operation, or facility.

threat analysis   The examination of all actions and events that might adversely affect a system or operation.

threat monitoring   The analysis, assessment, and review of audit trails and other data that are collected for the purpose of searching for system events that might constitute violations or attempted violations of system security.

ticket-oriented   A computer protection system in which each subject maintains a list of unforgeable bit patterns, called tickets, one for each object the subject is authorized to access. Compare list-oriented.

time-dependent password   A password that is valid only at a certain time of day or during a specified interval of time.

Time-Domain Reflectometer (TDR)   Mechanism used to test the effectiveness of network cabling.

TLA   Top Level Architecture

TLS   Transport Layer Security

token bus   A network that uses a logical token-passing access method. Unlike a token passing ring, permission to transmit is usually based on the node address rather than the position in the network. A token bus network uses a common cable set with all signals broadcast across the entire LAN.

Token Ring   A local area network (LAN) standard developed by IBM that uses tokens to control access to the communication medium. A medium access method that provides multiple access to a ring-type network through the use of a token. FDDI and IEEE 802.5 are Token Ring standards.

top-level specification   A non-procedural description of system behavior at the most abstract level; typically, a functional specification that omits all implementation details.

topology   A description of the network's geographical layout of nodes and links.

tranquility   A security model rule stating that the security level of an object cannot change while the object is being processed by an AIS.

transceiver   A device for transmitting and receiving packets between the computer and the medium.

Transmission Control Protocol (TCP)   A commonly used protocol in wide use for establishing and maintaining communications between applications on different computers. TCP provides full-duplex, acknowledged, and flow-controlled service to upper-layer protocols and applications.

Transmission Control Protocol/Internet Protocol (TCP/IP)   A *de facto*, industry-standard protocol for interconnecting disparate networks. Standard protocols that define both the reliable full-duplex transport level and the connectionless, "best effort" unit of information passed across an Internet.

transport layer   OSI model layer that provides mechanisms for the establishment, maintenance, and orderly termination of virtual circuits while shielding the higher layers from the network implementation details.

trap door   A hidden software or hardware mechanism that can be triggered to permit system protection mechanisms to be circumvented. It is activated in some innocent-appearing manner; for example, a special "random" key sequence at a terminal. Software developers often introduce trap doors in their code to enable them to re-enter the system and perform certain functions. Synonymous with back door.

Trojan horse   A computer program that has an apparently or actually useful function that contains additional (hidden) functions that surreptitiously exploit the legitimate authorizations of the invoking process to the detriment of security or integrity.

trusted computer system   A system that employs sufficient hardware and software assurance measures to enable its use for simultaneous processing of a range of sensitive or classified information.

Trusted Computing Base (TCB)   The totality of protection mechanisms within a computer system, including hardware, firmware, and software—the combination of which is responsible for enforcing a security policy. A TCB consists of one or more components that together enforce a unified security policy over a product or system. The ability of a TCB to correctly enforce a unified security policy depends solely on the mechanisms within the TCB and on the correct input of parameters by system administrative personnel (for example, a user's clearance level) related to the security policy.

trusted distribution   A trusted method for distributing the TCB hardware, software, and firmware components, both originals and updates, that provides methods for protecting the TCB from modification during distribution and for the detection of any changes to the TCB that might occur.

trusted identification forwarding   An identification method used in networks whereby the sending host can verify that an authorized user on its system is attempting a connection to another host. The sending host transmits the required user authentication information to the receiving host. The receiving host then can verify that the user is validated for access to its system. This operation might be transparent to the user.

trusted path   A mechanism by which a person at a terminal can communicate directly with the TCB. This mechanism can be activated only by the person or by the TCB and cannot be imitated by untrusted software.

trusted process   A process whose incorrect or malicious execution is capable of violating system security policy.

trusted software   The software portion of the TCB.

twisted-pair wire   Type of medium using metallic-type conductors twisted together to provide a path for current flow. The wire in this medium is twisted in pairs to minimize the electromagnetic interference between one pair and another.

U.S Federal Computer Incident Response Center (FedCIRC)   FedCIRC provides assistance and guidance in incident response and provides a centralized approach to incident handling across U.S. government agency boundaries.

U.S. Patriot Act of October 26, 2001   This law permits the:

- Subpoena of electronic records.

- Monitoring of Internet communications.

- Search and seizure of information on live systems (including routers and servers), backups and archives.

- Reporting of cash and wire transfers of $10,000 or more.

- Under the Patriot Act, the government has new powers to subpoena electronic records and to monitor Internet traffic. In monitoring information, the government can require the assistance of ISPs and network operators. This monitoring can even extend into individual organizations.

U.S. Uniform Computer Information Transactions Act (UCITA) of 1999   A model act that is intended to apply uniform legislation to software licensing.

UART   Universal asynchronous receiver transmitter. A device that converts parallel data into serial data for transmission, or it converts serial data into parallel data for receiving data.

untrusted process   A process that has not been evaluated or examined for adherence to the security policy. It might include incorrect or malicious code that attempts to circumvent the security mechanisms.

user   A person or process that is accessing an AIS either by direct connections (for example, via terminals), or by indirect connections (in other words, prepare input data or receive output that is not reviewed for content or classification by a responsible individual).

User Datagram Protocol   UDP uses the underlying Internet Protocol (IP) to transport a message. This is an unreliable, connectionless delivery scheme. It does not use acknowledgments to make sure that messages arrive and does not provide feedback to control the rate of information flow. UDP messages can be lost, duplicated, or arrive out of order.

user ID A unique symbol or character string that is used by a system to identify a specific user.

user profile Patterns of a user's activity that can be used to detect changes in normal routines.

V.21 An ITU standard for asynchronous 0-300 bps full-duplex modems.

V.21FAX An ITU standard for facsimile operations at 300 bps.

V.34 An ITU standard for 28,800 bps modems.

validation (in software engineering) To establish the fitness or worth of a software product for its operational mission.

vaulting Running mirrored data centers in separate locations.

verification The process of comparing two levels of system specification for proper correspondence (for example, a security policy model with top-level specification, top-level specification with source code, or source code with object code). This process might or might not be automated.

very-long-instruction word (VLIW) processor A processor in which multiple, concurrent operations are performed in a single instruction. Because multiple operations are performed in one instruction rather than using multiple instructions, the number of instructions is reduced relative to those in a scalar processor. However, for this approach to be feasible, the operations in each VLIW instruction must be independent of each other.

VIM Lotus' vendor-independent messaging system.

virus A self-propagating Trojan horse composed of a mission component, a trigger component, and a self-propagating component.

vulnerability A weakness in system security procedures, system design, implementation, internal controls, and so on that could be exploited to violate system security policy.

vulnerability analysis The systematic examination of systems in order to determine the adequacy of security measures, identify security deficiencies, and provide data from which to predict the effectiveness of proposed security measures.

vulnerability assessment A measurement of vulnerability that includes the susceptibility of a particular system to a specific attack and the opportunities that are available to a threat agent to mount that attack.

WAP Wireless Application Protocol. A standard commonly used for the development of applications for wireless Internet devices.

Wide Area Network (WAN) A network that interconnects users over a wide area, usually encompassing different metropolitan areas.

Wired Equivalency Privacy (WEP) The algorithm of the 802.11 Wireless LAN Standard that is used to protect transmitted information from disclosure. WEP is designed to prevent the violation of the confidentiality of data transmitted over the wireless LAN. WEP generates secret shared encryption keys that both source and destination stations use to alter frame bits to avoid disclosure to eavesdroppers.

wireless Describes any computing device that can access a network without a wired connection.

wireless metropolitan area network (wireless MAN)   Provides communications links between buildings, avoiding the costly installation of cabling or leasing fees and the down time associated with system failures.

WLAN   Wireless Local Area Network.

work breakdown structure (WBS)   Diagram of how a team will accomplish the project at hand by listing all tasks the team will need to perform and the products they must deliver.

work factor   An estimate of the effort or time needed by a potential intruder who has specified expertise and resources to overcome a protective measure.

work function (factor)   The difficulty in recovering the plaintext from the ciphertext as measured by cost and/or time. The security of the system is directly proportional to the value of the work function. The work function need only be large enough to suffice for the intended application. If the message to be protected loses its value after a short period of time, the work function need only be large enough to ensure that the decryption would be highly infeasible in that period of time.

write   A fundamental operation that results only in the flow of information from a subject to an object.

write access   Permission to write to an object.

X.12   An ITU standard for EDI.

X.121   An ITU standard for international address numbering.

X.21   An ITU standard for a circuit-switching network.

X.25   An ITU standard for an interface between a terminal and a packet-switching network. X.25 was the first public packet-switching technology, developed by the CCITT and offered as a service during the 1970s and still available today. X.25 offers connection-oriented (virtual circuit) service; and it operates at 64 Kbps, which is too slow for some high-speed applications.

X.400   An ITU standard for OSI messaging.

X.500   An ITU standard for OSI directory services.

X.75   An ITU standard for packet switching between public networks.

Index

Wiley Publishing, Inc.
End-User License Agreement

READ THIS. You should carefully read these terms and conditions before opening the software packet(s) included with this book "Book". This is a license agreement "Agreement" between you and Wiley Publishing, Inc. "WPI". By opening the accompanying software packet(s), you acknowledge that you have read and accept the following terms and conditions. If you do not agree and do not want to be bound by such terms and conditions, promptly return the Book and the unopened software packet(s) to the place you obtained them for a full refund.

1. **License Grant.** WPI grants to you (either an individual or entity) a nonexclusive license to use one copy of the enclosed software program(s) (collectively, the "Software" solely for your own personal or business purposes on a single computer (whether a standard computer or a workstation component of a multi-user network). The Software is in use on a computer when it is loaded into temporary memory (RAM) or installed into permanent memory (hard disk, CD-ROM, or other storage device). WPI reserves all rights not expressly granted herein.

2. **Ownership.** WPI is the owner of all right, title, and interest, including copyright, in and to the compilation of the Software recorded on the disk(s) or CD-ROM "Software Media". Copyright to the individual programs recorded on the Software Media is owned by the author or other authorized copyright owner of each program. Ownership of the Software and all proprietary rights relating thereto remain with WPI and its licensers.

3. **Restrictions On Use and Transfer.**

   (a) You may only (i) make one copy of the Software for backup or archival purposes, or (ii) transfer the Software to a single hard disk, provided that you keep the original for backup or archival purposes. You may not (i) rent or lease the Software, (ii) copy or reproduce the Software through a LAN or other network system or through any computer subscriber system or bulletin- board system, or (iii) modify, adapt, or create derivative works based on the Software.

   (b) You may not reverse engineer, decompile, or disassemble the Software. You may transfer the Software and user documentation on a permanent basis, provided that the transferee agrees to accept the terms and conditions of this Agreement and you retain no copies. If the Software is an update or has been updated, any transfer must include the most recent update and all prior versions.

4. **Restrictions on Use of Individual Programs.** You must follow the individual requirements and restrictions detailed for each individual program in the About the CD-ROM appendix of this Book. These limitations are also contained in the individual license agreements recorded on the Software Media. These limitations may include a requirement that after using the program for a specified period of time, the user must pay a registration fee or discontinue use. By opening the Software packet(s), you will be agreeing to abide by the licenses and restrictions for these individual programs that are detailed in the About the CD-ROM appendix and on the Software Media. None of the material on this Software Media or listed in this Book may ever be redistributed, in original or modified form, for commercial purposes.

5. **Limited Warranty.**

   (a) WPI warrants that the Software and Software Media are free from defects in materials and workmanship under normal use for a period of sixty (60) days from the date of purchase of this Book. If WPI receives notification within the warranty period of defects in materials or workmanship, WPI will replace the defective Software Media.

   (b) WPI AND THE AUTHOR OF THE BOOK DISCLAIM ALL OTHER WARRANTIES, EXPRESS OR IMPLIED, INCLUDING WITHOUT LIMITATION IMPLIED WARRANTIES OF MERCHANTABILITY AND FITNESS FOR A PARTICULAR PURPOSE, WITH RESPECT TO THE SOFTWARE, THE PROGRAMS, THE SOURCE CODE CONTAINED THEREIN, AND/OR THE TECHNIQUES DESCRIBED IN THIS BOOK. WPI DOES NOT WARRANT THAT THE FUNCTIONS CONTAINED IN THE SOFTWARE WILL MEET YOUR REQUIREMENTS OR THAT THE OPERATION OF THE SOFTWARE WILL BE ERROR FREE.

   (c) This limited warranty gives you specific legal rights, and you may have other rights that vary from jurisdiction to jurisdiction.

6. **Remedies.**

   (a) WPI's entire liability and your exclusive remedy for defects in materials and workmanship shall be limited to replacement of the Software Media, which may be returned to WPI with a copy of your receipt at the following address: Software Media Fulfillment Department, Attn.: The CISSP Prep Guide: Gold Edition, Wiley Publishing, Inc., 10475 Crosspoint Blvd., Indianapolis, IN 46256, or call 1-800-762-2974. Please allow four to six weeks for delivery. This Limited Warranty is void if failure of the Software Media has resulted from accident, abuse, or misapplication. Any replacement Software Media will be warranted for the remainder of the original warranty period or thirty (30) days, whichever is longer.

(b) In no event shall WPI or the author be liable for any damages whatsoever (including without limitation damages for loss of business profits, business interruption, loss of business information, or any other pecuniary loss) arising from the use of or inability to use the Book or the Software, even if WPI has been advised of the possibility of such damages.

(c) Because some jurisdictions do not allow the exclusion or limitation of liability for consequential or incidental damages, the above limitation or exclusion may not apply to you.

7. **U.S. Government Restricted Rights.** Use, duplication, or disclosure of the Software for or on behalf of the United States of America, its agencies and/or instrumentalities "U.S. Government" is subject to restrictions as stated in paragraph (c)(1)(ii) of the Rights in Technical Data and Computer Software clause of DFARS 252.227-7013, or subparagraphs (c) (1) and (2) of the Commercial Computer Software - Restricted Rights clause at FAR 52.227-19, and in similar clauses in the NASA FAR supplement, as applicable.

8. **General.** This Agreement constitutes the entire understanding of the parties and revokes and supersedes all prior agreements, oral or written, between them and may not be modified or amended except in a writing signed by both parties hereto that specifically refers to this Agreement. This Agreement shall take precedence over any other documents that may be in conflict herewith. If any one or more provisions contained in this Agreement are held by any court or tribunal to be invalid, illegal, or otherwise unenforceable, each and every other provision shall remain in full force and effect.